Windows® 7 ALL-IN-ONE FOR DUMMIES®

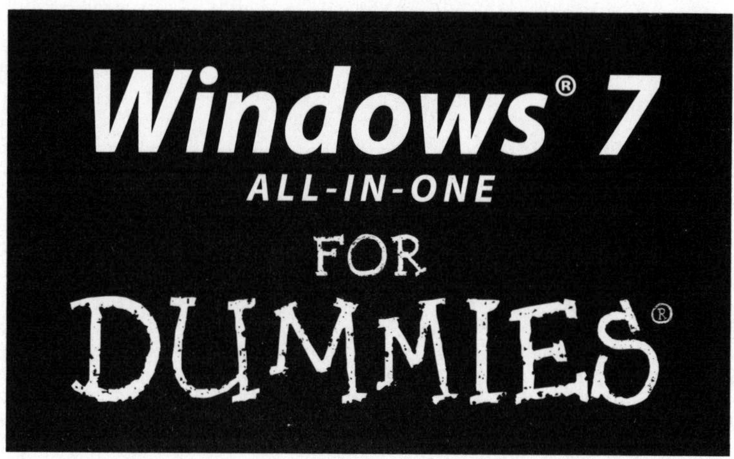

by Woody Leonhard

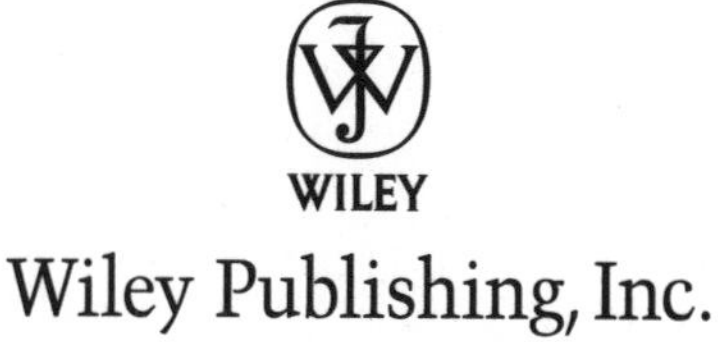

Wiley Publishing, Inc.

Windows® 7 All-in-One For Dummies®

Published by
Wiley Publishing, Inc.
111 River Street
Hoboken, NJ 07030-5774

www.wiley.com

Published by Wiley Publishing, Inc., Indianapolis, Indiana

Published simultaneously in Canada

For general information on our other products and services, please contact our Customer Care Department within the U.S. at 877-762-2974, outside the U.S. at 317-572-3993, or fax 317-572-4002.

For technical support, please visit www.wiley.com/techsupport.

Wiley also publishes its books in a variety of electronic formats. Some content that appears in print may not be available in electronic books.

Library of Congress Control Number: 2009932712

ISBN: 978-0-470-48763-1

Manufactured in the United States of America

10 9 8 7 6 5 4 3 2 1

About the Author

Curmudgeon, critic, and self-described "Windows victim," **Woody Leonhard** runs AskWoody.com, the Web's single best source of up-to-the-nanosecond news about Windows and Office — warts and all. He's also a contributing editor and secret leaker for the Windows Secrets newsletter, at `WindowsSecrets.com`.

With several dozen computer books under his belt, Woody knows where the bodies are buried. He's a Microsoft MVP, was one of the first Microsoft Consulting Partners, and was a charter member of the Microsoft Solutions Provider organization. He's a one-man, major Microsoft beta testing site and delights in being a constant thorn in Microsoft's side. Along with several coauthors and editors, he has won an unprecedented six Computer Press Association awards and two American Business Press awards.

Woody and his son, Justin, moved to Phuket, Thailand, in late 2000. Woody's dad, George, joined them in 2006. Woody, his wife Duangkhae Leonhard (better known as Add), and 33 talented Thai staff members run Khun Woody's Bakery and the Sandwich Shoppes in Patong, Laguna, and Chalong. Woody is the president of the Rotary Club of Patong Beach (RotaryPatong.org), a group best known for ongoing tsunami relief work and the support of more than 260 orphaned schoolchildren.

Most mornings, you can see Woody jogging on Patong Beach with his dad and then downing a latté and New Yawk bagel-n-Philly at the Shoppe. Feel free to drop by and say, "Sawadee krap!" Microsoft hit squads, please take a number and form a queue at the rear of the building.

Dedication

To Add, who had to shoulder so many burdens while I was locked up, plunking away on the computer.

And to Dad, who's always been happy to help.

Acknowledgments

My unending thanks to the entire editorial team — with Becky Huehls playing point. The flagship *All-in-One For Dummies* is an enormous undertaking, and I'm positively beaming at the result. Good show.

Thanks to Claudette Moore and Ann Jaroncyk, at Moore Literary Agency, the best agents a scribbler ever had.

Once again, Guy Wells has done yeoman work, with his fabulous UK-centric Media Center screen shots.

And, a particular thanks to the folks at Asus, who loaned me an Eee netbook running a full-fledged copy of Windows 7 Ultimate. I could hardly believe my eyes.

Publisher's Acknowledgments

We're proud of this book; please send us your comments at `http://dummies.custhelp.com`. For other comments, please contact our Customer Care Department within the U.S. at 877-762-2974, outside the U.S. at 317-572-3993, or fax 317-572-4002.

Some of the people who helped bring this book to market include the following:

Acquisitions and Editorial

Project Editor: Rebecca Huehls

Acquisitions Editor: Amy Fandrei

Copy Editor: Rebecca Whitney

Technical Editor: Kit Malone

Editorial Manager: Leah P. Cameron

Sr. Editorial Assistant: Cherie Case

Cartoons: Rich Tennant (`www.the5thwave.com`)

Composition Services

Project Coordinator: Katherine Crocker

Layout and Graphics: Ana Carrillo, Samantha K. Cherolis, Reuben W. Davis, Joyce Haughey, Melissa K. Jester, Christin Swinford, Ronald Terry

Proofreaders: Caitie Copple, John Greenough, Shannon Ramsey

Indexer: BIM Indexing & Proofreading Services

Special Help

Barry Childs-Helton, Jodi Jensen, and Elizabeth Kuball

Publishing and Editorial for Technology Dummies

Richard Swadley, Vice President and Executive Group Publisher

Andy Cummings, Vice President and Publisher

Mary Bednarek, Executive Acquisitions Director

Mary C. Corder, Editorial Director

Publishing for Consumer Dummies

Diane Graves Steele, Vice President and Publisher

Composition Services

Debbie Stailey, Director of Composition Services

Contents at a Glance

Table of Contents

Book VIII: Using Other Hardware 771

Chapter 1: Finding and Installing the Hardware You Need 773

Chapter 2: Using Device Stage 799

Chapter 3: Printing (Almost) Effortlessly 811

Index 825

Introduction

Welcome to *Windows 7 All-in-One For Dummies* — the no-bull, one-stop Windows 7 reference for the rest of us.

Step right up to the ab-so-lute-ly best-est Windows ever! Gorgeous graphics! Stranglehold security! Unsurpassed productivity! Audacious applications! And the greatest-est compatibility Windows has ever seen.

Ah, Phineas Barnum would've been proud.

Microsoft has been touting all those supposed improvements in the latest version of Windows for years: "seamless" graphics (whatever that means); rock-solid security (in yer dreams, Redmond); leaps and bounds in productivity enhancements (ever try to remove Antivirus 2009?); and peaceful coexistence with older hardware and programs (yeah, sure). Sometimes I think that the Microsoft marketing droids ran a global search-and-replace operation on their old ad copy, turning the term *Windows 98* or *Windows NT* into *Windows 7*.

Every version of Windows gets a little better than the preceding version. Usually. (Okay, we won't talk about Windows Me — or Vista. Yes, Vista draws a Bronx cheer in most circles. I said *usually*, eh?) But this time it looks like Microsoft has come up with a somewhat better-looking, marginally more secure, and substantially more compatible improvement on its previous version of Windows.

That's not all. In Windows 7, the search function *works* — which is more than I can say about Vista or XP. The Windows 7 backup program is worthy of the term *backup*. Networking — after you get used to strange new concepts such as HomeGroups — works better than Vista, and significantly better than XP.

Microsoft giveth and Microsoft taketh away. Vista victims, er, users may be surprised to discover that Windows 7 dumps the Windows Sidebar, which was once touted as one of the major reasons to upgrade from XP to Vista: All the old Sidebar functions now take place on the desktop itself, *in flagrante delicto*. The Windows Meeting Space in Vista bit the big bit bucket. And, a whole passel (I think that's the word for it) of old Windows applications have been yanked from the *corpus Windowi*, heart still beating, and cast out on the Net. There, you can find the as-yet-undead Windows Live Essentials and reunite them with Windows itself. Or not.

To many people — me included — Windows 7 is what Vista should've been.

Lest you think I've turned into Windows Fanboy 7.0, I readily admit that Windows 7 harbors a host of problems. Microsoft continues to rub me the wrong way, with its courtroom and regulatory shenanigans and vile business practices. I hate digital rights management, and I detest the way Windows 7 makes my life more difficult than it should be. Some of my old hardware doesn't work with Windows 7, either. I feel your pain.

But when you get right down to it, Windows 7 is a towering achievement, a more-than-worthy successor to all the Windows that have come before. It's literally awesome.

About This Book

Windows 7 All-in-One For Dummies takes you through the Land of the Dummies — with introductory material and stuff your grandmother could (and should!) understand — and then continues the journey into more advanced areas, where you can truly put Windows to work every day. I don't dwell on technical mumbo jumbo, and I keep the baffling jargon to a minimum. At the same time, though, I tackle the tough problems you're likely to encounter, show you the major road signs, and give you a lot of help where you need it the most.

Whether you want to set up a quick, easy, reliable network in your home office or publish provocative photos of your Boykin Spaniel on the Web, this is your book. Er, I should say *eight* books. I've broken out the topics into eight different minibooks, so you'll find it easy to hop around to a topic — and a level of coverage — that feels comfortable.

I didn't design this book to be read from front to back. It's a reference. Each chapter, and each of its sections, is meant to focus on solving a particular problem or describing a specific technique.

Windows 7 All-in-One For Dummies should be your reference of first resort, even before you consult Windows Help and Support. There's a big reason why: Windows Help was written by hundreds of people over the course of many, many years. Some of the material was written ages ago, and it's confusing as all get-out, but it's still in Windows Help for folks who are tackling tough "legacy" problems. Some of the Help file terminology is inconsistent and downright misleading, largely because the technology has changed so much since some of the articles were written. Finding help in Help frequently boggles my mind: If I don't already know the answer to a question, it's hard to figure out how to coax Help to help. The proverbial bottom line: I don't duplicate the material in Windows 7 Help and Support, but I point to it if I figure it can help you.

Conventions

I try to keep typographical conventions to a minimum:

- The first time a buzzword appears in text, I italicize it and define it immediately. That makes it easier for you to glance back and reread the definition.
- Whenever I want you to type something, I put the letters or words in bold. For example: "Type **William Gates** in the Name text box." If you need to press more than one key at a time on the keyboard, I add a plus sign between the keys' names; for example, "Press Ctrl+Alt+Delete to initiate a Vulcan Mind Meld."
- I set off Web addresses and e-mail addresses in monospace. For example, my e-mail address is `woody@AskWoody.com` (true fact), and my Web site is at `AskWoody.com` (another true fact). You may be accustomed to seeing Web addresses (commonly known as URLs) spelled out in their entirety, such as `http://www.dummies.com`. Mercifully, some printed media drop the (completely superfluous) `http://` and the most progressive printed sources drop the `www`. That's the convention you see in this book: I write `dummies.com` instead of `http://www.dummies.com`. If you type `dummies.com` into your Web browser and it comes back with `http://ww9.redirect.dummies.com/index.asp?lang=en,source=ohmy`, don't be too surprised, OK? Computers talk funny.

There's one other convention, though, that I use all the time: I always, absolutely, adamantly include the filename extension — the period and (usually) three letters at the end of a filename, such as `.doc` or `.vbs` or `.exe` — when talking about a file. Yeah, I know Windows 7 hides filename extensions by default, but you can and should change that setting. Yeah, I realize that Bill G. himself made the decision to hide the extensions and that Steve B. won't back off. (At least, that's the rumor.)

I also know that, years ago, hundreds — probably thousands — of *Microsoft employees* passed along the ILOVEYOU virus, primarily because they couldn't see the filename extension that would've warned them that the file was a virus. Uh, bad decision, Bill.

(If you haven't yet told Windows 7 to show you filename extensions, click the Start icon — the circle in the lower-left corner of the screen — and pick Documents. Press the Alt key on your keyboard. Choose Tools⇨Folder Options; then click to select the View tab. At the bottom of the Advanced Settings box, deselect the option marked Hide Extensions for Known File Types. Click OK, and then click the X (Close) button to close the Documents folder. [Sometimes I just say "X out of the dialog box."] For full details, take a gander at Book II, Chapter 1.)

What You Don't Have to Read

Throughout this book, I've gone to great lengths to separate "optional" reading from "required" reading. If you want to find out more about a topic or solve a specific problem, follow along in the main part of the text. You can skip the icons and sidebars as you go, unless one happens to catch your eye.

On the other hand, if you know a topic pretty well but want to make sure that you caught all the high points, read the paragraphs marked with icons and be sure that the information registers. If it doesn't, glance at the surrounding text.

Sidebars stand as "graduate courses" for those who are curious about a specific topic — or who stand knee-deep in muck, searching for a way out.

Foolish Assumptions

I don't make many assumptions about you, dear reader, except to acknowledge that you're obviously intelligent, well-informed, discerning, and of impeccable taste. That's why you chose this book, eh?

Okay, okay. The least I can do is butter you up a bit. Here's the straight scoop: If you've never used Windows, bribe your neighbor (or, better, your neighbor's kids) to teach you how to do three things:

- ✦ Play Solitaire.
- ✦ Get on the Web.
- ✦ Shut down Windows and make your PC sleep.

That covers it. If you can play Solitaire, you know how to turn on your computer, use the Start button, click, drag, and double-click. After you're on the Web, well, heaven help us all. And, if you know that you need to click the Start icon to stop, you're well on your way to achieving Dummy Enlightenment.

And *that* begins with Book I, Chapter 1.

Another assumption worth noting relates to the six versions of Windows 7. Yes, six. (I have the lowdown in Book I, Chapter 3.) One version is only for "emerging" countries (the Upper West Side?), and one is only available preinstalled on oh-so-incredibly-cute netbooks (see Book I, Chapter 1). One is available only by bulk licensing — typically, to large companies. That leaves three versions — Home Premium, Professional, and Ultimate — that most people need to think about (not counting the various European flavors, which may wax and wane depending on the negotiating capabilities of the Microsoft lawyers).

Most of this book is written for Windows 7 Home Premium. When a particular feature appears in Professional or Ultimate, but doesn't appear in Vista Home Premium, I don't tag the difference with an icon. Instead, I mention that fact loud and clear. If you find a feature that you can't wait to try, make sure that your version of Windows 7 supports it before you get carried away.

Organization

Windows 7 All-in-One For Dummies contains eight minibooks, each of which gives a thorough airing of a specific topic. If you're looking for information on a specific Windows topic, check the headings in the Table of Contents or refer to the index.

By design, this book enables you to get as much (or as little) information as you need at any particular moment. Want to know how to jimmy your Minesweeper score to amaze your boss and confound your co-workers? Look at Book III, Chapter 4. Want to activate the Windows 7 outbound firewall? Read why you shouldn't even try, in Book VI, Chapter 3. Also by design, *Windows 7 All-in-One For Dummies* is a reference that you will reach for again and again whenever a new question about Windows comes up.

Here's a description of the eight minibooks and what they contain:

Book I, Cranking Up Windows 7: With apologies to Dante, this book tells you what Windows can and can't do, and what's inside a PC and how Windows controls it. Do you truly need Windows 7? If you already know how to use Windows XP or Vista, what do you need to know about Windows 7? Which of the (many) versions is right for you? How do you upgrade? How do you find and install the missing Windows Live Essentials?

Book II, Windows 7 Boot Camp: Read this minibook to find out how to make Windows 7 work right whenever you add users (with a particular nod to security and the User Account Control bugaboo), manipulate files, use the Windows taskbar and shortcuts, make backups, and get help. I tell you all about the care and feeding of hard drives, how to burn CDs from Windows itself, and how to use the built-in applications for word processing and image manipulation.

Book III, Customizing Windows 7: Book III deals with fun stuff on your desktop: getting gadgets, using Glass, personalizing the desktop (with themes, colors, backgrounds, and the like), choosing mouse pointers, selecting screen savers, changing the Start menu, using the "super" taskbar, running searches easily and effectively, and beating the built-in Windows games. (Yeah, I know that's why you bought this book.)

Book IV, Joining the Multimedia Mix: Become aware of any Windows Media Player tricks and traps, and find out how to rip material from audio CDs and burn your own CDs and DVDs in Media Player. This minibook tells you how to capture Windows Media streams, mentions digital licensing, and describes what you can do to thwart encroaching Microsoft lockdowns. Discover how to handle iTunes and your iPod in a Windows 7 world, and find out about Windows Movie Maker, digital cameras, camcorders, and other video devices. Also, I tell you how to "unshake" your movies, set up Media Center, convert file formats, and use the essential Photo Gallery.

Book V, Windows 7 and the Internet: In Book V, I tell you why you need broadband, and I describe how to log in to your computer from the Internet, using Internet Explorer, Firefox, or Chrome. Find out how to get the most from your RSS feeds, how to search effectively on the Internet, and how to use Windows Live Mail. I also explain how to make cheap or free phone calls and Webcam calls with Windows Live Messenger.

Book VI, Securing Windows 7: Take a look at the Action Center, and then find out how to control the User Account Control and Windows Firewall, and use Windows Defender and its big missing piece. Get the scoop on letting Windows Update work automatically (or not!) and know when to avoid it. Get virus protection — free. I tell you what the bad guys already know and what you can do about it.

Book VII, Networking with Windows 7: Find out how to attach your computer to any network, anywhere. Get basic information about domains, workgroups, and the new HomeGroups. I describe the concepts behind peer-to-peer and client/server networking and tell you how to build your own network quickly, easily, and reliably. I discuss Wi-Fi and other ethereal wireless topics, and I tell you how to protect your network and your privacy.

Book VIII, Using Other Hardware: In this minibook, I throw a ton of items at you (not literally, of course): internal and external devices, cameras, scanners, printers, audio, memory, USB key drives, monitors, hard drives, and more. I also tell you how to choose the right products and get them to work. I tell you all about DeviceStage.

Icons

Some of the points in *Windows 7 All-in-One For Dummies* merit your special attention. I set off those points with icons.

When I'm jumping up and down on one foot with an idea so absolutely cool that I can't stand it any more, I stick a Tip icon in the margin. You can browse any chapter and hit its highest points by jumping from Tip to Tip.

Psst. Want to know the real story — not the stuff that the Microsoft marketing droids want you to hear but, rather, the kind of information that gives you some insight into this lumbering beast in Redmond? You see it all next to this icon, and on my eponymous Web site.

You don't need to memorize the information marked with this icon, but you should try to remember that something special is lurking.

Achtung! Cuidado! Thar be tygers here! Anywhere that you see a Warning icon, you can be sure that I've been burnt — badly. Mind your fingers. These are really, *really* mean suckers.

Okay, so I'm a geek. I admit it. Sure, I love to poke fun at geeks. But I'm a modern, New Age, sensitive guy, in touch with my inner geekiness. Sometimes, I just can't help but let it out, ya know? That's where the Technical Stuff icon comes in. If you get all tied up in knots about techie-type stuff, pass these paragraphs by. (For the record, I managed to write this whole book without telling you that an IP address consists of a unique 32-bit combination of network ID and host ID, expressed as a set of four decimal numbers with each octet separated by periods. See? I can restrain myself sometimes.)

Where to Go from Here

That's about it. It's time for you to crack this book open and have at it.

Don't forget to bookmark my Web site: `www.AskWoody.com`. It keeps you up-to-date on all the Windows 7 news you need to know — including notes about this book, the latest Windows bugs and gaffes, patches that are worse than the problems they're supposed to fix, and much more — and you can submit your most pressing questions, for free consultation from The Woodmeister hisself.

See ya! `woody@AskWoody.com`

Sometimes it's worth reading the Intro, eh?

Book I
Cranking Up Windows 7

"I really think the Home Basic version will work fine for you. Besides, there is no Yurt Basic version of Windows 7."

Contents at a Glance

Chapter 1: Windows 7 4 N00bs

In This Chapter

- **A newbie's quick guide**
- **Hardware is hard — and software is hard, too**
- **Windows' place in the grand scheme of things**
- **Those computer words that all the grade-schoolers understand**
- **Buying a Windows 7 computer**

Don't sweat it. We all started out as n00bs ("newbies").

All those high-falutin' technical words you have to memorize, eh?

So you're sitting in front of your computer and this thing called Windows 7 is staring at you. If more than one person is set up to use your computer, the screen you see — the one with the people's names on it — is a *Welcome screen,* but it doesn't say "Welcome" or "Howdy" or even "Sit down and get to work, Bucko." It has names and pictures only for people who can use the computer. Why do you have to click your name? What if your name isn't there? And why in the %$#@! can't you bypass all this garbage, log on, and get your e-mail?

Good for you. That's the right attitude.

Windows 7 ranks as the most sophisticated computer program ever made. It cost more money to develop and took more people to build than any previous computer program — ever. So why is it so blasted hard to use? Why doesn't it do what you want it to do the first time? For that matter, why do you need it at all?

Someday, I swear, you'll be able to pull a PC out of the box and plug it into the wall, turn it on, and get your e-mail — bang, bang, bang, just like that, in ten seconds flat. In the meantime, those of us who are stuck in the early 21st century have to make do with PCs that grow obsolete before you can unpack them, software that's so ornery you find yourself arguing with it, and Internet connections that surely involve turtles carrying bits on their backs.

If you aren't comfortable working with Windows and you still worry that you might break something if you click the wrong button, welcome to the club! In this chapter, I try to present a concise, school-of-hard-knocks overview of how all this hangs together, and what to look for when buying a Windows

PC. It may help you understand why and how Windows has limitations. It also may help you communicate with the geeky rescue team that tries to bail you out, whether you rely on the store that sold you the PC, the smelly guy in the apartment downstairs, or your eight-year-old daughter's nerdy classmate.

Hardware and Software

At the most fundamental level, all computer stuff comes in one of two flavors: hardware or software. *Hardware* is anything you can touch — a computer screen, a mouse, a CD. *Software* is everything else: e-mail messages, that letter to your Aunt Martha, digital pictures of your last vacation, programs like Microsoft Office. If you have a roll of film developed and put on a CD, the shiny, round CD is hardware — you can touch it — but the pictures themselves are software. Get the difference?

Windows 7 is software. You can't touch it. Your PC, on the other hand, is hardware. Kick the computer screen and your toe hurts. Drop the big box on the floor and it smashes into a gazillion pieces. That's hardware.

Chances are very good that one of the major PC manufacturers — Dell, Acer, HP/Compaq, IBM/Lenovo, Toshiba, or ASUS, for example — made your hardware. Microsoft, and Microsoft alone, makes Windows 7. The PC manufacturers don't make Windows. Microsoft doesn't make PCs, although it does make other kinds of hardware — video game boxes, keyboards, mice, and a few other odds and ends.

When you bought your computer, you paid for a license to use one copy of Windows on the PC you bought. The PC manufacturer paid Microsoft a royalty so that it could sell you Windows along with your PC. You may think that you got Windows from, say, Dell — indeed, you may have to contact Dell for technical support on Windows questions — but, in fact, Windows came from Microsoft.

Most software these days, most definitely including Windows 7, ask you to agree to an End User License Agreement. When you first set up your PC, Windows asked you to click a button labeled I Accept to accept a licensing agreement that's long enough to wrap around the Empire State Building. If you're curious about what agreement you accepted, a printed copy of the End User License Agreement (EULA) is in the box that your PC came in or in the CD packaging, if you bought Windows 7 separately from your computer.

If you can't find your copy of the EULA, here's how to retrieve it (and, at the same time, gain some experience in using the instructions in this book and in finding your way around the Windows Help system, which I talk about in Book II, Chapter 5):

1. **Click the big, round button in the lower-left corner of your screen.**

   I call that button the Start button because way back in the days of Windows XP, it bore the word *Start.* If you hover your mouse above the circle, a little box appears that says *Start,* too. You can call it an *orb,* if you like. I can think of several less-polite alternatives.

2. **On the right, at the bottom, click Help and Support.**

   The Windows Help and Support center springs into view.

3. **Type** eula **in the Search text box and press Enter (see Figure 1-1).**

   Windows shows you one or more results for your inquiry.

4. **Click the Read the Microsoft Software License Terms link.**

   Windows displays the EULA that you agreed to, back in your younger and more naïve days.

Now you know whom to blame, for sure.

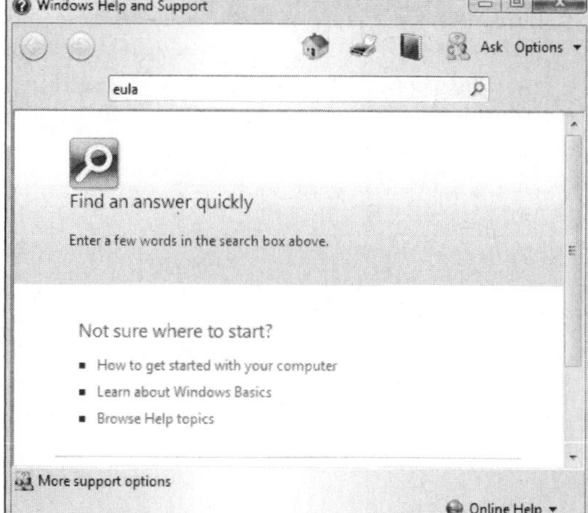

Figure 1-1: Recall what you agreed to in the End User License Agreement, or EULA.

Why Do PCs Have to Run Windows?

Here's the short answer: You don't have to run Windows on your PC.

The PC you have is a dumb box. (You needed me to tell you that, eh?) To get the dumb box to do anything worthwhile, you need a computer program that takes control of the PC and makes it do things such as show Web pages on the screen, respond to mouse clicks, or print résumés. An operating system controls the dumb box and makes it do worthwhile things, in ways that mere humans can understand.

Without an operating system, the computer can sit in a corner and count to itself or put profound messages on the screen, such as `Non-system disk or disk error. Insert system disk and press any key when ready.` If you want your computer to do more than that, though, you need an operating system.

Windows is not the only operating system in town.

Apple has made great strides running on Intel hardware, and if you don't already know how to use Windows or own a Windows computer, it makes a great deal of sense to consider buying an Apple computer and/or running Mac OS.

The big up-and-coming operating system, which has been up and coming for a couple of decades now, is Linux, which is pronounced "LIN-uchs." It's a viable contender for netbooks (covered in more depth at the end of this chapter). If you expect to use your PC only to get on the Internet — to surf the Web and send e-mail from the likes of your Gmail or Hotmail account — Linux can handle all that, and can do it with few of the headaches that remain as the hallmark of Windows. By using free programs such as Open Office and online programs like Google Docs (`docs.google.com`), you can even cover the basics in word processing, spreadsheets, presentations, contact managers, calendars, and more. Linux may not support the huge array of hardware that Windows offers — but more than a few wags will tell you, with a wink, that Windows doesn't support that huge array, either.

What do other people choose? It's hard to measure the percentage of PCs running Windows versus Mac versus Linux. One company, Net Applications, specializes in inspecting the online records of big-name Web sites and tallying how many Windows computers hit those sites, compared to Apple and Linux. Although the numbers are changing, Windows accounts for about 90 percent of all hits on major Web sites, Mac runs about 10 percent, and Linux kinda picks up the crumbs.

A Terminology Survival Kit

Some terms pop up so frequently that you'll find it worthwhile to memorize them, or at least understand where they come from. That way, you won't be caught flat-footed when your first-grader comes home and asks whether he can download a program from the Internet.

If you want to drive your techie friends nuts the next time you have a problem with your computer, tell them that the hassles occur when you're "running Microsoft." They won't have any idea whether you mean Windows, Word, Outlook, Live Messenger, Live Search, Defender, Media Center, or any of a gazillion other programs.

A *program* is *software* (see the first section in this chapter) that works on a computer. Windows, the *operating system* (see the second section), is a program. So are computer games, Microsoft Office, Microsoft Word (the word processor part of Office), Internet Explorer (the Web browser in Windows), Windows Media Player, those nasty viruses you've heard about, that screen saver with the oh-too-perfect fish bubbling and bumbling about, and others.

A special kind of program called a *driver* makes specific pieces of hardware work with the operating system. For example, your computer's printer has a driver, your monitor has a driver, your mouse has a driver, and Tiger Woods has a driver (several, actually, and he makes a living with them). Would that we were all so talented.

When you stick a program on your computer — and set it up so that it works — you *install* the program.

When you crank up a program — that is, get it going on your computer — you can say you *started* it, *launched* it, *ran* it, or *executed* it. They all mean the same thing.

If the program quits the way it's supposed to, you can say it *stopped, finished, ended, exited,* or *terminated.* Again, all these terms mean the same thing. If the program stops with some sort of weird error message, you can say it *crashed, died, cratered, croaked, went belly up,* or *GPFed* (techspeak for "generated a General Protection Fault" — don't ask), or employ any of a dozen colorful but unprintable epithets. If the program just sits there and you can't get it to do anything, you can say the program *froze, hung, stopped responding,* or *went into a loop.*

And then you have wizards. Windows comes with lots of 'em. *Wizards* guide you through complex procedures, moving one step at a time. Typically, wizards have three directional buttons on each screen: Back, Next (or Finish), and Cancel. Wizards remember what you've chosen as you move from step to step, making it easy to experiment a bit, change your mind, back up, and try a different setting, without getting all the check boxes confused.

A *bug* is something that doesn't work right. (A bug is not a virus! Viruses work as intended far too often.) US Navy Rear Admiral Grace Hopper — the intellectual guiding force behind COBOL and one of the pioneers in the history of computing — often repeated the story of a moth being found in a relay of an ancient Mark II computer. The moth was taped into the technician's logbook on September 9, 1947, with the annotation "1545 Relay #70 Panel F (moth) in relay. First actual case of bug being found."

The people who invented all this terminology think of the Internet as being some great blob in the sky — it's *up*, as in "up in the sky." So if you send something from your computer to the Internet, you're *uploading.* If you take something off the Internet and put it on your computer, you're *downloading.*

When you put computers together, you *network* them, and if your network doesn't use wires, it's *wireless*. At the heart of a network sits a box, commonly called a *hub* or a *router*, that computers can plug into. If the hub has rabbit ears on top, for wireless connections, it's usually called a *wireless router*. Yes, there are fine lines of distinction among all these terms. No, you don't need to worry about them. Book VII is your guide to networking.

If your Internet connection runs faster than a tortoise, you probably have broadband, which may run via *DSL* or *ADSL* over the phone lines or via *cable* (as in cable TV) or *satellite*. The DSL, cable, or satellite box is commonly called a modem, although it's really a router. In Book V, you find out more about going online with Windows 7.

Turning to the dark side of the force, Luke, the distinctions among *viruses*, *worms*, and *Trojans* grow more blurry every day. In general, they're programs that replicate and can be harmful, and the worst ones blend different approaches. *Spyware* gathers information about you and then phones home with all the juicy details. *Adware* gets in yer face, all too frequently installing itself on your computer without your knowledge or consent. I tend to lump the two together and call them *scumware* or *crapware* or something a bit more descriptive and less printable.

If a bad guy (and they're almost always guys) manages to take over your computer without your knowledge, turning it into a zombie that spews spam by remote control, you're in a *botnet*. (And yes, the term *spam* comes from the immortal Monty Python routine that's set in a café serving Hormel's SPAM luncheon meat, the chorus bellowing "lovely Spam, wonderful Spam.") Check out Book VI for details about preventing scumware and the like from messing with you.

The most successful botnets employ *rootkits* — programs that run "underneath" Windows, evading detection because normal programs, such as your antivirus program or Microsoft Security Essentials, can't see them. Rootkits rate as the wave of the future because they're hard to find and hard to remove and the person controlling a rootkit-based botnet can charge ungodly amounts of money to people who want to use the services of the botnet to distribute spam, collect data, ping the living daylights out of a Web site, or distribute even more malware.

Although it's true that some rootkits run on Vista PCs, and Windows 7 PCs are likely to be infected soon, the majority by far subvert Windows XP machines. It's considerably more difficult for a bad guy to get a rootkit installed on a Windows 7 or Vista machine than on one running XP, and keeping the rootkit's activities in the dark rates as a first-class pain. If you have Windows 7, be cautious about rootkits (see Book VI), but don't be overly paranoid. Yet.

This section should cover about 90 percent of the buzzwords you hear in common parlance. If you get stuck at a party where the bafflegab is flowing freely, don't hesitate to invent your own words. Nobody will ever know the difference.

Buying a Windows 7 Computer

Here's how it usually goes: You figure that you need to buy a new PC, so you spend a couple of weeks brushing up on the details — bits and bytes and kilobytes and megabytes and gigabytes — and comparison shopping. You end up at your local Computers Were Us shop, and the guy behind the counter convinces you that the absolutely best bargain you'll ever see is sitting right here, right now, and you'd better take it quick before somebody else nabs it.

Your eyes glaze over as you look at yet another spec sheet and try to figure out one last time whether a RAM is a ROM, how fast hard drive platters spin, and whether you need a SATA, SATA I, or SATA II. In the end, you figure that the guy behind the counter must know what he's doing, so you plunk down your plastic and pray you got a good deal.

The next Sunday morning, you look in the paper and discover you could've bought twice as much machine for half as much money. The only thing you know for sure is that your PC is hopelessly out of date, and the next time you'll be smarter about the whole process.

If that describes your experiences, relax. It happens to everybody. Take solace in the fact that you bought twice as much machine for the same amount of money as the poor schmuck who went through the same process last month.

Here's everything you need to know about buying a Windows 7 PC:

✦ **Comparison shop by using the Windows Experience Index.**

  The *Windows Experience Index* is a tool that takes a look at your computer components and then spits out a number that tells you how wonderful your Windows experience will be. Although the Windows Experience Index (see Figure 1-2) has its faults, it's an easily accessible, relatively unbiased measure of performance that should help you accurately size up a new computer. See Book II, Chapter 4 for details.

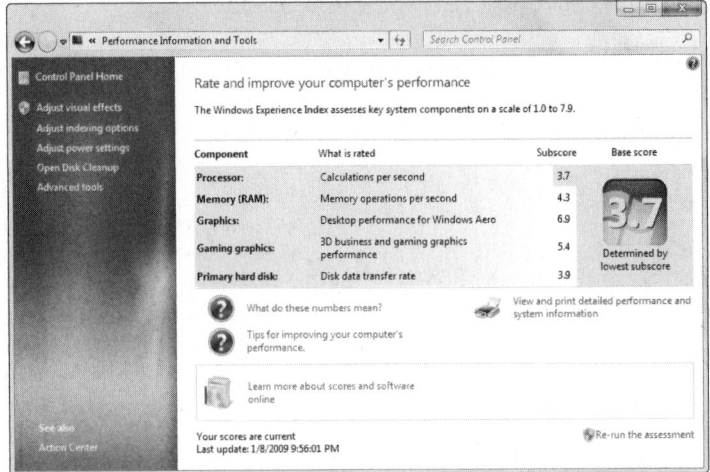

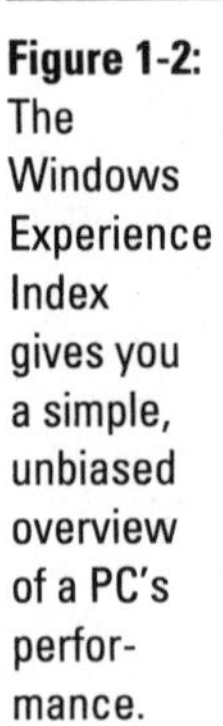
Figure 1-2: The Windows Experience Index gives you a simple, unbiased overview of a PC's performance.

- **Buy at least 2GB of memory.**

  Four gigabytes may be overkill. The section that talks about choosing 32 bits versus 64 bits is in Book I, Chapter 3.

- **Get a high-quality monitor, a solid keyboard, and a mouse that feels comfortable.**

  Corollary: Don't buy a computer online unless you know for a fact that your fingers will like the keyboard, your wrist will tolerate the mouse, and your eyes will fall in love with the monitor.

- **Go overboard with hard disk space.**

  It's cheap. You'll run through a terabyte (1,024GB) faster than you think, especially if you collect music, own a video camera, or record TV shows. Windows 7 itself swallows up 10 to 14GB or so — more if you install Windows Live Essentials (see Book I, Chapter 5).

- **Everything else they try to sell ya pales in comparison.**

If you want to spend more money, go for a faster Internet connection and a better chair. You need both items much more than you need a marginally faster computer.

In this section, I try to give you just enough information about the inner workings of your PC that you can figure out what you have to do with Windows. The details can change from week to week, but these are the basics.

Pay more to get a clean PC

I hate it when the computer I want comes loaded with all that nice, "free" crapware. I would seriously consider paying more to get a clean computer.

You don't need an antivirus and Internet security program preinstalled on your new PC. It'll just open and beg for money next month. And when you try to uninstall the program (I won't mention Norton by name), all the little bits and pieces stick around. You can get excellent antivirus protection for free — see Book VI, Chapter 5.

Browser toolbars? Puh-lease.

You can choose your own Internet service provider. AOL? Earthlink? Who needs ya?

And trialware? Whether it's Quicken or Office or any of a zillion other programs, if you have to pay for a preinstalled program in three months or six months, you don't want it. If you're looking for a new computer but can't find an option to buy a PC without all the "extras," look elsewhere. The big PC companies are slowly getting a clue, but until they clean up their act, you may be better served buying from a smaller retailer, who hasn't yet pre-sold every bit that isn't nailed down.

Inside the big box

The big box that your computer lives in is sometimes called a CPU, meaning central processing unit (see Figure 1-3). Right off the bat, you're bound to get confused, unless somebody clues you in on one important detail: The main computer chip inside that big box is *also* called a CPU. I prefer to call the big box "the PC" because of the naming ambiguity, but you have probably thought of a few better names.

Figure 1-3: The big box.

Courtesy of Dell, Inc.

The big box contains many parts and pieces (and no small amount of dust and dirt), but the crucial, central element inside every PC is the motherboard (see Figure 1-4).

You find the following items attached to the motherboard:

- **The processor, or CPU:** This gizmo does the main computing. It's probably from Intel or AMD or one of their competitors. Different manufacturers rate their CPUs in different ways. If you want to compare performance, at least to a first approximation, look at the Windows Experience Index for processor performance (refer to Figure 1-2).
- **Memory chips and places to put them:** Memory is measured in megabytes (1MB = 1,024K = 1,048,576 characters) and gigabytes (1GB = 1,024MB). Although Windows 7 can run on a machine with 512MB (I've done it), Microsoft recommends a minimum of 1GB. Unless you have an exciting cornfield to watch grow while Windows 7 saunters along, aim for 2GB or more. (See the section about choosing 32-bit versus 64-bit in Book I, Chapter 3.) Most computers allow you to add more memory to them, and boosting your computer's memory to 2GB from 1GB makes the machine much snappier, especially if you run memory hogs such as Office, PageMaker, or Photoshop. If you leave Outlook open and work with it all day and run almost any other major program at the same time, 2GB isn't overkill.

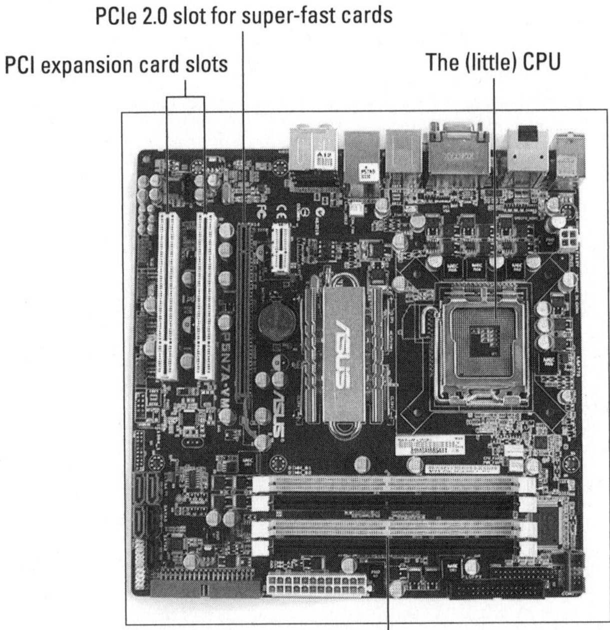

Figure 1-4: The motherboard sits in the middle of it all.

Courtesy ASUSTeK Computer Inc.

✦ **Video chipset:** Most motherboards include a built-in rudimentary video capability, which can be adequate if your video demands rarely rise above the mundane. Now that one of the major motherboard manufacturers — AMD — has acquired one of the major video chip manufacturers — ATI — we should see much more powerful video capabilities built into the motherboard itself. If you want more video oomph, you have to buy a video card and put it in a card slot.

✦ **Card slots (also known as expansion slots):** Laptops have very limited (if any) expansion slots on the motherboard. Desktops generally contain several expansion slots. Modern slots come in two flavors: PCI and PCI-Express (also known as PCIe or PCI-E). Most expansion cards use PCI, but very fast cards — including, notably, video cards — require PCIe. Of course, PCI cards don't fit in PCIe slots, and vice versa. To make things more confusing, PCIe comes in three sizes — literally, the size of the bracket and the number of bumps on the bottoms of the cards are different. The PCIe 1x is smallest, the relatively uncommon PCIe 4x is considerably larger, and PCIe 16x is just a little bit bigger than an old-fashioned PCI slot (refer to Figure 1-4). Most video cards these days require a PCIe x16 slot.

PCIe 2.0 runs twice as fast as the original PCIe. Fortunately, the cards are backward- and forward-compatible: You can run a PCIe 2.0 card in a PCIe 1.1 slot and vice versa. A new PCIe 3.0 standard is waiting in the wings, although the details weren't firm when this book went to press.

Don't get hung up on the alphabet soup, but avoid the older AGP standard. Windows 7 makes video cards work hard, and PCIe video cards invariably give you the best bang for the buck — or ruble.

✦ **Lots of other stuff:** You never have to play with this other stuff, unless you're very unlucky.

Here are a few upgrade dos and don'ts:

✦ **Don't** let a salesperson talk you into eviscerating your PC and upgrading the CPU: A 3.0 GHz PC doesn't run a whole lot faster than a 2.4 GHz PC, and a dual-quad-core ChipDuoTrioQuattroQuinto stuck in an old motherboard doesn't run much faster than your original slowpoke.

✦ When you hit 2GB in main memory, **don't** expect big performance improvements by adding more memory.

✦ On the other hand, if you have an older video card, **do** consider upgrading it to a faster card, or to one with 256MB or more memory. Windows 7 soaks it up.

✦ Rather than nickel-and-dime yourself to death on little upgrades, **do** wait until you can afford a new PC, and give away your old one.

If you decide to add memory, have the company that sells you the memory install it. The process is simple, quick, and easy — if you know what you're doing. Having the dealer install the memory also puts the monkey on his back if a memory chip doesn't work or a bracket snaps.

Screening

The *computer monitor* or *screen* — and LCD and plasma TVs — use technology that's quite different from old-fashioned television circuitry from your childhood. A traditional TV scans lines across the screen from left to right, with hundreds of them stacked on top of each other. Colors on each individual line vary all over the place. The almost infinitely variable color on an old-fashioned TV combined with a comparatively small number of lines makes for pleasant, but fuzzy, pictures.

By contrast (pun absolutely intended, of course), computer monitors and plasma and LCD TVs work with dots of light called *pixels.* Each pixel can have a different color, created by tiny, colored gizmos sitting next to each other. As a result, the picture displayed on computer monitors (and plasma and LCD TVs) is much sharper than on conventional TV tubes.

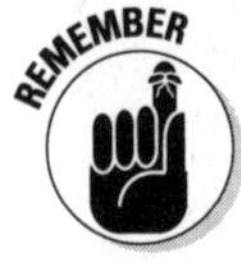

The more pixels you can cram on a screen — that is, the higher the *screen resolution* — the more information you can pack on the screen. That's important if you commonly have more than one word processing document open at a time, for example. At a resolution of 800 x 600, two open Word documents placed side by side look big but fuzzy, like caterpillars viewed through a dirty magnifying glass. At 1280 x 1024, those same two documents look sharp, but the text may be so small that you have to squint to read it. If you move up to wide-screen territory — 1680 x 1050 or even 1920 x 1200 — with a good monitor, two documents side-by-side look stunning.

A special-purpose computer called a *graphics processor* (or *GPU*), stuck on your video card, creates everything that's shown on your computer's screen. The GPU has to juggle all the pixels and all the colors, so if you're a gaming fan, the speed of the GPU's chip (and, to a lesser extent, the speed of the monitor) can make the difference between a zapped alien and a lost energy shield. If you want to experience Windows 7 in all its glory, particularly the see-through Aero glass interface, you need a fast GPU with at least 128MB (and preferably 512MB) of its own memory.

Computer monitors are sold by size, measured diagonally, like TV sets. Just like with TV sets, the only way to pick a good computer screen over a run-of-the-mill one is to compare them side by side or to follow the recommendation of someone who has.

Managing disks and drives

Your PC's memory chips hold information only temporarily: Turn off the electricity, and the contents of main memory go bye-bye. If you want to reuse your work, keeping it around after the plug has been pulled, you have to save it, typically on a disk. The following list describes the most common types of disks and drives:

- **Floppy disk**: The 1.44MB floppy disk drives that were ubiquitous on PCs for many years have bitten the dust. You have little reason to buy one nowadays. But —
- **SD/xD/CF card memory**: Even now, long after the demise of floppy disks, many computer cases have drive bays built for them. Why not use the open spot for a multifunction card reader? That way, you can slip a memory card out of your digital camera (or your Dick Tracy wristwatch, for that matter) and transfer files at will. SD card, xD card, CompactFlash, memory stick — whatever you have — the multifunction readers cost a pittance and read almost everything, including minds.
- **Hard drive:** Get the biggest, cheapest drive (or drives) you can. Electronic pictures swallow up an enormous amount of space, and the average teenager's music collection can easily consume as much storage as the first mission to the moon. Although it's generally true that more expensive hard drives are more reliable than cheaper ones, objective numbers are hard to come by and individual results can vary.

  Given the ability to *cache* — temporarily and quickly store data in the controller on the drive itself — speed doesn't matter nearly as much as it used to, unless you're transferring enormous amounts of data. Almost all hard drives these days run SATA 3Gb/s (sometimes called, erroneously, SATA II), although SATA 6Gb/s is on the horizon.

  Don't be afraid to stick a hard drive in a box and plug the box into your computer via a USB cable or an external SATA (eSATA) connection. External hard drives run reasonably fast, and they can be picked up and moved on a whim — and they don't contribute to your computer's heating problems. Plus, Windows 7 is smart enough to recognize when an external hard drive is plugged into a PC and to step you through the process of using it to create a backup (see Book II, Chapter 3).
- **Solid state drive:** This item gets cheaper and cheaper. You probably won't see solid state drives gain much market share during the reign of Windows 7, but they're undeniably out there on the horizon and may someday supplant the old whirling dervish drive. Solid state drives feature low power consumption and give off less heat. They have no moving parts, so they don't wear out, like hard drives. And, if you drop a hard drive and a solid state drive off the Leaning Tower of Pisa, one of them may survive. Or maybe not.

- **CD, DVD, or Blu-ray drive:** Of course, these types of drives work with CDs, DVDs, and the Sony Blu-ray discs, which can be filled with data or contain music or movies. CDs hold about 700MB of data; DVDs hold 4GB, or six times as much as a CD. Dual-layer DVDs (which use two separate layers on top of the disc) hold about 8GB, and Blu-ray discs hold 50GB, or six times as much as a dual-layer DVD.

  Unless you want to stick a high-definition movie on a single disc or play Blu-ray discs that you buy or rent in your local video store, 50GB of data on a single disc is overkill. Someday, the price of Blu-ray drives and discs will come down out of the stratosphere, but at least for now most Windows 7 users will do quite well with a dual-layer DVD-RW drive. You can always use a dual-layer drive to record regular (single-layer) DVDs or CDs. If you're nervous about installing a new drive, add an external USB version: Windows 7 loves external DVD drives, and it tolerates external Blu-ray drives.

  Many older audio CD players — like the one you may have in your car or home stereo — can play only CDs that are burned once, using the ISO format (see Book II, Chapter 4). If you reburn the CD, it doesn't play, so for those machines stick to CD-Rs rather than reburnable CD-RWs.

- **USB flash drive:** Treat it like it's a lollipop. Half the size of a pack of gum and able to hold an entire PowerPoint presentation or two or six, flash memory (also known as a jump drive, thumb drive, or memory stick) should be your first choice for external storage space or for copying files between computers. Pop one of these guys in a USB slot (see the next section in this chapter), and suddenly Windows 7 knows it has another drive — except that this one's fast, portable, and incredibly easy to use. Go for the cheapest flash drives you can find: Most of the "features" on fancy key drives are just, uh, Windows dressing.

This list is by no means definitive: New storage options are coming out every day.

Making PC connections

Your PC connects to the outside world by using a bewildering variety of cables and connectors. The most common are described in this list:

- **USB (Universal Serial Bus) cable:** This cable has a flat connector that plugs into your PC. The other end is usually shaped like a D, but different pieces of hardware have different terminators. ("I'll be back . . . Hasta la vista, baby. . . .") USB is the connector of choice for just about any kind of hardware — printer, scanner, MP3 player, Palm or pocket computer, portable hard drive, and even the mouse. If you run out of USB connections on the back of your PC, get a USB hub with a separate power supply and plug away.

WARNING!

Avoid USB 1.1, the older and considerably slower version of USB. There are still some awful, cheap, and awfully cheap USB 1.1 hubs floating around. They wouldn't even make good boat anchors.

- **LAN cable:** Also known as a CAT-5, CAT-6, or RJ-45 cable, it's the most common kind of network connector. It looks like an overweight telephone plug (see Figure 1-5). One end plugs into your PC, typically into a network interface card (or NIC, pronounced "nick"), a network connector on the motherboard. The other end plugs into your network's hub (see Figure 1-6) or switch or into a cable modem, DSL box, router, or other Internet connection–sharing device.
- **Keyboard and mouse cable:** More and more mice and keyboards (even cordless mice and keyboards) come with USB connectors. That's too bad, really, because most computers don't have enough USB ports, and most do have old-fashioned, round PS/2 ports. You can take advantage of your computer's PS/2 ports, and reduce the demand for USB ports, by buying USB-to-PS/2 adapters (see Figure 1-7) and plugging both mouse and keyboard into their respective PS/2 slots on the computer.

Figure 1-5: LAN connectors.

Courtesy of CablesToGo.com

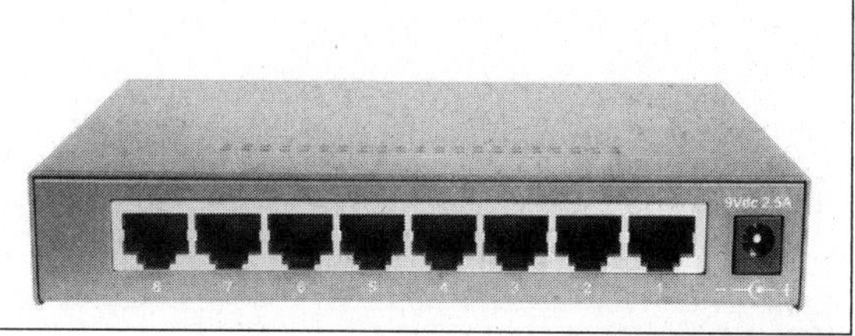

Figure 1-6: A network hub.

Courtesy of CablesToGo.com

✦ **DVI-D and HDMI connectors:** Although many older monitors still use legacy 15-pin HD15 VGA connectors, most monitors and video cards now use the DVI-D digital cable (see Figure 1-8). Given a choice, go with DVI-D: It's faster, and capable of delivering a much better picture. Some video cards and many TVs also support the small HDMI connector (see Figure 1-9), which transmits both audio and video over one cable. If you hope to hook up your new TV to your PC, consider getting a video card with an HDMI slot.

Figure 1-7: Convert your USB mouse and keyboard to use old-fashioned PS/2 ports.

Courtesy of CablesToGo.com

Figure 1-8: DVI-D has largely supplanted the old VGA video adapter.

Courtesy of CablesToGo.com

Figure 1-9: HDMI carries both audio and video signals.

Courtesy of CablesToGo.com

Old-fashioned serial (9-pin) and parallel (25-pin) cables are growing as scarce as hen's teeth. Hey, the hen doesn't need them, either.

Futzing with video, sound, and multitudinous media

Chances are pretty good that you're running Windows 7 on a PC with at least a little oomph in the audio department. In the simplest case, you have to be concerned about four specific sound jacks (or groups of sound jacks) because each one does something different. Your machine may not have all four (are you feeling inadequate yet?), or it may look like a patch board at a Korn concert, but the basics are still the same.

Here's how the four key jacks are usually marked, although sometimes you have to root around in the documentation to find the details:

- **Line In**: This stereo input jack is usually blue. It feeds a stereo audio signal — generally from an amplified source — into the PC. Use this jack to receive audio output into your computer from a cable box, TV set, radio, CD player, cassette player, electric guitar, or another audio-generating box.
- **Mic In:** This jack is usually pink. It's for unamplified sources, like most microphones or electric guitars. If you use a cheap microphone for Skype or another VoIP service that lets you talk long distance for free, plug in the microphone here. In a pinch, you can plug any of the Line In devices into the Mic In jack — but you may hear only mono sound, not stereo, and you may have to turn the volume way down to avoid some ugly distortion when the amplifier inside your PC increases the strength of an already-amplified signal.
- **Line Out:** A stereo output jack, usually lime green, that in many cases can be used for headphones or patched into powered speakers. If you don't have fancy output jacks (like the Sony-Philips SPDIF), this is the source for the highest-quality sound your computer can produce.
- **Rear Surround Out:** Usually black, this jack isn't used often. It's intended to be used if you have independent, powered rear speakers. Most people with rear speakers use the Line Out connector and plug it into their home theater systems, which then drives the rear speakers; or they use the HDMI cable (see preceding section) to hook up to their TVs.

Fancy sound cards can have full Dolby DTS or THX 5.1 output (that's left front, center front, right front, left surround, right surround, and a subwoofer). The 7.1 configuration uses two back surround speakers. Front panel output — where your sound card connects to jacks on the front of your PC, possibly a panel in a hard drive bay — makes connections easy. With a sufficiently bottomless budget, you can make your living room sound precisely like the 07L runway at LAX.

PC manufacturers love to extol the virtues of their advanced sound systems, but the simple fact is that you can hook up a rather plain-vanilla PC to a home stereo and get great sound. Just connect the Line Out jack on the back of your PC to the Aux In jack on your home stereo or entertainment center. Voilà!

Netbooks

I admit it. I'm hooked.

While writing this book, I managed to get an ASUS Eee PC 1000H netbook working with Windows 7 Ultimate — not the Starter edition, mind you, but rather the full-blown Ultimate version — and I love it. Several of the screen shots you see in this book were taken on the Eee PC 1000H (see Figure 1-10).

The combination of Windows 7 Ultimate and the Eee isn't sprightly, by any stretch of the imagination, and Windows turns off the Aero glass effect so that my window borders aren't transparent. I don't try to write books or balance the national debt with it. But while I'm performing normal netbook tasks — browsing the Web with Firefox, checking my e-mail on Gmail, dashing out a letter, or playing the occasional round of Minesweeper — Windows 7 does yeoman work in bringing all the features of the Eee to my fingertips, in a way that doesn't feel funny or foreign.

If you've ever considered buying a netbook but shied away because of performance or compatibility problems — and you just didn't want to learn how to use Linux — try a netbook running Windows 7. You'll be glad you did.

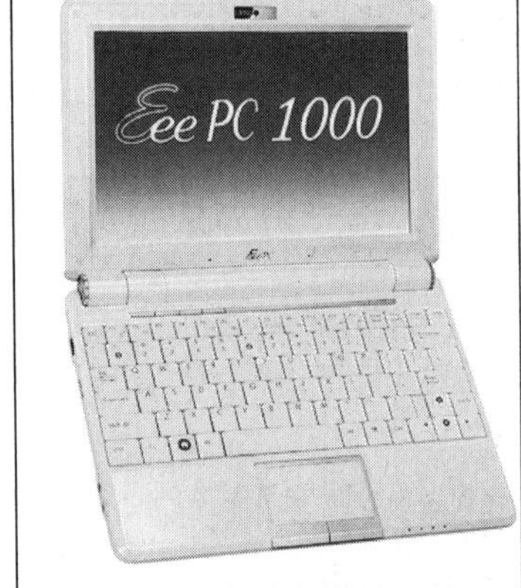

Figure 1-10: The ASUS Eee PC 1000H runs Windows 7, no sweat.

Courtesy of ASUSTeK Computer Inc.

Chapter 2: Windows 7 for the Experienced

In This Chapter

- What every experienced Windows user should know about Windows 7
- New tricks for Vista users
- What has changed for XP-ers
- How to know whether you truly need Windows 7 (the answer may surprise you)

If you're among the billion-or-so souls on the planet who have been around the block with Windows Vista or Windows XP, you're in for a shock. In many ways, Windows 7 looks and acts like Vista — and it isn't that far from XP with a bit of gussying-up around the edges. Many of the pieces of Windows 7 work much like their Vista and XP counterparts. But underneath the surface, much has changed.

Here's a quick guide to what's new — and what's still the same — with some down 'n' dirty help for deciding whether you truly need Windows 7.

What's New for Vista Victims

If you've struggled with getting Windows Vista to work on your computer, you can breathe a sigh of relief. Windows 7 isn't worse.

Yeah, that's definitely damning with faint praise. I don't deny it. Alexander Pope would've been proud.

Microsoft learned many lessons during the Vista Wars. It changed a lot of features in Windows 7. But it didn't change the *driver model* — the way hardware interacts with Windows. In fact, interaction with hardware in Windows 7 is almost indistinguishable from that in Vista Service Pack 1. So if you have hardware that works with Windows Vista, it will almost certainly work with Windows 7. No changes required. No new drivers, as long as you don't do something funny, like switch from 32-bit Vista to 64-bit Windows 7. (See "Choosing 32-bit versus 64-bit" in Book I, Chapter 3.)

Better performance

Incredibly, Microsoft tightened up Vista.

Windows 7 runs faster than Vista in most circumstances. It takes less memory. It occupies less space on your hard drive — even after you install Windows Live Essentials (see Book I, Chapter 5). Some savings and improvements are a tad illusory: Hard drive requirements fell because of a reduction in space reserved for shadow copies (see Book II, Chapter 3), for example. But most people who try Windows 7 find it faster, less of a hog, and more reliable than Vista.

There I go with that faint praise stuff again.

Improved interface

New versions of Windows invariably bring claims of improvements to the interface — and journalists join in on the "ooohs" and "aaaaahs" whenever Microsoft execs show off their flashy glittergrades — changes designed to show new sizzle, without really changing the steak. TechnoBling.

In Windows 7, some changes rate as genuinely useful. The new Taskbar (many of us still call it by its code name, Superbar) makes many daily tasks faster and easier to complete. See Book III, Chapter 2. The Aero Snap feature lets you drag a window to an edge of the screen and have it automatically resize to half-screen size — a boon to anyone with a wide screen.

Microsoft ditched the Windows Sidebar in Windows 7. (The Sidebar was one of the "oooh" and "aaaah" reasons proffered for upgrading from Windows XP to Vista.) Now gadgets — the little clock and stock ticker and the like — can float anywhere on the desktop (as shown in Figure 2-1). These gadgets could float in Vista, too, but few Vista users ever figured that out.

Windows 7 has many other glittery improvements:

- **Slide show:** You can use this feature for your desktop background.
- **Taskbar icons:** View pop-up thumbnails of running programs and right-click jump-list menu options.
- **Notification area:** Down by the clock, this feature can now be controlled, more or less.
- **Gadgets:** See them on your desktop by moving your mouse to the Aero Peek area, in the lower-right corner.
- **Font list:** It now looks better.

Be still, my beating heart.

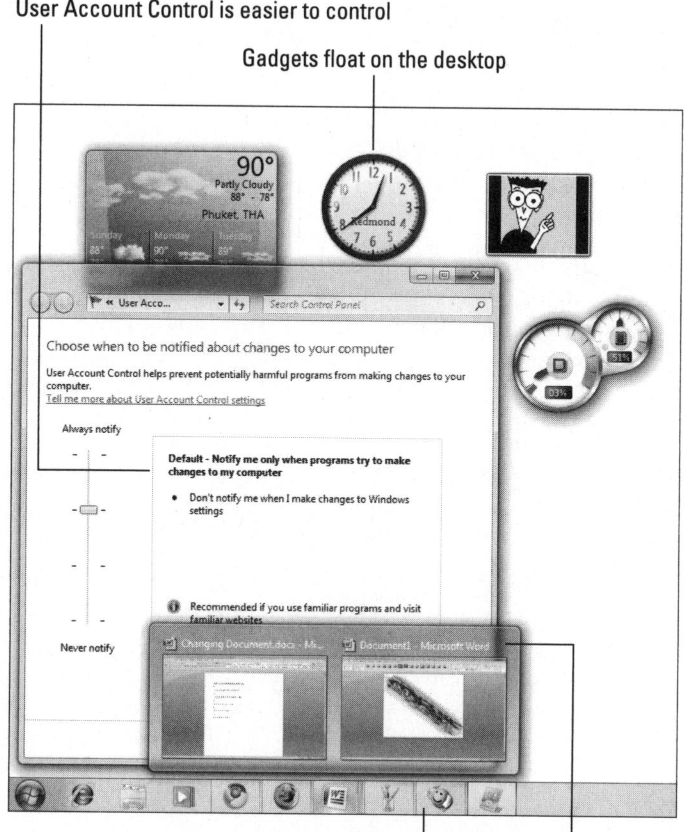
User Account Control is easier to control
Gadgets float on the desktop
90°
Partly Cloudy
88° - 78°
Phuket, THA
Redmond
User Acco...
Search Control Panel
Choose when to be notified about changes to your computer
User Account Control helps prevent potentially harmful programs from making changes to your computer.
Tell me more about User Account Control settings
Always notify
Default - Notify me only when programs try to make changes to my computer
Don't notify me when I make changes to Windows settings
Recommended if you use familiar programs and visit familiar websites
Never notify
Document1 - Microsoft Word
Icons stay put on the taskbar
Click a taskbar icon to see thumbnails of running programs

Figure 2-1: The Windows 7 desktop sports a few worthwhile changes.

Search that (finally!) works

If you read my earlier book, *Windows Vista All-In-One Desk Reference For Dummies* (Wiley), you saw me rail against the infuriating inconsistencies in Windows Search. I'm here to tell ya: Search in Windows 7 works and works well. Big difference.

Windows 7 lets you search data outside your computer using Federated Search and the OpenSearch standard. The new ability to build libraries — similar to the Vista Media Player audio libraries but extended to all kinds of files — makes organizing and searching simpler. Getting the hang of Search (see Book III, Chapter 3) is a little hard, but if you spend 10 to 15 minutes figuring it out, the Search feature's capabilities will repay your investment over and over again.

Security improvements

I'm told that Pliny the Elder once described the alarm system of ancient Rome by saying, "Even when the dogs sleep, the goose watches."

User Account Control — the goose of Windows Vista, if you'll forgive a transmillennia metaphor — has undergone significant changes in Windows 7. If you don't change the original setting, User Account Control security prompts you with the darken-your-screen-and-pray messages that bugged millions of Vista users. However, the prompts occur infrequently, and only when there seems to be genuine cause for concern. See Book II, Chapter 2.

Under the covers, Windows 7 has a few improved security features, but the ones you can see — such as HomeGroups (see Book VII, Chapter 1) and the revamped BitLocker drive encryption (Book VI, Chapter 1) — bundle old Vista security concepts differently and make them usable.

Mo' media and more

Windows Media Center gets a facelift in Windows 7, along with a whole bunch of support for different kinds of video and audio files and in-the-box capabilities to connect to CableCARD and clear QAM tuners.

Several of the tired, old (very old) Windows standbys — Calculator, Paint, WordPad — sport new interfaces and capabilities (see Figure 2-2). Windows 7 has better troubleshooting support, enhanced networking features especially for wireless networks, and hundreds of little improvements.

What you lose

On the flip side, several features in Vista went away in Windows 7. The old Sidebar bit the dust — don't need it. The Windows Defender Software Explorer program, which gave you some control over which programs automatically start on your computer, disappeared, no doubt the victim of enormous volumes of tech-support phone calls. Not to worry: You can find better, free alternatives — see Book VI, Chapter 4.

Several Vista programs (Windows Mail, Messenger, Movie Maker, Photo Gallery) have been moved out of Windows, repurposed as free downloads on the Internet. See Book I, Chapter 5 for an overview of these Windows Live Essentials.

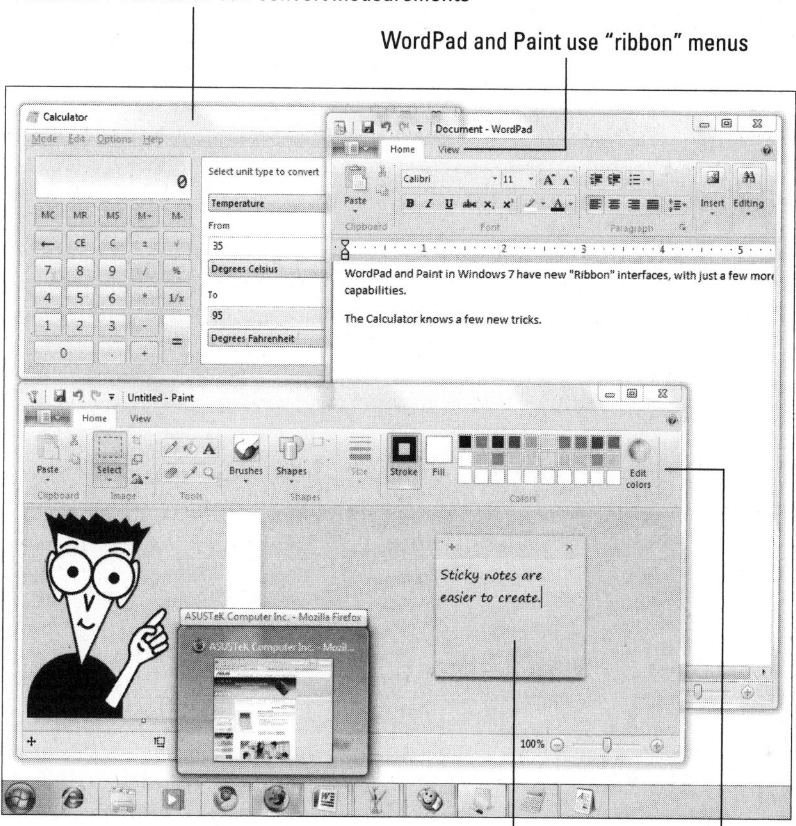

Figure 2-2: Several old Windows programs have pretty new faces.

What's New for the XP Crowd

If you didn't plunge into the Windows Vista madness, and instead sat back and waited for something better to come along, you should know that many improvements await in Windows 7.

Looking through the Aero Glass

As long as you run Windows 7 on a PC with some oomph in the graphics department, the Windows 7 Aero Glass interface (did you notice the see-through look in Figure 2-1) rates as a significant improvement over the boxy, now-antiquated look of Windows XP. (Windows 7 Starter Edition doesn't support Aero Glass.)

Microsoft marketeers insist on calling Aero Glass a *UX* (for User Experience). I guess they have a point — particularly if you can't get the %$#@#! thing to work. What an experience.

You can call Aero Glass a UX, if you like — heck, you can call it a Lifestyle Enhancement Package and tout its medicinal and neurolinguistic benefits. Under that pretty face, Aero Glass embodies a completely new way of making windows float and interact on the screen.

Aero Glass qualifies as much more than YAMG — Yet Another Microsoft Glittergrade — of which you have endured many over the years. Use it for a few hours, and you'll find benefits in these areas:

✦ **Window locations:** You can frequently locate the specific window you want faster, easier, and more accurately.

✦ **Window organization:** Organizing windows by stacking them on the desktop works better than in previous versions of Windows because you can peek through the edges.

✦ **Window switching:** Switching among windows feels less like a black art than it did in Windows XP.

Checking out improved video effects

Under the hood, Windows 7 intervenes between programs and the screen, by adding an extra layer of processing called the *Desktop Window Manager*. Historically, extra processing layers have gummed up Windows, so DirectX was invented specifically to bypass all the Windows overhead. Now, thanks to powerful processors on video cards, and more than a little bit of programming savvy, Windows 7 can intercede without bringing your computer to a grinding halt.

You see the effects of the Desktop Window Manager in the Windows 7 omniscient handling of all video. One example is the aforementioned glass effects: windows peeking out from under other windows, fast shading, transitional effects that smoothly roll a window onto the screen, the close (X) button that glows when the mouse cursor hovers over the button. You also see two features in Windows 7 that make skimming your open windows and finding the one you want much easier:

✦ Windows 7 shows you thumbnails of running programs when you hover your mouse over a program on the taskbar (see Figure 2-3).

✦ By activating the Windows Flip feature, you can leaf through running programs much like you riffle a deck of cards. Just hold down the Windows key and repeatedly press Tab (see Figure 2-4).

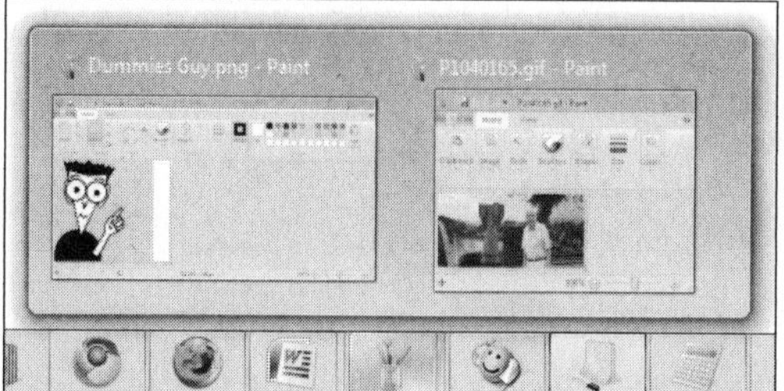

Figure 2-3: Two copies of Paint are running, so you see two different preview windows.

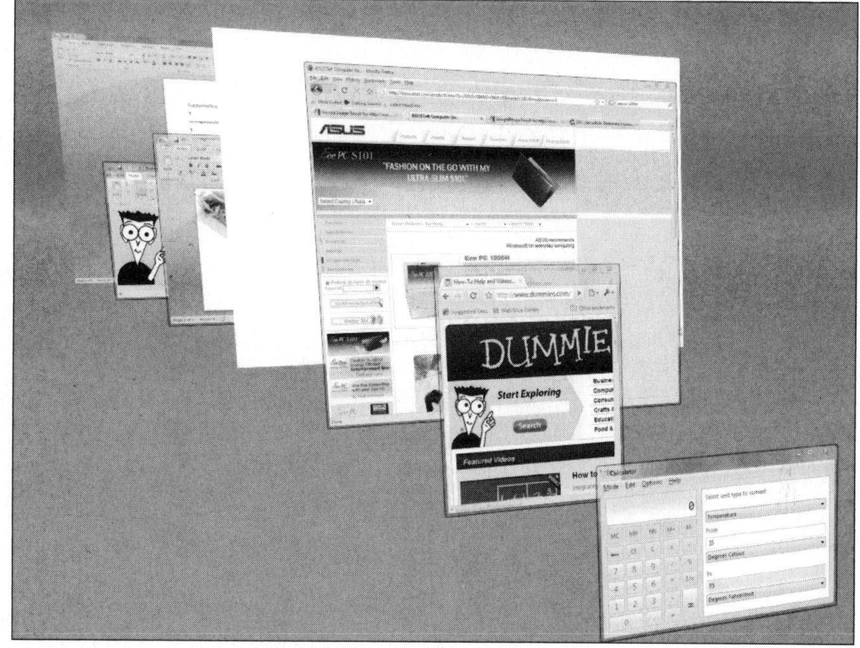

Figure 2-4: Windows Flip lets you riffle through running programs.

Interacting with gadgets

Microsoft tried to put "active" items on the Windows desktop for nearly a decade. Finally, Windows 7 has brought active content — otherwise known as gadgets — to the Windows desktop. Stability problems that dogged the Windows XP active desktop and performance problems in the original version of Vista are but a, uh, fond memory.

Gadgets can interact with you, with Windows, with files and folders, with your network, and with other gadgets. Windows 7 ships with a handful of moderately interesting gadgets — a clock (you can put more than one clock on your desktop, each set to a different time zone), weather forecaster, picture slide show, and PC performance monitor, all of which you can see earlier, in Figure 2-1.

To add gadgets to your desktop, follow these steps:

1. **Right-click an empty place on the desktop and choose Gadgets from the pop-up menu that appears.**
2. **In the Gadgets window, scroll to look through the built-in gadgets. To add one to your desktop, simply drag it onto your desktop.**

   The Media Center Gadget lets you play music or watch TV or movies, right there on your desktop. The other built-in gadgets may strike your fancy.

   But a whole new world awaits if you venture online for other gadgets.
3. **To peruse online gadgets, click the Get More Gadgets Online link, and you're transported to the Windows 7 Personalize Your PC page, which lists Gadgets galore.**

   Whether you need something to track your eBay bids, search for Xbox cheats, search for music based on what you're playing, hook into Windows Live Messenger, or give you a quick look at Twitter (see the Chirpr application) or Facebook, you'll find it.

Sizing up other improvements

The old Windows XP Media Center Edition was billed — and sold — as a separate operating system, almost exclusively available on new PCs. That always struck me as odd because Media Center is an application that runs on top of Windows just like, oh, Internet Explorer or Windows Media Player.

In Windows 7 Home Premium edition or higher (see Book I, Chapter 3), Media Center comes along for the ride. Chances are good that it's already installed on any computer you're going to buy — except some netbooks.

Many other features — less sexy but every bit as useful — put Windows 7 head and shoulders above XP. The standout features include everything mentioned in the preceding section for Vista users plus many other capabilities that Windows XP users should find worthwhile:

- **Backup worthy of the name:** Backup was a cruel joke in Windows XP. Vista did it better, but Windows 7 makes backup truly easy.
- **Second monitor support:** Although some video card manufacturers managed to jury-rig multiple monitor support into the Windows XP drivers, you need Windows 7 if you want to run more than one monitor.
- **Easy wireless networking:** All sorts of traps and gotchas live in the Windows XP wireless programs. Windows 7 does it much, much better.
- **Search:** In Windows XP, searching for anything other than a filename involved an enormous kludge of an add-on that sucked up computer cycles and overwhelmed your machine. In Windows 7, search is baked in.

Do You Need Windows 7?

Probably not. If you have a PC with Windows XP installed and it works well enough for what you want to do, leave it alone. Ain't broke. Don't fix. Keep your Windows XP machine updated with the latest security patches as soon as they're tested and found to be reliable (see `www.AskWoody.com`). But don't throw it in the trash heap yet. Even if you have a superfast, late-model Windows XP machine, you may have trouble getting Windows 7 drivers for all your hardware, and the demands (particularly graphic card demands) of Windows 7 may turn a zippy PC into a slug.

Besides, if you upgrade to Windows 7 on a Windows XP machine, you have to wipe out the hard drive and start all over. Microsoft doesn't offer a Windows 7 upgrade DVD that you can install over the top of XP. Save that kind of disk-trashing trauma for a big-payoff move, to a brand-new computer.

If you ignore my advice and want to see whether your current Windows XP PC can handle Windows 7, I suggest that you run the Microsoft Windows 7 Upgrade Advisor at `www.microsoft.com/windows/windows-7/get/upgrade-advisor.aspx`.

If you have a PC with Vista installed, you may just want to take the Windows 7 plunge. The upgrade isn't painless, and it isn't 100 percent foolproof. But my experience has been that most PCs upgrade just fine, and the performance benefits (if there are any) show up right away.

Don't change to Windows 7 just because you want one of the Windows Live Essentials. You can download and install them using the instructions in Book I, Chapter 5, and you get all the features — although they may be sluggish under Windows XP. The latest versions of many of the other Microsoft products — Windows Media Player 12, Internet Explorer 8, Microsoft Security Essentials, the Malicious Software Removal Tool (which runs every time you use Windows Update to fetch patches) — all work without a hiccup in Windows XP. You have no reason to upgrade to Windows 7 if you want just the latest Media Player.

Windows Live Movie Maker, on the other hand, is available only for Vista and Windows 7 users. If you have Windows XP and you want to run Live Movie Maker, do yourself a favor and buy a new Windows 7 PC. Your hardware will thank you.

Chapter 3: Which Version? Pick a 7, Any 7

In This Chapter

- **The five flavors of Windows 7**
- **Versions you don't want — and features you do want**
- **32-bit versus 64-bit**
- **The right version for you**

If you haven't yet bought a copy of Windows 7, you can save yourself some headaches and more than a few bucks by buying the right version the first time. And, if you're struggling with the 32-bit versus 64-bit debate, illumination — and possibly some help — is at hand. It's hard to keep track of all the various versions without a scorecard. That's where this chapter comes in.

Pick a 7 — Any 7

Windows 7 appears in five — count 'em, five — different versions. Four of those versions are available in 32-bit and 64-bit incarnations. That makes nine different versions of Windows 7 to choose from. Fortunately, most people need to concern themselves with only three versions, and you can probably quickly winnow the list to one. Contemplating the 32-bit conundrum may exercise a few extra gray cells, but with a little help you can probably figure it out easily.

In a nutshell, the five Windows 7 versions (and targeted customer bases) look like this:

- **Windows 7 Starter Edition,** a stunted version that's available only preinstalled on netbooks. It doesn't support the Aero Glass interface (see Book I, Chapter 2). It doesn't let you change your desktop background. Starter can't run automatic backups to another computer on your network. There's no Media Center, no Sticky Notes, and the Snipping Tool got, uh, cut. But it will definitely help keep the cost of Windows-powered netbooks out of the stratosphere.

Some of the Starter Edition limitations may be circumvented with simple changes to the Windows Registry. In particular, the inability to change your desktop background may drive you nuts. Keep an eye on `www.AskWoody.com` for the latest cracking news.

- **Windows 7 Home Basic** is available only in emerging countries, where the price of Windows typically exceeds the average gross monthly income of an experienced programmer with a college degree.

If you're accustomed to the old Vista version nomenclature, you may have noticed that in the process of moving to Windows 7, Microsoft swapped the names of its two least-capable versions: the old Vista Home Basic is now Windows 7 Starter, and the old Vista Starter is now Windows 7 Home Basic, at least to a first approximation.

- **Windows 7 Home Premium** ranks as the baseline system. Almost everybody who buys a new computer will buy Home Premium. It includes all the new interface goodies and Windows Media Center plus almost all the other features that you know as Windows 7. Two stinkers: Premium won't allow you to run automatic backups to another computer on your network, and you can't control a Windows 7 Home Premium computer with another computer by using Remote Desktop (see next).
- **Windows 7 Professional** includes everything in Home Premium plus the ability to attach the computer to a corporate domain network; the Encrypting File System (see the "Encrypting File System and BitLocker" sidebar, later in this chapter) for scrambling your hard drive's data; and the software necessary for your computer to act as a Remote Desktop host.
- **Windows 7 Enterprise** and **Windows 7 Ultimate** are two names for the same product. If your company has a corporate license, you get Enterprise. If you pay real money, you get Ultimate. Enterprise and Ultimate add support for BitLocker and BitLocker To Go (see the later sidebar "Encrypting File System and BitLocker") data encryption; all the language packs; BranchCache, for speeding file access on large, corporate networks; and the ability to boot from a virtual hard drive.

Before you tear your hair out trying to determine whether you bought the right version, or which edition you should buy your great-aunt Ethel, rest assured that choosing the right version is much simpler than it first appears. Flip to "Narrowing the choices," later in this chapter. If you're considering buying a cheap version now and maybe upgrading later, I suggest that you first read "Buying the right version the first time" before you make up your mind.

Buying the right version the first time

What if you aim too low? What if you buy, oh, Windows 7 Home Premium and decide later that you really want Windows 7 Professional? Be of good cheer. Switching versions ain't as tough as you think.

Microsoft chose the feature sets assigned to each Windows 7 version with one specific goal in mind: Maximize Microsoft profits. That's why you find plenty of upgrade routes and plenty of opportunity to spend more money in the Windows Anytime Upgrade program (see Figure 3-1).

All it takes is a credit card and a Windows Live ID to upgrade from Home Premium to Windows 7 Professional (or, less commonly, from Home Premium to Ultimate or from Professional to Ultimate). No, you can't downgrade and get a refund. Bonus points for thinking about it, though.

Upgrading is easy and cheap, but not as cheap as buying the version you want the first time. That's also why it's important for your financial health to get the right version from the get-go.

Windows Anytime Upgrades count as pure gravy for Microsoft: Follow the upgrade steps and Windows invites you to log on to the Internet, hand over your credit card number, and upgrade on the spot. You don't get a new box or a new CD. All you get is a new product key and a walk-through that installs the new version from media that's already in your possession. It's pure profit for the folks in Redmond. Smart.

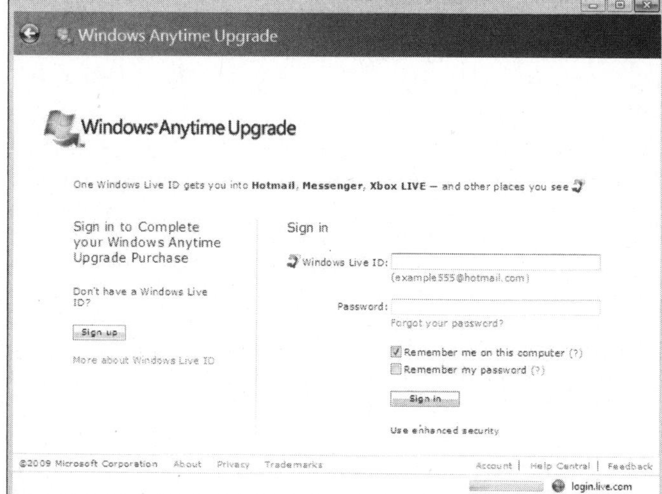

Figure 3-1: Windows Anytime Upgrade, ready to take your shekels at any time, 24-7.

Narrowing the choices

You can dismiss a couple of Windows 7 versions out of hand:

- **Windows 7 Starter Edition:** It's offered only with new PCs — typically, netbooks. If the company selling the netbook offers it with Windows 7 Home Premium, at a slightly higher price, you should take the Premium and not Starter. Why? Premium doesn't place much greater demands on the hardware, and it's packed with features you may want — including, notably, Media Center. The manufacturer should know if its netbook can handle Premium. In my experience, most can.

- **Windows 7 Home Basic:** Even if it's available where you live, you don't want it. With no Aero Glass and no Media Center, it isn't worth the effort. A very large percentage of all copies of Windows 7 Home Basic (and Vista Starter before it) are destined to be overwritten with a pirate copy of Windows 7 Ultimate.

That leaves you with Windows 7 Home Premium, unless you have a crying need to do one of the following:

- **Connect to a corporate network.** If your company doesn't give you a copy of Windows 7 Enterprise, you need to spend the extra bucks and buy Windows 7 Professional.
- **Play the role of the puppet — the *host* — in a Remote Desktop interaction**. If you're stuck with Remote Desktop, you have to buy Windows 7 Professional or Ultimate.

  Many businesspeople find that LogMeIn, a free alternative to Remote Desktop, does everything they need and that Remote Desktop amounts to overkill. LogMeIn lets you access and control your home or office PC from any place that has an Internet connection. Take a look at the Web site `logmein.com`.

- **Provide added security to protect your data from prying eyes or to keep your notebook's data safe even if it's stolen.** Start by determining whether you need Encrypting File System (EFS) or BitLocker or both (see the later sidebar "Encrypting File System and BitLocker"). EFS comes with Windows 7 Professional. Ultimate has both EFS and BitLocker — with BitLocker To Go tossed in for a bit o' lagniappe.
- **Change languages.** You can change the keyboard input language in any version of Windows 7 — you can easily type Cyrillic characters, for example, on a US English copy of Windows 7. But if you want to change all the menus, all the prompts, and all the Help files to Russian or some other language, you have to buy Ultimate.

Encrypting File System and BitLocker

EFS is a method for encrypting individual files or groups of files on a hard drive. EFS starts after Windows boots: It runs as a program under Windows, which means it can leave traces of itself and the data that's being encrypted in temporary Windows places that may be sniffed by exploit programs. The Windows directory isn't encrypted by EFS, so bad guys (and girls!) who can get access to the directory can hammer it with brute-force password attacks. Widely available tools can crack EFS if the cracker can reboot the, uh, crackee's computer. Thus, for example, EFS can't protect the hard drive on a stolen laptop/notebook. Windows has supported the Encrypting File System (EFS) since the halcyon days of Windows 2000.

BitLocker was introduced in Vista and has been improved in Windows 7. BitLocker runs *underneath* Windows: It starts before Windows starts. The Windows partition on a BitLocker-protected drive is completely encrypted, so bad guys who try to get to the file system can't find it.

EFS and BitLocker are complementary technologies: BitLocker provides coarse, all-or-nothing protection for an entire drive. EFS lets you scramble specific files or groups of files. Used together, they can be mighty hard to crack.

New in Windows 7, BitLocker To Go provides BitLocker-style protection to removable drives, including USB drives.

Choosing 32-Bit versus 64-Bit

If you've settled on, oh, Windows 7 Home Premium as your operating system of choice, you aren't off the hook yet. You need to decide whether you want the 32-bit flavor of Windows 7 Home Premium, or the 64-bit flavor of Windows 7 Home Premium. (Similarly, all the Windows 7 versions except Starter are available in a 32-bit model and a 64-bit model.)

Although the 32-bit and 64-bit flavors of Windows 7 look and act the same on the surface, down in the bowels of Windows, they work quite differently. Which should you get? The question no doubt seems a bit esoteric, but there are good reasons why, oh, five or six years from now, every new PC will be using 64-bit versions of Windows.

Although lots of technical mumbo jumbo is involved, the simple fact is that programs are getting too big and Windows as we know it is running out of room. Although Windows can fake it by shuffling data on and off your hard drive, doing so slows your computer significantly.

The 32-bit flavor of Windows — the flavor that all of us were using a few years ago and most of us use now — has a limit on the amount of memory that Windows can use. Give or take a nip here and a tuck there, 32-bit Windows machines can see, at most, 3.4 or 3.5 gigabytes (GB) of memory. You can stick 4GB of memory into your computer, but in the 32-bit world, anything beyond 3.5GB is simply out of reach. It just sits there, unused.

The 64-bit flavor of Windows 7 opens up your computer's memory, so Windows can see and use more than 4GB — much more, in fact. Whether you need access to all that additional memory is debatable at this point. Five years from now, chances are pretty good that 3.5GB will start to feel a bit constraining.

There's one more good reason for running a 64-bit flavor of Windows 7: security. Microsoft enforced some strict security constraints on drivers that are used to support hardware in 64-bit machines — constraints that just couldn't be enforced in the older, more lax (and more compatible!) 32-bit environment.

And that leads to the primary problem with 64-bit Windows: drivers. Many, many people have older hardware that simply doesn't work in any 64-bit flavor of Windows. Their hardware isn't supported. Hardware manufacturers sometimes decide that it isn't worth the money to build a solid 64-bit savvy driver, to make the old hardware work with the new operating system. You, as a customer, get the short end of the stick.

To run 64-bit Windows, your computer must support 64-bit operations. Here's an easy way to see whether your current computer can handle 64 bits: Go to Steve Gibson's SecurAble site, at `grc.com/securable.htm`. Follow the instructions to download and run the SecurAble program. If your computer can handle 64-bit operations, SecurAble tells you.

If you have older hardware that you want to use with your Windows 7 computer, do yourself a favor and stick with 32-bit Windows. It's unlikely that you'll start feeling the constraints of 32 bits until your current PC is long past its prime. On the other hand, if you're starting out with completely new hardware and you plan to run your current PC for a long, long time, 64-bit Windows 7 makes a lot of sense. You may end up cursing me when an obscure driver goes bump in the night. But in the long run, you'll be better prepared for the future.

Chapter 4: Upgrades, Clean Installs, Transfers

In This Chapter

- **Determining whether you can upgrade**
- **Performing an upgrade or a clean install**
- **Transferring your files and settings from another computer**
- **Activating Windows 7**
- **Cleaning the gunk off new PCs**
- **Did Windows die? Don't panic!**

If your current machine runs Windows Vista, you can upgrade to Windows 7 by simply starting Windows, inserting the Windows 7 CD into the CD drive, and following the instructions. "Upgrading" from Windows XP to Windows 7 is considerably more difficult than upgrading from Vista to Windows 7. The only way to upgrade from Windows XP to Windows 7 involves wiping out your hard drive. Before you upgrade from Vista or XP, take a few minutes to read this chapter. It may save you hours, days, or even months of headaches.

And, if you ever have the urge to throw in the towel, wipe out your hard drive, and install Windows 7 all over again, follow the nostrums here to minimize the chances of complete disaster.

Can Your Computer Handle Windows 7?

Before you install Windows 7 on a PC, it would behoove you to find out exactly what you're going to get. The primary question isn't whether Windows 7 can run on your PC, because requirements for the minimal existence of Windows 7 are surprisingly Spartan. If your computer is fewer than five years old, it can run Windows 7, to a greater or lesser extent.

What you need to know is whether your computer can handle the Glass interface (see Figure 4-1) — or whether Windows 7 will automatically turn it off. The answer to that question is by no means certain.

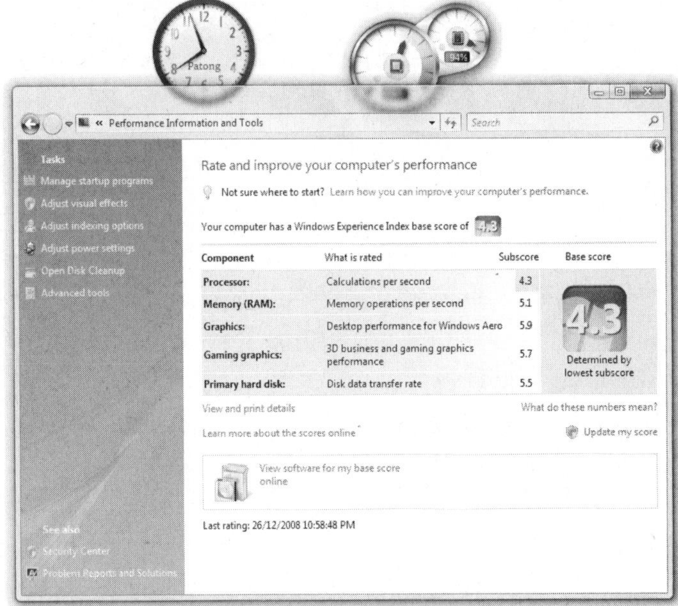

Figure 4-1: The Vista Windows Experience Index. Note the see-through Glass interface, identical to the one in Windows 7.

Upgrading a Vista computer

If you already have Vista running on the computer that you want to upgrade, you're in luck. The Windows Experience Index (WEI) in Vista gives you a good idea of what's ahead in a Windows 7 upgrade.

To see the Windows Experience Index on a Vista computer, follow these steps:

1. **Click Start⇨Control Panel.**
2. **Click the System and Maintenance link.**
3. **In the System group, click Check Your Computer's Windows Experience Index Base Score.**

   You see a rating screen like the one shown in Figure 4-1.

The Windows Experience Index in Windows 7 is considerably different from the one in Vista, but the Vista WEI can give you some important insight into what's in store for Windows 7. (Unfortunately, Windows XP doesn't have a Windows Experience Index.)

Here's what I've learned, after a lot of school-of-hard-knocking around:

- **If your Vista Windows Experience Index runs 2.0 or higher, you should be able to run Windows 7 reasonably well.** Windows 7 makes up its own mind about turning on Glass, though.

  Granted, you wouldn't want to use a PC with a Vista WEI rating of 2.0 for heavy graphics or gaming. But it's quite acceptable for Web browsing, light word processing, day-to-day spreadsheets, and the like.
- **If the first Graphics score, the one marked Desktop Performance for Windows Aero, exceeds 3.0, Windows 7 almost certainly turns on its Glass interface.** This happens *even if Vista turns it off.*
- **For most people, most of the time, the Memory (RAM), Gaming Graphics, and Primary Hard Disk scores don't mean much.** The processor score may make a difference in how Windows 7 behaves for you, but probably not as big a difference as you think.

When you're ready to take the plunge and upgrade your Vista computer to Windows 7, you get the most bang for the buck by having sufficient amounts of these few elements:

- **Memory:** You want to have at least 1GB of main memory, and it wouldn't hurt to put in 2GB or even 4GB. Memory's cheap. Have the dealer install it.
- **Graphics card:** If your computer's Graphics score is below 4.0 or so, you'll see a big improvement in Windows 7 performance by replacing your old graphics card with a cheap new one. That's assuming you *can* replace your old graphics card — not all notebook computers let you swap out old cards.
- **Hardware:** If you have old hardware that doesn't work with Vista, it probably doesn't work with Windows 7 either. Give up.

Upgrading a Windows XP computer

Unfortunately, unlike Vista, Windows XP doesn't have a Windows Experience Index program, so it's considerably more difficult to judge whether your Windows XP computer can run Windows 7 at anything more than a slug's pace.

As a rule of thumb, you can run Windows 7 on almost any PC made in the past five years — although you may have trouble finding drivers. That statement sounds innocuous, but finding drivers can present some real problems. For example, if you have a notebook with a built-in camera, you may find that you can run Windows 7 even though there's no way to make the camera work. If you have a desktop with a built-in sound card, you may find that the sound card doesn't work in Windows 7.

Upgrading your netbook

So you bought a netbook with Windows XP Home Basic or Linux (or both) preinstalled and you want to know whether you can upgrade to Windows 7 Home Premium edition. (Windows 7 Starter edition — the version that ships with new netbooks — isn't available at retail; it only comes preinstalled.) The quick answer: It depends.

If your netbook has 1GB of memory or more and at least 30 or 40GB of disk space, you can probably get away with upgrading. If you have Windows XP installed, you have to wipe out the hard drive in the process. If you have Linux installed, search at Google.com to see whether your particular flavor of Linux can peacefully coexist with Windows 7 using dual boot. Then you can decide every time you start your netbook whether you want to use Windows 7 or one of those penguin programs.

Don't expect to see the Glass interface. And, Windows 7 isn't anywhere nearly as snappy as Linux. But it looks and acts like good ol' Windows.

If you aren't sure about the existence of Windows 7 drivers for particular pieces of hardware — most certainly including hardware built-in to your computer — you should run to the manufacturer's Web site and search for the drivers you need. With rare exceptions, if the manufacturer has a Vista driver, it probably works in Windows 7.

Before you take the plunge and try to install Windows 7 on your Windows XP computer, keep a few guidelines in mind:

- **Just because you can run Windows 7 doesn't mean that you want to — or that you can live with yourself or your computer if you try.** In my experience, Windows 7 runs like a slug on an older Pentium computer with 512MB of memory.

- **Your computer has to be able to boot from a DVD drive.** If you don't have a DVD drive, you can buy a cheap external DVD drive — but your computer may or may not be able to boot from it.
- **If you want the Glass "experience," you need a video card that can take the strain.** If your video card has 128MB or more of its own memory (not shared memory — you have to look at the specs for the card), it can probably handle Glass.

Running the Windows 7 Upgrade Advisor

Microsoft's official take on your PC's upgradeability comes in the form of a program called the Windows 7 Upgrade Advisor. The Upgrade Advisor scans your Vista or XP computer and tells you, yea or nay, whether that particular computer can handle Windows 7.

To run the Windows 7 Upgrade Advisor on a Vista or Windows XP machine, follow these steps:

1. **Download the advisor from** `tinyurl.com/no4xb7` **(if you really want to type out the full address, it's** `microsoft.com/windows/windows-7/get/upgrade-advisor.aspx`**). Run the installer.**

2. **Double-click the Windows 7 Upgrade Advisor icon on your desktop. Click the Start Check button.**

   And wait. And wait. When the Advisor finishes, it shows you a summary report similar to the one in Figure 4-2.

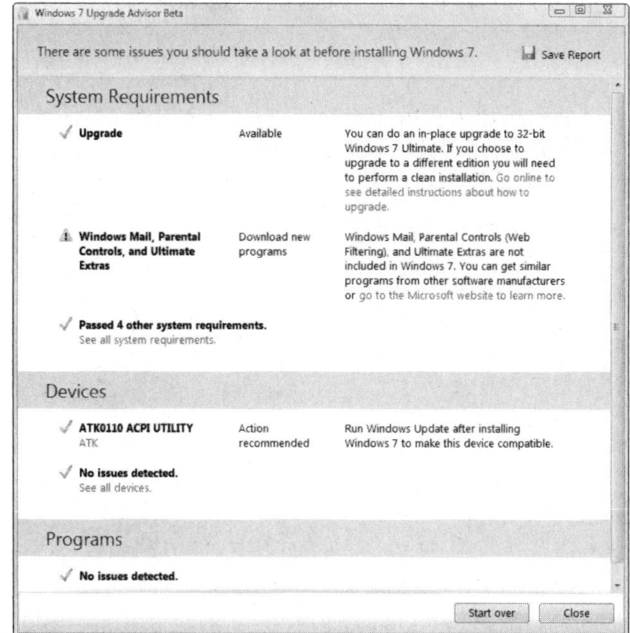

Figure 4-2: The Windows 7 Upgrade Advisor overview of potentially problematic hardware and software.

3. **In the System Requirements box, click the link that says See all System Requirements.**

   You see a list of minimal Windows 7 requirements, and how your computer stacks up against them.

Cleaning "free" programs off a new PC

Did you buy a new PC with Windows 7 preinstalled, only to discover that the manufacturer also included Norton Internet Security with Symantec Live Update and the trial version of WinDVD and Roxio and Quicken — oh! — this neat discount Earthlink and Napster and on and on?

If you find yourself with a hopelessly overburdened computer, a free-for-personal-use, nifty program might help: PC Decrapifier (you gotta love the name), from Jason York, at `pcdecrapifier.com/download`. The program doesn't claim to remove all the offal from your computer, but it does a remarkably good job with the junk it takes on, including, most notably, the Norton payola-ware. PC Decrapifier makes a restore point before it starts cleaning your Registry, so if something goes bump in the night, you can revert to a preprocessed state. See Book II, Chapter 1 for details.

4. **Back in the System Requirements box (Figure 4-2), click the link that says See All Devices.**

   The Upgrade Advisor returns with a detailed list of all the hardware devices attached to your computer, and lets you know if there are any missing drivers. This is a particularly comforting report because it verifies that (a) the Windows 7 installer can identify your hardware and (b) the drivers you need should be installed automatically.

5. **Click the X (Close) button to close the Upgrade Advisor.**

Performing a Clean Install

Windows 7 is an enormously complex program. In the best of all possible worlds, if you upgrade from your current version of Vista, the upgrade routines successfully grab all your old settings, get rid of the extraneous garbage that's floating around on your old machine, and install a stable, pristine copy of Windows 7, ready for you to take around the block.

Unfortunately, the world isn't always a pretty place, and your hard drive probably looks like a bit-strewn sewer. Historically, Windows has been considerably less stable for upgraders than for those who perform a clean install — wiping out the contents of the hard drive and starting over again. All the flotsam and jetsam that remain from an old version of Windows invariably muck up the works in the new version.

If you have a Windows XP computer and you want to turn it into a Windows 7 computer, you *have* to perform a clean install. That's the only option Microsoft allows — which is just as well. Trust me.

A clean install isn't for the faint of heart. No matter how hard you try, you will lose data, somewhere, somehow — it always happens, even to those of us masochists who have been running clean installs for a decade or two. If you value everything on your computer, go for the simple upgrade. If you want your PC to run more smoothly, think about a clean install.

The following is my general procedure for a clean install, in very broad terms:

1. **Download and install Revelation from SnadBoy Software at `www.snadboy.com` (see Figure 4-3).**

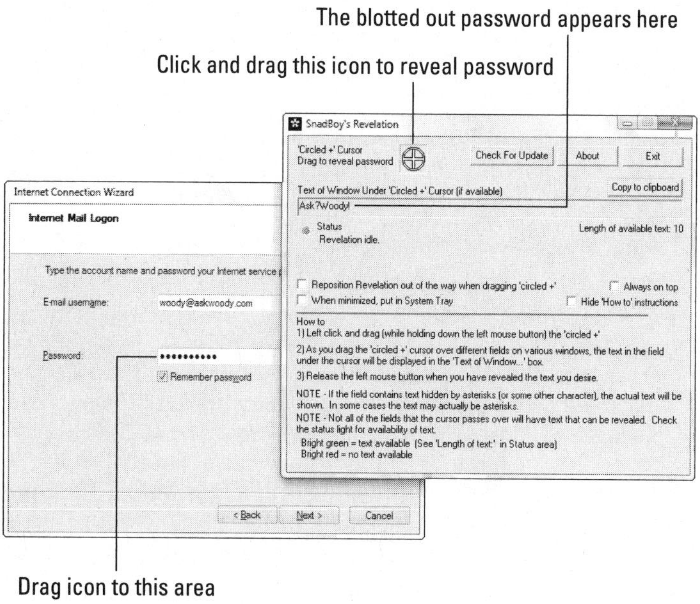

The blotted out password appears here

Click and drag this icon to reveal password

Drag icon to this area

Figure 4-3: The free SnadBoy program Revelation lets you see passwords that appear as ***** on the screen.

Revelation lets you look "underneath" the blocked-out asterisks (*****) in passwords in some Windows applications. In particular, it lets you retrieve the passwords you use in Outlook, Outlook Express, and Windows Mail to download your mail. Easy Transfer (see the next section in this chapter) is supposed to pick up e-mail settings, but it would behoove you to keep track of those passwords and any others you come across.

2. **Use Revelation for a few days (or weeks!) to grab any passwords it can find. Just click the icon, drag it over the password you want to see, and jot down the password that appears.**

   Revelation can't pick up passwords on Web pages, but it does a credible job of revealing many other passwords.

3. **If you use RoboForm (see Book V, Chapter 3) to keep track of your Web passwords, transfer your password file to a key disk and use that disk for a while to ensure that you have everything.**

   Take your time and retrieve all your passwords. They can be difficult to retrieve or re-create after a clean install.

4. **Make sure that you have current CDs for all the software you normally use.**

   If the programs require installation keys (sometimes called product keys, CD keys, or activation codes, among others), you need those keys, too. You can see the installation keys for Windows and Office by running the free Magical Jellybean Keyfinder, available at `magicaljellybean.com/keyfinder`.

   Make sure to write down your current Windows XP or Vista product key. (Magical Jellybean can tell you.) If Windows 7 goes to hades in a handbasket, at least you can reinstall your old version of Windows.

5. **Back up everything. Twice.**

   If you have a Windows 7 computer handy and you can attach it to the PC you're upgrading over a network or a direct-connect cable, you might want to try a Vulcan mind meld, er, a before-and-after Windows 7 Easy Transfer. The Windows 7 PC can act as an interim PC to hold all your files and settings while you upgrade your old PC. First, use Easy Transfer (see the "Using Easy Transfer" section, later in this chapter) on the Windows 7 computer to temporarily transfer all files and settings from the computer you're upgrading to the interim PC. Then upgrade your PC. Finally, follow the instructions again to move the files and settings from the interim PC back to your (freshly upgraded) original PC.

   With the price of hard drives falling like a Bakken rock, you might want to buy a new hard drive and replace your current C: drive with the new one before you install Windows 7 using the rest of the steps in this procedure. If you then turn off your computer and attach the old drive to another cable inside your computer, it will likely become your D: (or E: or F:) drive. That greatly simplifies the chore of backing up data — but it doesn't relieve you of the responsibility to write down all your passwords.

6. **Insert the Windows 7 installation disc in the DVD drive, and then choose Start⇨Shut Down to go through a full shutdown.**

   Windows 7 might offer to install itself while you're trying to shut down. If it does, click the Cancel button.

7. **Power off the PC and wait at least a full minute. Then turn on the power.**

8. **If the PC is capable of starting *(booting)* from the DVD drive, you see text on the screen that says something like `Press any key to boot from CD`. Press Enter.**

If the PC doesn't offer to boot from the DVD drive, you have to look in your PC's documentation for the correct setting in your PC's BIOS. If you're not familiar with your PC's BIOS, go to the Web site for your PC manufacturer and search for the terms *change boot sequence.*

9. **Complete the steps indicated by the installer. When asked what type of installation you want, choose the Custom (Advanced) option.**

The Windows 7 installer presents you with a list of hard drives that it recognizes. If you put a new hard drive in your computer, it shows up as Disk 0 Unallocated Space, as shown in Figure 4-4.

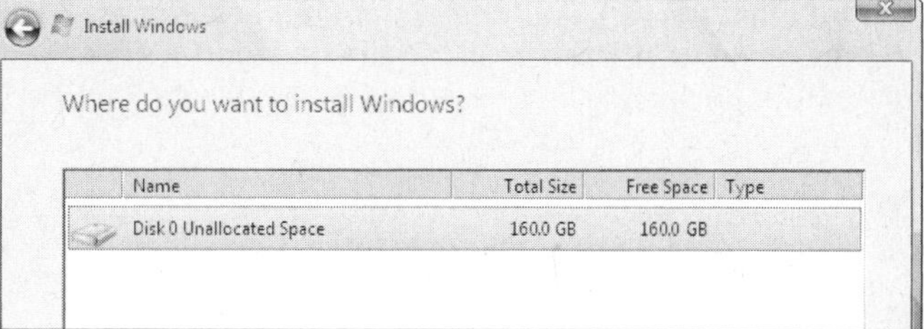

Figure 4-4: Disk 0 Unallocated Space (a new hard drive).

10. **Choose the disk where you want Windows 7 to live and then click Next.**

The installer wipes all the data from your old hard drive or reformats your new hard drive. Then the installer copies the files it needs in order to build your new system.

11. **Pick up your jaw from the floor, kick yourself twice for being so obstinate, pat yourself on the back for starting out fresh, and follow through with the rest of the installation.**

Windows 7 does a good job of taking you through the steps. The only truly tricky part of the installation: Windows might need to restart your PC a few times in the installation process. When that happens, you'll probably see the `Press any key to boot from the CD` message again. This time — the second time you see the message — ignore it. Let Windows start itself from the hard drive.

12. **When the installer asks for a username and a computer name, type them both and click Next.**

If you have a network, each computer's name has to be different. Personally, I use only letters and numbers for the name: you can make your life unnecessarily complex by using odd characters, punctuation marks, or spaces.

13. **The Windows 7 installer asks you for a password and a password hint. Type them both and click Next.**

    This password and hint are for the username you entered in Step 12. See Book II, Chapter 2 for advice on choosing passwords. Bonus points if you don't use one of the passwords that the Conficker worm recognizes.

14. **The installer then asks for your product key. If you don't have a product key, you needn't enter anything — but you have only 30 days to get a valid product key, lest Windows 7 curls up and dies. Click Next.**

WARNING!

    The Windows 7 installer then asks whether you want to send your Internet Explorer browsing history and details about what you're doing with Windows to the massive Microsoft database so that it can be mined in the future. The installer also wants to know whether it's okay for Microsoft to automatically push updates to your computer, without your knowledge or consent, even though Microsoft has a horrible track record of clobbering computers with buggy patches. Really, if you read the fine print in Figure 4-5, that's exactly what it says.

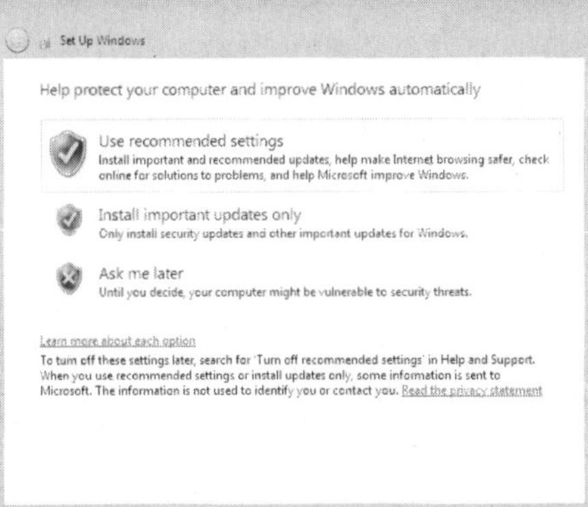
Set Up Windows
Help protect your computer and improve Windows automatically
Use recommended settings
Install important and recommended updates, help make Internet browsing safer, check online for solutions to problems, and help Microsoft improve Windows.
Install important updates only
Only install security updates and other important updates for Windows.
Ask me later
Until you decide, your computer might be vulnerable to security threats.
Learn more about each option
To turn off these settings later, search for 'Turn off recommended settings' in Help and Support. When you use recommended settings or install updates only, some information is sent to Microsoft. The information is not used to identify you or contact you. Read the privacy statement

Figure 4-5: Sending information about your Web browsing history and a log of what you're doing in Windows. Golly.

15. **Maybe you trust Microsoft a whole lot more than I do, but I strongly recommend that you choose Ask Me Later.**

ASKWOODY.COM

    Later, after you have Windows 7 running, Windows reminds you incessantly that you haven't turned on Automatic Updates. At some point, you should read the admonitions in Book VI, Chapter 4 and decide whether you want Windows to "notify but don't automatically install" security patches as they are pushed. That's what I do.

16. **If the installer can tell that you're connected to a network — sometimes it can have problems detecting an existing network if the right**

drivers aren't available — you're invited to select your computer's location (see Figure 4-6).

Windows 7 isn't interested in your location as much as it is in how you're going to use the computer when it's connected to the current network. Most people who are installing Windows 7 at home choose Home Network.

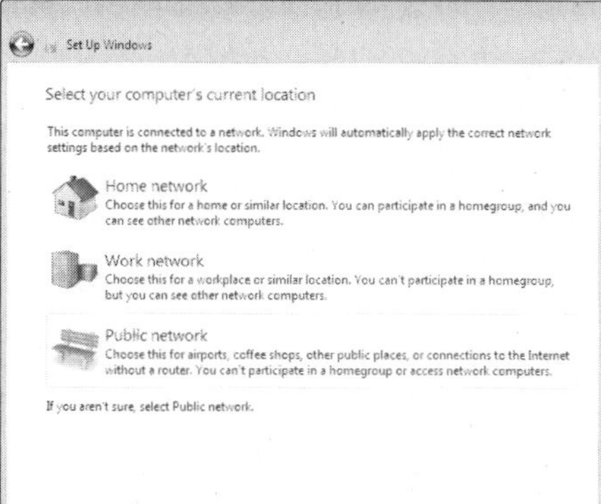

Figure 4-6: If Windows 7 detects that you're on a network, it sets the security levels based on your response.

17. **If you tell Windows 7 that you're connected to a home network and no HomeGroup is on the network already, you receive an invitation to create a HomeGroup (see Figure 4-7).**

    I talk about HomeGroups in Book VII, Chapter 1, but you can save yourself some reading now by just clicking Next and having a HomeGroup set up. Chances are good that you're going to want one. HomeGroups make it easy to share folders and printers with other computers on your network: they take the technical drudgery out of sharing what most people want to share.

    In Figure 4-7, I figure that other people on my network should be able to look at my documents, so I choose to share documents with the HomeGroup. You may or may not want to share your documents, depending on how well you trust people who can get on your network.

    The dialog box advises you to write down the password of your HomeGroup. Don't bother. You can get it again later.

18. **The installer whirs and clicks and clangs a bit, and you end up face-to-face with the Windows 7 desktop, ready to start.**

    If you see a box that says `View Important Message / Click to View Message`, go ahead and click the box. At the very least, you're badgered to install an antivirus package (see Book VI, Chapter 5), but you may also see important troubleshooting tips about failed hardware driver installations (see Book VIII, Chapter 1).

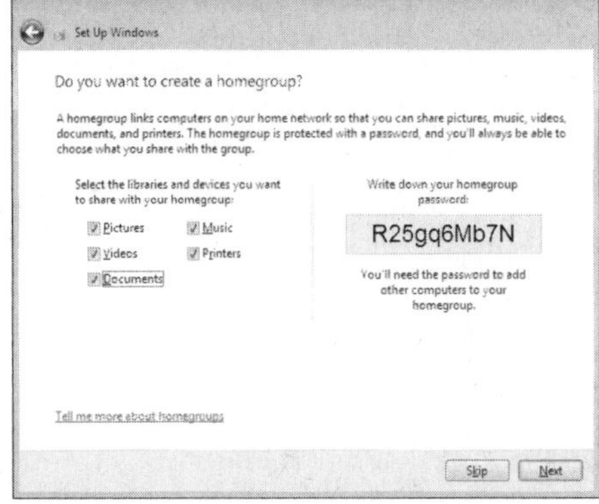

Figure 4-7: Set up a HomeGroup. You'll probably want to use it.

Using Easy Transfer

The Windows 7 Easy Transfer feature makes transferring certain kinds of settings and data files between two computers comparatively easy. It sounds great and works reasonably well, as long as you don't expect too much. You need to be aware of the following limitations:

- **The two PCs should be connected.** The instructions here are for Windows 7 PCs. The computer you're transferring files and settings to must be running Windows 7. If at all possible, the "To" PC should be connected to the PC that you're transferring settings from. The "From" PC can be running Windows XP, Windows Vista, or Windows 7.

Easy Transfer can send a humongous amount of data from one PC to another. You can schlep a USB drive from one machine to another, if you have a few spare hours (or days). A far better method, though, is to make both PCs talk to each other on a network. Failing that, you can connect the PCs with a USB cable, use an external hard drive, or even burn and then read CDs or DVDs. Easy Transfer can work with any of 'em.

- **Easy Transfer can't install your old programs on your new PC.** You have to do that yourself — manually and one at a time — generally from the programs' original CDs.

If you use Easy Transfer but you don't install all your old programs on your new PC, weird things can happen on the new PC. You might double-click a file in Windows 7, for example, and have Windows say that it can't find the program associated with the file. Outlook might have trouble displaying a file attached to a message. Nothing earth-shattering happens, mind you, but it can be annoying.

- **Easy Transfer picks up only data files, some settings, and Windows Registry entries** (see the next section). That means you can't expect it to pull across all your passwords, and some copy-protection schemes (on games, for example) might go haywire. Windows Easy Transfer doesn't pull across some third-party Internet and e-mail data and settings: For example, you have to move Firefox bookmarks and Thunderbird messages by yourself.

On the plus side, though, Windows Easy Transfer doesn't pick up much of the garbage that seems to accumulate in every Windows PC, such as vestiges of long-forgotten programs and Registry entries that lead nowhere, which means that you can use it without gumming up your new computer. Too much.

Knowing what will transfer

Here are the items that Easy Transfer should pick up in a transfer:

- **Data files:** If you're transferring from Windows XP, expect to see files from your Windows desktop, the My Documents folder (including My Pictures and My Music, if you have those in the My Documents folder), and the Shared Desktop and Documents folders. If you're transferring from a Vista machine or another Windows 7 machine, the folder names are different (for example, Documents rather than My Documents), but the usual suspects remain the same.
- **Windows settings:** These settings include user, desktop, screen saver, and taskbar options as well as settings for Windows Explorer, Internet Explorer (including your list of Favorites), Outlook Express (from XP), Windows Mail (from Vista), and Windows Live Mail (if you have it installed).

  Note that Windows 7 doesn't match up one-to-one with Windows XP or Vista, so the transferred settings might not have any effect, although you might see the more esoteric ones (say, the taskbar settings) if you dig deep into Windows 7.
- **All your Microsoft Office settings:** This one includes many of the Registry-based settings for other programs.

Making the transfer

Before you start Easy Transfer, it would behoove you to ensure that both the To and From computers are connected to reliable power supplies: plugging in notebook or netbook computers and a UPS (Uninterruptible Power Supply) wouldn't hurt for desktops and your network's hub. A Windows Easy Transfer can take a long time. It's disk intensive, too. The transfer goes considerably faster if you don't use wireless connections: Plug both computers into the same router, if humanly possible. After everything is plugged in, follow these steps:

1. **Make sure that Windows 7 is up and running on the To PC, and then log on to the To PC.**

   Check to make sure that your hardware is working, and run Windows 7 long enough to become familiar with it.

2. **Make sure that the connection between the To and From PCs is working.**

   If both the To and From PCs are connected to your network, choose Start➪Computer and click the Network link on the left side to make sure that the computers can see each other. If they aren't connected to the same network, attach a USB cable to the USB ports on both PCs or prepare that big stack of CDs.

3. **On the To PC, choose Start➪Getting Started➪Transfer Your Files.**

   The Windows Easy Transfer wizard shows itself.

4. **Click Next.**

   Windows Easy Transfer takes you through some easy questions, such as how you will transfer the files and whether you are on the To computer.

5. **Do one of the following, depending on your circumstances:**

   - *If your From computer isn't running Windows 7:* Windows Easy Transfer takes you through the process of copying Easy Transfer files to the From computer or a location that's accessible to both the To and From computers.

     After any setup files are transferred, you're instructed to go to the From computer and start the `MigSetup.exe` program in the `\WindowsEasyTransfer` folder.

     No, the instructions don't tell you which file to run — `MigSetup.exe` is the correct one.

   - *If the From computer is running Windows 7:* Go to the From computer and choose Start➪Getting Started➪Transfer Your Files.

6. **Regardless of which path you took in Step 5, click Next. Answer the easy questions again, by clicking Next until you arrive at the Windows Easy Transfer box, shown in Figure 4-8.**

7. **Go to the To computer, enter the Windows Easy Transfer key in the indicated location, and click Next.**

   Windows Easy Transfer ensures that the computers are connected, checks for updates to the program, and then grinds for a while and presents a list of user accounts that can be transferred, as shown in Figure 4-9.

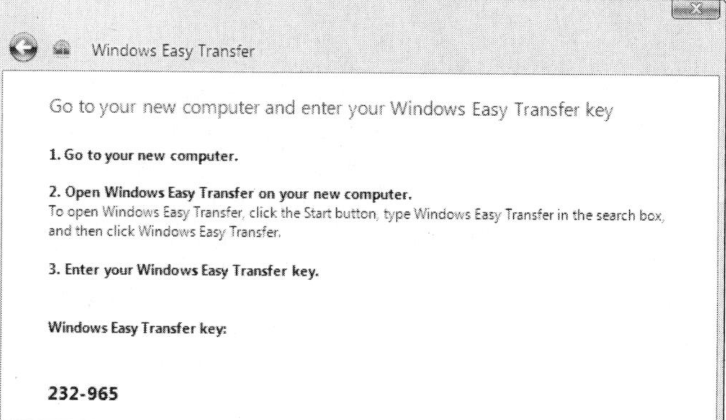

Figure 4-8: The Windows Easy Transfer key indicates that the From computer is ready to send data.

8. **Deselect the check boxes to the left of any user whose data you don't want to transfer. Click the Customize link for any user whose data you want to trim before the transfer (refer to Figure 4-9). Click Advanced for any user, and you can choose individual files or folders for that user.**

If you store data in a folder other than your Documents folder (or its subfolders, such as Pictures or Music) or the common Microsoft e-mail folders, you must click Advanced, find the folder, and select the check box next to it.

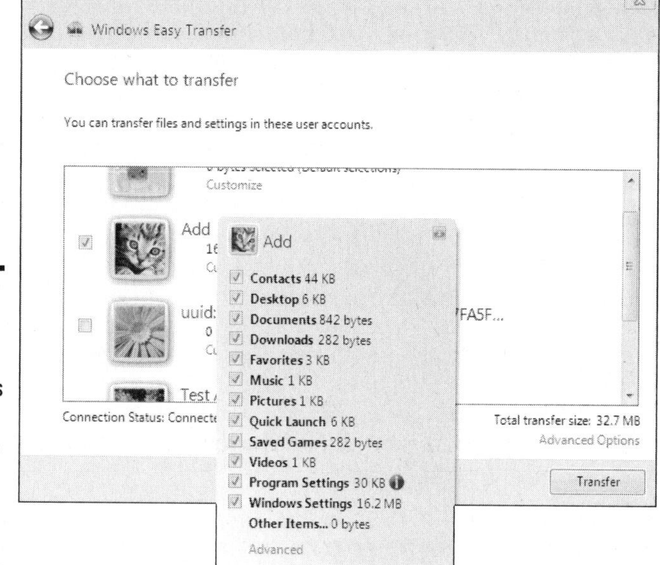

Figure 4-9: Windows Easy Transfer lets you specify which users to transfer to the To computer.

9. **Click Transfer.**

   Easy Transfer kicks in, warns you not to use either computer until the transfer is complete, and (sometimes hours later) finishes the transfer.

When Windows Easy Transfer works, it's great, but sometimes — far too frequently, in my experience — it just stalls in the middle of a transfer. You can try to run another Windows Easy Transfer, but after a couple of tries and stalls, you're better off digging into your computers and manually transferring the data and settings. You might consider hiring a pro.

If you decide to try transferring mano-a-mano, check out Brendon Chase's article for CNET Australia at `tinyurl.com/bepelv`. If you're comfortable using a more advanced approach, check out Ed Bott's approach to manual transfers at `blogs.zdnet.com/Bott/?p=553`.

Activating the Product

When you buy a copy of Windows 7 in a shrink-wrapped box, you're allowed to install it on one — and *only* one — PC. When you buy a new PC with Windows 7 preinstalled, Windows stays with the PC. You can't transfer Windows 7 from the original, bundled machine to a different machine. Microsoft uses the *BIOS locking* technique to ensure that the copy of Windows 7 that ships with a PC stays tied to that specific PC, forever and ever.

Some ifs, ands, and buts are floating around (for example, what if you upgrade to Windows 7 and the next day your PC suddenly dies?), but you generally can't copy Windows 7 and pass around pirated DVDs to your buddies or install a single copy on all the machines in your home. Actually, you *can* copy the Windows 7 DVD and install it, but unless you can cough up a product activation key within 30 days, Windows dies.

The precise actions taken by Windows to enforce the 30-day limit change from time to time, depending on the whims of Microsoft, but if you don't activate Windows 7 within 30 days, your use of the product is severely curtailed.

Ergo, if you have three PCs and you want to run Windows 7 on all of them, you have to buy three copies of Windows 7, either in shrink-wrapped boxes or preinstalled on new machines. If you pass around a Windows 7 DVD and all your friends install it, they have to come up with their own product keys or else their PCs will stop working. (Corporate licenses are a little different but beyond the scope of this book.) Or you can buy a Family Pack, if you qualify. It comes with three keys.

How Windows activates

Windows 7 enforces this one-Windows-one-PC licensing requirement by using the Windows Activation technique. Every time you start Windows 7, it checks to see whether it has been activated. Here's how the activation works:

✦ **If you bought a PC with Windows 7 preinstalled, it's activated already.**

That's easy. Your activation key is printed on a "birth certificate" sticker that's supposed to be stuck on the side or bottom of your PC. If you can't find a Windows birth certificate, talk — sternly — to the people who sold you the PC.

✦ **If you entered the 25-character activation key when you were installing Windows 7 and that key hasn't been used by anybody else, your PC is activated automatically soon after you log on for the first time.**

Windows 7 waits three days after your first logon before it tries to connect to the Internet, verify your product key with the Microsoft computers, and give your PC a clean bill of health. If you used a bad product key when you installed Windows 7, Windows doesn't start bellyaching about it until three days later. If you used a good product key — one that hasn't been used by anyone else — you see an activation notification saying that Microsoft vouches that your copy of Windows 7 is genuine, as shown in Figure 4-10.

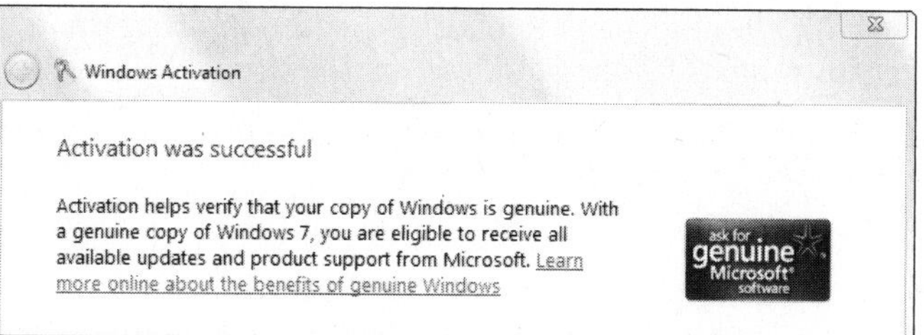

Figure 4-10: Congratulations! You passed activation.

✦ **If your copy of Windows 7 hasn't been activated, you see the message shown in Figure 4-11.** The latter half of this section walks you through the activation process.

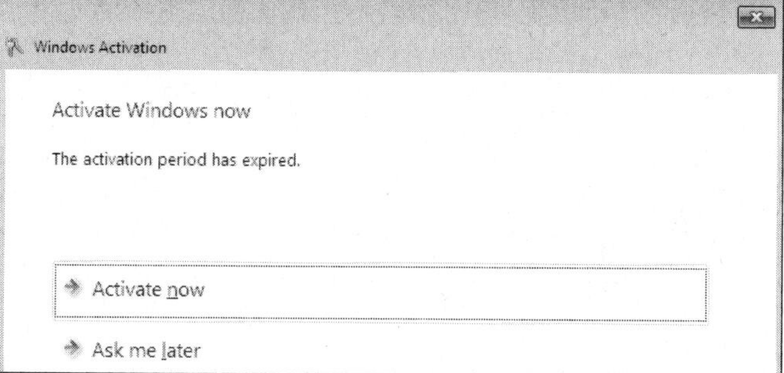

Figure 4-11: Activate Windows 7 or else it stops working.

To activate Windows 7 from the screen you see at start-up, follow these steps:

1. **Click the Activate Now link and Windows steps you through your options — namely, activating online or over the phone.**

   The easiest way for you to activate is online. (It's also the easiest way for Microsoft.)

2. **When prompted, type the unique 25-character code that's printed on the case of your Windows 7 CD.**

   If you activate by phone (perhaps your Internet connection isn't working or your unique situation requires some jawboning), you have to punch the installation ID into the phone.

   If you activate online, the installer prompts you. After you end your activation key, the Windows 7 Product Activation program then gets to work as follows:

   a. *Windows 7 Product Activation looks at various serial numbers inside your PC — the processor, network card, and disk drives, among others — and mixes them together, producing a second 25-character code that identifies your PC. Those 50 characters, taken together, are the installation ID.*

   b. *Your computer passes Microsoft the 50-character installation ID.*

   c. *Microsoft checks to see whether anybody else has submitted the 25-character code from the case of the Windows 7 CD.*

      If nobody else has activated that 25-character code from the CD case, or if the 25-character code has been activated with that specific installation ID (which means that you activated this particular copy of Windows Vista from the same PC twice), Microsoft sends back a 42-character confirmation ID. Both the installation ID and the confirmation ID are stored on your PC.

      If that 25-character code has already been used on a different PC, though, a polite message on your machine says that, according to the Microsoft records, the number of times you can activate Windows with this product key has been exceeded. You're asked to enter a different product key and then click Retry. You're given further instructions for contacting Microsoft, if you feel the need.

I've activated and reactivated various versions of Windows over the phone a dozen times and have always found the Microsoft reps to be courteous, fair, and understanding. If you have a good reason for reactivating Windows 7 — you bought and installed it on a PC that died or you changed a lot of hardware on an already activated PC — don't hesitate to follow the instructions and talk with a Microsoft rep over the phone. It takes a while, but you'll probably be pleasantly surprised.

Passing the Windows Activation process automatically approves your PC for the Windows Activation Technologies program.

Windows Activation Technologies

Windows Activation Technologies (formerly known as Windows Genuine Advantage; I used to call it Windows Genuine Spyware) has taken a hard rap over the years. It is the ultimate pirate buster in the Windows gang of thugs. Even if you followed the steps in the preceding section to activate your legitimate copy of Windows, there's a chance you might trigger an unwarranted Windows Activation Technology barb (especially if you make changes to your PC's essential hardware).

If you run into a WAT-related problem, you may experience flashing messages and limited Windows functionality, for example. Microsoft reserves the right to change just what the berserk behavior is at any time, but experience indicates that the penalties for running afoul of Activation requirements don't escape your attention. Consider the following:

- ✦ Microsoft once turned the screws to the point that WGA declared perfectly valid systems disingenuous, er, not genuine. The crackdown on presumably pirated copies of Windows left some perfectly legitimate Windows customers looking at frozen screens, unjustly accused.
- ✦ One time, the WGA servers broke down, so hapless Windows customers couldn't get their WGA-frozen computers to work.
- ✦ The original version of Vista entered an extreme "reduced functionality" mode if you tried to use it after the activation period expired: Basically, you could get at the data (in Safe mode) and use Internet Explorer for an hour, but that's about it.
- ✦ Vista Service Pack 1 backed off the draconian rules: If a Vista SP1 machine fails the Windows Genuine Advantage check, every hour Vista changes your computer's background to solid black and nags that "this copy of Windows is not genuine," but you can continue to use your computer normally. You can even revert the background to its original state, if you feel so inclined.

  At the time this book went to press, Windows Activation Technologies in Windows 7 reflected the same behavior as WGA in Vista SP1, and Microsoft had not announced any new differences, other than changing the name from Windows Genuine Advantage to Windows Activation Technologies.

Here's how the Windows 7 Activation Technology works — unless it has been changed recently:

Every couple of weeks, Windows 7 recalculates the 25-character code mentioned in the preceding section. If the code matches the one stored on your PC and the confirmation ID is good, Windows takes off. On the other hand, if the recalculated 25-character code doesn't match your original code, here's what happens:

- **If Windows decides that you made only a few changes to your PC:** If you replaced a hard drive, say, or even changed the motherboard, you can start Windows anyway, and you go on your merry way with everything right in the world.
- **If, on the other hand, Windows determines that you made too many changes:** Windows refuses to start and insists that you contact Microsoft for a new confirmation ID. That starts the activation cycle all over again.

Microsoft has full details at `www.microsoft.com/piracy/mpa.aspx`.

What If the Wheels Fall Off?

So what should you do if Windows 7 dies? Try this:

- If Windows 7 came bundled with a new PC, scream bloody murder at the vendor who sold you the %$#@! thing. Don't put up with any talk about "It's a software problem; Microsoft is at fault." If you bought Windows 7 with a new PC, the company that sold you the machine has full responsibility for making it work right. Period.
- If you upgraded from Vista to Windows 7 and you didn't go through a clean install, try that. You don't have much to lose, eh? Follow the instructions in the section "Performing a Clean Install," earlier in this chapter.
- If you completed a clean install and Windows 7 still falls over and plays dead, man, you have my sympathies. Check with your hardware manufacturer and make sure that you have the latest BIOS version installed. (Make sure to find an instruction book; changing the BIOS is remarkably easy, if you follow the instructions.) Visit the online newsgroups or drop by my lounge, at `www.wopr.com`, to see whether anybody there can lend a hand. If all else fails, admit defeat and reinstall your old operating system.

Life's too short.

Chapter 5: Getting Essentials: The Rest of Windows 7

In This Chapter

- **Understanding that Live Essentials are, uh, an essential part of Windows 7**
- **Knowing where Windows Live Essentials came from**
- **Winnowing out the not-so-essential Essentials**
- **Downloading and installing the Essentials**

So you have Windows 7 going — either on a brand-new computer or installed on an old workhorse — and you're raring to go. Good.

But wait a minute. You don't have all of Windows 7 yet. Microsoft, in its infinite wisdom, has lopped off big parts of Windows and stuck them up in the cloud, on the Internet. If you want Mail, Messenger, Photo Gallery, or Movie Maker (the more popular Essentials), you have to download and install them. This chapter steps you through the Essentials elements, helps you choose which ones you want, and deals out the straight scoop on installing them intelligently. If you're looking for detailed references for the individual Essentials, those come later, in the books and chapters that pertain to the topic at hand. I point you to each of them in this chapter, for your further edification and enjoyment.

There's one other "Essential" that qualifies as a horse of a different color: Microsoft Security Essentials, the free antivirus/antimalware product from Microsoft, isn't an official part of the Windows Live Essentials. Don't ask me why, but MS decided to borrow the "Essential" name for its free antivirus product, then distribute Microsoft Security Essentials in a completely different way, outside of the Windows Live Essentials channel. Microsoft Security Essentials doesn't look like any of the Windows Live Essentials; it doesn't install like the others; and it doesn't run like the others. The only way that Microsoft Security Essentials resembles Windows Live Essentials is in the name. If you like the idea of a free product from Microsoft that protects you from flaws in Windows, check out Microsoft Security Essentials, in Book VI, Chapter 5.

Understanding the Move to Downloadable Programs

Microsoft had to solve some specific problems on the road to Windows 7. It did so by lopping off four major applications in Windows — Mail, Messenger, Photo Gallery, and Movie Maker — and moving them to the cloud. Here's what happened:

- **Microsoft realized that it couldn't ship Windows 7 quickly unless it got rid of the four big, unwieldy (I didn't say *bloated*) applications.** So it took them out of the box and stuck them on the Internet.

- **All four of the programs are good candidates for "revving" independently.** There's no reason why you should have to wait for the next version of Windows to get the new MSN Messenger, er, Windows Live Messenger, or Mail.
- **Windows has a long production cycle.** Two or three or more months pass from the time the software is done until it appears in shrink-wrapped packages on store shelves. By putting the four Essentials on the Web, Microsoft got Windows out the door with enough time remaining to update the Essentials before Windows 7 was widely available.
- **The European Union can gripe about Microsoft's bundling of applications with Windows as an anticompetitive misuse of the Windows monopoly.** (Heaven knows that the U.S. Justice Department hasn't had the heart for it.) But if an anticompetitive part of Windows isn't part of Windows — it's available for free, as an independent download — who's to wail?
- **Microsoft has much better ways to make money from the programs available online.** Advertising is a prime example. You, as a Windows consumer, have come to expect advertising from Messenger, and you probably won't complain much if and when Live Mail, Photo Gallery, and Movie Maker start getting the advertising religion some day. But you'd raise a huge stink if Windows Explorer suddenly sported an advertising bar.

If the new Windows 7 Live Essentials can also work with Vista — or even Windows XP — so much the better, from the (Micro)Softie's point of view. Microsoft revenue from Windows 7 comes from selling software — Windows 7, Windows Server in various flavors, and Exchange, for example. The revenue model for the Live lineup involves advertising and commissions, so the more customers, the merrier.

Inventorying the Essentials

As of this writing, Microsoft advertises 11 Windows Live Essentials. Only 4 of them were in previous versions of Windows (or 5, if you stretch things a bit).

That means 6 or 7 of the new Live Essentials weren't so essential back in the prehistoric days of Vista.

Take it all with a grain of salt, okay?

Here's how I figure it. Almost every Windows 7 user will want three of the Windows Live Essentials:

+ **Windows Live Photo Gallery:** Shown in Figure 5-1, it runs rings around the Start⇨Pictures photo handling capabilities of native Windows 7. If you do anything with pictures — they don't have to be photos — it's worth your while to download and use Windows Live Photo Gallery to retrieve, tag, display, and manage your photos. (It works with Windows 7, Vista, and XP, although you need Windows 7 to get the full effects of the Picture Library. It's billed as a replacement for the Windows Vista Photo Gallery.)

Figure 5-1: Windows Live Photo Gallery lets you retrieve, tag, display, and manage photos or any other types of picture files.

+ **Windows Live Sync**: When you install Windows Live Photo Gallery, you also receive a copy of this full-featured folder synchronizer with a nascent interface. Microsoft bought the FolderShare program from ByteTaxi, Inc., in late 2005, added a user interface of sorts, and bundled the result with Windows Live Photo Gallery. *Et voilà.* You can synchronize pictures across different PCs or folders with just a few clicks.

See Book IV, Chapter 5 for the lowdown on Windows Live Photo Gallery.

+ **Windows Live Movie Maker:** For anyone who ever plays with video clips — indeed, anybody who wants to make a slide show without using

PowerPoint, this program (see Figure 5-2) is well worth the download. Or at least it will be worth the download, once Microsoft has fleshed it out a bit. Not as capable as the commercial video editing programs, it's still easy to use. And, it integrates well with Windows Live Photo Gallery. (Windows Live Movie Maker works on Vista and Windows 7. It's a replacement for the notoriously buggy and wimpy Vista Movie Maker.)

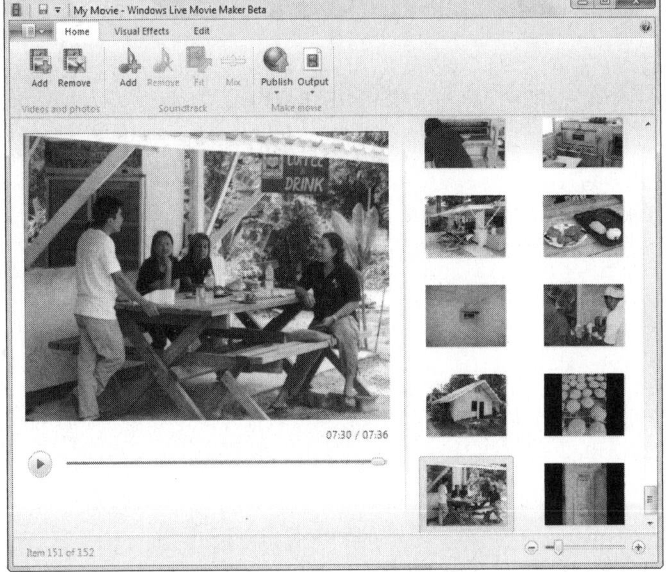

Figure 5-2: Windows Live Movie Maker lets you edit and stitch together clips like a pro.

See Book IV, Chapter 6 for more information about Windows Live Movie Maker.

In addition, many Windows 7 users will want two more Windows Live Essentials:

✦ **Windows Live Messenger** is the latest incarnation in a long line of Messengers, including MSN Messenger, .NET Messenger, Microsoft Messenger, and Windows Messenger. Now equipped with funny, rumbling icons for your chatting edification; easy voice and video capabilities; group chats (complete with home pages and group calendars); mobile phone tie-ins; and contact-harvesting capabilities with Bebo, Facebook, Hi5, LinkedIn, and Tagged, this ain't your grandfather's Messenger. Windows Live Messenger now works with Yahoo! Messenger, so your Yahoo! friends can chat with you, and you with them. Windows Live Messenger works with any version of Windows.

When you install Windows Live Messenger, something appears on your Start menu — Windows Live Call. As best I can tell, Windows Live Call isn't a program, Essential or not. It's just a hook into Windows Live Messenger that lets Messenger act like Skype. In other words, you can click Live Call to make a long distance phone call over the Internet to another person with Messenger or to someone's landline or mobile phone.

See Book V, Chapter 7 for more information on Windows Live Messenger.

✦ **Windows Live Mail** is the latest incarnation in a long line of free Microsoft mail programs that run on your computer. (If you don't have a reliable Internet connection, it may be better than Hotmail or Gmail.) If you've ever used Outlook Express (in Windows XP and earlier) or Windows Mail (which is almost identical to Outlook Express, in Windows Vista) or Windows Live Mail Desktop (a discarded name for the same thing), you've seen the progenitors of Windows Live Mail. Hotmail (er, Windows Live Hotmail) is different: For starters, it runs in your Web browser, not directly on your PC. Outlook is different, too: It costs money. Windows Live Mail (see Figure 5-3) not only grabs your "regular" e-mail but can also grab mail from your Hotmail, Gmail, and AOL mail accounts.

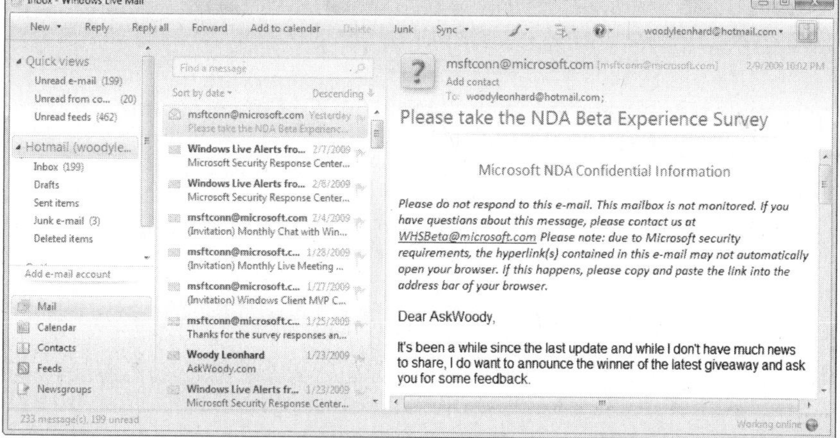

Figure 5-3: Windows Live Mail rates as a reasonably good, free mail program.

See Book V, Chapter 6 for more about Windows Live Mail.

Windows Live Essentials includes six additional components. I have no idea why Microsoft calls them *Essentials.* The list changes from time to time, but as of this writing, these are the six essential programs that few Windows 7 users will want:

- **Windows Live Writer** helps you write entries for your blog and post them, as long as you use one of the big-name services or products for your blog: Blogger, Live Journal, TypePad, Windows Live Spaces, WordPress, or (shudder!) the Microsoft SharePoint blog. Because the blogging service you're most likely to use — Blogger, TypePad, or WordPress, in particular — all have decent editors, it's hard to imagine why you would want to add another program in the middle of things. Word 2007 has a Publish As Blog option, if you feel like using a Bentley to do a Festiva job.
- **Windows Live Family Safety** presents the latest version of the Microsoft Web site and chat-blocking and -tracking software. It replaces the Family Safety features of Windows XP and Vista and the Family Safety component of Windows Live OneCare. The people involved work hard to make the Internet a safe place for kids to learn and play. Unfortunately, at least in my opinion, the job they've undertaken is intractable beyond a certain point. The American Academy of Pediatrics has an excellent overview of the challenges, and a lot of resource material, at `safetynet.aap.org`.
- **Windows Live Toolbar** — "Oh, goodie! Look, Mildred — *another* toolbar!" This one replaces the old MSN Search Toolbar, as though you missed it. Now you can make sure that you have *both* Microsoft Live and Windows Live Search available all the time — as long as you're using Internet Explorer (IE) and haven't upgraded to a better Web browser. How on earth anybody could call this an Essential boggles my mind. It works with any version of Windows, as long as you have (the toxic) IE 6 or later.
- **Microsoft Office Outlook (MOO) Connector** rates as essential because, uh, well, because Microsoft says it is. MOO Connector lets you download your Hotmail messages in Outlook 2003 and 2007. No, Hotmail isn't essential. No, Outlook 2003 and 2007 aren't essential. But the Microsoft Office Outlook Connector is like, totally, absolutely essential. Microsoft used to post instructions for hooking Outlook 2003 and Outlook 2007 into Hotmail (`support.microsoft.com/kb/287424`). The instructions are gone, replaced by a link to this essential product. Progress.
- **Microsoft Office Live Add-In** puts a new toolbar in Office XP, Office 2003, and Office 2007 ("Oh, goodie! Look, Mildred. . . ."). The toolbar's purpose is to "extend your Microsoft Office experience to the Web." (No, I don't make this stuff up.) Your experience is extended by the capability to save Word, Excel, and PowerPoint documents directly to Microsoft Office Live Workspace. I have no idea why this feature is essential to Windows 7 users. Some days, enlightenment eludes me.
- **Microsoft Silverlight** represents Microsoft's attempt to challenge Adobe Flash Player in the Web animation player market. You already have Flash Player — about 98 percent of all PCs do — and I can't think of a single good reason why you would want the Microsoft replacement. The Microsoft Silverlight site, `www.microsoft.com/silverlight`,

says that Silverlight offers a "seamless adaptive streaming experience" that you can, uh, you can, er, oh, never mind. The site advertises "the new MSN toolbar," so you can tell that these guys are (not) up-to-date. Essential? Meh.

That's the score. Of 11 Windows Live Essentials (this week, anyway), 2 are winners, 1 comes along for the ride, 2 may be useful for Windows 7 customers, and 6 aren't worth the bits to blast them to Ballmer.

Distinguishing Essentials from the Other Live Components

If you think that somebody came up with the list of Windows Live Essentials on the back of a cocktail napkin, well, you aren't alone. Before there were Essentials, Microsoft had already brought together a bunch of disparate programs and emblazoned them with the Windows Live brand.

So that you don't get confused, I list some of the Windows Live programs you may know. None of them is part of Windows Live Essentials (at least, not this week). None of them is a program that you download and run on your computer. You may want to use one or all of the Windows Live collection, but I don't discuss them in detail in this book. Here's the list:

- **Windows Live Hotmail** (`hotmail.com`), formerly just plain Hotmail and MSN Mail before that, offers a good-quality, free online e-mail service, comparable to Gmail (`mail.google.com`) or Yahoo! Mail (`mail.yahoo.com`).

  Think of it this way: The Windows Live Mail program runs on your computer; if you use it, your mail is stored on your computer. Windows Live Hotmail runs on the Internet — you can get to it by typing `hotmail.com` in a Web browser; if you use Hotmail, your mail is kept on the Internet.

- **Windows Live Spaces** (`spaces.live.com`), formerly MSN Spaces, offers free social networking with a bit of blogging. It sorta competes with Facebook, Flickr, LinkedIn, and MySpace as a social networking site.
- **Windows Live SkyDrive** (`skydrive.live.com`) gives you as much as 25GB of free online storage.
- **Windows Live Profile**, **Groups**, **Events**, and **Calendar** give you online contacts, scheduling, and the like.

If the Windows Live lineup doesn't inspire you, check back again in a few years. Microsoft will pour hundreds of millions of dollars into the Live bucket.

Installing Essentially

Want to install a couple of Live-ly ones? Here's how to get the Windows Live Essentials you want — and let the others sit and stew:

1. **Choose Start⇨Getting Started⇨Get Windows Live Essentials.**

   Windows 7 fires up (what else?) Internet Explorer and sends you to the Live Essentials download page, `download.live.com`. Alternatively, you can use any browser you like and go to the same page.

2. **Click the Download button on the right.**

   Choose to Save the file. The Windows Live Installer is transferred to your computer.

3. **Double-click the installer or do whatever you need to do (depending on your browser) to run it.**

   You see the Windows Live Installer, shown in Figure 5-4.

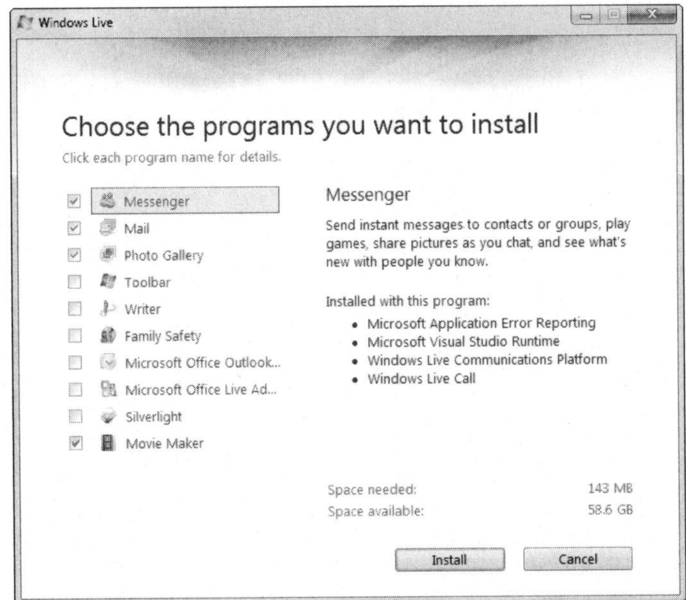

Figure 5-4: Pick the Essentials programs that are essential for you.

4. **Take a look at the list in the first section of this chapter and choose the Windows Live Essentials that strike your fancy. Click Install.**

   In Figure 5-4, I choose Windows Live Messenger, Mail, Photo Gallery, and Movie Maker. Your mileage may vary. The Windows Live Installer churns away for a while, and then comes back with a set of check boxes that ask you to set your search provider and home page and to "help improve Windows Live."

5. **Deselect all the check boxes and then click Continue.**

   Here's what Microsoft is trying to get you to agree to:

   If you select the first check box, the installer downloads the Choice Guard program, which changes the default search engine in both Internet Explorer and Firefox to Microsoft's own Live Search. (You can change the search engine anytime you like — see Book V, Chapter 2.) I find it creepy that Choice Guard looks for programs on your computer that might automatically change the default search engine to something else, and nullifies them, to ensure that Live Search is set as the default and stays there. Programs that change the default search engine are scummy by definition. Choice Guard protects against such scum — but only if you pick Windows Live Search as your default search engine.

   If you select the second check box, the installer downloads Choice Guard and sets both the Firefox and Internet Explorer home pages to `msn.com`. Golly, that's just the home page I always wanted. (See Book V, Chapter 2 to change it yourself.) Once again, Choice Guard roots out and nullifies any scummy competing programs that might change the home page back. Microsoft says that Choice Guard runs only once, so if you change your default search engine or home page, it doesn't come back to haunt you.

   The final check box lets you send all your Windows usage history, browser history, lists of songs you listen to and videos you watch, and just about anything else you do to Mother Microsoft so that the company can improve Windows Live. Ya gotta be kidding, right?

6. **When the final panel asks you to sign up for a Windows Live ID, ignore what it says and click Close.**

   If you have a Hotmail ID, a Messenger ID, or an Xbox Online ID, you already have a Windows Live ID. If you don't have one yet, follow the directions in Book V, Chapter 7 to get an anonymous Windows Live ID.

The Windows Live Essentials you chose are installed and ready to use. In fact, Windows Live Messenger is so pushy that you immediately see the sign-in screen, and if you click the X box to close Messenger, it informs you that it will continue to run so that you can be alerted if somebody tries to send you a message.

Microsoft. You gotta love it.

Book II

Windows 7 Boot Camp

Contents at a Glance

Chapter 1: Running Windows from Start to Finish

In This Chapter

- **Moving around the desktop**
- **Working with windows (*windows* with a wittle *w*)**
- **Stepping through the wondrous Taskbar**
- **Organizing files and folders**
- **Showing filename extensions**
- **Using libraries to extend your reach**
- **To sleep, perchance to dream**

This chapter explains how to find your way around the Windows windows. If you're an old hand at Windows, you know most of this stuff — such as mousing and interacting with dialog boxes — but I bet some of it will come as a surprise, particularly if you've never taken advantage of Windows 7 libraries or if the idea of using a background slide show appeals to you. You know who you are.

Most of all, you need to understand that you don't have to accept all the default settings. Windows 7 was designed to sell more copies of Windows 7. A lot of that folderol just gets in the way. What's best for Microsoft isn't necessarily best for you, and a few quick clicks can help make your PC more usable, and more . . . yours.

If you're looking for information on customizing the Windows 7 Start menu and the taskbar, skip ahead to Book III, Chapter 2.

A Few Quick Steps to Make the Desktop Your Own

As soon as you *log on* to the computer (that's what it's called when you click your name), you're greeted with an enormous expanse of near-nothingness, cleverly painted with a pretty picture. Your computer manufacturer might have chosen the picture for you, or you might see the default Microsoft screen.

Your Windows destiny, such as it is, unfolds on the computer's screen. The screen that Windows shows you every time you start your computer is the *desktop,* although it doesn't bear much resemblance to a real desktop. Try putting a pencil on it.

I talk about changing and organizing your desktop in Book III, Chapter 1, but every new Windows 7 user will want to make a few quick changes. In the end, your desktop should look something like Figure 1-1 — although you probably want a cool picture slide show on the desktop rather than a photo of my namesake.

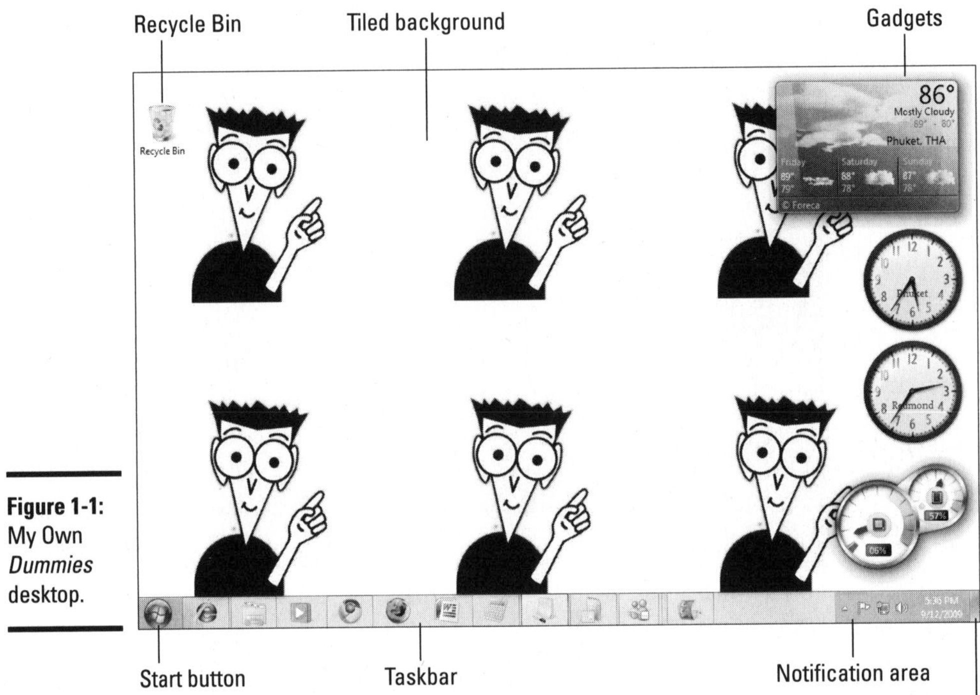

Figure 1-1: My Own *Dummies* desktop.

The Windows desktop looks simple enough, but don't fool yourself: Underneath that calm exterior sits the most sophisticated computer program ever created. Hundreds of millions of dollars went into creating the illusion of simplicity — something to remember the next time you feel like kicking your computer and screaming at the 7 gods.

Changing the background

Start taking your destiny into your own hands by changing the wallpaper (er, the *desktop background*). If you bought a new computer with Windows 7 installed, your background text probably says *Dell* or *Vaio* or *Billy Joe Bob's Computer Emporium / Dial 555-3765 for a good time.* Bah. Change your wallpaper by following these steps (note that Windows 7 Starter Edition owners can't change the wallpaper):

1. **Right-click an empty part of the desktop and choose Personalize.**

   Windows hops to the Control Panel's Personalization pane, shown in Figure 1-2.

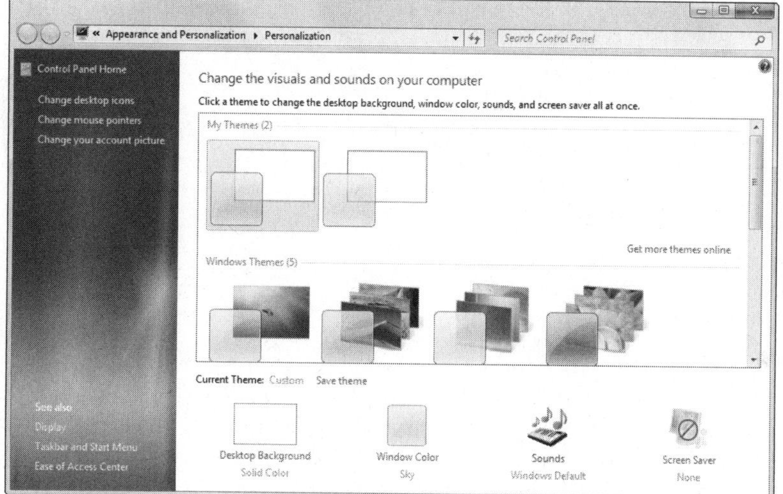

Figure 1-2: Choose your desktop background (even a slide show) here.

2. **If you see a theme you like (use the scroll bar on the right to make sure you see all of them, including the high contrast options), click one of the Windows themes.**

   Each of the Windows themes consists of a slide show of the pictures you see, shuffled every 30 minutes. Although themes can specify different sounds and screen savers, the built-in Windows themes don't modify the sounds and they don't include screen savers.

   If you want to see the details about each of the themes — in particular, if you *really* want to know where those gorgeous photos were shot — choose the theme and then click the Desktop Background link in the lower left corner. Hover the mouse over the picture to see its lineage.

3. **If you don't see a theme that tickles your fancy, or if you want to roll your own backgrounds, in the lower left corner click the Desktop Background link.**

   Windows responds with the Desktop Background window, shown in Figure 1-3, where you choose the pictures that you want to appear in a slide show by hovering the mouse over the picture and then selecting the box that appears.

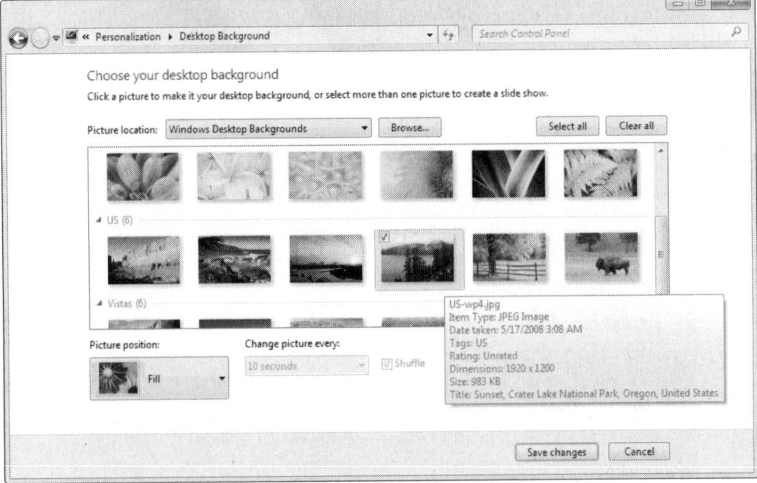

Figure 1-3: Choose the pictures that you want to appear in a slide show.

4. **Use the drop-down menu to tell Windows where to look for pictures or to select from the Windows 7 built-in collection of solid colors or photos or to pull out your highest-rated photos.**

   If you click a picture, it becomes your new desktop background. If you hover the mouse over a picture and select the check box in its upper left corner (refer to Figure 1-3), you add the picture to the Windows slide show collection.

5. **To enable the desktop wallpaper and background slide show, select more than one picture (or choose a theme that has more than one picture).**

   That's all it takes.

6. **(Optional) Change the speed of the slide show by selecting a forward speed in the Change Picture Every box.**

7. **At the bottom of the Desktop Background dialog box, in the Picture Position drop-down list, choose how you want to position the picture, if it's too small to cover your desktop.**

   Your options are

   - *Stretched to fill the screen*
   - *Centered in the middle of the desktop*
   - *Tiled over the desktop (refer to Figure 1-1)*

8. **In the Desktop Background dialog box, click the Save Changes button and then the Close (X) button to close the Control Panel's Personalization pane.**

   Your new wallpaper settings take effect immediately.

Getting gadgets

Gadgets started in Windows Vista, but they didn't catch on the way Microsoft thought they would, no doubt because of the clumsy way they were handled (saddled to the Sidebar but detachable) and the lack of compelling gadgets shipping with Vista.

Windows 7 improves on gadgets significantly, primarily by cutting out the middleman: Now, gadgets live on the desktop — and they aren't as prone to hobbling or even bringing down your computer, as they were before (although the Windows Media Center gadget sucks up cycles as eagerly as the media center itself).

To get your own gadgets, follow these easy steps:

1. **Right-click an empty part of the desktop and choose Gadgets.**

   Windows 7 lists its stock gadgets, as shown in Figure 1-4.

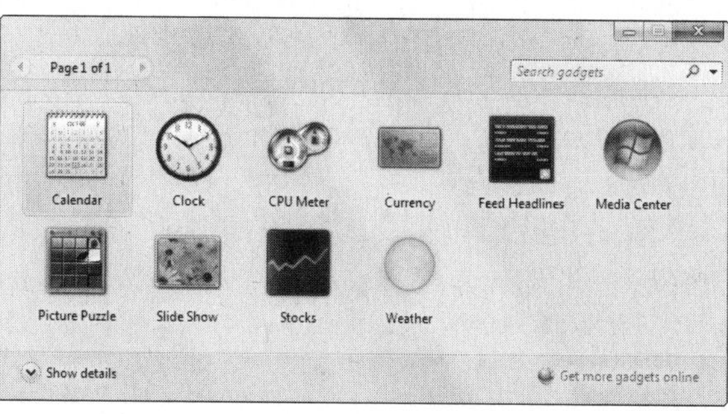

Figure 1-4: Built-in Windows 7 gadgets tell only a small part of the story.

2. **To put one of the built-in gadgets on your desktop, click and drag it onto the desktop. Or, skip to Step 3 to check out the wider selection of gadgets online.**

   When you drag the gadget onto the desktop, you see three or four controls to the right of the gadget, as shown in Figure 1-5.

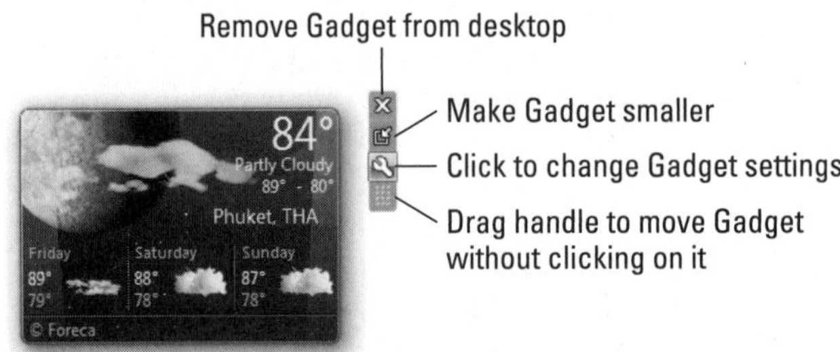

Figure 1-5: Most gadgets have three or four controls, which appear on the right when you drag the gadget.

3. **Click the Get More Gadgets Online link in the lower right corner to visit Microsoft Gadget Central at**

   ```
   windows.microsoft.com/en-us/Windows7/
      Personalize?T1=tab04
   ```

   Like most Microsoft sites, this one tries to sell you stuff you don't necessarily want, so make sure to read the fine print before you download a gadget or take a "computer wizard" test (". . . will recommend improvements to your computer automatically!" — puh-lease.) But if you stick to the gadgets marked Free, you might find some that are worthwhile.

   There *is* some potential for security holes in the Windows 7 gadget software. *Gadgets* are programs that run on your computer that constantly interact with the Internet, so they can't be completely bullet-proof — but I'm not aware of any breaches discovered to date. If you're curious about the technical details, look at `msdn.microsoft.com/en-us/library/bb498012.aspx`.

   Microsoft makes some of the Gadgets on offer, but many come from outside sources. The usual admonitions apply: While Microsoft undoubtedly vetted the Gadgets you see, it would be wise to limit yourself to Gadgets from people and companies you trust.

My favorite non-Microsoft gadgets are the Wired and Wireless Network Meters from Addgadget.com. They keep track of your up and down Internet speeds and watch your IP address. Very cool. Absolutely free.

4. **When you're done adding gadgets, click the Close (X) button to close your Web browser and then click X to close the gadget chooser.**

   To get rid of a gadget, just click the X in the upper right corner.

Cleaning up useless icons and programs

If you haven't yet taken control and zapped those obnoxious programs that your PC vendor probably stuck on your machine, now is the time to do it.

If you bought a new computer with Windows 7 preinstalled, the manufacturer probably sold some desktop real estate to a software company or an Internet service provider (ISP). (Oh yeah, the AOLs and Nortons of the world compensate the Sonys and Dells and HPs for services, and space, rendered.) The last thing you need is yet another come-on to sign up for AOL or an antivirus program that begs you for money every week.

- **To get rid of most icons,** simply right-click them and choose Delete.
- **To get rid of the icons' associated programs,** choose Start➪Control Panel➪Uninstall a Program (which appears in the Programs section). When the Uninstall or Change a Program dialog box opens, double-click a program to remove it.

Unfortunately, many scummy programs don't play by the rules: Either they don't have uninstallers or the uninstaller that appears in the Change a Program dialog box doesn't get rid of the program entirely. (I won't mention Norton Internet Security by name.) To get rid of the scummy stuff, look in Book I, Chapter 4 for information about PC Decrapifier, a program from Jason York. It's at `pcdecrapifier.com/download`.

Mousing with Your Mouse

For almost everybody, the computer's mouse serves as the primary way of interacting with Windows. But you already knew that. You can click the left mouse button or the right mouse button, or you can roll the wheel in the middle (if you have one), and the mouse will do different things, depending on where you click or roll. But you already knew that, too.

The Windows 7 Multi-Touch technology lets you act like Tom Cruise in *Minority Report,* if you have the bucks for the multiple-finger sensitive pad, the right application software, and the horsepower to drive it. But for those of us who put our gloves on one hand at a time, the mouse remains the input device of choice.

The best way to get the feel for a new mouse? Play one of the games that ships with Windows. Choose Start⇨Games and take it away. I recommend Minesweeper, Chess Titans, and Solitaire for mouse orienteering. Try clicking in unlikely places, double-clicking, or right-clicking in new and different ways. Bet you'll discover several wrinkles, even if you're an old hand at the games. (See Book III, Chapter 4 for more on Windows games.)

Inside the computer, programmers measure the movement of mice in units called *mickeys*. Nope, I'm not making this up. Move your mouse a short distance, and it travels a few mickeys. Move it to Anaheim, and it puts on a lot of mickeys.

What's up, Dock?

Windows 7 includes several "gesture" features that can save you a lot of time. Foremost among them: a half-window docking capability that Microsoft insists on calling *Aero Snap*.

If you click the title bar of a window and drag the window a-a-all the way to the left side of the screen, as soon as the mouse hits the edge of the screen, Windows 7 resizes the window so that it occupies the left half of the screen and the docks the window on the far left side. Similarly, *mutatis mutandis*, for the right side. That makes it two-drag easy to put a Word document and a spreadsheet side by side, or a PowerPoint presentation next to Photo Gallery, as shown in Figure 1-6.

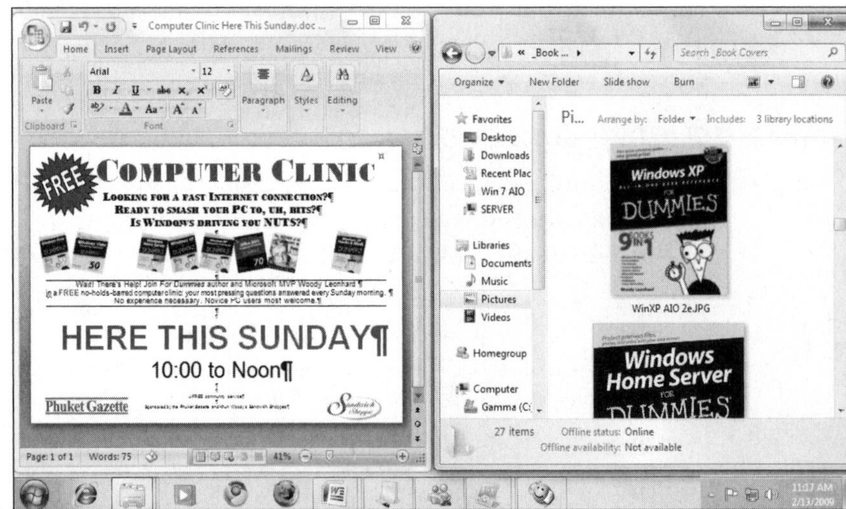

Figure 1-6: Two drags and you can have Windows arrange two different programs side by side.

Those aren't the only new gestures. If you drag a window to the top of the screen, it's *maximized,* so it occupies the whole screen. (Yeah, I know: You always did that by double-clicking the title bar.) And, if you click a window's title bar and shake it, all other windows on the screen move out of the way: They *minimize* themselves on the toolbar.

If you have rodentophobia, you can also do the mouse tricks explained in this section by pressing the following key combinations:

- **Aero Snap left:** ⊞+←
- **Aero Snap right:** ⊞ +→
- **Maximize:** ⊞+↑

Changing the mouse

If you're left-handed, you can interchange the actions of the left and right mouse buttons — that is, you can tell Windows 7 that it should treat the left mouse button as though it were the right button and treat the right button as though it were the left. The swap comes in handy for some left-handers, but most southpaws I know (including my son) prefer to keep the buttons as is because it's easier to use other computers if your fingers are trained for the standard setting.

The Windows ClickLock feature can come in handy if you have trouble holding down the left mouse button and moving the mouse at the same time — a common problem for notebook users who have fewer than three hands. When Windows uses ClickLock, you hold down the mouse button for a while (you can tell Windows exactly how long) and Windows locks the mouse button so that you can concentrate on moving the mouse without having to hold down the button.

To switch left and right mouse buttons or turn on ClickLock, follow these steps:

1. **Click Start. Immediately type mouse and press Enter.**

   Windows opens the Mouse Properties dialog box, shown in Figure 1-7.

2. **If you want to switch the functions of the left and right mouse buttons, select the Switch Primary and Secondary Buttons check box.**

3. **If you want to turn on ClickLock, check the Turn On ClickLock box and immediately click the Settings button.**

   You can then adjust the length of time you need to hold down the mouse button for ClickLock to kick in.

4. **Click OK.**

   The changes take place immediately.

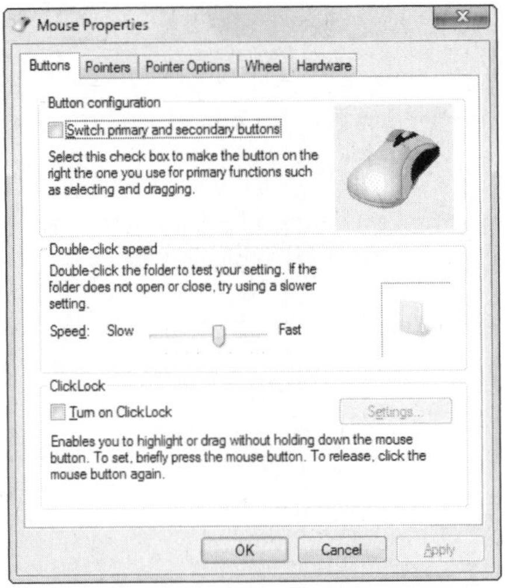

Figure 1-7: Reverse the left and right mouse buttons with one click.

Starting with the Start Button

The Windows 7 orientation rightfully starts in the lower left corner of the screen with the button that shows the Windows logo — the Start button, if you will.

Microsoft's subverting of the classic Rolling Stones song "Start Me Up" for Windows 95 advertising might be ancient history now, but the royal road to Windows still starts at the Start button. Click the Start button to open the Start menu, which looks something like the one shown in Figure 1-8.

The Start menu looks like it's etched in granite, but it isn't. You can change three pieces without even digging deep:

- **To change the name or picture of the current user,** see Book II, Chapter 2.
- **To remove a program from the list of pinned programs (upper left) or the recently used programs list (lower left),** right-click it and choose Remove from This List.
- **To add a program to the pinned programs list,** navigate to the program (by choosing Start⇨All Programs, for example), right-click the program, and choose Pin to Start Menu. Book III, Chapter 2 has more details on pinning.

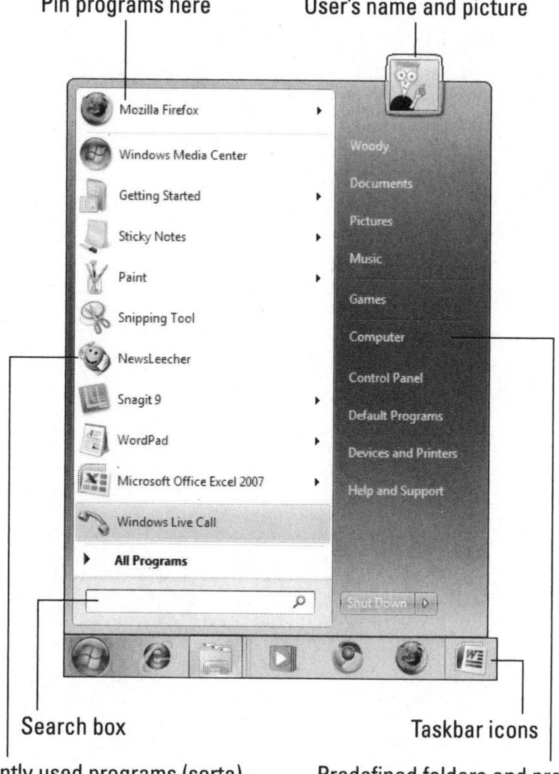

Figure 1-8: The Windows Start menu packs a wallop — and you can customize it, to some degree.

If you bought a new computer with Windows 7 preinstalled, the people who make the computer may have sold one or two or three of the spots on the Start menu. Think of it as an electronic billboard on your desktop. Nope, I'm not exaggerating. I keep expecting to bump into a Windows machine with fly-out Start menu entries that read, oh, "Statistics prove⇨Near and far⇨That folks who⇨Drive like crazy⇨Are⇨Burma Shave." (See `Burma-shave.org/jingles`.) You can always delete a pesky Start menu billboard by right-clicking it and choosing Remove from This List.

The right side of the Start menu contains an odd mélange of items:

- **Shortcuts to many of the Windows 7 predefined folders and libraries.** An introduction to libraries appears later in this chapter.
- **Quick access to features,** such as the Devices and Printers panel.

- **Entrée to the Control Panel,** which I discuss in Book II, Chapter 3, and the Help and Support Center, which I discuss in Book II, Chapter 5.
- **The means for putting your computer to sleep, locking it, restarting it, or shutting it off.** For details, see "Sleep: Perchance to Dream," later in this chapter.

You can modify most of the right side of the Start menu by using the Customize Start Menu dialog box (see Figure 1-9).

Select to make a Games fly-out menu.

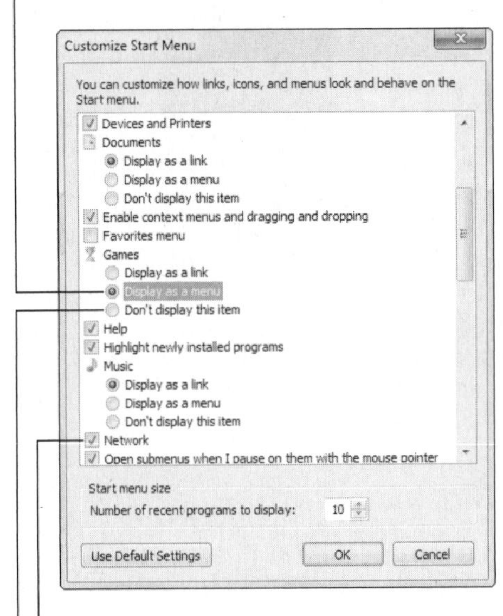

Check to add a direct link to a list of network devices.

Select to remove Games from Start menu.

Figure 1-9: Control the behavior of items on the right side of the Start menu.

Here's how to make the Start menu work your way:

1. Right-click the Start button and choose Properties.

   The Taskbar and Start Menu Properties dialog box appears.

2. On the Start Menu tab, at the top, click the Customize button.

   Windows 7 shows you the Customize Start Menu dialog box (refer to Figure 1-9).

3. Add or remove items, or change the way they behave, by selecting or deselecting the appropriate check boxes.

   The Display As a Menu option button enables a fly-out cascading menu, as shown in Figure 1-10.

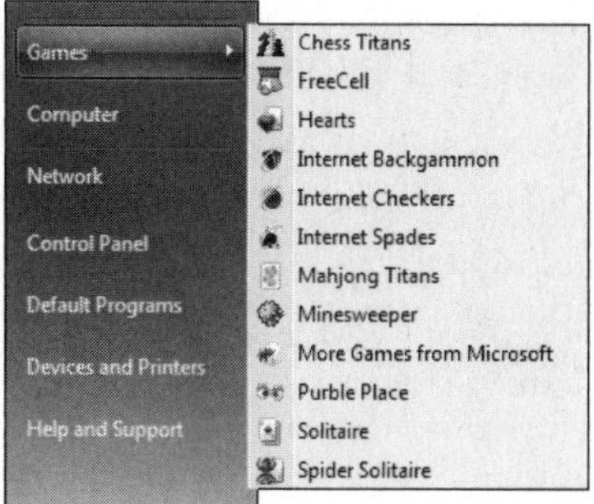

Figure 1-10: Example of a Display As a Menu fly-out menu.

4. When you're done, click the OK button twice.

   Windows 7 makes the changes immediately.

Old-timers used to have a Run item on the Start menu that allowed them to type a DOS command and have it executed directly. You can bring back the Run item by selecting the Run Command check box in the Customize Start Menu dialog box. Or (much easier), you can simply type your command in the Start Search box at the bottom of the Search menu and press Enter.

The old ⊞+R shortcut works in Windows 7, too: Press the two together and the Run dialog box appears.

Touching on the Taskbar

Windows 7 sports a highly customizable taskbar at the bottom of the screen (see Figure 1-11). I go into detail in Book III, Chapter 2.

Hover the mouse over a taskbar icon to see thumbnails.

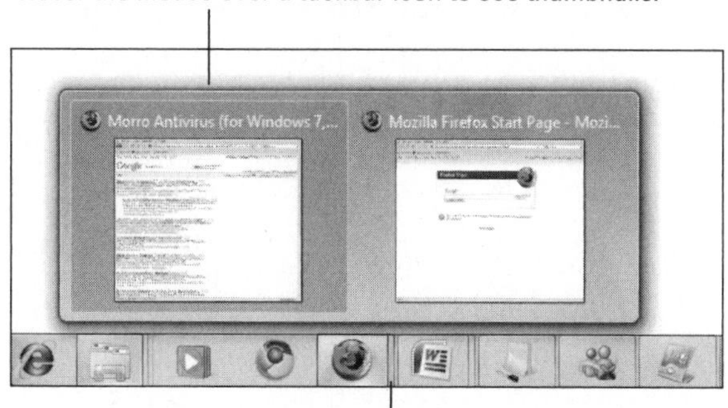

Subtle lines to the right indicate a program is running.

Figure 1-11: The Windows 7 Taskbar lets you pinpoint what's running and jump to the right location quickly.

Although the taskbar looks a lot like the Quick Launch toolbar that has been shipping with Windows since the days of Internet Explorer 4, there are a few important differences:

✦ **Hover your mouse over an icon to see what the program's running.** For example, in Figure 1-11 I hover my mouse over the Firefox icon and see that I have two open copies of Firefox. I can click either thumbnail to bring up the appropriate running copy.

Some applications, such as Internet Explorer 8, show each tab or open document in a separate thumbnail. Clicking a thumbnail brings up the application, along with the chosen tab or document. This nascent feature is implemented unevenly at this point — expect to see many more applications take advantage of this preview capability in the not-too-distant future.

✦ **Right-click an icon and you see the application's Jump List.** The Jump List may show an application's most recently opened documents. It may show a browser's history list. We're just starting to see how program writers will exploit this new capability, too.

If you click an icon, the program opens, as you would expect. But if you want to open a second copy of a program — say, another copy of Firefox — you can't just click the icon. You have to right-click and choose the application's name.

✦ **You can move the icons around on the taskbar by simply clicking and dragging.**

If you want to see all the gadgets on your desktop and relegate all open windows to shadows of their former selves, move your mouse to the far right edge of the taskbar.

The Windows taskbar has many tricks up its sleeve, but it has one capability that you may need, if screen real estate is at a premium. (Hey, you folks with 30-inch monitors need not apply, okay?)

Auto-Hide lets the taskbar shrink to a thin line until you bump the mouse pointer way down at the bottom of the screen. As soon as the mouse pointer hits bottom, the taskbar pops up. Here's how to teach the taskbar to auto-hide:

1. Right-click an empty part of the taskbar.
2. Choose Properties.

   The Taskbar tab should be visible.
3. Select the Auto-Hide the Taskbar check box and then click OK.

The taskbar holds many surprises. See Book III, Chapter 2.

Working with Files and Folders

"What's a file?" Man, I wish I had a nickel for every time I've been asked that question.

A file is a, uh, thing. Yeah, that's it. A thing. A thing that has stuff inside it. Why don't you ask me an easier question, like "What is a paragraph?" or "What is the meaning of life, the universe, and everything?"

A *file* is a fundamental chunk of stuff. Like most fundamental chunks of stuff (say, protons, Congressional districts, or ear wax), any attempt at a definitive definition gets in the way of understanding the thing itself. Suffice it to say that a Word document is a file. An Excel workbook is a file. That photograph your cousin e-mailed you the other day is a file. Every track on the latest Nine Inch Nails CD is a file, but so is every track on every audio CD ever made. Trent Reznor isn't that special.

WARNING!

Filenames and folder names can be very long, but they can't contain the following characters:

```
/ \ : * ? " < > |
```

Files can be huge. They can be tiny. They can even be empty, but don't short-circuit any gray cells on that observation.

Keeping folders organized

If you set folders up right, they can help you keep track of things. If you toss your files around higgledy-piggledy, no system of folders in the world can help. Unfortunately, folders have a fundamental problem. Permit me to illustrate.

Say you own a sandwich shop. You take a photograph of the shop. Where do you stick the photo? Which folder should you use? The answer: There's no good answer. You could put the photo in with all your other "shop" stuff — documents and invoices and payroll records and menus. You could stick the photo in the Pictures folder, which Windows 7 automatically provides. You could put it in the Public or Public Documents or Public Pictures folder so that other people using your PC, or other folks connected to your network, can see the photo of the shop. You could create a folder named Photos and file away the picture chronologically (that's what I do), or you could even create a folder named Shop inside the Photos folder and stick the picture in `\Photos\Shop`.

This where-to-file-it-and-where-to-find-it conundrum stands as one of the hairiest problems in all of Windows, and until Windows 7, you had only piecemeal help in keeping things organized. Now, using the Windows 7 libraries, and a Search function that (finally!) works the way you would expect, you stand a fighting chance of finding that long-lost file, especially if you're diligent in assigning tags to pictures and videos. See the section "Arranging Libraries," later in this chapter.

Folders hold files and other folders. Folders can be empty. A single folder can hold millions — yes, quite literally millions — of files and other folders.

To look at the files and folders on your machine that you probably use every day, choose Start➪Documents. A program named Windows Explorer appears, and it shows you the contents of your Documents library. As I explain later in this chapter (see the section "Arranging Libraries"), a library contains one or more folders, and the folders may contain any number of files or other folders. You see something like the list shown in Figure 1-12.

Windows Explorer shows you libraries. It can also show you the contents of a hard drive — folders and files — or a thumb drive or a CD/DVD drive. Windows Explorer can also help you look at other computers on your network, if you have a network. See the section "Using Windows Explorer," later in this chapter.

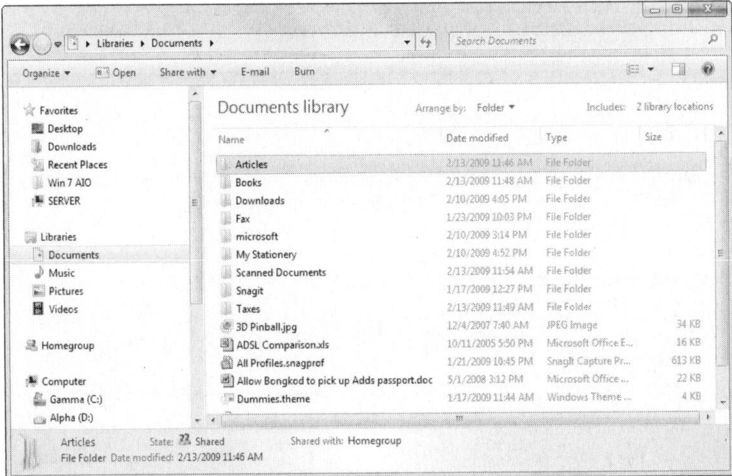

Figure 1-12: The files and folders in the Documents library, shown by Windows Explorer.

Creating files and folders

Usually, you create new files and folders when you're using a program. You make new Word documents when you're using Word, say, or come up with a new folder to hold all your offshore banking spreadsheets when you're using Excel. Programs usually have the tools for making new files and folders tucked away in the File➪Save and File➪Save As dialog boxes. Click around a bit and you'll find them.

But you can also create a new file or folder directly in an existing folder quite easily, without going through the hassle of cranking up a 900-pound gorilla of a program. Follow these steps:

1. **Move to the location where you want to put the new file or folder.**

   For example, if you want to stick the new folder Revisionist Techno Grunge in your Music folder, choose Start➪Music.

2. **Right-click a blank spot in your chosen location.**

   By "right-click a blank spot," I mean "don't right-click an existing file or folder," okay? If you want the new folder or file to appear on the desktop, right-click an empty spot on the desktop.

3. **Choose New (see Figure 1-13) and pick the kind of file you want to create.**

   If you want a new folder, choose Folder.

   Windows creates the new file or folder and leaves it with the name highlighted so that you can rename it by simply typing.

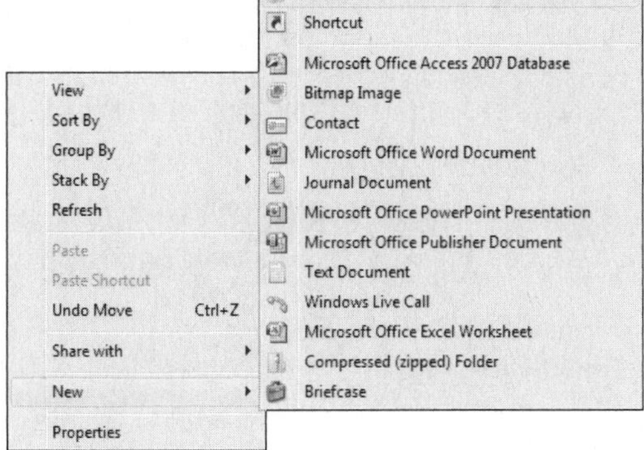

Figure 1-13: Right-click an empty location and choose New to create a new file or folder.

Modifying files and folders

As long as you have permission (see the section "Sharing folders," later in this chapter), modifying files and folders is easy — rename, delete, move, or copy them — if you remember the trick: Right-click.

To copy or move more than one file (or folder) at a time, select all the files (or folders) before right-clicking. To select more than one file:

- Hold down Ctrl while clicking.
- Click and drag around the outside of the files and folders to "lasso" them.
- Use the Shift key if you want to choose a bunch of contiguous files and folders — ones that are next to each other. Click the first file or folder, hold down Shift, and click the last file or folder.

Bringing back previous versions

Windows 7 uses a fancy method to keep track of previous versions of all files you open and change, as long as the file is located on the hard drive that contains Windows. Windows doesn't actually store a snapshot of all states of your lovely files. Instead, it uses a very sophisticated method to keep track of changes to your files. In geek-speak, it "stores the deltas."

These previous versions (also commonly called *shadow copies)* are stored whenever your computer creates a restore point. Because Windows 7 creates restore points, by default, once a day, chances are good that you can pick up several earlier versions of a file.

If you want to know which versions of a modified (even a deleted!) file exist in the Windows restore point maw and bring it back, follow these steps:

1. **Navigate to the munged file or folder — the one you want to bring back from the crypt — and right-click it.**

   If you accidentally deleted the file and can't bring it back from the Recycle Bin (see the section "Recycling," later in this chapter), right-click the folder that used to contain the file.

2. **Choose Restore Previous Versions.**

   Windows shows you the Properties dialog box for the file or folder you selected, opened to the Previous Versions tab, as shown in Figure 1-14.

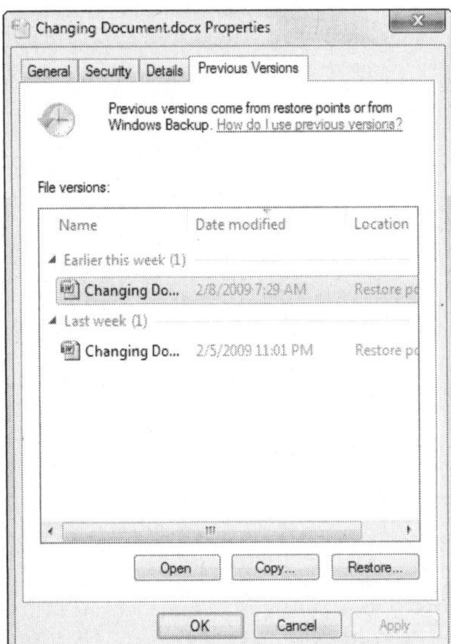

Figure 1-14: Previous versions can save your tail.

3. **Click the Open or Copy button and copy the older version of the file onto your desktop.**

Avoid the temptation to click the Restore button. This button overwrites whatever you may have — a hasty decision, at best, because even the most munged file or folder may have usable bits inside.

4. **Work with the restored version for a while and make sure that it's what you want.**

When you're happy with the result, copy the file to its original location.

A few key restrictions can jump up and bite you:

- Previous versions don't work continuously: If you saved a file in the morning, saved it again in the afternoon, and saved it at night, too, Windows 7 stores only the version that existed when it created a restore point — typically around midnight.
- A file has to be closed when Windows runs a restore point in order to get the current version saved. If you leave a file open overnight, you don't get a previous version that night.

- If a file is located on a drive other than the Windows system drive (typically C:), Windows doesn't save previous versions of the file unless you specifically tell it to include the drive in its previous version runs.

To tell Windows 7 to include other drives in its previous version runs, follow these steps:

1. **Choose Start, right-click Computer, and choose Properties.**

   You see the Control Panel's System pane.

2. **On the left, click the link to System Protection.**

   Windows opens the System Properties dialog box, on the System Protection tab, as shown on the left in Figure 1-15.

3. **Click the drive you want to include in previous versions, and then click Configure.**

   Windows opens the System Protection dialog box for the selected drive, as shown on the right in Figure 1-15.

4. **Click the button marked Only Restore Previous Versions of Files.**

   Consider setting aside more space for restore points by moving the slider. Personally, I leave it at the default.

5. **Click OK twice.**

   Starting tonight, Windows will create previous versions of all files on the chosen drive.

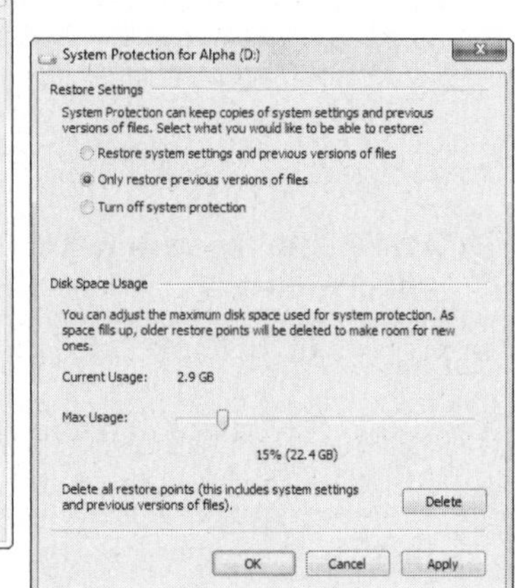

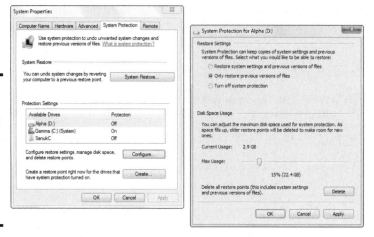

Figure 1-15: Include other drives in the Previous Versions brigade by using this dialog box.

Showing filename extensions

If you're looking at the Documents library on your computer and you can't see the period and three-letter suffixes of the filenames (such as `.doc` and `.xls` and `.jpg`) that are visible in Figure 1-12, don't panic! You need to tell Windows to show them — electronically knock Windows upside the head, if you will.

In my opinion, every single Windows 7 user should force Windows to show full filenames, including the (usually three-letter) extension at the end of the name.

I've been fighting Microsoft on this topic for many years. Forgive me if I get a little, uh, steamed — yeah, that's the polite way to put it — in the retelling.

Every file has a name. Almost every file has a name that looks more or less like this: `Some Name or Another.ext`.

The part to the left of the period — `Some Name or Another`, in this example — generally tells you something about the file, although it can be quite nonsensical or utterly inscrutable, depending on who named the file. The part to the right of the period — `ext`, in this case — is a filename *extension,* the subject of my diatribe.

Filename extensions have been around since the first PC emerged from the primordial ooze. They were a part of the PC's legacy before anybody ever talked about "legacy." Somebody, somewhere decided that Windows wouldn't show filename extensions any more. (My guess is that Bill Gates himself made the decision, about ten years ago, but it's only a guess.) Filename extensions were considered dangerous: too complicated for the typical user, a bit of technical arcana that novices shouldn't have to sweat.

Garbage. Pure, unadulterated garbage.

The fact is that nearly all files have names like `Letter to Mom.doc`, `Financial Projections.xls`, or `ILOVEYOU.vbs`. But Windows, with rare exception, shows you only the first part of the filename. It cuts off the filename extension. So you see `Letter to Mom`, without the `.doc` (which brands the file as a Word document), `Financial Projections` without the `.xls` (a dead giveaway for an Excel spreadsheet), and `ILOVEYOU` without the `.vbs` (which is the filename extension for Visual Basic programs).

I really hate it when Windows hides filename extensions, for four big reasons:

✦ **If you can see the filename extension, you can usually figure out which kind of file you have at hand and which program will open it.** People who use Word 2003, for example, may be perplexed to see a `.docx` filename extension — which is generated by Word 2007 and can't be opened by bone-stock Word 2003.

✦ **It's almost impossible to get Windows to change filename extensions if you can't see them.** Try it.

✦ **Microsoft Outlook forbids you from sending or receiving specific kinds of files, based solely on their filename extensions.** You can find a list of 88 dangerous filename extensions, blocked by Outlook 2003, at `office.microsoft.com/en-us/assistance/HA011402971033.aspx`.

✦ **You bump into filename extensions anyway.** No matter how hard Microsoft wants to hide filename extensions, they show up everywhere — from the `Readme.txt` files mentioned repeatedly in the official Microsoft documentation to discussions of `.jpg` file sizes on Microsoft Web pages and a gazillion places in between.

Take off the training wheels, okay? To make Windows show you filename extensions the easy way, follow these steps:

1. **Open Windows Explorer by choosing Start⇨Documents.**
2. **Press Alt to show the menu; then choose Tools⇨Folder Options and click the View tab.**

   You see the Folder View's Advanced Settings box, shown in Figure 1-16.

Figure 1-16: Make Windows show you filename extensions.

3. **Deselect the Hide Extensions for Known File Types check box.**

While you're here, you may want to change two other settings if you can avoid the temptation to delete or rename files that you don't understand. Select the Show Hidden Files, Folders and Drives option button if you want Windows to show you all files on your computer. Also consider deselecting the Hide Protected Operating System Files (Recommended) check box — showing Protected files tends to clutter the screen, so use your own discretion. Sometimes you need to see all your files, even if Windows wants to hide them from you.

4. **Click the OK button.**

Take a look at your unveiled filename extensions.

Sharing folders

Sharing is good, right? Your mom taught you to share, didn't she? Everything you need to know about sharing you learned in kindergarten — like how you can share your favorite crayon with your best friend and get back a gnarled blob of stunted wax, covered in mysterious goo.

Windows 7 supports two very different ways for sharing files and folders:

- **Move the files or folders that you want to share into the `\Public` folder.** The `\Public` folder is kind of a big cookie jar for everybody who uses your PC: Put a file or folder in the `\Public` folder so that all the other people who use your computer can get at it. The `\Public` folder is available to other people in your HomeGroup, if you have one, but you have little control over who, specifically, can get at the files and folders. (HomeGroups make it easier to set up sharing among Windows 7 computers on a network; see Book VII, Chapter 1 for details.)

- **Share individual files or folders, without moving them anywhere.** When you share a file or folder, you can tell Windows 7 to share the folder with everyone in your HomeGroup, or you can specify exactly who can access the file or folder and whether they can just look at it or change or delete it. I talk about the details in the section "Sharing and permissions," later in this chapter.

Using the \Public folder

You might think that simply moving a file or folder to the `\Public` folder would make it, well, public. At least to a first approximation, that's exactly how things work.

Any file or folder that you put in the `\Public` folder, or any folder inside the `\Public` folder, can be viewed, changed, or deleted by anybody who's using your computer, regardless of which kind of account they may have and whether they're required to log on to your computer. In addition, anybody who can get into your computer through the network will have unlimited access. The `\Public` folder is (if you'll pardon a rather stretched analogy) a big cookie jar, open to everybody who is in the kitchen.

(For more details, and important information about Public networks and big-company domains, check out *Networking All-In-One For Dummies,* by Doug Lowe [Wiley].)

Follow these easy steps to move a file or folder from one of the built-in libraries (Documents, Music, Pictures, or Videos) into its corresponding location in one of the `\Public` folders:

1. **Use Windows Explorer by choosing Start⇨Documents or Start⇨Pictures to navigate to the file or folder that you want to move into the `\Public` folder.**

   In Figure 1-17, I chose Start⇨Pictures to go to the Pictures library.

2. **If you can't see the `\Public` folder that you want to use, navigate to it. For example, to show the `\Public Pictures` folder, click on Pictures. Then click the folder (or file) that you want to move and drag it down to the `\Public` folder area.**

   In Figure 1-17, I drag the Leonhard Family Photos folder to the Public Pictures area.

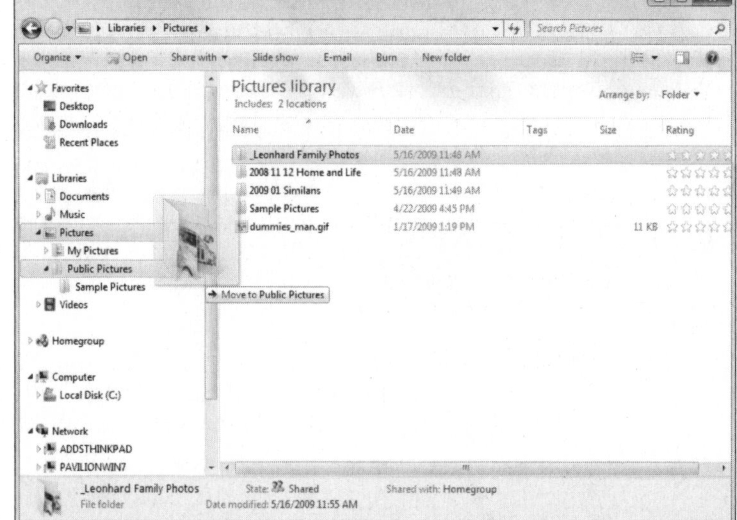

Figure 1-17: Moving a folder to the `\Public` folder is easy, if you know the trick.

3. **When the notification to the right of the dragging icon says Move to Public Pictures (or Documents, Music, or Videos), release the mouse button.**

   The folder moves to its new location, at which point it's available to anybody who uses your computer and to people who connect to your computer using HomeGroups. (It may also be available to other computers connected to your network, workgroup, or domain, depending on various network settings. See the rest of this chapter and *Networking All-In-One For Dummies* for specific examples.)

You can move other files and folders into the `\Public` folder by using Windows Explorer the old-fashioned way. Navigate to the folder (you typically choose Start⇨Computer and work from there), right-click it, choose Cut, and then go to the `Public` folder (choose Start⇨Computer and double-click C: and then Users and then Public) and right-click Paste into the folder you want.

Sharing on mixed HomeGroup and workgroup networks

Say you have a mixed network with Windows 7, Windows Vista, and Windows XP computers. The Windows 7 computers use a HomeGroup. The Vista and Windows XP computers use a workgroup. (As noted in Book VII Chapter 1, Vista and Windows XP computers don't recognize HomeGroups.) HomeGroups and workgroups coexist rather peacefully on the same network, in general, but you need to know the username and password for an account on the Windows 7 computer before you can get into its `\Public` folders.

If you have a Windows 7 computer that's attached to a HomeGroup and you try to access the `\Public` folder on that Windows 7 computer from Windows XP, you *usually* see a challenge like the one shown in Figure 1-18. You have to provide a username and password that are recognized on the Windows 7 computer before you can get into the `\Public` folder.

Figure 1-18: To get into a Windows 7 computer's `\Public` folder, provide a recognized username and password.

I say *usually* because there's one trick: If you set up an administrator account on both the Windows XP computer and the Windows 7 computer, both with the same username and password, Windows 7 passes you through without a challenge.

Vista works similarly. If you have a Windows 7 computer that's attached to your network and you try to get into the `\Public` folder of another Windows 7 computer that's part of a different HomeGroup, you have to provide a username and password, the same as in Vista and XP.

Unfortunately, having one account on two computers with the same username and password can pose all sorts of security problems. In the worst case, any bad program that runs on one computer may be smart enough to reach out to other computers on the network and infect them: The Conficker worm, which spread in early 2009, took advantage of that exact weakness.

Having said that, Microsoft uses this approach with Windows Home Server. WHS encourages you to share the same usernames and passwords on multiple computers in a home network. Go figger.

Sharing and permissions

Using the `\Public` folder, as described in the preceding section, constitutes a quick 'n' dirty approach to sharing: Everybody using your computer gets full access to all the `\Public` files, and people coming in from the network either get in or they don't. You have a little bit of fine control over who gets in and what they can do, but by and large, `\Public` is a blunt object.

You have fairly complex ways to force people accessing the `\Public` folder from the network to provide a password before opening the folder. If you set a password, anybody on your computer can get at the `\Public` folder without hindrance, but someone coming in from the outside has to provide the password. You can also establish read/write permissions for people accessing the `\Public` folder from the network. See Book VII, Chapter 1 for details.

The Windows 7 ability to establish sharing permissions for individual folders on your PC gives you much finer control. You can assign fine-grained permissions for your HomeGroup, or for individual users with Windows 7 built-in permission levels, which come in two flavors:

- **Read** allows the chosen individuals or groups to open or copy the file, but not change or delete them.
- **Read/Write** lets the designated user or group do anything to the files: open, change, delete, move.

This kind of fine-grained sharing is a minefield that you should not undertake unless you're willing to keep permissions updated. You should also be tolerant of many potential problems because I guarantee you'll bump into them. Rather than assign detailed sharing permissions to a folder, you might find it smarter (and much easier) to put the files you want to share in `\Public` and use read-only or read/write passwords to control access to the data in those files. All Office applications, and many others, have heavy-duty password protection available.

If you're convinced that using folder sharing permissions is the way to go, here's how to set up fine-grained sharing for a folder that's not in the `\Public` folder:

1. **Navigate to the folder you want to share.**

   In Figure 1-19, I go to the Articles folder on my D: drive.

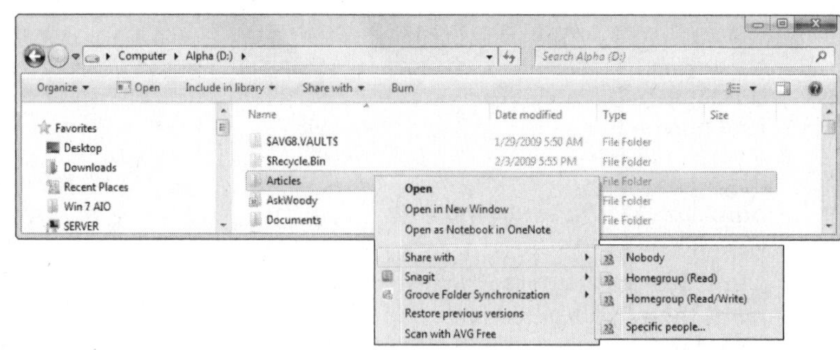

Figure 1-19: You can easily assign sharing restrictions for your HomeGroup, and it's only slightly harder for individual users to do so.

2. **Right-click the folder and choose Share With.**

   Share With appears on the right-click context menu only if you have sufficient rights to change access to the folder.

3. **Choose one of these options:**

   - *Nobody* so that nobody other than you can access the folder
   - *Homegroup (Read)* so that anyone in the HomeGroup can open or copy the file
   - *Homegroup (Read/Write)* for full permission in the HomeGroup
   - *Specific People* to set Read or Read/Write permission for individual users on your computer

   If you choose Specific People, Windows opens another dialog box that lets you choose users identified on the computer and assign them rights.

   Anyone accessing your computer from the network who isn't in the HomeGroup has to know a username and password that works on the computer. That's the username that Windows uses to assign permissions, in this dialog box.

4. **After you successfully share the folder, a small icon with tiny people on it appears below the name of the folder.**

   You can see the "sharing" icon overlay in Figure 1-19, on the AskWoody folder.

Recycling

When you delete a file, it doesn't go to that Big Bit Bucket in the Sky. An intermediate step exists between deletion and the Big Bit Bucket. It's called purgatory — oops. Wait a sec. Wrong book. (*Existentialism For Dummies*, anybody?) Let me try that again. Ahem.

The step between deletion and the Big Bit Bucket is the Recycle Bin.

When you delete a file or folder from your hard drive — whether by selecting the file or folder in Windows Explorer and pressing Delete or by right-clicking and choosing Delete — Windows doesn't actually delete anything. It marks the file or folder as being deleted but, other than that, doesn't touch it.

Files and folders on key drives, SD cards, and network drives don't go into limbo when they're deleted. The Recycle Bin doesn't work on key drives, SD cards, or drives attached to other computers on your network. That said, if you accidentally wipe out the data on your key drive or camera memory card, there is hope. See the sidebar on recovering lost photos in Book IV, Chapter 4.

To rummage around in the Recycle Bin, and possibly bring a file back to life, follow these steps:

1. **Double-click the Recycle Bin icon on the Windows desktop.**

   Windows Explorer opens to the Recycle Bin, shown in Figure 1-20.

2. **To restore a file or folder (sometimes Windows calls it *undeleting*), click the file or folder and then click Restore the Selected Items in the upper left corner.**

   You can select a bunch of files or folders by holding down Ctrl as you click.

Windows 7 maintains shadow copies of previous versions of many kinds of files. If you can't find what you want in the Recycle Bin, follow the steps in Book II, Chapter 3 to see whether you can dig something out of the Windows Time Machine.

To reclaim the space that the files and folders in the Recycle Bin are using, click the Empty the Recycle Bin link. Windows asks whether you really, truly want to get rid of those files permanently. If you say Yes, they're gone.

Figure 1-20: Restore files one at a time or en masse.

Getting Around

Your PC is a big place, and you can get lost easily. Microsoft has spent hundreds of millions of dollars to make sure that Windows 7 points you in the right direction and keeps you on track through all sorts of activities.

Amazingly, some of it actually works.

If you don't want to hunt around for the mouse — or if your mouse has suddenly gone out to lunch — Windows 7 has the Windows Flip feature, which lets you switch among running programs while (insert your best W.C. Fields impression here) your fingers never leave your hands . . . er, your fingers never leave the keyboard. Wink, wink. Just hold down Alt and press Tab. When you see the program you want, release Alt. Bam!

Using Windows Explorer

If you're going to get any work done, you have to interact with Windows. If Windows is going to get any work done, it has to interact with you. Fair 'nuff.

Microsoft refers to the way Windows interacts with people as the *user experience.* Gad. Windows Explorer lies at the center of the, er, user experience. When you want to work with Windows 7 — ask it where it stuck your wedding pictures, show it how to mangle your files, or tell it (literally) where to go — you usually use Windows Explorer.

If you choose Start⇨Documents, Start⇨Pictures, or Start⇨Music or Computer or Games, Windows Explorer jumps to your command like an automated bird dog, pointing at whatever location you selected. When you run a search by choosing Start⇨Search, Windows Explorer takes the reins.

Navigating

Windows Explorer helps you get around in the following ways:

- **Click a folder to see the files you want.** On the left side of the Windows Explorer window (see Figure 1-21), you can click a real folder (such as Desktop or Downloads); a shortcut you dragged to the Favorites list on the left (Server, for example); one of the Windows 7 libraries, including the predefined Documents, Music, Pictures, or Videos; other computers in your HomeGroup; other drives on your computer; or other computers on the network.
- **Use the "cookie crumb" navigation bar to move around.** At the top of the Windows Explorer window (refer to Figure 1-21), you can click the wedges to select from available folders.

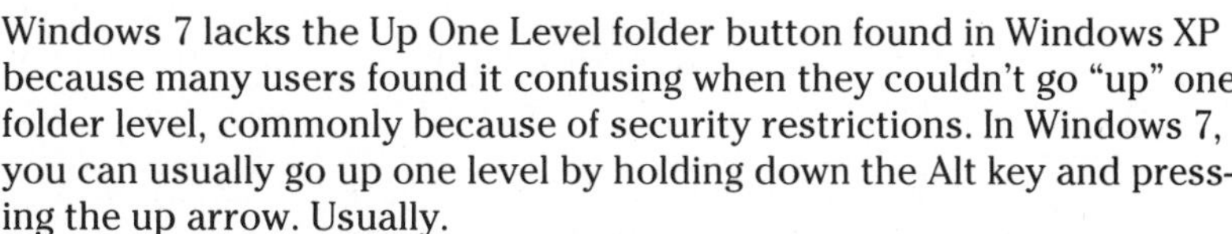

Windows 7 lacks the Up One Level folder button found in Windows XP because many users found it confusing when they couldn't go "up" one folder level, commonly because of security restrictions. In Windows 7, you can usually go up one level by holding down the Alt key and pressing the up arrow. Usually.

- **Details appear below.** If you click a file or folder once, details for it appear in the Details box at the bottom of the Windows Explorer window. If you double-click a folder, it becomes the current folder. If you double-click a document, it opens. (For example, if you double-click a Word document, Windows fires up Word and has it start with that document open and ready for work.)

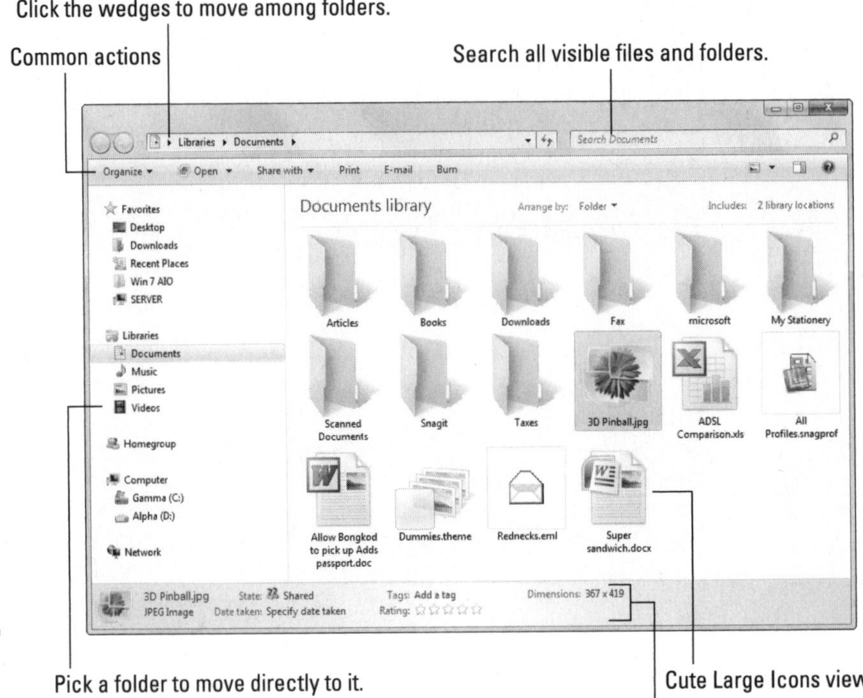

Figure 1-21: Windows Explorer helps you move around.

✦ **Many of the actions you might want to perform on files or folders show up in the command bar at the top.** Most of the other actions you might want to perform are accessible by right-clicking the file or folder.

✦ **To see all options, press Alt.** Windows Explorer shows you an old-fashioned command bar (File, Edit, View, Tools, Help) with dozens of functions tucked away.

✦ **Open as many copies of Windows Explorer as you like.** That can be very helpful if you're scatterbrained like I am — er, if you like to multitask and you want to look in several places at once. Simply choose Start⇨Documents (or Computer, whatever), and a totally independent copy of Windows Explorer appears, ready for your finagling.

Viewing

Large Icons view (refer to Figure 1-21) is, at once, visually impressive and cumbersome. If you grow tired of scrolling (and scrolling and scrolling) through those icons, click the Views button and choose Details. You see the succinct list shown in Figure 1-22.

Windows 7 offers several picturesque views — dubbed Extra Large Icons, Large Icons, Medium Icons, Small Icons, and Infinitesimal Eyestraining Icons (okay, I got carried away a bit) — that can come in handy if you're looking through a bunch of pictures. In most other cases, though, the icons only get in the way. Besides, if you're looking at pictures, you should be using Windows Live Photo Gallery (see Book I, Chapter 5) or Picasa.

In Details view, you can sort the list of files by clicking one of the column headings — Name or Date Modified, for example. You can right-click one of the column headings and choose More to change what the view shows (get rid of Type, for example, and replace it with Tags).

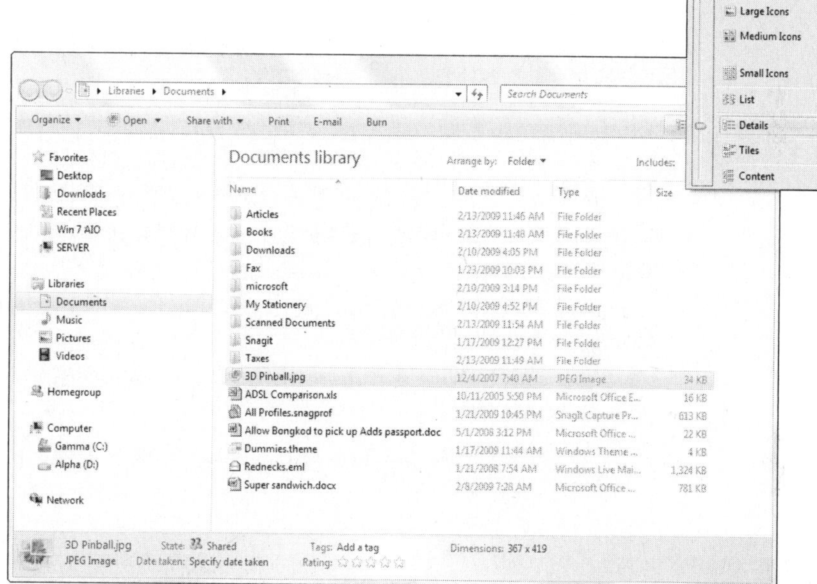

Figure 1-22: Details view has more meat, less sizzle.

Preview

Every Windows Explorer window has a button in its upper right corner, next to the Help question mark, that lets you turn on the Preview pane — a strip along the right side of the window that, in many cases, shows a preview of the file you selected.

Some people love the preview feature. Others hate it. A definite speed hit is associated with previewing — you may find yourself twiddling your thumbs as Windows 7 gets its previews going. The best solution is to turn off the preview unless you absolutely need it. And use the right tool for the job — if you're previewing a lot of picture files, fire up Windows Live Photo Gallery (see Book I, Chapter 5) or Picasa.

You can set the preview pane, and all other Windows Explorer panes, by clicking the Organize button in the upper left corner.

Arranging Libraries

Windows 7 brings a powerful new concept to the table: libraries. Think of them as easy ways to mash together the contents of many folders: You can work with a collection of folders as easily as you work with just one folder, no matter where the folders live. You can pull together pictures in ten of the folders on your desktop plus the ones in your computer's `\Public` folder plus the ones on that external terabyte drive and the `\Public` folder on another computer connected to your network, and treat them all as though they were in the same folder.

Recent versions of Windows Media Player (WMP), Windows Media Center (WMC), and Vista Photo Gallery all keep libraries. In Windows 7, Microsoft has unified the concept (WMP and WMC used to keep their own, distinct libraries!) and extended it, with good results.

Here's how you can customize your Documents library:

1. **Choose Start⇨Documents to bring up the Documents library.**
2. **In the upper right corner, click the box that says Includes: 2 Library Locations.**

   Windows 7 invites you to change where the library looks for its contents, as shown in Figure 1-23.
3. **Click the Add button and then navigate to a folder that you want to include in the library.**

   In Figure 1-24, I move to my D: drive, where I want to add a folder named Documents. (Clever, eh?)

Libraries go better with tags

Whereas most music files have (at least rudimentary) tags associated with them, photos don't come with tags. Nor do videos. To keep massive amounts of media sorted out, you have to come to grips with *tags,* the index data (or *metadata)* that you can stick on every file you own.

Windows Media Player and Live Photo Gallery both have good tools for handling tags. In general, you can assign your own tags to just about any file (except GIFs) by locating the file in Windows Explorer, clicking it once, and editing the tags in the pane at the bottom (refer to Figure 1-21). Many free programs are available for editing tags on MP3 files, too.

Don't be intimidated: If you want to find a file, put a tag on it!

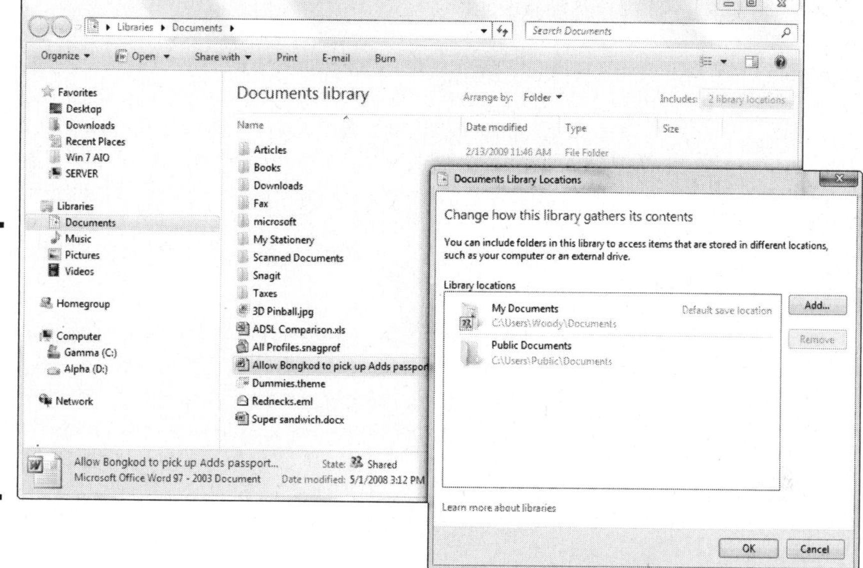

Figure 1-23: Windows aggregates folders in different locations to build its libraries.

4. **Select the folder you want to add to the library and click Include Folder.**

   Back in the Library Locations dialog box, you see that the new folder has been added.

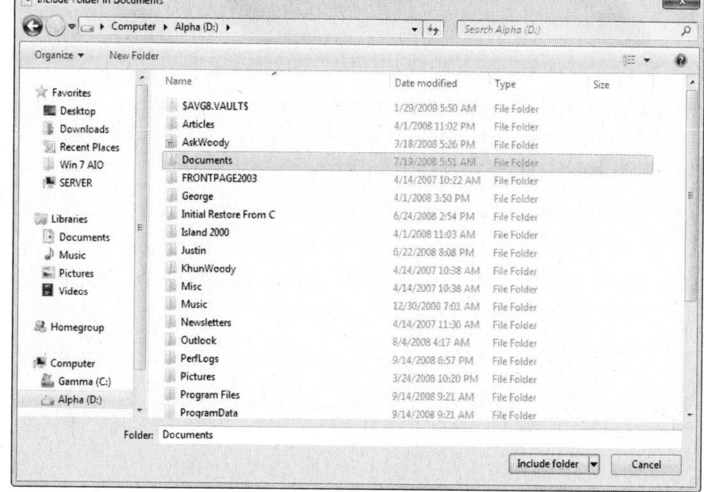

Figure 1-24: Add any folder — even folders on your network — to the library.

5. **Click OK to go back to the library.**

   In this case, my Documents library now includes all the items in the `D:\Documents` folder.

One nice feature of libraries is that you can drag and drop files or folders into them — the library acts a lot like a superfolder. When you drag a file or folder into a library, Windows knows where to put the file physically. The reason is that you tell Windows where you want the file, by changing the Default Save Location item, which you can see in the Library Locations dialog box (refer to Figure 1-23).

Libraries work fabulously with HomeGroups. Libraries make it very easy to share music, pictures, and videos in particular. In fact, when you join a HomeGroup, those libraries are automatically updated on your computer so that you can "discover" music and pictures on other computers without lifting a finger.

Creating Shortcuts

Sometimes life is easier with shortcuts. (As long as the shortcuts work, anyway.) So, too, in the world of Windows, where shortcuts point to things that can be started. You may set up a shortcut to Word and put it on your desktop. Double-click the shortcut and Word starts, the same way as if you chose Start⇨All Programs⇨Microsoft Word.

You can set up shortcuts that point to the following items:

- Programs, of any kind
- Web addresses, such as `www.dummies.com`
- Documents, spreadsheets, databases, PowerPoint presentations, and anything else that can be started in Windows Explorer by double-clicking it
- Specific chunks of text (called *scraps*) inside documents, spreadsheets, databases, and presentations, for example
- Folders (including the weird folders inside digital cameras, the Fonts folder, and others that you may not think of)
- Drives (hard drives, CD drives, and key drives, for example)
- Other computers on your network, and drives and folders on those computers, as long they're shared
- Printers (including printers attached to other computers on your network), scanners, cameras, and other pieces of hardware
- Network connections, interface cards, and the like

You have many different ways to create shortcuts.

Say that you use the Windows Calculator all the time, and you want to put a shortcut to the Windows Calculator on your desktop. Here's an easy way to do it:

1. **Choose Start⇨All Programs⇨Accessories.**

   Windows 7 shows you a list of Windows programs that Microsoft loosely describes as "accessories."

2. **Right-click Calculator and then choose Send To⇨Desktop (Create Shortcut).**

   Windows places an icon of the Windows Calculator on your desktop. The icon has an arrow, a kind of visual hint that the icon exists as a shortcut to the Calculator.

Anytime you double-click the Windows Calculator shortcut on your desktop, the Calculator comes to life.

You can use a similar procedure for setting up shortcuts to any file, folder, program, or document on your computer or on any networked computer.

Believe it or not, Windows thrives on shortcuts. They're everywhere, lurking just beneath the surface. For example, every single entry on the Start menu is a (cleverly disguised) shortcut. The icons on the taskbar are all shortcuts. Most of Windows Explorer is based on shortcuts — although they're hidden where you can't reach them. So don't be afraid to experiment with shortcuts. In the worst-case scenario, you can always delete them. Doing so gets rid of the shortcut but doesn't touch the original file.

Sleep: Perchance to Dream

Aye, there's the rub.

A fundamental dichotomy exists in the way computers store information, and the difference dictates how well and how fast a PC can spring back to life.

Main memory is relatively small (your computer probably has 1 or 2 gigabytes) and very fast but *volatile* — if you turn off the juice, everything disappears. Hard drives, on the other hand, are massive (100GB? 500GB? 1 terabyte?) and slow, but data that is written to a hard drive sticks around for years, with no power required.

That's why, when you click the Start button and then the arrow next to the Shut Down button and then Sleep, you set off a rather complex sequence of events:

1. Windows 7 copies the programs, documents, and anything else that's running from memory to the computer's hard drive.
2. Windows *freezes* the contents of memory, putting a "blanket" around everything so that it can be revived quickly.
3. Windows winds down the hard drive, the monitor, and anything else that drains power, keeping a little trickle going to the memory, to maintain it as long as possible.

Think of it as a modern version of two logs crossing. If the, uh, powers that be manage to maintain a constant supply of electricity to the computer, when you start Windows again, it only needs to unwrap the blanket and kick-start your system. On the other hand, if the juice runs out — whether the batteries run down, the UPS goes belly up, or the cat finally gnaws all the way through the power cord — Windows 7 can retrieve a snapshot of memory from the hard drive and get going in fairly short order.

Most of the time, sleep is good enough. But at least once a week — possibly once a day — you should restart your computer. Why? Windows should have an opportunity, from time to time, to start with a clean slate. Follow these steps to restart your computer:

1. **Click the Start button.**

   In the lower right corner of the Start menu, you see a Shut Down button with a right-pointing wedge next to it.

2. **Click Shut Down if you want to turn off your computer, or click the wedge and then choose Restart to turn it off and back on again.**

   If other people are using your computer, Windows 7 warns you, but if not, the computer goes away and then comes back.

You should always turn off your computer the "official" way, by following the preceding steps. If you just flip off the power switch, unplug the machine, or press the reset switch, Windows can accidentally zap files and leave them unusable. (Yes, pressing the power switch or reset switch is supposed to initiate the appropriate shutdown sequence inside Windows. No, it doesn't always work the way it's supposed to.) Windows needs time to make sure that everything is in order before turning off the lights. Make sure that it gets the time it needs by choosing Shut Down.

To verify your computer's power settings, follow these easy steps:

1. **Choose Start⇨Control Panel⇨Hardware and Sound.**

   You see the Control Panel's Hardware and Sound pane.

2. **Under Power Options, click the Change Power-Saving Settings link.**

   You see the Power Options settings, shown in Figure 1-25.

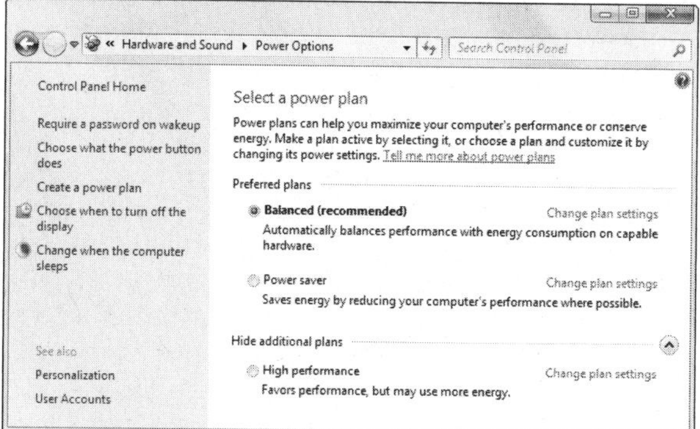

Figure 1-25: Most people find the Balanced settings adequate, but to truly save energy, you have to dig deeper.

3. **Choose the power plan you prefer, or modify the plan by clicking a link to Change Plan Settings. When you're done, click the X button to close the pane.**

   On a desktop computer, the Balanced plan turns off the monitor after 10 minutes and puts the computer to sleep after 30 minutes. The Power Saver plan turns off the monitor after 5 minutes and puts the computer to sleep after 15.

Microsoft recently published some recommendations that I found fascinating. To truly conserve energy with a desktop computer, be very aggressive with the monitor idle time — 2 minutes or fewer — and make sure that you don't have a screen saver enabled. If you want to conserve energy with a notebook or netbook, your top priority is to reduce the screen brightness.

I talk about power conservation and the many paths to greenness in *Green Home Computing For Dummies*, which I co-wrote with Katherine Murray (Wiley). (Hi, Kathy!) It's packed with important information for anybody with a PC and a conscience.

Chapter 2: Controlling Users

In This Chapter

- Logging on
- Controlling the User Account Control
- Adding users
- Preventing specific users from changing the computer
- The (in)security of it all

Microsoft reports that 70 percent of all Windows PCs have just one user account. That's a startling figure. It means that 70 percent of all Windows PCs run at the most permissive security level, all the time. It means that, on 70 percent of all Windows PCs, little Billy can install Internet Antivirus 2009 — a notorious piece of scumware — and have it bring down the whole family with a couple of simple clicks. "Sorry, Dad, but it's an anti-virus program and it said that we really need to install it, and it's just $49.95 for a three-month subscription. I thought you said that antivirus was good. They wouldn't lie about stuff like that, would they?"

Although it's undoubtedly true that many PCs are used by just one person, I think it's highly likely that people don't set up multiple user accounts on their PCs because they're intimidated. Not to worry. I take you through the ins and outs.

This chapter explains how to take control of users on a Windows 7 PC. You'd think it would be simple. No way. Like it or not, user control has all sorts of implications for security and sharing and other issues you get to manage on your PC.

Even if you're the only person who ever uses your PC, you might want to create a second account — another user, as it were — even if the second user is just you. (As Pogo said, "We have met the enemy and he is us.") Then again, you might not. And therein lies this chapter's story.

If you're running Windows 7 Professional, Enterprise, or Ultimate and your PC is connected to a big corporate network (in the parlance, a *domain*), you have little or no control over who can log on to your computer and what a logged-on user can do after she's on the machine. That's a Good Thing, at least in theory: Your company's network administrator gets to worry about all the security issues, relieving you of the hassles of figuring out whether the guy down the hall should be able to look at payroll records or the company Christmas card list. But it can also be a pain in the neck, especially if you have to install a program, like, right now, and you don't have a user account with sufficient capabilities. If your computer is attached to a domain, your only choice is to convince (or bribe) the network admin to let you in.

The nostrums in this chapter apply only to PCs that are connected to small networks (*HomeGroups* or *workgroups*, in Microsoft-speak) or to stand-alone PCs. If you're on a big network, you must pay homage to the network gods. Pizza, beer, and a smile can help.

Logging On

Windows 7 assumes that, sooner or later, more than one person will want to work on your PC. All sorts of problems crop up when several people share a PC. I set up my screen just right, with all my icons right where I can find them, and then my son comes along and plasters the desktop with a shot of Alpha Centauri. He puts together a killer teen Media Player playlist and "accidentally" deletes my Grateful Dead playlist in the process.

It's worse than sharing a TV remote.

Windows helps keep peace in the family — and in the office — by requiring people to log on. The process of *logging on* (also called *signing on*) lets Windows keep track of each person's settings: You tell Windows who you are, and Windows lets you play in your own sandbox.

Having personal settings that are activated whenever you log on to Windows 7 doesn't create heavy-duty security, at least on a stand-alone PC or one connected to a peer-to-peer HomeGroup or workgroup network. (Big networks — *domains* — running Active Directory rate as a cabal of the first order.) Unless your Windows 7 PC is a slave to a big Active Directory domain network, your settings can get clobbered, and your files deleted, if someone else with access to your computer or your network tries hard enough. But as long as you're reasonably careful and follow the advice in this chapter, Windows 7 security works surprisingly well.

If someone else can put his hands on your computer, it isn't your computer any more. That can be a real problem if someone swipes your laptop, if the cleaning staff uses your PC after hours, or if a snoop breaks into your study. Unless you use BitLocker (in the Enterprise and Ultimate versions of Windows 7), anybody who can restart your PC can look at, modify, or delete your files or stick a virus on the PC. How? In most cases, a miscreant can bypass Windows directly and start your PC with another operating system. With Windows 7 out of the picture, compromising a PC doesn't take much work.

When Windows 7 is ready to get started, it greets you with a Welcome screen — variously called a *logon screen* or a *sign-on screen* — like the one shown in Figure 2-1. The screen lists all users who are signed up to use the computer. It may also show a catchall user named Guest. (I guess that sounds better than Other or Hey, You!)

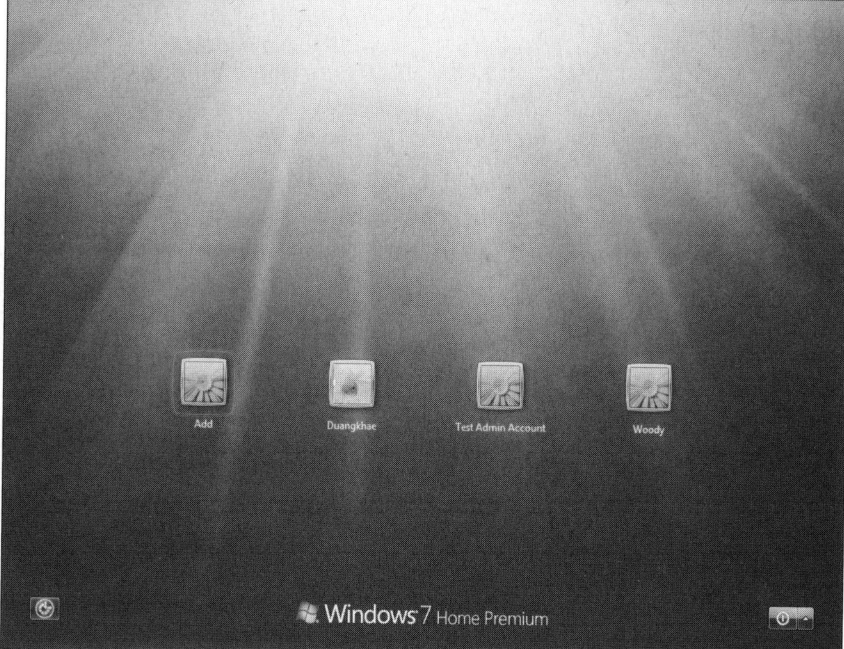

Figure 2-1: The Welcome screen helps sort out the settings attached to each user account.

I explain how to set up new users and, optionally, the Guest account in the sections "Adding Users" and "Enabling the Guest Account," later in this chapter.

Unless you assign a password to a specific account, nothing prevents anyone who's sitting at your computer — friend, foe, or mother-in-law — from clicking one of the other icons and logging on under an assumed identity: In general, Windows 7 (unless it's connected to a big corporate network domain) relies on the gentlemanly conduct of all participants to keep its settings straight.

If you can't rely on gentlemanly conduct, you need to set up a password for your account, although a password doesn't give you *that* much protection. I talk about the vagaries of password-protected accounts in the section "Changing other users' settings," later in this chapter.

Choosing Account Types

When dealing with user accounts, you bump into one existential fact of Windows 7 life over and over again: The type of account you use puts severe limitations on what you can do.

Unless you're hooked up to a big corporate network, user accounts can generally be divided into two groups: the haves and the have-nots. (Users attached to corporate domains are assigned accounts that can exist anywhere on the have-to-have-not spectrum.) The have accounts are *administrator* accounts. The have-nots are *standard* accounts. That's it. "Standard." Kinda makes your toes curl just to think about it.

What's a standard account?

A person running with a standard account can do only, uh, standard tasks:

- Run programs that are installed on the computer, including programs on key drives.
- Use hardware that's installed on the computer.
- Create, view, and use documents, pictures, and sounds in the `Documents/Pictures/Music` folders as well as in the PC's `Public` folders (see Book II, Chapter 1).
- If your computer is part of a HomeGroup, a standard user can also create, view, and use any files in the `Public` folders of computers that are part of your HomeGroup. A standard user can also access any shared folders on other computers in the HomeGroup.
- Change his password or switch back and forth between requiring and not requiring a password for his account.
- Change the picture that appears next to his name on the Welcome screen and the Start menu, change the desktop wallpaper, resize the Windows toolbar, add items to the Start menu and toolbar, and make other small changes that don't affect other user accounts.

In most cases, a standard user can change system-wide settings, install programs, and the like, but only if he can provide the username and password of an administrator account.

If you're running with a standard account, you can't even change the time on the clock. It's quite limited.

What's an administrator account?

People using administrator accounts can change almost anything, anywhere, at any time. (Certain folders remain off limits, even to administrator accounts, and you have to jump through some difficult hoops to work around the restrictions.) People using administrator accounts can even change other user accounts' passwords — a good thing to remember if you ever forget your password.

If you start Windows 7 with a standard account and you accidentally run a virus or worm or some other piece of bad computer code, the damage is limited: The malware can delete files in your `Documents` folder, and probably in the `Public` folders, but that's about the extent of the damage. Usually. In particular, the virus can't install itself into the computer, so it can't run repeatedly, and it may not be able to replicate. Poor virus.

Someone with an administrator account can get into all the files owned by other users: If you thought that attaching a password to your account and putting a top-secret spreadsheet in your `Documents` folder would keep it away from prying eyes, you're in for a rude surprise. Anybody who can get into your machine with an administrator account can look at it. Standard users, on the other hand, are effectively limited to looking only at their own files.

Choosing between standard or administrator accounts

Administrator accounts and standard accounts aren't set in concrete. In fact, Windows 7 helps you shape-shift between the two as circumstances dictate:

✦ If you're using a standard account and try to do something that requires an administrator account, Windows 7 prompts you to provide an administrator account's name and password (see Figure 2-2).

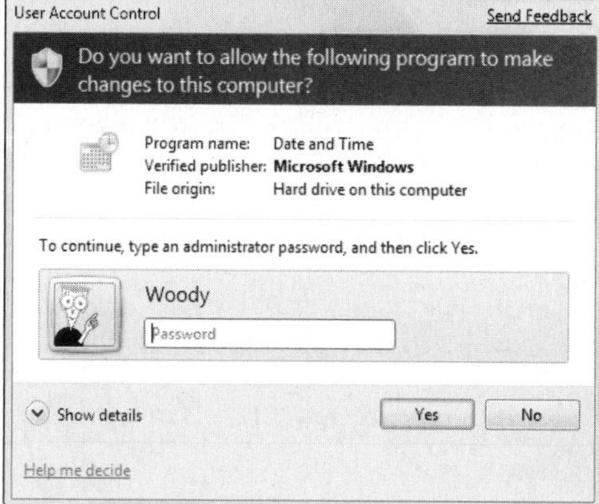

Figure 2-2: Windows 7 asks permission before performing administrative actions.

If the person using the standard account selects an administrator account without a password, simply clicking the Yes button allows the program to run.

✦ Even if you're using an administrator account, Windows 7 normally runs as though you had a standard account, in some cases adding an extra hurdle when you try to run a program that can make substantial changes to your PC — and *substantial* is quite a subjective term. You have to clear the same kind of hurdle if you try to access folders that aren't explicitly shared (see Figure 2-3). That extra hurdle helps prevent destructive programs from sneaking into your computer and running with your administrator account, doing their damage without your knowledge or permission.

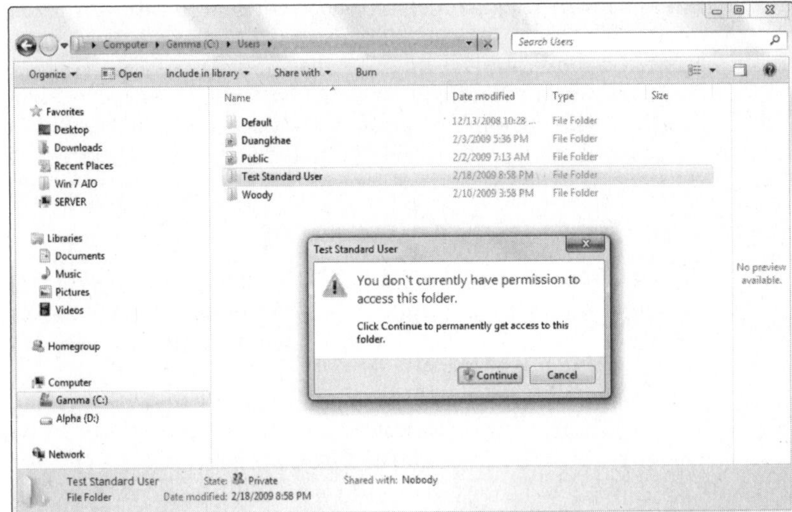

Figure 2-3: Even if you're using an administrator account, Windows lays down a User Account Control challenge before you dive into another user's folder.

Most experts recommend that you use a standard account for daily activities and switch to an administrator account only when you need to install software or hardware or access files outside the usual shared areas. Most experts ignore their own advice: It's the old do-as-I-say-not-as-I-do syndrome. It's also a bit of a head-in-the-sand approach because you're given a chance to shoot yourself in the foot (er, run programs that make substantial changes) as though you were using an administrator account, by simply filling in the administrator password and clicking the Yes button in the dialog box shown in Figure 2-2. Owning an administrator account but forcing yourself to use a standard account just doesn't make sense. I believe the term is *self-deluding*.

In addition, an inherent problem with passwords appears in spades here. Someone running with a standard account needs an administrator username and password to "elevate" the security clearance high enough to make substantial changes to the PC. But if you give a standard user an administrator password, that standard user can basically do anything an administrator can do — including simply logging off and logging on with that administrator account.

When you give away an administrator password (or create an administrator account without a password), you give away the keys to the executive washroom. The only way to get them back is to log on with that administrator account and change the password.

Here's the best compromise I've found: Stick with administrator accounts on PCs that will be used by people who are moderately aware of the dangers of running unknown programs, and are sufficiently jaded to question the wisdom of running any program they don't understand. But if you have users who might not be so circumspect — or if folks use your computer who don't have any business digging around in other users' files — give them standard accounts and lock out any administrator accounts with passwords. Then jealously guard the passwords.

Controlling User Account Control

Does User Account Control (UAC) — this incessant prompting for passwords, or requests to confirm actions you want to take — drive you nuts? Have you finally reached the point where you never look at the UAC dialog boxes — whenever your screen goes dark, you just click the Continue button to get the stupid thing out of the way?

Yeah. Me, too. (See the nearby sidebar, "What went wrong with UAC?")

In Windows Vista, your only real choice (give or take a waffle or two) is to disable UAC completely. With Windows 7, Microsoft has seen the light and given you a simple slider that lets you control your User Account Control destiny.

To bring up the slider and adjust your computer's UAC level, follow these steps:

1. **Choose Start⇨Control Panel⇨System and Security.**
2. **Under the Action Center heading, click the Change User Account Control Settings link.**

   You see the slider shown in Figure 2-4.
3. **Adjust the slider according to Table 2-1 and then click OK.**

   Perhaps surprisingly, as soon as you try to change your UAC level, Windows hits you with a User Account Control prompt (refer to Figure 2-2). If you're using a standard account, you have to provide an administrator username and password to make the change. If you're using an administrator account, you have to confirm the change.

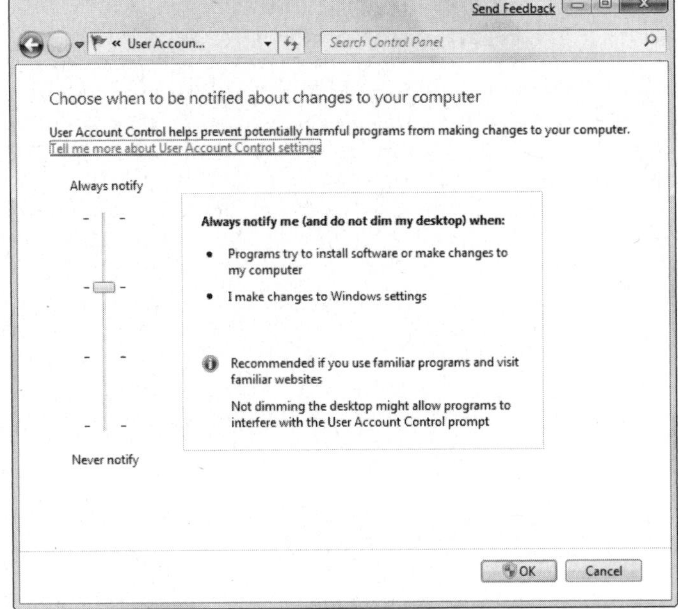
Send Feedback
« User Accoun...
Search Control Panel
Choose when to be notified about changes to your computer
User Account Control helps prevent potentially harmful programs from making changes to your computer.
Tell me more about User Account Control settings
Always notify
Always notify me (and do not dim my desktop) when:
Programs try to install software or make changes to my computer
I make changes to Windows settings
Recommended if you use familiar programs and visit familiar websites
Not dimming the desktop might allow programs to interfere with the User Account Control prompt
Never notify
OK
Cancel

Figure 2-4: Windows 7 allows you to change the level of UAC intrusiveness.

4. **Click Yes and then the X button to close the slider dialog box.**

   Your changes take effect immediately.

If you're using a standard account, you can set the slider to only Level 1 or Level 2.

Table 2-1 User Account Control Levels

Slider	*What It Means*	*Recommendations*
Level 1	Always brings up the full UAC notification whenever a program tries to install software or make changes to the computer that require an administrator account, or when you try to make changes to Windows settings that require an administrator account. You see these notifications even if you're using an administrator account.	This level offers the highest security but also the highest hassle factor.
Level 2	Brings up the UAC notification whenever a program tries to make changes to your computer that require an administrator account, but there's no notification when you make changes to Windows settings. This is the default setting in Windows 7.	This level strikes a good balance between security and hassle factor.

Slider	What It Means	Recommendations
Level 3	This level is the same as Level 2 except that the UAC notification doesn't take over the PC and dim the screen. Dimming is only part of the equation: When the screen isn't dimmed, UAC isn't in complete control of your computer, and a running program can "send keys" or otherwise monkey with the UAC prompt.	When you tell Windows "don't dim," a sneaky program can jump in and "click" the dialog box for you — not a good choice.
Level 4	UAC is disabled — programs can install other programs or make changes to Windows settings, and you can change anything you like, without triggering any UAC prompts. Note that this doesn't override other security settings: For example, if you're using a standard account, you still need to provide an administrator's ID and password before you can install a program that runs for all users.	Choosing Level 4 automatically turns off all desktop gadgets — not recommended.

This description sounds simple, but the details are quite complex. Consider. Microsoft's Help system says that if your computer is at Level 2, the default setting in Windows 7, "You will be notified if a program outside of Windows tries to make changes to a Windows setting." So how does Windows 7 tell when a program is "outside of Windows" — and thus whether actions taken by the program are worthy of a UAC prompt at Levels 2 or 3?

UAC-level rules are interpreted according to a special Windows 7 security certificate. Programs signed with that certificate are deemed to be part of Windows. Programs that aren't signed with that specific certificate are "outside of Windows" and thus trigger UAC prompts if your computer is at Level 1, 2, or 3.

What went wrong with UAC?

User Access Control originated as a cure for a fundamental design decision made by the originators of Windows 20 years ago. From the beginning, Windows was designed to let programs pull each other's strings: You could double-click a folder, for example, but in a similar way, a program running on your computer could "double-click" the same folder. Anything you can do, a program can do: Send e-mail, reformat a hard drive, or ping `www.whitehouse.gov`. Twenty years ago, that was cool. Now it's considered dangerous, and for good reason.

I believe that Microsoft missed the boat on UAC. I fear that the Windows 7 designers, and

(continued)

(continued)

Vista designers before them, by tackling the problem from a programmer's point of view, didn't look hard enough from the user's point of view.

Windows 7 designers will tell you that UAC has to verify that you're the one who started the potentially dangerous program. In Figure 2-3, for example, using an administrator account, I clicked a folder that belongs to a standard user. Windows let me in, no problem, but I have to click through another prompt to get into the folder. The Windows 7 folks note, correctly, that a program could've done the same thing. Thus, the UAC dialog box confirms that you — not some scummy program — are the one trying to look in the folder.

As far as I'm concerned, that's a disingenuous and short-sighted approach. Windows 7 has many ways to verify that I was the one who did the clicking: input buffers and counters, screen coordinates, draw commands, and much more. Windows 7 hooks directly into the hardware. If Windows 7 is smart enough to draw the folders on the screen, smart enough to know that I clicked the screen, and smart enough to know that the place I clicked was on top of a specific folder, why isn't it smart enough to remember that I was the one who clicked it and then just let me in?

The answer, of course, is that Windows 7 isn't designed to remember such things. The records are there, but they're buried deep, and it would take a major reworking of Windows to make that kind of interface tracking both accessible and secure.

Adding Users

After you log on by clicking your name on the Welcome screen, you can add more users quite easily. The Getting Started item near the top of the Start menu invites you to add new users, but you don't need an invitation to add them at any time. Here's how:

1. **Choose Start⇨Control Panel and, under the User Accounts and Family Safety heading, click the Add or Remove User Accounts option.**

   You see the Manage Accounts window, shown in Figure 2-5.

2. **Click the Create a New Account option.**
3. **Type a name for the new account.**

   You can give a new account just about any name you like: first name, last name, nickname, titles, abbreviations. No sweat, as long as you don't use the characters / \ [ ] " ; : | < > + = , ? or *.

4. **Tell Windows whether you want the account to be a standard user account or an administrator account.**

   The choice of standard versus administrator account status isn't nearly as straightforward as the Microsoft description would lead you to believe. See the section "Choosing Account Types," earlier in this chapter.

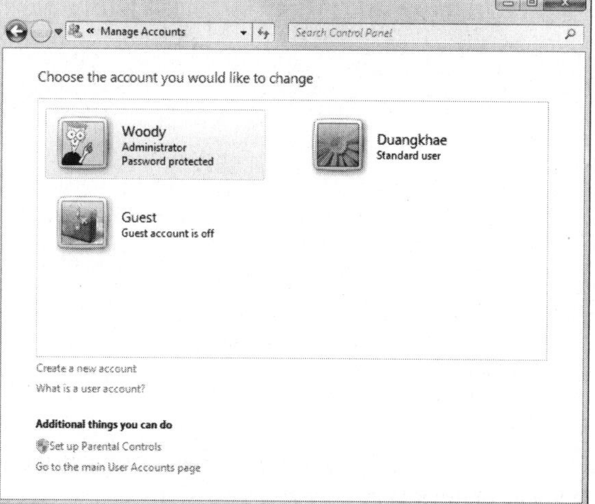

Figure 2-5: Perform all kinds of account maintenance in the Manage Accounts window.

5. **Click the Create Account button.**

   You're done. Rocket science. The name now appears on the Welcome screen.

This topic is more than a bit confusing, but you aren't allowed to create a new account named Administrator. There's a good reason why Windows 7 prevents you from making a new account with that name: You already have one. Even though Windows 7 goes to great lengths to hide the account named Administrator, it's there, and you bump into it if you ever have to restore your system. For now, don't worry about the ambiguous name and the ghostly appearance. Just refrain from trying to create a new account named Administrator.

Enabling the Guest Account

The *Guest* account is a special standard account that comes in handy if many different people need to use a computer but you don't want any of them to be able to get at important information — or run potentially destructive programs. To make the Guest account available on your computer, follow these steps:

1. **Choose Start➪Control Panel and, under the User Accounts and Family Safety heading, click the Add or Remove User Accounts option.**

   You see the Manage Accounts dialog box (refer to Figure 2-5).

2. **Click the Guest icon.**

   Windows asks whether you want to turn on the Guest account.

3. **To enable the Guest account, click the Turn On button.**

   From that point, Windows shows Guest as an account on the Welcome screen.

If you only have a few people who sporadically use your PC, take the time to set up standard accounts for each of them. That way, your PC can save their settings and make them available the next time each person logs on. But if you have more than a handful of guests, enable the Guest account and have all of them use the Guest account.

Don't enable the Guest account unless you need it. One more account is just one more potential hole for a slobbering cretin virus writer to exploit.

If you ever encounter instructions on the Internet that show you how to get rid of the Guest account, ignore them. The Guest account, which exists on every Windows 7 PC, is used for all sorts of behind-the-scenes stuff. You need the Guest account lurking in the background, even if you don't enable it and it isn't visible on the Welcome screen — no matter what those self-appointed experts might say.

Changing Accounts

If you have an administrator account, you can reach in and change every detail of every single account on the computer — except one.

Changing other users' settings

If you can't already see the Manage Accounts window (refer to Figure 2-5), log on to Windows with an administrator account, choose Start➪Control Panel, and then click the Add or Remove User Accounts link under User Accounts and Family Safety.

On the Manage Accounts screen, click the account you want to change.

Windows immediately presents you with several options (see Figure 2-6).

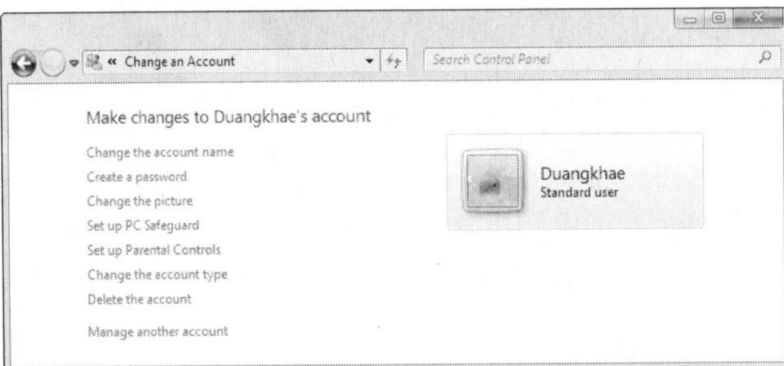

Figure 2-6: Maintain another user's account.

Here's what the options entail:

✦ **Change the Account Name:** This option modifies the name displayed on the Welcome screen and at the top of the Start menu while leaving all other settings intact. Use this option if you want to change only the name on the account — for example, if Little Bill wants to be called Sir William.

✦ **Create/Change/Remove a Password:** If you create a password for the chosen user, Windows 7 requires a password to crank up that user account. You can't get past the Welcome screen (using that account) without it. This setting is weird because you can change it for other people: You can force Bill to use a password when none was required before, you can change Bill's password, or you can even delete the password.

Passwords are cAse SenSitive — you must enter the password, with uppercase and lowercase letters, precisely the way it was originally typed. If you can't get the computer to recognize your password, make sure that the Caps Lock setting is off. That's the number one source of logon frustration.

If you decide to put a password on another user's account, tell that person to take a couple of minutes to run the Forgotten Password Wizard, as described in the next section.

Much has been written about the importance of choosing a secure password, mixing upper- and lowercase letters with punctuation marks, ensuring that you have a long password, blah blah blah. I have only two admonitions: First, don't write your password on a yellow sticky note attached to your monitor; second, don't use the easily guessed passwords that the Conficker worm employed to crack millions of systems (see Table 2-2, at the end of this list).

✦ **Change the Picture:** To change the picture that appears next to the user's name on the Welcome screen, the Start menu, and in the User Accounts areas, choose this option. You can choose a picture from any of the common file types: BMP, GIF, JPG, or PNG. Windows offers a couple dozen pictures to choose from, but you can reach out and grab any picture, anywhere. If you pick a big picture, Windows automatically scales it down to size.

✦ **Set Up PC Safeguard:** Think of PC Safeguard as a time machine for standard accounts. If PC Safeguard is turned on for a user, whenever the user logs off, the entire PC reverts to the same state it was in before the user logged on. That means any documents he created are deleted; any changes he made to the system are thrown away; and new programs he installed are ripped out by the tonsils. This can be a Very Good Thing, as you might imagine.

A little bit of a waffle is built in to PC Safeguard: You can turn off the Safeguard feature for select hard drives, if you want. That lets the PC

Safeguarded user save files to a specific location. Click the Lock Hard Disk Drives (Advanced) link for details.

- **Set Up Parental Controls:** This link takes you to a stunted set of controls for limiting the times a user can use the computer, turn off games, or block specific programs. If you're the least bit interested in parental controls, forget this setting and download Windows Live Family Safety, described in Book I, Chapter 5.
- **Change the Account Type:** You can use this option to change accounts from administrator to standard and back again. The implications are somewhat complex; I talk about them in the section "Choosing Account Types," earlier in this chapter.
- **Delete the Account:** Deep-six the account, if you're that bold (or mad, in all senses of the term). Windows offers to keep copies of the deleted account's `Documents` folder and desktop, but warns you quite sternly and correctly that if you snuff the account, you rip out all the e-mail messages, Internet Favorites, and other settings that belong to the user — definitely not a good way to make friends.

Table 2-2 The Most Frequently Used Passwords*

000	0000	00000	0000000	00000000	0987654321
111	1111	11111	111111	1111111	11111111
123	123123	12321	123321	1234	12345
123456	1234567	12345678	123456789	1234567890	1234abcd
1234qwer	123abc	123asd	123qwe	1q2w3e	222
2222	22222	222222	2222222	22222222	321
333	3333	33333	333333	3333333	33333333
4321	444	4444	44444	444444	4444444
44444444	54321	555	5555	55555	555555
5555555	55555555	654321	666	6666	66666
666666	6666666	66666666	7654321	777	7777
77777	777777	7777777	77777777	87654321	888
8888	88888	888888	8888888	88888888	987654321
999	9999	99999	999999	9999999	99999999
a1b2c3	aaa	aaaa	aaaaa	abc123	academia
access	account	Admin	admin	admin1	admin12

admin123	adminadmin	administrator	anything	asddsa	asdfgh
asdsa	asdzxc	backup	boss123	business	campus
changeme	cluster	codename	codeword	coffee	computer
controller	cookie	customer	database	default	desktop
domain	example	exchange	explorer	file	files
foo	foobar	foofoo	forever	freedom	f**k
games	home	home123	ihavenopass	Internet	internet
intranet	job	killer	letitbe	letmein	login
Login	lotus	love123	manager	market	money
monitor	mypass	mypassword	mypc123	nimda	nobody
nopass	nopassword	nothing	office	oracle	owner
pass	pass1	pass12	pass123	passwd	password
Password	password1	password12	password123	private	public
pw123	q1w2e3	qazwsx	qazwsxedc	qqq	qqqq
qqqqq	qwe123	qweasd	qweasdzxc	qweewq	qwerty
qwewq	root	root123	rootroot	sample	secret
secure	security	server	shadow	share	sql
student	super	superuser	supervisor	system	temp
temp123	temporary	temptemp	test	test123	testtest
unknown	web	windows	work	work123	xxx
xxxx	xxxxx	zxccxz	zxcvb	zxcvbn	zxcxz
zzz	zzzz	zzzzz			

** From the Conficker worm, Bowdlerized with an asterisk (*) as a fig leaf*

Changing your own settings

Changing your own account is just a little different from changing other users' accounts. Follow these steps:

1. **Choose Start⇨Control Panel and then, under the User Accounts and Family Safety heading, click the Add or Remove User Accounts option.**

   You see the Manage Accounts dialog box (refer to Figure 2-5).

2. **Click the icon next to your own username.**

   You see the Change an Account dialog box.

Most of the options for your own account mirror those of other users' accounts, as described in the preceding section. One key difference is that you can't delete your own account. Another is that you can't turn yourself into a standard user if only one administrator account is on the computer Windows has to protect itself. Every PC must have at least one user with an administrator account. If Windows 7 lost all its administrators, no one would be around to add users or change existing ones, much less to install programs or hardware, right?

Creating a password reset disk

If you put a password on your own account (or somebody else does it for you), you must create a password reset disk. To do so, follow these steps:

1. **Make sure you have a USB drive handy (or another type of removable media, such as an SD card).**

   The password reset disk routine writes a tiny text file on the drive.

2. **Choose Start➪Control Panel. Click the User Accounts and Family Safety link and then click the User Accounts link.**

   Windows 7 shows you the User Accounts dialog box.

3. **On the left, click the link that says Create a Password Reset Disk.**

   This step launches the Forgotten Password Wizard, which creates a "password reset disk." This nifty little program creates a file that you can use to unlock your password and get into your account, even if your precocious seven-year-old daughter changes it to MXYPLFTFFT.

4. **At the final step of the wizard, click Finish.**

   Store that USB drive someplace safe. If you ever forget your password — or if someone changes it for you — you can use the drive to log on to your account.

Switching Users

Windows 7 allows you to have more than one person logged on to a PC simultaneously. That's convenient if, say, you're working on the family PC and checking Billy's homework when you hear the cat screaming bloody murder in the kitchen and your wife wants to put digital pictures from the family vacation in the `Public Pictures` folder while you run off to check the microwave.

The ability to have more than one user logged on to a PC simultaneously is called Fast User Switching, and it has advantages and disadvantages:

- **On the plus side:** Fast User Switching lets you keep all your programs going while somebody else pops onto the machine for a quick jaunt on the keyboard. When she's done, she can log off, and you can pick up precisely where you left off before you got bumped.
- **On the minus side:** All idle programs left sitting around by the inactive ("bumped") user can bog things down for the active user, although the effect isn't drastic. You can avoid the overhead by logging off before the new user logs on.

You probably won't be surprised to find that you have to click the Start button to log off or switch users. Simply click the Start button, click the right-wedge to the right of the Shut Down button, and then click the Switch User option or the Log Off option.

Chapter 3: Maintaining Your System

In This Chapter

- **Using the Windows 7 automatic recovery options**
- **Coping with Start-Up Problems**
- **Using backups, previous versions, and more**
- **Working with drives**
- **Using System Restore and Restore Points**
- **Scheduling boring tasks so that your computer does them automatically**
- **Storing more and spending less with Zip files**
- **Monitoring your computer resources**
- **Controlling the Control Panel**

Onto every glass window a little rain must fall.

Or something like that.

Windows 7 is a computer program, not a Cracker Jack toy, and it will have problems. The trick lies in making sure that *you* don't have problems, too.

This chapter walks you through all the important tools you have at hand to make Windows 7 do what you need to do, to head off problems and to solve problems as they (inevitably!) occur.

I start this chapter with a discussion of Windows 7's little-known system repair disc to cajole you into creating one. Right now. Read on.

Coping with Start-Up Problems

Can't get Windows to start? Welcome to the club.

Windows is notorious for crashing and freezing, making it impossible to start the computer, or garbling things so badly that you'd think the screen went through a garbage disposal. Microsoft has poured a lot of time, effort, and money into teaching Windows how to heal itself. You can take advantage of all that work — if you know where to find it.

If you read nothing else in this chapter, follow my advice in this section and get Windows 7 to make you a system repair disc. You're welcome.

Creating a system repair disc

Right now, while you're thinking of it, have Windows 7 make you a system repair disc. It's easy and it's free, if you can spare a blank CD. (Yes, the disc fits on a CD — no DVD required.)

The system repair disc allows you to boot your PC, even if you can't get anything else to work. After it's booted, you have several repair options (see Figure 3-1). The system repair disc isn't a copy of Windows 7: You can't install Windows 7 from the disc. It isn't an image of your computer's hard disk or (shudder!) the kind of "recovery" disk shipped by some PC manufacturers that installs Windows along with all the scumware that came with your new PC. Its sole purpose is to allow you to boot when all else fails, and then present you with several options to help get Windows 7 working again.

Figure 3-1: Your options when booting from the system repair disc.

The options look like this:

- **Startup Repair:** Automatically scan the parts of Windows involved in getting your computer started — the files needed to *boot* Windows 7. Detected problems are fixed automatically. If you don't have a system repair disc but you can see the Windows 7 boot screen, you can run Startup Repair by pressing the F8 key while Windows starts. If you can boot from a Windows 7 installation disc (which you may or may not have received when you bought your new computer), you can run Startup Repair by booting from the installation CD and choosing Repair Your Computer.

Sometimes PC manufacturers monkey with the Startup Repair program, so if you can't make it work, blame your PC's manufacturer.

✦ **System Restore:** Choose a System Restore point and reset your PC to that point. See the section "Using System Restore and Restore Points," later in this chapter.

This option is a good one if you just installed a new piece of hardware and Windows doesn't restart. Pick the System Restore point that was created automatically immediately before installing the hardware. (The installer should have created one for you.) Then you can roll back without even booting Windows.

✦ **System Image Recovery:** Wipe out your hard drive and replace the contents with an image backup copy — a *ghost,* if you will. See the section "Working with Backups," later in this chapter.

✦ **Windows Memory Diagnostic Tool:** Run a small program that thoroughly tests your memory. This Microsoft diagnostic runs continuously until you stop it — helpful for detecting intermittent memory problems.

✦ **Command Prompt** opens `cmd.exe`, a program that offers a DOS-style command prompt within a Windows window. Be careful with this option. *Thar be tygers here.* If you want to shoot yourself in the foot, er, explore your options, take a look at the TechNet listing of available commands at `technet.microsoft.com/en-us/library/bb491071.aspx`.

To create a system repair disc, follow these steps:

1. **Choose Start⇨All Programs⇨Maintenance⇨Create a System Repair Disc.**
2. **Select your CD drive from the drop-down menu and insert a CD when you're prompted, as shown in Figure 3-2.**
3. **After you slap a CD in the indicated drive, click Create Disc.**

   Windows copies about 140MB of data.

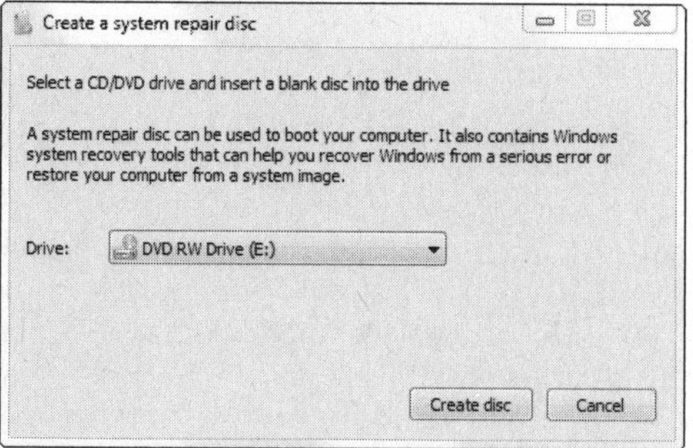

Figure 3-2: Creating a system repair disc is easy — if you do it while your computer's working.

4. **When Windows finishes, click X to close the dialog box.**

   Your system repair disc is ready to use.

Using the system repair disc

Here's how to run the system repair disc:

1. **Boot from the system repair disc.**

   Usually, all you have to do is put the system repair disc in a drive and then press any key when Windows says "Press Any Key to Boot from CD or DVD." In case you don't see the Press Any Key message, About.com has a good discussion of the problem and its solution at `tinyurl.com/6osf4a`.

   If the Windows Boot Manager appears, proceed with Step 2. If you don't see the Boot Manager, the system repair disc asks you for your keyboard layout, and you can continue with Step 4.

2. **In Windows Boot Manager, choose Windows 7 as your operating system choice and press Enter.**

   The Boot Manager shows you another text screen, titled Advanced Boot Options (see Figure 3-3). For details about the advanced boot options, see Table 3-1.

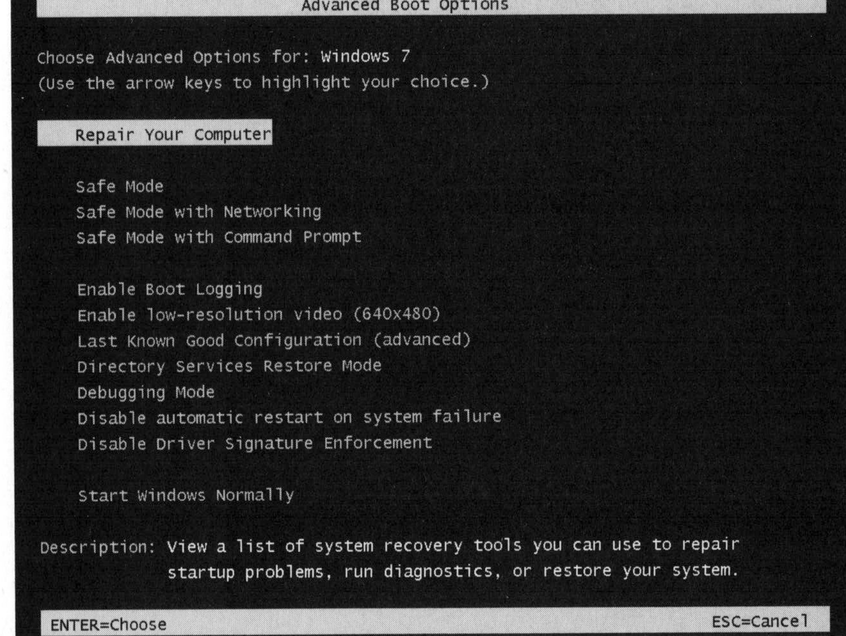

Figure 3-3: If you choose Repair Your Computer, Windows offers the options shown in Figure 3-1.

3. **Choose the first option, Repair Your Computer, and press Enter.**
4. **When the System Recovery routine kicks in, choose your keyboard layout (typically, US).**

   The System Recovery routine asks for a username and password. (If your computer has an administrator account with no password, you don't see the prompt.)
5. **Type a username and password that are valid on this computer.**

   You can use all the System Recovery options if you supply an administrator's name and password. If you use a standard account, System Recovery doesn't let you get to the Command Prompt.

Table 3-1 What the Advanced Boot Options Really Mean

Option	*What It Does*
Repair Your Computer	If you booted from the system recovery disc, you can see this option. Congratulations! Choose this line to see the system repair options shown earlier, in Figure 3-1.
Safe Mode	Starts Windows 7 with a minimal set of drivers, including the bone-stock VGA video driver. In Safe Mode, you can run most Windows programs and try to narrow down the problems pestering your PC. See the following sidebar, "Running in Safe Mode."
Safe Mode with Networking	Starts Windows 7 in Safe Mode and loads all drivers necessary for Windows to connect to your network. That should include the ability for you to get on the Internet.
Safe Mode with Command Prompt	Starts Windows 7 in Safe Mode, but you end up at a DOS-style command line. This is different from the Command Prompt option on the system recovery disc because, with this option, all of Windows is running.
Enable Boot Logging	As drivers are loaded, Windows lists them in the file `c:\windows\ntbtlog.txt`. If Windows doesn't start properly, you can look at the log and see where it died.
Enable Low-Resolution Video	Loads your current video driver and puts it in low-resolution, 640 x 480 mode.
Last Known Good Configuration	Rolls back your computer to the previous restore point (see "Using System Restore and Restore Points," later in this chapter) and then tries to boot normally.

(continued)

Table 3-1 *(continued)*

Option	*What It Does*
Debugging Mode	You don't want to go there.
Disable Automatic Restart on System Failure	If you hit a Blue Screen of Death, Windows doesn't automatically restart. This option is useful if Windows is in an endless loop of BSODs.
Disable Driver Signature Enforcement	If you know that you have a good drive but Windows 7 doesn't accept it, try this option to force-feed the driver.
Start Windows Normally	Uh, starts Windows normally.

Working with Backups

Of course you make backups. Doesn't everybody?

Seriously, you should back up your data periodically — and store the major backups off-site (that's computer lingo for "anyplace that's far enough away from your computer that a fire doesn't take out your computer and your backup, unless you live next to Mrs. O'Leary's cow").

Windows 7 backups fall into four categories:

- **Shadow copies** (also called *previous versions* and, confusingly, backup copies) of your data files, which Windows 7 keeps for you automatically.
- **Data backups** are partial backups in which you use the File and Folder Backup Wizard to make copies of a subset of everything on your drives.

  You find details about shadow copies and data backups a little later in this section.
- **System restore points** back up most of your computer's internal settings, drivers, and certain key system files. Windows 7 automatically creates a system restore point daily. Windows 7 also usually creates a restore point before installing new software. Restore points are quite different from data backups; see "Using System Restore and Restore Points," later in this chapter, for details.
- **Image backups** are snapshots of the entire contents of your drives. Image backups are also called system images, Complete PC backups (that's Vista terminology), system backups, complete backups, ghosts — in deference to Norton Ghost, the granddaddy of image backup software — and several other imaginative appellations. Confused yet? Details on image backups appear later in this section.

Running in Safe Mode

Windows Safe Mode dates to Windows 95. Ancient history. Way back then (according to 'Softie Raymond Chen, who was there), Safe Mode was designed to disable potentially problematic drivers — long the bugaboo of the Windows development classes — and correct weird problems, like missing desktop icons, that could make it hard to get your computer working.

Although it's hard to describe Safe Mode as obsolete, Microsoft has worked hard in the intervening decade-plus to make Windows startup problem detection and correction much more automatic. That's why I recommend you try the system recovery disc approach discussed in this section or roll back to an earlier restore point (see "Using System Restore and Restore Points," later in this chapter) before you try the venerable Safe Mode.

If you're absolutely convinced that Safe Mode will solve a problem that the automated fixers don't fix, you can find a good overview of Safe Mode and its care and feeding on the PCStats site, `www.pcstats.com/articleview.cfm?articleID=1643`.

If you have a Windows Home Server PC on your network, you have no need to run Windows 7 backups. Really. Windows Home Server takes care of everything — shadow copies, image backups, the whole nine yards — and it does so in a way that's technically superior to Windows 7 capabilities. Windows Home Server has a lot of cool capabilities. I'm a fan. To see why, check out *Windows Home Server For Dummies* by, uh, Woody Leonhard (Wiley).

Restoring a file with shadow copies (previous versions)

Unless you change things (see the next section for details), Windows 7 automatically keeps shadow copies of every folder and document on your main hard drive.

Shadow copies (also called "previous versions") live on the same hard drive that contains the original data, so they don't protect you from disasters that take out the drive, like an errant ball bearing rolling to meet its maker or a talented cup of coffee performing a swan dive into your computer's case. Instead, shadow copies exist to help you recover if you accidentally delete or otherwise screw up an important file.

To understand the real world benefits and shortcomings of shadow copies, it's important to realize that different programs save changes in different ways — and the differences can cost you hours of frustration. For example:

- When you're using Microsoft Word and you save a Word document, Word puts the updated information on disk but saves all your intermediate steps. As long as you don't close the document, you can undo any mistakes you made. If you mess up a document and you catch the problem in time, you can click the Undo button and move back to any previous state. After you close the document, though, Word forgets all the undo steps.

- By contrast, when you're using Microsoft Excel and you save an Excel spreadsheet, Excel puts the updated information on disk, but it then immediately forgets all your undo steps. If you mess up an Excel spreadsheet and discover the error of your ways immediately after you save, the best you can hope for (with apologies to Kenny Rogers) is to die in your sleep — to a first approximation, anyway.

Windows 7 makes shadow copies of your data files sporadically. At the very least, you should have an automatically generated shadow copy (er, previous version) of every data file on your main hard drive, and at any given moment, that shadow copy should be no more than 24 hours old.

If you suddenly get that "oops" feeling and want to recover your data, follow these school-of-hard-knocks steps:

1. **If you're working on a document (spreadsheet, whatever) and you get the sinking feeling that something has gone awry, *don't* panic, *don't* save the document, *don't* close the document, and *don't* shut down the application.**

Back up to the cloud?

If you have a fast Internet connection and you don't mind storing your data on a gigantic company's computer, consider backing up to the Internet. At the time this book was published, several companies appeared poised to enter the backup biz, including, notably, Google with its soon-to-be-released product code-named GDrive.

Advantages to storing over the Internet include being able to retrieve your data from anyplace you can run a Web browser. All your backups are offsite, by definition, so Mrs. O'Leary's cow is less likely to take out your computer and your backup, too.

It remains to be seen what kind of software Google will ship with its backup program — or how much, if anything, the company will charge. But for many, back up to the cloud is an idea whose time has come. (Yes, I know, Mozy has been doing it for years — but GDrive will bring cloud backup to the masses.)

Disadvantages of backing up to the Internet include the necessity of an Internet connection to make it work — the "cloud" Achilles heel. It should also give you pause that a large company has access to your data, a fact that's rife with all sorts of privacy and legal implications. What happens if Google gets subpoenaed on your behalf?

2. **Click the application's Undo button.**

   Almost all Office applications, and many other applications, have a drop-down arrow next to the Undo button that lets you group undo actions and apply many of them at once. See whether you can restore the document to the state you want by undoing.

3. **If you can't undo your way out of the mess, don't save or close the screwed-up document.**

   Leave it open, right where it is, in case you can use some of the jumbled mess to make an older version of the document right.

4. **Choose Start⇨Documents and navigate to the document that's causing you problems. Right-click the document and choose Restore Previous Versions.**

   Windows 7 shows you the Previous Versions tab for the afflicted file (see Figure 3-4).

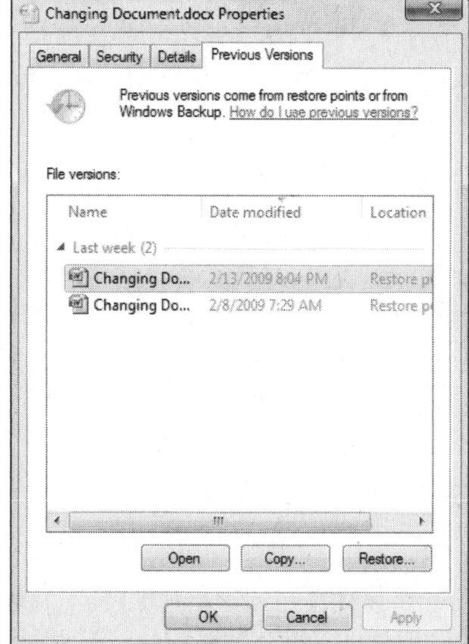

Figure 3-4: Previous versions of a file in trouble.

5. **Click the Copy button (*don't* click the Open button), and put the copy of the old version of the file in a location you can remember.**

   Clicking Open in the Previous Versions dialog box can cause all sorts of confusion — and you may not know that you have a problem until you try to save or close the recovered file.

   WARNING! If the Open and Copy buttons are both grayed out, avoid using the Restore button. Instead, click the red X to close the Previous Versions dialog box, go back into the original application, and choose File⇨

Save As to save the screwed-up version of the file, giving it a new name. Then repeat Steps 1 to 4, and use the Previous Versions dialog box to open the older version of the file. Yes, it's complicated. A scorecard helps.

6. **Open the previous version.**

If you're restoring an Excel spreadsheet, you have to manually change the name of the previous version file before opening it — Excel doesn't allow you to open two spreadsheets with the same name at the same time. That's crazy, but that's Excel.

You can now copy and paste between the previous version and the screwed-up version of the document. When you're done, close and delete the screwed-up version.

Shadow copies can also be useful if you accidentally delete a file — although I recommend that you use the Recycle Bin, if at all possible (double-click the Recycle Bin on the desktop, select the file you want to restore, and then click the Restore button). The Recycle Bin is much less confusing. Book II, Chapter 1 introduces the Recycle Bin.

To bring back a deleted file (or folder) using shadow copies/previous versions, right-click the folder that used to contain the file (or folder) and choose Restore Previous Versions. Then click the version of the folder you want to resurrect and drag it to the desktop. At that point, you can open the folder and rummage around inside — your deleted files (and folders) are still there.

Maintaining previous versions on different drives

By default, Windows 7 maintains shadow copies/previous versions for all files on the main Windows hard drive — typically, the C: drive. The shadow copies are stored along with all the information that's stored in a restore point (see the section "Using System Restore and Restore Points," later in this chapter.) If you have other drives and you want Windows to keep previous versions of files on the other drives, you have to warn Windows.

Actually, previous versions are maintained separately for each partition. So if you have one hard drive with two partitions, C: and D: drive, and Windows is on the C: drive, the C: files are protected automatically, but you have to tell Windows that you want it to keep shadow copies of the D: files.

For reasons that elude me, Microsoft calls this automatic storage of shadow copies "system protection." When you want to tell Windows that it should keep shadow copies of all the files and folders on your D: drive, for example, you're "enabling system protection on D:" in Microsoft-speak. These computer guys sure do talk funny.

Here's how to tell Windows that you want to keep shadow copies of files and folders on your D: drive:

1. **Choose Start⇨Control Panel⇨System and Security, and then click the System link.**

   Windows shows you the View Basic Information about Your Computer dialog box. (Yeah, I know, it's weird, but that's where you need to go.)

2. **On the left, click the link that says System Protection.**

   You see the System Properties dialog box, shown in Figure 3-5.

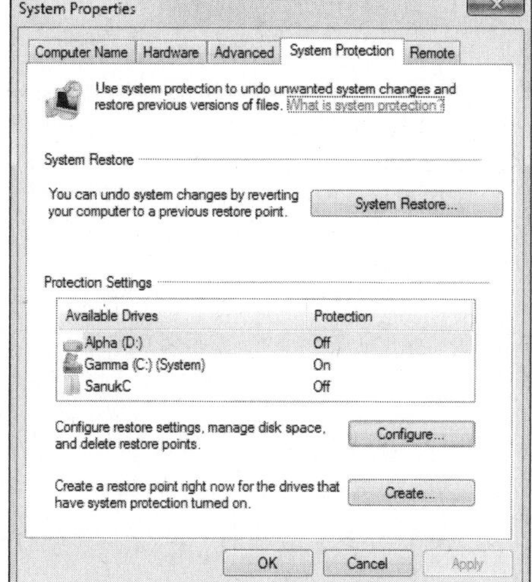

Figure 3-5: Choose the drive where you want shadow copies.

3. **In the Protection Settings area, select the drive where you want Windows to generate shadow copies and click Configure.**

   Windows shows you the System Protection dialog box for the drive (see Figure 3-6).

4. **Select the button that says Only Restore Previous Versions of Files. Consider adjusting the disk space reserved for shadow copies (yes, the default is a whopping 15 percent of the hard drive's capacity), and then click OK.**

5. **Click the X Close button to close the System Properties dialog box.**

   Windows starts gathering shadow copies with its next automatically generated restore point — typically, around midnight.

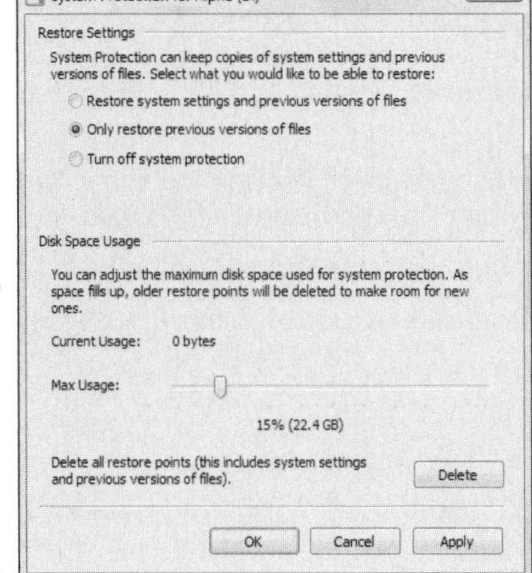

Figure 3-6: For drives other than C:, keeping previous versions is sufficient.

Creating data backups

Unless your computer is attached to a network with reliable backup services (for example, if you have a Windows Home Server network or your computer is attached to a network storage device that automatically performs backups), you should take advantage of Windows 7's abilities to make copies of your key files — and then ensure that those files are stored off-site, away from the computer from whence they came.

Here's how to get backups going on your computer:

1. **Choose Start⇨Getting Started⇨Back Up Your Files.**

   If you've never performed a backup, Windows responds with a Backup and Restore Center dialog box, informing you of that fact.

   You may also see this dialog box if you plug an external hard drive into your computer and choose Use This Drive for Backup.

2. **Click Set Up Backup.**

   Windows starts its backup software. That can take awhile. When the scampering chipmunks come back up for air, you see the dialog box shown in Figure 3-7.

3. **If you have a network, and you're running windows 7 Professional or Ultimate, you should store the backup on another computer's hard drive, so click the Add Network Location button and follow the instructions.**

   Windows 7 Starter and Home Premium editions don't allow you to automatically back up to a different computer on your network.

You have to provide a valid username and password for the computer that will take your backups out on the network.

The username and password have to be valid on the backup computer *when the backup program runs.*

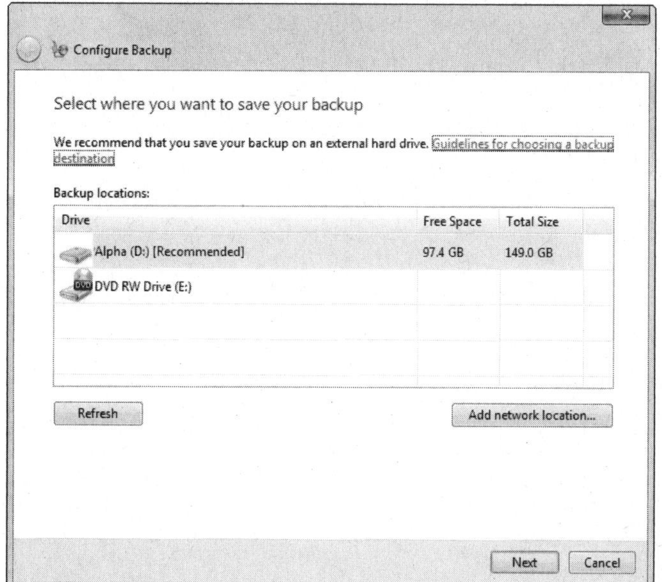

Figure 3-7: Choose your own backup location.

4. **Click the location that you want to hold your backups, and then click Next.**

   You see the Configure Backup dialog box, shown in Figure 3-8.

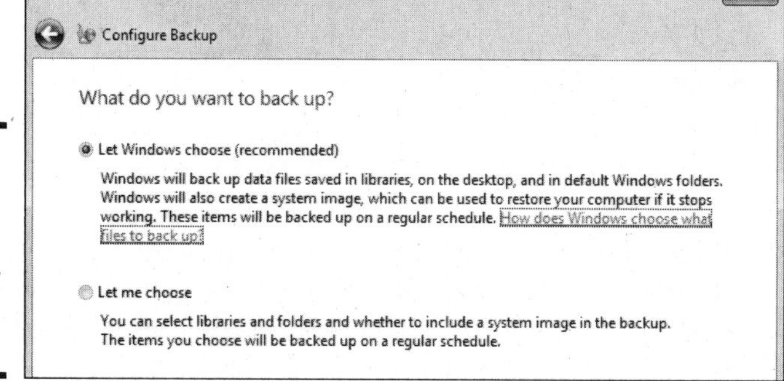

Figure 3-8: Windows can choose files for you, or you can go it alone.

5. **Specify whether you want to select the list of folders for backup or whether you trust Windows to do the dirty deed. (See the following sidebar, "What does Windows want to back up?" for details.) Click Next.**

If you elect to choose your own files for backup, Windows 7 gives you an opportunity to select file locations, but not file types. So, for example, you can say that you don't want to back up anything in a user's Videos library — but you can't tell Windows 7 that you want to include (or exclude) particular kinds of files.

The Configure Backup Wizard presents you with the criteria it intends to use, as shown in Figure 3-9.

6. **Click the Change Schedule link at the bottom to change the scheduled backup time.**

Generally it's a good idea to choose a schedule that doesn't interfere with your normal work schedule. If you commonly surf the Lonely Hearts sites until 3:00, go for 4:00.

7. **When you're ready to run a backup — and it can take a while — click the button marked Save Settings and Run Backup.**

The backup routine needs to transfer a lot of data, so don't expect your computer to be particularly, uh, sprightly in the interim.

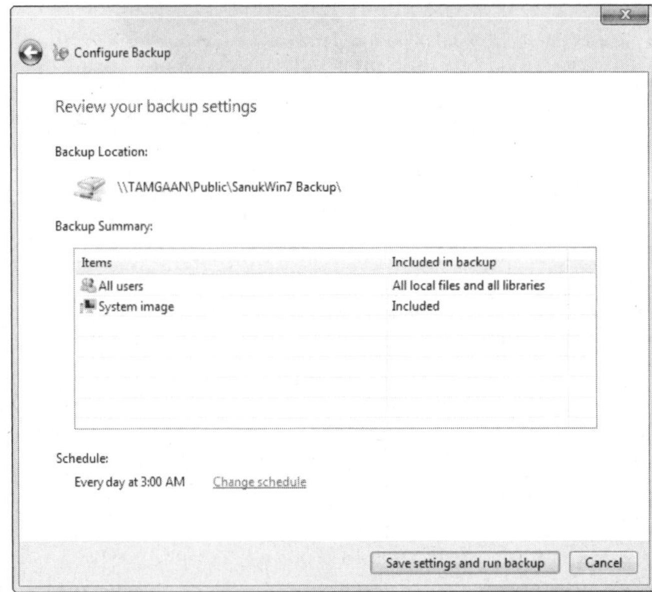

Figure 3-9: Full details for your backup settings.

What does Windows want to back up?

If you let Windows choose which files get backed up, you get a whole lotta data.

For every user on the computer (not just you, but everybody), all the data files (pictures, documents, music, video, e-mail, zips) that are in libraries are backed up. So if you added a folder to, oh, your Music library, the songs in that folder are backed up, too. All the data files in the Windows default folders get backed up, as do all the data in the Public folders.

That's just part of the story. The lion's share of the space required for a backup, using Windows defaults, is for a complete *ghost* image backup (Microsoft also calls it a *system image*) of everything on your hard drive.

Unless you specifically opt otherwise, Windows creates an image backup for the drive that contains Windows (typically, the C: drive). If you want to add more drives to the melee, follow the instructions in the earlier section "Maintaining previous versions on different drives" and tell Windows to put the other drives in the system protection pool.

The Windows 7 backup routine packs a whole bunch of smarts. It backs up only files that have changed since the previous backup, and if only part of a file has changed, just the "deltas" are transferred. It stores the backups as regular, old, everyday Zip files, in locations that you can find, understand, and get to. Recovering backed-up files takes only a few clicks. All in all, the wizard's a remarkable achievement, incorporating features that other backup programs have had for, oh, a decade or more.

When it comes to backup, how often is often enough? I dunno. How long is a string? I back up every night, and I let the wizard do the heavy lifting, but then again I don't have to worry about running out of drive space or swapping DVDs. If you have data that changes frequently — in my case, I'm a slave to e-mail — consider backing up nightly, too.

Even if you feel secure about your fancy automatic shadow copies and previous versions (see the preceding sections), here are two good reasons for running this more mundane style of backup:

- From time to time, you definitely want to store backups someplace other than the drive on which the original data resides. Unless you (or your company's network administrator) have changed things, shadow copies go on the same drive as the original data.
- Having a full set of file backups at your beck and call can get you out of some very tight spots. I speak from personal experience.

Managing and restoring data backups

With all that backed-up data floating around on your machine, you might think that restoring a backed-up file would prove daunting at best. Not so. The Backup and Restore Center gives you several tools to make managing and restoring data backups — the kind you created in the preceding section — surprisingly easy.

Windows 7 automatically keeps shadow copies/previous versions of your data files, but they sit on the same hard drive as the original file: If the drive goes belly-up, the shadow copies go down hard.

Data backups usually go on some drive other than the original hard drive — possibly on a network drive, or a USB drive, burned on a DVD, or a second hard drive attached to your computer. Data backups keep growing and growing and if you don't prune them back, they'll take up all the space they can.

Windows provides you with a one-stop center for pruning data backups. Here's all you have to do:

1. **Choose Start⇨Control Panel. Under the System and Security heading, click the Back Up Your Computer link.**

   The Windows 7 Backup and Restore Center appears.

2. **Click the Manage Space link.**

   The Backup and Restore Center shows you a full analysis of the room occupied by your data backups and system image ("ghost") backups. (See Figure 3-10.) (Shadow copies/previous versions aren't listed here because they're stuffed into each drive's system restore area.)

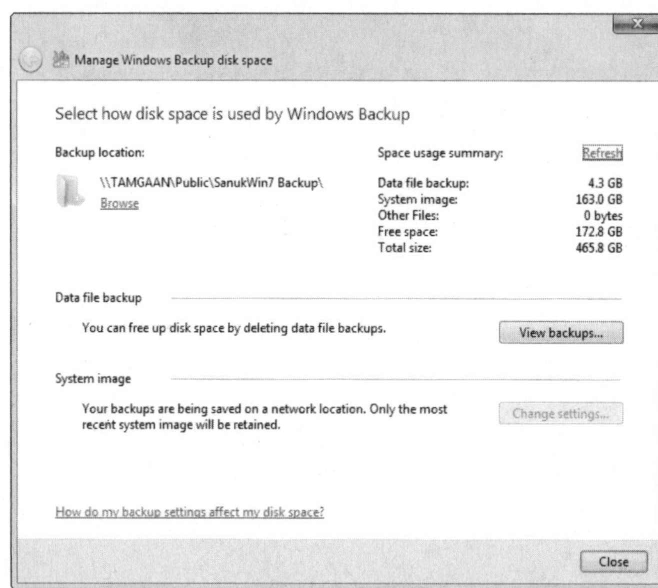

Figure 3-10: The Backup and Restore Center shows you what you need to know about the space used by all your backups.

3. **Click the View Backups button.**

   The Backup and Restore Center shows you a list of all backups that have taken place recently, noting the size of the backup.

4. **If you want to delete a backup, click it once and then click Delete.**

   If you're trying to reclaim significant amounts of space on a hard drive, search for the really old, really big backups. Remember that you're only deleting the backup, not the original data.

5. **Click Close, and then click X to close the Backup and Restore Center.**

   Backups can take a lot of room.

To restore a file from a data backup, follow these steps:

1. **Choose Start⇨Control Panel. Under the System and Security heading, click the Back Up Your Computer link.**

   The Windows 7 Backup and Restore Center appears

2. **Click the Restore My Files button.**

   The Backup and Restore Center has you specify which files you want to restore by either browsing or searching.

3. **Choose Browse for Files, Browse for Folders, or Search, and add all the files or folders you want to restore. When you're done, click Next.**

   The Backup and Restore Center lets you specify whether you want the files restored to their original location or to a new location of your choosing.

4. **Unless you have an overwhelming reason to overwrite your current files, pick a new location for the restored files. Click Restore.**

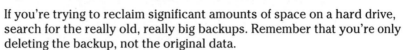

   By restoring the file to a location other than its original location, you eliminate the possibility (indeed, the likelihood) of shooting yourself in the foot by confusing restored files with any original files.

   Windows restores each selected file and folder. When it's done, a final dialog box tells you that the files have been restored.

5. **When the wizard presents you with the final dialog box, click the Finish button.**

6. **Immediately open the restored file, and make sure that you got what you thought you were going to get.**

   If you got the right file, you can feel comfortable about moving it to its original location, possibly zapping out a screwed-up version.

   If you have the wrong file, repeat Steps 1-3 and, in Step 3, select the Files from an Older Backup option.

Going back more than one generation is a tricky job, fraught with potential errors. Work slowly, and don't overwrite anything until you're sure you have the correct file.

Getting back the image backup (don't give up the ghost)

A *ghost,* or image backup, takes a full snapshot of your hard drive and stores it away so that you can restore your system in the event of a calamitous crash.

Unlike the other backup methods discussed in this chapter, restoring a system image backup obliterates everything on your hard drive, replacing the whole works with the saved copy. It's a drastic, scorched-earth approach that most Windows 7 users should employ only in the most dire circumstances — typically, when malware has so completely taken over your system that you can't get it to work and you don't care whether you have to throw out all the data you acquired after the last good image backup.

Yes, in some circumstances, propeller heads need ghosts, er, image backups: If you're running more than one copy of Windows on the same machine or if you swap out hard drives like burgers at McDonald's, ghosting can save you quite a bit of time. For the typical user, restoring a full system image rarely cures anything and always obliterates much.

To restore a full-disk ghost backup, you must have either of the following two items, and your computer has to be able to boot from the DVD or CD:

- An original Windows 7 installation DVD
- A system repair disc (see "Creating a system repair disc," earlier in this chapter, for instructions on burning a repair CD).

If you bought a computer with Windows 7 preinstalled, some manufacturers put System Repair hooks on the restore CDs or DVDs that come in the box. Other manufacturers add system repair options to their panic restore kits, which often live in a hidden partition on your hard drive. In either case, you may be able to do a full-disk image restore by following the manufacturer's instructions. Good luck.

With the CD or DVD in hand, your next challenge is to wade through the lousy, inconsistent terminology. You may think that Windows has six different ways to back up an entire hard drive, but in fact all these terms mean exactly the same thing: *image backup* (the term you see in most parts of Windows 7), *system image* (which you also see in Windows 7), *Complete PC backup* (the term used in Vista), *system backup* (another one scattered throughout Windows 7), *system image backup,* and *complete backup.*

Personally, I prefer the term *ghost*, referring to the original Norton Ghost product, which set the standard in entire disk drive backup for many years.

If you went through the Windows 7 backup routine and accepted all the defaults, you already have a ghost image backup (at least one) hanging around. See the section "Creating data backups," earlier in this chapter, for details.

If you have an image backup available — either on a network drive, a drive inside your computer, a bunch of burned DVDs, or embossed in cuneiform on a USB stone tablet, here's how to wipe out your hard drive and replace it with an older version:

1. **Do one of the following, depending on whether you have a system repair disc:**

   - *If you have a system repair disc* (see "Creating a system repair disc," earlier in this chapter), follow the steps in the earlier section "Using the system repair disc" to open the System Recovery Options dialog box.
   - *If you don't have a system repair disc but you have a Windows 7 Installation disc,* boot from that disc, select your language preference, and then click Repair Your Computer. In the next dialog box, select Microsoft Windows 7 and then click Next.

   In either case, you see the System Recovery Options dialog box (refer to Figure 3-1).

   If you bought Windows 7 preinstalled on a PC, the System Recovery Options, and the methods for invoking them, may have been changed by the manufacturer. If you don't have a system repair disc or a genuine Windows 7 Installation disc, you have to follow the manufacturer's directions, if you can find them.

2. **Click the System Image Recovery link.**

   Windows 7 System Recovery shows you the Re-Image Your Computer Wizard.

3. **Do one of the following, depending on which one applies to your circumstances:**

   - *If you backed up your drive to another computer on the network,* the wizard tells you, "Windows Cannot Find a System Image on This Computer." Hey, no problem. Click Cancel and then select Restore a Different System Image. Proceed to Step 4.
   - *If the wizard finds the backup you want to use,* select Use the Latest Available System Image. Then click Next and proceed to Step 6.

4. **Click Next.**

   The wizard asks you to select the location of the backup.

5. **If your backup is on a different computer, connected to the network, click the Advanced button and follow the instructions to find the backup. Select the backup location you want to use and click Next.**

   After you choose a location, the wizard wants you to choose among the ghosts, er, image backups available in the location.

6. **Choose the backup you want to restore and click Next.**

   You can choose to reformat and repartition your hard drives at this point. Click Next, confirm that you have the right restore point, and then click Finish. The wizard chunks away — possibly for hours — and reboots the computer as soon as it's done.

Maintaining Drives

E pur, si muove. Even so, it does move.

—Galileo, to his inquisitors, April 30, 1633

Drives (floppies, hard drives, CDs, DVDs, and other types of storage media) seem to cause more computer problems than all other infuriating PC parts combined. Why? They move. And, unlike other parts of computers that are designed to move — printer rollers and keyboard springs and mouse balls, for example — they move quickly and with ultrafine precision, day in and day out.

As with any other moving mechanical contraption, an ounce of drive prevention is worth ten tons of cure. Unlike other moving mechanical contraptions, a good shot of WD-40 usually doesn't cure the problem.

If you're looking for help installing a new hard drive, you're in the wrong place. I talk about adding new drives and getting Windows 7 to recognize them in Book VIII, Chapter 1.

Hard drives die at the worst possible moments. A hard drive that's starting to act flaky can display all sorts of strange symptoms: everything from long, long pauses when you're trying to open a file to completely inexplicable crashes and other errors in Windows itself.

Windows 7 comes with a grab bag of utilities designed to help you keep your hard drives in top shape. One of these utilities runs automatically every time your system shuts down unexpectedly, like when the dog finally chews through the power cord: The next time you start your system, Windows scans your hard drives to see whether any pieces of files were left hanging around.

What is formatting?

Drives try to pack a lot of data into a small space, and because of that, they need to be calibrated. That's where formatting comes in.

When you format a drive, you calibrate it: You mark it with guideposts that tell the PC where to store data and how to retrieve it. Every hard drive (and floppy disk, for that matter) has to be formatted before it can be used. The manufacturer probably formatted your drive before you got it. That's comforting because every time a drive is reformatted, everything on the drive is tossed out, completely and irretrievably. Everything.

You can format or reformat any hard drive other than the one that contains Windows by choosing Start⇨Computer, right-clicking the hard drive, and choosing Format. (To format a floppy disk, insert a disk into the floppy drive, right-click, choose Format.) You can also "format" rewritable CDs, DVDs, USB (key) drives, and SD or other removable memory cards — delete all the data on them — by following the same approach. To reformat the drive that contains Windows, you have to reinstall Windows. See the instructions for a clean Windows install in Book I, Chapter 4.

You can spend a lot of time futzing around with your hard drives and their care and feeding if you want, but as far as I'm concerned, just three utilities suffice: Check Disk, Disk Cleanup, and Disk Defragmenter. You have to be a designated administrator (see the section on using account types in Book II, Chapter 2) to get them to work.

In addition to running an error check from time to time, I use the Windows Task Scheduler to periodically remove temporary files that I don't need; I use the Disk Cleanup utility. I tell you how to do that in the section "Scheduling the Task Scheduler," later in this chapter.

Running an error check

If a drive starts acting weird — for example, you see error messages when trying to open a file, or Windows crashes in unpredictable ways — run the Windows error-checking routines.

If you're an old hand at Windows — or an even older hand at DOS — you probably recognize the following steps as the venerable CHKDSK routine, in somewhat fancier clothing.

Follow these steps to run Check Disk:

1. **Choose Start⇨Computer.**
2. **Right-click the drive that's malfunctioning and choose Properties.**

3. **On the Tools tab, click the Check Now button.**

   You may have to click through a User Account Control dialog box, providing it with an administrator account username and password, but ultimately the Check Disk dialog box appears (see Figure 3-11).

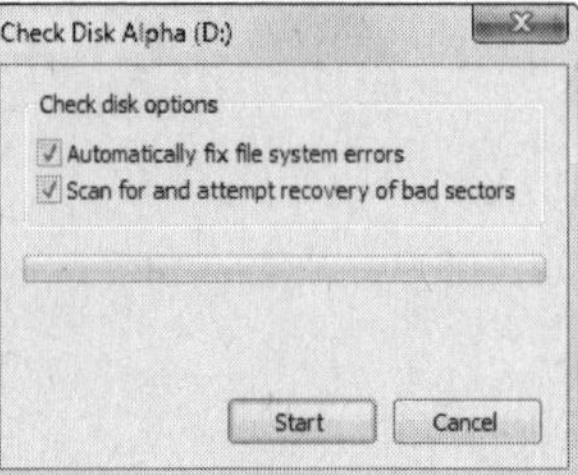

Figure 3-11: Check Disk performs a complete surface scan.

4. **In most circumstances, you select the Scan For and Attempt Recovery of Bad Sectors check box and then click the Start button.**

   If you don't want to sit and wait and wait for Windows to finish, you probably want to select the Automatically Fix File System Errors check box, too.

As long as you aren't using any files on the hard drive that Windows is scanning, Windows performs the scan on the spot and reports on what it finds. If you're using files on the hard drive, however — and that always happens if you're scanning the drive that contains Windows itself — Windows asks whether you want to schedule a scan to run the next time you restart your machine. If you say yes, you have to turn off the computer and then turn it back on again before Windows runs the scan. (Note that merely logging off isn't sufficient.)

Defragmenting a drive

Once upon a time, defragmenting your hard drive — instructing Windows to rearrange files on a hard drive so that the various parts of a file all sit next to one another — rated as a Real Big Deal. Windows didn't help automate running defrags, so few people bothered. As a result, drives started to look like patchwork quilts with pieces of files stored higgledy-piggledy. On the rare occasion that a Windows user ran the defragmenter, bringing all the pieces together could take hours — and the resulting system speed-up rarely raised any eyebrows, much less rocketed Windows fans into hyperthreaded bliss.

Windows 7 changes that by simply and quietly scheduling a disk defragmentation to run every week. You don't need to touch a thing.

Windows 7 doesn't run automatic defrags on solid state drives — which is to say, flash memory drives that don't have any moving parts. (You probably don't have one yet, but they're becoming more common every year.) Solid state drives don't need defragmentation. They also have a finite lifespan, so there's no need to overwork the drives with a senseless exercise in futility.

If you're curious about how your computer's doing in the defrag department, choose Start➪All Programs➪Accessories➪System Tools➪Disk Defragmenter. Disk Defragmenter gives you a full report (see Figure 3-12), allowing you to make scheduling changes if you so desire. You can also choose which drives you want to defrag.

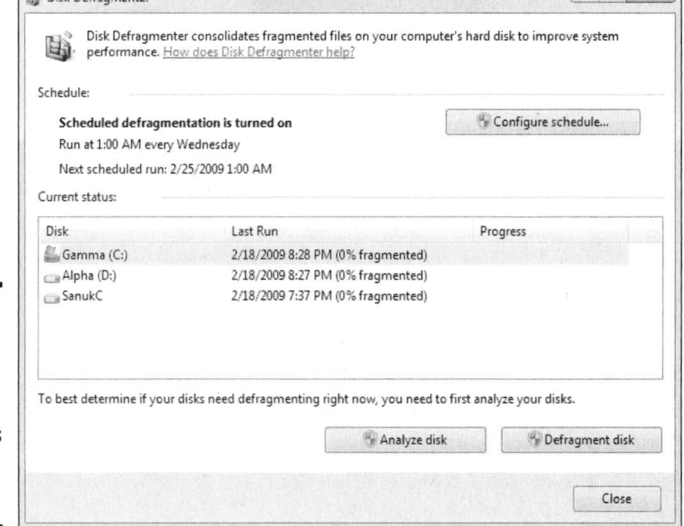

Figure 3-12: Windows 7 automatically defragments once a week.

Using System Restore and Restore Points

Ever get the feeling that things were going right?

Moments later, did you get the feeling that something must be wrong because things are going right?

Now you understand the gestalt behind System Restore. If you take a snapshot of your PC's settings from time to time, when things are going right, it's relatively easy to go back to that "right" time when the wolves come howling at the, uh, Gates.

Windows 7 automatically takes System Restore snapshots — called *restore points* (or, confusingly, *checkpoints*) — once a day. It also automatically saves a restore point every time you successfully start Windows. A restore point contains Registry entries and copies of certain critical programs including, notably, drivers and key system files — a "snapshot" of crucial system settings and programs. When you *roll back* (or, simply, *restore*) to a restore point, you replace the current settings and programs with the older versions.

When Windows 7 can tell that you're going to try to do something complicated, such as install a new network card, it sets a restore point. Unfortunately, Windows can't always tell when you're going to do something drastic — perhaps you have a new CD player and the instructions tell you to turn off your PC and install the player before you run the setup program. So it doesn't hurt one little bit to run System Restore from time to time, and set a restore point, all by yourself.

Creating a restore point

Here's how to create a restore point:

1. **Wait until your PC is running smoothly.**

   No sense in having a restore point that propels you out of the frying pan and into the fire, eh?

2. **Make sure that you're using an administrator account (see Book II, Chapter 2).**

3. **Choose Start, right-click Computer, and choose Properties. On the left, click the System Protection link.**

   Windows 7 shows you the System Protection tab, shown earlier in this chapter, in Figure 3-5.

4. **In the lower-right corner, click the Create button.**

   Windows 7 asks you to fill in a description for this manually generated restore point (see Figure 3-13). Type something that describes the reason for creating a restore point.

5. **Type a good description, and then click Create.**

   Windows advises that it's creating a restore point. When it's done, it shows a message that says `The restore point was created successfully.`

System Protection

Create a restore point

Type a description to help you identify the restore point. The current date and time are added automatically.

Before installing PCI-X card

Create | Cancel

Figure 3-13: Type something you'll remember.

6. **Click Close on the message, and then click the X button to close the System Properties dialog box.**

   Your new restore point is ready for action.

Rolling back to a restore point

If you ever want to manually restore your computer to a previous state, follow these steps:

1. **Save your work and then close all running programs.**

   System Restore doesn't muck with any data files, documents, pictures, or anything like that. It only works on system files. Your data is safe. But it can mess up settings, so if you recently installed a new program, for example, you may have to install it again.

2. **Choose Start➪All Programs➪Accessories➪System Tools➪System Restore.**

   Windows 7 recommends that you restore to a recent system-generated restore point, as shown in Figure 3-14.

3. **If you're willing to accept System Restore's recommendation, click Next. But if you want to take a look around and see what options are available, select Choose a Different Restore Point and click Next.**

   System Restore presents a list of recent available restore points, shown on the left in Figure 3-15.

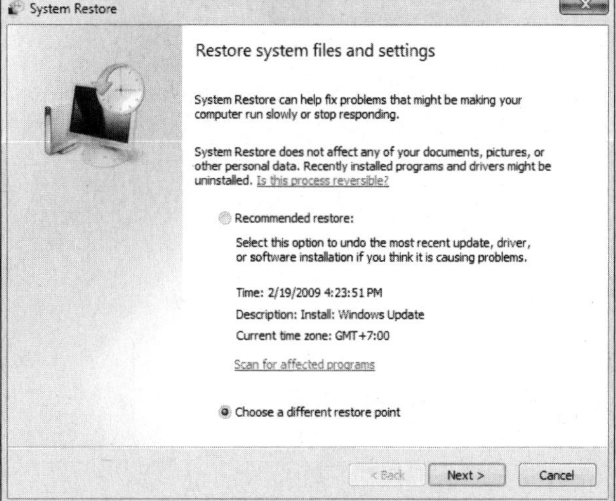

Figure 3-14: The recommended restore point isn't always the best restore point.

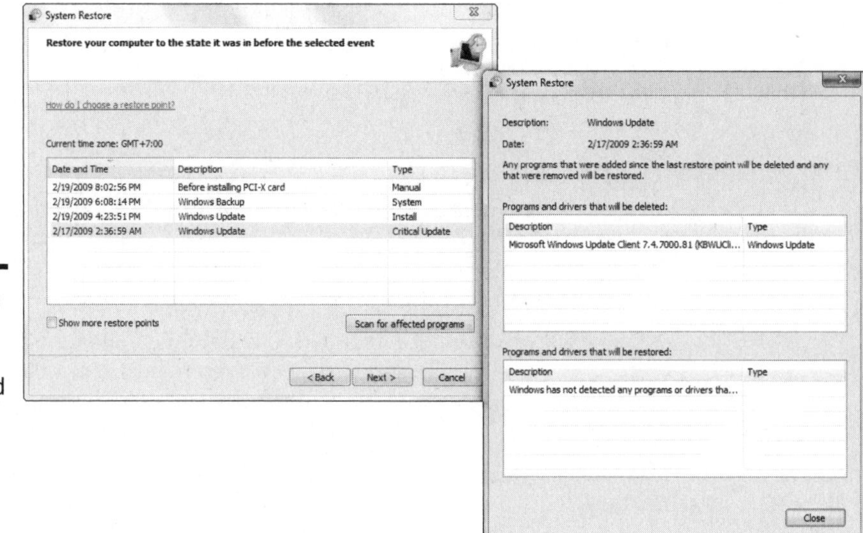

Figure 3-15: Pick a restore point — and see which programs will be affected.

4. **Before you roll your PC back to a restore point, click it once and then click the Scan for Affected Programs button.**

   System Restore tells you which programs and drivers have system entries (typically in the Registry) that will be altered and which programs will be deleted if you select that specific restore point. Refer to the right side of Figure 3-15.

5. **If you don't see any major problems with the restore point — it doesn't wipe out something you need — click Next.**

   System Restore asks you to confirm your restore point. You're also warned that rolling back to a restore point requires a restart of the computer, and that you should close all open programs before continuing.

6. **Click Finish.**

   True to its word, System Restore reverts to the selected restore point and restarts your computer.

System Restore is a nifty feature that works very well.

Scheduling the Task Scheduler

Windows 7 has a built-in scheduler that runs just about any program according to any schedule you specify — daily, weekly, monthly, middle of the night, or on alternate blue moons.

The scheduler comes in handy in three very different situations, when you want to

- ✦ **Always do something at the same time of day every day, week, or month:** Perhaps you always want to start Outlook at 6:15 every morning so that your machine is connected and your mail's ready by the time you drag your sorry tail into your desk chair. Or maybe you want to run a PowerPoint presentation every morning at 7:30 so that your boss hears the telltale sounds as she walks by your cubicle. (And who said Dummies aren't devious?)
- ✦ **Make sure that the computer performs some mundane maintenance job when it won't interfere with your work time:** Thus, you may schedule disk cleanups every weekday at 2:00 in the afternoon because you know you'll always be propped up in the mop closet, taking a snooze.
- ✦ **Do something every time you log on or when your computer starts:** You can even have the Task Scheduler send an e-mail message to your boss every time you log on. Interesting possibilities there.

TIP

Any discussion of scheduled tasks immediately conjures up the old question "Should I leave my computer running all night, or should I turn it off?" The fact is that nobody knows which is better. You can find plenty of arguments on both sides of the fence, although Microsoft's progress with Sleep mode has taken some wind out of the sails of those who insist that PCs need to be turned off. Suffice it to say that your computer has to be on (or sleeping) for a scheduled task to run, so you may have to leave your computer on at least one night a week (or a month) to get the maintenance work done.

I go into more detail on the environmental consequences in *Green Home Computing For Dummies*, which I wrote with Katherine Murray (Wiley).

You find absolutely no debate about one "should I leave it on" question, though. Everybody in the know agrees that running a full surface scan of your hard drive daily is a bad idea (specifically running Check Disk; see the "Running an error check" section, earlier in this chapter). A full scan simply inflicts too much wear and tear on the hard drive's arms. It's kind of like forcing yourself to fly every morning just to keep your shoulders in shape.

One of the most important uses of the Task Scheduler is driving a Windows file cleanup program called, imaginatively, Disk Cleanup. Here's how to get Disk Cleanup scheduled — and how to use the Task Scheduler in general.

Starting with your parameters

First, you need to set the Disk Cleanup parameters. Because Disk Cleanup can be run in many different ways, Windows 7 allows you to store many different sets of parameters, each set identified by a number. In this case, I (completely arbitrarily) call this set of parameters 9. Follow these steps to set your Disk Cleanup parameters:

1. **Choose Start. Immediately type** cleanmgr /sageset:9 **in the Search box and press Enter.**

   Be sure to put a space before the slash, but don't type spaces anywhere else. This command runs Windows 7 Disk Cleanup, saving your settings as "number 9," just like on The Beatles' *White Album.*

   The Disk Cleanup Settings dialog box appears (see Figure 3-16).

Figure 3-16: Make your Disk Cleanup choices here.

2. **Select the check boxes that correspond to the types of files you want Windows 7 to delete.**
3. **Click OK.**

   Windows doesn't run a disk cleanup. It merely saves your Disk Cleanup settings, identifying them as "number 9."

Scheduling a task

With Disk Cleanup configured properly, you can set it to run every night, by following these steps:

1. **Choose Start⇨All Programs⇨Accessories⇨System Tools⇨Task Scheduler.**

   The Task Scheduler appears, as shown in Figure 3-17.

2. **On the right, select the Create Basic Task option.**

   The Create Basic Task Wizard appears (see Figure 3-18).

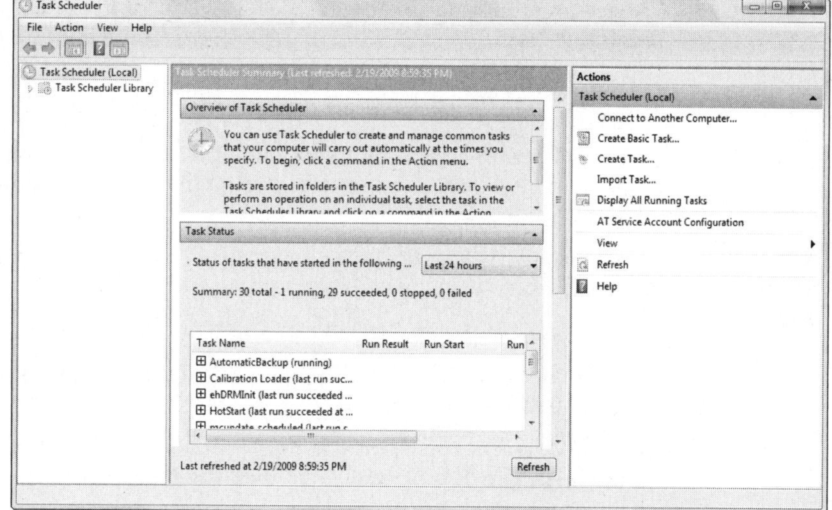

Figure 3-17: In spite of its intimidating appearance, the Task Scheduler can help you schedule almost any repetitive task.

3. **Type a name for the task, and then click the Next button.**

   The wizard asks for a trigger — geek-speak for "Under what circumstances do you want the scheduled task to run?"

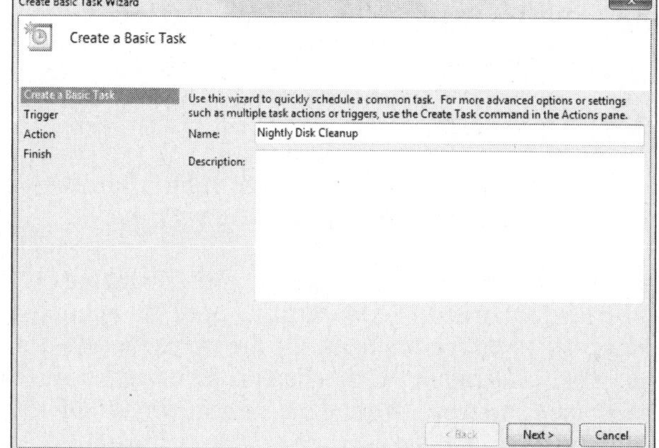

Figure 3-18: Give the scheduled task a descriptive name.

4. **Choose Daily if you want the cleanup to run every day, and then click the Next button.**
5. **Set the time of day that you want the cleanup to run, and click Next.**

6. **Choose an action. In this case, select the Start a Program option, and then click Next.**

   The Task Scheduler asks you for the program you want to run, `cleanmgr.exe`.

7. **To run Windows 7 Disk Cleanup, click the Browse button, navigate to** `\Windows\System32\cleanmgr.exe`**, click the program once, and click the Open button.**

   You can similarly run any other program with the Task Scheduler by clicking the Browse button, navigating to the program, and clicking Open.

8. **In the Add Arguments (Optional) box, type** **`/sagerun:9`**

   As you probably guessed, this step tells Windows 7 Disk Cleanup to use the "number 9" parameters.

9. **Click Next, select the Open the Properties Dialog for This Task When I Click Finish check box, and then click the Finish button.**

   The Task Scheduler Wizard adds your cleanup run to its list of active tasks. You can verify it by clicking the Refresh button at the bottom of the Task Scheduler window and then scrolling through the active tasks.

10. **In the Task Properties box, select the Run Whether User Is Logged On or Not option, and then click OK. If prompted for a password, type it and click OK.**

    You have to complete this final step in the Task Properties dialog box so that the cleanup can run whether you're logged on or not.

Zipping and Compressing

Windows 7 supports two very different kinds of file compression. The distinction is confusing but important, so bear with me.

File compression reduces the size of a file by cleverly taking out parts of the contents of the file that aren't needed, storing only the minimum amount of information necessary to reconstitute the file — extract it — into its full, original form. A certain amount of overhead is involved because the computer has to take the time to squeeze extraneous information out of a file before storing it, and then the computer takes more time to restore the file to its original state when someone needs the file. But compression can reduce file sizes enormously. A compressed file often takes up half its original space — even less, in many cases.

How does compression work? That depends on the compression method you use. In one kind of compression, known as Huffman encoding, letters that occur frequently in a file (say, the letter *e* in a word-processing document) are massaged so that they take up only a little bit of room in the file, whereas letters that occur less frequently (say, x) are allowed to occupy lots of space. Rather than allocate eight 1s and 0s for every letter in a document, for example, some letters may take up only two 1s and 0s and others could take up 15. The net result, overall, is a big reduction in file size. It's complicated, and the mathematics involved get quite interesting.

The two Windows 7 file compression techniques are as follows:

- Files can be compressed and placed in a Compressed (zipped) Folder, with an icon to match.
- Files, folders, or even entire drives can be compressed by using the built-in compression capabilities of the Windows 7 file system (NTFS).

Here's where things get complicated.

NT File System (NTFS) compression is built into the file system: You can use it only on NTFS drives, and the compression doesn't persist when you move (or copy) the file off the drive. Think of NTFS compression as a capability inherent to the hard drive itself. That isn't really the case — Windows 7 does all the sleight-of-hand behind the scenes — but the concept can help you remember the limitations and quirks of NTFS compression.

Although Microsoft would have you believe that Compressed (zipped) Folder compression is based on folders, it isn't. A Compressed (zipped) Folder is really a file — not a folder — but it's a special kind of file, called a *Zip file.* If you ever encountered Zip files on the Internet (they have a `.zip` filename extension and are frequently manipulated by using programs such as WinZip, `www.winzip.com`), you know exactly what I'm talking about. Zip files contain one or more compressed files, and they use the most common kind of compression found on the Internet. Think of Compressed (zipped) Folders as being Zip files, and if you have even a nodding acquaintance with Zips, you'll immediately understand the limitations and quirks of Compressed (zipped) Folders. Microsoft calls them Folders because that's supposed to be easier for users to understand. You be the judge.

If you have Windows show you filename extensions — see my rant about that topic in the section on showing filename extensions in Book II, Chapter 1 — you see immediately that Compressed (zipped) Folders are, in fact, simple Zip files.

Table 3-2 shows a quick comparison of NTFS compression and Zip compression.

Table 3-2 NTFS Compression versus Compressed (Zipped) Folders Compression

NTFS	Zip
Think of NTFS compression as a feature of the hard drive itself.	Zip technology works on any file, regardless of where it is stored.
The minute you move an NTFS-compressed file off an NTFS drive — by, say, sending a file as an e-mail attachment — the file is uncompressed, automatically, and you can't do anything about it: You'll send a big, uncompressed file.	You can move a Compressed (zipped) Folder (it's a Zip file, with a `.zip` filename extension) anywhere, and it stays compressed. If you send a Zip file as an e-mail attachment, it goes over the ether as a compressed file. The person who receives the file can view it directly in Windows 7, or he can use a product such as WinZip to see it.
A lot of overhead is associated with NTFS compression: Windows has to compress and decompress those files on the fly, and that sucks up processing power.	Very little overhead is associated with Zip files. Many programs (for example, antivirus programs) read Zip files directly.
NTFS compression is helpful if you're running out of room on an NTFS-formatted drive.	Compressed (zipped) Folders (that is to say, Zip files) are in a near-universal form that can be used just about anywhere.
You have to be using an administrator account to use NTFS compression.	You can create, copy, or move Zip files just like any other files, with the same security restrictions.
You can use NTFS compression on entire drives, folders, or single files. They cannot be password protected.	You can zip files or folders, or (rarely) drives, and they can be password protected.

If you try to compress the drive that contains your Windows folder, you can't compress the files that are in use by Windows.

Compressing with NTFS

To use NTFS compression on an entire drive, follow these steps:

1. **Make sure that you're using an administrator account (see Book II, Chapter 2).**
2. **Choose Start⇨Computer and right-click the drive you want to compress. Choose Properties and then click the General tab.**

3. **Select the Compress This Drive to Save Disk Space check box. Then click the OK button.**

   Windows asks you to confirm that you want to compress the entire drive. Windows takes some time to compress the drive — in some cases, the estimated time is measured in days. Good luck.

To use NTFS compression on a folder or single file, follow these steps:

1. **Make sure that you're using a full-fledged administrator account (see Book II, Chapter 2).**
2. **Navigate to the folder or file you want to compress (for example, choose Start⇨Documents or Start⇨Computer). Right-click the file or folder you want to compress. Choose Properties and click the Advanced button on the General tab.**

   The Advanced Properties dialog box appears.
3. **Select the Compress Contents to Save Disk Space check box, and then click the OK button.**

   To uncompress a file or folder, reopen the Advanced Properties dialog box (right-click the file or folder, choose Properties, and then click the Advanced button) and deselect the Compress Contents to Save Disk Space check box.

Zipping the easy way with Compressed (zipped) Folders

The easiest way to create a Zip file, er, a Compressed (zipped) Folder is with a simple right-click. Here's how:

1. **Navigate to the files you want to zip. (For example, choose Start⇨Documents or Start⇨Computer and go from there.)**
2. **Select the file or files that you want to zip together. (You can Ctrl+click to select individual files or Shift+click to select a bunch.) Right-click any of the selected files and choose Send To⇨Compressed (Zipped) Folder.**

   Windows responds by creating a new Zip file, with a `.zip` filename extension, and placing the selected files in the new Zip folder.

   The new file is just like any other file — you can rename it, copy it, move it, delete it, send it as an e-mail attachment, save it on the Internet, or do anything else to it that you can do to a file. (That's because it *is* a file.)
3. **To add another file to your Compressed (zipped) Folder, simply drag it onto the zipped folder icon.**

4. **To copy a file from your Zip file (uh, folder), double-click the zipped folder icon and treat the file the same way you would treat any "regular" file.**

5. **To copy all files out of your Zip file (folder), click the Extract All Files button on the command bar.**

   You see the Windows 7 Compressed (Zipped) Folders Extraction Wizard, which guides you through the steps.

The Compressed (Zipped) Folders Extraction Wizard places all copied files into a new folder with the same name as the Zip file — which confuses the living bewilickers out of everybody. Unless you give the extracted folder a different name from the original Compressed (zipped) Folder, you end up with two folders with precisely the same name sitting on your desktop. Do yourself a huge favor and feed the wizard a different folder name while you're extracting the files.

Using the Windows 7 Resource Monitor and Reliability Monitor

Ever want to look under the hood?

The Windows 7 Resource Monitor lets you peek into the inner workings of the beast, with graphs and statistics galore. If you're having trouble with a program taking over your computer, or if you're curious to see how much of its memory is being used, the Resource Monitor knows all, sees all, tells all.

To peruse the internal behavior of your system, follow these steps:

1. **Choose Start⇨All Programs⇨Accessories⇨System Tools⇨Resource Monitor.**

   They buried it deep, eh? To get there quickly, click Start, type **resmon**, and hit Enter.

   The Windows 7 Resource Monitor appears, in its Overview state (see Figure 3-19).

2. **To keep a watch on which programs are hogging the CPU, click the Average CPU column heading.**

   That column presents a 60-second running average of CPU utilization. The hogs float to the top.

If a program has stopped responding, right-click it here and choose Analyze Process. You may be able to glean some worthwhile information that helps you whack the program upside the head.

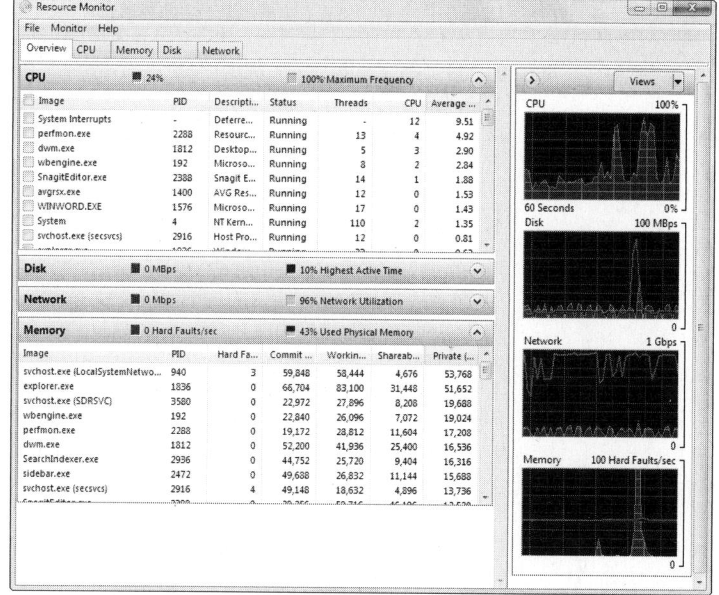

Figure 3-19: The Resource Monitor shows you what's running.

3. **If you're curious about how your computer's memory is being used, click the Memory tab.**

   The Resource Monitor's memory tracker appears. The bar graph at the bottom may surprise you, particularly if you have 4GB installed on a 32-bit Windows 7 system: A sizable chunk of memory isn't accessible, and this graph tells you how much.

   In general, if Windows reports many page faults (the graph marked Hard Faults/sec), you may be able to increase your computer's performance significantly by increasing its amount of memory.

4. **When you're done, click the X Close button to close the Resource Monitor.**

   I could spend hours watching it.

By contrast, the Windows 7 Reliability Monitor gives you an eagle-eye view of the problems your PC has encountered, with some insight as to the causes. I talk about the Reliability Monitor in Book II, Chapter 5.

Controlling the Control Panel

The inner workings of Windows 7 reveal themselves inside the mysterious (and somewhat haughtily named) Control Panel. Choose Start➪Control Panel to plug away at the innards (see Figure 3-20).

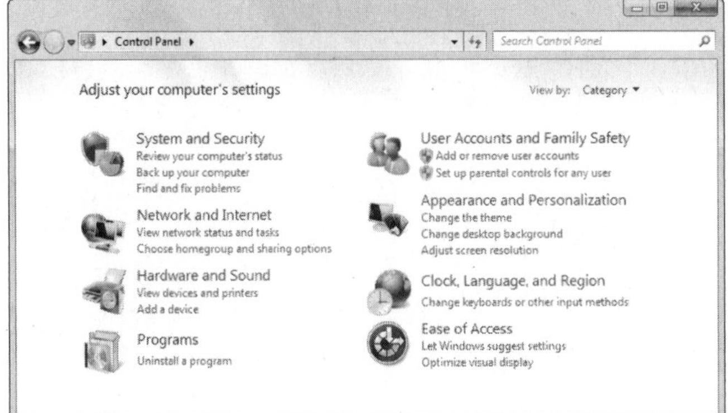

Figure 3-20: The packed Windows 7 Control Panel.

I cover various Control Panel components at several points in this book, but an overview appears in this chapter.

The main categories of the Control Panel span the breadth (and plumb the depth) of Windows 7-dumb:

- **System and Security:** Use an enormous array of tools for troubleshooting and adjusting your PC, backing up your data, controlling how Windows conducts searches, checking your performance rating, and generally making your PC work when it doesn't want to. Check out the components of the Windows 7 mighty security arsenal, including Windows Firewall (at least, the inbound part of Windows Firewall; see Book VI, Chapter 3), Windows Defender (Book VI, Chapter 5), and the efficacy of your antivirus software. This is also the place to make changes to the Internet Explorer security settings (Book V, Chapter 3). Unfortunately, this category also includes all the tools you need to shoot yourself in the foot, consistently and reliably, day in and day out. Use this part of the Control Panel with discretion and respect.
- **Network and Internet:** Set up a network or a HomeGroup. Set up Internet connections, particularly if you're sharing an Internet connection across a network, or if you have a cable modem or digital subscriber line (DSL) service. Deal with conflicting wireless networks. Configure synchronization between computers. Many security settings in this category duplicate those in the Security category.
- **Hardware and Sound:** The "all other" category. Add or remove printers and connect to other printers on your network. Troubleshoot printers. Install, remove, and set the options for scanners and digital cameras, mice, game controllers, joysticks, keyboards, and pen devices. Power settings are here, too.

- **Programs:** Add and remove specific features in some programs (most notably, Windows 7 and Office). Uninstall programs. Change the association between filename extensions (see Book II, Chapter 1) and the programs that run them (so that you can, for example, have iTunes play WMA audio files). Microsoft also kindly gives you an easy way to buy new programs online. Gawrsh.
- **User Accounts and Family Safety:** Add or remove users from the Windows Welcome screen. Enable the Guest account (see Book II, Chapter 2). Change user account characteristics, including passwords. A couple of rudimentary parental controls appear here, but for the more advanced choices, you need to download and install Windows Live Family Safety (see Book I, Chapter 5).
- **Appearance and Personalization:** Turn on the Glass effect and make your windows translucent. Change what your desktop looks like — wallpaper, colors, mouse pointers, screen saver, and icon size and spacing, for example. Set the screen resolution (for example, 1280 x 1024 or 2048 x 1280) so that you can pack more information onto your screen — assuming that your eyes (and screen) can handle it. Make the Windows taskbar hide when you're not using it, and change the items on your Start menu. Change what Windows Explorer shows when you're looking at folders. Add or remove fonts.
- **Clock, Language, and Region:** Set the time and date — although double-clicking the clock on the Windows taskbar is much simpler — or tell Windows to synchronize the clock automatically. You can also add support for complex languages (such as Thai) and right-to-left languages, and change how dates, times, currency, and numbers appear.
- **Ease of Access:** Change settings to help you see the screen, use the keyboard or mouse, or have Windows flash part of your screen when the speaker would play a sound. Also set up speech recognition.
- **All Control Panel Items:** Flip the Control Panel back into its Windows XP form, with many little icons jumbled together.

Many Control Panel settings duplicate options you see elsewhere in Windows 7, but some capabilities that seem like they should be Control Panel mainstays remain mysteriously absent. You have at least 157 different ways in the Control Panel to turn on Windows automatic updating, for example (okay, so I exaggerate a little), but you don't find the controls for adjusting the Windows 7 outbound firewall anywhere in the long Control Panel list.

If you want to change a Windows setting, by all means try the Control Panel, but don't be discouraged if you can't find what you're looking for. Instead, look in this book's table of contents or index.

Removing and changing programs

Windows lives only to serve — or so I'm told — and, more than anything, Windows serves programs. Most of us spend our time working inside programs such as Outlook or Word or Adobe Photoshop or QuickBooks. Windows acts as traffic cop and nanny but doesn't do the heavy lifting. Programs rule. Users rely on Windows to keep the programs in line.

Installing programs is easy. When you want to install a program, you typically insert a CD into your CD drive and follow the instructions or double-click a downloaded program. You've done that a hundred times.

Removing well-behaved programs is just as easy, if you follow the instructions in this section. Changing programs, on the other hand, is a different kettle of fish, as you will soon discover.

Windows 7 includes a one-stop shopping point for removing and making massive changes to programs. To get to it, choose Start⇨Control Panel, and then under the Programs heading, click the Uninstall a Program link. You see the dialog box shown in Figure 3-21.

Some programs let you change installed features

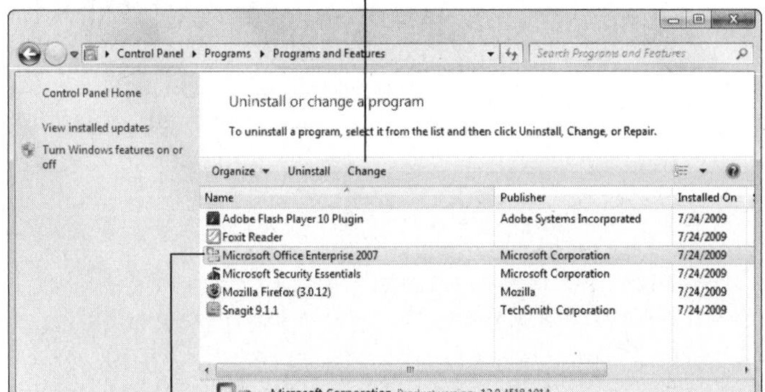

Double-click a program to start its uninstall

Figure 3-21: Remove a program the proper way.

When Windows 7 talks about changing programs, it isn't talking about making minor twiddles — this isn't the place to go if you want Microsoft Word to stop showing you rulers, for example. The Uninstall or Change a Program dialog box is designed to activate or deactivate big chunks of a program — graft on a new arm or lop off an unused head (of which there are many, particularly in Office). In the Uninstall or Change a Program dialog box for Office 2007, for example, you may tell Excel that you want to use its Analysis ToolPak add-in for financial analysis. Similarly, you may use the Uninstall or Change a Program dialog box to obliterate the Office speech recognition capabilities. That's the kind of large-scale capability I'm talking about.

Yes, it's true. If you want to install a big chunk of a program, you have to click the Uninstall a Program link in the Control Panel. The terminology stinks. Windows 7 really should say something like "Bring up a program's installer or uninstaller." But I guess speaking the truth plainly would be too confusing.

Windows 7 itself doesn't do much in the Uninstall or Change a Program dialog box. Windows 7 primarily acts as a gathering point: Well-behaved programs, when they're installed, are supposed to stick their uninstallers where the Uninstall or Change a Program dialog box can find them. That way, you have one centralized place to look in when you want to get rid of a program. Microsoft doesn't write the uninstallers that the Uninstall or Change a Program dialog box runs; if you have a gripe about a program's uninstaller, you need to talk to the company that made the program.

A few school-of-hard-knocks comments pertain:

- If you want to remove a program and it isn't listed here, there's a 99 percent chance that the program you want to remove is a piece of scumware. Hop onto Google and search for the name of the program — make sure you copy it precisely — and add the term *uninstall.* You may be in for some interesting times.
- You rarely use the Uninstall or Change a Program dialog box to remove parts of a program. Either you try to add features in a program that you forgot to include when you originally installed the program — most commonly with Office — or you want to delete a program entirely, to wipe its sorry tail off your hard drive.

  Why sweat the small stuff? When you install a program, install all of it. With large hard drives so cheap that they're likely candidates for a landfill, it never pays to cut back on installed features to save a few megabytes. In for a penny, in for a pound.
- Many uninstallers, for reasons known only to their company's programmers (I don't mention Adobe by name), require you to insert the program's CD into your CD drive before you uninstall the program. That's like requiring you to show your dog's vaccination records before you kick it out of the house.

When you start a program's uninstaller, you're at the mercy of the uninstaller and the programmers who wrote it. Windows doesn't even enter into the picture.

Removing Windows patches

If you install a Windows patch and discover a minute (or a day or week) later that the patch causes more problems than it solves, you may — *may* — be able to roll back the patch.

To see whether the fix that bedevils you can be exorcised, choose Start➪Control Panel➪Programs, and under Programs and Features, click View Installed Updates.

Windows 7 presents you with a list of all patches that have been applied to your system. Click the one that's the most likely source of your problems, and then click the Remove button. If you're allowed to uninstall the patch, Windows 7 does it for you.

Chapter 4: Getting the Basic Stuff Done

In This Chapter

- **Burning CDs and DVDs**
- **Using Windows Experience Index to beef up your machine**
- **Word processing, calculating, painting, and more**
- **Sticking sticky notes**
- **Lots of boring stuff that you need to know anyway**

You bought your PC to get things done, right? I guess it depends on what you mean by *things*. You need to know how to write a letter, even if you don't have Microsoft Office installed on your PC. You should figure out how to use the Windows Calculator, even if the thought of employing a $1,000 tool to solve a two-bit problem leaves you feeling a little green.

Hey, I have to talk about that stuff somewhere.

This chapter also digs into the truly cool Windows 7 support for burning CDs and DVDs, and what you can (and can't!) do to improve your performance rating, er, experience index.

You know. Stuff.

Burning CDs and DVDs

Windows 7 includes simple, one-click (or two- or three-click) support for burning CDs or DVDs — *burning,* or writing, is the process of putting stuff on a CD or DVD. You can burn music, video, recorded TV shows, photos, and all kinds of data — pyromania on a platter.

You need a CD recorder (a CD-RW drive) or DVD recorder (variously, DVD-RW, DVD+RW, DVD+-RW) to make your own CDs or DVDs, of course, but most PCs these days have optical drives (that's what they're called) with recording capabilities built in. If you don't like the optical drive in your PC and you buy a cheap, dual-layer DVD+-RW drive that attaches to your PC via a USB cable, your most difficult job is pulling it from its Styrofoam padding. See Book VIII, Chapter 2, for more about installing external devices.

Burn with Windows or Media Player?

When you insert a blank CD into your CD/DVD drive, you may be stumped when Windows asks whether you want to "burn an audio CD using Windows Media Player" or "burn files to disc using Windows Explorer." When you stick a blank DVD into your CD/DVD drive, you're asked if you want to "Burn files to disc using Windows Explorer" or "Burn a DVD video disc using Windows DVD Maker."

There's a reason why Windows presents you with such obfuscated choices. Here's the scorecard:

If you want to burn an old-fashioned audio CD — the kind you can stick in an old-fashioned CD player — you must use a blank CD, and you must use Windows Media Player. You end up with one album on one CD, give or take a fudge or two.

If you want to burn a DVD video — the kind you can stick in a DVD player — you must use a blank DVD (or Dual Layer DVD or Blu-ray disc), and you must use Windows DVD Maker.

Here's where it gets murky. If you want to put music on a CD and you're going to play that music on any modern CD player, you should stick MP3 music files on the disc. (That way, you can fit ten albums or so on a single CD.) Windows calls a CD with MP3 files a music *data disc,* and you can create data discs with either Windows Explorer or Windows Media Player.

If you want to put an AVI file on a DVD — some DVD players can play AVI files — you have to use Windows Explorer. But you can also put smallish AVI files on CDs, and many DVD players play them just fine. For that matter, you can stick a ton of MP3s on a DVD, and some CD players play them.

If you want to stick your MP3s on a CD, Windows Media Player has a few features that help: For example, WMP keeps track of how much data fits on the CD and warns you if you have accumulated too much. (I hate the way WMP makes it hard to change the sequence of folders being burned.) If you're going to put music on a CD, I suggest you look at the chapter that covers WMP in depth: Book IV, Chapter 1.

In this chapter, I talk about using Windows Explorer to burn CDs and DVDs. Those CDs and DVDs may contain MP3 or AVI files, or data, programs, and the like. If you want to learn how to use Windows Media Player to burn old-fashioned audio CD or music data discs, see Book IV, Chapter 1. If you want to use Windows DVD Maker to burn a video DVD, see Book IV, Chapter 6.

Many people use the software that shipped with their computers (which, in turn, probably came from the companies that made the drives) to burn CDs and DVDs. In almost all cases, though, Windows 7 itself does yeoman work, and it doesn't suffer from the Windows compatibility problems that dog other manufacturers' software.

You may have Nero on your PC, compliments of the PC manufacturer or the CD/DVD drive manufacturer. Personally, I don't install Nero on new PCs: It hooks into all sorts of places in Windows, and it's devilishly difficult to remove completely. But if you have it, you should give it a try.

Not surprisingly, CD-R discs cost less than the others, and DVD-RW discs cost the most. CDs can hold about 700MB of data. DVDs go up to 4.7GB — or six-and-a-half times as much.

Confused yet? Allow me to make things worse. Dual-layer DVD-RW drives work with special discs that hold up to 8.5GB of data. Before you burn a dual-layer DVD, though, be sure that the disc is destined for another dual-layer drive. You can't play or read a dual-layer DVD in a "normal" DVD drive.

Blu-ray discs hold up to 50GB of data, but both the players and the discs themselves (as of this writing anyway) can send shivers down your pocketbook. If you really want to watch the latest movies in full, glorious high definition — HD files are so big that you need a Blu-ray-size disc to hold them — buying a Blu-ray player (or Blu-ray-friendly PlayStation) may make some sense. But for day-to-day burning and schlepping, stick to DVD-RW.

What to burn

DVDs and CDs hold bits — 1s and 0s. There's nothing particularly mysterious about it.

Unfortunately, confusingly, the bits can be interpreted in different ways, and the different interpretations can be hard to follow:

- **Audio tracks** are (by computer standards) an ancient art form. When you buy an audio CD from a music store, the CD (usually) contains audio tracks. Every audio CD player I've ever seen understands standard audio, the progenitor of all CD formats.

  To a first approximation, tracks on an audio CD are very similar to WAV files. The main difference is this: Audio tracks have a layer of error-correcting codes on the CD. Regardless of what Windows may tell you, no "files" exist on an audio CD: If your computer shows you `.cda` files on an audio CD, it's acting like a Jedi knight, creating a beneficent illusion.

  The process of converting audio tracks into data files that a computer can handle more readily is *ripping*. I talk about ripping extensively in Book IV, Chapter 1.

- **Video tracks** may not be as ancient as audio tracks, but they're certainly growing long in the tooth. When you buy or rent a movie, the DVD contains video tracks. The process of converting video tracks into data files that a computer can handle more readily is, uh, ripping. Is there an echo in here?

- **Data files** can take on any form — literally anything you can put in your computer can go on a CD or DVD. Someday the world will wean itself off audio and video tracks, and we'll only have to deal with data files. But it won't happen any time soon.

The mother lode of all CD-R information sits on the Web (where else?) in Andy McFadden's CD-R FAQ, www.cdrfaq.org. If you go to that site, An has information for downloading and reading the massive tome. For DVD information, check out Jim Taylor's www.dvddemystified.com/dvdfa html, an invaluable and authoritative reference. And for ultimate Blu-ray coverage, including a mighty FAQ, see www.blu-ray.com.

Understanding -R and -RW

Sorry, Marshall. When it comes to DVDs, the medium isn't the message. T get a handle on all this CD/DVD/HD-DVD/Blu-ray bafflegab, it's easiest to start with the disc itself, the silvery piece of coated plastic that's just one short step away from becoming a coffee table coaster.

Before you burn a CD or DVD, you should understand the fundamental di ference between R and RW. Most optical drives these days can burn DVD and DVD-RWs as well as CD-Rs and CD-RWs: The main question is whethe you should spend extra money for more-capable discs. Silver for silver, as it were. You have to choose the kind of disc that suits your situation, as I describe in the following list:

- **CD-Recordable (CD-R):** Can be played in CD players or read on compu ers, but the data on them cannot be erased. Although it's physically possible to record on a CD-R disc more than once, the "old" data isn't erased — "new" data is added to the end of the CD-R, in groups called *sessions* (see the following sidebar, "Close that session!"). Many audio CD players don't recognize data beyond the first session.

  If you're trying to burn a regular old, everyday audio CD that can work in most old-fashioned audio players, CD-R is your best (and cheapest!) choice — but if the burn goes awry, you end up with a coaster that car be fixed.

- **CD-Record/Write (CD-RW):** Can be erased, and the erased area can be rewritten with new stuff. CD-RW discs do not work in some audio CD players, particularly older ones, but most newer players swallow CD-R discs with aplomb. You can rewrite CD-RW discs hundreds of times before they wear out.
- **DVD-Recordable (DVD-R or DVD+R):** Can be played in almost any DVD player but cannot be erased. A technical distinction exists between the + and the – that enters into the picture only if you have an older DVD player. For most purposes, DVD-R, DVD+R, and DVD+-R work the same.
- **DVD-Record/Write (DVD-RW or DVD+RW):** Can work in almost any DVD player and can be erased. Again, the distinction between + and – is largely academic, although some players can be picky. These discs put up with hundreds of rewrites.

When you rip audio tracks and turn them into data files, the resulting files can come in many different flavors — MP3, WMA (the Microsoft proprietary format), AAC (the Apple proprietary format), OGG, and many more. Video tracks can turn into WMV format (Microsoft again), M4V (playable on iPods, not proprietary), MPG, AVI, and many others.

What's a *proprietary format*? It's a method of storing and interpreting bits that's owned lock, stock, and barrel by a company. Microsoft hopes to control the format of our music and video files with its proprietary WMA and WMV formats — and make money by selling licenses to companies that make CD and DVD players, among many others. See my discussion of C.R.A.P. music (a term coined by ZDNet's David Berlind) in Book IV, Chapter 1.

Newer CD players can handle CDs that contain MP3 and WMA files. Some can even handle DVDs with MP3 and WMA files. That's an RBD, er, a Real Big Deal because Windows 7 makes it surprisingly easy to burn DVDs chock-full of MP3 files. Consider this: A typical audio CD, filled with audio tracks, holds about an hour's worth of music — say, 15 songs. But if you rip the songs and store them as MP3s, and then burn the MP3s to a CD, that same-size CD can hold, oh, about 100 to 150 songs. A single DVD can hold 1,000 songs. Mind-boggling. For a look at the economics of the situation, see Table 4-1.

Table 4-1 How Much to Burn a Song?

Disc Type	*Data Type*	*Number of Songs*	*Media*	*Disc Price*	*Cost per Song*
CD	Audio tracks	15	One-time	$0.30	$0.0200
			Rewritable	$1.00	$0.0670
CD	MP3 files	150	One-time	$0.30	$0.0020
			Rewritable	$1.00	$0.0067
DVD	MP3 files	1,000	One-time	$0.50	$0.005
			Rewritable	$1.00	$0.0010

Mastered or Live File System?

You have many different ways to arrange data on a CD or DVD, but most folks need only concern themselves with the following two (sets of) standards:

- ✦ **Mastered formatting** (sometimes called *ISO*), the older version, works with almost any kind of drive. Windows 7 calls this standard "With a CD/DVD Player." If you're going to burn a CD or DVD that will be used in an older CD or DVD player, you should use Mastered.

When you burn a Mastered disc, you have to choose all the files you're going to burn and then burn them all at once. Windows 7 performs a kind of preprocessing step to convert all the files to the ISO format and then writes all the files continuously onto the disc.

- **Live File System formatting** (sometimes called, confusingly, *File System* or *UDF*), the new version, is a good choice for discs that are used in computers running Windows XP, Windows Vista, or Windows 7. Windows 7 calls it "Like a USB flash drive" even though it isn't much like a USB flash drive at all. At this writing, some (but by no means all) audio CD players or DVD players can accept UDF/Live File System–formatted discs.

  When you burn a Live File System disc, Windows 7 writes the data one file at a time, without preprocessing each file. You can burn a few files on the disc today and a few more tomorrow.

Windows 7 contains a lot of Help documentation (some of it is confusing!) about making a choice between "With a CD/DVD Player/Mastered/ISO" and "Like a USB flash drive/Live File System/UDF." Until more players can use Live File System/UDF, the choice is pretty easy: If you're creating a CD or DVD to absolutely, positively use on a Windows XP, Windows Vista, or Windows 7 computer, go ahead and use Live File System/UDF. Otherwise, given a choice, stick with Mastered/ISO.

What's the best way to get a feel for the differences between Mastered and File System formatting? Go through the process of burning CDs in each format, following the steps in the next section.

Burning with Windows 7

The first time you try to burn a CD (or DVD) with a new CD (or DVD) drive, work with data files instead of music or video. Start out with the easiest possible scenario (simple data files) before you work your way up to the most complex (high-definition video DVDs). That increases your chances of finding and solving problems when they're easiest to tackle. When you have a CD-R, CD-RW, DVD-R, or DVD-RW drive installed and working, transferring your files to CD or DVD couldn't be simpler.

If you're accustomed to the Windows XP way of burning discs, the Windows 7 method may feel a bit uncomfortable until you get the hang of it. Many folks who grew up with XP tend to choose the files they want to burn first, mark them for burning, insert a blank disc, and then sit back while XP does the dirty deed.

In Windows 7, you find it much easier to work the other way around: Put a blank CD or DVD into the drive before you pick your files. When you insert the blank disc up front, Windows 7 can tell how much space is on the disc. It can also ask whether you want to burn in Mastered/ISO or Live File System/UDF format, and prepare the CD or DVD appropriately in response to your choice.

If you want to burn music files, don't follow these instructions. Use Windows Media Player (WMP). I show you how to use Windows Media Player in Book IV, Chapter 1. WMP has all sorts of bells and whistles that are specific to music, and it does a fine job of burning music CDs with all the ancillary information, including playlists.

Close that session!

Ready for the advanced course? You can write multiple times on a CD-R (or DVD-R) disc. It's confusing. If you've never had to wrangle with multiple CD-R sessions, count yourself lucky. (This applies only to CD-R and DVD-R discs; you can write to CD-RW and DVD-RW discs till the cows come home.)

When you burn a CD-R using the Mastered (ISO) format, Windows preprocesses the files you have chosen to burn and then writes them all to the CD-R (or DVD-R) at one time. Invariably, some unused space exists at the end of the CD-R, so you can have Windows gather more files, preprocess them, and burn the next bunch, all at once. Each bunch of files constitutes a session.

Here's where the terminology gets confusing — the manufacturers themselves don't completely agree on the names of things, so watch out. You can close a session and increase the chances that another computer can read your CD-R or DVD-R (see the next paragraph). Windows 7 automatically closes each session after it's written. You can also finalize a disc, which not only closes the last session but also marks the CD-R as complete: After you finalize a CD-R or DVD-R, you can't add any more data to it. Ever.

Here are two infuriatingly simple rules for Mastered (ISO) CDs:

- A CD-R (or DVD-R) drive that is not an RW drive usually can't read a CD-R (or DVD-R) unless it has been closed. Because audio CD players (and movie DVD players) usually can't record, you almost always have to close a CD-R (or DVD-R) before it can be played in a traditional player (but, again, Windows 7 closes each session for you automatically).
- Most audio CD players can only read the first session on a CD.

CDs burned with the Live File System, uh, File System, er, UDF format, on the other hand, may need to be closed before the CD can work on other computers. You can close the same CD or DVD many times; each clump of data between two "closes" constitutes a session. I cover that procedure in the nearby section "Burning with Windows 7."

Here's the bottom line: CDs are cheap. Don't try to fool Mother Nature and record multiple sessions on a CD-R that's destined to be played in a "normal" audio CD player. Ditto for DVD. But if you want to experiment, hey, it's a lot of fun getting closer to the hardware.

Burning a CD in the Mastered/ISO style

Follow these steps to burn a CD (or DVD) with data files using the Mastered/ISO format:

1. **Pick the kind of CD or DVD you want to use and stick it in the drive.**

   See the section "Understanding -R and -RW," earlier in this chapter, for tips on picking the right disc for the job.

   When you put a blank CD in the drive, Windows 7 responds with the AutoPlay dialog box, shown in Figure 4-1. (A blank DVD brings up a similar AutoPlay dialog box, labeled Burn a DVD Video Disc Using Windows DVD Maker.)

Figure 4-1: Insert a blank disc before selecting files.

2. **Click the Burn Files to Disc Using Windows option.**

   Windows 7 responds with the Burn a Disc dialog box, shown in Figure 4-2. This is the point where you have to choose between using UDF and ISO formats.

Figure 4-2: Choose a format for burning a disc.

3. **Since you decided to burn a Mastered CD/DVD, choose With a CD Player/Mastered (ISO).**

4. **Type a label for the disc in the Disc Title box, and then click Next.**

   Windows 7 takes a couple of seconds to verify the size of the CD or DVD in the drive and then shows you a Windows Explorer window (the "burn" window) that says Drag Files to This Folder to Add Them to the Disc, as in Figure 4-3. Windows 7 doesn't write anything to the disc.

If Windows 7 shows you a bogus AutoPlay dialog box offering to "Open the folder to view files using Windows Explorer," click the X Close button to close it. As far as I'm concerned, that's a bug.

Note the Burn to Disc option

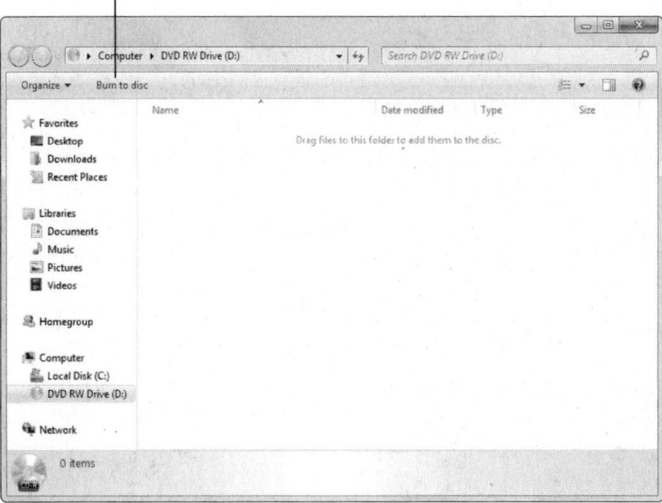

Figure 4-3: The Windows Explorer burn window for a Mastered (ISO) disc.

5. **Navigate to the files you want to copy (for example, choose Start⇨Pictures or Start⇨Music), click the files, and drag them to the burn window. Or, select the files you want to put on the CD and click the Burn button.**

   Windows 7 copies the files you select into a sort of holding area on your hard drive. A note appears in the notification area, down near the clock, that says "You Have Files Waiting to be Burned to Disc." If you try to drag more files into the holding area than can fit on the disc you're burning, or if you select more data than will fit on the disc and click Burn, Windows 7 doesn't warn you (see Step 7, when Windows 7 finally gets smart).

6. **In the Mastered/ISO burn window, click the Burn to Disc button.**

   Windows 7 opens the first window in the Mastered/ISO disc burning wizard, filled in with the title you typed in Step 4 (see Figure 4-4).

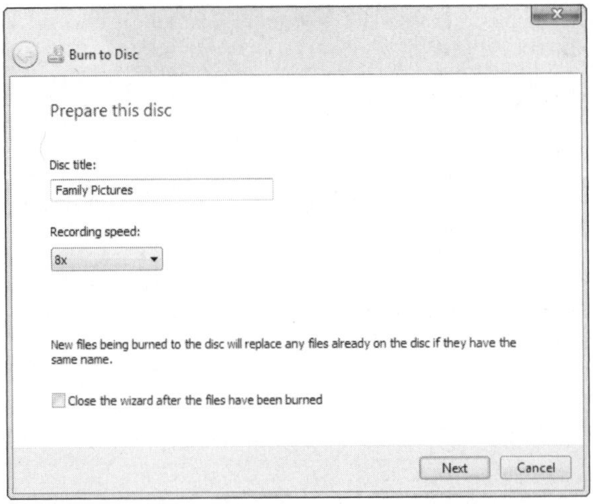

Figure 4-4: A wizard guides you through the steps to burn a Mastered/ISO CD.

7. **Change the disc title, if you like, and then click the Next button.**

   If you dragged too much data into the ISO burn window, Windows 7 bellyaches at this point that you need to remove files. Do so.

   When you delete temporary files from the CD/DVD writer's holding area, Windows 7 asks "Are you sure you want to move this folder (or file) to the Recycle Bin?" Not to worry. Windows 7 doesn't delete your original folder or file. It just wants your permission to delete the copy sitting in the holding area.

   Windows 7 takes ages to write the data. First, it constructs a disc image that's suitable for burning on the CD, and then it transfers the image, thus copying to the CD the files you dragged into the burn window. Even on a relatively fast CD drive, it can take 15 minutes to burn a full CD.

   When Windows 7 finishes, you see the ISO disc-burning wizard message, shown in Figure 4-5.

8. **Don't click the Finish button yet. Take the CD out of the burner, and try to read it on a different machine.**

   If you have no other machine, take it out of the drive and try to read it on the same machine.

9. **If it looks like all the files were burned correctly, click the Finish button in the Burn to Disc dialog box (refer to Figure 4-5). But if it looks like you have a useless piece of plastic on your hands, select the Yes, Burn These Files to Another Disc check box and then click the Finish button.**

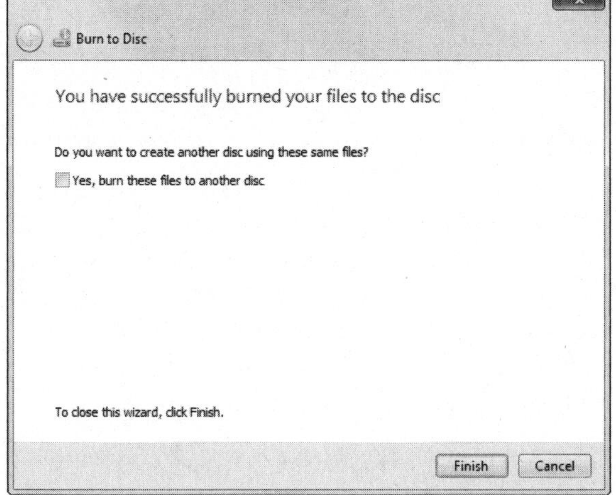

Figure 4-5: Make sure that the burn went well before clicking the Finish button.

You can add files to a Mastered/ISO CD-R (as long as the disc isn't full):

1. **Slide the CD-R into your drive and copy files to the drive using any of the myriad Windows 7 methods (see Figure 4-6).**
2. **When you have all the new files that are fit to burn, click the Burn to Disc button.**
3. **Follow along from Step 6 in the preceding set of steps.**

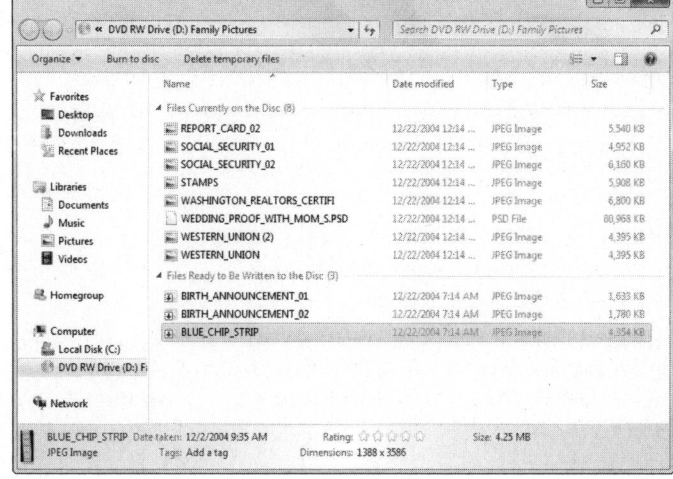

Figure 4-6: To add more files to a Mastered/ ISO CD-R, drag them to the drive's folder.

Burning a CD in the Live File System/UDF format

Follow these steps to burn a CD (or DVD) with data files using Live File System/UDF format:

1. **Pick the kind of CD or DVD you want to use, and stick it in the drive.**

   See the section "Understanding -R and -RW," earlier in this chapter, for tips on picking the right disc for the job.

   When you put a blank CD in the drive, Windows 7 responds with the AutoPlay dialog box (refer to Figure 4-1). (A blank DVD prompts a similar AutoPlay dialog box to open, labeled Burn a DVD Video Disc Using Windows DVD Maker.)

2. **Click the Burn Files to Disc Using Windows option.**

   Windows 7 responds with the Burn a Disc dialog box (refer to Figure 4-2).

3. **Choose Like a USB Flash Drive/Live File System (UDF) formatting.**

   Use the guidelines in the section "Mastered or Live File System?" earlier in this chapter. If you know that the CD or DVD will be used only in Windows XP or Windows 7 computers, Like a USB Flash Drive/Live File System/UDF is a good choice.

   In spite of what Figure 4-2 says, recording to a random-access USB flash drive is nothing like burning to a sequential CD. Using Live File System/UDF on a CD is much more like writing to a giant floppy drive or an extremely slow and small hard drive.

4. **Type a label for the disc in the Disc Title box, and then click Next.**

   Windows 7 formats the CD or DVD by writing guiding marks on the disc. The process can take many minutes, especially if you're using a DVD. The disc title you specify in Figure 4-2 becomes the newly formatted disc's name. Windows 7 presents you with a Windows Explorer burn window (see Figure 4-7). If you compare this to Figure 4-3, be sure to note three important differences: The Burn to Disc button is replaced with Close Session and Eject buttons, and the CD title already appears on the disc.

   If Windows 7 shows you a bogus AutoPlay dialog box offering to "Open the folder to view files using Windows Explorer," click the X button to close it. As far as I'm concerned, that's a bug.

5. **Navigate to the files you want to copy (for example, choose Start⇨Pictures or Start⇨Music), click the files, and drag them to the burn window, or select the files you want to put on the CD and click the Burn button.**

   Windows 7 immediately copies the files you drag into the folder — or the files you selected before clicking Burn — directly onto the CD (or DVD). If you try to put too much data on the CD (or DVD), Windows 7 warns you that you don't have enough space, as shown in Figure 4-8.

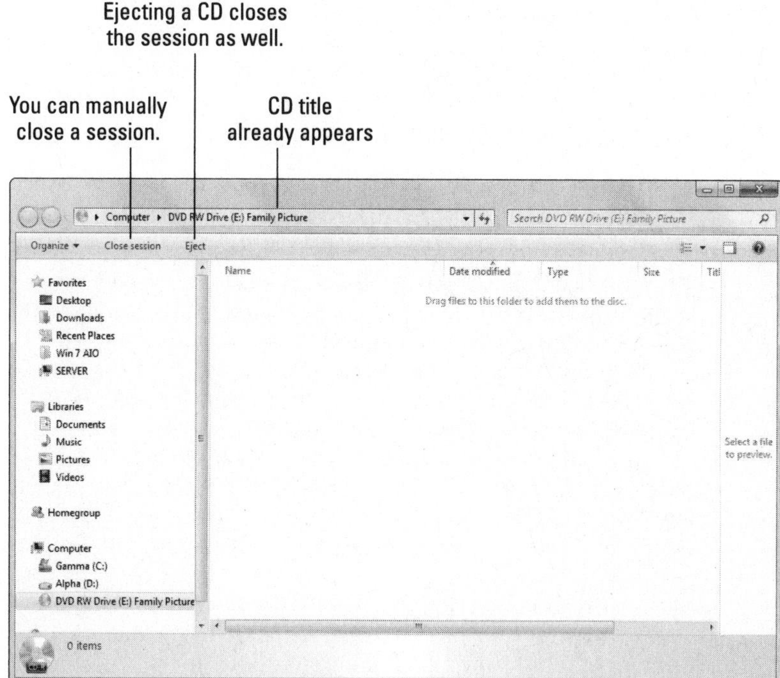

Figure 4-7: The burn window for a Live File System/UDF disc.

6. **If you don't have enough space, per the warning message, you can delete files on the CD or move them off the CD back onto your hard drive.**

   That's true even with a CD-R disc, as long as you're using the UDF format.

7. **Eject the CD by using the appropriate buttons.**

   When you eject a Live File System/UDF CD or DVD from the drive, by default Windows 7 closes the session (see the sidebar "Close that session!" in this section). When Windows 7 is done, you see a message in the notification area, next to the clock, that says Safe to Remove Hardware. Closing the session zaps 20MB from the amount of free data on the CD but also increases the chances that your CD (or DVD) can be read on other drives.

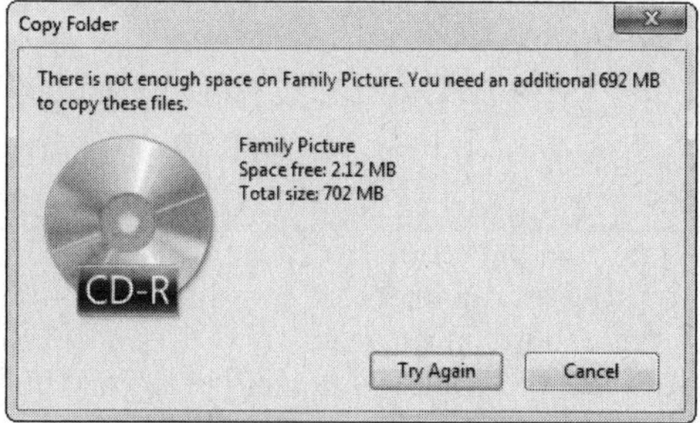

Figure 4-8: With UDF, Windows 7 warns that the CD has too much data.

You can remove the Live File System/UDF CD or DVD and store it away, take it to another computer, or use it as a fashionable coaster or even-more-fashionable ear-lobe extender. Anytime you want to add data to it (or delete data, for that matter), slip the disc back into the drive and use Windows Explorer in the usual way.

Improving Your Experience Index

Hardware benchmarks have suffered a long, checkered history. Once the mainstay of the computer magazine industry ("Buy a GefilteFlop because it rates 7.9 on the FlippIndex and its competitor rates only a 7.7"), hardware manufacturers since the dawn of the Bronze Age have tweaked and mangled and goosed their designs to boost meaningless benchmark numbers. Scandals erupted when manufacturers cooked their products to increase ratings at the big-name computer magazines, frequently sacrificing overall performance to gain a slight advantage with a specific test. Once the quantification of the PC Holy Grail, over time benchmarking became enormously complex and arcane and gradually fell out of favor with the general computer-buying public.

Microsoft turned that all around with the advent of Vista and its simple numerical ratings for processor speed, memory, video, and storage. In the Land of Windows 7, every computer completes a battery of tests, and ultimately receives a number between 1.0 and 7.9 that represents the PC's Windows Experience Index. (That's like calling the U.S. 1040 Tax Form a Wealth Assistant.) Microsoft says the Windows Experience Index isn't a benchmark. Yeah, sure.

Burning ISO files

For many, many years, dyed-in-the-white geeks have begged Microsoft to put something in Windows that would allow them to burn ISO files. In Windows 7, our plaintive pleas have been answered.

An ISO file contains an *exact* image of a CD — all the bits, the name of the CD, the internal tables — everything. Software manufacturers commonly distribute ISO files to testers: The person receiving the file can burn an exact CD (or DVD) image of the original by using the ISO file. Copying files to a CD doesn't accomplish the same thing.

If you ever encounter an ISO file — and they're becoming more popular as a way of distributing large pieces of software — all you have to do is right-click the ISO file and choose Burn Disc Image, stick a CD (or DVD) in your CD drive, and click Burn. Slick.

Getting a faster Internet connection trumps anything and everything Windows 7 has to offer.

When you look at your computer's Windows Experience Index (WEI), and when you comparison-shop for products based on their WEIs, remember that benchmarks always lie, but the best ones don't lie as much. A 20 percent difference in any single WEI score isn't perceptible to any normal human. More than that, the WEI scores are calculated in a way that, in some cases, defies any sort of logic I can discern. But there's learning to be had from WEI, if you know when to pay attention to it and when to tune it out. In the following sections, I offer up the details of my, uh, experience.Checking your Windows Experience score

Before you waste time and money chasing an elusive performance boost, make sure you understand the numbers and their limitations.

To see how your system stacks up, follow these steps:

1. **Choose Start⇨Control Panel⇨System and Security.**
2. **Then, under the System icon, click the Check Your Computer's Windows Experience Index Base Score option.**

   You should see the Performance Information and Tools dialog box, with a big number for the overall rating and with five smaller numbers delineating Microsoft's take on your computer's performance in five key areas (see Figure 4-9). The big number — your *base score* — is simply the lowest of the five component scores.

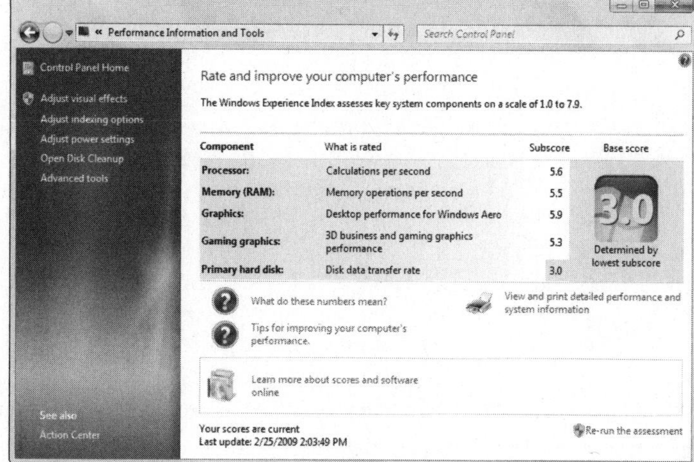

Figure 4-9: An overall performance rating, er, Experience Index of 3.0.

3. **If you think that your system hasn't been given a fair shake, click the Re-run the Assessment link.**

   Windows 7 runs through all its performance benchmarks, recalculates the component ratings, and comes up with a new number. Unless you changed hardware lately, or somebody jimmied the system, the new number is precisely the same as the old number.

Interpreting the numbers

At this moment, every component on every computer receives a rating between 1.0 and 7.9, except for hard drives, which all run from 2.0 to 7.9. You could install the fastest overclocked gigacore pipelined processor on the planet with ten terabytes of L2 cache and your CPU score wouldn't hit 8.0. You could have two chipmunks spinning hard drive platters for peanuts and your disk wouldn't fall below 2.0.

Microsoft has scaled the scores. Over time, the maximum values increase, but for now 7.9 is as good as it gets. Think of the open-ended Richter scale, where we haven't seen a big enough quake yet.

A higher number is better. That part's easy. Understanding the rest of the numbers isn't nearly as straightforward. Here's what the performance scores *really* measure:

- The **processor** score measures how quickly your processor runs a battery of CPU-intensive tests such as compressing and decompressing data, encryption and decryption, and encoding video. It doesn't attempt to measure many compute-intensive activities that you see in other processor benchmarks, such as recalculating huge spreadsheets or repaginating *War and Peace* or morphing Bill Clinton's old publicity stills. Depending on the kind of work you do, the Vista benchmarks may or may not reflect your kind of work.
- In spite of what Figure 4-9 says, the **memory** component doesn't take into account "memory operations per second" at all. Instead, Windows looks at how much memory you have on your system, subtracts the amount of memory dedicated to graphics, and gives you a score based on Table 4-2.
- The **graphics** component score emphasizes two-dimensional performance, with specific tests geared to the Desktop Windows Manager (the program that controls the Aero Glass interface), video memory bandwidth, and video decoder capability. If your graphics card doesn't support the Windows Display Driver Model (WDDM), your score is capped at 1.9.
- The **gaming graphics** component, confusingly, deals with 3D graphics. Internally, it's the *D3D* score, short for Direct3D, Microsoft's proprietary set of commands for high-performance 3D picture rendering. The

benchmark measures blending and shading performance. If your graphics card doesn't support the Pixel Shader 3.0 spec, the score is clipped at 4.9, no matter how fast your card.

- The **primary hard disk** component tests your hard drive by measuring read speeds while overflowing the hard drive with changed data that needs to be written to disk. In my opinion, for most Windows 7 users, most of the time this number doesn't mean much (see the nearby sidebar "What happened to my Vista performance?").

Table 4-2 Maximum Memory Component Scores

Amount of Memory	*Score*
Less than 256MB	1.0
Less than 500MB	2.0
Less than 512MB	2.9
Less than 704MB	3.5
Less than 960MB	3.9
Less than 1.5GB	4.5
Less than 3GB	5.5

The *Windows System Assessment Tool* is a program (it's a big bunch of programs) that runs all the benchmarks and boils down the results to the WEI numbers you see on the screen. The raw scores are stored in XML files in the folder `c:\Windows\Performance\WinSAT\DataStore`.

Turning the numbers into real improvement

Used properly, the WEI scores can help you assemble a kick-butt Windows 7 system for a very low price. As with any good benchmark, the Windows Experience Index tells you how well a piece of hardware works. Forget the salesdroid's palaver. Toss the glossy brochure in the trash. The WEI can tell you if a piece of hardware delivers the goods — or if it's all hat and no cattle, if yaknowhatimean.

While I was writing this book, I hopped down to my friendly local PC dealer, looking for a dirt-cheap PC to run Windows 7. I found a discontinued HP Pavilion — dozens of them — that the retailer had marked down to $225. Very basic stuff: Dual core Pentium, 1GB of memory, 160GB hard drive, integrated Intel GMA 3100 video driver, PCI Express slots, running Vista Home Basic. The bone-stock Vista WEI came in at a toe-curling 1.0 (see Figure 4-10). The WEI told me at a glance that my graphics and gaming graphics scores were the trouble spots: Both scores were several points below the others.

What happened to my Vista performance?

Many Vista owners who upgrade to Windows 7 have a hard time understanding the changes in hard drive performance numbers. Their beef? Some hard drive numbers plummet: That trusty big name hard drive that rates a 5.5 or more under Vista, may come up a paltry 2.9 under Windows 7. Same drive. Same computer. Much lower number.

Since the overall WEI base score reflects the lowest-rated component, some people with denigrated hard drives who upgrade from Vista to Windows 7 have watched their PCs go from a 5 to a 2.9 while their performance has noticeably *improved* under Windows 7. The machine runs faster, but the benchmark goes way down.

Kinda makes you wonder about benchmarking, doesn't it?

Microsoft has details about the changes in hard disk benchmarking on its Engineering Windows 7 blog (`tinyurl.com/956xqq`), but it all boils down to this: As long as your disk activity falls within the limits of the hard drive's ability to store changes in its small internal memory (its *cache*), you experience blindingly fast performance. It's only when you make a whole lot of changes to your files, and you try to send them to the hard drive in a bunch, and you try to pull in more data from the hard drive, and do all those things at once, that you see degraded performance. I don't think hard drive cache run problems affect most Windows users, most of the time. As things stand with the Windows 7 benchmark, I wouldn't spend a sous for a 5.6 hard drive over a 2.9 hard drive.

Bravely pursuing Windows 7 enlightenment, I tore open the case and installed a used video card that I had lying around the office. It sports an NVIDIA GeForce 8600 GT chip with 256MB of memory. You can buy the same card at many discount shops for $50 or less. I also added one 2GB stick of memory, worth about $20, to bring the total memory up to 3GB.

I installed Windows 7 on the same machine and ran the WEI again, with the results shown earlier in this chapter (refer to Figure 4-9). Note how my hard drive score went from a 5.6 under Vista to a 3.0 under Windows 7. Same hard drive. No changes.

If it weren't for the totally bogus hard disk score of 3.0, my souped-up $295 Pavilion would rate an impressive 5.3 in the Windows 7 test. That makes it almost as fast as my (ridiculously expensive) two-year-old production machine.

Moral of the story: Even a cheap PC can make a great Windows 7 computer, providing you use a decent video card. And the hard drive speed? Fuhgeddaboutit.

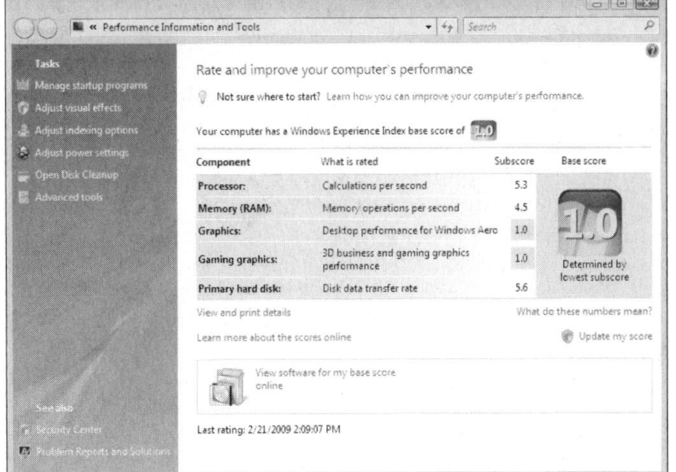

Figure 4-10: My wimpy new Pavilion, with a Vista WEI of 1.0.

Getting Word Processing — Free

If you're serious about word processing, you undoubtedly have Microsoft Word (and probably even Microsoft Office) installed already. Word is a great program — and one that can serve you well, along with the other useful programs in the Office suite. Personally, I've been swearing at Office for almost a decade — my first four books were about it.

On the other hand, if you only mess around the periphery of word processing, with an occasional letter to Mom or a diatribe to the local newspaper, good, free alternatives for word processing abound. They include OpenOffice.org Writer (`www.openoffice.org`), Zoho Writer (`zoho.com`), and Google Docs (`http://docs.google.com`).

Windows 7 ships with two — count 'em, two — free programs that help you with text: WordPad and Notepad. Although WordPad and Notepad aren't word processing powerhouses like Word, they can help a little bit — as long as you don't have any great expectations, anyway.

Running Notepad

Reaching back into the primordial WinOoze, Notepad was conceived, designed, and developed by programmers, for programmers — and it shows. Although Notepad has been vastly improved over the years, many of the old limitations pertain. Still, if you want a fast, no-nonsense text editor (certainly nobody would have the temerity to call Notepad a word processor), Notepad's a decent choice.

Notepad understands only plain, simple, unformatted text — basically the stuff you see on your keyboard. It wouldn't understand formatting like bold or an embedded picture if you shook it by the shoulders, and heaven help ya if you want it to come up with links to Web pages.

On the other hand, Notepad's shortcomings are, in many ways, its saving graces. You can trust Notepad to show you exactly what's in a file — characters are characters, old chap, and there's none of this froufrou formatting stuff to mess things up. Notepad saves only plain, simple, unformatted text; if you need a plain, simple, unformatted text document, Notepad's your tool of choice. To top it off, Notepad is fast and reliable. Of all the Windows programs I ever met, Notepad is the only one I can think of that has never crashed on me.

The following tidbits of advice are all you'll likely ever need to successfully get in and around Notepad:

✦ To start Notepad, choose Start➪All Programs➪Accessories➪Notepad, or double-click any text (`.txt`) file in Windows Explorer. You see something like the file shown in Figure 4-11.

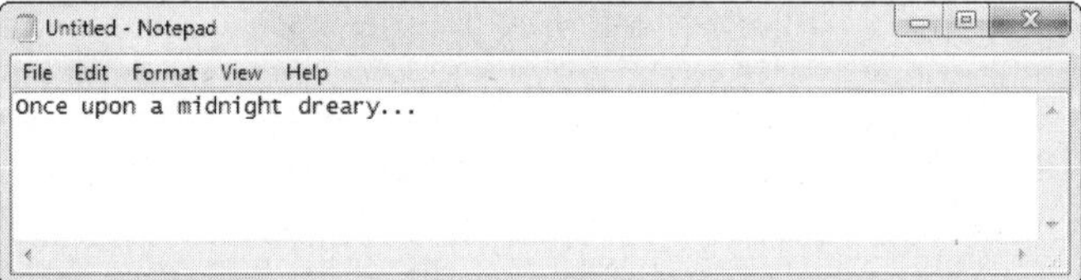

Figure 4-11: Notepad rocks in a geriatric sort of way.

✦ Notepad can handle files up to about 48MB in size. (That's not quite the size of the *Encyclopedia Britannica*, but it's close.) If you try to open a file that's larger, a dialog box suggests that you open the file with a different editor.

✦ You can change the font, sorta. When you first start Notepad, it displays a file's contents in the 10-point Lucida Console font. That font was chosen by Notepad's designers because it's relatively easy to see on most computer monitors.

Just because the text you see in Notepad is in a specific font, don't assume for a moment that the characters in the file itself are formatted. They aren't. The font you see on the screen is just the one Notepad uses to show the data. The stuff inside the file is plain-Jane, unformatted, everyday text.

If you want to change the font that's displayed on the screen, choose Format➪Font and pick from the offered list. You don't need to select any text before you choose the font because the font you choose is applied to all text on the screen — and it doesn't affect the contents of the file.

The default Notepad font is monospaced — all the characters are the same width. If you change the font, text files that are designed for a fixed-width world can look very odd.

- ✦ You can wrap text, too. Usually text extends way off the right side of the screen. That's intentional. Notepad, ever true to the file it's attached to, skips to a new line only when it encounters a line break — usually that means a carriage return (or the Enter key), which typically occurs at the end of every paragraph.

  Notepad allows you to wrap text on-screen, if you insist, so that you don't have to go scrolling all the way to the right to read every single paragraph. To have Notepad automatically break lines so that they show up on the screen, choose Format➪Word Wrap.

- ✦ Notepad has one little geeky timestamp trick that you may find amusing — and possibly worthwhile. If you type .LOG as the first line in a file, Notepad sticks a time and date stamp at the end of the file each time it's opened.

Many, many alternatives to Notepad exist: Programmers need text editors, and many of them take up the mantle to build their own. To see one of the best, check out Caditor at `caditor.sourceforge.net/releases`.

Writing with WordPad

If you really want and need formatting — and you're too cheap to buy Microsoft Word or too lazy to download OpenOffice — Windows 7 WordPad will do. If you've been locked out of Word by the nefarious Microsoft Office (De)Activation Wizard, you'll no doubt rely on WordPad to keep limping along until Microsoft can reactivate you.

If you find yourself reading these words because Office has slipped into "reduced functionality mode" (gawd, I love that phrase!), take heart, but be forewarned: If you aren't careful, you can clobber your Word files by saving them with WordPad. If you have to edit a Word 97, 2000, 2002, 2003, or 2007 `.doc` file with WordPad, always follow these steps:

1. **Make a copy of the Word document, and open the copy in WordPad.**

   Do not edit original Word documents with WordPad. You'll break them as soon as you save them. Do not open Word documents in WordPad, thinking that you'll use the Save As command and save with a different name. You'll forget.

2. **When you get Word back, open the original document, choose Tools➪Compare and Merge Documents, pick the WordPad version of the document, and click the Merge button.**

   In Word 2007, it's Review➪Compare➪Combine and then choose the WordPad version.

The resulting merged document probably looks like a mess, but it's a start.

3. **Use the Revisions toolbar (which is showing in Word 2003 and earlier) or the Review tab (in Word 2007) to march through your original document and apply the changes you made with WordPad.**

   This is the only reliable way I know to ensure that WordPad doesn't accidentally swallow any of your formatting.

WordPad works much the same as any other word processor, only less so. Its feature set reflects its price: You can't expect much from a free word processor — at least, not from Microsoft. That said, WordPad isn't encumbered with many of the confusing doodads that make Word so difficult for the first-time e-typist, and it may be a decent way to start figuring out how simple word processors work.

To get WordPad going, choose Start➪All Programs➪Accessories➪WordPad (see Figure 4-12).

Some people like the Ribbon interface across the top of the WordPad window. I find it familiar (like Word 2007) but annoying (like, uh, Word 2007).

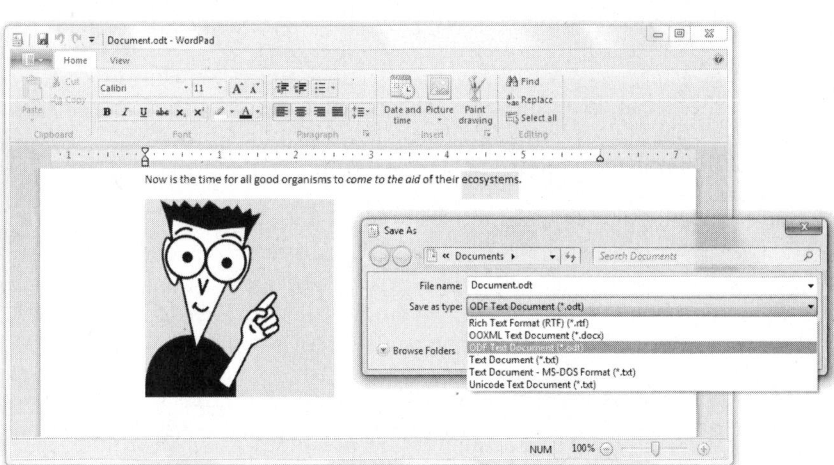

Figure 4-12: WordPad includes rudimentary formatting capabilities as well as the ability to embed images for free.

WordPad lets you save documents in any of the following formats:

- **Rich Text Format** (RTF) is an ancient, circa-1987 format developed by Microsoft and the legendary Charles Simonyi (yes, the space tourist) to make it easier to preserve some formatting when you change word processors. RTF documents can have some simple formatting, but nothing nearly as complex as Word 97, for example. Many word processing programs from many different manufacturers can read and write RTF files, so RTF is a good choice if you need to create a file that can be moved to a lot of places.

- **OOXML Text Document** (`.docx`) is the new Microsoft document standard file format, introduced in Word 2007.

Note that WordPad can read and write `.docx` files. Unfortunately, Word Pad takes some, uh, liberties with the finer formatting features in Word: If you open a Word-generated `.docx` file in WordPad, don't expect to see all the formatting. If you subsequently save that `.docx` file from WordPad, expect it to clobber much of the original Word formatting.

- **ODF Text Document** (`.odt`), the OpenDocument format, is the native format for OpenOffice.
- **Text Document** (`.txt`) strips out all pictures and formatting and saves the document in a Notepad-style regular old everyday text format. The two alternatives — MS-DOS format and Unicode — control the way WordPad handles non-Roman characters in the document.

If you're just starting out with word processing, keep these facts in mind:

- To format text, select the text you want to format; then choose the formatting you want from the Font part of the Ribbon. For example, to change the font, click the down arrow next to the font name (it's Calibri in Figure 4-12) and choose the font you like.
- To format a paragraph, simply click once inside the paragraph and choose the formatting from the Paragraph part of the Ribbon.
- General page layout (such as margins and whether the page is printed vertically or horizontally, for example) is controlled by settings in the Page Setup dialog box. To open it, click the down arrow next to the icon that looks like a piece of paper. (It's the one above the Paste icon.) Then choose Page Setup.
- Tabs are complicated. Every paragraph starts out with tab stops set every half inch. You set additional tab stops by clicking in the middle of the ruler. (You can also set them by clicking the tiny side arrow to the right of the word *Paragraph* and then clicking the Tabs button.) The tab stops you set up work only in individual paragraphs: Select one paragraph and set a tab stop, and it works only in the selected paragraph; select three paragraphs and set the stop, and it works in all three.

WordPad treats tabs like any other character: A tab can be copied, moved, and deleted, sometimes with unexpected results. Keep your eyes peeled when using tabs and tab stops. If something goes wrong, click the Undo icon (to the right of the diskette-like Save icon) or press Ctrl+Z immediately and try again.

WordPad has a few features worthy of the term: bullets and numbered lists; paragraph justification; line spacing; super and subscript; indent. WordPad lacks many of the features that you may have come to expect from other word processors: You can't even insert a page break, much less a table. If you spend any time at all writing anything but the most straightforward documents, you'll outgrow WordPad quickly.

Taming the Character Map

Windows 7 includes the Character Map utility, which may prove a lifesaver if you need to find characters that go beyond the standard keyboard fare — "On Beyond Zebra," as Dr. Seuss once said. Using the Character Map, you can ferret odd characters out of any font, copy them, and then paste them into whatever word processor you may be using (including WordPad).

Windows ships with many fonts — collections of characters — and several of those fonts include many interesting characters that you may want to use. To open the Character Map, choose Start⇨All Programs⇨Accessories⇨System Tools⇨Character Map. You see the screen shown in Figure 4-13.

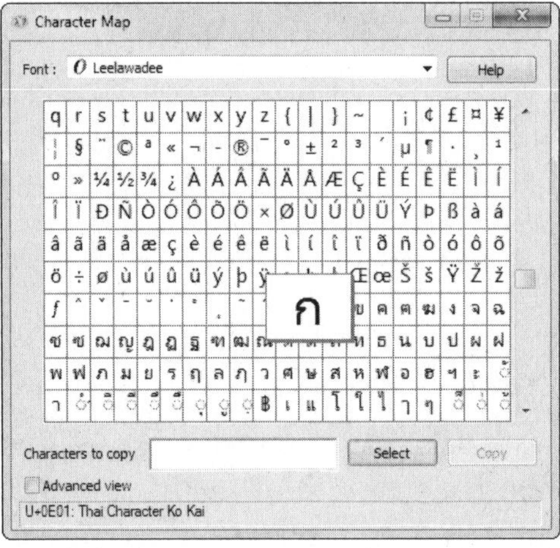

Figure 4-13: Need a character from a different language? Use the Windows 7 Character Map.

You can use many characters as pictures — arrows, check marks, boxes, and so on — in the various Wingdings and Webding fonts. Copy them into your documents, and increase the font size as you like.

Calculating — Free

Windows 7 includes a capable calculator. Actually, it contains four capable calculators, with several options in each one. Before you run out and spend 20 bucks on a scientific calculator, check out the two you already own!

To run the Calculator, choose Start➪All Programs➪Accessories➪Calculator. You probably see the standard calculator, or one of its gussied-up forms, as shown in Figure 4-14.

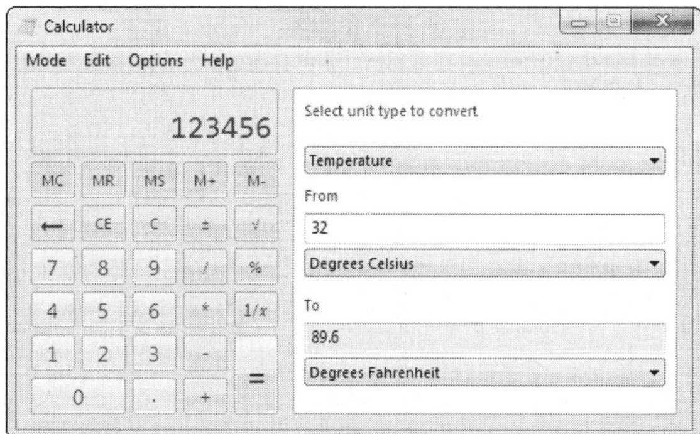

Figure 4-14: The standard calculator, showing its Unit Conversion option.

To use the Calculator, just type whatever you like on your keyboard and press Enter when you want to carry out the calculation. For example, to calculate 123 times 456, you type `123 * 456` and press Enter.

The Calculator comes in four modes: Standard, Scientific (which adds sin and tan and *x* to the *y* and the like), Programmer (hex, octal, Mod, Xor), and Statistics (averages, summations). You can also choose three options, which appear as a separate slide-out calculator to the right of the "real" calculator. The Unit Conversion option appears in Figure 4-14. Date Calculation makes you choose dates from built-in calendars. The Templates option gives you a quick way to calculate gas mileage, lease payments, and simple mortgage amortization.

Personally, I use Google for all the options. You can type `32 C in F` in Google and get the answer back immediately. (Google can calculate `1.2 euro per liter in dollars per gallon`, in one step — way beyond Windows Calculator.) Do a Google search for mileage, lease payment, or amortization and you can find hundreds of sites with far more capable calculators.

A few Calculator tricks:

- ✦ You can use your mouse to "press" the keys on the Calculator — an approach that's quite slow and error-prone.
- ✦ Nope, an X on the keyboard doesn't translate into the times sign. I don't know why, but computer people have had a hang-up about this for decades. If you want to say "times," you have to press the asterisk key on the keyboard — the *, or Shift+8.
- ✦ You can use the number pad, if your keyboard has one, but to make it work you have to get Num Lock going. Try typing a few numbers on your number pad. If the Calculator sits there like a dodo and doesn't realize that you're trying to type into it, press the Num Lock key. The Calculator should take the hint.

Of all the applications in Windows, you'd think that the %$#@! Calculator would let you select the number in the readout window so that you could copy it or paste over it, using any of the Windows-standard methods. Uh-uh. No way. But in the Windows 7 version, you can finally copy a history of your calculations, like running a tape on a manual calculator. To start the History function, choose View➪History. Then to retrieve the History, choose Edit➪History➪Edit.

Painting

The Windows Paint program has taken a lot of hard knocks for a lot of years, but it can actually do a few things that you might need. It's a just-barely-good-enough application for manipulating existing pictures, and it helps you convert among the various picture file formats (JPEG or GIF, for example). But it's certainly no competition for a real drawing tool like CorelDRAW or Adobe Illustrator, or even a free graphics editor like IrfanView (`www.irfanview.com`). And, if you want to correct red-eye or adjust for a bad exposure, Windows Live Photo Gallery or Picasa have tools that you need (see Book IV, Chapter 5).

That said, you can have a lot of fun with Windows Paint. To bring it to life, choose Start➪All Programs➪Accessories➪Paint. You see a screen like the one shown in Figure 4-15.

Opening, saving, and closing pictures in Paint is a snap; it works just like any other Windows program, once you figure out that you have to click the down arrow to the right of the icon that looks like a piece of paper. (It's above the Paste icon.)

Figure 4-15: Paint offers a handful of useful features.

Scanning pictures into Paint goes like a breeze (click the down arrow to the right of the icon that looks like a piece of paper, and then choose From Scanner or Camera). To draw one of the prebuilt shapes, just click the shape and then click and drag the drawing paper to adjust the size. Crop, resize, or rotate by choosing the corresponding icon in the Image part of the Ribbon. Easy.

Where you're bound to get in the most trouble is in free-form drawing, which can be mighty inscrutable until you understand the following points:

- ✦ You select a line color (used by all the painting tools as their primary color) by clicking the Stroke icon and then clicking the color in the Colors part of the Ribbon.
- ✦ You select a fill color (used to fill the inside of the solid shapes, such as the rectangle and oval) by clicking the Fill icon and then choosing a color in the Colors part of the Ribbon.
- ✦ Many painting tools let you choose the thickness of the lines they use — in the case of the spray can, you can choose the heaviness of the spray — in the Size drop-down list on the Ribbon.

General rules for editing are a lot like what you see in the rest of Windows — select, copy, paste, delete, and so on. The only odd editing procedure I've found is for the Free-form Selection tool, which hides behind the Select icon on the Image part of the Ribbon. If you click this tool and draw an area on the picture, Paint responds by selecting the smallest rectangle that encloses the entire line you drew. It's . . . different.

You can specify the exact size of your picture by clicking the down arrow to the right of the icon that looks like a piece of paper and then choosing Properties.

Sticking Sticky Notes

One of the really useful new features in Windows 7, Windows Sticky Notes warrants a bit of your time — unless you already use Outlook's Sticky Notes. Here's how to make a note to yourself:

1. **Choose Start⇨All Programs⇨Accessories⇨Sticky Notes.**
2. **Start typing.**

   Really. That's all there is to it.

Your new sticky note appears, as shown in Figure 4-16.

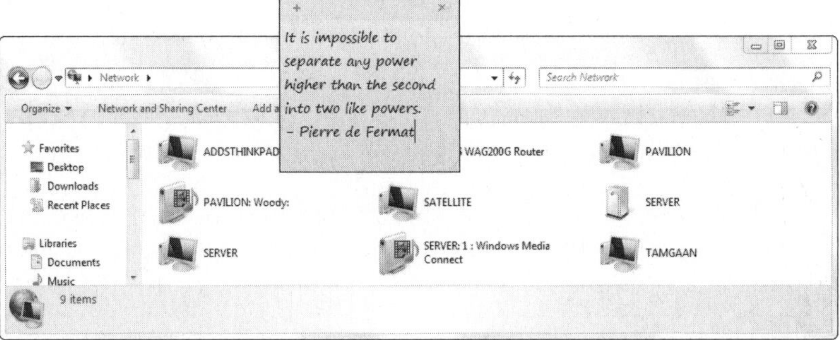

Figure 4-16: Sticky notes are cool — but the margin is too small for the proof, eh?

Sticky notes live on your desktop. You can drag and move them like any other denizen of the desktop. They're easy to resize. You can change the color by right-clicking the note. You can show all sticky notes on your desktop by clicking the Sticky Notes icon on the toolbar.

As of this writing, Microsoft was hinting that it might make a tool available so that you can change the font used on the notes. If I hear of anything, I'll let you know on AskWoody.com. In the interim, you're stuck.

Using Sneaky Key Commands

Windows 7 includes two well-buried key commands that everyone should know about. Neither of the key combinations works if your machine is hopelessly frozen, but in most normal circumstances, they should help a lot, especially if a program isn't behaving the way it should.

Conjuring up the Task Manager

Windows 7 has a secret command post that you can get to if you know the right handshake, uh, key combination. Whatever. The key combination works all the time — unless Windows is seriously out to lunch — as long as you're a designated administrator. (For a discussion of administrators, see the section on using account types in Book II, Chapter 2.)

To open the Task Manager, press Ctrl+Alt+Delete. Windows 7 comes up with a screen that looks suspiciously like the Welcome screen. Click the Start Task Manager link. The Task Manager should appear with a list of all running applications (see Figure 4-17).

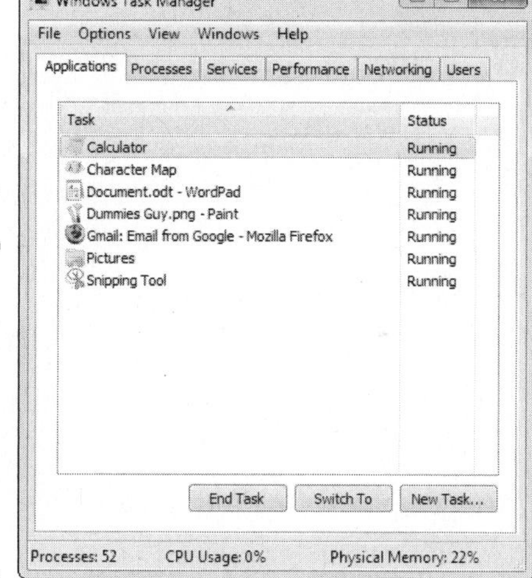

Figure 4-17: Windows 7 Task Manager lets you control running programs.

With the Task Manager, you can do the following things:

- ✦ **Click an application and then click the End Task button to initiate an orderly shutdown of the application.** Windows tries to shut down the application without destroying any data. If it's successful, the application disappears from the list. If it isn't successful, it presents you with the option of summarily zapping the application (called End Now to the less imaginative) or simply ignoring it and allowing it to go its merry way.
- ✦ **Click an application and then click the Switch To button, and Windows opens the switched-to application.** This is convenient if you find yourself stuck somewhere — in a game, say, that doesn't "let go" while it's taken control of your system — and you want to jump over to a different application.

The Task Manager goes way beyond application control. For example, if you have a somewhat dominant techie gene (it runs in the family), you may be tickled to watch the progress of your computer on the performance monitor, which is in the Task Manager on the Performance tab (see Figure 4-18).

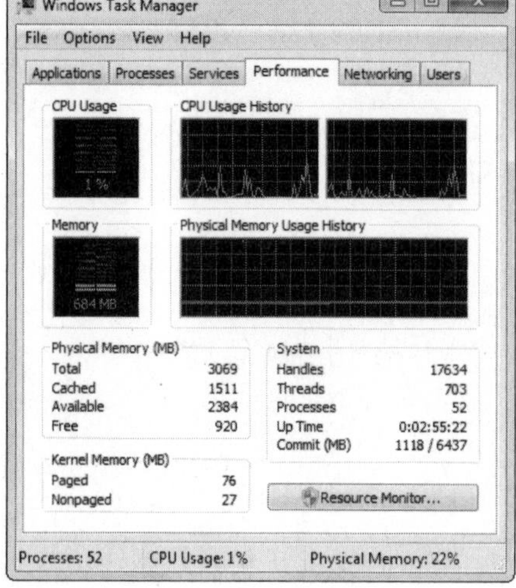

Figure 4-18: Windows Task Manager lets you take a peek inside your machine.

If the Task Manager's Performance tab gets your juices going, try this trick: Click the Resource Monitor button. Whoa. The Windows 7 Resource Monitor shows you every imaginable performance detail, in real time. You could spend a lifetime in there. See the section about using the Windows 7 Resource Monitor in Book II, Chapter 3.

Switching coolly

Windows includes a quick, easy way to switch among running applications without diving for the mouse to click the Windows taskbar. It's known as the CoolSwitch (yes, that's the technical term for it), and it works on any computer, any time, unless Windows is totally out to lunch, which happens sometimes.

To use the CoolSwitch, hold down Alt and press Tab. You see something like the screen shown in Figure 4-19.

As you press Tab repeatedly, Windows cycles through the running programs. When you arrive at the program that you want to run, simply release the Alt key, and the selected program comes to life.

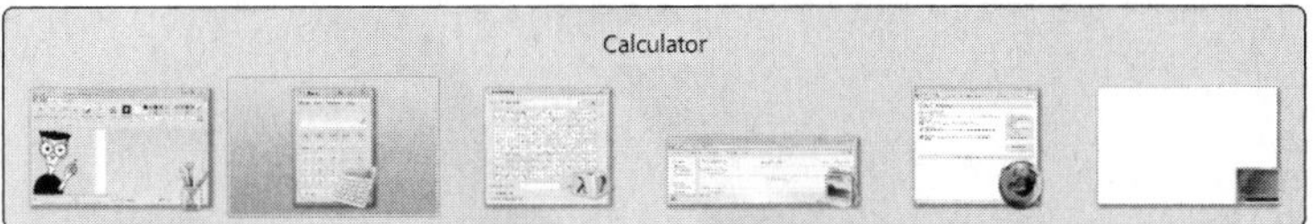

Figure 4-19: Windows 7 CoolSwitch lets you leaf through running programs easily.

By simply sliding over to the Windows key — the one with the Microsoft Windows logo on it — and repeatedly pressing Tab, you launch Windows 7 into one of its most famous poses, Flip 3D. You can do the same thing by clicking the Switch between Windows icon, to the right of the Start button. I'm not sure that Flip 3D works any better than CoolSwitch, but it sure draws a lot of attention. Cool, eh?

Chapter 5: Troubleshooting and Getting Help

In This Chapter

- Using the Windows 7 troubleshooting tools
- Checking your system's stability
- Working with Windows Help and Support
- Snapping your problems
- Getting help from other folks with Remote Assistance
- Getting help on the Web — effectively

Windows Explorer has encountered a problem and needs to close.

Wish I had a nickel for every time I've seen that message. People write to me all the time and ask what caused the message, or one like it, to appear on their computers. My answer? Could be anything. Hey, don't feel too bad: Windows couldn't figure it out, either, and Microsoft spent hundreds of millions of dollars trying to avoid it.

Think of this chapter as help on Help. When you need help, start here.

Windows 7 arrives festooned with automated tools to help you pull yourself out of the sticky parts. The troubleshooters really do shoot trouble, frequently, if you find the right one. The error logs, event trackers, and stability graphs can keep you going for years — even the experts scratch their heads. Windows 7 abounds with acres and acres — and layers and layers — of Help. Some of it works well. Some of it would work well, if you could figure out how to get to the right help at the right time.

This chapter tells you when and where to look for help. It also tells you when to give up and what to do after you give up. Yes, destroying your PC is an option. But you may have alternatives. No guarantees, of course.

This chapter also includes detailed, simple, step-by-step instructions for inviting a friend to take over your computer, via the Internet, to see what is going on and lend you a hand while you watch. I believe that this Remote Assistance capability is the most powerful and useful feature ever built into any version of Windows.

This chapter shows you what you can do when you're ready to tear your hair out.

Troubleshooting in the Action Center

If something goes bump in the night and you can't find a discussion of the problem and its solution in this book, your first stop should be the Action Center. They don't call it Action fer nuthin'.

Windows 7 originally shipped with a handful of troubleshooters. Troubleshooters, as the name implies, take you by the hand and help you figure out what's causing problems — and, just maybe, solve them.

Microsoft intends to add to the collection as time permits. New troubleshooters are downloaded to your computer from time to time, typically as part of "non-security updates." In addition to new troubleshooters, the troubleshooters you see today may not work the same way as the ones you see tomorrow because, well, because the troubleshooters need to be troubleshot, too. Fixed. Repaired. Sent in for an overhaul.

If you run into a problem and you're stumped, see whether Microsoft has released a pertinent troubleshooter by following these easy steps:

1. **Choose Start⇨Control Panel. Click the System and Security Link. Then, under Action Center, click the Find and Fix Problems (Troubleshooting) link.**

   No, they don't really mean you should take the initiative to go out and find problems. The problems tend to find you, yes?

   You see the Troubleshooting screen, shown in Figure 5-1.

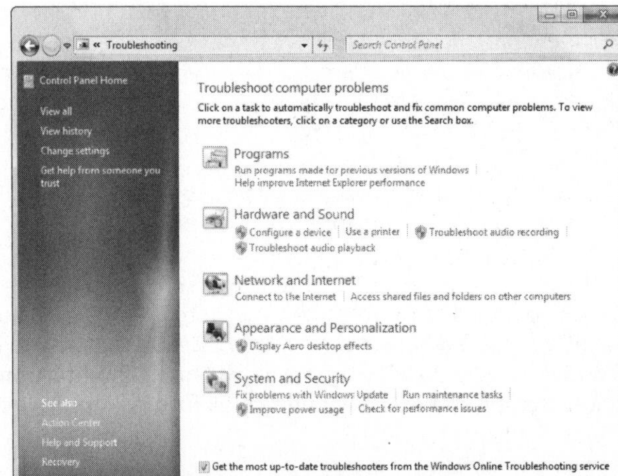

Figure 5-1: Troubleshooting wizards can cut to the heart of a problem, if you can find one.

2. **Make sure that the Get the Most Up-to-Date Troubleshooters check box is selected.**

   This step keeps you updated.

3. **If you see a troubleshooter that seems to address your problem, click it.**

   The selection is limited, but if you're lucky, the Troubleshooting Wizard steps you through the entire process of fixing the problem.

Frequently, troubleshooters just can't shoot the trouble, and they end up with an error message dialog box that says something like, `This error cannot be automatically repaired.`

You can click Next and end up with informative messages such as "The Error '5' was encountered." (I don't make this stuff up — that's exactly the error message I received while running this connection troubleshooter.)

If you're wondering where the Network Troubleshooter log, which features prominently the error message dialog box, is located, the answer is that it's buried in your system log. You can unearth content from your systems log using the Event Viewer, a topic that's beyond the scope of this book.

Tracking Your System's Stability

A useful tool can help pinpoint problems that you can only vaguely identify. Say your computer suddenly starts getting those messages saying "Windows Explorer has encountered a problem and needs to close." You know for sure that your PC didn't have those problems last week. But something happened in the past few days, and now, suddenly, Windows Explorer encounters more problems than Kiefer Sutherland in a season of *24*.

Windows watches, knows all, sees all — and keeps a record. It's a System Stability Report, and you can see yours in a nonce. Click Start, type **reliability**, and hit Enter. (You have several other ways to get there, including using the Action Center Maintenance section.) You see a graph like the one shown in Figure 5-2.

The Reliability Monitor calculates an aggregate score, based on how many problems appear in this graph, taken as a rolling (or in some cases, roiling) average.

If you take the Stability score with a small grain of salt, you may be able to glean some useful information from the graph. For example, if you install a new driver and your system goes from 10 to 5 that day, you can bet that the driver had something to do with the decline. The Reliability Monitor shows you significant events for each day and leaves it to you to draw inferences.

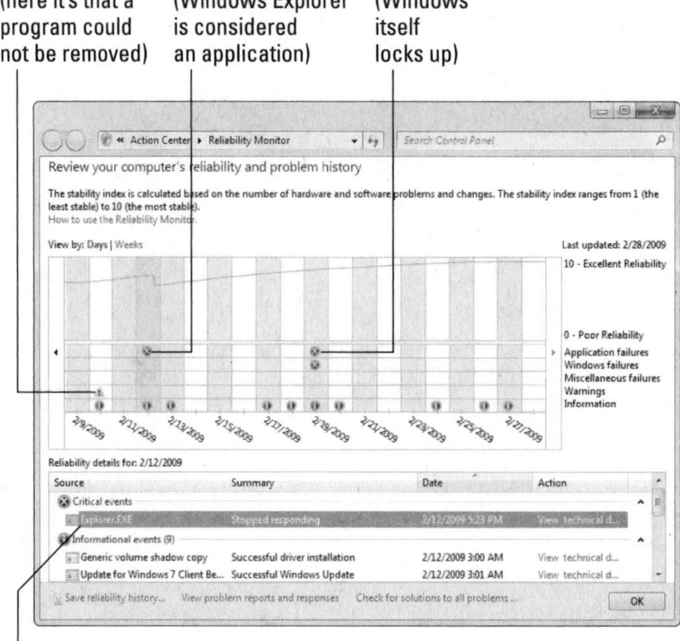

Figure 5-2: Windows tracks major problems that it encounters.

Tackling Windows Help and Support

When you choose Start➪Help and Support, Windows 7 presents you with an entry point to a wide array of Help and Support documentation (see Figure 5-3). Microsoft hopes to make finding what you need easier for you, even if you don't know the answer to your question in advance — a common problem in all versions of Windows Help.

The problem(s) with Windows Help

Windows Help and Support offers only the Microsoft party line. If a big problem crops up with Windows 7, you find only a milquetoast report here. If you want searing insight or unbiased evaluations, look elsewhere — like, oh, in this book.

Windows Help and Support exists primarily to reduce Microsoft support costs, which is both good and bad. Microsoft has tried hard to enable you to solve your own problems, and to help you connect with other people who may be willing to volunteer. That's good. At the same time, Microsoft has made it difficult to figure out how to pick up the phone and chat with somebody in Product Support Services. That's bad. I spill the beans — and give you some much better alternatives — in the next section of this chapter.

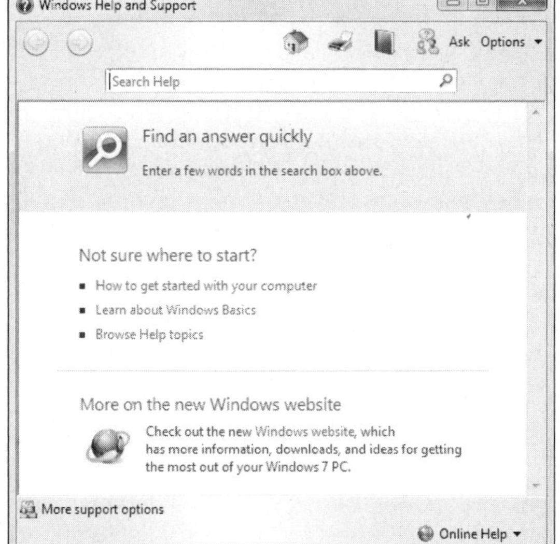

Figure 5-3: The main entry point into the Windows 7 Help system.

Windows Help and Support puts a happy face on an otherwise sobering (and bewildering!) topic. After you click past the sugarcoating, you find the following gotchas that you should know about:

- **You can't configure the Help and Support search engine.** The Windows 7 Help and Support engine already looks in all the places it can. Your only option is to cut off online searches — which makes about as much sense as cutting off your clicking finger. You don't have anywhere near as many choices as with, say, a standard Google search (see "Getting Help on the Web," later in this chapter).
- **Live, one-on-one support from Microsoft is notoriously uneven.** One day you reach a support rep who can solve your problem in the blink of an eye. The next day, you spend hours on hold, only to be told that you need to reformat your hard drive and reinstall Windows. If you get bumped up to Level 2 live support, you're more likely to find someone who knows what she's doing, but you have to persist to Level 3 before you get to talk to a real, live, breathing guru. Few customers have the patience or the savvy to convince Microsoft product support droids to escalate their problem to Level 3.

It never hurts to run a System Restore checkpoint when Windows is firing on all cylinders. The worst possible time to create a checkpoint? When your system has gone to the dogs. Right now, while you're thinking about it and Windows makes you smile from ear to ear, follow the instructions in Book II, Chapter 3 to run a checkpoint. That way, when the inevitable falling out occurs, you have something to fall back on.

Using different kinds of help

Windows 7 Help has been set up for you to jump in, find an answer to your problem, resolve the problem, and get back to work.

Unfortunately, life is rarely so simple. So too, with Help. You probably won't dive into Help until you're feeling lost. And when you're there, well, it's like the old saying, "When you're up to your <insert favorite expletive here> in alligators, it's hard to remember that you need to drain the swamp."

Windows Help morsels fall into the following categories:

- **Overviews, articles, and tutorials:** Explanatory pieces aimed at giving you an idea of what is going on, as opposed to solving a specific problem.
- **Tasks:** Step-by-step procedures for solving a single problem or changing a single setting.
- **Walk-throughs and guided tours:** Marketing demos . . . uh, multimedia demonstrations of capabilities that tend to be, uh, light on details and heavy on splash.
- **Troubleshooters:** Walks you through a series of (frequently complex) steps to help you identify and resolve problems. I talk about troubleshooters earlier in this chapter.

Staying online

If you aren't connected to the Internet when you open Windows Help and Support, Windows 7 falls back to a stunted version of the Help system. If you really need help with almost anything that's fairly complex, you have to be online.

The Windows 7 Help system has few options that you can set, but you should check the one key setting that keeps Help talking to the mother ship. Follow these steps:

1. **Choose Start⇨Help and Support.**

   Windows 7 shows you the Windows Help and Support main page (refer to Figure 5-3).

2. **In the upper-right corner, choose Options⇨Settings.**

   Windows 7 Help has just two settings, but one of them is vital.

3. **Ensure that the box marked Improve My Search Results by Using Online Help (Recommended) is checked. Click OK and then click the X button to close Windows Help.**

   When Help is connected to the Internet, you see the Online Help icon in the lower-right corner of every Help screen.

Choosing the index versus search

Just as this book has an index, so too does the Windows Help and Support Center. To find the index, click the Browse Help icon, the one in the upper-right corner of the Help and Support main page that looks like a book (refer to Figure 5-3).

The Windows Help index is quite thorough but, like any index, relies heavily on the terminology being used in the Help articles themselves. That leads to frequent chicken-and-egg situations: You can find the answer to your question quite readily if you, uh, know the answer to the question — or if you know the terminology involved (which is nearly the same thing, eh?).

Generally, typing keywords in the Search Help text box is the best way to approach a problem, but the index comes in handy from time to time. Don't hesitate to use it.

How to Really Get Help

You use Windows Help and Support when you need help and support, right? Well, yes. Sorta.

In my experience, Help and Support works best in the following situations:

- When you want to understand what functions the big pieces of Windows 7 perform, and you aren't overly concerned about solving a specific problem (for example, "What is Windows Live Photo Gallery?")
- When you have a problem that's easy to define ("My printer doesn't print")
- When you have a good idea of what you want to do but you need a little prodding on the mechanics to get the job done ("How do I change my desktop's picture?")

Help and Support doesn't do much for you if you have only a vague idea of what's ailing your machine, if you want to understand enough details to think your way through a problem, if you're trying to decide which hardware or software to buy for your computer, or if you want to know where the Windows 7 bodies are buried.

For example, if you type the question `what are fonts?`, the eight answers you see talk about Internet Explorer and WordPad — but nothing all about fonts.

For all that, and much more, you need an independent source of information — this book, for example.

My Web site, AskWoody.com, can come in handy, especially if you're trying to decide whether you should install the latest Microsoft security patch of a patch of a patch. AskWoody.com links to The Lounge, where hundreds of volunteers help thousands of bewildered Windows 7 victims! You'll find more than half a million searchable posts, absolutely free. Drop by from time to time to see what's happening.

If you can't find the help you need in Windows Help and Support or at AskWoody.com, expand your search for enlightenment in this order:

1. **Far and away the best way to get help involves simple bribery. Buttonhole a friend who knows about this stuff, and get her to lend you a virtual hand. Promise her a beer, a pizza, a night on the town — whatever it takes. If your friend knows her stuff, it's cheaper and faster than the alternatives.**

   If you can cajole your machine into connecting to the Internet — and get your friend to also connect to the Internet — Windows 7 makes it easy for a friend to take over your computer while you watch with the Remote Assistance feature, which I discuss a little later in this chapter.

2. **If your friend is off getting a tan at Patong Beach, you may be able to find help elsewhere on the Internet.**

   See the section "Getting Help on the Web," later in this chapter.

3. **If all else fails, you can try to contact Microsoft by e-mail.**

   You may qualify for free e-mail support using something called Microsoft E-mail Support, or Chat Support. The best way to find out whether you qualify, and connect with a support droid if you do, is to jump through the following hoops:

   i. *Choose Start⇨Help and Support.*

   ii. *In the upper-right corner, click the Ask button. Then choose Microsoft Customer Support.*

      You're taken to the Microsoft Support Web site.

   iii. *On the Microsoft Support Web site, on the left (unless they moved it last week), click the link that says Understand Your Support Options.*

   iv. *Follow through and answer the questions.*

      When the site asks whether Windows 7 was installed on your computer when you purchased it, be sure to tell the truth — but if you can't remember, say No.

      At that point, you see your no-charge support options.

4. **As a last resort, you can try to contact Microsoft by telephone.**

   Heaven help ya.

Microsoft offers support by phone — you know, an old-fashioned voice call — but some pundits (including yours truly) have observed that you'll probably have more luck with a psychic hotline. Be that as it may, the telephone number for tech support in the United States is (425) 635-3311; in Canada, it's (905) 568-4494.

Snapping and Recording Your Problems

Raise your hand if you've heard the following conversation:

Overworked Geek (answering the phone): "Hi, honey. How's it going?"

Geek's Clueless Husband: "Sorry to call you at work, but I'm having trouble with my computer."

OG: "What kind of trouble?"

GCH: "I clicked on the picture and it went into Microsoft, you know, and I tried to look at this report my boss sent me, but the computer said it couldn't."

OG: "Huh?"

GCH: "I'm sure you've seen this a hundred times. I clicked on the picture but the computer said it couldn't. How do I look at the report?"

OG: "Spfffft!"

GCH: "What's wrong? Why don't you say anything? You have time to help the other people in your office. Why can't you make time for me?"

OG wonders, for the tenth time that day, how she ever got into this bloody business.

At one time or another, you may have been on the sending or receiving end of a similar conversation — probably both, come to think of it. In the final analysis, one thing's clear: When you're trying to solve a computer problem, being able to look at the screen is worth ten thousand words. Or more.

Windows 7 includes the magical new application Problem Steps Recorder (PSR), which lets you take a movie of your screen. To a first approximation, anyway — it's a series of snapshots, but you'd never notice the difference. You end up with a file that you can e-mail to a friend, a beleaguered spouse, or an innocent bystander, who can then see which steps you've taken and try to sort things out. To read the file, your guru has to be running Internet Explorer.

PSR's fast and easy, and it works like a champ.

Here's how to record your problems, er, your screen:

1. **Make sure you remember which steps you have to take to make the problem appear.**

   Practice, if need be, until you figure out just how to move the whatsis to the flooberjoober and click the thingy to get to the sorry state that you want to show to your guru friend.

   Realize that anything appearing on the screen, even fleetingly, may be recorded, and your friend may be able to see it. So don't send out your salary information, okay?

2. **Click Start, immediately type** `psr`**, and press Enter.**

   `psr` stands for Problem Steps Recorder. You can start it from the Control Panel, but this method is a whole lot easier.

   The Problem Steps Recorder, which resembles a full-screen camcorder, springs to life (see Figure 5-4). It isn't recording yet.

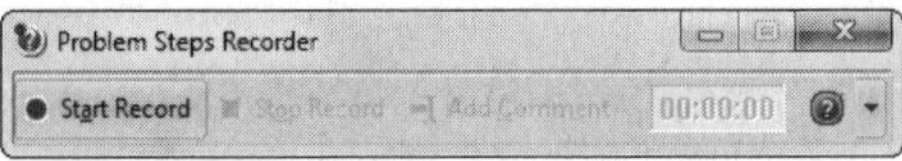

Figure 5-4: The Problem Steps Recorder.

3. **Click Start Record.**

   The recorder starts. You know it's going because the title flashes "Problem Steps Recorder — Recording Now."

4. **If you want to type a description of what you're doing or why or anything else you want your guru friend to see while she's looking at your home movie, click the Add Comment button.**

   The recording pauses and the screen grays out a bit. A box appears at the bottom of the screen that says Highlight Problem and Comment. Click the screen wherever your problem may be occurring, and drag the mouse to highlight the problematic location. Type your edifying text in the box and click OK. Recording continues.

5. **When you're done with the demo, click Stop Record.**

   PSR responds with the Save As dialog box, as shown in Figure 5-5.

6. **Type a name for the file (it's a regular Zip file) and click Save.**

7. **Send the file to your guru friend.**

   Sneakernet works.

Figure 5-5: Save the recording as soon as you finish it.

8. **When your friend receives the Zip file, have her double-click it and then double-click the MHT file inside.**

   MHT is a Microsoft-proprietary "Web archive" file format.

   Internet Explorer appears and shows the MHT file. You have several options; my favorite is to show the file as a slide show (see Figure 5-6).

9. **When you're done, click the red X button to close the Problem Steps Recorder.**

   Magical. Okay, Snagit does the screen recording shtick better, but still.

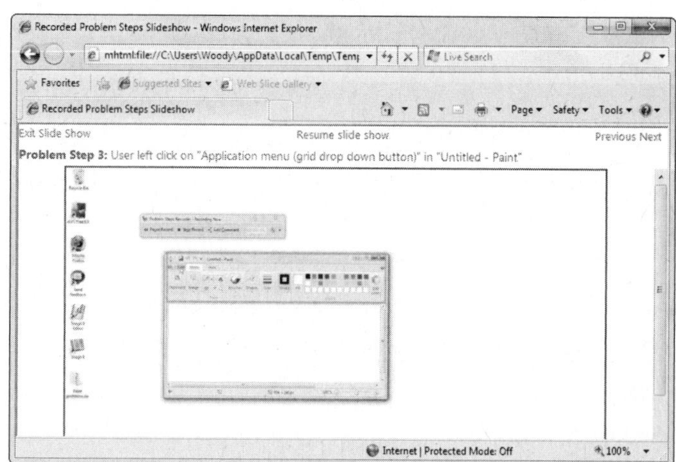

Figure 5-6: The recording appears as a series of snapshots, with detailed accounts of what has been clicked and where.

Connecting to Remote Assistance

Windows has long boasted the Remote Assistance feature, which lets a person on one computer control a second computer, long distance, while both watch what's on the screen. It's a great puppet/puppetmaster capability that allows someone to solve your problems remotely, while you watch. (Or, if you're a guru merely dressed as a Dummy, it allows you to solve others' problems while they watch.)

Understanding the interaction

Windows 7 includes the Remote Assistance feature, which lets you call on a friend (or friendly guru) to take over your PC. The interaction goes something like this:

1. **You create an invitation for your guru friend, asking him to take a look at your computer. You put a password on the invitation.**
2. **You send the message to your guru friend, either by e-mail or giving your friend a file. You also have to tell your friend the password.**

   The file can go any way you can imagine: Attach it to an e-mail message, send it via an instant messaging program that allows you to transfer files, put it on a network shared drive, post it on your company's intranet, stick it on a USB key drive, or burn it on a CD. You can even (gasp!) stick it on a floppy disk. It's just a text file. Nothing fancy.
3. **Your guru friend receives the message or file and responds by clicking a specific link and then typing the password.**
4. **Your PC displays a message saying that your guru friend wants to look at your computer.**
5. **If you give the go-ahead, your guru friend can see what you're doing.**
6. **Your guru friend may ask whether he can take over your computer. If you give your permission, he takes complete control of your machine. You watch as your friend types and clicks, just as you would if you knew what the heck you were doing. Your friend solves the problem as you watch.**
7. **Either of you can break the connection at any time.**

The thought of handing your machine over to somebody on an Internet connection probably gives you the willies. I'm not real keen on it either, but Microsoft has built some industrial-strength controls into Remote Assistance. Your guru friend must supply the password that you specify before he can connect to your computer. He can take control of your computer only if he requests it and you specifically allow it. And you can put a time limit on the invitation: If your friend doesn't respond within an hour, say, the invitation is canceled.

Making the connection

When you're ready to set up the connection for Remote Assistance, here's what you need to do. (I'm writing this from the point of view of the Dummy requesting assistance from a guru. If you're the guru in the interaction, you have to kind of stand on your head and read backward, but, hey, you're the guru and no doubt you knew that already, huh?)

1. **Make sure that your guru friend is ready.**

   Call him or shoot him an e-mail and make sure that he will have his PC on, connected to the Internet, and running Windows 7, Windows Vista, Windows XP, Windows Server 2003, or Windows Server 2008. Also, make sure that he has his Instant Messenger program cranked up, will check e-mail frequently, or will wait for you to hand him a file or make one available on your network.

   Make sure that you can contact your guru friend using your selected method: If you're using e-mail, make sure that he's in your address book and send him a test message to make sure that you have his e-mail address down pat; if you're going to send a floppy disk by carrier pigeon, make sure that the pigeon knows the route and has had plenty of sleep.

2. **When you contact your guru friend, make up a password and give it to him.**

   It doesn't have to be fancy — any text that's six or more characters long is fine — and it shouldn't be a password you use for anything else. It's a one-timer that's valid for only this single Remote Assistance session.

3. **Start your machine (the PC that your Remote Assistance friend, the guru, will take over), and make sure that it's connected to the Internet.**

   Make sure you aren't running any programs that you don't want the guru to see. Yes, that includes the Sudoku with the lousy score.

4. **Choose Start⇨All Programs⇨Maintenance⇨Windows Remote Assistance.**

   The Windows Remote Assistance Wizard appears, as shown in Figure 5-7.

5. **Click Invite Someone You Trust to Help You.**

   You don't actually have to *trust* them but, well, you get the idea.

   Remote Assistance responds with the dialog box shown in Figure 5-8.

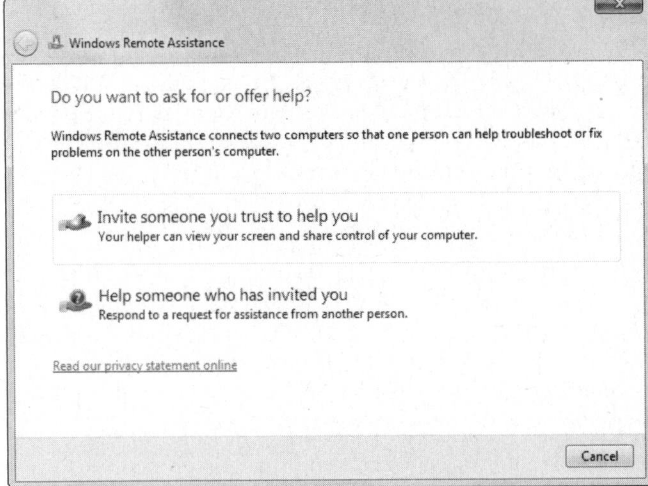

Figure 5-7: Windows Remote Assistance wants to know whether you're giving or getting advice.

6. **Choose Save this Invitation As a File.**

   Even if you're going to e-mail the file, it's easier to save the file first and then attach it to an e-mail message.

   Remote Assistance opens the Save As dialog box and prompts you to save the file `Invitation.msrcIncident`. You can change the name, if you like, but it's easier for your guru friend if you keep the filename extension `msrcIncident`.

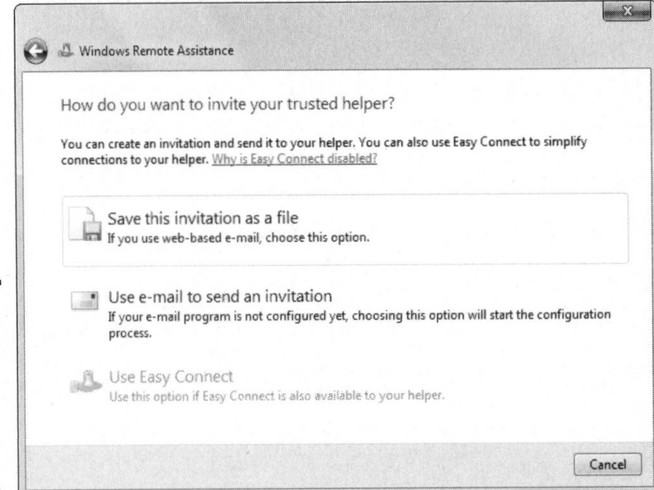

Figure 5-8: Always choose to save the invitation as a file.

7. **Save the file in a convenient place.**

   Remote Assistance responds with an odd-looking dialog box, the Windows Remote Assistance control bar, shown in Figure 5-9. It advises you to provide your helper (that's your guru friend) with the invitation file and the automatically generated 12-character password.

   Windows waits for your guru friend to contact you. You can continue to work, swear, play Minesweeper, or do whatever it takes to keep you sane until your friend can connect.

8. **Send the invitation file to your guru friend.**

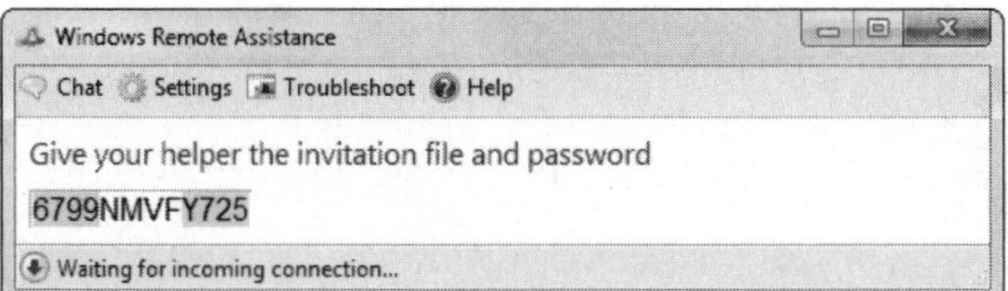

Figure 5-9: The Windows Remote Assistance control bar.

9. **Your friend should double-click the invitation file to initiate the Remote Assistance session.**

   Windows 7 asks for the password you created and gave to your guru friend. He types it in the indicated box and clicks the OK button.

   Windows Remote Assistance then asks whether it's okay to allow your guru friend to connect to your computer (see Figure 5-10).

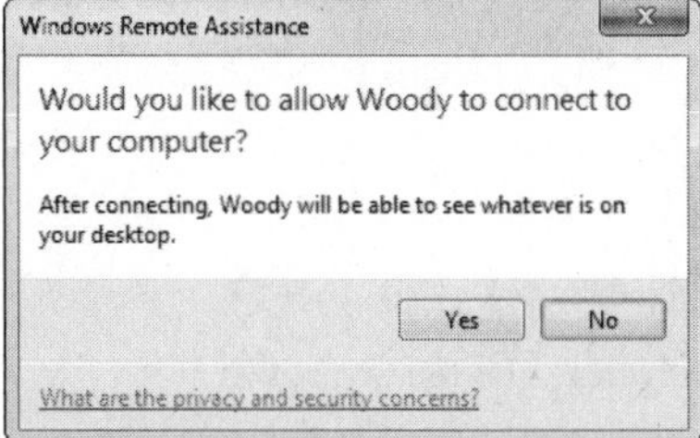

Figure 5-10: Remote Assistance requires your explicit permission.

10. **When you click the Yes button, two things happen simultaneously:**

    Your computer's Remote Assistance bar shows that you're connected, as shown in Figure 5-11.

    Your guru friend's computer sets up a window that shows him everything on your computer (see Figure 5-12).

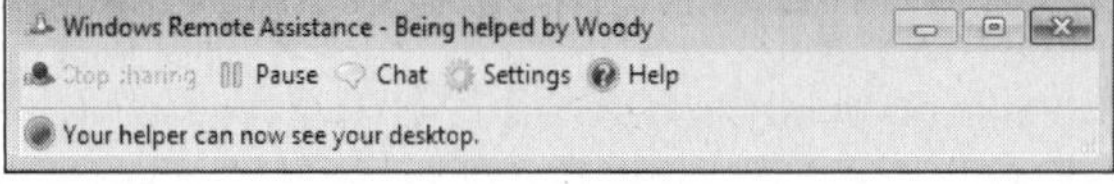

Figure 5-11: Your computer gets this Remote Assistance bar.

11. **If your guru friend wants to take control of your PC, he needs to click the Request Control icon on the Remote Assistance bar.**

    If he does that, your machine warns you that your guru friend is trying to take control (see Figure 5-13) and asks whether you want to let your guru friend respond to User Account Control prompts. (If you're having a technical problem, you probably do.)

    If you allow your guru friend to respond to User Account Control prompts, he has to know an administrator username and password that's valid on your machine.

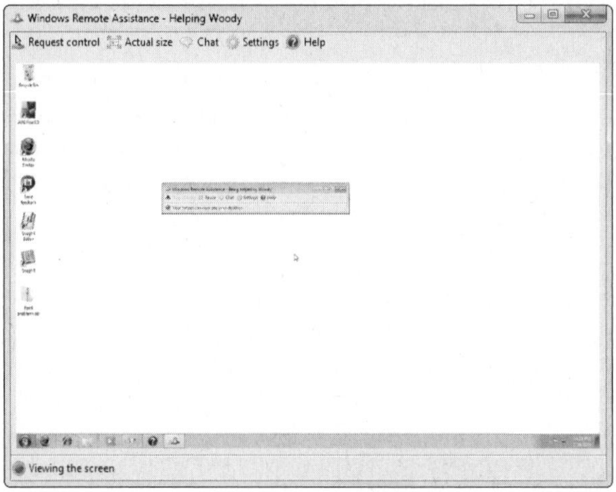

Figure 5-12: Your guru friend sees your entire desktop, in a special Remote Assistance window.

12. **On your machine, click Yes to allow your guru friend to take control of your PC.**

13. **Your guru friend can now control your computer, move the mouse, and type on the keyboard while you watch. Anytime either of you wants to sever the connection, click the Disconnect icon on the Remote Assistance bar.**

    In addition, you — the person who requested the session — can cancel the session at any time by pressing Esc.

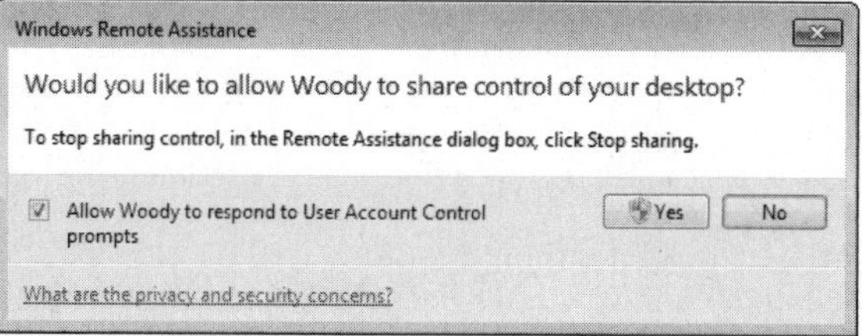

Figure 5-13: Allow your guru friend to take over.

After a Remote Assistance session is under way and you release control to your friend, your friend can do anything to your computer that you can do — anything at all except change users. (If either of you logs off, the Remote Assistance connection is canceled.) Both of you have simultaneous control over the mouse pointer. If either or both of you type on the keyboard, the letters appear on-screen. You can stop your friend's control of your computer by pressing Esc.

Your friend can rest assured that this is a one-way connection. He can take control of your computer, but you can't do anything on his computer. He can see everything that you can see on your desktop, but you aren't allowed to look at his desktop. Whoever said life was fair?

Limiting an invitation

Unless you change things, an invitation that you send out requesting Remote Assistance expires after six hours. To change the expiration time, follow these steps:

1. **Choose Start➪Control Panel➪System and Security.**
2. **Under the System icon, click the Allow Remote Access link.**

   You may have to click through a User Access Control message.

3. **Make sure that the Remote tab is showing, and in the box marked Remote Assistance, click the Advanced button.**

4. **In the Invitations box, choose the amount of time you want invitations to remain open. Click the OK button twice, and then click the red X to close the Control Panel.**

Troubleshooting Remote Assistance

Plenty of pitfalls lurk around the edges of Remote Assistance, but it mostly rates as an amazingly useful, powerful tool. The following are among the potential problems:

- ✦ You and your guru friend have to be connected to the Internet or to the same local network. If you can't connect to the Internet — especially if that's the problem you're trying to solve — you're outta luck.
- ✦ Both of you have to be running Windows XP, Windows Vista, Windows 7, Windows Server 2003, Windows Server 2008, or another operating system that supports Remote Assistance.
- ✦ You have to be able to give (or send) your guru friend a file so that he can use the invitation to connect to your PC:
- ✦ If a firewall sits between either of you and the Internet, it may interfere with Remote Assistance. Windows Firewall (the firewall that's included in Windows 7 and Windows Vista, as well as Windows XP Service Pack 2 and later) doesn't intentionally block Remote Assistance, but other firewalls may. If you can't get through, either contact your system administrator or dig into the firewall's documentation and unblock "Port 3389" — the communication channel that Remote Assistance uses.

You — the person with the PC that will be taken over — must initiate the Remote Assistance session. Your guru friend can't tap you on the shoulder, electronically, and say something like this (with apologies to Dire Straits): "You an' me, babe, how 'bout it?"

Getting Help on the Web

Of course, the single greatest source of information about Windows 7 is the single greatest source of information about everything — the Web. Windows 7 Help and Support weaves in and out of the Web in a multitude of ways. As long as you're connected (see the section "Staying online," earlier in this chapter), Windows 7 pulls in information from the Microsoft servers on the Internet with no assistance required on your part.

If Windows 7 Help doesn't work out, one source of information stands head and shoulders above the rest: Google. Spend a little time to understand Google's nuances and you can save all sorts of headaches when you're trying to track down a problem.

No book can have all the answers, particularly to Windows problems. Even though my AskWoody Lounge (`AskWoody.com/askforhelp.php`) has 600,000 posts, it represents only a small slice of the collective wisdom of millions of Windows users. Google has volume on its side — all you have to do is separate the wheat from the chaff, eh?

Here's what you need to know about Google:

- **Search for something relatively unique and concrete.** You get the best results this way. Typing `Error BCCode 1000008e` gets good results; typing `Windows stops working` doesn't accomplish much.
- **If you're looking at an error message, type the important parts of the precise message into Google:** Typing `Windows Explorer has encountered a problem and needs to close` returns millions of hits. If you see that message, click the Details button and try googling the precise error message: `AppName: explorer.exe AppVer: 6.0.2900.2180 ModName: msvbvm60.dll ModVer: 6.0.96.90 Offset: 000ef6bd`. That narrows it right down.
- **To save time when you're wading through the Google results, first check results from sites that you know and trust**. A search on a QuickTime error that returns results from `www.apple.com` and `www.billyjoebobsmufflershop.com` should be an easy call.
- **Play with quotes.** If you put quotation marks around a phrase, Google gives extra weight to Web sites with that precise phrase. Sometimes that helps you narrow a search. Sometimes it gets too narrow.
- **Don't forget the newsgroups.** If you aren't having any luck with a standard Google search, switch over to the newsgroups: From the main Google page, at the top, click More and then Groups. That gives greater emphasis to listings in the newsgroups. Newsgroups are generally wide-open forums where people post messages. Newsgroups generally adhere to a specific topic, although a cursory glance at most of them reveals that posters commonly veer way off the main topic. Newsgroups are a world unto themselves. For more information, see *The Everyday Internet All-In-One Desk Reference For Dummies*, by Peter Weverka (Wiley).
- **If you can find reference to a Microsoft Knowledge Base article, type** `kb` **followed by the article number in the Firefox or Internet Explorer address bar.** For example, type `kb 960715`. (The Knowledge Base is the mother lode, the source of information that all Microsoft tech-support people use.)

Book III

Customizing Windows 7

Contents at a Glance

Chapter 1: Personalizing Your Desktop

In This Chapter

- Taking control of each desktop level
- Traipsing through themes
- Starting a screen saver in a flash
- Finding the real story on how Windows puts together your desktop

It's your desktop. Do with it what you will.

You might think it'd be easy for a computer to slap windows on the screen, but it isn't. In fact, Windows 7 uses six separate layers to produce that Windows 7, er, vista — and you can take control of every layer. I show you how in this chapter.

I also include a discussion of desktop themes, backgrounds in Windows Explorer, and the deservedly famous (but oh-so-derivative) Windows 7 gadgets. Pretty cool stuff.

Most importantly, I include instructions for creating a Super Boss Key in the later section "Selecting Screen Savers." Whenever you press a key combination that you choose — say, Alt+F10 — a Windows 7 screen saver immediately springs into action. If you've ever been surprised when the boss walked in as you were dusting off your résumé, day trading, or playing a mean game of Minesweeper, you now know how to cover your tracks. You're welcome.

Recognizing Desktop Levels

The Windows 7 desktop — that is, the collection of stuff you see on your computer screen — consists of six layers (see Figure 1-1, which shows five of the six layers).

For a quick change of pace, desktop themes change five of the six layers, all at once. I talk about desktop themes in the section "Using Desktop Themes," later in this chapter.

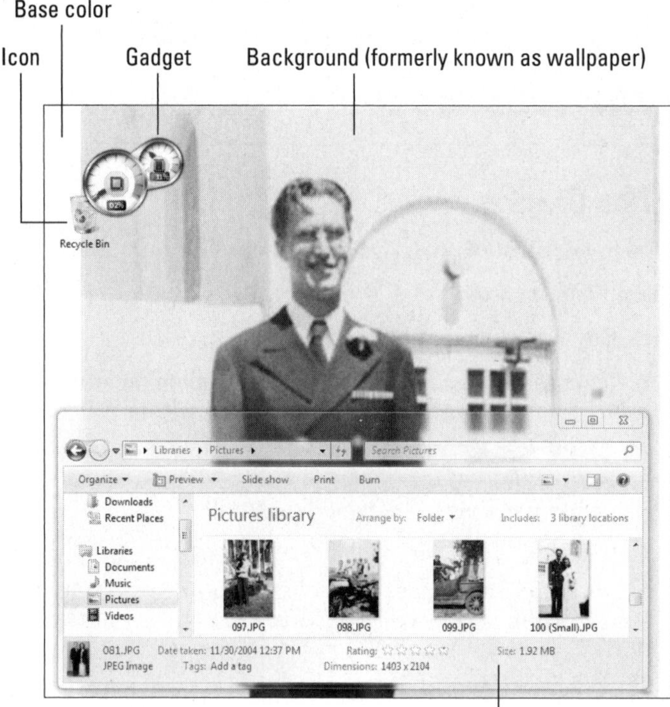

Figure 1-1: The Windows 7 desktop, showing the Glass transparency effect.

These six layers control how Windows dishes up your desktop:

- **Level 1:** At the bottom, the Windows 7 desktop has a base color, which is a solid color that you see only if you don't have a desktop background picture or if your chosen background doesn't fill the entire screen. Most people never see their Windows base color because the background usually covers it up. I tell you how to set the base color and all the other Windows colors — for dialog boxes, the taskbar, the works — in the next section of this chapter.
- **Level 2:** Above the base color lives the Windows desktop background. (Microsoft used to call it wallpaper, and you see that name frequently.) In Figure 1-1, my dad's photo appears as the desktop background. It isn't stretched to fit the full screen, which is why you can see the base color.

  The people who sold you your computer may have placed some sort of dorky ad on the desktop. I tell you how to get rid of the ad and replace it with a picture you want in the section "Picking a Background," later in this chapter.

- **Level 3:** Windows puts all its desktop icons on top of the background layer and underneath everything else. Bone-stock Windows 7 includes only one icon — the Recycle Bin. If you bought a PC with Windows 7 pre-installed, the manufacturer probably put lots of additional icons on the desktop, and you can easily get rid of them. I tell you how in the section "Controlling Icons," later in this chapter.
- **Level 4:** Above the icons you find (finally!) the program windows — the ones that do *work* — you know, in little programs such as Word, Excel, and Media Player. Windows 7 ships with Aero, a specific program window style. If your graphics card is sufficiently capable, the edges of the Aero windows are translucent — the Glass effect. That's the origin of the term Aero Glass. For more information and many non-Aero non-Glass options, see the next section in this chapter. (See Book I, Chapter 2 to find out more about video cards and Windows 7.)

  Program windows share a layer with Windows gadgets — those incredibly useful little tools such as clocks, currency converters, calculators, performance monitors, and slide shows — that everybody and his brother seem to produce nowadays. You can slide a gadget on top of a program window, or you can slide a program window on top of a gadget. I show you how to get the most from your gadgets in the section in Book II, Chapter 1 about getting gadgets.
- **Level 5:** Then you have the mouse, which lives on the layer above the program windows. In case you want to change the picture used for the pointer, I talk about fancy mouse pointers in the section "Changing Mouse Pointers," later in this chapter.
- **Level 6:** At the top of the desktop food chain sits the screen saver. It kicks in only if you tell Windows that you want it to appear when your computer sits idle for a spell. I talk about that beast in the section "Selecting Screen Savers," later in this chapter.

If you have more than one user on your PC, each user can customize every single part of the six layers to suit her tastes, and Windows 7 remembers every setting, bringing it back when the user logs on. Much better than getting a life, isn't it?

Setting Color Schemes in Windows 7

Windows 7 ships with 16 prebuilt designer color schemes; the "Sky" blue version of Aero is the scheme of choice. You can change to a different designer scheme or invent one all your own. To change color schemes, follow these steps:

1. **Right-click any empty part of the Windows desktop and choose Personalize.**

   The Change the Visuals and Sounds on Your Computer dialog box appears.

2. **At the bottom, click the link that says Window Color.**

   Windows 7 opens the Window Color and Appearance dialog box (see Figure 1-2).

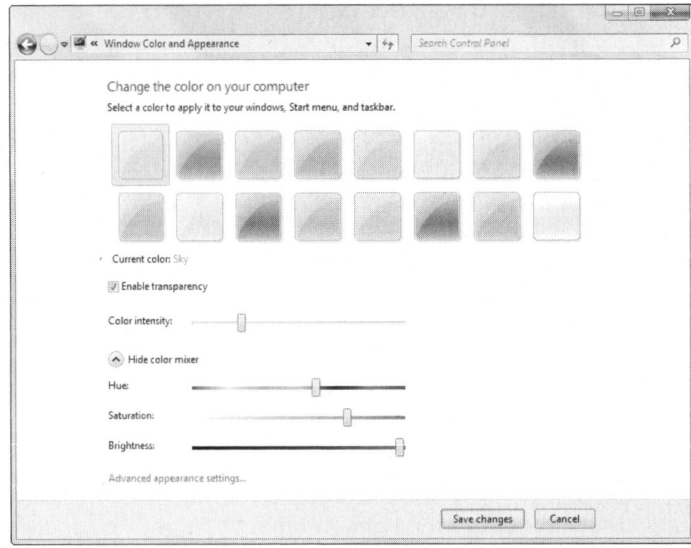

Figure 1-2: The 16 designer color schemes — and a nearly infinite array of alternatives — appear here.

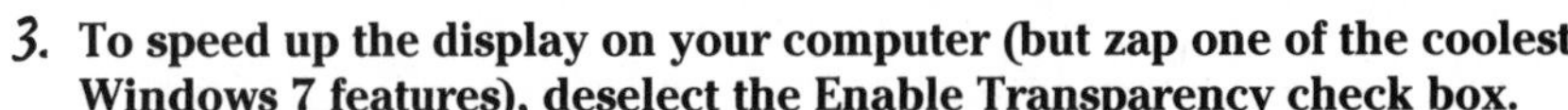

3. **To speed up the display on your computer (but zap one of the coolest Windows 7 features), deselect the Enable Transparency check box.**

   The transparency feature (you can see its effect around the Windows Explorer box in Figure 1-1) is named Glass, for reasons that escape me at the moment. When Windows Vista came out, everybody oooh'ed and aaah'd about something named Aero Glass. It was billed as one of the top new Windows Vista features. As you can see from this dialog box, Aero is now named Sky — it's one of 16 color schemes on offer — and Glass equates to a check box labeled Enable Transparency (the same as in Vista). I commonly hear the terms Aero, Glass, Aero Glass, and Time Flies Like an Aero used interchangeably. *Sic transit gloria computerii.*

   If your PC can't run the Glass interface — either you don't have a powerful enough video card to run the Glass interface or you got conned into buying Windows 7 Starter edition — you may not see the choices in Figure 1-2. See Book I, Chapter 3 for the maddening details.

4. **Be sure to click the Show Color Mixer down arrow and then, in the Pick a Color box, click the default Sky, Twilight, Sea, Leaf, or Lime icon or whichever color scheme appeals to you.**

The Hue, Saturation, Brightness, and Transparency sliders move when you click new color schemes. The eight designer color schemes are just recommendations for specific transparency, hue, saturation, and brightness settings.

5. **Choose one of the prebuilt color schemes, or mix and match your own by moving the Transparency, Hue, Saturation, and Brightness sliders. When you're done, click the OK button.**

Your chosen color scheme takes effect immediately.

To make Windows 7 look a little bit like the older versions of Windows, you can click the Advanced Appearance Options link. That opens the old-fashioned Windows Color and Appearance dialog box (see Figure 1-3), which hasn't changed much since the days of Windows 95.

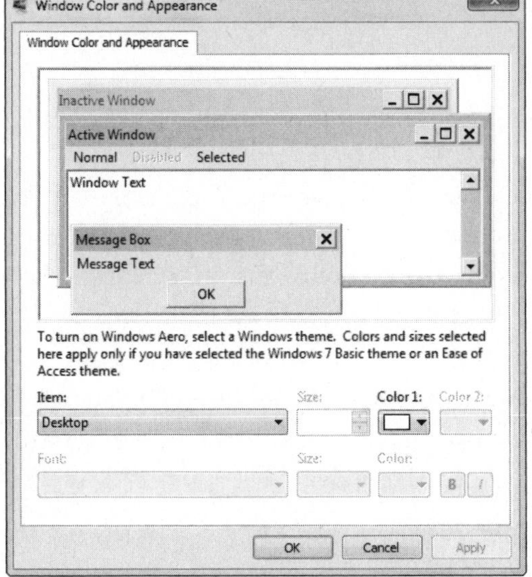

Figure 1-3: Appearance settings for truly retro shenanigans.

If you want to change the Windows base color — Level 1, in my earlier discussion "Recognizing Desktop Levels" — you can do so by changing the Color 1 box for the Desktop item (refer to Figure 1-3).

By and large, the Advanced settings there haven't changed much since Windows 3.1. (Yes, the same old bugs are still there.) Windows 7 doesn't warn you about one key feature of these advanced settings: Everything here is virtually obsolete. You can make changes till you're blue in the face, but you see little effect in Windows 7 itself. Buggy-whip stuff.

Picking a Background

If you installed Windows 7 from a CD, you had a chance to choose your initial wallpaper, er, desktop background.

If you bought a PC with Windows 7 preinstalled, the manufacturer chose your background — maybe the manufacturer's own logo or something a bit more subtle, like Buy Wheaties. Don't laugh. The background is up for sale. PC manufacturers can include whatever they like. You probably have an AOL icon on your desktop. Same thing. Guess who bought and paid for that?

There's nothing particularly magical about the desktop background. In fact, Windows 7 can put any picture on your desktop — big one, little one, ugly one — even a picture stolen straight off the Web. Here's how to personalize your desktop:

1. **Right-click any empty part of the Windows desktop and choose Personalize.**

   The Change the Visuals and Sounds on Your Computer dialog box appears.

   If you want to use one of Windows' built-in combinations of desktop background, window color, sound scheme and screen saver, you can simply choose among the Aero Themes or High Contrast Themes on offer.

2. **At the bottom, click the link marked Desktop Background.**

   Windows 7 shows you the Choose Your Desktop Background dialog box, shown in Figure 1-4.

3. **Click the Picture Location drop-down box and choose from many different wallpapers that ship with Windows 7. You can also click the Browse button and choose any picture you like.**

   If you hover your mouse over a picture, Windows shows you a description of the picture, and a check box appears in the upper left corner. If you select the check box, Windows adds that particular picture to its background slide show. You can put dozens, hundreds, or even thousands of pictures in your slide show collection. And, at the bottom of the screen, you can change the speed of the slide show.

Keep in mind that cycling through desktop backgrounds quickly can create noticeable delays in your daily activities. Notebook and netbook owners should avoid setting the delay to high levels because of the additional, completely unnecessary, battery drain.

Figure 1-4: Pick a wallpaper or a collection of wallpapers.

The Solid Colors category changes the *base* color of the desktop (see the section "Recognizing Desktop Levels," earlier in this chapter) — the color that shows through if your desktop background doesn't fit the whole screen.

4. **If your picture is too big or too small to fit on the screen, you need to tell Windows how to shoehorn it into the available space. Use the drop-down Picture Position list.**

   Details are in Table 1-1.

5. **Click the OK button and then the red X button to close the Personalize Appearance and Sounds dialog box.**

   Your desktop slide show begins immediately.

Windows 7 lets you right-click a picture — a JPG or GIF file, regardless of whether you're using Windows Explorer or Internet Explorer or even Firefox — and choose Set As Desktop Background (in Windows Explorer) or Use As Background (in Internet Explorer or Firefox). When you do so, Windows 7 makes a copy of the picture and puts it in the `C:\Users\username\AppData\Roaming\Microsoft` folder and then sets the picture as your background.

Table 1-1 Picture Position Settings

Setting	*What It Means*
Fill	Windows 7 expands the picture to fit the entire screen and then crops the edges. The picture doesn't appear distorted, but the sides or top and bottom may get cut off.
Fit	The screen is *letterboxed.* Windows 7 makes the picture as big as possible within the confines of the screen and then shows the base color in stripes along the top and bottom (or left and right). No distortion occurs, and you see the entire picture, but you also see ugly strips on two edges.
Stretch	The picture is stretched to fit the screen. Expect distortions.
Tile	The picture is repeated as many times as necessary to fill the screen. If it's too large to fit on the screen, you see the Fill options.
Center	This one is the same as the Fit setting except that the letterboxing goes on all four sides.

Controlling Icons

Straight out of the box, Windows 7 ships with exactly one icon: the Recycle Bin. Microsoft found that most people appreciate a clean desktop, devoid of icons — but it also found that hiding the Recycle Bin confused the living daylights out of all its guinea pigs (er, usability lab test subjects). So Microsoft compromised by making the desktop squeaky clean except for the Recycle Bin: Aero Glass and a Recycle Bin. Who could ask for more?

If you bought a PC with Windows 7 preloaded, you probably have so many icons on the desktop that you can't see straight. That desktop real estate is expensive, and the manufacturers receive a pretty penny for dangling the right icons in your face. Know what? You can delete all of them, without feeling the least bit guilty. The worst you'll do is delete a shortcut to a manufacturer's tech support software, and if you need to get to the program, the tech support rep can tell you how to find it from the Start menu.

Windows 7 gives you several simple tools for arranging icons on your desktop. If you right-click any empty part of the desktop, you see that you can

- ✦ Choose Sort By and sort icons by name, size, or type (folders, documents, and shortcuts, for example) or by the date on which the icon was last modified.
- ✦ Choose View and autoarrange icons — that is, have Windows 7 arrange them in an orderly fashion, with the first icon in the upper-left corner, the second one directly below the first one, the third one below it, and so on.

- ✦ Choose View, and if you don't want to have icons arranged automatically, at least you can choose Windows Align to Grid so that you can see all the icons without one appearing directly on top of the other.
- ✦ You can even choose View and then deselect the Show Desktop Icons check box. Your icons disappear — but that kinda defeats the purpose of icons, doesn't it?

In general, you can remove an icon from the Windows desktop by right-clicking it and choosing Delete or by clicking it once and pressing Delete.

Some icons are hard wired: If you put a Word document on your desktop, for example, the document inherits the icon — the picture — of its associated application, Word. The same goes for Excel worksheets, text documents, and recorded audio files. Icons for pictures look like the picture, more or less, if you squint hard.

Icons for shortcuts, however, can be changed at will. (I talk about shortcuts in Book II, Chapter 1.) Follow these steps to change an icon — that is, the picture — on a shortcut:

1. **Right-click the shortcut and choose Properties.**
2. **In the Properties dialog box, click the Change Icon button.**
3. **Pick an icon from the offered list, or click the Browse button and go looking for icons.**

   Windows abounds with icons. See Table 1-2 for some likely hunting grounds.
4. **Click the OK button twice.**

   Windows changes the icon permanently.

Table 1-2 Places to Look for Icons

Contents	*File*
Windows 7 and Vista icons	C:\Windows\system32\imageres.dll
Everything	C:\Windows\System32\shell32.dll
Computers	C:\Windows\explorer.exe
Household	C:\Windows\System32\pifmgr.dll
Folders	C:\Windows\System32\syncui.dll
Old programs	C:\Windows\System32\moricons.dll

Lots and lots of icons are available on the Internet. Use your favorite search engine to search for the term **free Windows icons**.

Changing Mouse Pointers

Believe it or not, Microsoft has spent many thousands of person-hours honing its mouse pointers. The pointers you see in a standard Windows 7 installation have been selected to give you the best possible visual "clues," without being overly distracting.

What? You think they're boring? Yeah, me too.

You can control your mouse pointer destiny in three different ways:

- **Choose a new desktop theme that includes pointers.** The themes that ship with Windows 7 all use the same mouse pointers, but other themes are available that change your pointers, sounds, and the like. (If you ever saw the Microsoft Dangerous Creatures theme with its poisonous frog mouse pointer, you'll never forget.) I talk about desktop themes in the section "Using Desktop Themes," later in this chapter.
- **Select and change individual pointers.** Then you can turn, say, the Windows "I'm busy but not completely tied up" mouse pointer (named Working in Background in Windows) into, oh, a dinosaur.
- **Change all your pointers, wholesale, according to schemes that Microsoft has constructed.**

To change individual pointers or to select from the prefab pointer schemes, follow these steps:

1. **Right-click any empty part of the desktop and choose Personalize. On the left side of the screen, click the Change Mouse Pointers link.**

   The Mouse Properties dialog box appears, with the Pointers tab showing (see Figure 1-5).

2. **Modify your pointers in any of these ways:**
   - *To change all pointers at the same time,* pick a new pointer scheme from the Scheme drop-down list.
   - *To change an individual pointer,* click the pointer in the Customize box and then click the Browse button.

     Windows shows you all available pointers — which number in the hundreds. Choose the pointer you want, and click the Open button.
   - *To bring back the original scheme,* choose Windows Aero (System Scheme), which is probably the one you started with.
   - *To change an individual pointer back to the original pointer for the particular scheme you have chosen,* click the pointer in the Customize box and then click the Use Default button.

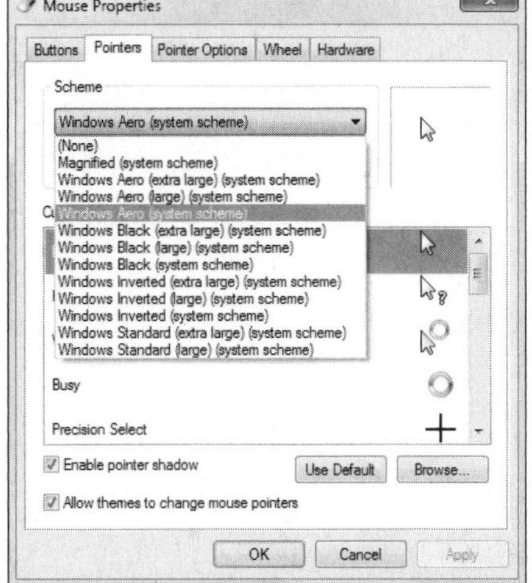

Figure 1-5: Change mouse pointers individually or en masse.

3. **When you settle on a set of pointers that appeal to you, click the Save As button and give your new, custom scheme a name so that you can retrieve it at any time.**
4. **Click the OK button.**

   Windows starts using the pointers you chose.

Selecting Screen Savers

Windows screen savers are absolutely, totally, utterly, 100 percent for fun. Ten or 15 years ago, screen savers served a real purpose — they kept monitors from "burning in" the phosphors in frequently used parts of the screen. Nowadays, monitors aren't nearly as prone to burn-in (or burnout — as can be the case with humans!), and saving screens rates right up there with manufacturing buggy whips on the obsolescence scale. Flat-panel LCD monitors (such as a laptop's screen) don't have phosphors, so there's nothing to burn.

Now that Windows itself can run a slide show of desktop backgrounds, the demand for screen savers has taken a big hit.

Still, screen savers are amusing, and if you follow the tricks in the following sections, they serve one truly important function: A screen saver makes an excellent front for a Super Boss Key — a key you can press whenever Da Boss makes an unexpected, unwanted appearance.

Changing the screen saver

Follow these steps to select a screen saver:

1. **Right-click any empty part of the desktop and choose Personalize. In the lower-right corner of the screen, click the Screen Saver link.**

   Windows 7 shows you the Screen Saver tab (see Figure 1-6).

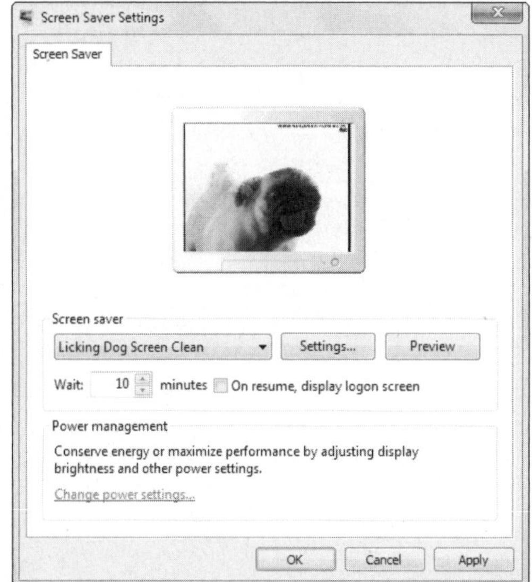

Figure 1-6: Choose a screen saver here.

2. **Choose a screen saver from the Screen Saver drop-down box. Click the Settings button and take the screen saver for a test drive.**

   Don't like it? Pick another one.

3. **Select or deselect the On Resume, Display Logon Screen check box.**

   This setting can be a bit confusing. Basically, it controls what happens when the computer "wakes up" after the screen saver kicks in:

   - *When the On Resume, Display Logon Screen check box is selected:* When the computer wakes up, it shows the Windows logon screen. If the user who was logged on has an account that requires a password, she must reenter her password to get back into Windows. (I talk about passwords in the section on changing user settings in Book II, Chapter 2.)

- *When the On Resume, Display Logon Screen check box is deselected:* When the computer wakes up, it returns to the state it was in when the screen saver started. The user who was logged on remains logged on.

4. **When you're happy with your screen saver settings, click the OK button.**

   The screen saver kicks in whenever a sufficient length of time passes with no activity.

To get rid of your current screen saver, right-click an empty spot on the desktop, choose Personalize, click the Screen Saver link at the bottom, and select None in the Screen Saver drop-down list. Click the OK button, and your screen will never be saved again.

If you want to download screen savers from the Internet, be aware of one painful fact: The overwhelming majority of "free" screen savers you find on the Web carry spyware, adware, and various kinds of scumware, which are installed when you install the screen saver. To minimize the chances of hauling dreck into your computer, make sure that you have the Firefox Attack Site feature or Internet Explorer malware protection working. Personally, I like the selection at `wincustomize.com`.

What's with the pug?

All right. I confess. If you look at Figure 1-6 closely, you see that I too run a screen saver. I bet you've seen it: A little dog — a pug — licks the inside of your screen and keeps trying to get it clean but never quite makes it. I identify with the pug's Sisyphean-ness, if that's a word that can be repeated in a family publication.

The screen saver has a fascinating story behind it. I first bumped into the version posted by Tim Lester, publisher of the *Midwestern Bio-Ag Bio-News,* on his Web site, `Nuganics.com.au`. Nuganics stands for *nu*trition-based or*ganics*. Tim's very involved in efforts aimed at stopping genetically modified food, and other healthy-farming issues, from his base near Marcoola, Queensland, in Australia.

It ends up that Tim got the video of the dogs from the Web — but after days of trying, I couldn't find the original source of the footage. An early version is at `www.linein.org/blog/2008/01/11/free-screen-cleaner`. Linein credits the Warner Brother's film *Must Love Dogs,* at `www2.warnerbros.com/mustlovedogs/downloads.html`. Whatever its origins, the screen saver is one of the most popular of all time, right up there with the 3D aquarium and its gurgling fish. You can download the dog screen saver for free from `www.nuganics.com.au/2008/01/25/screen-cleaner-screen-saver`. It works well on Windows 7. And, yes, there's a cat version — four different dogs, at last count.

Setting up a Super Boss Key

Here's the trick you've been waiting for — the reason you turned to this chapter in the first place. You can use screen savers to create a *Super Boss Key* — a key combination, such as Alt+F10, that you can press to make the PC immediately switch over to running the screen saver. The Super Boss Key runs independently of the usual Windows screen saver stuff: The Super Boss Key doesn't affect the screen saver you set up to run on your computer when it's idle. The screen saver is just a handy program that doesn't look the least bit suspicious if your boss glances at your PC's monitor.

Setting up the Super Boss Key is quite simple because Microsoft fixed the Search function in Windows 7. (In Vista, you had to jump through all sorts of hoops.) Here's how:

1. **Choose Start➪Computer. In the Search box, in the upper-right corner, type** *.scr **and press Enter.**

   Windows responds with a list of all `.scr` files — all the screen savers — on your computer, as shown in Figure 1-7. (If you don't see `scr` at the end of the filenames, rap your knuckles for me and look at the section on showing filename extensions in Book II, Chapter 1.)

2. **Right-click the screen saver you want to use for the Super Boss Key, and choose Send To➪Desktop (Create Shortcut).**

   Most filenames are obviously associated with specific screen savers, but a couple of them are tricky. Table 1-3 lists the screen savers that ship with Windows 7.

   A shortcut to the corresponding `.scr` file appears on your desktop.

Table 1-3 Screen Savers and Their Program Files

Screen Saver	*File*
3D Text	ssText3d.scr
Aurora	Aurora.scr
Blank	scrnsave.scr
Bubbles	Bubbles.scr
Mystify	ssmyst.scr
Photos	PhotoScreensaver.scr
Ribbons	Ribbons.scr
Windows Energy	ssBranded.scr
Windows Logo	logon.scr

3. **On the desktop, right-click the new shortcut and choose Properties.**

The Shortcut Properties dialog box appears, as shown in Figure 1-8.

Yes, yes, I use the pug licking screen cleaner. You caught me. The boss likes dogs. Heh-heh-heh.

4. **Click once in the Shortcut Key field, and then press the key combination you want to use to activate the Super Boss Key, er, screen saver.**

In Figure 1-8, I chose Alt+F10 (that is, hold down the Alt key and then press F10).

5. **Click the OK button, and your Super Boss Key is complete.**

Test it — press the key combination you chose. The puppies take a little while to get going; the built-in screen savers spring to life much faster.

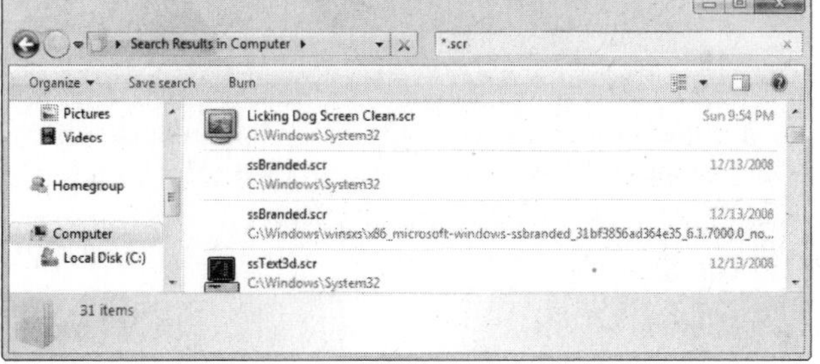

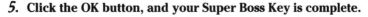

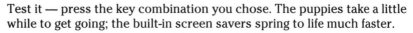

Figure 1-7: Search for all the .scr files on your computer.

Figure 1-8: Change the automatically generated shortcut to your anointed screen saver.

A few programs "swallow" certain odd key combinations — if such a program is running, it grabs the key combinations and doesn't hand them over to Windows, so Windows doesn't know that you want to run your Super Boss Key screen saver. I haven't found many programs that swallow Alt+F10, but some undoubtedly exist. Test the Super Boss Key in all your favorite clandestine situations before you really need to use it, okay? If you find that your chosen key combination doesn't work with an important program (the worst offenders are games), try different key combinations until you find one that makes the Super Boss Key work.

If you want to gussy up your Super Boss Key screen saver, right-click the shortcut and choose Configure. You can change all the screen saver's settings.

Using Desktop Themes

Windows desktop themes incorporate many settings in one easy-to-choose package. The themes revolve around specific topics that frequently (and refreshingly) have nothing to do with Windows — say, cars with carapaces, cavorting carnivores, or carnal caruncles. A theme includes five of the six desktop levels I discuss in this chapter plus a few extra goodies — a base color for the desktop, a background, settings for fonts and colors of the working windows, pictures for the reserved Windows icons (Recycle Bin and Documents, for example), a set of mouse pointers, and a screen saver. A theme can also include a set of custom sounds associated with various Windows events.

To bring in a new theme, follow these steps:

1. **Right-click any open spot on the desktop and choose Personalize.**

   Windows shows you the Change the Visuals and Sounds on Your Computer dialog box.

2. **On the right, click the Get More Themes Online link.**

   Windows opens the Microsoft Windows 7 personalization home page. At least as of this writing, it contains free themes that work well with Windows 7, along with a host of other Windows 7-centric items, including gadgets.

3. **If you can find a theme you like, click the download link underneath it. In Firefox, tell the downloader that you want to open the file by using the themepackfile program. In Internet Explorer, just click Open, then Allow when prompted.**

   The themepackfile program adds the downloaded theme you selected to the My Themes collection, as shown in Figure 1-9.

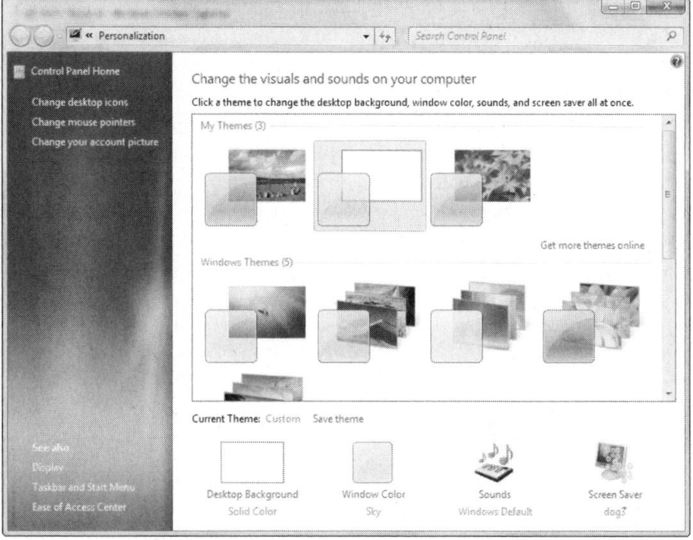

Figure 1-9: Adding new themes is easy, if you choose from Microsoft stock.

4. **After the new theme has been downloaded, go back to the Change the Visuals and Sounds on Your Computer dialog box and choose the theme you like.**

   Safely back in the Change the Visuals and Sounds on Your Computer dialog box, you can make whatever changes you like.

When you bring in a theme, it might contain five of the six desktop levels I discuss in this chapter, plus a new sound scheme: Some themes have only a few of those items; some have all. If you switch themes, the old background, icon pictures, mouse pointers, and screen savers all remain on your PC — the new theme doesn't delete them — but if you want to get any of them back, you have to go through the customization steps you followed earlier.

Zillions of Windows desktop themes are available on the Web, many of them quite good, and most of them can work with Windows 7. My comment in the screen saver section of this chapter applies here in spades: Watch out for scumware. To be on the safe side, visit `wincustomize.com` or `themeworld.com` for thousands of free themes.

Seeing Your Desktop Clearly

The best, biggest monitor in the world "don't mean jack" if you can't see the text on the screen. Windows 7 contains a handful of utilities and settings that can help you whup your monitor upside the head and improve its appearance.

With apologies to Billy Crystal, sometimes it *is* more important to look good than to feel good.

Setting the screen resolution

I don't know how many people ask me how to fix this new monitor they just bought. The screen doesn't look right. Must be that %$#@! Windows, yes? The old monitor looked just fine.

Nine times out of ten, when somebody tells me that a new monitor doesn't look right, I ask whether the person adjusted the screen resolution. Invariably, the answer is No. So here's the quick course — the answer to one of the questions I hear most.

If you plug in a new monitor (or put together a new computer) and the screen looks fuzzy, the most likely culprit entails a mismatch between the *resolution* your computer expects and the resolution your monitor wants. To a first approximation, a screen resolution is just the number of dots that appear on the screen, usually expressed as two numbers: 1680 x 1050, for example. Every flat-panel screen has exactly one resolution that looks right and a zillion other resolutions that make things look like you fused your monitor with the end of a Coke bottle.

Setting the screen resolution is easy: Right-click any empty place on the desktop and choose Screen Resolution. You see the Screen Resolution dialog box, shown in Figure 1-10. (If you have more than one monitor, or certain kinds of video cards, you might see multiple monitors in the top box.)

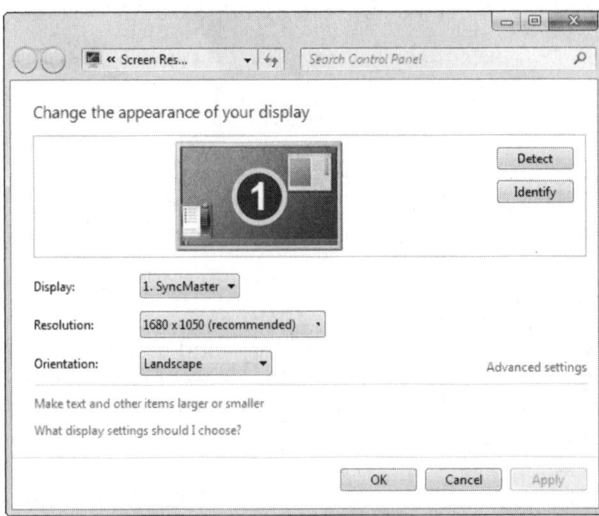

Figure 1-10: Tell Windows which screen resolution works best on your monitor.

Changing the screen resolution is as simple as clicking the Resolution drop-down list and picking the resolution you want. That's the easy part.

The hard part? Figuring out which resolution your monitor likes: its *native resolution*. Some monitors have the resolution printed on a sticker that might still adhere to the front. (Goo Gone works wonders.) All monitors have their native resolutions listed in the manual. (You *do* have your monitor's manual, yes? No, I don't either.)

If you don't know your monitor's native resolution, Google is your friend. Go to `www.google.com` and type **native resolution** followed by your monitor's model number, which you can (almost) always find engraved in the bezel or stuck on the side. For example, typing `native resolution 226BW` immediately finds the native resolution for a Samsung 226BW monitor.

Activating and adjusting ClearType

Misbehaving text can make your monitor look fuzzy, too.

Not too many years ago, *ClearType* — the proprietary Microsoft method of sharpening the appearance of text on a screen — was considered a bleeding-edge technology that just didn't work right on some monitors.

Times have changed. Now, every monitor, without exception, is designed to work well with ClearType. Monitor manufacturers put it in their design specs.

If you have an older CRT "tube" monitor, you might want to turn off ClearType because it can make fonts look fuzzy. But almost every flat-screen monitor can benefit from what ClearType has to offer. (Industry icon Steve Gibson has an excellent description of ClearType and its supremacy on LCD displays at `grc.com/cleartype.htm`.)

You can adjust ClearType so that it works best on your monitor, under your lighting conditions. To open the ClearType Text Tuner, choose Start⇨Control Panel⇨Appearance and Personalization and then, at the bottom under Fonts, click the Adjust ClearType Text Settings link.

Showing larger fonts

If your eyes aren't what they used to be — and mine never were — you might want to tell Windows to increase the size of text and other items on the screen. It's just enough boost to help, particularly if you're at an Internet café and forgot your glasses.

To adjust the size of fonts (actually, everything), choose Start⇨Control Panel⇨Appearance and Personalization. Under the Display icon, click the Make Text and Other Items Larger or Smaller link. You see the choices shown in Figure 1-11.

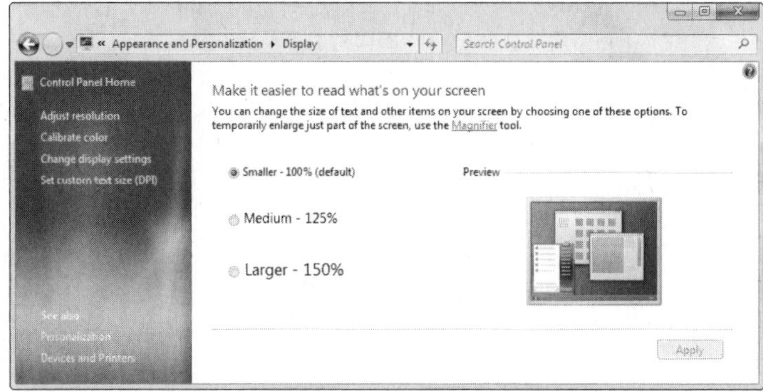

Figure 1-11: Windows itself has a setting that resembles the "zoom" you find in many programs.

Using magnification

If you need more "zoom" than the font enlarger can offer, click the Magnifier link (refer to Figure 1-11; the link is in the first paragraph), and the Windows Magnifier appears. The Magnifier lets you zoom the entire screen by a factor of 200, 300, or 400 — or as high as you like.

Note that magnifying doesn't increase the quality or resolution of text or pictures. It makes them bigger, not finer. That CSI "David, can you make the picture sharper?" thing doesn't work with Windows. Sorry, Grissom.

If these nostrums don't do the job, you should take advantage of the Windows 7 high-contrast themes. They use color to make text, in particular, stand out. High-contrast themes are available from the Theme list, shown in Figure 1-9 and described in the section "Using Desktop Themes," earlier in this chapter.

Chapter 2: Organizing Your Interface

In This Chapter

- **Taming the super Taskbar**
- **Harnessing the power of the Start menu**
- **Getting at your most recently used documents quickly**
- **Starting your favorite programs with just a click**
- **Making workhorse programs start automatically**

Windows 7 contains an enormous variety of self-help tools that can make your working (and playing!) days go faster. As you become more comfortable with the Windows inner world, you find shortcuts and simplifications that really do make a difference.

This chapter shows you how to take off the training wheels.

Tricking Out the Taskbar

Microsoft developers working on the Windows 7 taskbar gave it a secret internal project name: the Superbar. Although one might debate how much of the *Super* in the bar arrived compliments of Mac OS, there's no doubt that the Windows 7 taskbar runs rings around its predecessors.

The Windows 7 Super, uh, taskbar, appears at the bottom of the screen, as in Figure 2-1.

If you hover your mouse over an icon and the icon is associated with a program that's running, you see thumbnails of all the copies of the program. For example, in Figure 2-1, three different instances of Firefox are running, each sitting at a different Web site. Hover your mouse over the Firefox icons and you can see which sites are up for grabs. Slide your mouse over a thumbnail and click once, and Firefox appears with a site loaded and ready for bear.

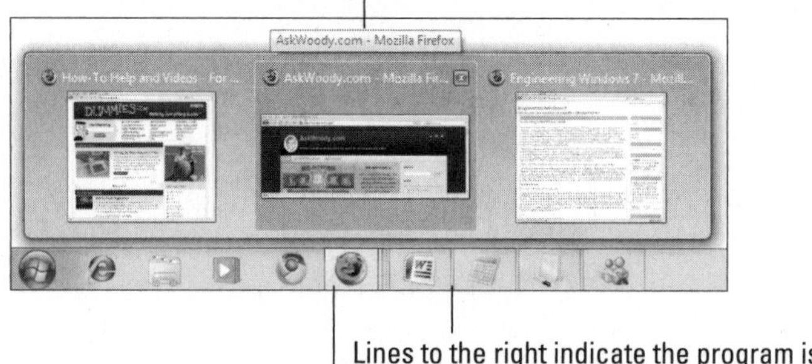
Thumbnails of running windows
Lines to the right indicate the program is running.
Hover your mouse over a taskbar icon to see thumbnails.

Figure 2-1: The taskbar juggles many different tasks.

Anatomy of the taskbar

The Taskbar consists of two different kinds of icons:

- **Icons that have been pinned there:** Windows 7 ships with three icons on the taskbar — one apiece for Internet Explorer, Windows Explorer, and Windows Media Player. You can see them on the left in Figure 2-1. If you install a program and tell the installer to put an icon on the taskbar (or on the now-defunct Quick Launch toolbar), an icon for the program appears on the taskbar. You can also pin programs of your choice on the taskbar.
- **Icons associated with running programs:** Every time a program starts, an icon for the program appears on the taskbar. If you run three copies of the program, only one icon shows up. When the program stops, the icon disappears.

In general, you can't differentiate between the pinned icons and the ones that are just coming along for the ride, except by noting which ones are on the right (the running programs) and which are on the left (the pinned programs). You *can*, however, tell which icons represent running programs: Windows puts little vertical lines to the left and right of the icon for any running program. If you have more than one copy of the program running, you see more than one line on the right. It's subtle. In Figure 2-2, the first icon doesn't have a running program. All the others do.

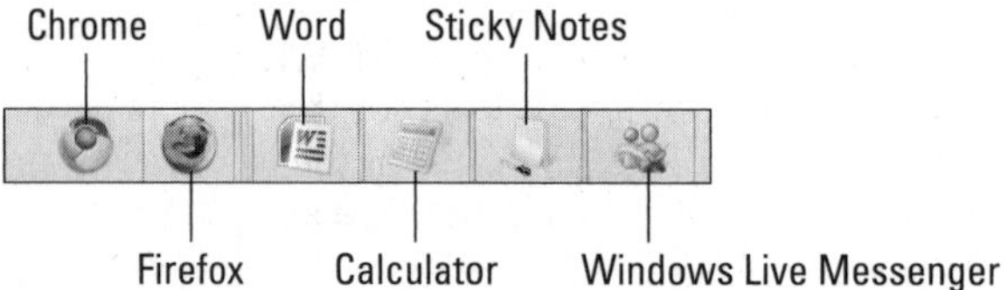
Chrome
Word
Sticky Notes
Firefox
Calculator
Windows Live Messenger

Figure 2-2: All but one icon has a running program.

In Figure 2-2, Chrome isn't running (there's no vertical stripe on the left). Three different versions of Firefox are running, as shown in Figure 2-1. There's one copy apiece of Word and the calculator. I have Sticky Notes on my desktop. And Windows Live Messenger is running, but not signed in. See how that works?

Jumping

If you right-click any icon in the taskbar — pinned or not — you see a bunch of links called a *Jump List*, as in Figure 2-3.

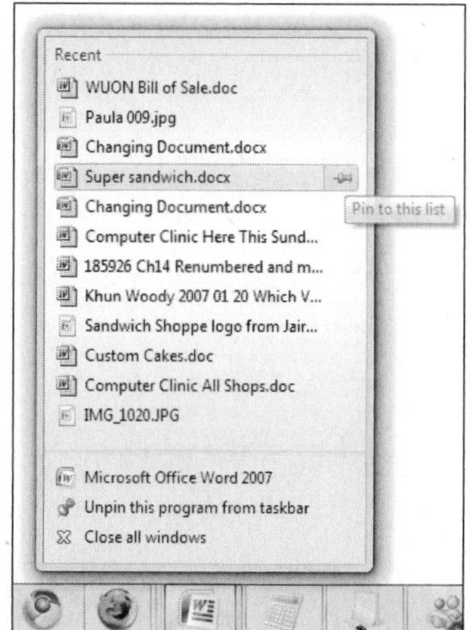

Figure 2-3: The Jump List in Word.

The contents of the Jump List vary depending on the program that's running, but the bottom pane of every Jump List contains the name of the program and the entry Unpin This Program from Taskbar.

Jump Lists are new in Windows 7 and more than a little half-baked. Here are your Jump List basics:

- **Jump Lists may show you recently opened file history.** For example, the Word Jump List (refer to Figure 2-3) shows you the same Recent Documents list that appears inside Word. The currently open document(s) appear at the top of the list.

- **It's easy to pin an item to the Jump List.** When you pin an item, it sticks to a program's Jump List whether or not that item is open. To pin an item, run your mouse out to the right of the item you want to pin and click the stick pin. That puts the item in a separate pane at the top of the Jump List. In Figure 2-3, if I click the pin next to `Super sandwich.docx`, that document gets pinned to the top of the list. In the future, if I want to open `Super sandwich.docx`, I just right-click the Word icon and select the document.

The Jump List has one not-so-obvious use. It lets you open a second copy of the same program. Say you want to copy a handful of albums from the music library to your thumb drive on `F:`. You start by clicking Start⇨Music. Windows Explorer opens the Music Library. Cool.

You could do the copy-and-paste thang — select an album, press Ctrl+C to copy, use the list on the left of Windows Explorer to navigate to `F:`, and then press Ctrl+V to paste. But if you're going to copy many albums, it's much faster and easier to open a second copy of Windows Explorer, and navigate to `F:` in that second window. Then you can click and drag albums from the Music folder to the `F:` folder.

To open a second copy of a running program (Windows Explorer, in this example), you have two choices:

- Hold down the shift key and click the icon.
- Right-click the icon and choose the program's name.

In either case, Windows starts a fresh copy of the program.

Changing the toolbar

The toolbar rates as one of the few parts of Windows that's highly malleable. You can modify it till the cows come home:

- **Pin any program on the toolbar** by right-clicking the program (say, in the Start⇨All Programs list) and choosing Pin to Toolbar. Yes, you can right-click the icon of a running program on the toolbar.
- **Move a pinned icon** by clicking and dragging it. Easy. You know — the way it's supposed to be. You can even drag an icon that isn't pinned into the middle of the pinned icons. When the program associated with the icon stops, the icon disappears and all pinned icons move back into place.
- **Unpin any pinned program** by right-clicking it and choosing Unpin from Toolbar. Rocket science.

Unfortunately, you can't turn individual documents or folders into icons on the toolbar. But you *can* pin a folder to the Windows Explorer Jump List, and you *can* pin a document to the Jump List for whichever application is associated with the document. For example, you can pin a song to the Jump List for Windows Media Player.

Here's how to pin a folder or document to its associated icon on the taskbar:

1. **Navigate to the folder or document that you want to pin.**

   You can use Start➪Pictures, say, to open your Pictures library. You can even make a shortcut to the folder or document.

2. **Drag the folder or document (or shortcut) to the taskbar.**

   Windows tells you where it will pin the folder, document, or shortcut, as in Figure 2-4.

Figure 2-4: Pinning a folder, file, or shortcut.

3. **Release the mouse button.**

   That's all it takes.

Making your own little toolbars

You can turn your own folder into a toolbar, which sits on the taskbar. It's a cool tool if you frequently need to navigate around a hornet's nest of folders and don't want to do the navigating from inside a specific program (such as Word or Excel). Instead, you can put a pop-up menu — a new *toolbar*, in Windows parlance — on the taskbar. This toolbar whisks you directly to a folder, and from that point, subfolders turn into submenus. You can navigate through the folder maze to individual files.

The terminology here is confusing because the custom pop-up toolbar you create sits on top of the Windows taskbar. Your folder doesn't show up as an icon; it appears on the right side of the taskbar with the name of the folder. When you click the name of the folder, you see a navigable list of all subfolders and documents. Confused? Take a look at Figure 2-5.

For example, in Figure 2-5, I put a shortcut to my Khun Woodys Reserve folder on the taskbar. Digging into that folder is as easy as clicking a toolbar button.

Most people don't need the extra cascading toolbar: You can navigate your program's usual File➪Open menu with no problem or choose Start➪Documents and you're on your way. For most of us, this fancy custom toolbar just takes up room on the Windows taskbar — where space is in short supply anyway. But if you have a bunch of folders that you navigate frequently, it can save a lot of time.

In a toolbar, each folder is associated with a flyout menu.

Items in the flyout menu match items in the folder.

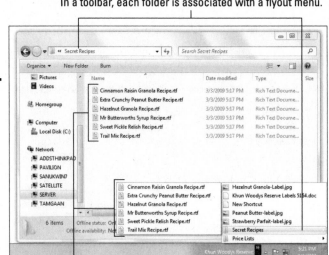

Figure 2-5: When you create your own toolbar, the entries on the toolbar match the underlying folder structure.

To put a new toolbar on the Windows taskbar:

1. **Right-click any unused part of the taskbar and choose Toolbars⇨New Toolbar.**

   You see the New Toolbar dialog box, shown in Figure 2-6.

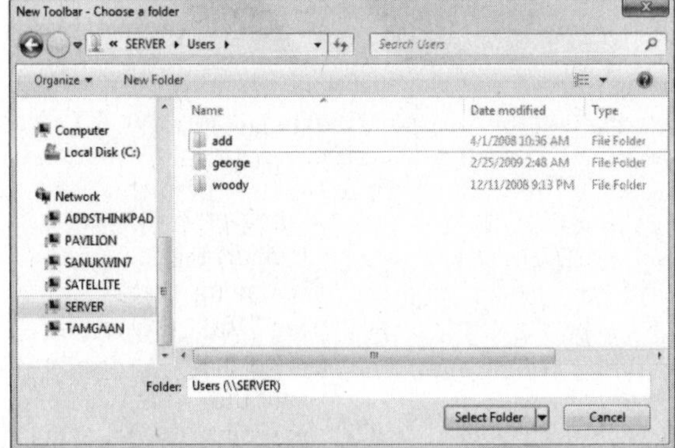

Figure 2-6: Choose the root folder for the taskbar.

2. **Navigate to the folder you want as the root of the pop-up menu, and click Select Folder.**

The contents of this folder appear on your new toolbar. Figure 2-5 shows the result of my placing the `Khun Woodys Reserve` folder on my taskbar.

3. **If you want to try to relocate the toolbar, make sure the taskbar is unlocked (right-click an empty part of it and deselect the Lock the Taskbar option). Then click and drag your new toolbar wherever you want.**

   If you play with the toolbar, you see that Windows restricts the placement and sizing of the toolbar quite drastically — and it has a habit of dragging out subfolders and files.

4. **When you're happy with the result, right-click an unused spot on the taskbar and select the Lock the Taskbar check box.**

   Try using the new toolbar and see if you get used to it.

If you change your mind and want to get rid of the new toolbar, right-click an open place on the taskbar, choose Toolbars, and deselect the option that mentions the new toolbar.

Bring back the Quick Launch toolbar

It's hard to wax nostalgic about an old Windows feature, but the old Quick Launch toolbar has been around since 1997, and plenty of people mourn its passing in Windows 7. Quick Launch works differently from the new taskbar, and if you want to continue to use it, you're in luck.

Here's how to bring it back:

1. **Choose Start, immediately type** gpedit.msc **and press Enter.**

   This step opens the Windows Group Policy Editor, one of those weird, geeky internal things your mother warned you about.

2. **On the left, choose User Configuration⇨Administrative Templates⇨Start Menu and Taskbar.**

3. **Near the bottom of the Setting list, double-click Show Quick Launch on Taskbar.**

4. **Choose Enabled and click OK.**

5. **Back in Windows, right-click the taskbar and choose Toolbars⇨New Toolbar.**

6. **Navigate to the folder** `c:\users\<your name>\AppData\Roaming\Microsoft\Internet Explorer\Quick Launch` **and click Select Folder.**

   Quick Launch appears as a new toolbar on your taskbar.

You can drag programs on and off the Quick Launch toolbar, just as you did in Windows XP and Vista. Use the tricks described in the earlier section "Making your own little toolbars," to expand the toolbar. If you decide that you no longer want the Quick Launch toolbar, follow the Group Policy Editor steps again and this time, rather than choose Enabled, choose Not Configured.

Working with the taskbar

I've discovered a few tricks with the taskbar that you may find worthwhile:

- When you hover your mouse over an icon, you see thumbnails of the running copies of the program (refer to Figure 2-1). Normally, the thumbnails disappear when you move the mouse, but if you click the icon once, the thumbnails stay until you click somewhere else.
- Sometimes you want to shut down all (or most) running programs, and you don't want Windows to do it for you. It's easy to see what's running, by looking at the vertical lines to the right of the icons (refer to Figure 2-2). To close down all instances of a particular program, right-click its icon and choose Close Window or Close All Windows.

  The terminology is a bit screwy here. Normally, you would say "Exit the program" or "Choose File⇨Exit" or "Click the red X" or some such. When you're working with the taskbar, you say "Close all windows." Different words, same meaning.
- To get a quick look at all running programs, slide your mouse along the row of taskbar icons.
- To bring up the last window that was open in a particular program, hold down the Ctrl key and click the program's icon. For example, if you Ctrl+click the Word icon, Word appears with the most recently viewed document open.

I have no idea why Microsoft calls it Aero Peek (marketing Kool-Aid, no doubt), but if you swing your mouse down to the lower-right corner of the screen — at the right end of the taskbar — Windows 7 turns all open windows transparent so that you can "see through" the open windows and view the icons and gadgets below. Elsewhere, Windows calls the same feature Show Desktop and Desktop Preview — both of which sound better, to me, than Twin Peaks, er, Error Peek.

If you drag your mouse to the lower-right corner and then click, Windows minimizes all open windows. Click again, and Windows brings back all minimized windows.

Controlling the notification area

Windows 7 finally (finally!) gives you some specific control over the contents of the notification area — the glob of icons down near the clock that used to be known as the system tray.

Windows 7 ships with a small handful of visible notification icons — for the Action Center, the Network Center, and the master audio volume control slider. That's it. If you see any additional icons, your computer's manufacturer probably put them there. When you install a new program that has an icon for the notification area, the icon is placed in the box that you can see when you click the up arrow at the left edge of the icons.

If you're tired of seeing a useless icon in the notification area — or if you know that you want to see an icon all the time — you can take control. Here's how:

1. **Click the up arrow at the left edge of the icons.**

   If you see an icon in the box that you absolutely must have visible all the time, simply click and drag it into the notification area, near the clock.

   If you later change your mind, you can click and drag the icon back from the notification area into the box.

2. **Choose Customize.**

   Windows shows you the Notification Area Icon Zapper box — that's what I call it, anyway (see Figure 2-7).

3. **Find the icon you want to zap and, in the drop-down box, choose Hide Icon and Notifications (to turn off the beast completely) or Only Show Notifications (shows the balloon warnings but doesn't show the icon).**

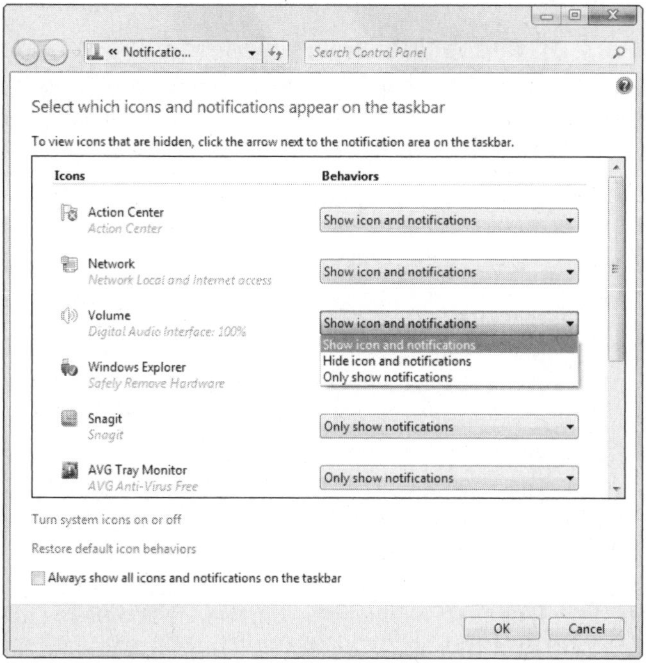

Figure 2-7: Control notification area icons here.

4. **Click OK.**

   The icon changes its wayward ways immediately.

Customizing the Start Menu

I give you a brief overview of the Start menu in Book II, Chapter 1. In this chapter, I take a look at the beast in far greater detail by explaining what makes it tick and how you can use this newfound information to practice a little Start menu mind control so that the menu reflects the way you use your PC.

The tricks you find in this section should appeal to you especially if you bought your PC with Windows 7 preinstalled, because the PC manufacturer probably stuck some programs on the Start menu that didn't originate with Microsoft. If you want to take control of your Start menu, follow the steps in this chapter to get rid of the stuff you don't want or need. It's your Start menu. You can't break anything. Take the, uh, bull by the horns.

To change the Start menu for everyone who uses your computer, you need to be a designated administrator. Find out more about becoming an administrator in the section on choosing account types in Book II, Chapter 2.

Genesis of the Start menu

Although the Start menu looks like it sprang fully formed from the head of some malevolent Windows god, in fact Windows creates much of the Start menu on the fly, every time you click the Start button. That's why your computer takes a little while between the time you click the Start button and the time you see the Start menu on the screen.

Here's where the various pieces come from, looking from top to bottom (see Figure 2-8):

- The name and picture in the upper-right corner are taken from the Windows sign-on screen. You can change them by following the procedure described in the section on changing user settings in Book II, Chapter 2.
- You can pin a program or shortcut to the upper-left corner of the Start menu. After being pinned, it stays there until you remove it. I go into pinning details in the next section of this chapter.
- The recently used programs list maintained by Windows goes on the left side of the Start menu, at the bottom. Although you have a little bit of control over this list, Windows (or your PC manufacturer) may stack the deck, by loading favored programs first, whether you use them or not. Most of the time, you probably let Windows take control of the

list — after you figure out how to unstack the deck. I talk about the way Windows maintains this list in the section "Reclaiming most recently used programs," later in this chapter.

✦ At the bottom of the menu, All Programs connects to folders on your hard drive. This is the part of the Start menu that was designed by Microsoft to be easy to modify. You can add submenus and change or delete items to your heart's content — all of which is really easy. I talk about these features in the section "Changing the All Programs menu," later in this chapter.

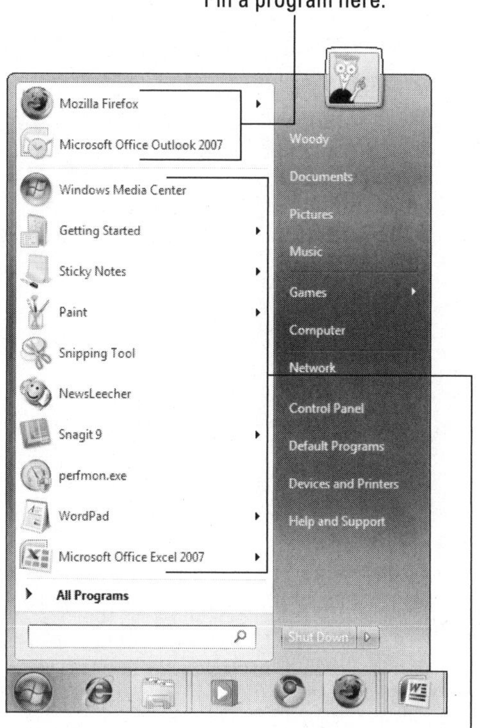

Figure 2-8: A typical Start menu.

Although you can make many little changes to the items on the right side of the Start menu (see the section "Making minor tweaks to the Start menu," later in this chapter), you should definitely spend a few minutes deciding whether any of the changes is worthwhile for you. The big change on the right side is the inclusion of a Recent Items list. Some people love it. Some people hate it. Read the "Making minor tweaks to the Start menu" section, later in this chapter, and decide for yourself.

Pinning to the Start menu

Do you have one or two programs that run your life? Yeah, me too: Word and Outlook. I use them day in and day out. I dream in Word. Sad, but true.

If you have Microsoft Office installed on your computer, the Office installer probably pinned Outlook on your Start menu as your e-mail program. Windows 7 enables you to easily put other programs of your choice way up at the top, in the upper-left corner of the Start menu. That's the high-rent district, the place my mouse gravitates to every time I click Start.

I don't know why, but Microsoft calls this *pinning* — kind of a wimpy name for the most powerful feature on the Start menu, eh?

Beginning adventures in pinning

When you're ready to start pinning away, here are some handy things to know about customizing this area of the Start menu:

✦ **The easiest place to pin from is the All Programs menu.** Choose Start⇨All Programs; then right-click the program and choose Pin to Start Menu.

In Figure 2-9, I chose to pin Word 2007.

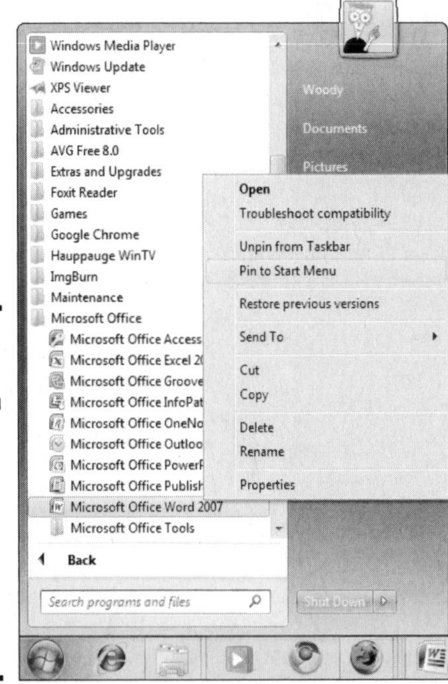

Figure 2-9: Right-click any program anywhere on the Start menu and pin it in the upper-left corner — the high-rent district.

✦ **If the program you want to pin isn't already on the All Programs menu, you can use Windows Explorer or Search to find it.** After you find the program file, simply right-click it and choose Pin to Start Menu. But of course, finding a program isn't always as easy as it sounds because many program filenames don't bear much resemblance to the program itself. For example, you can easily find `Outlook.exe`, the Outlook program file, with a standard Windows search (see the next chapter), but you may be hard-pressed to identify `Winword.exe` as the progenitor of Word. You can find many program filenames by choosing Start⇨Computer, double-clicking the main hard drive, and digging into the Program Files folder.

✦ **Pinning a program doesn't move it from its original location.** If you pin a program on the Start menu by right-clicking it and choosing Pin to Start Menu, Windows creates a second entry on the Start menu for the pinned copy. Your original — the program you right-clicked — stays where it was.

✦ **You can also drag and drop a program, file, or folder from anywhere in Windows onto the pinned list.** The program, file, or folder isn't moved anywhere: Windows 7 is smart enough to put a shortcut to the item on the Start menu.

✦ **You can put pinned programs in any order you like.** When the program, file, or folder gets pinned, it appears at the bottom of the pinned pile — which is to say, below your Web browser and e-mail program. To change all that, just click the program and drag it to any other spot in the pinned list.

✦ **If you like, give your pinned programs names that you can live with.** Right-click the program and choose Properties. On the General tab, change the name in the top box to whatever you want to show on the Start menu. Figure 2-10 shows Word at the top of the pinned list, with the names shortened from Microsoft Office Outlook 2007 to Outlook 2007 and from Microsoft Office Word 2007 to plain ol' Word 2007.

Figure 2-10: Outlook and Word, renamed the way I want, appear at the top.

Removing an item pinned to the Start menu

You can remove any program from the pinned part of the Start menu. If you right-click either of the built-in pinned programs (marked Internet and E-mail) and choose Remove from This List, the program disappears from the pinned programs area. If you right-click any other pinned programs (presumably ones you place in the high-rent district, or ones that your computer's manufacturer graciously added to the list), choose Unpin from Start Menu and the item goes away.

Note that unpinning a program removes it only from the pinned list in the upper-left corner of the Start menu. The program itself stays right where it is. So do any other shortcuts to the program, whether they're elsewhere on the Start menu or somewhere else in your computer, such as on your desktop. Unpin with impunity, sez I.

Changing the pinned Internet and e-mail programs

You can change the Internet and e-mail programs listed at the beginning of the pinned list if you have more than one Web browser or e-mail program installed. To change the Internet or e-mail program (or default media player, instant messaging program, or default Java Virtual Machine), follow these steps:

1. **Make sure you have your new favorite Internet or e-mail program installed.**

   If you want Chrome and Thunderbird, start by installing those programs; otherwise, Windows can't find them and doesn't offer them.

2. **Choose Start⇨Default Programs. Then click the bottom link, Set Program Access and Computer Defaults.**

   You see the Set Program Access and Computer Defaults dialog box, shown in Figure 2-11.

3. **Click the Custom down arrow and choose your default Web browser (Firefox?), e-mail program (Outlook?), media player (iTunes?), instant messenger (Trillian?), and, if you're feeling brave, Java Virtual Machine.**

   Selecting the default not only sticks the expected icon on the Start menu but also sets the default browser, e-mail program, and media player. If you click a link in a document, your default browser pops up and opens the Web site.

4. **Click OK.**

   Your changes take effect immediately. Run over to the Start menu and check it out.

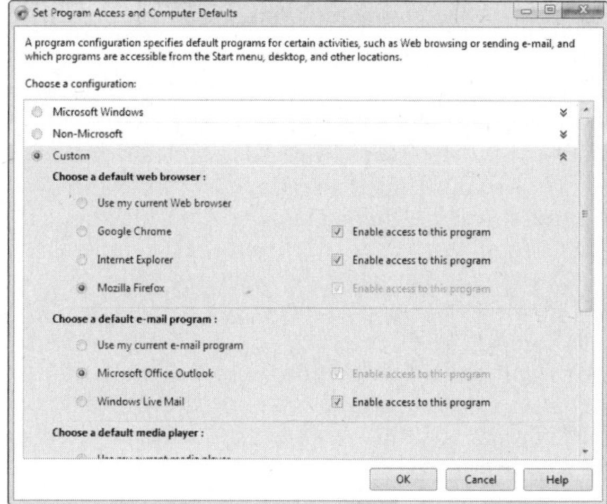

Figure 2-11: Changing the default program moves it to the pinned area of the Start menu, replacing whatever was there.

Pinning taskbar items to the Start menu

If you want to pin a program on the Start menu, you just open the program (usually by choosing Start⇨All Programs), right-click the program, and choose Pin to Start Menu.

Unfortunately, that doesn't work for items on the taskbar. If you right-click a taskbar icon, you see the Jump List (refer to Figure 2-3, earlier in this chapter) and other unhelpful choices, such as Unpin This Program from the Taskbar.

You could hunt and peck your way around the All Programs list to find the program you want to pin on the Start menu: Items on the All Programs menu can be stuck on the Start menu with a simple right-click. But you can also drill down into the buried list of Windows 7 taskbar programs. Here's how:

1. **Click Start⇨Computer and navigate to `c:\users\<your name>\AppData\Roaming\Microsoft\Internet Explorer\Quick Launch\User Pinned\Taskbar`.**

   In that location, you find all the programs you pinned to the taskbar.

   A whole lotta history is in that folder list. You can see that the "Super" taskbar is based on the old Quick Launch toolbar (which I show you how to resurrect in the sidebar "Bring back the Quick Launch toolbar," earlier in this chapter). Most people don't realize it, but the Quick Launch toolbar originally came from Internet Explorer 4, not from Windows.

2. **Pick the program that you want to stick on the Start menu, right-click it, and choose Pin to Start Menu.** ***Voilà!***

   The program shows up at the bottom of the Pin List, which is in the upper-left corner of the Start menu.

Geeky bonus trick: If you installed an older Vista (or Windows XP) program and it told you that it was putting an icon on the Quick Launch toolbar, you can find that icon down in these latitudes. You can even move the icon to the new Windows 7 taskbar, which is probably where you wanted it anyway. Here's how: Go to `c:\users\<your name>\AppData\Roaming\Microsoft\Internet Explorer\Quick Launch`, right-click the icon you want to stick on your taskbar, and choose Copy. Then drill down farther, to `Quick Launch\User Pinned\TaskBar`, right-click, and choose Paste. Log off and log back on again, and there's your old icon, all shiny and new, sitting exactly where you expected.

Reclaiming most recently used programs

Directly above the Start button, in the lower-left corner of the Start menu, you find a list of the programs you've used most recently. This list can be handy: It's updated dynamically as you use programs, so you have a decent chance to see the program you need right there on the list.

When you run a program that's pinned to the upper-left corner of the Start menu (see the preceding section), it doesn't count: The most recently used list includes only programs that aren't at the top of the Start menu.

At least, that's the theory. In fact, the most recently used programs list — like so many things in Windows 7 — does a little bit more (or less?) than first meets the eye. Unless your hardware manufacturer has jiggered things, the first time you start Windows 7, you see these programs in the most recently used area:

- ✦ Getting Started
- ✦ Windows Media Center
- ✦ Sticky Notes
- ✦ Snipping Tool
- ✦ Calculator
- ✦ Paint

In fact, the most recently used counter that controls what shows up in the most recently used programs box isn't quite kosher. If you play with the list for a while, you discover that the programs higher on the list tend to stay on the list longer — whether you've used them or not. I had to run one program a dozen times before it bumped Media Center off the top of the list.

There's no reason on earth why you should keep Microsoft advertising (or your PC manufacturer's either, for that matter, if your list varies from the standard one) on your Start menu. Fortunately, you can easily get rid of all the built-in most recently used programs and start out with a clean slate. Just follow these steps:

1. **Right-click the Start button and choose Properties.**

   Windows 7 opens the Taskbar and Start Menu Properties dialog box, shown in Figure 2-12.

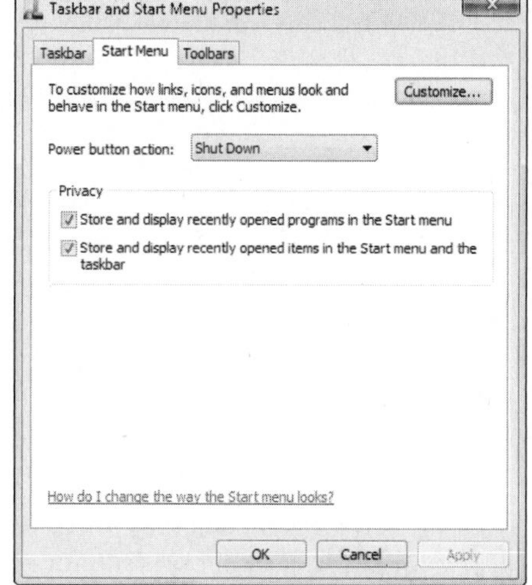

Figure 2-12: Clear the most recently used programs list here.

2. **Deselect the Store and Display a List of Recently Opened Programs check box. Then click the Apply button.**

   That clears the list.

3. **Select the Store and Display a List of Recently Opened Programs check box. Then click the OK button.**

   By clearing the list and then telling Windows 7 to start showing it again, you get rid of all the bad karma, er, salted programs, and Windows 7 starts keeping track of the programs you use.

Sometimes Windows 7 doesn't quite keep up with the programs you open. To whip it back into shape, try these tips:

- ✦ If you don't see your most recently used list updating properly, try logging off (click the Start button, click the right-facing arrow next to the picture of the lock, and choose Log Off) and logging back on again.
- ✦ Windows maintains the most recently used programs list on its own: You cannot drag and drop items on the list. You can, however, remove programs from the list. Just right-click an offending program and choose Remove from This List.

Changing the All Programs menu

When you choose Start⇨All Programs, Windows assembles the list of "all" programs by combining these two separate folders on your hard drive:

- ✦ The `Start Menu\Programs` folder for you, which is in the `C:\Users\<your name>\AppData\Roaming\Microsoft\Windows` folder
- ✦ The `Start Menu\Programs` folder for Windows itself, which is in the `C:\ProgramData\Microsoft\Windows` folder

If you can't see the AppData folder, you haven't told Windows 7 to show you hidden and system folders. Follow the instructions in Book II, Chapter 1, to get Windows 7 to show you all your data.

If you look at your own folders and compare then to your Start menu, you can see that files inside the folders turn into menu entries. Some folders appear on both lists: When that happens, the contents of both folders go on the All Programs menu.

Everything on the All Programs menu comes from one or the other of the two `Start Menu\Programs` folders (or, much less commonly, from one or the other of the two parent `Start Menu` folders).

You can perform plenty of prestidigitation with the All Programs programs (say that ten times fast) without digging into the folders that spawn the entries. For example, you can

- ✦ Right-click a program, folder, or file and drag it to the All Programs list. (You have to hover the mouse over the Start button and then hover over All Programs.) When you release the mouse button, choose Create Shortcut Here and the program, folder, or file will always appear on your All Programs list.

✦ Right-click a program, folder, or file and choose Rename to change the name that appears in the list.

✦ Right-click a program, folder, or file and choose Delete to remove the item from the list.

If you right-click a program, folder, or file and drag it to the All Programs list, Windows 7 puts a shortcut to the program (or folder or file) in your `Start Menu\Programs` folder. That means the shortcut appears only on your All Programs list — other folks using your computer can't see it. If you want to make a shortcut available to everybody on your computer, you need to move it to the Windows `Start Menu\Programs` folder, `C:\ProgramData\Microsoft\Windows\Start Menu\Programs`.

Making minor tweaks to the Start menu

You can make a number of additional changes to the Start menu. Some of them are actually useful, particularly if you frequently jiggle things inside your computer. To tweak, follow these steps:

1. **Right-click the Start button and choose Properties.**

   You see the Taskbar and Start Menu Properties dialog box.

2. **On the Start Menu tab, click the Customize button.**

   Windows 7 shows you the Customize Start Menu dialog box, shown in Figure 2-13.

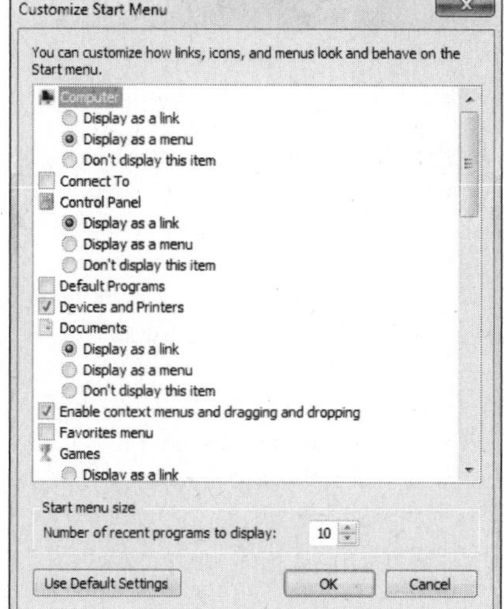

Figure 2-13: Change the behavior of the right side of the Start menu.

3. **Select or deselect the features you want to enable or disable.**

   Here's a quick guide to the bafflegab:

   - *Display As a Link* means that a link appears on the Start menu; click it and you get to your destination. Almost all items on the Start menu are displayed as links.
   - *Display As a Menu* shows the item as a fly-out menu. Normally, Games appears as a fly-out menu.
   - *Don't Display This Item* takes the entry off the Start menu.

   My recommendations are in Table 2-1.

4. **Click the OK button twice when you're done.**

   Take your new Start menu for a ride (see Figure 2-14).

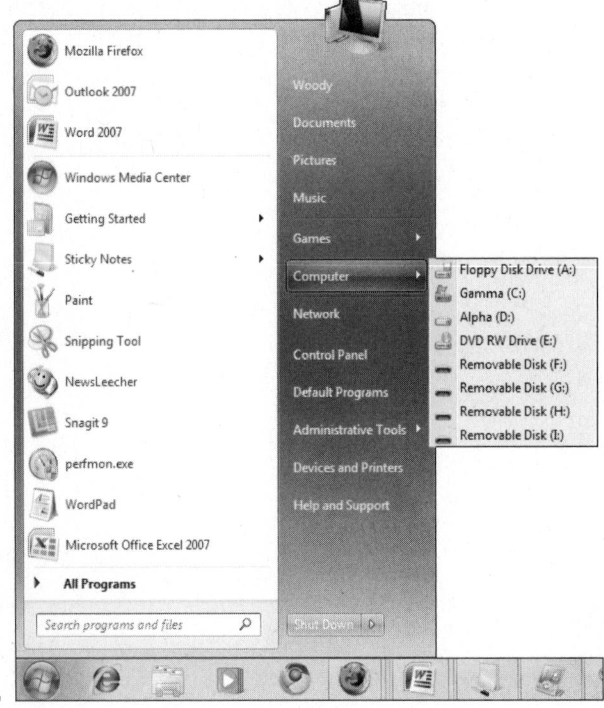

Figure 2-14: My Start menu, after the makeover in Table 2-1, showing the fly-out menu for the Computer item.

Table 2-1 Woody's Favorite Start Menu Settings

Start Item	*My Setting*	*Reason It's a Favorite*
Computer	Display As a Menu	Having a fly-out menu to show all my drives saves time.
Connect to	Unchecked	Useless. It just opens the same Network Connection notice that I can see by clicking the Network icon in the notification area.
Control Panel	Display As a Link	If you choose Display As a Menu, you get to wade through a zillion Control Panel applets. Wotta mess.
Default Programs	Checked	This setting provides an easy, quick way to change the program associated with a filename extension. If I ever ran out of room on the right side of the Start menu, this one would be the first to go.
Devices and Printers	Checked	Marvelously useful. See Book VIII, Chapter 1.
Documents	Display As a Link	The Display As a Menu option gets overwhelming.
Enable Context Menus and Drag/Drop	Checked	Of course.
Favorites Menu	Unchecked	Golly. Internet Explorer can show its Favorites on my Start menu — not.
Games	Display As a Menu	The list on my PC is fairly limited, so what the heck.
Help	Checked	Be it ever so humble, there's no place like Windows Help and Support.
Highlight Newly Installed Programs	Checked	Some people find this one a pain in the neck, but occasionally I want Windows to highlight programs that I just installed on the Start menu.
Music	Display As a Link	Same setting and same reason as for the Documents entry.
Network	Checked	It's a bit redundant because a full Network listing is on the left side of most Windows Explorer windows, but it doesn't hurt to have another way to create a list of all computers attached to the network.

(continued)

Table 2-1 *(continued)*

Start Item	*My Setting*	*Reason It's a Favorite*
Open Submenus When I Pause on Them	Checked	Gets in the way sometimes but generally useful.
Personal Libraries	Display As a Link	Windows is referring to the link in the upper-right corner of the Start menu that almost always shows your name. I never use it, but it's nice to have my name at the top so that I can tell quickly if I'm using a different account.
Pictures	Display As a Link	Same setting and same reason as for the Documents entry.
Recent Items	Unchecked	Some people love it, and others hate it. I hate it. The Jump Lists on the taskbar icons are plenty of recent item memory for me.
Recorded TV	Don't Display This Item	I don't record a lot of TV with Windows Media Center. If you do, you might want to show the item.
Run Command	Unchecked	It's the old Start⇨Run box, popular in Windows XP. You can do the same thing with the Search box — just click Start and type. Who needs ya, baby?
Search Other Fields and Libraries	Search with Public Folders	Why bother searching if you intentionally miss a place that's likely to contain what you want? See Book III, Chapter 3 for details.
Search Programs and Control Panel	Checked	This feature lets me get rid of the old Run box (see the Run Command entry).
Sort All Programs Menu by Name	Checked	Actually, Windows doesn't sort the menu by name (the programs appear above the folders), but I would have a devil of a time finding anything if it weren't sorted.
System Administrative Tools	Display on All Programs and Start	Heavens, yes, Martha! Why have all those wonderful tools and make it difficult to use them?
Use Large Icons	Checked	Small icons on the taskbar make me dizzy and turn my mouse finger twitchy.
Videos	Don't Display This Item	This option links to the Videos library. I don't use it often enough to take up the space.

Chapter 3: Searching Your Computer

In This Chapter

- Nailed it: Sorting through the search maze
- Controlling indexes and indexing
- Using Search settings
- Saving and reusing searches

Want to know my first reaction to Windows 7, after I played with the interface for about five minutes?

Yesssss! Microsoft finally — finally — fixed Search.

I had to find a document on my home server, like, really fast. I tried using Vista and just couldn't locate the stupid thing. So I switched over to Windows 7 and, in a matter of seconds, found the document.

Yesssss!

You may not be as easily impressed as I, but I've collected a bunch of screen shots over the years showing Windows Vista missing searches — simple searches that should've resulted in easy hits, passed over for some unknown reason or possibly no reason.

I'll never use Vista to search again. (I never *did* rely on Windows XP.) Search alone is reason enough for me to upgrade to Windows 7. True fact.

Even so, searches don't always go the way you probably expect. This chapter explains how to use the Windows 7 search features in ways that don't leave you scratching your head (or other parts of your anatomy). First check out the section "Searching Basics," which provides tips to find which search tools offer the best results. It also helps to know a little about what's going on under the hood — search quirks, which I translate into plain-English advice for you. If you're the tinkering sort, check out the section on twiddling with the search index settings. (The index is the brain behind the Windows search beast.) And last but not least, if you get lost searching for a must-have file, flip to the section near the end of this chapter, "Finding Files That Got Lost," which walks you through the progressively powerful arsenal of search-and-recovery tools available to you in the big, bad world of lost files.

If you want to understand how Windows *really* performs searches, you have to be able to see filename extensions — the short (usually three-letter) suffix of each file's name that identifies the file's type, such as `.doc` and `.jpg`. Windows 7 doesn't show you filename extensions unless you specifically tell it to. To make heads or tails out of anything in this chapter, make Windows show you filename extensions by following the steps I outline in Book II, Chapter 1.

Searching Basics

Maybe you need to find all the handouts you typed for your Porcine Prevaricators seminar. Maybe you remember that you have a recipe with tarragon in it but you can't remember where in the world you put it. Maybe you accidentally moved or deleted all the pictures of your trip to Cancun or Windows Media Player suddenly can't find your MP3s of the 1974 Grateful Dead tour.

Good. You're in the right place.

People generally go looking for files or folders on their computers for one of two reasons. Perhaps they vaguely remember that they used to have something — maybe a Christmas letter, a product description, or a great joke — and now they can't remember where they put it. Or, they have been playing around with Windows Explorer, and whatever they thought was sitting in a specific place isn't there any more. In either case, the solution is to make Windows 7 do the work and go searching for your lost files or folders.

Engaging your brain before the search

All the search engines in the world can't help until you have your act together. You can save a lot of time and frustration by following these suggestions:

- **Visualize exactly what you want.** Don't search for *lightning* if you're looking for *lightning bug*.
- **Know your tools.** The Windows 7 search engine works in mysterious ways, but you can increase your chances of finding what you want quickly if you accommodate the foibles of Windows 7. This chapter can help.
- **Narrow the search ahead of time.** You can easily create massive lists of files that match specific search criteria. But if you're looking for a file where *Woody* is the author, why search for all files?
- **Stay flexible.** If you keep typing the same search string, you keep receiving the same answers — guaranteed. Any idea how many different ways you can spell Shakespeare — correctly?

✦ **Use every trick in the book.** This book, of course.

Remember the First Law of Searching. *If you know where the file you desire might be located, navigate to the folder before you start the search.* For example, if you know that the file you want is inside the `\Documents\Invoices` folder, open that folder before you type the search argument (or arguments) in the search bar.

✦ *Corollary I:* If you're searching for an e-mail message, search from inside your e-mail program. That effectively restricts the scope of the search.

✦ *Corollary II:* If you're searching for a picture or video, use Windows Live Photo Gallery (see Book IV, Chapter 5). For a song, use Windows Media Player (or iTunes or Winamp or whichever player happens to ring your chimes). For a video, use Windows Media Center. The tools there are much better — aw, you get the idea.

Stepping through a basic search

Windows 7 packs Search boxes everywhere, most noticeably at the bottom of the Start menu and in the upper-right corner of every Windows Explorer window.

The example in this section focuses on searching from an Explorer window, although you can use the Start menu box with the steps as well. Note, however, that the Start menu Search box has a few extra peculiarities worth knowing. I explain them in the section "Searching from the Start menu," later in this chapter. Ahem.

If you type something in a Search box, Windows 7 immediately runs to the index, looking for matches in the current folder and all folders underneath the current folder. It searches for all kinds of files — documents and text files, of course, but also pictures and music, e-mail messages, and even the contents of Web pages.

The result frequently reminds me of listening for a specific conversation in a packed room — or in a mosh pit.

Here's a simple example of a relatively tame search:

1. **Choose Start⇨Documents.**

   Windows Explorer opens your Documents library.

2. **In the upper-right corner, where it says *Search,* type a word that might appear inside your Documents library or one of the subfolders of the folders in the library.**

Although there are exceptions (see the section, "What Windows can (and can't) find"), the word generally can

- *Be inside a file, if Windows 7 recognizes the file type*
- *Appear at the beginning of the filename*
- *Exist as a tag or other metadata, such as the author or artist attached to a file*

In Figure 3-1, I typed `adsl` and Windows 7 found all files in my Documents library (and its subfolders) that contain the text *adsl* or where *adsl* appears at the beginning of the filename or in a file's metadata.

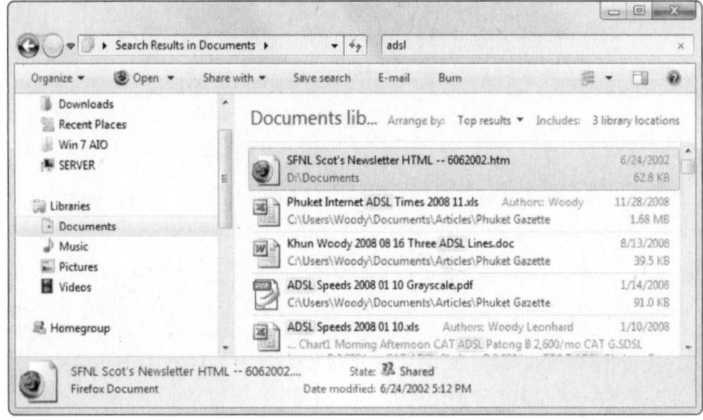

Figure 3-1: The Search box finds files in the current folder or library and all its subfolders.

3. **If you don't find what you seek, scroll to the bottom of the results list (see Figure 3-2), where you can choose to rerun your search in one of these spots:**

   - *All Libraries:* Goes after the contents of your Documents, Music, Pictures, and Videos libraries all at the same time.
   - *All shared folders on computers in your HomeGroup:* If you have a HomeGroup set up with other Windows 7 computers on your network (see Book VII, Chapter 1), Windows can automatically search all the locations accessible to the HomeGroup.
   - *The whole computer:* That can take some time, particularly in areas that aren't indexed (see the later section "Indexing for Fun and Profit").
   - *Selected locations:* If you think you're running the search on the wrong folders, it's usually faster to navigate to a different location and run the search from there. If you like, this option allows you to choose locations all over your computer.

- *The Internet:* If you can't find what you want on your computer, perhaps there's something on the Internet that can help. You can open your default Web browser and feed your default search provider the search criteria. In this case, on my PC, if I click the Internet icon, Windows launches Firefox (my default browser) and runs a Google search (my default search provider) for *adsl.* See Book V, Chapter 5 for details.

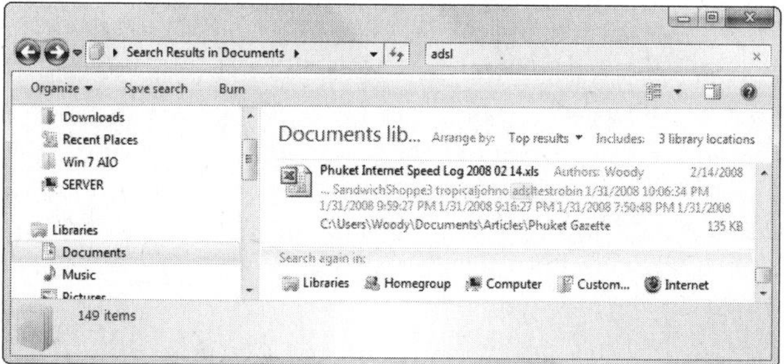

Figure 3-2: You can easily repeat the search, but in a different location.

4. **Alternatively, you can use the Boolean operators AND, OR, and NOT to further refine your search.**

   Check out the section "Adding Boolean operators to a search," later in this chapter. If you're feeling wild, check out the section on wildcard characters.

5. **As another alternative, you can search on metadata (which is to say, data attached to the file).**

   For example, Office documents have a piece of metadata named `author` that's supposed to contain the author's name. Thus, you can search for *adsl authors:woody*. Or, you can search for dates, sizes, and artists' aunts' middle names.

   See a discussion of this Advanced Query Syntax on the Microsoft site at `tinyurl.com/2nuk2n`. (If you've never used a Tinyurl before, type it into your Web browser's address box and you end up in the right place. It beats typing a verrrrry long address.)

What Windows can (and can't) find

Here's what I found, after hours of exhaustive testing, and even more hours of struggling with the Microsoft Party Line. You don't find this information in any manual:

The stuff you type in the Search box is treated differently, depending on whether Windows is looking at the contents of a file or looking at a filename. Suppose that you type `dummy` in the Search box. Here are the results you see:

- **When searching for filenames,** `dummy` matches any file with `dummy` appearing at the beginning of the filename, or any file where `dummy` appears in the filename after a space or period. So you get matches on `dummy.doc`, `dummy2.xls`, `Any dummy can type.pdf` and `some.dummy`. But you don't get a hit on `mydummy.doc` or `adummy.xlsx`.
- **When searching for file contents,** `dummy` matches any file that contains `dummy` at the beginning of a word. (Capitalization doesn't matter.) If you have a Word document that contains the sentence `this dummy doesn't know`, the document is a match, as is a spreadsheet with a cell that contains the word `dummytotal`. But a spreadsheet containing a cell that says `dodummy` or an e-mail message with `udummy` doesn't match.

If your searches don't work the way you think they should, make sure that you haven't run afoul of Windows 7 search's limitations. Don't go looking for `dummy` if you really want `udummy`. You won't find it.

Your search options settings (and the list of locations included in the Windows 7 index) have an enormous influence on what can be found and what will appear in the search results. If you can't find a file that you know must be on your PC, check your options.

Adding Boolean operators to a search

Boolean operators give the Windows search hamster (or dog — remember Rover, the old Search Companion pooch?) special instructions, and you can use them to refine your search queries. For example:

- If I search on `adsl OR provider`, Windows finds a match on any file that contains either the term `adsl` (which can be capitalized any way) or the term `provider`.
- Whereas OR expands a search, AND narrows it, requiring that both terms be in a file before a match occurs.
- And NOT is, well, NOT.

For reasons known only to Microsoft, the Boolean operators have to be capitalized. If you search for `adsl or provider`, you see a list of all files with `adsl` or `or` or `provider`.

Not surprisingly, you can also use quotes in the search string — `"adsl provider"` turns up only documents in which `adsl` and `provider` appear next to each other, separated by a space. You can also use parentheses:

`muffin AND (blueberry OR banana)` matches documents that have the word `muffin`, and in addition to `muffin` the doc must have either `blueberry` or `banana` or both. Some people get all caught up in this stuff.

Breaking out the wildcard characters

Since the Dawn of DOS (somebody should write a book with that title), searches have employed special characters commonly called *wildcards*. The most common wildcard is an asterisk: *. When you type an asterisk in any search, you're telling the search engine "match any number of characters of any kind" before matching whatever comes next — it's the "don't care" of the search string business.

Except. Except Windows 7 doesn't quite work that way.

When you type an asterisk in a Windows 7 Search box, Windows uses the characters following the asterisk to match any part of a filename. Permit me another example. If you type `*dum` in a Windows 7 Search box, here's what happens:

- Windows looks inside files for the text dum, but the text has to appear at the beginning of a word. Thus, you find matches on files that contain the words `dumb` and `dumber`, but there's no match on files with the words `tadum` or `ridumcowboy`.
- Windows scans filenames and matches any file that has the characters `dum` in its filename. For example, you get a hit on `madum.txt` and `some.dummy` and `anotherdumbexcuse.ppt`. But you don't get a hit on `du.mht`.

To put it another way, if you search for `*exe`, you get all the files that end with the `.exe` filename extension, as you might expect, but you also get `hexen.com`.

Caveat searchor.

Searching from the Start menu

When you click the Windows 7 Start button, you can immediately type in the Start Search bar and have Windows 7 look for the text you type.

You can change the way the Start Search bar behaves, but only in a limited way. Here's how:

1. **Right-click the Start button and choose Properties.**

   Windows 7 shows you the Taskbar and Start Menu Properties dialog box.

2. **At the top, next to the Start Menu label, click the Customize button.**

   Windows 7 shows you the Customize Start Menu dialog box, shown in Figure 3-3.

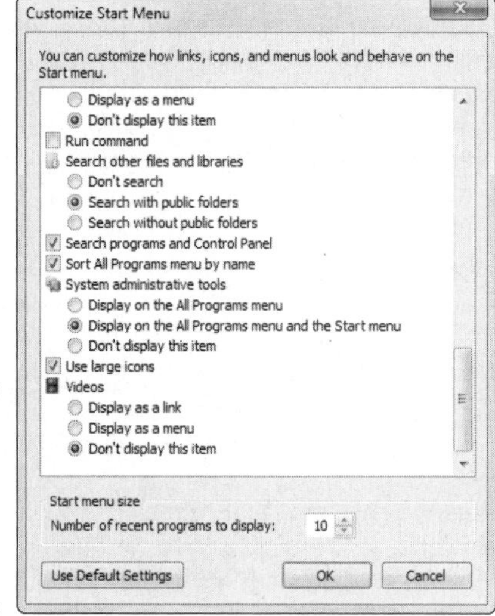

Figure 3-3: Change the Start menu Search bar behavior.

   I discuss the Customize Start Menu dialog box at length in Book III, Chapter 2.

3. **In the Customize Start Menu dialog box, you have these options:**

   - *Choose Don't Search:* The Search bar no longer appears above the Start button.
   - *Choose Search with (or without) Public Folders:* Include (exclude) the folders under the `Public` folder in the search results.

   You might want to choose Search without Public Folders if you have a lot of items in your public folders that you never want to access from the Start menu.

4. **Click OK twice.**

   Your changes take effect immediately.

Note that these changes to the Start Menu Properties dialog box affect only the way the Start menu Search bar acts. Changes here have no effect on other kinds of search in Windows 7.

If you type in the Start Search bar and press Enter, the Windows 7 reaction depends on the results you can see at that point. If the results include any programs or Control Panel applets, Windows 7 runs the top program on the list when you press Enter. If the results don't include any programs, pressing Enter throws you into a simple search, covering everything in the Windows 7 search index, as shown in Figure 3-4. Note that the search shown in the figure covers all indexed locations — it isn't tied to a particular folder or library.

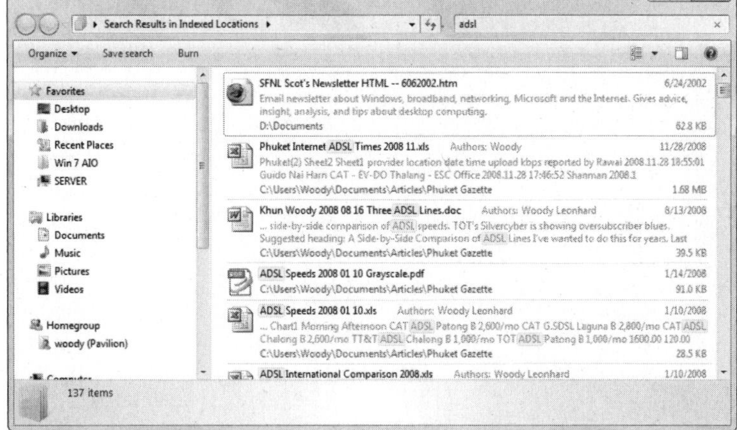

Figure 3-4: A full search that started in the Start menu.

Indexing for Fun and Profit

At the heart of the Windows 7 search feature sits the index. Much like the index in this book, the Windows 7 index stores references to the book's contents. If you're looking for information about the taskbar, check the index in the back of this book and you're directed to pages x, y, and z (and this page, too, for that matter).

Similarly, if you tell the Start menu's Search bar to look for the word *water,* Windows 7 consults its index and knows more or less immediately that your computer has a bunch of matching entries, as you can see in Figure 3-5.

Building an index takes time, and maintaining an index can put quite a strain on your computer. Windows 7 watches specific folders on your computer (and a few on your network) and updates the index only when it has to. A short delay can occur between the time you change a file and the time the index is updated.

Windows 7 index doesn't include every item from every file on your computer: You wouldn't want to index, oh, the text of Windows warning messages or the patterns of bits inside picture or music files.

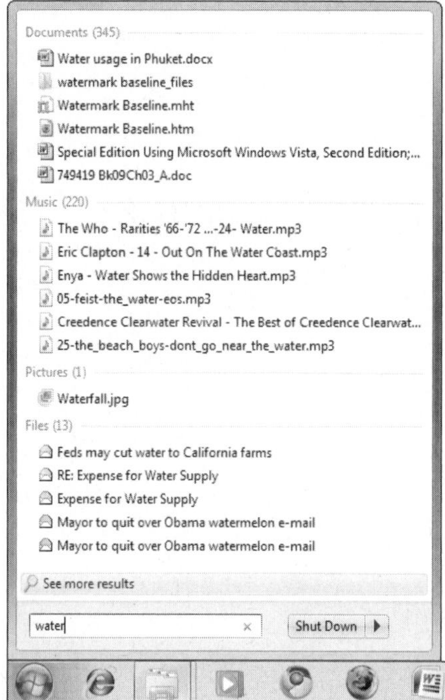

Figure 3-5: A Start menu search for the word *water.*

On the other hand, you *do* want the indexer to look at files that you're likely to go searching for. Scanning the index takes seconds. Scanning your unindexed files — looking through them, character by painful character — can take hours. Or years.

Thus, the indexing dilemma: What should Windows 7 incorporate into the index, and what can be safely left aside?

When Windows 7 builds and maintains its index, it keeps track of the files going into and being removed from specific locations on your computer. When a file is added or removed from one of the locations that the indexer tracks, Windows 7 looks to see whether the file type (which is to say, if the filename extension for the file) is on the list of file types that the indexer is supposed to index. Then, and only then, is the file added to the index.

You have control over both processes:

- ✦ Tell Windows 7 to look in specific locations for files it should index.
- ✦ Tell Windows 7 that it should or should not index specific filename extensions.

The rest of this section goes into details.

Goodbye scanning, hello-o-o-o (improved) indexing

You have two fundamentally different ways of looking for information on a computer:

- **Scanning:** Involves looking through each file, one by one, and trying to find what you're looking for. Think of Diogenes walking through the marketplace of Athens, in broad daylight, with a lantern, seeking an honest man. Sometimes Windows 7 stumbles upon the things you seek. Sometimes it doesn't. Every time, it takes forever.
- **Indexing:** Involves digesting the contents of your computer and maintaining a list, not unlike the index in the back of this book. When you have to find an honest man, you needn't walk through the marketplace. You just look under H in the Athens Yellow Pages, eh?

In principle, indexing is pretty simple: The computer waits until you aren't doing anything; then it starts looking, methodically, at every file on your hard drive (or drives). Say the computer's looking at a file named `Woody da Dummy.doc`. Inside the file, the computer discovers the words *jumping jack flash.* It builds an index entry that says, among other things, "The word *jumping* is in `Woody da Dummy.doc`." Then it builds another index entry that says, "The word *jack* is in `Woody da Dummy.doc`." And so on. When you ask for all files that contain the word *jack,* any program looking at the index realizes immediately that `Woody da Dummy.doc` should be included on the list.

In practice, indexing is one whole heckuvalot more difficult than you might imagine. The biggest problem Microsoft had, for years, was the intrusiveness of the bloody indexer: You'd be typing along, pause a few seconds to think, and — WHAM! — all of a sudden, this crazy program had taken over your machine. Resume typing, and you had to wait an eternity to regain control of your PC. That situation has improved significantly in Windows 7. Really. A good discussion of the techniques involved is on the Microsoft Engineering Windows 7 blog at `tinyurl.com/3mdfs4` and a learned white paper at `tinyurl.com/b3r4j2`.

Setting index file type options

The Windows 7 indexer keeps track of filenames, various file properties (for example, the day it was created or modified or viewed), most other *metadata* that's assigned to the file (author, tags, star rating, artist), and in some cases the contents of the file itself.

Windows 7 indexes files based on their filename extensions. (Another reason to show filename extensions, eh?) For each filename extension that Windows 7 recognizes, you can tell the indexer to

- **Ignore all files with that particular filename extension.** The ignored files, their filenames, properties, other metadata, and contents never make it into the index.

- **Index only the filename, file property information, and other metadata.**
- **Index the filename, information, other metadata, and the contents of the file.** To index the contents, Windows 7 must have a program — a *filter* — available to look inside that particular kind of file and retrieve its contents.

You can't pick and choose the specific file information and other metadata to be indexed: It's an all-or-nothing issue.

By and large, the Windows 7 choices for indexing make a lot of sense. In particular, if you install Adobe Acrobat or Adobe Reader to look at PDF files, Windows 7 takes advantage of the Adobe filter to index the contents of all PDF files in the areas of your hard drive that get indexed. (See the next section, "Adding locations to the index.") RSS feeds are indexed, too (see Book V, Chapter 3), as are Rich Text Format (RTF) files and the titles of pages in the `Internet Explorer Favorites` and `History` folders.

If you don't want to index a particular kind of file, or if you want to tell Windows 7 to index only the file information and other metadata for a particular type of file, ignoring the contents, making a change is easy. Here's how:

1. **Choose Start, immediately type** index**, and press Enter.**

   You see the Indexing Options dialog box.

2. **Click the button marked Advanced, provide an administrator account name and password if necessary, and then click the File Types tab.**

   Windows 7 shows you the File Types dialog box, shown in Figure 3-6.

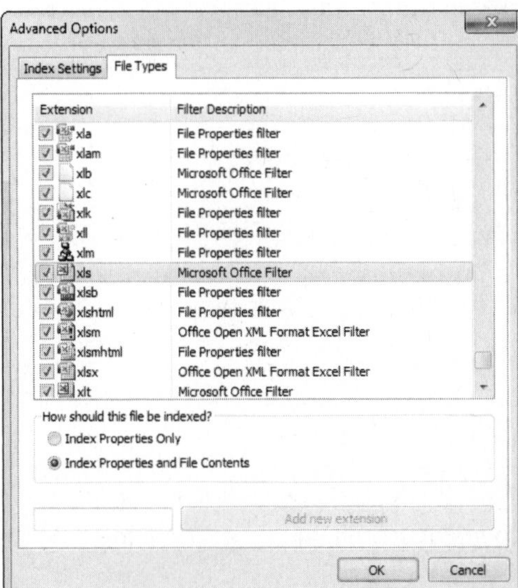

Figure 3-6: Indexing options listed by filename extension.

3. **If you want to stop indexing a particular kind of file, deselect the box next to the filename extension.**

If you elect to remove a filename extension from the indexing list, Windows 7 goes back and rebuilds the entire index. Although in theory the reindexing should take place in the background without interrupting your work, in practice you find that your machine frequently slows to a crawl. Remove a file type from the index only when you're ready to take a *very* long break.

4. **Click the filename extension for the type of file you want to have indexed differently. At the bottom, choose either Index Properties Only or Index Properties and File Contents.**
5. **When you're done, click OK.**

   New items are indexed immediately, give or take a minute or two.

Adding locations to the index

The Windows 7 indexer doesn't even look at a file unless it's in one of the locations you chose — or, more frequently, one of the locations that was chosen for you.

The depth and breadth of folders that have been selected for you differ depending on which applications you installed. The computer I used to shoot Figure 3-4, earlier in this chapter, has both Outlook 2007 and Windows Live Mail. Your mileage may vary.

Unless you use Outlook or Windows Live Mail, indexing of e-mail is *not* a given: Each e-mail program works differently. Note that e-mail indexing works only if the mail sits on your computer. If you use Gmail or Hotma — er, Windows Live Mail or Yahoo Mail or AOL Mail, Windows 7 indexing doesn't help one whit.

Note the entry in Figure 3-4 for the Start menu. Windows 7 indexes all files in the All Users Start Menu folder (`c:\Program Data\Microsoft\Windows\Start Menu`) and all the individual user's Start Menu folders (`C:\Users\<username>\AppData\Roaming\Microsoft\Windows\Start Menu`).

Why index the contents of the Start menus? That way, the Windows 7 search engine picks up the programs and systems that you expect it to find.

It may not be obvious, but the indexer picks up all folders in all libraries for all users. Yes, it even indexes folders on network drives, as long as the folders are part of one user's Documents, Music, Pictures, or Videos library. Want to add more folders to the index? That's a common situation for advanced users, who might store indexable files in locations other than in the Documents library.

The easiest way to add a folder to the index is to simply add the folder to a library. Choose Start⇨Documents (or Music or whatever), click the Library Locations link in the upper right corner, and add the folder. Yes, you can add folders out on your network, if you have one, and they're indexed too.

If you don't want to add the folder to a library, you can manually add the folder to the index — but only if the folder is on your computer. You can't manually add networked folders. Here's how to make it so:

1. **Wait until you can leave your computer alone for a few hours. Or overnight.**

   Indexing a big folder can take a long time.

2. **Choose Start, immediately type index, and press Enter.**

   Windows 7 shows you the Indexing Options dialog box.

3. **Click the Modify button.**

   Windows shows you the Indexed Locations dialog box.

4. **In the upper panel, click the arrows next to the drives that contain the folders you want to add. Select the check boxes next to the folders. When you're done, click OK.**

   Windows 7 wheezes and moans and indexes the locations you picked.

Using Advanced Search Settings

Most Windows 7 users want and need the default search settings that Microsoft built into the search feature. Some people, though, find Windows 7 search too slow or not thorough enough.

It's easy enough to change several search parameters — for example, you can tell Windows 7 to search exclusively for file names, and not file contents — but there are consequences to any changes you may make. Make sure you understand the benefits and drawbacks to any search modifications before you make them. Else, you may find yourself looking for a needle in a field of electronic haystacks.

Here's how to change the default simple search settings:

1. **Choose Start⇨Documents. In the upper-left area, click the down-arrow next to Organize. Choose Folder and Search Options. Select the Search tab.**

   You see the Search options, shown in Figure 3-7.

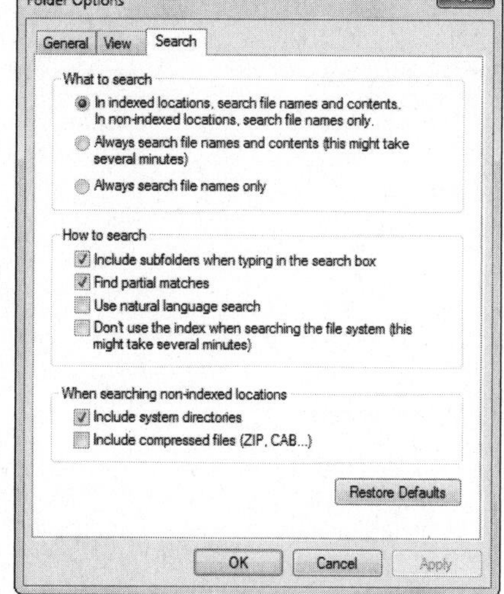

Figure 3-7: One of the most confusing dialog boxes in all of Windows 7 — dumb.

2. **Use the tips in Table 4-1 to make any changes to the Windows 7 search options.**

   Remember that altering the settings here can make all your searches painfully slow.

3. **When you're happy with the results, click OK.**

   The settings apply to any new simple searches you may make.

Table 4-1 Search Options

Setting	*What It Means*	*Recommendation*
In indexed locations, search filenames and contents. In non-indexed locations, search filenames only.	Windows 7 looks for filenames and, in addition, contents for file types you have chosen (refer to Figure 3-5).	You probably want to pick this setting.
Always search filenames and contents (might be slow).	Ignore the index and crawl through the contents of every file in the current folder and its subfolders.	Slow isn't the right term — try *glacial.* If you use this option more than once, modify the index using the method described in "Adding locations to the index," earlier in this chapter.

(continued)

Table 4-1 *(continued)*

Setting	*What It Means*	*Recommendation*
Always search filenames only	It looks exclusively at filenames, ignoring file contents, properties, and other metadata.	This is the Windows XP approach. If you can live with it, results appear much faster, but most people need (and are willing to wait for) the full text search.
Include subfolders when typing in the Search box.	Windows 7 looks in the current folder and subfolders, as described elsewhere in this chapter.	Leave the check box selected.
Find partial matches.	Match anywhere in the word (but see the section "What Windows can (and can't) find," earlier in this chapter).	Leave the check box selected.
Use natural language search.	You can type search strings in a less structured way. For example, if you select this check box, you can type `by Woody` and Windows 7 retrieves everything with *Woody* listed as author.	If you select this check box, you can still use "regular" searches, but sometimes Windows 7 gets confused. I leave the option deselected. *And* I talk funny.
Don't use the index when searching the file system (might be slow).	Ignore the index entirely.	You can use this setting if you think your index is broken, but otherwise don't select the check box.
Include system directories.	Include system folders when searching for files.	If you commonly search for system files and you don't want to navigate to `c:\Windows` before initiating every search, this setting can help.
Include compressed files (ZIP or CAB, for example)	Look at the filenames of the files inside compressed (ZIP and CAB) files, which are normally ignored by the indexer.	Select the check box, if you like, but realize that a performance hit occurs when Windows 7 scans the files inside zip files. If the file is in an indexed location, both the filename and its contents are indexed by default.

Finding Files That Got Lost

Wish I had a nickel for every time people ask me why Windows stole their files. The story always goes like this: "Woody, I used to have a whole bunch of important files in `Documents\Someplace`, and now they're gone! What did Windows 7 do with them?"

Oy.

When you discover that your files are lost, save yourself a lot of time and headaches and remember that there are only four possibilities:

- ✦ You moved them somewhere (probability: 90 percent).
- ✦ You deleted them, and they're still available (probability: 9 percent).
- ✦ You permanently deleted them and it's difficult, but probably not impossible, to get them back (Probability: less than 1 percent).
- ✦ Little green men broke into your office in the middle of the night and ate them (Probability: varies).

First, don't panic

If you suddenly discover that some of your files are "lost," here's the fastest, most reliable way to get them back:

1. **Don't panic.**

   Douglas Adams' sage advice pertains.

2. **Don't create any new files or delete any existing ones.**

   Do not choose this particular moment to defragment your hard drive. Even when you "permanently" delete a file, all the data remains on your disk until it's overwritten.

3. **Open Windows Explorer (choose Start⇨Documents or Start⇨Computer) and look at the folders near the one that used to contain the "lost" files.**

   Chances are very good that you accidentally moved the files while you were using Explorer. Accidentally dragging a bunch of files to a nearby folder is easy. If you go back to the scene of the crime, you may be able to retrace what went wrong.

4. **Run Search to find one of the lost files.**

   Don't bother trying to find all lost files at the same time. Just look for one of them. With a little luck, you can remember something unique about one lost file's name, or part of a name, or some of the data inside.

5. **If you find one of the lost files, right-click the filename and choose Open File Location. If the files (or file) are in a regular, everyday folder, select them, right-click, and choose Cut. Navigate back to where they belong. Right-click and choose Paste.**
6. **If that doesn't work, take a chill break and continue with the next section.**

Second, get determined

If you can't find the files by making a simple search, it's time to haul out the big guns. Or at least the bigger guns:

1. **Go to your desktop and double-click the Recycle Bin icon.**

   Windows brings up the contents of the Recycle Bin. Any files you deleted are probably there.
2. **Scan the Recycle Bin for your lost file.**

   You already tried searching, but maybe you didn't spell the name exactly right — the Achilles heel of searches. A little bit of eyeballing might turn up the culprit. Usually it's fastest to look at the most recently deleted items first. To do so, click the More Options icon near the upper right area and choose Details. Then click the Date Deleted column heading.
3. **If you find the lost files, select them and click the button marked Restore This Item (or These Items).**
4. **If that still doesn't work, shut down your machine and go buy a file recovery program.**

   Even if you "permanently" deleted a file, its remnants remain and can frequently be put back together. Norton Utilities has long been the product of choice for undeleting files, but it has dozens of competitors, all of which basically do the same thing. It's important that you follow the instructions precisely in order to maximize your chances of getting your file back. I talk about using the free program Recuva in my *Phuket Gazette* computer column, at `tinyurl.com/cwt4f6`.
5. **If you still can't find the file and no suspicious green men are lurking about and you're willing to spend many hundreds of dollars getting your data back, look for a data recovery company.**

   These folks can scan every bit on your hard drive and bring seemingly lost files back from the dead. Here's the best way to find a data recovery company, short of a recommendation from a satisfied customer: Go to Google (`google.com`) and search on the phrase *data recovery services.*

Chapter 4: Beating and Cheating Windows 7 Games

In This Chapter

- Playing the Windows 7 games
- Beating the Windows 7 games
- Cheating the Windows 7 games

The real reason you bought this book is because you heard it had all the game cheats, isn't it? C'mon, admit it.

If your boss doesn't like for you to play games on the company PC, just remind her that Windows games are, singularly, the best way to brush up on your mousing skills, take your mind off work for a brief spell, and take a break from all the typing. How do you spell *repetitive motion syndrome?*

Windows 7 Home Premium ships with 11 games installed (see Figure 4-1), many of which are quite good. If you can't see all the games, and your network administrator hasn't blocked them, you may be able to retrieve some by choosing Start⇨Control Panel⇨Programs⇨Turn Windows Features On or Off and selecting the appropriate check boxes in the Games category.

If you played games in Vista — which had nine built-in games — you probably don't lament the passing of InkBall. But I bet you'll like the three new Internet games Backgammon, Checkers, and Spades. Windows XP had older versions of all three, and the new versions work even better: You can choose your own skill level and be matched up with a randomly selected opponent.

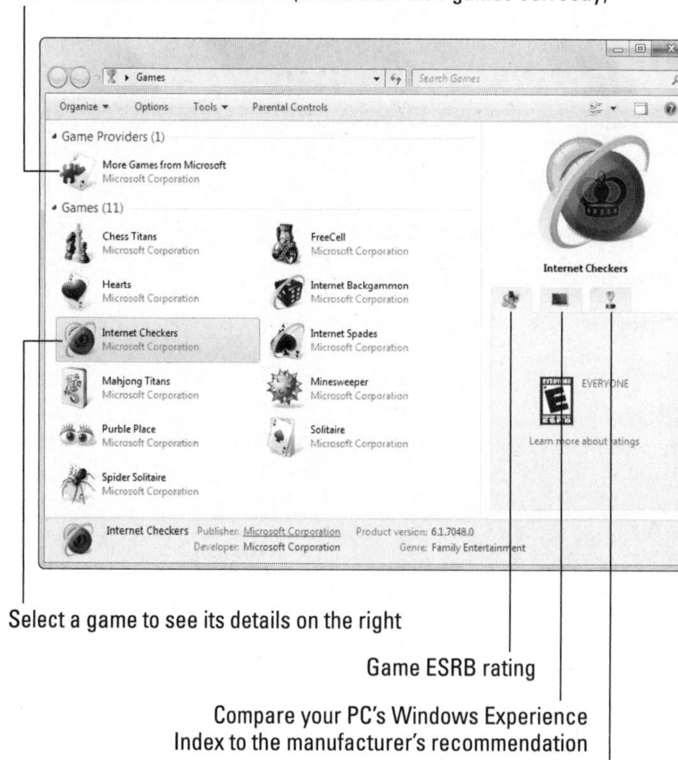

Figure 4-1: Windows 7 games range from kid-friendly to utterly fiendish.

Get Yer Games Goin'

The first time you click Start⇨Games, Windows 7 asks whether you want to check automatically for game updates (see Figure 4-2).

I personally have no problem with the games' Automatically Check Online for Updates and News setting. (See Book VI, Chapter 4 for analogous "Check but don't install" settings for Windows as a whole.) But your situation may be different from mine:

✦ **I don't run any pirate games.** If you have a pirate/ripped-off/un-genuine game, or a game from a dubious source, installed on your computer and you elect to have Windows check for updates, a small amount of information (specifically, your Internet connection's IP address, at least) is sent to the game manufacturer. Hard to say how that information could be used, but with all the data mining going on, you can never tell.

- **I don't take notification as gospel.** If Windows tells me that an update is available, I always check online, before installing, to see whether people are having problems with it.
- **I'm relatively immune to Microsoft exhortations to spend more money.** Wading through advertising, in the form of upgrade notifications or "special offers from our partners," doesn't rankle: My X click reflexes are well honed.

If you can stick to those three points, you're a good candidate for having Windows automatically check (but not install!) game updates.

Sometimes I leave the Collect Most Recently Played Game Information check box deselected because I hate to be reminded of my (manifest) gaming shortcomings. Usually, though, I check it and resign myself to the muffled guffaws of anyone looking over my shoulder. Your mileage may vary.

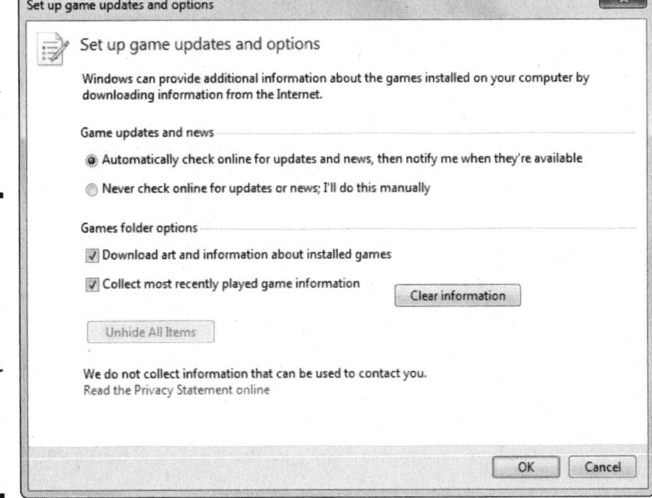

Figure 4-2: Windows checks automatically to see whether your games need updating.

After you set your options, every subsequent time you click Start⇨Games, Windows opens the specialized Games Explorer viewing pane (refer to Figure 4-1).

You can change those options at any time by clicking the Options button at the top of the Games Explorer.

Solitaire

The venerable classic Solitaire, the oldest Windows game (see Figure 4-3) — dating back to the prehistory of Windows 3.0 — still captures the hearts and spare cranial cycles of millions. To get it going, choose Start➪Games and double-click the Solitaire icon. (Or, you can take the express train: Click Start, immediately type `sol`, and press Enter.) But you've probably done that a hundred times already, haven't you?

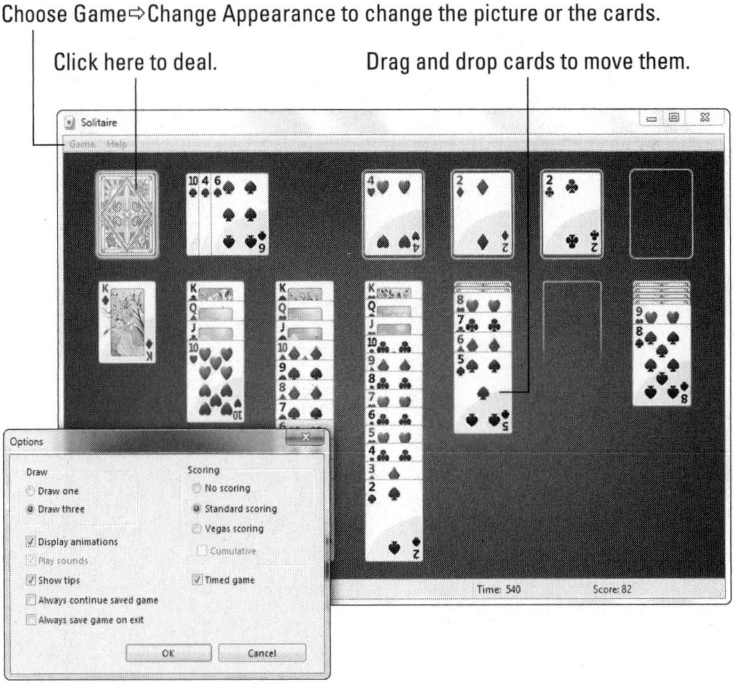

Choose Game➪Change Appearance to change the picture or the cards.

Click here to deal.

Drag and drop cards to move them.

Figure 4-3: Windows Solitaire, the mother of all Windows games.

If you don't know the general rules for Solitaire, ask the guy sitting next to you on your next flight. The Windows version of Solitaire has a few wrinkles:

- ✦ It doesn't let you pull a card from inside a stack, but it lets you move a card (other than an ace) from one of the suit stacks back to the playing table.
- ✦ It lets you undo any move or group of moves by pressing Ctrl+Z. After you undo, you can't redo.
- ✦ It lets you put only kings in open stacks.

You probably know that if you double-click a card that's eligible to be placed on a suit stack, Windows moves the card for you. But you probably don't know that if you press Ctrl+A or right-click the playing table, Windows moves all eligible cards from the main playing table to the suit stacks. It's a cool, quick way to perform the *coup de grace* if you have all the cards turned over and just want to watch the grand display at the end.

Solitaire can give you a hint, if you want it: Press H. Just don't expect a good hint. Many times, Solitaire overlooks perfectly legitimate moves. Solitaire's advice comes free. It's worth every penny.

If you press H and you like the suggested move, push Enter and Solitaire performs the move for you.

Scoring a Solitaire game makes cricket look like child's play. To select a scoring option, choose Game⇨Options to see the Options dialog box (refer to Figure 4-3).

Standard scoring

Solitaire standard scoring goes like this:

- ✦ Add 5 points when you move a card off the deck or turn over a card.
- ✦ Add 10 points when you move a card to a suit stack.
- ✦ Subtract 15 points when you return a card from a suit stack to the playing table. (Note that if you press Ctrl+Z to undo a move, you lose the points from only that move.)
- ✦ By choosing the Draw Three option (see the Options dialog box in Figure 4-3), you can flip through the deck three times with no penalty, and then you lose 20 points every additional time.
- ✦ Using the Draw One option, you can flip through the deck once with no penalty, and then you lose 100 points every additional time.

- ✦ In a timed game, you lose 2 points every 10 seconds, but the size of a bonus awarded at the end of the game depends on how quickly you finish. (You earn no bonus points if the game lasted less than 30 seconds; if it lasted more than 30 seconds, you earn a bonus of 700,000 divided by the number of seconds.) According to Microsoft, the highest possible score is 24,113.

ASKWOODY.COM

Using standard scoring, you earn a bonus if you can move a card from the deck to the main playing table (5 points) and from there to the suit stack (an additional 10 points, for a total of 15) rather than move a card straight from the deck to the suit stack (which scores only 10 points).

If you use the Draw Three option, a cheat is available that allows you to turn over one card at a time. If you press Ctrl+Alt+Shift and then click the deck, Windows turns over one card at a time. If you're using standard scoring and use this trick, you can turn over every card in the deck three times before Windows sticks you with the 20-point-per-deck penalty.

Vegas scoring

Vegas scoring is simpler to explain — but harder to master. When you start a Vegas game, you "pay" the house $52. Every time you move a card to a suit stack, you "make" $5. That's all there is to it.

Using the Draw Three option (refer to the radio button in Figure 4-3), you can flip through the deck three times. Using the Draw One option, you flip through only once.

The Ctrl+Alt+Shift cheat for standard scoring also works for Vegas scoring, but in a different way: If you press Ctrl+Alt+Shift and click the deck, Windows turns over one card at a time. If you use the Ctrl+Alt+Shift trick and turn over one card at a time, you can flip through the entire deck three times — a boon for Vegas scorekeeping.

FreeCell

FreeCell, Microsoft's first Solitaire variant, mimics the card game of the same name. To get it going, choose Start⇨Games and double-click the FreeCell icon. (The result is shown in Figure 4-4.)

Game play in FreeCell resembles "regular" Solitaire in several ways:

- ✦ You try to expose aces, moving them to one of the upper-right suit stacks; after you start a stack with an ace, you build each stack sequentially, with a two, three, four, and so on.
- ✦ You can move a card at the bottom of a column so that it sits on top of a card that's one position higher in rank and of the opposite color, much like playing "regular" Solitaire.
- ✦ You can move a card from the bottom of a column to an empty slot in the upper-left corner of the table.
- ✦ You can move any free card to an empty column on the table. (Some people mistakenly believe that you can move only kings. Not so. Any card can be moved to an empty row.)

You can find a detailed explanation of the rules, along with a step-by-step example, at `www.solitairelaboratory.com/tutorial.html`.

Park your cards here.

Stack cards in order here.

Add cards to columns, as in classic Solitaire.

Figure 4-4: FreeCell should stimulate a few more gray cells.

Like Solitaire, FreeCell has a help function: just press the H key. As in Solitaire, the help isn't always good help. (FreeCell has a nasty habit of moving the same card back and forth between the same locations.) If you press H and then immediately press Enter, FreeCell makes the recommended move for you.

FreeCell lets you replay the same hands, over and over, by assigning numbers to specific starting-card combinations. To play hand number 50,000, for example, choose Games⇨Select Game, type **50000**, and click the OK button. That's a nifty trick if you want to play the same hand at home and then do it again at work, or if you want to challenge a friend on a different machine to a duel.

The Windows 7 version of FreeCell supports hands numbered from 1 to 1,000,000 — which should keep you rather well occupied. You also find four additional, fascinating, symmetrical hands, numbered –1, –2, –3, and –4. Games –1 and –2 can't be won. Games –3 and –4 win all by themselves: Just drag an ace onto one of the suit stacks, and Windows takes care of the rest.

All hands numbered from 1 to 1,000,000 are winnable, except for the eight hands 11,982, 146,692, 186,216, 455,889, 495,505, 512,118, 517,776, and 781,948 (and, of course, –1 and –2). Yes, some people study these things. No, they don't have lives. (Hey, I was a mathematician too, in a previous lifetime.) See Michael Keller's incredibly thorough analysis at `solitairelaboratory.com/fcfaq.html`.

FreeCell keeps track of how many hands you won and lost, and the length of your current winning (or losing) streak. To see the scores, choose Game➪Statistics. You see a list like the one shown in Figure 4-5.

Figure 4-5: FreeCell keeps tabs, but you can stack the deck.

What's the easiest way to run up your winning statistics? Play a whole bunch of games using hands numbered –3 and –4. You don't need to finish the game to have it show up as a win. Simply drag an ace onto one of the suit stacks and wait for the cards to start crashing against the bottom of the screen. Then choose Game➪Select Game, and you'll rack up another effortless win.

Windows 7 stores your FreeCell scores in the file `C:\Users\<username>\AppData\Local\Microsoft Games\FreeCell\FreeCellSettings.xml`. If you're feeling adventurous, you can try to hack your way to a breathtaking score. I haven't figured out how to alter the file and still get FreeCell to open it — I think Microsoft (more accurately, Oberon Games, which did the programming) has some sort of checksum buried in the file. If you figure out how to crack it, shoot me an e-mail, okay? It's `Woody@AskWoody.com`.

Spider Solitaire

When you get the hang of it, Spider Solitaire is every bit as addictive as its two older Windows Solitaire siblings. Get Spider going by choosing Start➪Games and double-clicking the Spider Solitaire icon.

The easiest way to learn to play Spider Solitaire is to start with a single suit — Spider gives you that option when you start. Basically, you have to move cards around in descending order (see Figure 4-6), and you can mix and match suits to your heart's content (pun intended). When you have a descending sequence (from *K* to *A*) in a single suit, the entire sequence is removed. When you get stuck, click the Spider card deck and Spider Solitaire deals another row of cards.

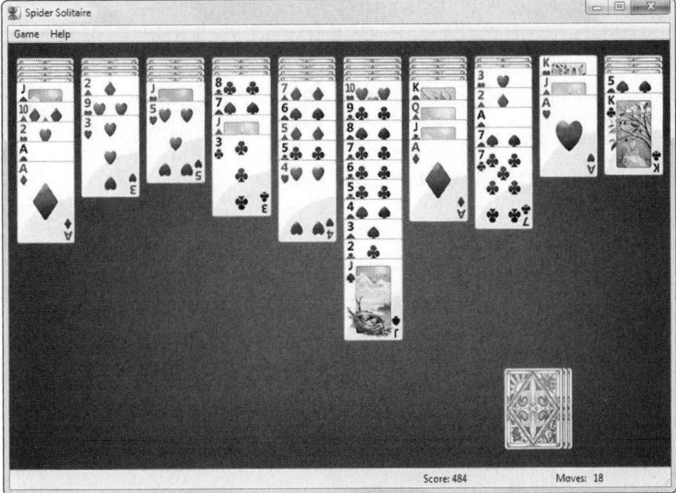

Figure 4-6: In Spider Solitaire, you mix suits in intermediate steps, but ultimately match them to win.

As in FreeCell, Windows 7 stores your Spider scores in `C:\Users\<username>\AppData\Local\Microsoft Games\Spider Solitaire\SpiderSolitaireSettings.xml`. I had very little luck hacking that file, but you may be able to crack it.

Even experts say that four-suit Spider Solitaire rates high on the "can't win and can't get ahead" scale. Two-suit hands can be won consistently with practice, but even the best Spider players succeed, at most, one in four hands with the four-suit variation.

If you don't like the way the cards were dealt, you can press F2 before moving any cards and Spider Solitaire deals again — without adding a loss to your statistics.

Like Solitaire and FreeCell, Spider Solitaire has a Help function: Just press H. As in Solitaire, the help isn't always good help — building out lines isn't always the best strategy. If you press H and then immediately press Enter, Spider Solitaire makes the recommended move for you.

Minesweeper

One of the simplest, most absorbing games ever created — and a longtime personal favorite of Bill Gates — Minesweeper has been around since the days of Windows 3.1.

The concept is simple: Click a square and a number appears, indicating the number of adjacent squares that contain mines (see Figure 4-7). (The Intermediate level is discussed later in this section.) Click a square that contains a mine and you lose. Play against the clock.

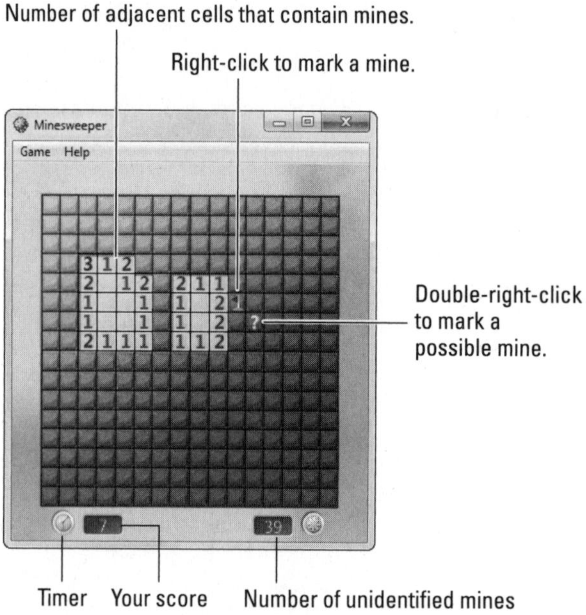

Number of adjacent cells that contain mines.

Right-click to mark a mine.

Double-right-click to mark a possible mine.

Timer

Your score

Number of unidentified mines

Figure 4-7: The Intermediate Minesweeper playing field.

The Windows 7 version of Minesweeper includes a kinder, gentler face — a flower garden, optionally played on a green field — that you can summon by choosing Game➪Change Appearance.

If you've never tried Minesweeper, you're in for a treat — even inveterate computer-game-haters take a liking to this one.

Minesweeper holds oodles of options:

✦ Click Game➪Options and choose from Beginner (a 9-x-9-box playing field with 10 mines), Intermediate (a 16-x-16 field with 40 mines), and Expert (16 x 30 with 99 mines). Minesweeper automatically keeps high-score figures for each level. Alternatively, you can tell Minesweeper how many squares you want to see and how many mines should be scattered on the field.

✦ If you think a square contains a mine, and you want to, uh, remind yourself of that fact, right-click the square. A flag appears, warning you that you figure a mine sits right there (or, at least, you thought there was a mine there, at some point in the past). If you found a mine, Minesweeper reduces by one the mine count in the lower-right corner.

✦ Right-click the same square a second time and you plant a question mark on the square. Question marks are good to remind you that you once thought a mine was there, and maybe you ought to click the sucker to see whether it blows up. Right-click the square a third time and it goes back to normal.

Whenever you want to see the best times and who holds the records, choose Game⇨Statistics.

It's easy to "stop the clock" in Minesweeper. Minimize the Minesweeper window by clicking the Minimize icon in the upper-right corner or by pressing ⊞+D. Then do the "3D flip" by holding down the Windows key (⊞) and pressing Tab repeatedly. You may have to squint a bit, but you should be able to make out the details. When you figure out where you want to click next, bring the screen back up by either clicking the Minesweeper button on the Windows taskbar or releasing the Windows key.

Minesweeper cheats in your favor. Your first click is free: Minesweeper always arranges things so that you never hit a mine on your first click (unless you choose to restart a game, in which case the mines appear in the same location as in the previous game).

Think you have a good score? Ha! Take a look at `www.minesweeper.info/worldranking.html` for the best-ever Minesweeper scores. And make sure that your jaw is firmly attached before you hit the page.

Minesweeper allows you to replay a game, which has raised havoc in the Minesweeper community, particularly among the speed record holders. After all, if you replay a game that you already played, it's kinda like catching a fish you already caught, if you know what I mean. Such unfair prior knowledge — UPK — has disqualified Windows 7 Minesweeper from world record consideration.

The Internet Games

Everything old is new again.

Windows XP was shipped with several games that allowed you to play opponents on the Internet. No charge. No hassles. And, in Windows Vista, no way.

My guess is that Microsoft figured it would try to make money with games on the Internet (or it was worried about competition with the Xbox), so it yanked the games from Vista. Don't know about you, but I haven't heard anything about Microsoft's stock price going up because of Internet Checkers.

In Windows 7, they're back. They're free and visually compelling, and they work pretty well.

Here's the lineup:

- ✦ Internet Backgammon
- ✦ Internet Checkers
- ✦ Internet Spades

Each of the games follows a similar rhythm:

- ✦ When you start the game, you set your own skill level — beginning, intermediate, or advanced. Microsoft computers use your self-assessment to match you with a partner on the Internet who gives herself the same skill level. (You can change your skill level self-assessment at any time: Just choose Game➪Skill Level.)
- ✦ Your computer connects to the Microsoft server, which runs out and finds an opponent. When the matchmaking is done, you see the game screen.
- ✦ If you give up, you can click the Resign button and your opponent is informed of the win. But if you (or your opponent) wait a long time to respond, Microsoft computers take over, and you (or your opponent) end up playing against the computer.

The Chat function is lame, as you might expect: You can choose from a list of canned and extremely inoffensive exclamations, and your opponent can do the same. Golly. If you feel like venting a little, you have to just yell at your screen.

That's about it. You can see your own win-loss record (choose Games➪Statistics) and change the background (choose Game➪Change Appearance). But there's no way you can ask to play against a specific player, and no way to compare your results with anyone else. (Guess they'll have to leave the double-elimination contests for Windows 14.)

The Other Games

Windows 7 comes with several additional games that are worthy of your perusal — or hours of introspection, as the case may be. The stellar cast includes

- ✦ **Chess Titans** combines a very strong chess-playing engine with admirable 3D graphics. You can play against a human opponent or against the computer, and the computer can be set to one of ten different levels of difficulty. Yes, you can castle on both the king and queen sides, and pawns can capture *en passant*.

- In **Hearts**, you play one hand and Windows plays the other three. (Amazingly, even though Spades works over the Internet with four live players, Hearts only has one, uh, beating heart.) Does the computer cheat? Er, take unfair advantage of its knowledge of the contents of your hand? That's a good question. See `mrsbsbrilliantblog.blogspot.com/2008/05/does-microsoft-hearts-cheat.html` for some interesting insight.
- **Mahjong Titans** is a solitaire game loosely based on the traditional Mahjong tile game (the game you hear clacking at all hours of the day and night on the side streets of Hong Kong). At least you can understand the rules of Mahjong Titans. Your goal is to remove all tiles by matching pairs of exposed tiles, which is to say — tiles that have empty spaces to the left or right. Like Solitaire, FreeCell, and Spider Solitaire, Mahjong Titans gives you a hint if you press H and completes the hint if you then press Enter.
- **Purble Place** consists of three different games for the preschool and elementary crowd. Pattern recognition, memory stretches, and elimination exercises can keep kids going for hours.

Book IV

Joining the Multimedia Mix

"I had a little trouble with the automatic video tracking camera, so during the video conference, before speaking, say 'Here Rollo!' and wait for Rollo to get his paws up on your knees before beginning to speak."

Contents at a Glance

Chapter 1: Jammin' with Windows Media Player

In This Chapter

- **Understanding C.R.A.P. music and video formats**
- **Setting up Windows Media Player for *your* benefit — not Microsoft's**
- **Buying music that won't bite**
- **Ripping music from an audio CD**
- **Copying music to a CD or digital player**
- **Finding the Media Library: where your music is kept**

Windows Media Player (WMP) is da *man*. Er, uh. Wait a sec. Let me start over. WMP *sucks*. No, that's not what I meant. Hold on. I have this loud thud coming from my speakers, the Water Ambience visualization looks like smoke in Godzilla's eye, and Trent Reznor is screaming "You can't take it away from me." Lemme turn the volume down. There. Yeah. That's better.

What I meant to say is that Windows Media Player sucks you in from the moment you start it. As the Windows 7 built-in boom box, it plays CDs, of course, but it also lets you play, organize, and generally enjoy almost any kind of music and most videos stored on your computer, whether the tunes or "vids" came from CDs, an online store, the Internet, or that smelly guy with a big baseball cap at the flea market.

Wait! Before you buy more music or try to rip a DVD, you need to know something: the industry's dirty little secret. Some of the music you buy and many DVDs and recorded TV shows are protected by digital rights management (DRM), and the companies that pull the strings can not only dictate how and when you listen to the music (or view the videos) but also change the rules, retroactively, and you can't do a thing about it. I talk about the broadcast protection flag — the mechanism that prevents you from viewing recorded TV shows — in Book IV, Chapter 4. The rest of it is, if you'll pardon the expression, C.R.A.P.

What You Need to Know about C.R.A.P.

Digital Rights Management doesn't add any value for the artist, label (who are selling DRM-free music every day — the Compact Disc), or consumer; the only people it adds value to are the technology companies who are interested in locking consumers to a particular technology platform.

— Ian Rogers, Yahoo! Music blog

ZDNet Executive Editor David Berlind calls it C.R.A.P. — Content Restriction, Annulment, and Protection (`blogs.zdnet.com/BTL/?p=2428`). You may know it by the politically correct *digital rights management,* or DRM. Whatever its name, you're the one getting nailed. Don't buy C.R.A.P.

Music and video come in many different formats — think of them as different methods for converting sight and sound into bits. The formats are all different, and translating a video or song from one format to another can really put a crimp on the quality of the recording.

Back in the dark ages, if you wanted to record music on a computer, you used the MP3 format. It wasn't (and isn't) the fanciest format on the street; it makes files that are bigger than they need to be, and it doesn't support some truly cool capabilities in newer formats (such as Dolby-style 5.1 or 7.1 channel recording). Despite all its shortcomings, MP3 took off and became the universal language of digital music. If you have a device that plays digital music — whether it's an old PC, an ancient portable audio player (they're called "MP3 players" for a reason), a 200GB iPod, or a Galactic Zune — it understands MP3.

In the video arena, AVI and MPG file formats play a similar role: They're long-established (okay, old-fashioned) and blissfully DRM free.

AVI, MP3, and MPG files aren't just DRM-free. They're *DRM-impossible:* The file format doesn't support any attempts to lock you out of your own music or videos. If you buy an MP3 file, for example, you know from the get-go that it doesn't bear any digital rights restrictions — nobody else has control over your music. There are no hidden restrictions, such as limitations on whether you can burn the song on a CD, or whether you can play the song on a specific Windows PC.

DRM-locked C.R.A.P. music is disappearing. Consumers wised up. Companies that used to peddle locked-up music now sing the praises of DRM-free, with all the fervor of a saved sinner caught with his hand in the till.

iTunes leads the way

Apple opened its iTunes store in April 2003. For more than five years, iTunes.com stood as the preeminent cash cow, er, source of online music and videos. And, for more than five years, every single song or clip you bought from iTunes was C.R.A.P. These days, the digital rights management restrictions that Apple placed on its products would make an executive blush. Or maybe make them nostalgic, I suppose.

Along came Amazon. In January 2008, Amazon launched its version of an online music store, named Amazon MP3 and — you guessed it — sold only MP3 (and other DRM-free) files. Amazon MP3 wasn't the first online shop for, uh, music that isn't C.R.A.P. — `eMusic.com` has been selling DRM-free stuff for years. But it was big and it was aggressive, and the world sat up and took notice. (At least, the United States and United Kingdom sat up — folks in other countries still can't buy MP3s from Amazon.) iTunes started to bleed money. Their old, locked M4P music files didn't look inviting at all to folks who knew the whole story.

Apple took a look at its bottom line, twisted the arms of recalcitrant music distribution companies, and announced that, starting in January 2009, it would sell some DRM-free music. Golly. The response was so overwhelming (which means that Apple suddenly started selling some music again) that the folks in Cupertino removed all DRM restrictions in April 2009. iTunes calls it iTunes Plus. I call it "Wake up and smell the roses, turkeys." The files iTunes sells are still in AAC format, but they work just like MP3s, and they'll play in most MP3 players.

With a little luck, DRM in the audio world will go the way of the dodo, although you may be stuck with DRM-laden dreck that you got suckered into paying for months or years ago. Video's a different story. See the later sidebar "Why can't I rip a DVD?" or the long, sorry story of recorded TV in Windows, in Book IV, Chapter 4.

Adjusting WMP Privacy Settings

Microsoft releases new versions of WMP about as often as Steve Sinofsky changes suits. Windows Media Player 12 shipped with the original version of Windows 7, but a new version may be available by the time you read this book. If you haven't specifically gone fishing for the latest version of Windows Media Player (affectionately known as WiMP to its fans), you should take a look and see what Microsoft has available. Drop by `www.microsoft.com/windows/windowsmedia` and make sure that you have the latest and greatest.

The competition

Windows Media Player isn't the only game in town. Although WMP excels in some respects, two other competitors deserve your attention — if not your ears.

Lots of folks swear by Winamp, a mercifully compact, surprisingly capable player from Nullsoft (`www.winamp.net`). The basic player is free. If you want to add MP3 ripping and fast CD burning, it costs all of $19.95 — and you aren't pestered until the day you die to buy and download songs from a proprietary library. I use the free version of Winamp to feed my iPod. It works great. Yes, you read that right. You *don't* need iTunes to put music on your iPod. The free version of Winamp does everything you need to care for and feed an iPod, and then some.

Apple iTunes once ruled the roost in the music-playing biz, but I'm still leery of iTunes: I've had older versions of Apple QuickTime freeze on Windows machines so often that I could scream — and iTunes uses QuickTime. See Chapter 2 of this minibook for some school-of-hard-knocks advice.

My other favorite media program? A free, open source, low-overhead player named VLC, created and maintained by the VideoLAN Project (`www.videolan.org/vlc/download-windows.html`). Don't let its name fool you: VLC isn't just for LANs any more, although it works great over home networks. Mostly, I use VLC when I don't want to stare at the gussy Windows Media Player interface, or when WMP just doesn't work. You'd be amazed at how many different video files, in particular, are a hassle to play in WMP but play immediately with VLC.

The download is free — you already paid for Windows Media Player when you bought Windows 7. More to the point, Microsoft keeps adding new "features" to WiMP that try to sell you something, so the upgrades come frequently and invariably at no charge. If you find a newer version of WMP, download the file and run it.

Setting options when you install WMP

If you haven't run WMP yet, here's how to get off on the right foot:

1. **Choose Start⇨Windows Media Player or Start⇨All Programs⇨ Windows Media Player.**

   The installer appears, as shown in Figure 1-1.

2. **Click the Custom Settings button, and then click the Next button.**

   WMP shows you the Select Privacy Options dialog box, shown in Figure 1-2. Considering the checkered past of Windows Media Player, I think it's a good idea to limit its snooping.

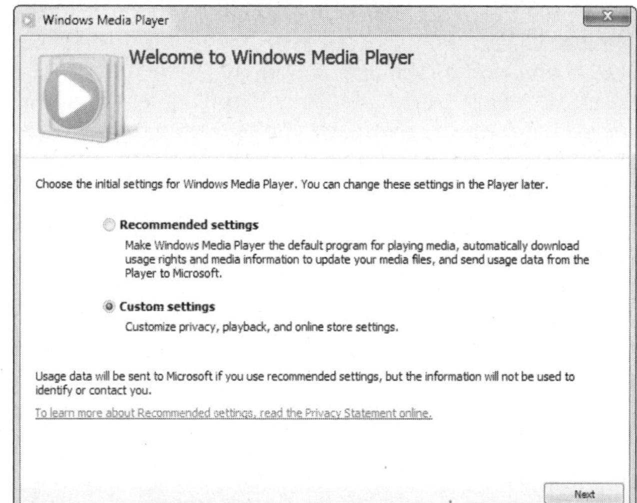

Figure 1-1: If you value your privacy, don't accept the Microsoft-recommended settings.

Windows Media Player

Select Privacy Options

Privacy Options | Privacy Statement

Enhanced Playback Experience

Display media information from the Internet

Update music files by retrieving media information from the Internet

Download usage rights automatically when I play or sync a file

Note: Media information that is retrieved may not be in your language.

Enhanced Content Provider Services

Send unique Player ID to content providers

Click Cookies to view or change privacy settings that affect cookies Cookies

Windows Media Player Customer Experience Improvement Program

I want to help make Microsoft software and services even better by sending Player usage data to Microsoft

History

Store and display a list of recently/frequently played:

Music Pictures Video Radio Playlists

Back Next

Figure 1-2: Big Brother wants your permission.

3. **Select or deselect the various check boxes, depending on your preferences.**

Microsoft has a long, tumultuous history of using Windows Media Player to gather all sorts of personal information about you and your media-playing habits. Approach this dialog box with skepticism. I select only the Display Media Information from the Internet and the Update Music Files by Retrieving Media Information from the Internet check boxes.

You may want to send Microsoft more, but unless you have an overwhelming reason to do so, I suggest that you limit your exposure. Of course, if you choose the option Display Media Information from the Internet, Microsoft keeps tabs on you, too. I guess it all boils down to a question of how much privacy you're willing to give up to get cool features such as automatically downloaded album covers and correct song titles.

If you select the Download Usage Rights Automatically When I Play or Sync a File check box, every time you try to play or sync a protected file (typically, a song in the Microsoft proprietary WMA format or a video in WMV format) on your computer, if the rights have expired, Windows Media Player goes out to the company that owns the copyright on the file and asks for a license. (See the section "What You Need to Know about C.R.A.P.," earlier in this chapter, for details.) In other words, if you try to play a protected WMA file that you don't have rights to play, Microsoft and the copyright holder are notified. Part of the notification includes a number that identifies your computer uniquely and your IP address, which may or may not identify your location uniquely. You usually end up on a Web page that asks you to buy something. Bah. Humbug. Turn off this option so that WMP asks for your permission before it goes out to retrieve rights information. That way, you know in advance that you're trying to play C.R.A.P. music, before Windows Media Player phones home.

4. **When you're comfortable with your privacy choices, click the Next button.**

   WMP then asks whether you want it to be used as the default music and video player. I use WMP as my default player, but you may prefer VLC or Winamp (see the earlier sidebar "The competition").

5. **Choose whether you want WMP to be your default player, and click the Finish button.**

   WMP springs to life with some free sample music (in MP3 format!) in the library, as shown in Figure 1-3.

WMP immediately begins scanning your Music Library, adding songs as it bumps into them. (I talk about libraries in general, and the Music Library in particular, in Book II, Chapter 1.) Initially, your Music Library includes your own `Music` folder, plus the `Music` folder in your computer's `Public` folder. Later in this chapter, I show you how to expand the library's reach.

The sample music provided by WMP sits in your `\Public\Public Music\Sample Music` folder.

Figure 1-3: Windows Music Player opens, shouting "Put me in, Coach! I'm ready to play, today."

Tweaking options after installation

If you already installed WMP or the latest version came preinstalled on your PC, take a moment now to turn off the $#@! Acquire Licenses setting. Follow these steps to do so:

1. **Start Windows Media Player.**
2. **Press Alt to open the main menu. (If you used an older version of WMP, I bet you wondered where it was hidden.) Then choose Tools⇨Options and click the Privacy tab (see Figure 1-4).**
3. **In particular, make sure the Download Usage Rights Automatically When I Play or Sync a File check box isn't checked. Personally, I deselect all check boxes except for the first two (refer to Figure 1-4).**

   You might be wondering about the Automatically Check If Protected Files Need to Be Refreshed and the Set Clock on Devices Automatically check boxes. Both of those are related to subscription services — where you pay by the month for the ability to play music (or video) files. The first check box tells WMP that it should check to see whether you paid for your subscription before the right to play the music expires. The second check box tells WMP that it should set the secure clock on MP3 players as soon as they're attached to your PC — an important step in verifying that you paid your subscription fee and can continue to play the music you're renting, you scofflaw.

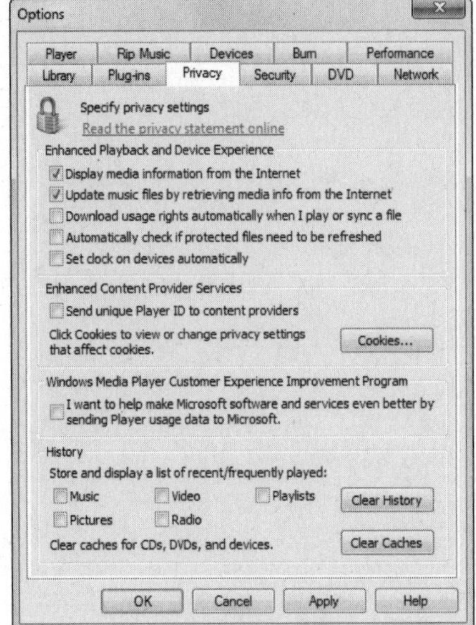

Figure 1-4: Control WMP privacy settings.

If you rent your music, you probably want to select both check boxes. If you don't, the boxes don't mean anything. I turn them off.

4. **Click the OK button.**

   Your changes take effect immediately — although, if you didn't make these changes soon enough, Microsoft may already have your unique player ID on file. That isn't a horrible lapse of personal security, but it does add to the stockpile of personal information Microsoft has on file.

If you have questions about the other tabs in the Options dialog box, see the section "Customizing WMP," later in this chapter.

Playing with Now Playing

To start Windows Media Player, choose Start⇨All Programs⇨Windows Media Player, or (much easier) click the WMP icon on the taskbar. It looks like a Play button.

You control Windows Media Player by using the three tabs in the upper-right corner of the window, and you control the music by using the bar at the bottom.

The first time you start WMP, it scans all the music in your Music Library — unless you added folders to your Music Library, it consists of your `\Music` folder and the computer's `\Public\Music` folder. WMP also reaches out across your network and HomeGroup, to see whether any media collections have been made available. The scanning process can take quite awhile, and in the interim you may not be able to see all your media.

Double-click an album, and you see something like Figure 1-5.

This address bar behaves differently from the Windows Explorer address bar.
Navigation pane
Album and songs
Control WMP with these tabs.
Controls for playing the media
Current playlist
Switch to Now playing mode.

Figure 1-5: Library view, where you can leaf through your music.

Many Windows Media Player components aren't quite what they seem. Here's the scorecard so that you can keep count:

✦ WMP isn't overly concerned with the location of your media files. Instead, it takes the contents of your Music Library (or Videos Library, Pictures Library, or Recorded TV Library) and mashes all the media in the library into one big blob. Your Music Library, if you haven't changed it, consists of your personal `\Music` folder plus the `\Public\Music` folder. WMP melds the contents of both without regard to location.

Melding the contents can be confusing if you're looking for an album and can't find it. It's particularly vexing when you take music off a CD and stick it in your computer — a process called *ripping* — and other people who use your computer can't find the music. See the section "Copying from a CD (Also Known As Ripping)," later in this chapter.

✦ The address bar doesn't work like the Windows Explorer address bar. Windows Explorer is concerned about the location of your files: When you navigate, you move from folder to folder. By contrast, Windows Media Player doesn't care, with one exception, about the location of your media. It doesn't jump from folder to folder. Instead, the WMP address bar lets you choose a type of media and, in the case of music, navigate to specific albums. The location of the music on your hard drive doesn't matter; as long as an album is in your Music Library, WMP picks it up.

The exception? This part is confusing, but WMP *does* make a distinction between music residing in the Music Library on your computer, as opposed to the music library or libraries on other computers on your network. It also makes a distinction between music in your Music Library and music on a CD or USB drive you attached to your computer.

In Figure 1-5, if you click the wedge to the left of the word *Library,* you see something like the arrangement shown in Figure 1-6. Note how the computer's Music Library appears at the top of the list (it's named Library); music in a CD player appears next; followed by libraries taken from MP3 players and USB drives; and then each exposed music library on your network appears afterward.

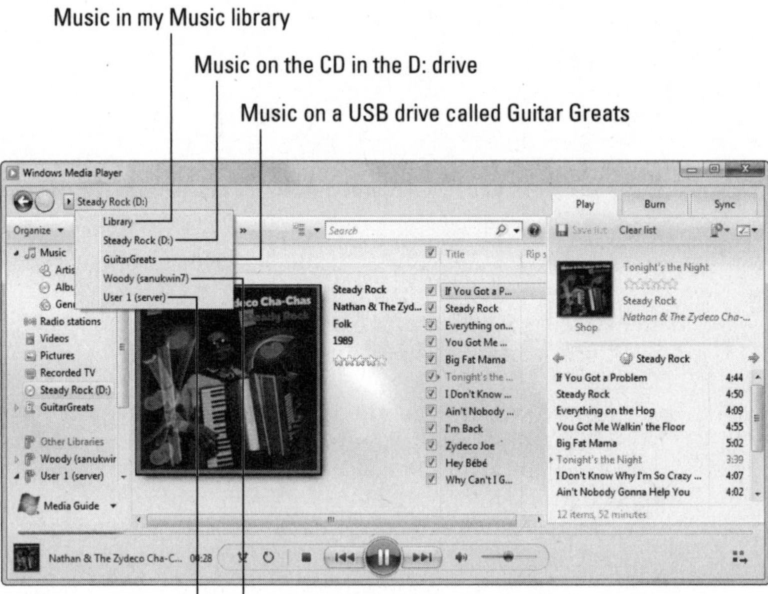

Figure 1-6: Where the different libraries come from.

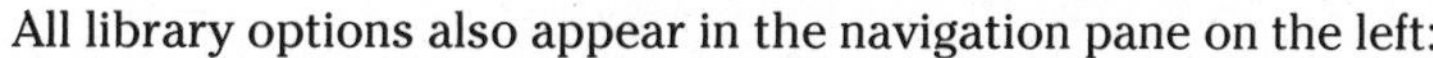

All library options also appear in the navigation pane on the left:

- Windows Media Player mashes together all the music in your Music Library, but it doesn't include the albums (or video tracks or recorded TV shows) outside your Music Library (or Video Library or Recorded TV Library). To see music from a CD, USB drive, MP3 player, or any of the exposed music libraries on your network, you must pick that specific library in the navigation pane on the left or click the wedge to the left of the word *Library* and choose a different source.
- The right side of the Now Playing window displays a playlist, which is just a sequence of tracks. You can create your own playlists or rely on the ones built into WMP. The Now Playing playlist, for example, is the list of tracks that are queued up to play, one after the other. To play a different track from the current playlist, double-click the track down in the list of playlist contents.

If you click the small bunch of squares in the lower-right corner of WMP (refer to Figure 1-5), the program shrinks to an appearance that Microsoft calls Now Playing mode. If you minimize WMP and hover your mouse on the WMP icon, you see an even smaller version of Now Playing mode (see Figure 1-7).

Figure 1-7: The Taskbar pop-up (on the left) and Now Playing mode (on the right) offer similar controls.

Playback buttons

The buttons along the bottom of the library window (refer to Figure 1-6) and both flavors of the Now Playing windows (refer to Figure 1-7) are similar to the buttons on a conventional CD player. See Table 1-1.

Table 1-1 Playback Buttons for Windows Media Player

Button	*What It Does*
	The Pause button pauses the playback. When playing is paused, the Pause button toggles to a Play button. Click it again to make playing resume.
	The Stop button stops the playing. Click the Play button to start playing again. Unlike Pause/Resume, the Stop/Start button returns to the start of the track. To start a different track, double-click that track in the playlist.
	The Previous Track button skips to the start of the previous track. From the first track in the playlist, it skips to the beginning of the last track on the playlist.
	The Next Track button skips to the start of the next track. From the last track in the playlist, it skips to the first.
	The Mute button silences the sound. Click the button again to restore the sound. Unlike the Pause button, the Mute button does not halt playing. If you mute the sound for ten seconds, you miss hearing ten seconds of the track. If you mute Eminem for ten seconds, you get unwrapped (heh-heh-heh).
	The little slider to the right of the buttons controls the volume.
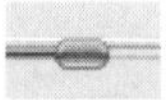	The skinny slider above the buttons shows the WMP position in the current track. As the track progresses from beginning to end, the slider moves from left to right. While WMP is playing a track, you can shift it to any point in the track by clicking that point on the track or by dragging the slider control to that point.

That's about all you need to know to play music from a playlist. Rocket science.

Playing a CD

Want to play a CD? That's hard, too. Here's how:

1. **Take the CD out of its plastic case, if it's in one.**
2. **Wipe the pizza stains off the shiny side. (Don't worry about the other side.)**

   The correct method: hold the CD with one finger in the hole in the middle, the other on the edge, and wipe gently from the middle to the outside. Start with a clean soft cloth and if that doesn't work, try rubbing alcohol or plain ol' soap and water.

3. **Stick the CD in the PC's drive and close it.**

   Chances are good that the CD will just start playing with WMP in its Now Playing incarnation (refer to Figure 1-7).

4. **If Windows asks whether you want to Play Audio CD Using Windows Media Player (see Figure 1-8), click the No, I'd Rather Clip My Toenails — What Did You Think I Wanted to Do? button and then click the OK button.**

Figure 1-8: Do you want to play the CD you just inserted into your CD drive? Yes, you probably do.

If WMP isn't running already, it starts all by itself. Then you wait a few seconds and WMP starts playing the first track, using the Now Playing visage (refer to Figure 1-7).

To Media Player, the CD *is* a playlist. It's also a library, all by itself. If you click the Switch to Library button in the upper-right corner of the Now Playing window, you can see in the library that the tracks on the CD appear in the playlist area on the right side of the window. Look at the drop-down list of playlists in the upper-right corner of the window; the name of the CD appears as the selected item.

How does WMP know what's on the CD? After it identifies the CD from information encoded along with the recorded tracks, it gets the CD's description and track titles over the Web, from a database maintained for that purpose.

If a CD is quite obscure — or really good — it may not be in the Microsoft database. Then WMP can display only the information it finds on the CD itself: the number of tracks and the playtime of each track. If a CD isn't in the Microsoft database, you can enter the names of the songs manually. (To do so, right-click any song and choose Edit, and then type a new name.)

Buying Music and Videos Online

Last night I went to the Phuket Blues and Rock Festival (`phuketblues festival.com`) and saw an absolutely riveting performance by Eric Bibb, a tremendous blues guitarist and singer. Today I dropped by my friendly local music shoppe and couldn't find a single CD by Eric Bibb. So I hopped on Amazon and was listening to Eric's latest album in a few minutes. Here's how:

1. **Point your Web browser to** `amazon.com`**.**
2. **At the top of the Amazon page, in the Search box, choose MP3 Downloads, and on the right, type the name of the artist or album you're looking for. Click Go.**

   I searched for Eric Bibb, and Amazon responded with 130 songs and eight albums from Eric Bibb (see Figure 1-9). I peeled myself off the floor.

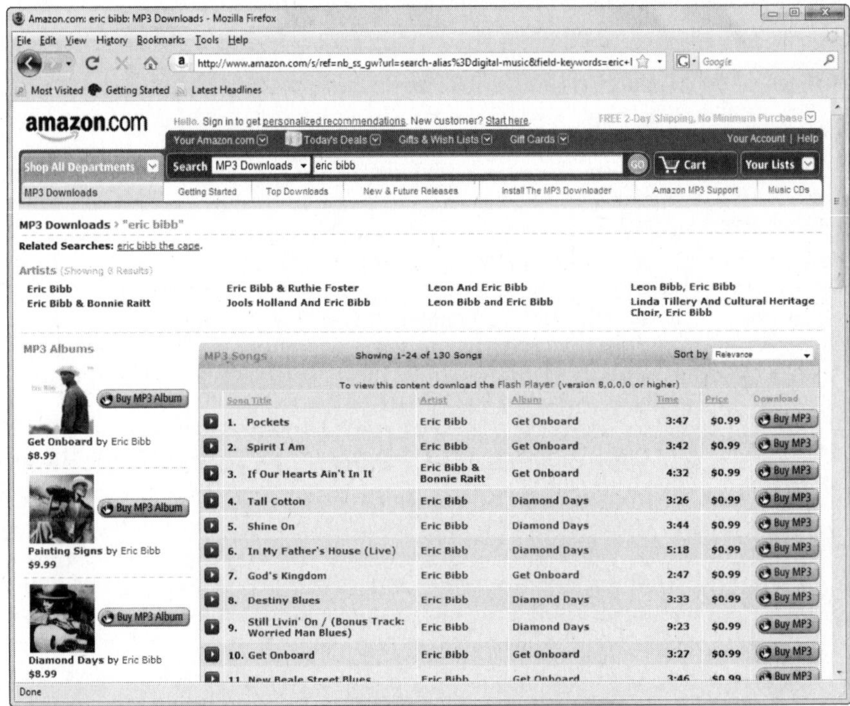

Figure 1-9: Amazon boasts an extensive collection of MP3s.

3. **On the left, click Buy MP3 Album next to the album you want to buy.**

   I chose Get Onboard.

4. **Amazon asks whether you have an account and a password. If so, enter the password; if not, you can sign up for an account in no time.**

   Amazon says I must install the Amazon MP3 Downloader.

5. **Follow the instructions and install the downloader.**

   It takes about 30 seconds. You have to click through a User Account Control message, but eternal vigilance is the price you pay for liberty, eh?

6. **After the downloader is installed, Amazon prompts you to click the Download Album button. Do so.**

   If you don't already have an account, you can set one up with almost any kind of credit card. Online verification takes another 30 seconds.

   Amazon begins the download, with a message like the one shown in Figure 1-10.

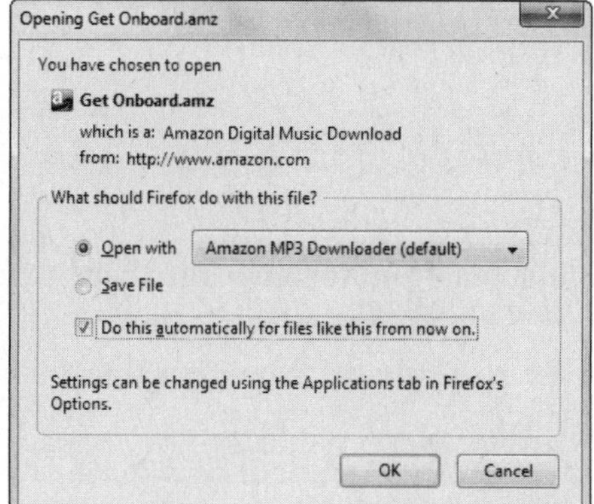

Figure 1-10: Start the download.

7. **Select the check box marked Do This Automatically for Files Like This from Now On so that you never have to mess with the installer again. Click OK.**

   It may take a few minutes, but ultimately the Amazon downloader downloads all the tracks and puts them in your `\Music` folder, in a newly created folder named `\Amazon MP3`. In this case, I found a new folder named `\Music\Amazon MP3\Eric Bibb\Get Onboard` that contains MP3s for all songs in the album.

One little problem. Two, actually. First, other users on my computer can't play the music: It's stuck in *my* `\Music` folder and they can't see the folder. Second, other people on my home network can't see the new songs, either. Fortunately, I have an easy solution: Move the album to the `Public\Music` folder. Here's how:

1. **Choose Start⇨Music.**

   Windows shows you the Music Library.

2. **On the left, click the wedge next to Music, under the Libraries heading.**

   This step shows you the folders in your `My Music` folder, as in Figure 1-11.

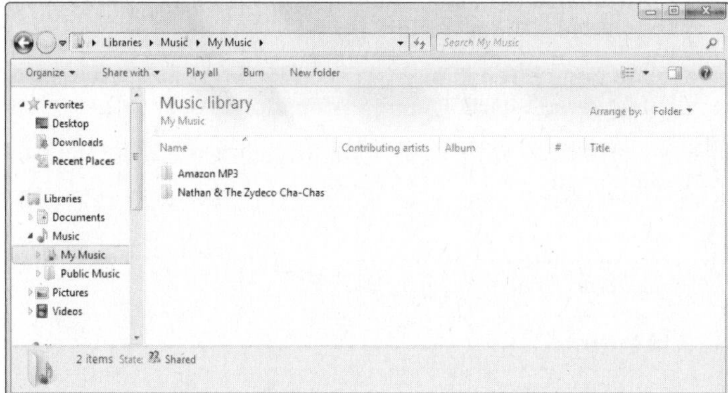

Figure 1-11: Amazon puts downloaded music in the `Amazon MP3` folder, under your personal `Music` folder.

3. **Drill down to the album you want to move into the `Public Music` folder, right-click it, and choose Cut.**

   In this case, I double-click Amazon MP3 and then Eric Bibb. I right-click the folder named `Get Onboard` and choose Cut.

4. **On the left, click Public Music. Then right-click in an empty area on the right and choose Paste.**

   This step finishes the transfer of the entire album from your personal `Music` folder to the computer's `Public Music` folder. From there, anybody should be able to find the music.

Thank heaven for MP3 files: No restrictions on where they can go. No restrictions on who can play them.

Copying from a CD (Also Known As Ripping)

Before you copy music from a CD onto your computer, take a few minutes to find out more about MP3 and the reason why you don't want to add to the world's accumulation of C.R.A.P. music. See the section "What You Need to Know about C.R.A.P.," earlier in this chapter.

Here's how to rip a CD — that is, convert the audio tracks on the CD into files that your computer can work with:

1. **Put the audio CD that you want to copy into the CD drive.**

   If this is the first time you ever inserted an audio CD in your computer, Windows Media Player jumps in and immediately starts to play it. On the other hand, if you've used CDs in the past, Windows 7 may ask whether you want to play the CD or rip it — or if you've used Media Player or other players, you may see a much more complex dialog box (see Figure 1-12).

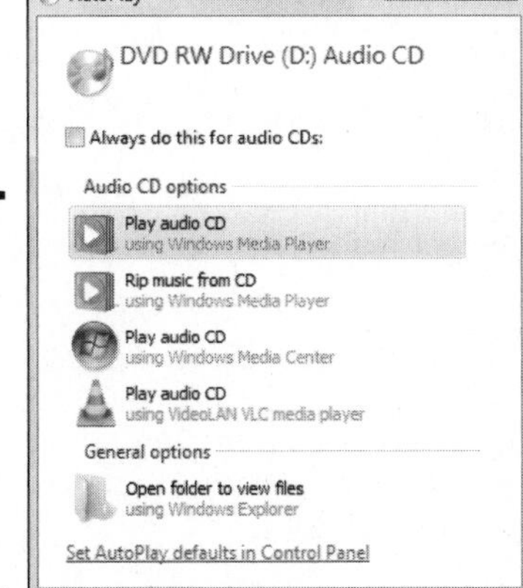

Figure 1-12: When you insert an audio CD in the drive, you may see many options.

2. **The first time you rip, don't click the Rip Music from CD Using Windows Media Player icon, which starts the ripper without giving you a chance to choose your settings. Instead, choose to play the CD using Windows Media Player.**

   The Rip settings are "sticky," so after you set them correctly, there's no need to reset them. Thus, the second time you rip a CD (and all subsequent times) you can click Rip Music from CD and rip away.

3. **When your CD starts playing, click the Play tab.**

4. **On the menu, next to the Organize, Stream, and Create Playlists items, click Rip Settings and then click More Options.**

   You see the Rip Music Options dialog box, shown in Figure 1-13.

5. **(Optional) In the Rip Music to This Location box, click the Change button. Navigate to your `Public Music` folder (refer to Figure 1-13) and click OK.**

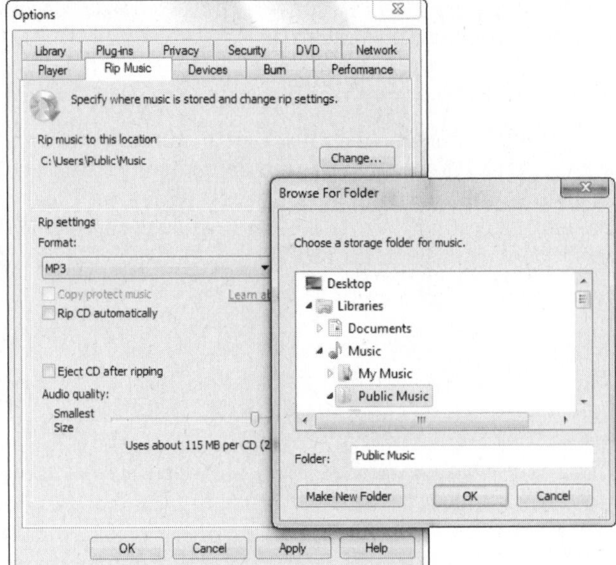

Figure 1-13: Set rip parameters before you start ripping.

This step ensures that the audio files you rip end up in your computer's `Public Music` folder, where other people using your computer, and other people on your network, can find them.

Of course, if you're the only one who listens to the music on your computer, you can skip this step.

6. **In the Rip Settings Format drop-down box, choose MP3.**

   This step ensures that the music you create isn't — and can't be — the victim of digital rights management. Microsoft wants you to record in the Microsoft proprietary WMA format so that it can collect royalties from MP3 player hardware manufacturers. Some MP3 players don't play WMAs.

7. **Slide the Audio Quality slider over to 192 Kbps or 256 Kbps. Click OK.**

   At 192 Kbps, the quality of the songs you rip is close to the original quality of the CD recording. If you don't mind making your files bigger for higher-quality songs, choose 256 Kbps or even 320 Kbps (which is, in my opinion, indistinguishable from the original).

   See Table 1-2 for a thumbnail comparison of sound quality and file size.

8. **Back in Windows Media Player (see Figure 1-14), make sure that Windows Media Player has correctly identified the name of the album and all the tracks, er, songs.**

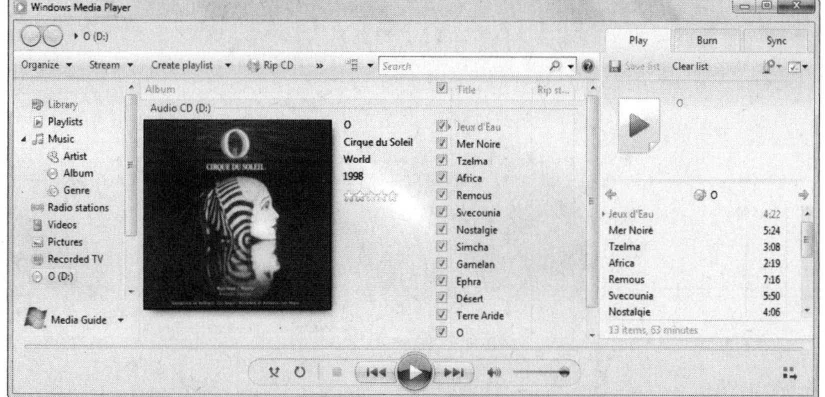

Figure 1-14: Windows Media Player is ready to let 'er rip.

If any information is missing — rare, in my experience, even with obscure CDs — right-click the incorrect entry and choose Find Album Info. WMP phones home and retrieves as many matches for the album as it can find. You can then choose the correct album or right-click the track, choose Edit, and type your own information.

9. **(Optional) If you want to choose specific songs to copy, select the check boxes to the left of each track that you want to copy and deselect the check boxes next to the ones you want to leave behind.**

   To rip all tracks (er, copy all songs) on the CD, you don't need to do anything.

10. **Click the Rip CD link.**

    Windows Media Player dutifully copies the tracks you selected, placing the "ripped" files in the default folder, which (if you followed Step 5) is your `Public Music` folder.

Table 1-2 Number of CDs That Fit On an 8GB iPod

MP3 Quality	*Sound Quality*	*Number of CDs*
128 Kbps	Excellent on a portable player and so-so on good sound equipment	More than 140
192 Kbps	Very good on normal consumer audio systems	More than 90
256 Kbps	Indistinguishable from the original CD	More than 70
320 Kbps	As good as it gets	More than 50

To a first approximation, WMP makes a folder for each artist, and inside the artist's folder, it makes a subfolder for each album. The music tracks go into the album's folder. (Things get a little hairy when two artists collaborate on a song. In that case, WMP puts all the songs in one folder, and that folder usually goes under the name of the artist who performed most of the album. If WMP can't decide, you may find a folder named Various Artists or Unknown Artist. Frequently, classical music is filed under the name of the composer, not the artist performing the piece.)

Why can't I rip a DVD?

I once had dinner with a senior Microsoft exec who told me, point blank, "As far as Bill's concerned, ripping any DVD is illegal." Full stop.

That's why Microsoft doesn't make tools that allow you to rip DVDs. Microsoft doesn't want the legal hassles. It doesn't want to alienate movie companies. It doesn't want to be viewed as soft on copyright violation. There's a whole lotta upside to being friendly with movie companies, and exactly zero potential profit in providing DVD-ripping software.

The legalities of the situation vary depending on where you live, but in my opinion, everyone should be able to create digital backups of DVDs they own. DVDs die. Bits don't. Or, at least they don't die as frequently as DVDs. My observation may be against the law in your neck of the woods — or it may be legal today and illegal tomorrow. To be sure, ask your lawyer how she rips her DVDs. If ripping DVDs is illegal where you live this week, please take a thick black pen and mark out the rest of this sidebar.

There's nothing particularly unique about a DVD movie disc. The movie consists of a handful of files. A typical DVD movie disc contains two folders: `AUDIO_TS` and `VIDEO_TS`, and the `AUDIO_TS` folder is usually empty. The `VIDEO_TS` folder contains files with names ending in BUP, IFO, and VOB. All the video tracks, including the sound tracks and subtitles, are in the VOB files. Each VOB file runs about 15 minutes.

If you run VLC (see the sidebar "The competition," earlier in this chapter), you have everything you need to watch VOB files: Simply start VLC, click Media➪Open File, and open the VOB. You can choose the language track and subtitles by using the VLC menu. Fifteen minutes later, when the first VOB is finished, open the next one. It's that simple.

For those with VLC who don't mind interruptions every 15 minutes, you can copy an entire DVD by just clicking the VOB filenames and dragging them to your computer.

If you want something a little more sophisticated — a way to meld the VOB files, or to burn the ripped movie onto a blank DVD, check out the tools on the Lifehacker page `lifehacker.com/355281/dvd-rip-automates-one+click-dvd-ripping`. If the powers that be have prevailed on Lifehacker to drop the article, remember that Google is your friend. Try searching for *free dvd ripping software.* Just remember that almost every scummy software company in the world claims to offer free DVD ripping software.

If you're connected to the Internet, WMP grabs all associated album information — track titles, album cover art, and artist — and sticks it in the folder along with the music. Very sweet.

Because you ripped the album into your `Public Music` folder, your newly ripped album appears in the Music Library list, and in the Windows Media Player Library list, for you, for other people who use your computer, and for anyone who can connect to your `Public Music` folder. Smart, eh?

Organizing Your Media Library

WMP uses the Windows 7 libraries — Music, Video, Pictures, and Recorded TV — to organize soundtracks, videos, TV shows, and so on. When you understand how Windows libraries work, you can organize your music just the way you want. I talk about Windows 7 libraries in Book II, Chapter 1, and I discuss the way Windows Media Player uses libraries in the section "Playing with Now Playing," earlier in this chapter.

Leafing through the library

When you start WMP, it's in Library mode, which displays a window split into three panes, with the library's structure on the left, the contents of the selected item on the right, and the current playlist also on the right, as shown in Figure 1-15.

Figure 1-15: My Music Library, or at least a small part of it, seen through the eyes of Windows Media Player.

WMP shows the media-related Windows 7 libraries along the left side: Music, Videos, Pictures, and Recorded TV. It also shows several additional categories, which are specific to (and handled by) Windows Media Player. You can choose from among the categories by clicking the category. Here's the rundown of categories you find:

✦ **Music**: Contains all the audio tracks in your Windows Music Library, such as those you ripped from CDs. You can have WMP sort and gather audio tracks by artist, album, or genre (rock, classical, comedy, folk, jazz, dance, or Cajun, for example).

As mentioned in the section "Playing with Now Playing," earlier in this chapter, the Music Library contains only items in your Windows Music Library. If you haven't changed anything, that includes your `Music` folder and your computer's `\Public\Music` folder. If you want to look in other libraries in your HomeGroup or network, you have to click the specific library, as listed under Other Libraries, at the bottom of the list.

✦ **Pictures:** Contains various kinds of image files that happen to be located in your Windows Pictures Library. WMP may be the worst place to work with pictures. See the discussion of Windows Live Photo Gallery in Book IV, Chapter 5.

✦ **Video:** Contains the contents of your Windows Video Library, which I discuss in Book IV, Chapter 6. WMP can play video files in many formats, including ASF, AVI, MPG, WMV, and many others — but not the Apple-protected M4V format, and not in the native DVD movie VOB format. (See the earlier sidebar "Why can't I rip a DVD?")

✦ **Recorded TV:** Includes all TV shows you recorded using Windows Media Center Edition. Shows are listed by title, series, genre, date recorded, actors, or your star ratings.

Windows Media Center uses the weird file format DVR-MS for recorded television programs (`.dvr-ms` files). You may find it difficult to play those files on anything other than a PC running a version of Windows Media Center.

✦ **Other devices:** MP3 players, for example.

✦ **Other libraries:** Automatically detected by Windows 7 on your HomeGroup or network.

Finding the tracks you want

The Windows Media Player library folders are powerful tools for keeping your recordings organized because they offer so many different ways of looking at the same information.

It behooves you to keep your data clean. Misfiled and misidentified songs lead to endless frustration when you can't find a song that you know should be in the library. If you want to change the data associated with a bunch of songs (for example, if the songs are all by the same artist or on the same album), follow these steps:

1. **Find them in the library, and get the library to list the individual songs. (Typically, you can do that by double-clicking an album.)**
2. **Select the songs (Ctrl+click to select individual songs or Shift+click to select a group of songs).**
3. **Right-click one of the fields (for example, Album or Artist) and choose Edit.**
4. **Type the new value and press Enter.**

   All selected songs are changed at the same time.

Rating songs

One of the most powerful WMP capabilities, the ability to create and manipulate playlists based on your own ratings of individual songs (or movies or TV shows), works only if you take the time to rate your songs! To rate any track or album at any time, right-click it, choose Rate, and give it a rating from 1 to 5 stars. You can even select multiple tracks or albums and rate them all in one fell swoop.

If you have WMP show you albums rather than individual songs, the really cool rating system doesn't work as well. When WMP rates an album, it uses the average rating of all the songs in the album. So, if you have an absolutely great song inside a rather dull album, if you sort the albums by rating, you might not even get around to that truly great song. The only solution? Lie. Rate all songs in the album with five stars. That way, the album floats to the top of the charts.

Sorting songs

You have a great deal of flexibility in the ways you can sort. If you want to look at all your rap and hip-hop albums, for example, make sure that you're looking at the Music category (in the upper-left area) and then double-click Album to list all albums by album name. Now click the top of the Genre column to sort the list of tracks by genre, from *A* to Z. Click Genre again to sort the list backward.

If your collection of recordings is large, sorting the list in different ways can help you find items you want. Microsoft claims that Windows Media Player can handle tens of thousands — even hundreds of thousands — of tracks. Go ahead. Put it to the test.

Searching

You can search the Music Library (or any of the other libraries, for that matter) for items that have certain words in their titles or for artist names, album names, composer names, conductor, date, or genres. When your collection of recordings becomes too large to inspect easily, this is a convenient way to find things in it.

Searching the Music Library is much like searching in Windows Explorer — no doubt because they use the same search engine. To find what you want, simply start typing in the Search box, in the upper-right part of the screen. WMP responds immediately, narrowing its list of found items as you type. In Figure 1-16, my search for blue brought up Diana Krall's song "Almost Blue," as I would expect, but also Eric Bibb's *Get Onboard* album. Why? The album is filed under the genre Blues.

Figure 1-16: Searches look for titles, artist names, album names, genres, composers, and other ancillary meta information.

Depending on where you perform the search, WMP may display a list of how many artists, albums, or songs match the search criteria. In that case, simply click the underlined link to view the results.

You can use the Windows 7 search tricks, which I describe in Book III, Chapter 3. For example, AND, OR, and NOT work in the Search box: A search on *Willie Nelson* AND *minuet* brings up Willie's "Bach Minuet in G" from his album *The Promiseland.* No, I'm not kidding.

Managing Playlists

Er, maybe that should be *mangling* playlists.

WMP gives you all sorts of control over which songs you hear, and it does so through playlists. Did you ever want to rearrange the order of the songs on The Beatles' *White Album*? My son just about croaked when he found out he could burn a CD that plays Britney Spears' "Oops! . . . I Did It Again" immediately after Eminem's homage "Oops! . . . The Real Slim Shady Did It Again." You've got the power. Hmmm. That's a catchy tag line, isn't it?

Windows Media Player helps you create your own playlists, and you can modify them to your heart's content.

Creating a new playlist

If you have a favorite set of tracks that you like to hear in a particular order and the tracks are in the Music Library (or Video Library), you can build a playlist that gives you precisely what you want. It's like being able to create your own, custom CD.

In fact, you can use a playlist to make your own, custom CD, if you have a CD burner (er, recorder). Nothing to it. The section "Burning CDs and DVDs," later in this chapter, explains how.

To make your own playlist, follow these steps:

1. **Make sure that the Music Library is showing (on the left edge). If the Playlist area on the right has a bunch of music in it, click the Clear List link at the top of the Playlist area.**

   Windows Media Player invites you to drag items to create a new playlist, as shown in Figure 1-17.

Figure 1-17: Build a new playlist by dragging tracks to the area on the right.

2. **On the left, navigate to each song that you want to have on the playlist and then drag it to your preferred location on the right.**

   You can use any of the navigation tools — choose an artist, album, or genre, or use the search box — everything's fair game.

   WMP adds the track to the playlist. In Figure 1-18, I build a playlist of rock songs by the Thai-American artist Tata Young.

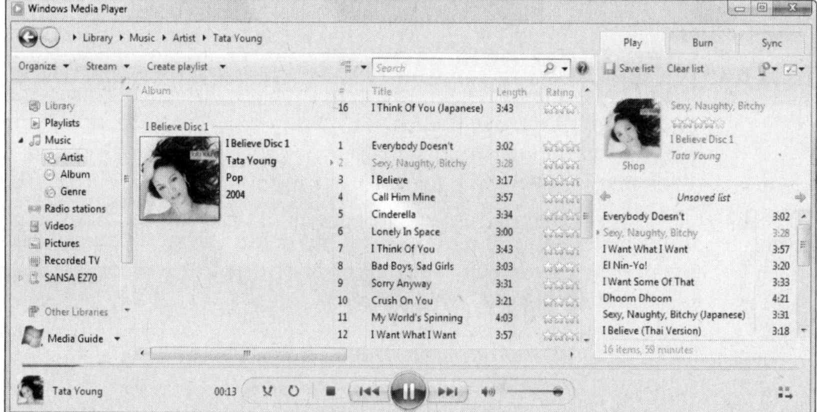

Figure 1-18: Various tracks from my favorite Thai rock singer.

3. **If you decide that you don't want a specific song on the playlist, right-click it and choose Remove from List.**

4. **Click and drag to move the songs up and down on the playlist.**

5. **When you're happy with your playlist, click the Save List button at the top of the Playlist area.**

   WMP highlights the Untitled Playlist text box, inviting you to type a name for the new playlist.

6. **Type a name for your new playlist in the Untitled Playlist text box and press Enter.**

   WMP saves your new playlist. It appears anywhere playlists appear, anywhere in Windows Media Player.

That's how easy it is to create a new playlist.

Note how Windows Media Player shows you the common decency of not arbitrarily rearranging the order of the songs.

Adding a track to a playlist

In the library, you can add a track to any playlist, at any time. Just follow these steps:

1. **Find the track.**

   You can use any of the navigation tricks.

2. **Right-click the track and choose Add To, and then choose the playlist.**

   It's that easy.

Alternatively, you can open a playlist so that it appears on the right (say, by double-clicking a playlist on the left) and then drag new tracks into the playlist. Just remember to click the Save List link when you're done.

You can add the same track to any number of playlists. Just right-click it again, choose Add To, and pick a different playlist.

Don't worry about using up storage space. Playlists take almost no room. No matter how many playlists you add a track to, Windows Music Library maintains just one copy of the track. Playlists are like headings in a library catalog: No matter how many headings a particular book is indexed under, just one copy of the book exists.

Renaming and deleting playlists

To change a playlist's name, you can right-click the playlist name on the left, in the Playlists list, and choose Rename. Or, you can simply click the playlist name near the top of the Playlist area on the right, and type the new name.

To delete a playlist, follow these steps:

1. **Right-click the playlist in the Playlists list (say that ten times really fast) and choose Delete. Or, just click the playlist and press Delete.**

   WMP responds with a confusing dialog box, as shown in Figure 1-19.

   Don't worry. Removing a playlist does *not* remove the songs from your computer. Where the dialog box says Delete from Library and My Computer, it isn't referring to the songs. The songs stay on your computer no matter which choice you make. The dialog box is referring to the playlist — and you can delete a playlist from your computer with no ill effect.

2. **Choose either the Delete from Library Only or the Delete from Library and My Computer check box, and then click OK.**

   There's essentially no difference between the two choices, unless you want to copy playlists from computer to computer.

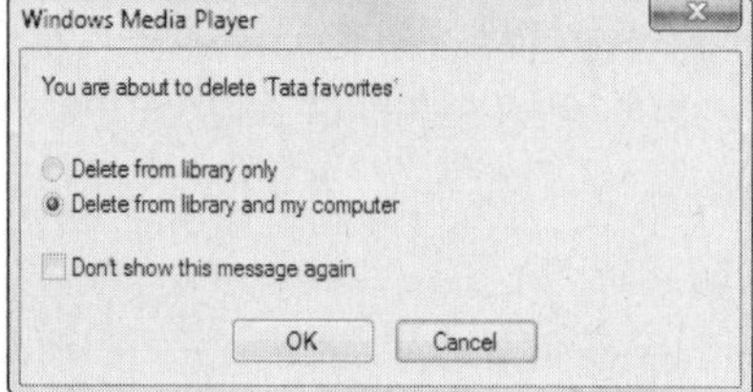

Figure 1-19: Select an option to delete a playlist.

Managing the contents of playlists

Just as you can manage playlists, you can manage the contents of a playlist. You have these options:

- To make any type of change to a playlist, double-click the playlist in the left pane of the library and then make your changes in the right pane.
- To delete a track from the playlist, right-click the track and choose Remove from List, or select the track and press Delete. That doesn't delete the song. It removes the song from the playlist.
- To change a track's position in the playlist, just drag the track to the position you want.

Deleting tracks from the library

No matter how many playlists a track is added to, your hard drive still contains just one copy of the track. The reverse is just as true: Even if you delete a track from every playlist that contains it, the track is still on your hard drive, and the Music Library still has a record of the track.

However, you *can* remove a track from the Music Library (or Video Library or Recorded TV Library).

If you right-click a track, an album, or even an artist or genre, and choose Delete, WMP asks whether you want to delete the track (album, whatever) from only the library or from both the library and your computer, as shown in Figure 1-20. This dialog box looks exactly like the one you see when deleting a playlist (refer to Figure 1-19), but it's not nearly as innocent. When you click a track (as opposed to a playlist), selecting the Delete from Library and My Computer check box deletes the song itself from your computer.

This concept is complicated. If you choose to Delete from Library Only, Windows Media Player doesn't delete the track (clip, whatever) from the Windows Music Library. Instead, it marks the track so that Windows Media Player doesn't show it again. If you select Delete from Library Only, the track still shows up when you choose Start⇨Music. But it doesn't appear in Windows Media Player. No, I don't know why.

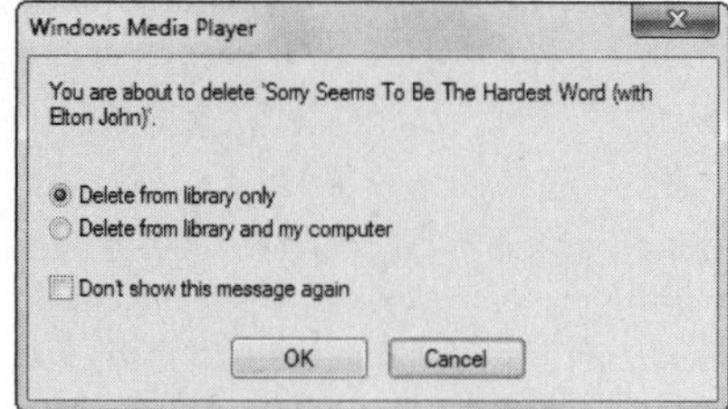

Figure 1-20: This dialog box asks whether you want to delete the song itself.

Rarely do you want to delete a track from your computer — although if you have 200GB of tracks (and I don't mention a certain author by name), you might want to free hard drive space by working from inside Windows Media Player. In general, choose to delete the track from the player (so that it doesn't clutter things when you're looking for stuff you really want to play), but don't delete the track from your computer.

Burning CDs and DVDs

If your computer has a CD writer, you can create an audio CD by using tracks in the Music Library. Windows Media Player makes it easy.

Of course, you can also burn CDs and DVDs by using Windows 7 itself — see the nearby sidebar "Burn with Windows or Media Player?" But if you want to make an audio CD — that is, a CD that you can stick into any old CD player — you need to use Windows Media Player. Just as ripping (see the section "Copying from a CD (Also Known As Ripping)," earlier in this chapter) changes audio sound tracks into files that the computer can understand, burning with Windows Media Player transforms those files back into audio sound tracks that any CD player can play.

You may also want to use Windows Media Player to burn a data CD or DVD — which is to say, a CD or DVD that contains MP3 (or WMA) files. If you have your music organized into playlists, or if you want to burn more than one CD-ful or DVD-ful of music files, using WMP runs rings around the Windows-based click-and-drag method — and it's much, much easier to maintain the sequence of songs you specify.

Burning video DVDs — that is, transferring movies to a DVD writer — is an entirely different can of worms. I talk about burning DVDs in Book IV, Chapter 6.

Burn with Windows or Media Player?

When you insert a blank CD into your CD/DVD drive, you may be stumped when Windows asks whether you want to burn an audio CD using Windows Media Player or burn files to disc using Windows Explorer. When you stick a blank DVD into your CD/DVD drive, you're asked whether you want to burn files to disc using Windows Explorer or burn a DVD video disc using Windows DVD Maker.

There's a reason why Windows presents you with such obfuscated choices. Here's the scorecard:

If you want to burn an old-fashioned audio CD — the kind you can stick in an old-fashioned CD player — you must use a blank CD and you must use Windows Media Player. You end up with one album on one CD. Give or take a fudge or two.

If you want to burn a DVD video — the kind you can stick in a DVD player — you must use a blank DVD (or Dual Layer DVD or Blu-ray disc), and you must use Windows DVD Maker.

Here's where it gets murky. If you want to put music on a CD and you're going to play that music on most modern CD players, you want to stick MP3 music files on the disc. (That way, you can squish ten albums or so on a single CD.) Windows calls a CD with MP3 files a music "data disc," and you can create data discs with either Windows Explorer or Windows Media Player.

If you want to put an AVI file on a DVD — some DVD players can play AVI files — you have to use Windows Explorer. But you can also put smallish AVI files on CDs, and many DVD players play them just fine. For that matter, you can stick a ton of MP3s on a DVD and some CD players play them.

If you want to stick your MP3s on a CD, Windows Media Player has a few features that help: For example, WMP keeps track of how much data fits on the CD and warns you if you have accumulated too much. (Although I hate the way WMP makes it hard to change the sequence of folders being burned.) If you're going to put music on a CD, this chapter is the one you want to read.

In Book II, Chapter 4, I talk about using Windows Explorer to burn CDs and DVDs. Those CDs and DVDs may contain MP3 or AVI files, or data, programs, and the like.

Burning an audio CD

To a first approximation, if you're going to create an audio CD, you should use a blank CD-R disc, as opposed to a (more expensive) CD-RW rewritable disc. It maximizes the chances that your burned CD can work in almost any sentient CD player. I go into very gory detail about various ways to make your burning life more complicated in Book II, Chapter 4. If you just want to burn an audio CD, don't read that chapter. Grab a plain old CD-R disc, follow the instructions here, and forget about the complicated stuff.

The process of writing data to a CD is called *burning*. Rip and burn. Rip and burn. WMP enables you to burn a plain, old-fashioned, everyday audio CD very, very easily. Here's the quickest way I know to put together a dynamite audio CD:

1. **Stick a blank CD-R disc in your CD drive.**

   Assuming that you have a CD drive that's capable of burning CDs, Windows 7 responds with the AutoPlay dialog box, shown in Figure 1-21.

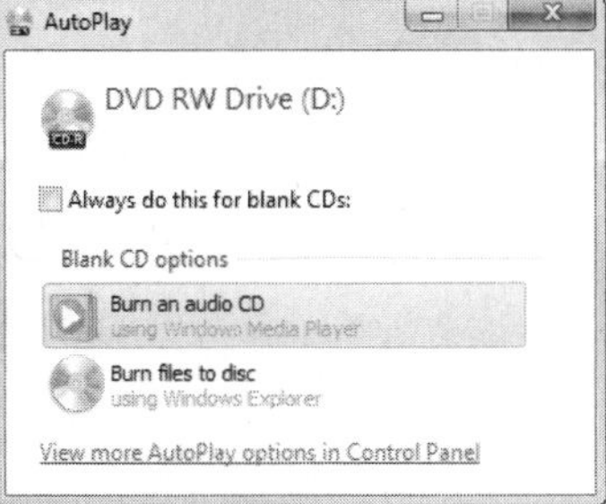

Figure 1-21: The fastest way to burn a plain, old-fashioned audio CD.

2. **Click the Burn an Audio CD Using Windows Media Player icon.**

   Windows 7 opens WMP and starts a burn list for you on the right (see Figure 1-22).

Figure 1-22: Ready to create a burn list.

3. **Using any tricks you can muster (listing by artist or album, sorting, searching, pulling up an existing playlist — whatever), click and drag the tracks you want to burn, and arrange them on the right, in the burn list.**

   Keep an eye on the "Remaining" number at the top of the list. WMP has been known to overestimate the available room on a CD, so it's a good idea to leave a minute or two or three, unused, on the CD.

If you try to put too much music on a CD, WMP breaks out the burn list, with horizontal lines marking the current disc, the next disc, the next disc, and so on. When you burn a multidisc list, you just have to keep feeding CDs into the drive. Easy.

4. **As a precaution, if you just created a unique playlist, save it by clicking the name Burn List at the top of the playlist on the right (see Figure 1-23) and typing a new name.**

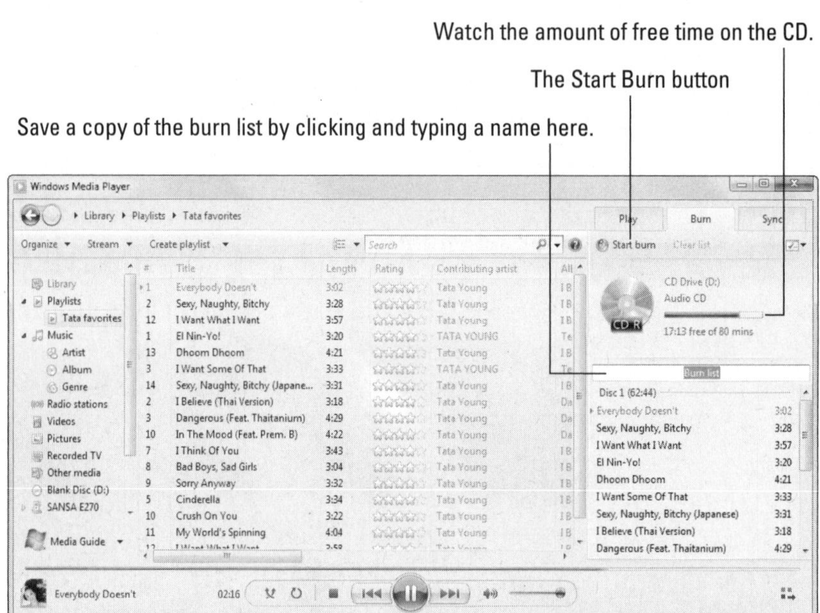
Watch the amount of free time on the CD.
The Start Burn button
Save a copy of the burn list by clicking and typing a name here.

Figure 1-23: Save your Burn List in case you need it later.

The saved playlist can come in handy if a problem crops up with the burn that you don't find out about for a day or two or three. You can select your saved playlist rather than redo the working of choosing and arranging the tracks just the way you want them.

5. **Before you burn, double-check the burn options so that you don't, uh, get burned. In the upper-left corner, choose Organize➪Options and then click the Burn tab.**

   The Burn Options are listed in Figure 1-24.

6. **Follow the advice in Table 1-3 to set up the burn the way you want it.**

7. **When you're happy with your choices, click the OK button.**

   WMP goes back to the main Burn window (refer to Figure 1-23).

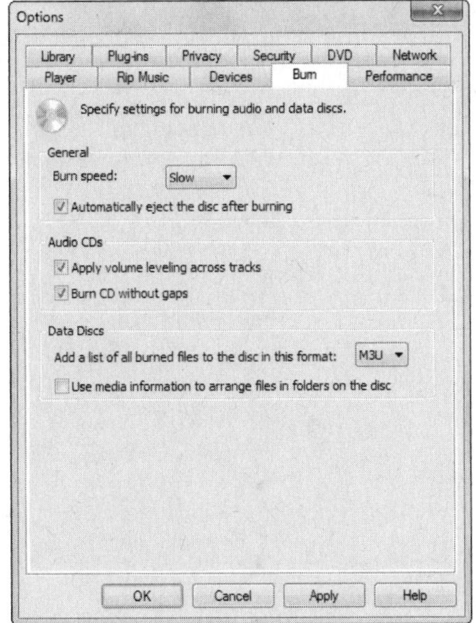

Figure 1-24: Set the basic burn characteristics.

8. **Click the Start Burn button, at the top of the burn list.**

   WMP processes each track in turn, converting it from a music file into data that's required on an audio CD and, when it's done converting, writing each one to the CD.

   It's truly that simple. When WMP is done, pull the CD out of the CD burner and plop the CD into any CD player. The magic's the music.

Table 1-3 Recommended Burn Options

Setting	*Recommendation*	*Reason*
Burn Speed	Slow	Greatly reduces the chances of turning out a coaster. If it takes longer, it takes longer, okay?
Apply Volume Leveling Across Tracks	Check	It takes more time but ensures that you don't get blasted by a rogue song.
Burn CD without Gaps	Check	If you deselect this check box, WMP inserts an additional 2-second gap between each track.
Add a List of All Burned Files	M3U	Use M3U, the universal playlist format. WPL is the Microsoft format.

(continued)

Table 1-3 *(continued)*

Setting	*Recommendation*	*Reason*
Use Media Information to Arrange Files	Unchecked	Keep this option deselected so that WMP leaves the sequence of your tracks the way you set them when you burn a "data disc" — a disc full of MP3 files. (Note that WMP *always* honors your sequencing when you burn an old-fashioned audio CD.) If you select the box, WMP groups data disc songs by album, no matter how you laid out the tracks in the burn list. The files appear in `\Music\Artist\Album` folders, where the artist and album information is pulled from each individual track.

The copying process takes, oh, a third to a fifth of the time it would take to play the copied tracks, the exact time depending on the speed of your CD writer.

If you interrupt the writing process by clicking the Stop Burn button or by removing the CD from the writer before the burn is complete, WMP goes bananas and the whole process stops. A fried CD-R ain't good for anything but a coaster.

Burning data CDs and DVDs with Media Player

The procedure for burning data CD-Rs, CD-RWs, DVD-Rs, and DVD-RWs with Windows Media Player is essentially the same as that described in the preceding section, except that . . .

. . . you can fit a whole lot more music on a data CD than on an audio CD. In spite of that fact, the burning process for a data CD can go faster than that for an audio CD. Why? WMP doesn't have to preprocess data files — it doesn't need to convert them into a form that works with audio CD players.

If you already set the data disc's options in Step 6 (refer to Table 1-3), you've done everything you need to do to produce top-notch MP3 (er, data) CDs and DVDs. Just remember to click the check box icon above the burn list and choose Data CD or DVD, as shown in Figure 1-25.

Figure 1-25: To burn a data disc (full of MP3s), be sure to choose Data CD or DVD before you start the burn.

Syncing with a Portable Player or Mobile Phone

Call it an MP3 player, if you will. Call it a Zune. (The folks at Microsoft do, but they kinda have a vested interest.) Or, call it a portable digital audio player or a personal digital device. Moving your songs from your computer to an MP3 player has never been simpler. Most mobile phones are just as easy.

Audio is only part of the story, though. The new generation of portable video machines — whether you call the device a Portable Media Center (a term trademarked by Microsoft, of course), MP4 player, fancy phone, video jukebox, digital video player, or that dern MTV thingy — seems poised to take over the toy market.

Windows Media Player handles both audio and video (including recorded TV) with aplomb. In fact, when WMP works right, transferring files to your portable player is every bit as easy as burning a CD. It's easier, actually, because you don't have to put a blank CD in the drive.

If you can't get WMP to work with your particular MP3 player or phone, you may have to resort to using the software that came with the machine. That's a pity, really, and the number of nonconformist players and phones has fallen off in recent years. But realize that the WMP way isn't the only way, and you may have to fall back on the Sony or LG or Nokia or Samsung software that came with your machine. If you have an iPod, you can't use Windows Media Player, either. The iPod has a weird internal format, and syncing with WMP doesn't add songs to iPod playlists. You have to use iTunes, Winamp, or another iPod-speaking media program. See Book IV, Chapter 2 for details.

The very best, very latest players and phones (except the iPod family) work with the phenomenal Windows 7 Device Stage. If you have a new player or phone and the advertising says that it works with Device Stage, don't hang around here. Hop over to Book VIII, Chapter 2 and revel in your wondrous purchase.

Moving tracks to the player

Here's how to get your tunes and flicks onto your MP3 or video player:

1. **Attach your player/phone/whatever to one of your computer's USB ports and turn it on.**

   Windows 7 should identify the player with the Found New Hardware Wizard. If all else fails, read the player's instruction manual and run the program on the CD that came with the player to get the drivers working. You may need to visit the manufacturer's Web site to download the latest drivers. This technology is changing fast, and drivers become obsolete overnight.

   If your MP3 player holds more than 4GB of data and your music collection is less than 4GB, Windows Media Player asks your permission as soon as you plug in your player and then automatically syncs your player, copying all your music from your computer to your player. Personally, I don't worry about it too much. My music collection hasn't measured less than 4GB since about 1993. Bet you're in the same boat.

2. **Start Windows Media Player if Windows 7 doesn't start it for you. Click the Sync tab if it isn't already showing.**

   Windows 7 shows you the MP3 device in the upper-right corner (see "Sansa e270" in Figure 1-26) and sets up a sync list for you.

Figure 1-26: Syncing with an MP3 player is easy.

3. **Use whatever tricks are at your disposal (clicking entries on the left, sorting, searching) to find tracks that you want to transfer to the MP3 player. Click each track and drag it to the Sync List on the right.**

   See the section "Finding the tracks you want," earlier in this chapter, for details.

   Watch the "remaining" counter to fill your MP3 player as far as possible. If you drag too many songs to the sync list, right-click any you want to remove and choose Remove from List.

4. **To save your new playlist (and you should), click Sync List at the top of the sync list and type a new name.**

5. **Click the Start Sync button.**

   WMP copies the files in your playlist to your portable player.

   If your MP3 player didn't have enough room, Windows Media Player simply states that the track or tracks weren't copied.

   Note that nothing on your MP3 player gets deleted. Syncing with WMP is quite different from syncing with iTunes (see Book IV, Chapter 2).

6. **When the copying is done, unplug your portable player and have at it.**

   Transferring songs, video, and TV shows is truly that simple, as long as your media files are the kind your player understands.

If you need to convert files on your computer into formats that your player can understand, remember that Google is your friend. For example, to search for converters that can change QuickTime MOV files into AVI files (which essentially all portable video players can understand), search Google for *convert MOV AVI free.*

Moving tracks from the player to your PC

If you have tracks on your player that you want to copy to your PC, this section is the one for you — unless you have an iPod.

If you have an iPod, copying music from your iPod to your computer involves a trip through Windows Explorer, with hidden files displayed. It isn't difficult, but it's a pain in the neck. See Book IV, Chapter 2 for details. The method I explain in that chapter works for copying files from any other kind of MP3 player to your computer too, but why bother? Windows Media Player makes it easy to "reverse sync" your music.

To reverse-sync your music from your player to your PC using Windows Media Player, follow these steps:

1. **Plug your MP3 player into your computer.**

   Windows Media Player may appear, showing the Sync tab.

   If this doesn't happen, start Windows Media Player and click the Sync tab. You should see an invitation to drag songs off your MP3 player and stick them on your computer, as shown in Figure 1-27.

Figure 1-27: WMP offers to sync tracks on your MP3 player, sticking them on your computer.

2. **On the left, click the name of your MP3 player and then click the `Music` folder underneath.**

3. **Navigate to the songs you want to copy to your PC.**

   You can use any of the typical tricks, including a search.

4. **Click and drag the songs you want to retrieve to the sync list on the right.**

   The Start Sync link magically turns into a Copy from Device link.

5. **After you gather all the songs you want to copy to your PC, click the Copy from Device button.**

   WMP lists each song and lets you know when they've been copied.

The songs end up in your computer's `Public Music` folder or whichever folder you designated as your default folder for ripped music. See the section "Copying from a CD (Also Known As Ripping)," earlier in this chapter.

Deleting tracks from your player

What? You're tired of listening to the same Weird Al Yankovic song a hundred million times? Does it make you break out in hives? Zap it!

WMP makes it surprisingly easy to manually delete any song you like. But before you make any rash decisions — sorry, Al — why not create a backup copy of the song, before you send it to that big bit bucket in the sky? Here's how:

1. **Follow the steps in the preceding section to copy to your PC the songs you want to delete from your player.**

   If a particular song is already on your PC and you try to reverse-sync it, WMP simply tells you that the song is already in the library. No biggie.

2. **When WMP finishes copying all the songs to your PC, right-click the song in the Copy from Device list on the left and choose Delete (see Figure 1-28).**

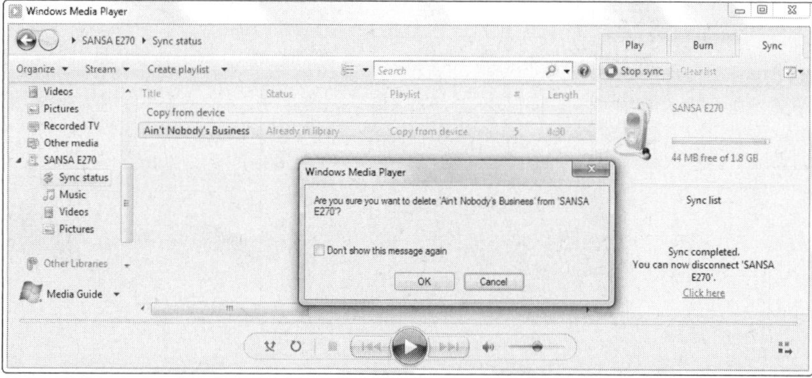

Figure 1-28: Deleting songs from your MP3 player is easy, too — if you know the trick.

3. **When WMP asks for confirmation that you want to delete the song from the MP3 player, click the OK button, and it's gone.**

Sharing Your Windows Media Player Media

Windows Media Player can make media in its libraries available to other computers on your network by using the *streaming* technique. To a first approximation, streaming involves using your Windows 7 PC to send signals to a digital media player, which can then play the music or show a movie on a television. That can be mighty handy if you want to hook up an Xbox 360, or some other network digital media player, to play songs or movies.

The mechanics for setting up a network in your house or small office are straightforward. The mechanics for sharing things over the network aren't quite so easy.

I talk about networking and sharing all sorts of things in Book VII, Chapter 2.

If your Windows 7 computer is part of a HomeGroup (see Book VII, Chapter 1) and you haven't changed any settings, your computer automatically shares everything in its media libraries (Music Library, Video Library, Recorded TV Library, Picture Library) with all other computers in the HomeGroup and with every user on every computer in the HomeGroup.

If you have an Xbox 360 or some other kind of networked digital media player that doesn't understand HomeGroups, you should hop into Windows Media Player and give Windows permission to share your media — assuming that you *want* to share your media.

Here's how to share all your media:

1. **Start Windows Media Player and click the Play tab.**
2. **In the upper-left corner, click Stream➪More Streaming Options.**

   You see the Media Streaming Options dialog box. Depending on how many computers you have connected to your network, it looks more or less like Figure 1-29.

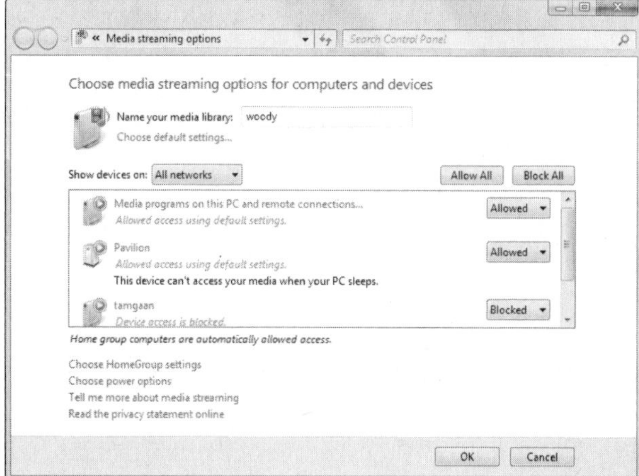

Figure 1-29: Media sharing options.

3. **In the Show Devices On drop-down box, choose All Networks.**
4. **Click the button marked Allow All.**

   This step sets up streaming for any device now connected to your network. It also opens your media libraries to other computers on your network. Windows Media Player on those other computers shows your media libraries under the Other Libraries entry on the left side of the main Windows Media Player window.

If you get stuck with C.R.A.P. media that plays only on your computer, streaming in this way may be a viable option — if your network is fast enough to handle the load.

Customizing WMP

You can customize WMP in a large number of ways. You get to most of the settings by choosing Organize➪Options. This command displays a dialog box with a bunch of tabs for customizing many aspects of WMP behavior:

- ✦ **Player:** Controls general aspects of WMP behavior, such as checking for automatic updates.
- ✦ **Rip Music:** Controls aspects of the copying process, including, most importantly, the format of ripped CDs (which you set to MP3 already, right?). You can also control the amount of data compression to apply when copying a CD. (More compression makes the copied tracks occupy less space, but reduces sound quality.) It also controls the folder to which music is copied. (You changed it to your computer's `Public Music` folder, right?)
- ✦ **Devices:** Lists available devices that WMP can use (such as CD drives and portable players) and enables you to control certain aspects of their behavior. If you tend to rip CDs with lots of scratches, click the Devices tab, click your DVD drive, and then click Properties. In the Rip section at the bottom (see Figure 1-30), select the Use Error Correction check box and click OK. That makes ripping go slower, in some circumstances, but increases the chances that you perform a clean rip, even from an iffy CD.

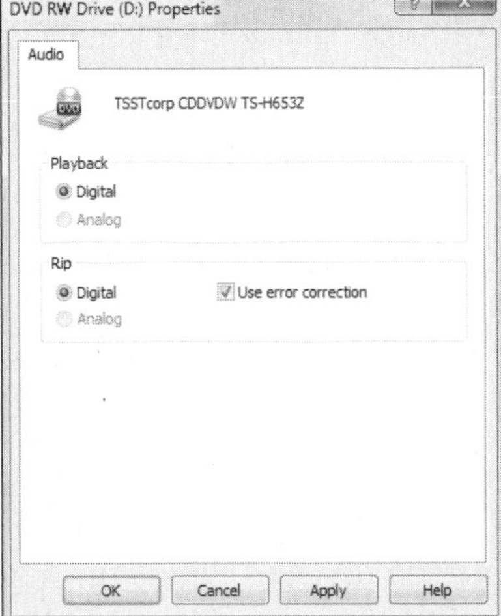

Figure 1-30: Tell Windows to keep trying, over and over, to produce a high-quality rip.

- **Burn:** A subject I talk about extensively in the section "Burning CDs and DVDs," earlier in this chapter.
- **Performance:** Lets you control how WMP handles streaming media.
- **Library:** Controls whether WMP looks for video files in the Pictures Library, whether volume-leveling information should be calculated for new files, and how WMP retrieves information from the Internet.
- **Privacy** and **Security:** Primarily controls how much information you send to Microsoft every time you use WMP. See the section "Adjusting WMP Privacy Settings," earlier in this chapter.

  My privacy settings are shown at the beginning of this chapter (refer to Figure 1-4). If you decide to give Microsoft more information than the amount shown in that figure, I strongly recommend that you click the Read the Privacy Statement Online link and read the information with a thoroughly jaundiced eye.

- **DVD:** Sets the default language that's used when playing DVDs.
- **Network:** Lets you select the network protocols that WMP may use to receive streaming media. It also lets you control proxy settings, which you may have to change if your computer is on a local-area network protected by a separate firewall.

It would take an advanced degree in computer science to even begin to understand many of these settings. Come to think of it, I have an advanced degree in computer science and I don't understand some of those settings. It's a good policy to change one of the options only if you understand it well and keep careful notes so that you can restore the original setting if anything goes wrong.

There's no harm in looking at the options, though. You can discover a lot by rummaging through each tab of the Options dialog box.

Chapter 2: iPod and iTunes in Windows 7

In This Chapter

- Getting your iPod to work
- Getting your iPod to work right
- Copying songs from your iPod to your computer
- Solving the problems everyone has with iPods and Windows

So you went out and splurged on a brand-new iPod, eh? Yeah. Me, too — six times, at last count. That teensy, tiny Shuffle is positively o-o-o-zes cool.

No doubt you've discovered that the iPod works fine with Windows — as long as you use Apple software and buy from the Apple music store, and you don't want to do anything Apple doesn't want you to do. B-o-r-i-n-g.

Look. You bought your iPod. You paid for your music (or you got it for free, legitimately). You bought your PC. You paid for Windows 7. So why in the heck are you treated like a criminal every time you want to do something reasonable?

As Windows 7 hit the stands, Apple and the iTunes Store were experiencing a traumatic transition: Before 2009, Apple controlled the music you bought in the iTunes Store, and you had few options and no rights. Because most iPod owners bought their music from the Apple iTunes Store, Apple called the tune and set the rules for what you can and can't do with your purchase. It's all about C.R.A.P. music; see Book IV, Chapter 1 for details.

By the time Windows 7 arrived in the fall of 2009, Apple had seen the error of its ways (and the plummeting of its income) and converted almost all its iTunes tunes to the MP3 format, which can't be controlled.

You, too, can convert your digital-rights-encumbered iTunes tracks to so-called iTunes Plus music (the *Plus* means "C.R.A.P.-free") for 30 cents per song. (See `www.apple.com/itunes/whatsnew`.) So, if you made a mistake and paid Apple for digital-rights-locked music, you can pay them again and get the music unlocked. Golly.

Because upward of 5 *billion* Apple-locked songs are running around, this chapter has to cover the unsavory, and increasingly obsolete, restrictions that Apple still imposes on its old songs. The restrictions are going away gradually, but if you can't figure out why iTunes prevents you from performing perfectly reasonable actions with your own songs, the tricks in this chapter should help.

What You Can't Do

I bet you've shed more than a few tears (and sworn more than a few syllables) trying to figure out why these things happen:

- **You can't use Windows Media Player to put music on your iPod.**

  Why? No way will Microsoft do anything to support iPod. Well, okay, maybe if UFOs invade Lake Washington and a hundred little green aliens march into Bill G's living room, chanting "I pod, you pod, we all pod for iPod. . . ."

- **You can't upload music from your iPod to your PC, using either iTunes or Windows Media Player.**

  Why? Apple wants you to buy more music from the iTunes Store. Microsoft wants you to buy more from the MSN Music store (or whatever front it's using this week). Neither Microsoft nor Apple nor the music companies want you to use your iPod to move music from one PC to another, even if you bought and paid for the music. Ka-ching. But a solution exists. See the section "Copying Songs to Your PC," later in this chapter.

- **You can play MP3s on your iPod and play music you bought from iTunes on your iPod, but you can't play music that you bought from other services on your iPod — unless, of course, you were smart enough to buy MP3 music.**

  Why? Because every place that sells music other than MP3s is banking on customer ignorance to keep the suckers — er, customers — tethered. My favorite example: Microsoft's old PlaysForSure campaign. If you bought music from Microsoft that "plays for sure," you got hoodwinked — the music *doesn't* play, for sure, on most MP3 players.

  If you have unprotected WMA files (that's the Microsoft proprietary music format), iTunes gleefully translates them into AACs (to a first approximation that's Apple's proprietary format), and the translated files play on your iPod.

- **You can't add music from two computers to the same iPod.**

  Why? When you connect an iPod to a computer it becomes "tethered" to that computer. As long as you only plug it into the same computer, everything (usually) works as advertised. But when you move the iPod to a second computer, iTunes wants to erase all the old music and sync with the music on the second computer. Of course, Apple stands to make more money that way, but you have a rather easy (and not well known) way to get around the restriction.

✦ **You plug your iPod into your computer, and all of a sudden, some songs that you had on your iPod disappear.**

  Why? Apple built it that way, to enforce its digital rights management scheme. It's called auto-sync. I talk about how to disable it — or at least make it work for you, instead of against you — in the sidebar "The downside of automatically syncing," later in this chapter.

✦ **You can't play any music you bought from the iTunes Store before 2009 on another computer. (If you're really unlucky, or just weren't paying attention, this problem can happen with music you bought after 2009, too.)**

  Why? Apple built it that way, to enforce its digital rights management scheme. (Do you hear an echo in here?) Actually, you can copy and play the music you bought on as many as five different computers (if you know the trick), but you can't mix 'n' match — all five computers have to be "locked in" to the same iTunes Store account. See the sidebar "The five-PC limit for older iTunes songs," later in this chapter.

  But you can play regular old MP3 music files on your iPod, even if you borrowed those files from your maiden aunt's long-suffering hairdresser's underworked and overpaid boyfriend.

  Why? Because Apple would lose most of its market share overnight if it blocked the most popular open music file format.

Does it cost $30,000 to fill an iPod?

Touting its Zune Pass service, Microsoft claims that it costs $30,000 to fill a 120GB iPod with music and costs only $15 a month for unlimited music on a Zune Pass (see `zunepass.net`). It's a sobering thought — but the devil lies in the details.

Though it's true that a 120GB iPod can hold 30,000 songs, give or take ten thousand or so, few people go out and buy 30,000 songs in one fell swoop. Of course, after you buy MP3 songs, you can play them anywhere, on any computer, or burned, sliced, and diced to the owner's content.

You pay $15 per month for Zune Pass, but if you stop paying, your songs die. *Bye-bye, Miss American Pie.* You have to download your entire collection once a month. Microsoft lets you keep ten songs a month, but at that rate it would take 250 years to fill your 120GB Zune with tunes. You can play the downloaded music on as many as three PCs or Macs and as many as three Zune players. But you can't burn any of the songs on CD or DVD, and Microsoft retains full control over the music: You play by Microsoft's rules, or you don't play at all.

The subscription model has too many restrictions for my tastes, but you may well disagree. Choose whatever feels right and vote with your pocketbook.

Using Winamp to feed your iPod

iTunes ain't the only game in town. If you own an iPod, you can't use Windows Media Player to fill it with music — but you *can* use Winamp (`winamp.com`). The free version includes full iPod support, without many of the "weirdities" that Apple retains to try to sell you more music.

Copying songs from Winamp to your iPod takes three steps: Add the music you want to a playlist; select the playlist; and right-click and choose Send To⇨your iPod. It's that simple.

Best of all, your iPod isn't married to a single computer. Though you have to perform your updates manually in Winamp, all the legacy junk that Apple has to keep around for its nefarious digital rights management (DRM) scheme doesn't even appear in Winamp.

It's surprisingly difficult to get surprisingly simple things done, eh?

Fortunately, decent workarounds exist for all those problems, and many more.

The rest of this chapter not only explains the "official" way to work with your iPod but also takes you behind the scenes to see how the pros make iPods dance the hurdy-gurdy, whether the folks in Redmond or Cupertino like it or not.

iPod the Apple Way

So you pulled your iPod out of its cavernous box and you're ready to boogie. Fine. Just don't bother slipping the iPod driver CD into your computer. The stuff on the CD is obsolete by now, and you want the latest.

Even if you already installed anything and everything that Apple has to offer, your first stop should be the Apple Web site.

In the following sections, you find out the best way to break in your new iPod by getting the software you need, setting up iTunes, and filling the iPod with songs.

Installing the iTunes program

The *iTunes* program runs on your PC. It uses another Apple program, QuickTime — a video-playing program that I've sworn at for many years. When you install iTunes, you install QuickTime, whether you want to or not.

From time to time, Apple also tries to get you to install other pieces of ju — er, software, such as Safari, Bonjour Services, the Apple Updater, MobileMe, and they've been known to use sneaky techniques to convince you to install the other ju — er, software. So keep your guard up, and keep your clicking finger at bay. The idea is to install iTunes because you have to — and nothing extra. If that friendly Apple update reminder appears miraculously on your screen three months from now and says you need to install *another* wonderful Apple product, you have my permission to guffaw and obliterate the reminder.

Over the years, Apple PC software has repeatedly driven me nuts. Bonjour, in particular, has been known to cause major headaches with corporate virtual private network (VPN) connections. Look before you leap.

You need to make sure that you have the latest version of the internal iPod software *(firmware)* and the latest version of iTunes. You don't need to do this every week, but you probably should check things out every few months. Here's how to keep on top of the latest:

1. **Crank up your favorite browser and head to** `www.apple.com/itunes/download`**.**

   You might shield your eyes before you hit Enter. The site's a bit, uh, overwhelming.

2. **On the left, choose between Windows 64-bit and Windows 32-bit (probably marked Windows XP or Vista). Click Download Now.**

   If you aren't sure whether your copy of Windows 7 is 32-bit or 64-bit, click Start, right-click Computer, and pick Properties. The, uh, bittedness of your computer appears at the bottom of the list marked System.

   You can elect to put your e-mail address on the special Apple mailing list, thereby ensuring a constant run of ju — er, informative e-mails — that keep you up to date with Apple news and the latest information. Submit your e-mail address, if you like, but realize that you don't need to give Apple anything more. You've already given it your money.

   Windows warns you that Apple is trying to invade your system. Actually, it says that you have chosen to open `iTunesSetup.exe`. Depending on your browser, save the file or open it. After you save it, double-click the file and press whichever placating buttons are necessary to run it.

   The iTunes installer appears, as shown in Figure 2-1. Remember that installing iTunes also brings along QuickTime, a movie-playing program from Apple that I've been swearing at for a decade.

3. **Click Next to start the installation and then click through the End User License Agreement (EULA).**

   You see the Installation Options dialog box, shown in Figure 2-2. iTunes asks permission to bug you, for not only iTunes but also any other program that Apple wants to throw your way.

4. **Deselect the check box marked Automatically Update iTunes and Other Apple Software. Also, deselect the check box marked Use iTunes As the Default Player for Audio Files.**

   In the past, Apple has used the update "permission" to bother iTunes users into installing Safari and putting ten new icons on the desktop.

   If you let iTunes take over all your audio files, it appears in all sorts of weird places and does things that aren't at all intuitive — to me, anyway.

5. **Click Install.**

   The installer splashes an ad on your screen, does its thing, and ends several minutes later with a Congratulations! message.

6. **Click Finish.**

   You can quit at this point, or you can continue on to start iTunes for the first time. See the next section.

Figure 2-1: Installing iTunes gives you a QuickTime bonus.

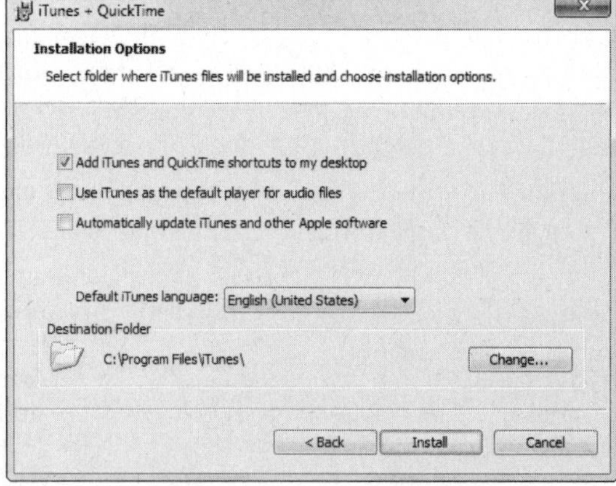

Figure 2-2: iTunes asks permission to bug you.

Setting up iTunes

Before you use iTunes for the first time, you get to run through the iTunes Setup Assistant program. Here's how to minimize your ongoing headaches:

1. **If you quit immediately after iTunes is installed (see the preceding section) or if iTunes was preinstalled on your PC, double-click the iTunes icon to run iTunes for the first time. (Otherwise, you automatically come to this step after iTunes has been successfully installed.)**

   After you click through another license agreement, which is only slightly shorter than the U.S. Constitution, the iTunes Setup Assistant appears, as shown in Figure 2-3.

Figure 2-3: Yes, iTunes has an installer *and* a Setup Assistant.

2. **Click Next.**

   The assistant presents you with the dialog box shown in Figure 2-4. *Don't* let iTunes scan just yet.

   The Setup Assistant offers to scan your music library (or at least part of it), looking for MP3 and AAC files, to add them to the iTunes catalog. The Setup Assistant also offers to scan for WMA (Microsoft format) files and convert them to AAC (Apple format) files: The WMA files aren't touched, but AAC copies appear on your hard drive in the iTunes library.

3. **Deselect both check boxes — don't let iTunes scan for existing music just yet. Then click the Next button.**

   Later, in Steps 6 and 7, you can change the automatic scanner so that it generates MP3 files (which can be used anywhere) rather than Advanced Audio Coding (AAC) files (which are good only in the Apple world, really) when it automatically converts Microsoft-formatted (WMA) music files. You don't need to run the scan now and create a bunch of files you'll never use.

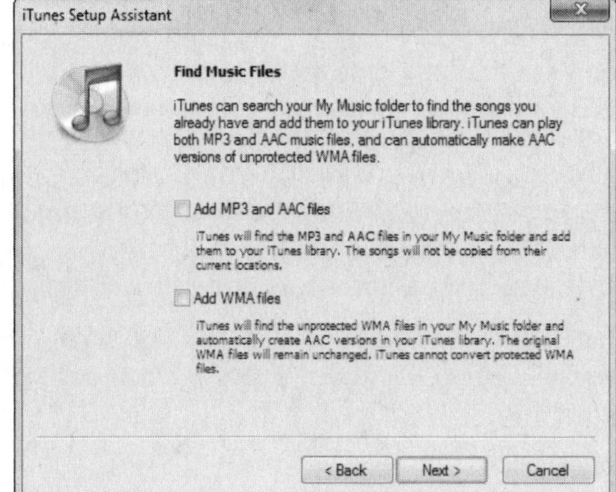

Figure 2-4: Don't let iTunes scan for existing music yet.

Whenever you convert file formats, the quality of the recording suffers. If you have a bunch of WMA files that were ripped from CDs by Windows Media Player, it would behoove you to take the time to rip the same CDs again, but into MP3 format. You won't notice the quality difference on your portable boom box, but if you listen carefully on good-quality equipment — even on an iPod — you can tell the difference between converted WMA files and those ripped directly to MP3. See Book IV, Chapter 1 for details.

The assistant asks whether you want iTunes to maintain its own music folder.

4. **Select the Yes, Keep My iTunes Music Folder Organized check box and click the Next button.**

   Allowing iTunes to maintain its own music folder (which is kept in your `\Music\iTunes` folder) can help keep things straight on your iPod. iTunes is quite good about not creating extraneous copies of music files — the folder is used only when you convert music file formats or change the names of songs.

   The Setup Assistant explains that iTunes can automatically download album covers for you, but you have to create an iTunes Store account in order to enable the feature. If you plan to buy MP3 files from iTunes that are free of digital rights management, that isn't a bad idea. You don't need to do anything right now.

5. **Click Finish.**

   iTunes appears in all its naked glory — without a song to be seen but offering to sell, sell, sell, as shown in Figure 2-5.

6. **Immediately choose Edit⇨Preferences. In the dialog box that appears, on the General tab, click the Import Settings button.**

You see the Import Settings dialog box, shown in Figure 2-6. Switch around the iTunes importer so that it rips and converts imported WMA files to the MP3 — not AAC — format.

7. **In the Import Using drop-down list, select MP3 Encoder. For Setting, use Higher Quality (192 kbps). Select the check box marked Use Error Correction When Reading Audio CDs. Then click the OK button.**

   By doing so, you ensure that iTunes always rips songs into MP3 format. (See Book IV, Chapter 1 for a description of why that's beneficial.) You also ensure that when iTunes encounters a WMA file that hasn't been locked up with digital rights management, it converts the WMA file into an MP3 file. (WMA is the Microsoft proprietary music format.)

Figure 2-5: iTunes finally appears and invites you to spend money the Apple way.

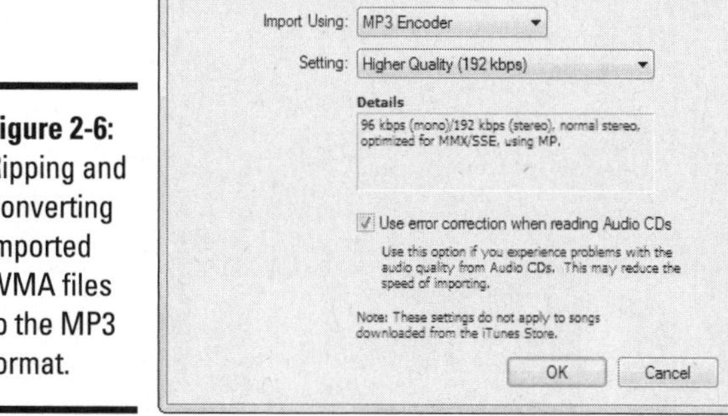

Figure 2-6: Ripping and converting imported WMA files to the MP3 format.

I strongly recommend that you use error correction when ripping audio CDs, even if it takes more time, because it minimizes your chances of coming up with ripped tracks that are screechy and skippy. Ya know — like peanut butter?

Now it's time to import your music into iTunes. (Note that your music hasn't moved — iTunes just collects pointers to the song files.)

8. **Choose Start➪Music, click any albums or songs that you want to add (or press Ctrl+A to select everything in your `Music` folder), and drag the albums into the left pane in iTunes.**

   If iTunes bumps into songs in WMA format, it warns you (see Figure 2-7). Click the Convert button, and iTunes automatically creates an MP3 version of the song, placing it in the `iTunes` folder `<your username>\Music\iTunes\iTunes Music`.

   Your WMA file remains intact — iTunes doesn't touch it.

9. **Gather all the music you like — and avoid the music that you don't particularly want on your iPod. (You can use Windows Media Player to mess around with that stuff.)**

   In the end, you should have a sizable collection of music. If you gather more than can fit on your iPod (as you can confirm by the status bar at the bottom of the iTunes window; see Figure 2-8), not to worry: iTunes can help.

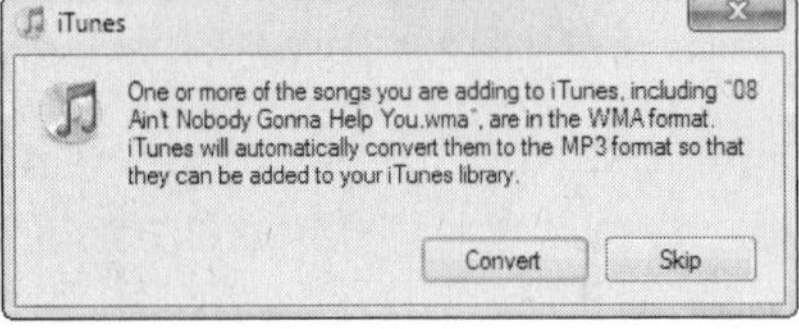

Figure 2-7: Converting WMA songs to MP3 format.

Figure 2-8: iTunes now has 2.32GB of songs, according to the status bar.

The five-PC limit for older iTunes songs

Back before Apple got the MP3 religion, music sold in the iTunes Store was restricted to playing on five computers. If you have old iTunes music and don't want to pay Apple to release its chains, you may still have music that lives under the bad, old rules. Here's how it works.

Each computer (PC or Mac) gets branded with an Audible Account ID (which does double duty as an iTunes Store account number). As many as five computers can be branded with the same Audible Account ID. Songs can be played only on computers branded with the original, downloading computer's Audible Account ID. Confused? Yeah, me too.

Say you buy a song at the iTunes Store with an Audible Account ID of `myaccount@someplace.com` and the password `123456789`. Here's a hypothetical scenario to show you how the limit might affect your use of that song:

- **Sharing a song with another computer requires authorization (or branding).** Keeping with the example, you give a copy of the song to your son to play on his computer. When he tries to play it, iTunes asks for authorization. Your son has to type `myaccount@someplace.com` and the password `123456789`, and his computer is then "branded" with that account number. (Not so coincidentally, he now has your iTunes Store ID and password.) Now, you and your son can share songs bought using that iTunes Store account number 'til the cows come home. You can copy the file without restriction. But the song doesn't play on any PC unless the person who tries to play the file can provide the correct authorization — `myaccount@someplace.com` and password `123456789`.
- **Because a computer can be branded with only one Audible Account ID, you can't mix and match songs.** If your computer is branded with `myaccount@someplace.com`, you can't play songs that were bought with, oh, `anotheraccount@someplaceelse.com`. It's an either-or situation.
- **Only five PCs, at any one time, can be branded with that Audible Account ID.** To deauthorize a computer, go to iTunes, choose Advanced➪Deauthorize Audible Account, type your Audible Account ID and password, and click the OK button. That frees one of the five available copies.

If you ever discover that iTunes failed to pick up a new song — one that you ripped from a CD, downloaded from the Internet, or bought from an online service — simply locate the song file or album folder and drag it into iTunes, precisely as you did in Step 8.

Now would be a good time to run through the Apple iPod tutorial. Even if you've been using an iPod for years, you might pick up on some nuances that could prove to be fun — or even useful. Start at `www.apple.com/support/ipod/tutorial` and click the Click to Play link.

With the latest versions ready, and a bit of Apple party line orientation under your belt, it's time to fill your iPod.

Moving music to your iPod

Have all the songs you want in your iTunes library? Good. It's time to transfer them to your iPod. Here's how:

1. **Wait until you have enough time to fill up your iPod.**

   If you have a lot of music, it can take an hour. You don't have to sit next to the iPod while it's transferring music, but you should stick around and check on it occasionally, like it's a five-year-old.

2. **Get iTunes going and plug your iPod into your USB port.**

   If you see an AutoPlay notice, click the red X to get rid of it.

   The iPod setup page appears, as shown in Figure 2-9.

Figure 2-9: Set up your iPod for the first time.

3. **Give your 'Pod a good name.**

4. **Consider whether you want your iPod to be updated automatically, and select or deselect the check boxes accordingly.**

   I have iTunes update my iPod automatically. Why? Because I use Windows Media Player to work with most of my music. I put only the songs I want on my iPod in one specific playlist in iTunes. (The next section shows you how.) I add or remove songs from the playlist as the mood strikes. And, I tell iTunes to sync only this specific playlist. That way, when I plug my iPod into my computer, I know exactly which songs will get synced.

   There's a downside to automatically updating your songs, as I explain in the nearby sidebar, "The downside of automatically syncing."

If you choose to update your iPod manually, you just need to click the Sync button in iTunes before your songs are synced.

You probably don't want to sync your photos, unless you have only a few photos inside iTunes — otherwise, your photo collection takes over your Pod.

5. **Click Done.**

   If you selected the check box marked Automatically Sync Songs to my iPod, iTunes takes off and immediately begins copying songs to the iPod.

   You see the iPod Summary tab, shown in Figure 2-10.

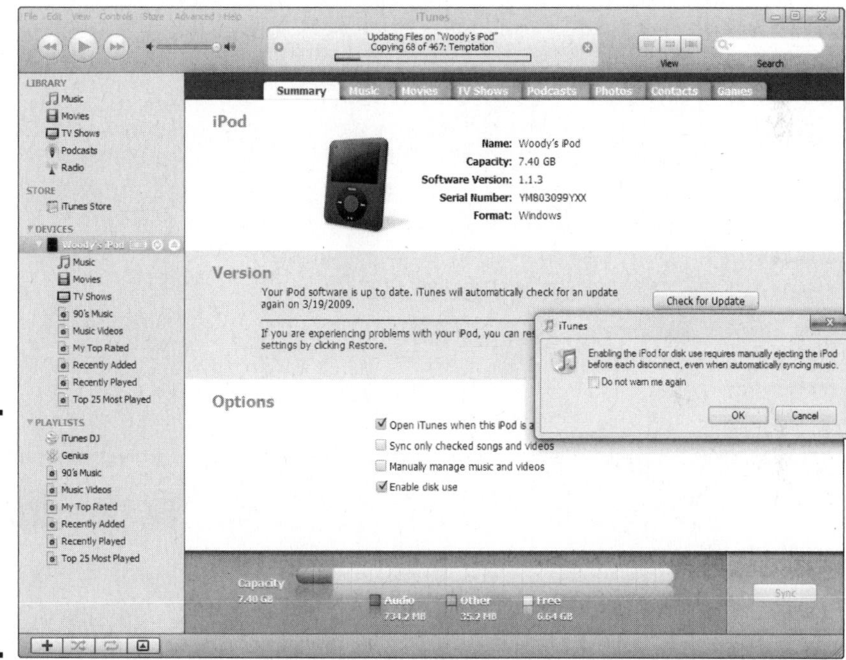

Figure 2-10: iTunes immediately starts copying music to your iPod.

6. **If you want to take control of your iPod — including being able to copy music from the iPod to your PC, as I explain later in this chapter — select the Enable Disk Use check box.**

   iTunes warns you that enabling the iPod for disk use means that you have to eject the Pod — if you simply yank the cord, some data may get scrambled.

7. **Click OK to dismiss the warning.**

8. **If you have too much music to fit into the iPod, iTunes detects a blivet condition (that's a technical term — never mind) and asks whether it can choose a selection of songs to copy to the iPod. If you see that dialog box, click the Yes button.**

If you tried to put more music on your iPod than the iPod can handle, iTunes automatically creates a new playlist named `<your iPod's name> Selection`. (In my case, it's `Woody's iPod Selection`.) The program trims the list of songs you tried to put on the 'Pod, removing songs from the bottom of the list, and that truncated list of songs becomes the new playlist, `<your iPod's name> Selection`. iTunes then automatically sets itself up so that it synchronizes the `<your iPod's name> Selection` playlist with your iPod.

The process sounds complicated, but it's about the only thing iTunes can do. If you ever wondered why your iPod synchronizes with a weird playlist that you didn't personally create, now you know why.

When iTunes finishes syncing — copying the songs from iTunes to the iPod — it tells you, in the box at the top of the iTunes window, that the sync is complete, as shown in Figure 2-11.

iTunes

iPod sync is complete.
OK to disconnect.

Figure 2-11: Start grooving!

The downside of automatically syncing

During a sync, iTunes reigns: What's on iTunes is synced to your iPod, according to the settings you selected in iTunes. If you choose to automatically sync, you can't count on your iPod to be your backup if something goes awry in iTunes. For example, if you remove a song from iTunes (even accidentally), or if something catastrophic happens to your iTunes database, the next time you plug your iPod into your computer, it's synchronized quite precisely: Any songs that are in your iPod, but aren't in iTunes, disappear.

If you backed up your PC (as you should; see Book II, Chapter 3), you should have copies of your music. Or, if you chose to sync manually, you have a chance to grab the songs off your iPod before you sync (see "Copying Songs to Your PC," later in this chapter).

Controlling syncing with playlists

I've played with iPods for years now and have finally settled on a way of syncing that works for me. I bet it'll work for you, too. I have a whole lot of music — much more than will fit on the iPod. And, I don't trust any automated gizmos — not even the Genius feature — to choose the right music for me. Here's how I set up iTunes to sync <ahem> "My-y-y-y Wa-a-a-y."

Gad. I didn't really say that, did I?

The trick is to set up playlists and then tell iTunes to sync only those playlists. Here's how it works:

1. **Start iTunes. Click the Music Library, in the upper-left corner. Choose File⇨New Playlist.**

   iTunes opens a new, blank playlist.

2. **Click and drag into this new playlist the songs you want to put on your iPod.**

   Fill 'er up! A status bar at the bottom tells you how much space remains.

3. **On the left side, scroll down to the bottom of the Playlists list, click the text *untitled playlist,* and type a good name for your sync playlist.**

   In Figure 2-12, I name my new playlist Stuff to Sync.

   If you want, you can create multiple playlists to break your songs into categories. (You might have a playlist of fast-paced songs for the gym and another for relaxing in the dentist's waiting room before your root canal surgery.) Just repeat Steps 1 through 3.

Figure 2-12: Give your iPod sync list a name.

4. **When you're done dragging songs into the playlist, on the left, under Devices, click your iPod and then click the Music tab.**

   You see a list of all your playlists, as shown in Figure 2-13.

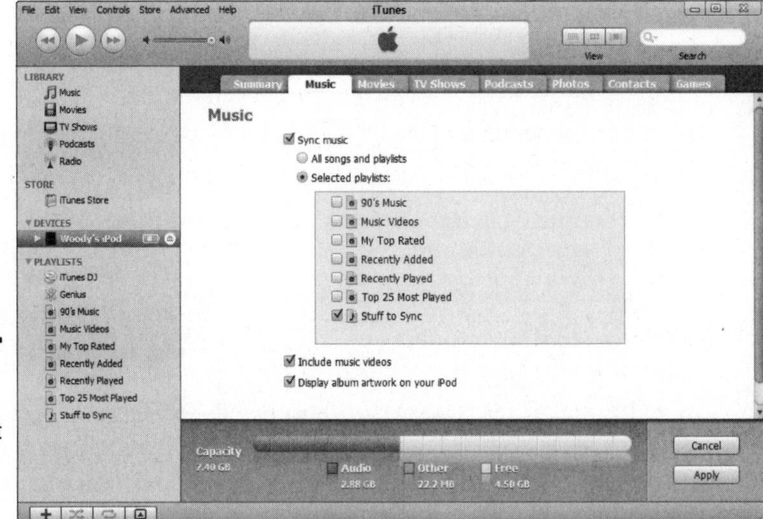

Figure 2-13: Choose playlists that sync automatically.

5. **Select the button marked Selected Playlists, and then select the check box next to the name of the sync playlist you just put together.**

   This step tells iTunes that you want it to sync only this specific playlist (or playlists).

6. **Click Apply. Then click the Summary tab and click Apply again.**

   iTunes syncs to your new playlist. The next time you plug your iPod into the computer, it syncs to the same playlist.

Sometimes your iPod flashes a "Do not disconnect" message while iTunes says "iPod update is complete / OK to disconnect." (It's a bit of iPodding cognitive dissonance, eh?) If that ever happens to you, click the Eject iPod icon to the right of the name of your iPod. Give it a few seconds, and as long as the battery's charged, the iPod should say "OK to Disconnect."

Copying Songs to Your PC

Here's one question I hear over and over: How do I take songs off the iPod and copy them back to my PC?

It's very easy. In fact, if you follow my instructions in Book II, Chapter 1 and tell Windows 7 that you want to see hidden files, you're basically done. Here's how to copy songs back to your PC:

1. **Make sure your iPod is set to Enable Disk Use.**

   See Step 6 in the section "Moving music to your iPod," earlier in this chapter. You may have to plug your iPod into your computer, start iTunes, and double-click the name of your iPod under Devices on the left, in order to see the Enable Disk Use option.

2. **If your iPod isn't connected to your computer, plug it in. If you receive an AutoPlay notification, click the Open Folder to View Files Using Windows Explorer link.**

   If your iPod is already connected, or you don't see an AutoPlay notification, choose Start➪Computer and double-click your iPod "drive."

   If you don't see a drive letter for your iPod, go back to Step 1. You have to select the Enable Disk Use setting for your iPod or else it doesn't show up in Windows Explorer.

   Windows Explorer should look like Figure 2-14, with your music in the hidden folder `iPod_Control`.

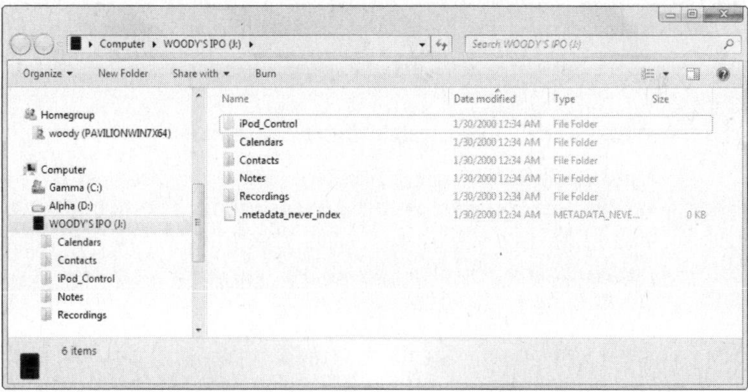

Figure 2-14: Your music is in the hidden folder `iPod_Control`.

3. **If you can't see the `iPod_Control` folder, press Alt and then choose Tools➪Folder Options➪View. Select the Show Hidden Files and Folders check box, and then click OK.**

   While you're here anyway, deselect the Hide Extensions for Known File Types check box. Click the OK button.

   The details are in Book II, Chapter 1, but every Windows 7 user needs to be able to see her hidden files and folders and her full filename extensions. I hate to say it, and I don't mean to nag, but I toldja so.

4. **Double-click to navigate to the `iPod_Control\Music` folder and then double-click one of the subfolders.**

   On an iPod nano, they're marked F00, F01, and so on.

5. **Right-click one of the columns and choose More. Select the Album and Title check boxes. Click the OK button.**

   Windows Explorer shows you the (inscrutable) iPod filename, plus the album title and the song's title, as shown in Figure 2-15.

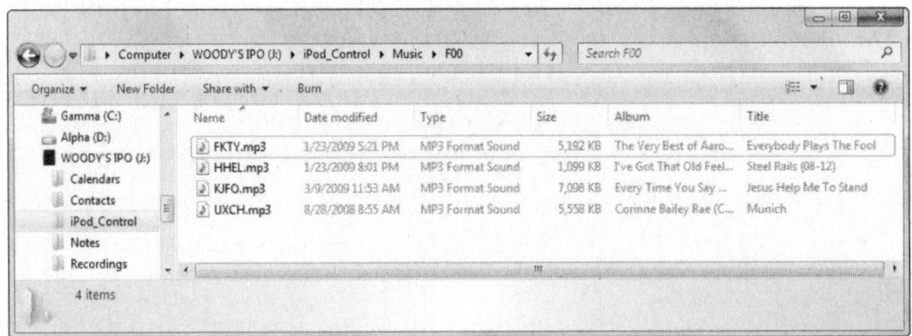

Figure 2-15: A track name and an album title for every song.

6. **Select, click, drag, copy, and so on to copy the files back to your PC.**

   You can treat the files on your iPod like any other files. But don't move or delete them! The iPod keeps its own database. It ain't nice to fool with Mother Nature. If you want to remove a song, use iTunes.

7. **When you're done, click the red X to exit Windows Explorer.**

8. **Double-click the Safely Remove Hardware icon, in the system tray — er, notification area — next to the clock. Then choose your iPod.**

   The Safely Remove Hardware icon looks like a USB plug with a green check mark on it; you may have to click the up-wedge in the notification area before you can see it.

   After you select your iPod, Windows displays the Safe to Remove Hardware balloon in the notification area. At that point, you can unplug your iPod, even if it still shows the Do Not Disconnect icon.

Taking a Look at the iPod Ecosystem

An entire industry has grown up around the iPod: cute little fuzzy things that warble and squeak; cases that can withstand a point-blank blast from an Abrams M1A2 tank; and lots of software that can turn your iPod into an air-traffic control system — or a puddle of useless iron. It's a cool puddle, yes, but a puddle nonetheless.

If you're interested in keeping up on the latest, permit me to recommend a couple of Web sites:

- ipodhacks.com does a good job of dishing out iPod news. It's a bit Mac-centric for my tastes, but that's just me. Its forums cover just about every nook and cranny of iPod-dom.
- ilounge.com covers the news, but more from an industry perspective. Its free Buyer's Guide to iPod and iPhone Accessories is well worth the download. You'll find lots of information.

If you have an iPod, you should also read *iPod & iTunes For Dummies*, 6th Edition, by Tony Bove (published by Wiley). You can also check out articles, tips, and videos to help you get started with iPod and iTunes at www.dummies.com.

Chapter 3: Discovering Digital Cameras and Recorders

In This Chapter

- Choosing a camera
- Buying a camera
- Moving photos and movies to your PC
- Sharing your shots

Microsoft spent a lot of time and money adding rudimentary but capable photo and movie features to Windows 7. The result won't impress anyone who's accustomed to working with, say, Photoshop. But for most of us, the Windows 7 photo and video capabilities are good enough, and they're remarkably easy to use. They also tie in, reasonably well, with Windows Live Photo Gallery, which I discuss in detail in Book IV, Chapter 5 and Windows Live Movie Maker, which you can find in Book IV, Chapter 6.

The Windows 7 video/photo shtick is composed of three programs that work together, more or less:

- ✦ The **Import Pictures and Videos** program moves digital photos (and movies) from your camera to your computer's hard drive.
- ✦ The **Windows Live Photo Gallery** works with photos on your computer (or on your network). You can adjust, crop, rotate, print, or burn photos to CD or adjust them for red-eye reduction. The Live Photo Gallery also lets you run a bunch of photos you choose as a slide show. I talk about Windows Live Photo Gallery — one of those "Live" programs that you need to download — in Book IV, Chapter 5.

Technically, Windows Photo Gallery supports JPG, TIF, and WPD files, and can support camera RAW files in many cases. (See the nearby sidebar "What about RAW?") GIF and BMP files — typically, clip art — aren't handled.

Although the Photo Gallery can show you videos, you can't do much with them.

✦ **Windows Movie Maker** provides tools for creating movies, editing and stitching together clips and photos, and adding sound, titles, and other elements. I talk about Windows Live Movie Maker — another one of those "Live" programs — in Book IV, Chapter 6.

In this chapter, you discover a basic introduction to choosing a digital camera and the ins and outs of hooking it up to your PC, and moving pictures from the camera to the PC, where you can store, edit, and print them with just a couple of clicks.

Buying a Camera or Camcorder: The Bottom Line

Here's my 60-second guide to buying a digital camera or camcorder, assuming you don't have a few minutes to hop over to Hong Kong:

1. **Decide whether you want a still camera or a camcorder.**

   Unless you can afford both a good digital camera and a good digital camcorder, this decision may be the most difficult. Ultimately, you have to decide how you want to use the pictures. Still cameras take lousy videos. Camcorders take lousy stills. If you want a mobile phone, pick the phone on its own merits; digital photos just come along for the ride.

2. **Narrow your choices to two or three models.**

   I recommend that you take a look at reviews in the major magazines and on Web sites such as `cnet.com` and `dpreview.com`. Photo magazine pieces are helpful, too, but unless you look at a side-by-side review that compares many cameras, you may be swayed by a tiny new feature that may or may not be all it's cracked up to be.

3. **Search the Web for comments.**

   A few minutes spent with Google — particularly, Google Groups — can save you days of headaches. Although you can't believe everything you read online, if you see ten complaints about picture quality under low-light conditions, think twice about buying it.

4. **Search the Web for prices and keep a list of the lowest ones.**

   When you have a short list of cameras you're interested in, you can easily run a quick price comparison. Everybody has favorite shopping sites, but I always check these:

   - `www.mysimon.com`
   - `www.shopping.com`

- www.pricegrabber.com
- www.nextag.com
- www.bizrate.com

I also drop by www.amazon.com, to see what customers say and to see whether its prices are competitive.

Don't overlook www.nextag.com. This site shows you historical prices for the camera so that you can see how rapidly the price is decreasing (see Figure 3-1). A recent, fast descent may mean that the camera's ready to be replaced with a newer model.

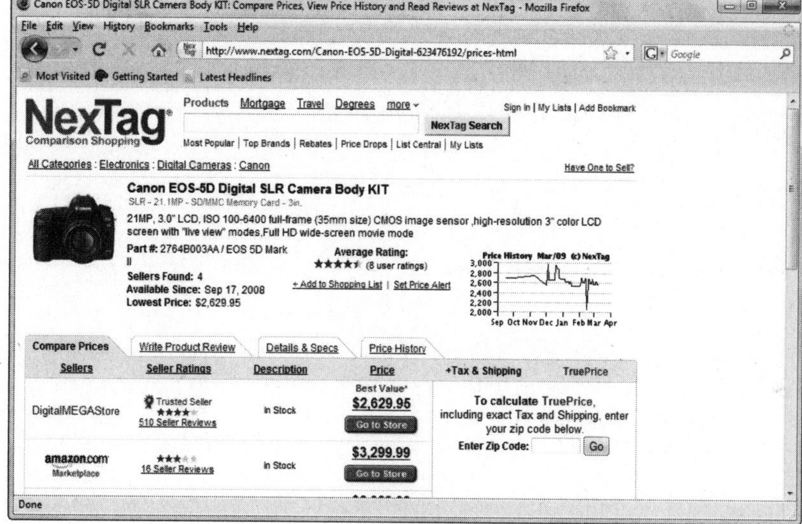

Figure 3-1: Nextag.com includes a price history graph that speaks volumes about price trends.

5. **After you have a good idea of what you want and how much it costs, you can shop anywhere with confidence.**

   Local discount stores may have the camera cheaper (don't forget to factor in shipping costs). Camera shops might charge a few dollars more, but their help — and the knowledge that you're supporting a local business — could well be worth spending a few extra dollars.

Come to think of it, those steps apply particularly *if* you hop over to Hong Kong — or 47th Street.

Don't forget the batteries

Digital cameras eat batteries for lunch. The Energizer Bunny might last only 20 minutes in a normal camera, particularly one being used at night. Throwaway batteries — especially if they're alkaline — don't last long, and they're murder on the environment. You need rechargeable batteries.

If you have a choice in the type of battery you buy, consider the following:

- **Lithium-ion (Li-ion):** These batteries recharge faster and hold their charge longer. But they cost more, and you can't recharge them as many times as other types of batteries.
- **Nickel-metal hydride (NiMH):** These batteries are slow on the uptake and discharge quickly, but they aren't as expensive as some other types and can be recharged many more times than Li-ion batteries. NiMH batteries are measured in milliamp-hours (mAh) per charge: A 1,800 mAh battery lasts 12.5 percent longer than a 1,600-mAh battery on one charge.
- **Nickel-cadmium (NiCad):** These batteries are the dogs — slow to charge and quick to die; they degenerate (each progressive charge gets less effective) and die much sooner than Li-ion or NiMH.

Also, consider spending extra for a fast recharger. If you have to wait eight hours to recharge your batteries and each set lasts 20 minutes — well, you do the math.

Moving Images to Your Computer

How you transfer images to your computer depends on the type of camera you're using.

If your brand-spanking-new camera came with a CD and a dire warning to install the camera manufacturer's program before trying to transfer pictures to your PC, fuhgeddaboutit. In my experience, file transfer applications from camera manufacturers are buggy, slow, and error-prone, and a general pain in the neck. It's far better to use the program that comes with Windows 7.

If you're using a conventional camera and your images were scanned by the photofinisher, transferring images is easy: Simply put the CD-ROM in a handy CD drive and copy the files, or go to the photofinisher's Web site and follow its directions. Rocket science.

If you're using a video camera, you should first try the interface in Windows Live Movie Maker, which I discuss in Book IV, Chapter 6. If you bump into a problem and you're looking for answers, start with the camera manufacturer's Web site (see Table 3-1).

Table 3-1	Major Camera Manufacturers
Manufacturer	*U.S. Web Site*
Canon	www.usa.canon.com
Casio	www.casio.com
Fuji	www.fujifilm.com
Kodak	www.kodak.com
Logitech	www.logitech.com
Nikon	www.nikonusa.com
Olympus	www.olympusamerica.com
Panasonic	www.panasonic.com/consumer_electronics
Sony	www.sony.com

You can use any one of three procedures to bring images from digital cameras and Internet cameras into your PC:

✦ **Webcams and digital cameras supported by Windows 7:** Plug the camera into your PC and use the Import Pictures and Videos program (see the steps that follow this list).

✦ **Any digital camera:** You can use the file transfer application provided with the camera, but I don't recommend these apps.

✦ **Any digital camera that uses memory cards:** You can transfer images by putting the card — say, an SD or a CompactFlash card — into a memory card reader. Sticking the card in a reader opens the Import Pictures and Videos program, and you can proceed in the same manner as though you had plugged the camera itself into the PC.

Use the Import Pictures and Videos program to transfer to your PC any images stored in the memory of a digital camera (or to capture still images from a Webcam). Follow these steps:

1. **Plug the camera into the appropriate port on your computer or, better, take the camera's memory card out of the camera and stick it in the computer.**

   If it's a digital camera, turn it on. You may have to move the camera's controls to a particular setting; consult the camera's instructions for transferring images.

Windows 7 should stumble for a few seconds, put a bubble in the notification area (near the clock) saying that it's installing the new device, and then confirm that the device is installed.

When Windows 7 comes back up for air, it shows you an AutoPlay dialog box, like the one shown in Figure 3-2.

Figure 3-2: Windows 7 is ready to transfer pictures.

2. **Click the Import Pictures Using Windows icon.**

   Windows responds with the main dialog box for the Import Pictures and Videos program, as shown in Figure 3-3.

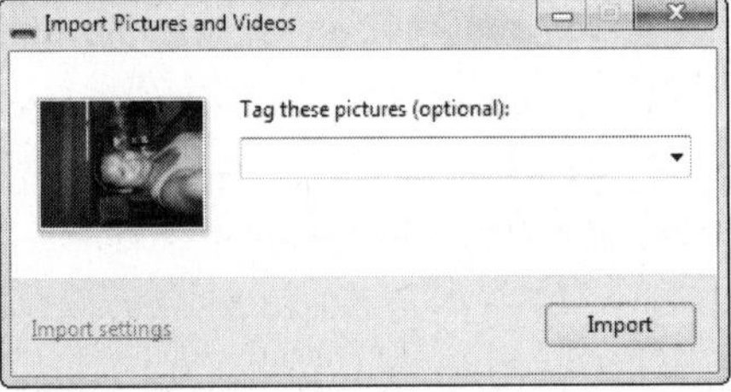

Figure 3-3: Modify the settings before you import!

3. **Click the Import Settings link.**

   The Import Pictures and Videos import settings dialog box appears, as shown in Figure 3-4.

   Personally, I change the image import folder to my `Public Pictures` folder: `c:\Users\Public\Public Pictures`. That way, anybody else on my computer — or anybody in my HomeGroup or on my network who has permission — can take a look at the imported pictures.

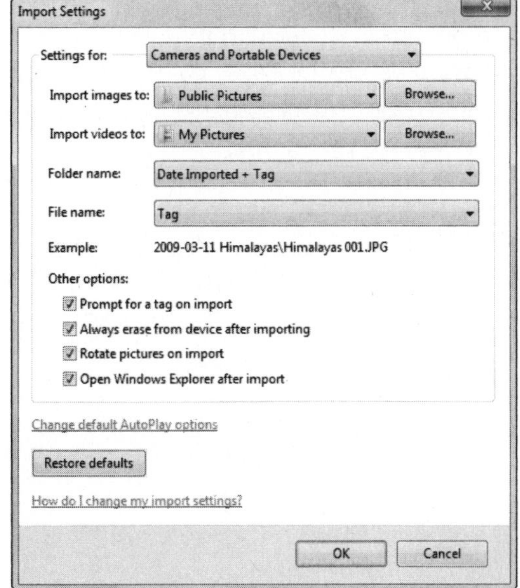

Figure 3-4: Tell Windows what to do with the imported pictures.

I also select the Always Erase From Device after Importing check box.

Selecting the Always Erase check box requires a small leap of faith, but after you use the Import Pictures and Videos program a couple of times, you'll probably let Windows do the deleting. If something goes bump in the night and you accidentally delete photos on your camera memory card, don't panic: See Book II, Chapter 1 for instructions on how to "undelete" the photos using a program named Recuva.

4. **Make the changes you feel comfortable with, and then click OK.**

   The Import Pictures and Videos program returns to the main dialog box (refer to Figure 3-3).

5. **Type a good tag for your pictures and click Import.**

   Windows 7 copies all pictures on the camera and puts them in a folder labeled with the current date and the tag you typed in Step 5. In Figure 3-5, I imported the pictures on March 11, 2009, and gave them the tag Phuket, so Windows 7 created a new folder named `\Pictures\2009-03-11 Phuket` and put all the pictures there.

   The imported pictures receive filenames based on the tag I typed in Step 5. In this case, they're named Phuket 001.JPG, Phuket 002.JPG, and so on. In addition, all the pictures are tagged with `Phuket`.

   If you chose to erase after importing in Step 4, Windows 7 then goes into your camera and deletes all imported pictures.

Mission accomplished, the Import Pictures and Videos program then opens Windows Explorer to show you the results.

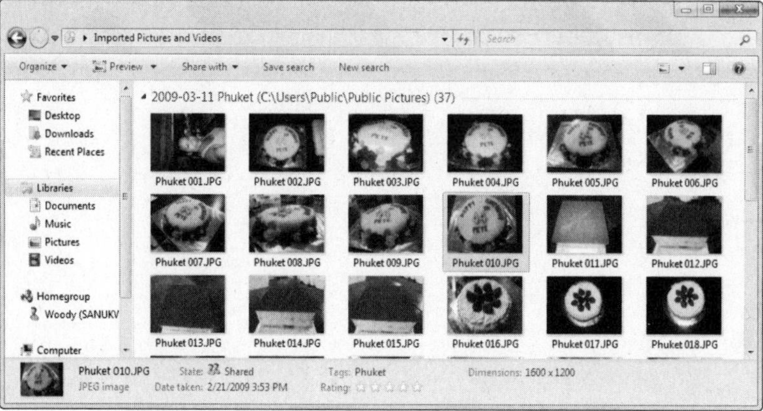

Figure 3-5: Pictures are automatically tagged and stored in a specifically generated folder.

If Windows 7 doesn't recognize your memory card, or if the camera stores data in a way that you can't get at directly (for example, on a hard drive), you may have no choice but to try the software that shipped with the camera to transfer images from the camera to your PC. Most digital cameras come with this type of application. Install it and follow its instructions. Good luck.

What about RAW?

Traditionally, most cameras save pictures in JPG format. JPG represents a decent balance between image quality and file size, and just about every kind of software recognizes JPG. It's a *lossy* format — some of the detail of the picture gets zapped in the process of crunching the bits.

Not so with RAW. The RAW file format (actually, it's a loosely defined bunch of formats) captures information from every single pixel inside the camera. When it comes to quality, what RAW sees is what you get. Full stop.

Unfortunately, every camera manufacturer creates RAW files in different ways, and the files themselves can be big — say, two to ten times the size of a good-quality JPG file. But if you work in the, uh, RAW, you can edit every detail that the camera can muster directly, without bumping into the pre-editing that's inherent in JPG.

RAW files are a pain in the neck. Not every camera can generate RAW files, and for daily use, you won't want to hassle with them. Nikon and Canon now have *codecs* (filters) that help you work with RAW files in Windows Live Photo Gallery and Picasa (the photo editing program from Google), although problems abound. RAW files produce tremendous results, however, and they're just one more reason why megapixels don't tell the whole story.

Sharing Your Pictures on the Web

When you have some nice pictures on your computer, naturally you want to share them with other interested people. As I mention in the next chapter, you can easily use Windows Live Photo Gallery to send pictures by e-mail or to burn pictures to a CD.

Many Internet service providers maintain Web servers where subscribers can post their Web sites with personal material. You can use this type of Web site to "publish" your pictures. Anyone who knows where to look can see them, of course, which you may or may not consider a good thing.

Check your service provider's Web site for information about its file hosting policies and instructions for uploading files.

More and more people are using free or inexpensive Web sites to share pictures. It makes a lot of sense: You don't need to clog your friends' inboxes with big pics when they can browse yours on Facebook or Flickr, download what they like — or ignore you.

These are the most popular picture-sharing sites:

- **Facebook (`facebook.com`):** As of this writing, Facebook leads the pack with more than 10 billion photos available online. Like all other major photo sites, Facebook makes its money (such as it is) from advertising. Although it's billed as a social networking site, the Facebook Photos feature is its most popular application. Facebook has extensive tools for limiting access to your profile and for inviting people to view your pictures or chat. You can upload a nearly unlimited number of photos to Facebook with no charge.
- **Photobucket (`photobucket.com`):** Unlike Facebook, Photobucket was designed from the ground up for photos. Photobucket automatically resizes photos you send that are too big for the site (1MB). Many people complain about the ubiquitous Photobucket advertising.
- **Flickr (`flickr.com`):** Yahoo!'s Flickr, the granddaddy of free photo-sharing sites, still offers a free account, limited to 20MB of uploads per month. You can specify who can see your pics or open them to the world, and uploading photos from your camera is easy. Tags and an "interestingness" filter help you find photos from other people that might ring your chimes.
- **Picasa Web Albums (`picasa.com`):** Google's Picasa Web Albums work as an extension to the Picasa photo handler. You get room for 1GB of photos for free. Blissfully ad free, Picasa Web albums are popular among people who work with lots of photos. (I talk about Picasa in Book IV, Chapter 5.)

Many other, smaller picture-sharing sites are worthy of your consideration. Shutterfly (`shutterfly.com`), Fotki (`fotki.com`), Kodak EasyShare (`kodakgallery.com`), and imeem (`imeem.com`) each have their strong points. Don't be afraid to shop around.

I cover digital photography extensively (and even answer questions!) on my Web site, AskWoody.com. You can also pick up *Digital Photography For Dummies,* 6th Edition, by Julie Adair King (published by Wiley).

Chapter 4: Managing Pics with Windows Live Photo Gallery

In This Chapter

- **Organizing with the Photo Gallery**
- **Fixing photos**
- **Taking advantage of Photo Gallery quirks**
- **Tagging with verve and alacrity**

Remember that photo I took of Dad falling out of the fishing boat? You know, the one from 1998? Or was it 1996? Wait a sec. Gimme a minute. I have it right here. Uh, no, it must be over here. Hmmm, maybe it's in this folder down here. Is it on the network drive? Er, where in the %$#@! did I put that thing?

Windows Live Photo Gallery brings a handful of sophisticated tools to the thorny problems of gathering, fixing, and, most of all, finding pictures on your computer.

Unfortunately, WLPG (as it's known to its friends) can't read your mind. If you want to retrieve that shot of Dad falling out of the fishing boat, you need to *tag* (mark) the picture with some pertinent keywords that you can later find. I don't know about you, but it'd take me a year or two to go through all my old shots and sort them out. By the time I was done, I'd have to start all over again with new shots. Like the hare and the tortoise, I'd probably never finish.

That's the fundamental problem with the fancy WLPG indexing methods. Windows Live Photo Gallery can't create indexes out of thin air. You have to do the work before you can reap the rewards — and it's debatable whether all the time you might invest in cataloging your pictures will ever pay off.

You have to put the garbage in before you can take it out, eh?

Windows Live Photo Gallery is one of the Windows Live Essentials, which I talk about in Book I, Chapter 5. It's designed to work with Windows 7, but it isn't part of Windows 7. Sorta.

Picasa versus Photo Gallery

Microsoft updates Windows Live Photo Gallery frequently. Which is just as well, because Google is on Microsoft's heels with an alternative, free, very capable photo handling program named Picasa (picasa.google.com).

When people ask me which is better — Windows Live Photo Gallery or Picasa — I ask them, "What week is it?" Features in both programs change constantly: When either Photo Gallery or Picasa runs out ahead with a new feature, the other catches up within a month or two.

I suggest that you choose between the two based on the fact that Photo Gallery has better hooks into Windows 7 and Picasa ain't Microsoft. WLPG connects with Flickr online, but Picasa hooks into Picasa Web Albums. That seems to sum up the enduring differences between the two products.

Feel comfortable in the fact that you aren't stuck with either: A Windows Live Photo Gallery plugin named Picasa Publisher lets you "publish" your pics to Picasa. And, Picasa ties right in with the Windows 7 Picture Library.

De gustibus non est disputandum: you can choose either Picasa or Windows Live Photo Gallery and feel good about your decision. Pick one or the other and get to know it well. The trick's in the learning curve.

Getting the Gallery Going

Can't find Windows Live Photo Gallery on your computer? That's okay. Even if you see WLPG on your Start⇨All Programs menu, it's a good idea to run out and grab the latest version.

Here's how to get the latest and greatest:

1. **Choose Start⇨Getting Started⇨Get Windows Live Essentials. If you can't find Getting Started, look under Start⇨All Programs⇨Accessories.**

   Windows 7 starts Internet Explorer and sends you to the Live Essentials download page, `download.live.com`.

   If you prefer, you can use any browser you like and go to `download.live.com`. In Figure 4-1, I use Firefox.

2. **Click Download.**

   The Windows Live Installer, `wlsetup-web.exe`, is transferred to your computer. Double-click it or do whatever you need to do (depending on your browser) to run it.

3. **Select the box marked Photo Gallery and deselect the others. Then click Install.**

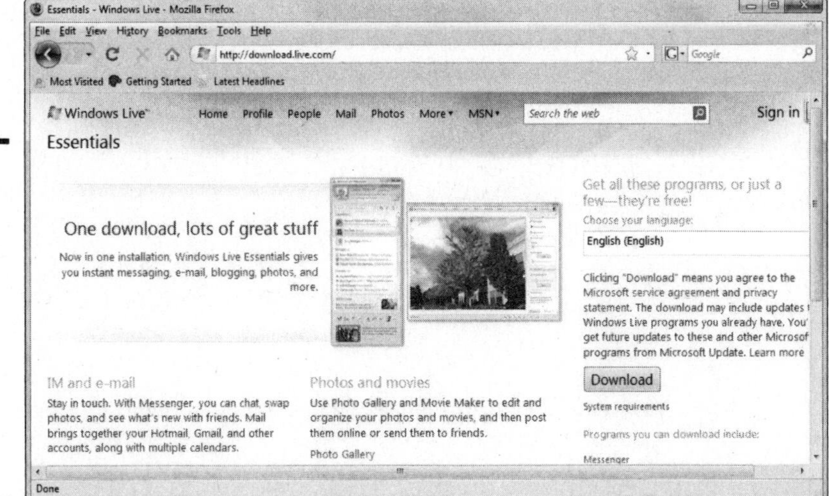

Figure 4-1: The Windows Live download page includes all the Microsoft "Live" offerings.

The Windows Live installer downloads WLPG and sticks it on your computer. Time to grab a latté.

Then (as I describe in detail in Book I, Chapter 5), Microsoft asks you to let it take over your Web browsing, uh, experience — and keep track of all your Windows activities — with the dialog box shown in Figure 4-2. Cheeky, huh?

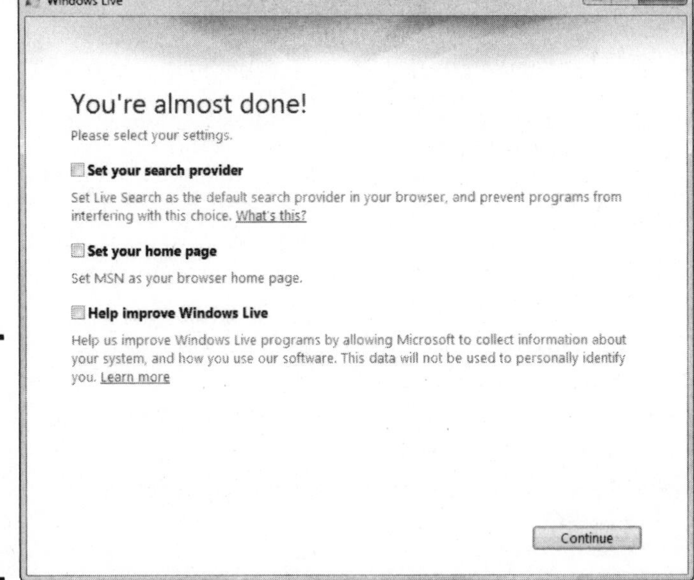

Figure 4-2: Microsoft wants to take over your computer. Just say no.

4. **Select the check box labeled Hey, Man, You Gotta Be Kidding, Why on Earth Would I Let Microsoft Do That? (or deselect all three check boxes, whichever is easier) and click Continue.**

   The final panel asks you to sign up for a Windows Live ID.

5. **If you want to post your pictures on Flickr (or on Microsoft Live Spaces) and you don't already have a Windows Live ID, click Sign Up and follow the instructions in Book V, Chapter 7 to create a completely bogus ID.**

   If you have a Hotmail ID, a Messenger ID, or an Xbox Online ID, you already have a Windows Live ID.

6. **Click Close.**

   Windows Live Photo Gallery is now installed on your computer. You can't see it yet, but it's there.

Leafing through the Gallery

Here's how to get started with Windows Live Photo Gallery for the first time:

1. **Choose Start➪All Programs➪Windows Live➪Windows Live Photo Gallery.**

   The first time you start WLPG, it asks for your Windows Live ID and password.

2. **If you want to publish your picks on Flickr or Windows Live Spaces, the interaction is easier if you give WLPG your ID. Go ahead and type your Windows Live ID and password and then click Next.**

   WLPG asks whether you want to use Windows Live Photo Gallery to open BMP, ICO, JPG, PNG, TIF, and WDP files. See Table 4-1 for a description of each file type.

   Note that Windows Live Photo Gallery doesn't work with GIF, PCX, or WMF files.

3. **Chances are good that you will want to open each of those file types with WLPG, so click Yes.**

   WLPG scans the contents of your `\Pictures`, `\Videos`, `\Public\Pictures`, and `\Public\Videos` folders and shows them on the screen.

   At the time this book was printed, WLPG still didn't integrate with the Windows 7 Pictures library or Videos library. By the time you read this chapter, WLPG may be smart enough to pull in all the pictures and videos from them — but maybe not. For now, you have to add any other library folders to WLPG by hand. (See the section "Adding photos from a different folder," later in this chapter.)

You should see something like Figure 4-3. The Windows Live Photo Gallery shows all pictures and videos that sit in folders you add to the collection. It doesn't automatically pick up Windows 7 libraries.

Table 4-1 File Types That WLPG Can Handle

Filename Extension	*Relative File Size**	*Description*
JPG	1MB	When you take photos on a camera, they're usually created in JPG format. JPG is *lossy,* which means that this kind of file can be manipulated by the computer (or camera) to make it smaller, even though the quality suffers. If you edit and reedit a JPG file, the quality of the file may decrease substantially.
TIF	10MB	This *lossless* format is almost universal. Its file sizes are big, but the quality never changes. It's commonly used for scans and archive and fax files.
PNG	6MB	The PNG (pronounced "ping") lossless format is easier to compress than TIF, but it isn't as universally recognized: Many programs can't handle PNG. In fact, WLPG can show you PNG files, but it won't help you edit them.
WDP or HDP	Varies	Windows Media Photo, also known as WMPhoto or HD Photo, is a Microsoft proprietary format that can be lossy or lossless. It isn't widely used.
BMP	10MB	The Windows bitmap is lossless and used mostly for screen shots nowadays. WLPG can show you BMP files, but it won't help you edit them.
ICO	N/A	Windows icon files typically contain many icons. Windows Live Picture Gallery can "handle" them — in the sense that you can double-click an ICO file and WLPG steps you through all the icons in the file. WLPG doesn't show the file in the Gallery, though, and it doesn't help you edit the icons.

** Compares the sizes of a typical 10MB photo.*

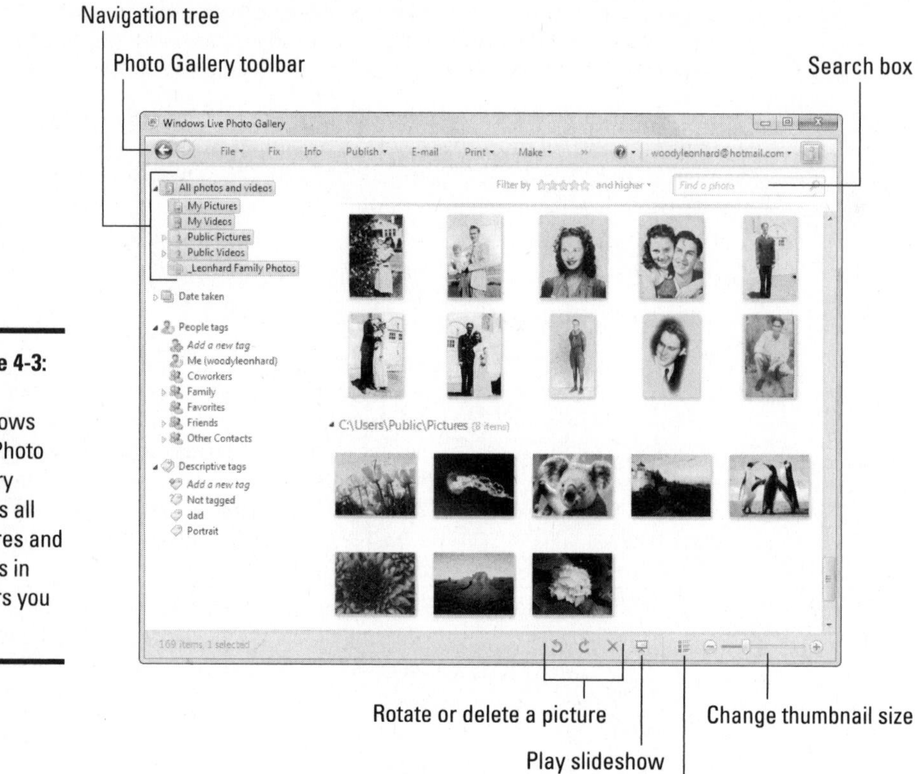

Figure 4-3: The Windows Live Photo Gallery shows all pictures and videos in folders you add.

The WLPG development team likes to say that Windows Live Photo Gallery is designed to store your "digital memories." Gag me with a RAMDAC. What they're really saying is that Windows Live Photo Gallery works with only the kinds of picture files that are commonly produced by digital cameras — JPG and MPG (and to a lesser extent, TIF) files. You can use RAW format pictures, but only if the camera manufacturer has a program (a codec) that can pass them on to WLPG. You can't use Photo Gallery to look at GIF, PCX, or WMF files — another reason why it's important to have Windows show you filename extensions (see Book II, Chapter 1).

If you want WLPG to show you a GIF file, simply right-click the file and rename it to JPG — if the file is named, oh, `Dummy.gif`, you can rename it to `Dummy.jpg` and it magically appears in the Photo Gallery. WLPG won't help you edit the file, but you can see it in the gallery.

You can have WLPG show you more or less of the gallery in the ways you would expect, by hopping through the navigation pane on the left: Click, oh, Public Pictures, and WLPG shows you only the pictures in the `\Public\`

`Pictures` folder. Choose Date Taken➪2008➪January and you see only pictures that have been branded as taken in January 2008. It's a similar situation for tags, including people tags (which are just a particular kind).

All this *metadata* (the date taken, people tags, descriptive tags) lives inside the picture files, and you can change the tags by using the tools described in the "Tagging Pictures" section, later in this chapter.

If you double-click a picture, Windows Live Photo Gallery flips into a single-picture view, like the one shown in Figure 4-4.

Tag all people in the picture to make searching easier

General tags go here

Revert to Gallery view (shown in Figure 5-13)

Previous or next picture

Zoom slider

Zoom to actual size

Figure 4-4: WLPG showing a single picture.

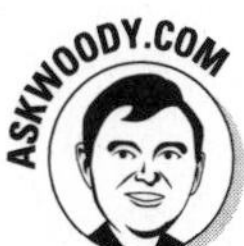

If you want to edit a file that's in a format WLPG can't edit (GIF-renamed-to-BMP, JPG, or PNG), double-click the file to go into single picture view and choose File➪Make a Copy. Windows Live Photo Gallery lets you save the file in JPG, TIF, or WDP format, all of which are editable in WLPG.

Adding Photos to the Photo Gallery

You can put photos in the Photo Gallery in three ways:

- ✦ Use the Picture and Video Import program to pull them off a camera and add them to the Photo Gallery automatically.
- ✦ Copy or move a picture (which is to say, a BMP, JPG, MPEG, MPG, PNG, or TIF file) to your `Pictures` folder, your `Public Pictures` folder, or any folder within the `Pictures` or `Public Pictures` folders.
- ✦ Point the Photo Gallery at a folder, on either your computer or your network (if you have one), and tell Photo Gallery to add the photos in that folder to the gallery.

Importing photos

When you transfer photos from your camera to your PC, you can use the Windows Picture and Video Import program (see Book IV, Chapter 3), but you'll probably have better results if you use the (considerably smarter!) importer in Windows Live Picture Gallery.

Here's how to import pictures a better way:

1. **Insert your camera's memory card into your PC.**

   If you don't have a memory card reader that takes your camera's kind of cards, go out and buy one! If all else fails, you may be able to use a USB cable attached to your camera (see Book IV, Chapter 3 for details).

   If Windows Live Photo Gallery is installed on your computer, you see an AutoPlay notification, like the one shown in Figure 4-5.

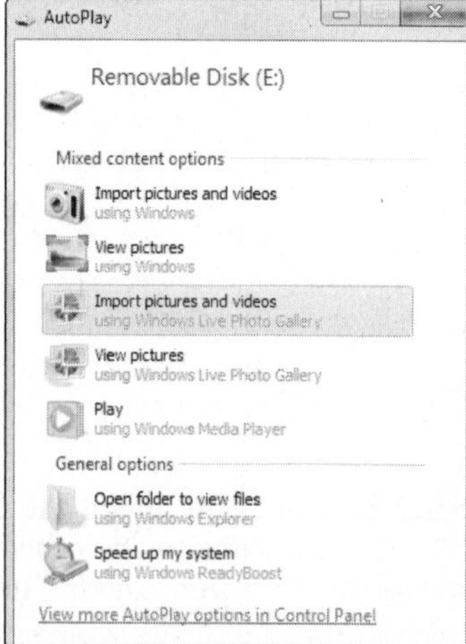

Figure 4-5: Given a choice, import through the Windows Live Photo Gallery.

2. **Click the link labeled Import Pictures and Videos Using Windows Live Photo Gallery.**

   The Import Photos and Videos program offers to Review, Organize, and Group Items to Import (see the left side of Figure 4-6).

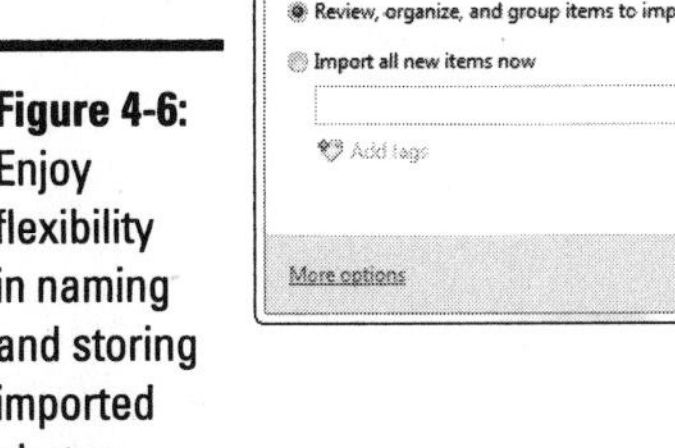

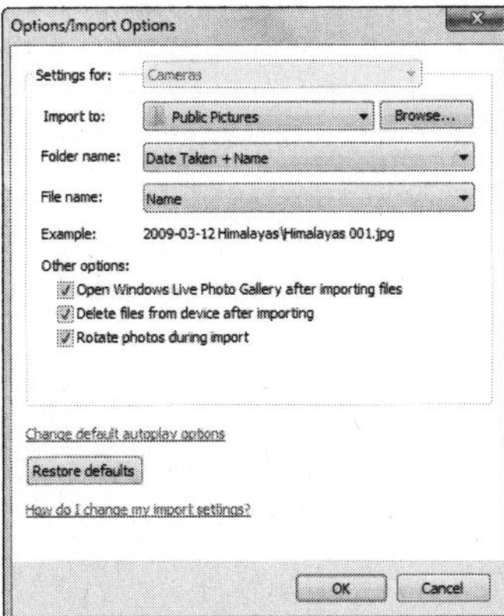

Figure 4-6: Enjoy flexibility in naming and storing imported photos.

3. **Click More Options.**

   You see the Options/Import Options box on the right in Figure 4-6.

4. **Type (or navigate to) a location where you want to put your imported pictures.**

   Personally, I change the image import folder to my `Public Pictures` folder, `c:\Users\Public\Public Pictures`. That way, anybody else on my computer — or anybody in my HomeGroup or on my network who has permission — can take a look at the imported pictures.

   I also select the check box labeled Delete Files from Device after Importing.

   Selecting the Delete Files from Device after Importing box requires a small leap of faith, but after you use the Import Pictures and Videos program a couple of times, you'll probably let Windows do the deleting. If something goes bump in the night and you accidentally delete photos on your camera memory card, don't panic. File undelete programs such as Recuva (`www.recuva.com`) take advantage of the fact that the data — your picture — isn't deleted until the camera needs to reuse the space on the memory card. With a bit of luck, you can recover pictures that you took a long, long time ago.

   Finally, I like to give my pictures filenames that reflect the name I assign to the group of pictures (see Step 6), and I like to stick them in separate folders for each date on which the pictures were taken. The result is what you see in Figure 4-7.

5. **When you're happy with your import settings, click OK.**

   The Import Photos and Videos window returns, as shown on the left side of Figure 4-6.

6. **Click Next.**

   The Import Photos and Videos program analyzes the photos and videos on the camera, groups them by the date and time the pictures were shot, and presents you with the results shown in Figure 4-7.

   If you don't like the way the import program breaks up your pictures into groups, you can change the sensitivity of the time grouping by moving the Adjust Groups slider in the lower-right corner.

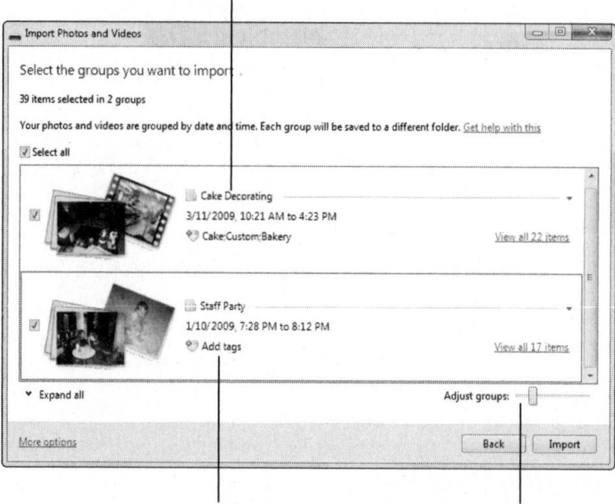

Figure 4-7: WLPG makes an educated guess about which photos belong with the others.

7. **Click next to the folder icon and type a name for the folder. Then click the Add Tags link and type your custom tags. When you're happy with the results, click Import.**

   The Import Photos and Videos program copies the photos into the appropriate locations, tags them per your instructions, and (optionally) erases them from the camera's data card.

   You end up in Windows Live Photo Gallery, looking at your newly imported photos (see Figure 4-8).

Recuva lost photos

If you find yourself in a tight spot, download and install Recuva (it's free). When you install it, make sure you don't opt for the Yahoo! Toolbar or any other junk that comes along for the ride. If you have a card reader attached to your PC, take the card out of the camera and flip the write-protect Lock tab so that nothing can be written to the card, and then put it in the card reader. Choose Start⇨All Programs⇨Recuva⇨Recuva. The Recuva Wizard opens. Click Next, and then follow the steps in the wizard to retrieve the lost files. It may take a while, but in the end Recuva presents you with a list of recoverable files. Select the check boxes next to the files you want to recover and click the Recover button.

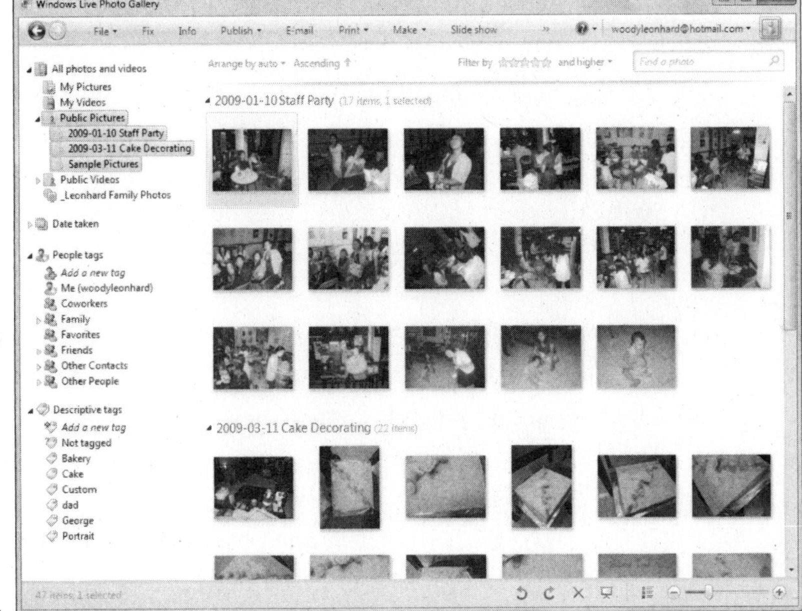

Figure 4-8: The imported pictures are tagged and stored in folders you specify.

Copying photos to the Pictures folder

If you already have pictures on your computer or network (and I would bet you do), the mere act of copying them or moving them to your `Pictures` folder, or any folder within the `Pictures` folder, adds them to the Photo Gallery. Similarly, copying or moving videos to the `Videos` folder adds them to the Photo Gallery.

Also, copying or moving pictures to the `\Public\Pictures` folder or the `\Public\Videos` folder — the folders that Windows Live sets up in your "public" shared folder — also adds them to the Photo Gallery. You don't need to lift a finger.

The Photo Gallery doesn't work with — doesn't even recognize — GIF or WMF files. If you move a GIF file to your `Pictures` folder, you can't see it in the Photo Gallery.

Perhaps surprisingly, if you click and drag a file — any file — into the Photo Gallery window, the file is copied to your Pictures folder. That's true even if the file you drag isn't a picture file. Note that the file is *copied,* not moved.

Adding photos from a different folder

So you have photos stored on a network drive? Yeah, me too.

Fortunately, you can easily tell WLPG to add those photos to the gallery — without copying them to your `Pictures` or `\Public\Pictures` folder. Here's how:

1. **If Windows Live Photo Gallery isn't running, start it by choosing Start⇨All Programs⇨Windows Live Photo Gallery.**

   The Photo Gallery appears, showing multiple pictures (refer to Figure 4-3, earlier in this chapter).

2. **Choose File⇨Include a Folder in the Gallery.**

   WLPG opens a dialog box that lets you navigate to the folder you want.

3. **Locate the folder you want to add, and click the OK button.**

   WLPG warns you that it will take a while and that Photo Gallery might run a bit slowly, as shown in Figure 4-9. Click the OK button and go grab a latté. By the time you come back, the Photo Gallery should show all the new pictures.

When you use this approach, the photos stay where they are — Windows Live Photo Gallery doesn't copy them or touch them in any way.

Include a Folder in the Gallery

This folder has been added to the gallery.

Photo Gallery may run slower while your files are being added to the gallery.

Don't show this message again — OK

How do I control which folders appear in the gallery?

Figure 4-9: Successfully adding a folder to the gallery.

If you delete a photo from the Photo Gallery, Windows Live deletes the file — so the picture not only disappears from the Gallery but also disappears, period — even if the photo is located on a networked drive! If you accidentally delete a picture on your computer, you can pick it back up in the Recycle Bin. But if you delete a picture on a network drive, it's gone. Bye-bye.

Scanning photos

You can scan photos (or anything else, for that matter) directly into Windows Live Photo Gallery. WLPG uses the same scanning routines that you see throughout Windows. Details may vary depending on which kind of scanner you have installed.

Here's the fast, easy way to scan a photo into your computer:

1. **Choose Start⇨All Programs⇨Windows Live Photo Gallery**

   You see the main Photo Gallery, uh, gallery.

2. **Click File⇨Import from a Camera or Scanner.**

   You see the Import Pictures and Videos dialog box, and it should list your scanner, as shown in Figure 4-10.

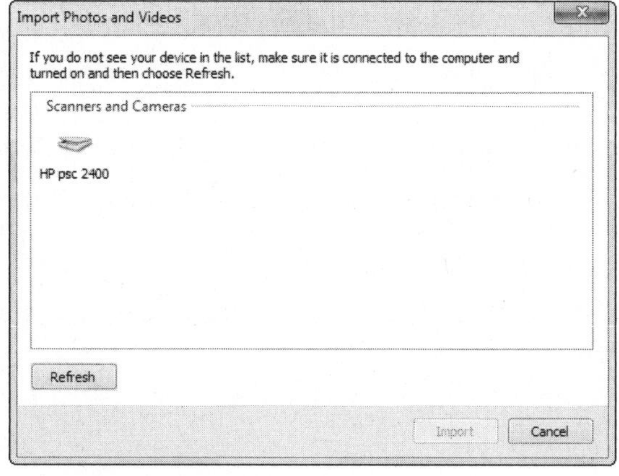

Figure 4-10: If your scanner doesn't show up, make sure it's plugged in and turned on.

3. **Click your scanner if it isn't already selected, and click the Import button.**

   WLPG shows you the New Scan dialog box, shown in Figure 4-11.

4. **Stick the page you want to scan into your scanner and click Preview.**

   The scanner hums and screeches — softly, of course — and a picture of the page appears onscreen.

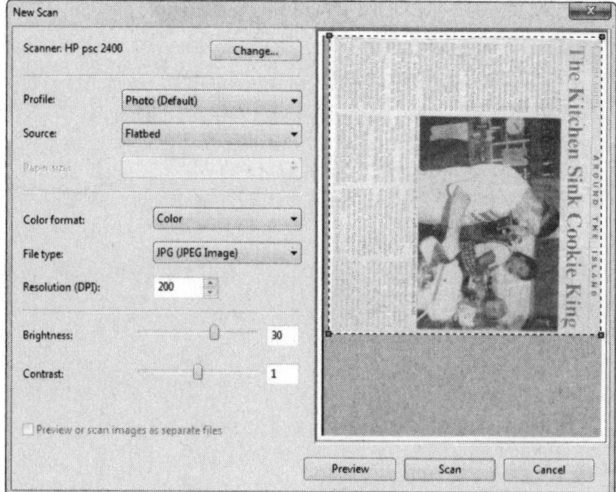

Figure 4-11: WLPG scanning is a piece of cake.

5. **If you want to zoom in on a specific location, click and drag the resizing handles at the corners. If you feel so motivated, adjust the Brightness and Contrast sliders and then click Preview again.**

   In Figure 4-11, I zoom in on a newspaper article with a photo I want to scan, and brighten it a bit.

6. **When you're happy with the preview, click Scan.**

   The scanner hums again. Then Photo Gallery invites you to tag the pictures, as shown on the left side of Figure 4-12.

7. **Click Import Settings.**

   You see the Import Settings dialog box on the right in Figure 4-12. Scanner settings for the WLPG importer bear more than a striking resemblance to those for photos.

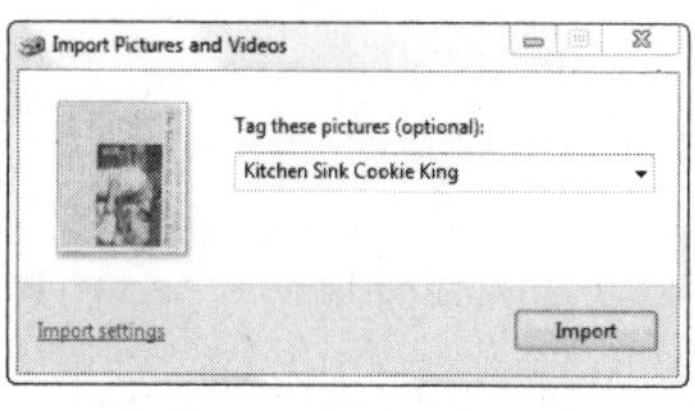

Figure 4-12: An invitation to tag pictures and the Import Settings dialog box.

8. **When you're happy with your import settings, click OK.**

   I put all scans inside `Public Pictures` in a folder named, imaginatively, Scans, `c:\Users\Public\Pictures\Scans`. That way, Windows Live Photo Gallery picks up the scan automatically, and anybody else on my computer — or anybody in my HomeGroup or on my network who has permission — can take a look at the scans.

   I have no idea why Microsoft includes an Always Erase option. It doesn't make any sense with a scanner. Ah, well. A foolish inconsistency is the hobgoblin of Windows 7 minds.

   Speaking of little minds — the Import Settings dialog box (like the WLPG importer; refer to Figure 4-6) gives you almost no flexibility in establishing folder names. I haven't found any way to set up automatic folder naming beyond the extremely limited choices in the Folder Name drop-down box.

   The Import Photos and Videos window returns (refer to the left side of Figure 4-12).

9. **Click Import.**

   The Scanner kicks in and deposits your scan in the location you chose in Step 8. The indicated tags are applied, and you're ready to scan again. That's it.

   You end up in Windows Explorer (*not* in Windows Live Photo Gallery), looking at your new scan.

Tagging Pictures

If you've spent more than ten minutes looking for a photo, you already know that browsing for pictures based on their location on disk can drive you nuts in no time. That's why tags were invented.

Skipping through tags

When you tag your pictures, the Photo Gallery keeps an index that makes it lightning-quick to find any pic with the specific tag. The problem, of course, is that you have to type a tag or two or three before Photo Gallery has anything to find.

Windows Live Photo Gallery draws a distinction between people tags and descriptive tags. It's a useful distinction, as you can see later in this section, but don't let the distinction fool you. Deep down at heart, a *people tag* is a descriptive tag, where the tag is just the name of the person.

Say you took a picture of your dad falling out of a fishing boat. You might want to tag the picture with a people tag of `George` (hey, that's my dad's name) and, oh, `fishing` and `boat`. After you tag a hundred thousand pictures or so, you can tell Photo Gallery to show all pics that have the name tag `George` or the descriptive tag `boat` and narrow your choices considerably.

Tagging a picture

To add a tag to a picture or group of pictures, follow these steps:

1. **Open WLPG, if it isn't already open, by choosing Start⇨All Programs⇨Windows Live Photo Gallery.**
2. **Click the pictures you want to tag.**

   To give a bunch of pictures the same tag or tags, hold down Ctrl while clicking each picture. Alternatively, if the pictures are contiguous (one after another), you can click the first picture, hold down Shift, and click the last picture, or you can "lasso" them by clicking and dragging a box over the pictures you want to select.

   WLPG shows selected pictures with a gray border around them, as shown in Figure 4-13.

Figure 4-13: Tagging photos of the Songkran Festival in Phuket.

3. **On the left, click the Add a New Tag icon, type the first tag that you want to apply to all selected pictures, and press Enter. To add more tags to the same group of pictures, click the Add Tags icon again, type the next tag, and press Enter. Repeat until you give your selected pics all the tags you like.**

In Figure 4-13, I apply two tags to the selected pictures: `Songkran` and `Phuket`. That way, I can display all the pictures I have of the Songkran Festival, no matter which city; and I can display pictures of Phuket, whether they cover the Songkran Festival or not.

People tags work similarly: Select the pictures you want to tag and, rather than choose Add a New Tag under the Descriptive Tags list, select Add a New Tag from the People Tags list.

Tags you assign to a picture travel with the picture. If you tag a photo as `George`, `fishing`, and `boat` and you send a copy of the picture to your brother, and your brother then puts the picture in his `Pictures` folder, he can use Windows Live Photo Gallery to find the picture by using any of the tags.

Tagging en masse

Tired of typing tags? Yeah, after you have a couple dozen of them, you find yourself typing the same thing over and over.

Fortunately, you can easily assign an existing tag to a picture or group of pictures. Here's how:

1. **Select the pictures.**

   All the usual methods apply: Click, Ctrl+click, Shift+click, and lasso.

2. **Drag the selected pictures to the tag you want to use.**

   When you release the mouse button, the pictures are tagged with the tag you chose.

Rearranging the tag list

Tags are like coat hangers: Ignore them for a day or two, and all of a sudden you have hundreds of 'em. Tags help you manage pictures. Windows Live Photo Gallery helps you manage tags.

You can click and drag tags in the navigation pane, creating a hierarchy of tags. Simply click a tag and drag it to the location you want. Grouping tags in ways that make sense to you decreases the amount of hunting and clicking necessary to find the right tag.

For example, in Figure 4-14, I organized a bunch of tags that I used to keep track of pictures taken in Thailand: individual cities, places within the cities, and festivals, for example. Clicking a higher-level tag displays all pictures associated with the tag and all lower-level tags. So, if I click `Phuket`, I also see pictures of Chalong, Laguna, and Patong. It's a powerful capability.

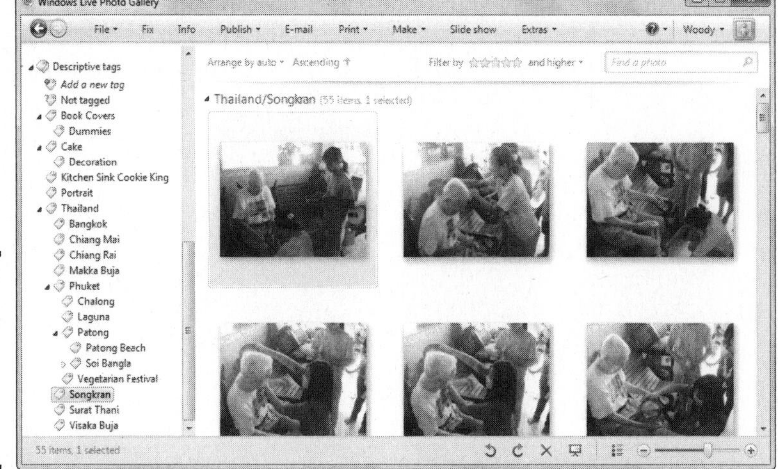

Figure 4-14: Organize tags to make them easier to find.

Finding a tagged picture

If your tags are in good shape, Windows Live Photo Gallery can find the tagged pictures in a split second. You have two choices:

- **In the search box, type the tags that interest you.** If you type more than one tag, Photo Gallery retrieves all pictures that match any of the tags — in Boolean terms, the search is an OR search (such as find George OR mountain OR boat).

  When you search using the search box, Photo Gallery looks for tags, and it looks for filenames. So if you have a picture named `Georgeanne.jpg` and a tag named `George`, searching for *George* brings up both the tagged pictures and the pic named `Georgeanne.jpg`.

  Typing on the search bar performs a search only on items that you can see. For example, if you're viewing items tagged *George* and you search for *Rubye*, you see only results tagged with both *George* and *Rubye*.

- **In the navigation pane, on the left, click the tag.** Photo Gallery shows you all pictures that have the specific tag.

You can combine tags with other entries in the navigation pane. For example, if you click the `George` tag and then Ctrl+click the Date Taken entry 2005, Photo Gallery shows you all pictures with the `George` tag that were taken in 2005. In other words, Photo Gallery performs an AND search.

Confusingly, if you Ctrl+click to select two different tags, Photo Gallery performs an OR search. So, if you click the `George` tag and Ctrl+click the `Woody` tag, Photo Gallery shows you all pictures with the `George` tag, plus all pictures with the `Woody` tag — you see pictures with either `George` OR `Woody` (or both).

Touching Up Pictures

Windows Live Photo Gallery offers a small set of the most-used photo touch-up tools, specifically designed to be easy to use and not particularly intimidating — or powerful. You may find them useful, especially if you don't have a more capable program at hand.

The Photo Gallery "fix" tools can permanently change a picture. If you mess things up, you can usually retrieve a version of the picture that's more than 24 hours old (see the discussion of shadow copies in Book II, Chapter 3), but it's a pain in the neck. For that reason, I strongly recommend that you make a backup copy of a picture before you apply fixes.

Here's how to safely and effectively touch up your pictures:

1. **In WLPG, click a picture and then click the Fix button on the toolbar.**

   Windows Live Photo Gallery shows you the touch-up tools on the right side of the screen, as shown in Figure 4-15.

Figure 4-15: The "fix" tools appear on the right.

2. **Immediately choose File⇨Make a Copy and save a copy of the original, giving it a name you can remember.**

   The copy gets saved; you continue to work on the original.

3. **To let Photo Gallery try to adjust everything on its own, click the Auto Adjust icon.**

   Windows Live Photo Gallery analyzes the picture and automatically adjusts the brightness, contrast, and color. It also straightens out the photo, if it seems a little skewed.

   If you don't like what Photo Gallery did to your picture, click the Undo button at the bottom of the Fix pane.

4. **To adjust your photo manually, click the Adjust Exposure icon to set brightness and contrast and click the Adjust Color icon to set color temperature, tint, and saturation (see Table 4-2).**

5. **To crop the picture (cut off the edges), click the Crop Photo icon. When you're happy with your croppin', click the Apply button.**

   You can then set the crop location manually or click the Proportion drop-down list (see Figure 4-16) to crop for specific print sizes (actually, aspect ratios).

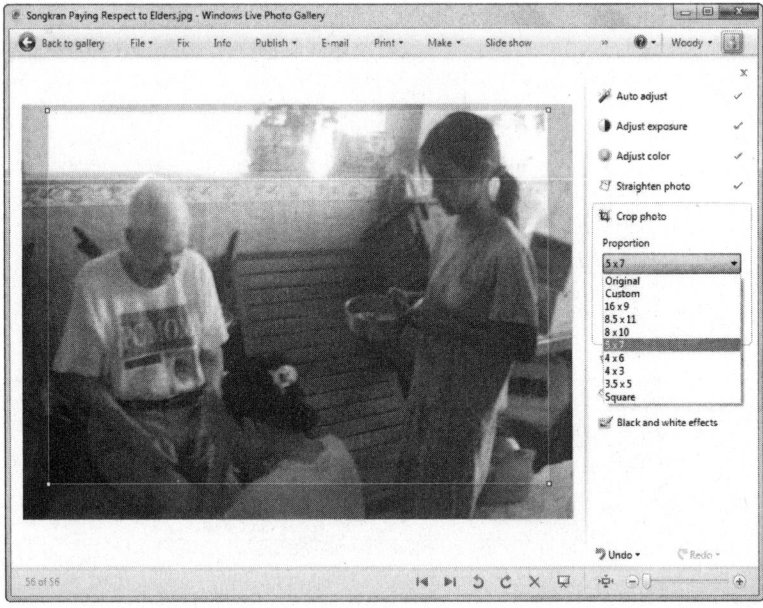

Figure 4-16: You can easily crop to fit a specific print size.

If you want to use still photos in your movies, keep in mind that the typical wide-screen aspect ratio is 16:9 and standard TV is 4:3. Windows Live Movie Maker (see Book IV, Chapter 6) likes those sizes.

6. **To fix the red-eye effect (see the nearby "Here's red in your eye" sidebar), click the Fix Red Eye icon and then drag a box around the eye that's red.**

   To get the most accurate red-eye correction, you usually need to zoom in so that you can pick out the bad eye. To do so, click and drag the slider in the lower-right corner of the window. Then hold down Alt while you click and drag the picture, moving it around so that you can reach the eye. When you have the eye in, uh, sight, release Alt and click and drag a box around the eye. Make the box as small as you can while still getting all the red. Release the mouse button, and Windows Live does its level best to get the red out.

   When you're done, click Back to Gallery. Your changes are saved automatically, which is why you made a copy of the original in Step 2, eh?

The touch-up tools are designed to be used in order, from top to bottom.

Table 4-2 A Layperson's Guide to Color

Term	*What It Does*
Brightness	Makes all pixels in the picture lighter or darker, by the same amount.
Contrast	Changes the relative darkness of individual pixels.
Temperature	Makes reds look more blue (sliding to the right) or blues look more red.
Tint	Adjusts the green and red.
Saturation	Makes colors more or less intense.

Here's red in your eye

That devilish glint of red in a photographed eye arises because your camera's flash happened so quickly that the iris of the eye didn't have a chance to close the pupil. Light from the flash gets focused by the eye's lens onto the retina, at the back of the eye. The lens then focuses the light back to the camera. All the blood in the retina results in a vivid red color.

Animals get red-eye, too. Pictures of cats can have "red" eye, but it's usually green because of a coating in the cat's eyes.

Most modern cameras have red-eye reduction modes that cause the flash to go off multiple times before the real picture is taken. Those preliminary blasts suffice to close the pupil.

Red-eye occurs only when the flash goes straight into the eye and straight back. If you have a lot of problems with red-eye, try to bounce your flash — aim the flash at the ceiling or a wall — or have the person look away from the camera.

Stitching a Panoramic Photo

Have you ever taken a series of shots, side by side, trying to convey the vastness of a scene? Windows Live Photo Gallery can "stitch" side-by-side shots, tying them together automatically. It's so easy that you won't believe your eyes.

Here's how to stitch together a bunch of photos:

1. **Get the photos into Windows Live Photo Gallery.**

   You can use any of the methods discussed in the section "Adding Photos to the Photo Gallery," earlier in this chapter.

   In Figure 4-17, I import five photos, taken from left to right, from my office balcony.

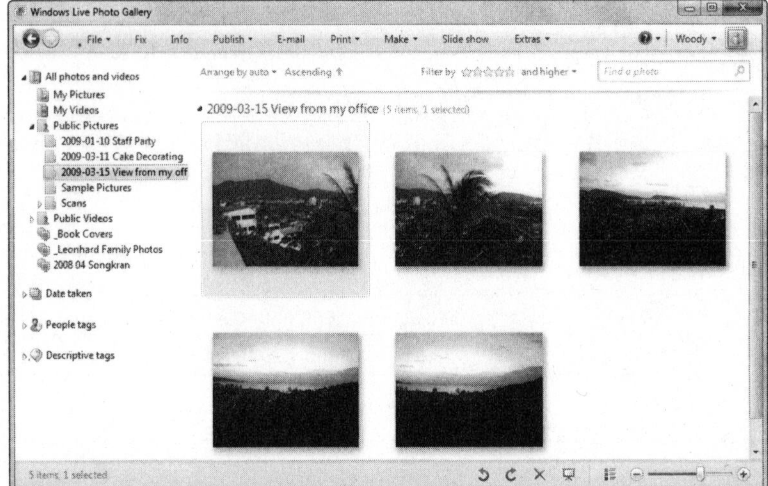

Figure 4-17: Five photos, taken from left to right, from my office in Patong.

2. **Select the photos that you want WLPG to stitch.**

   In this case, I press Ctrl+A and select all five shots.

3. **Choose Make⇨Create Panoramic Photo.**

   WLPG asks you to verify which pictures you want to have stitched.

4. **Type a name for the stitched picture and click Save.**

   WLPG takes a few minutes and then produces a fabulous stitched result, as shown in Figure 4-18.

Figure 4-18: WLPG stitches together the pictures — and you don't have to lift a finger.

Getting Your Photos into Flickr

Microsoft has established a "special relationship" with Yahoo!, the people who own the Flickr social networking Web site. One of the fortunate side effects of that relationship is that you can use Windows Live Photo Gallery to feed photos directly to your own space on Flickr.

Flickr accounts are free, unless you want to post a lot of pictures — check out the details and sign up at `flickr.com`. After you have an account, here's how hard it is to move photos from WLPG to your personal Flickr page:

1. **In Windows Live Photo Gallery, select the pictures you want to transfer to Flickr.**

   As always, you can use the click, Ctrl+click, Shift+click, or lasso methods.

2. **Choose Publish⇨More Services⇨Publish on Flickr.**

   WLPG puts up a message saying that you must give your authorization before you can publish your photos on Flickr.

3. **Click Authorize.**

   Your favorite Web browser pops up and asks you to log on to Yahoo!.

4. **Type your Yahoo! ID and password, and click Sign In.**

   Flickr tells you that you must give your authorization to allow Windows Live Photo Gallery to connect to your Flickr account (see Figure 4-19).

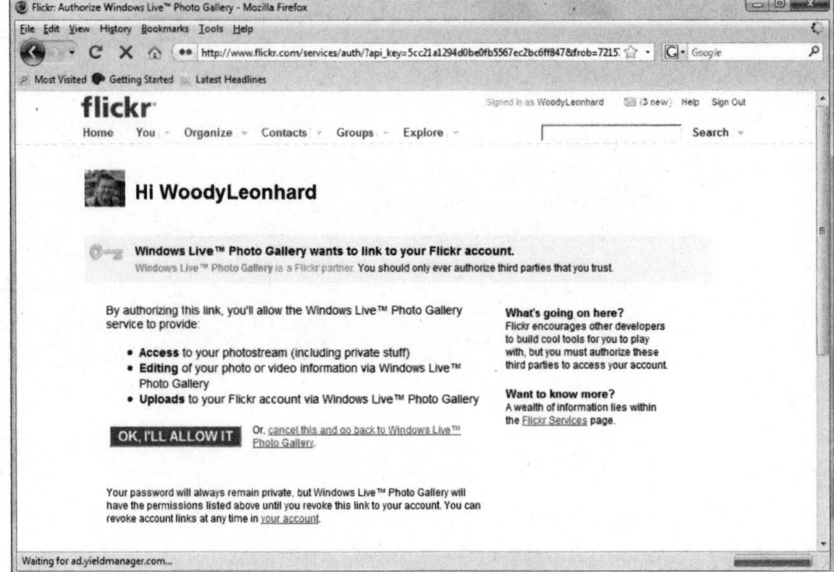

Figure 4-19: You have to tell Flickr that it's okay to connect to Windows Live Photo Gallery.

5. **In Flickr, click OK, I'LL ALLOW IT. (Yahoo! REALLY! LIKES! CAPITALS! and! EXCLAMATION! points!)**

   Flickr says that you have successfully authorized Windows Live Photo Gallery to access your Flickr account.

6. **Close the browser. Back in WLPG, click Next.**

   WLPG shows you the Publish on Flickr dialog box, shown in Figure 4-20.

Figure 4-20: Moving photos from WLPG to Flickr is incredibly easy.

7. **If you want to create a new photo set (an "album," if you will), click the drop-down box below Photo Sets and choose accordingly. Adjust the Photo Size to whatever you like and choose the correct permissions. Then click Publish.**

   That's all it takes. Your photos are uploaded to Flickr, stuck in the album, er, photo set you specify, and given the permissions you requested — even the tags you assigned in WLPG are intact. And, the photos are made available immediately to anyone who can open your Flickr page.

In the future, you don't have to jump through the authorization hoops. Uploading photos to Flickr is almost as fast as copying them to another computer.

Chapter 5: Lights! Action! Windows Live Movie Maker

In This Chapter

- **Recording and editing video**
- **Bringing in narration and background sounds**
- **Creating transitions**
- **Burning your own DVDs — within limits, anyway**

No, you can't go down to Blockbuster, rent a DVD, take it home, and make a copy of it using Windows Live Movie Maker (WLMM). There. That answers about 80 percent of the questions I get about WLMM.

Yes, you can take that TV program you recorded in Windows Media Center — you know, that hu-u-u-u-ge hour-long 4GB WTV file — convert it to DVR-MS, run it through WLMM, and save the program as a 400MB WMV file. The trip through WLMM takes more than an hour of computer time. But it reduces the size of the file by 80 percent to 90 percent. You may have trouble recording the show (see the discussion of broadcast flags in Book IV, Chapter 4), but after you get it into unencrypted form on disk, you can use WLMM to put it on DVD. That answers about 80 percent of the questions I *should* get about WLMM.

Windows Live Movie Maker brings a stunted but barely usable video-editing workshop to your PC. You can use it to create anything from a few seconds of action — say, to dress up an e-mail message — to a full-length documentary about your kid's first birthday party. Get the sound synchronization right and you could even toss together a decent music video, sell it to iTunes, and turn into an overnight sensation.

Just remember where you got the idea, huh?

This chapter covers two different programs that fit together like a hand and glove. Windows Live Movie Maker helps you turn *stills* (that's pictures, to the uninitiated) and *clips* (short stretches of video) into a movie. Windows DVD Maker puts the movie on a DVD so that you can play it in any DVD player.

Windows DVD Maker can take a series of stills (er, photos) and turn them into a slide show that plays in any DVD player. Windows Live Movie Maker can do the same thing, but it has better tools.

With that single exception, almost everyone who uses WLMM also uses DVD Maker: You build the movie in WLMM and burn it to DVD with DVD Maker so that folks can watch the movie on a DVD player. Makes sense, eh?

Here's the funny part (funny strange, not funny-funny): Windows Live Movie Maker is part of the Windows Live Essentials — the programs I discuss in Book I, Chapter 5 that you have to download from the Internet. WLMM isn't part of Windows 7 and doesn't even ship with Windows. Contrariwise, Windows DVD Maker ships as part of Windows 7; you can't download it. Go figger.

Installing Windows Live Movie Maker

What? You don't see Windows Live Movie Maker on your computer? That's because you have to download and install it before you can use it. Even if you do see WLMM on your Start⇨All Programs menu, you should try to grab the latest version.

Here's how to get the latest and greatest:

1. **Choose Start⇨Getting Started⇨Get Windows Live Essentials. If you can't see Getting Started, choose Start⇨All Programs⇨Getting Started.**

   Windows 7 starts your Web browser and sends you to the Live Essentials download page, `download.live.com`.

   If you prefer, you can use any browser you like and go to `download.live.com`. In Figure 5-1, I use the Google Chrome browser.

2. **Click Download.**

   The Windows Live Installer, `wlsetup-web.exe`, is transferred to your computer. Double-click it or do whatever you need to do (depending on your browser) to run it.

3. **Select the box marked Movie Maker and deselect the others. Then click Install.**

   The Windows Live installer downloads WLMM and sticks it on your computer. If you don't yet have Windows Live Photo Gallery, you get a copy of that, too (see Book IV, Chapter 5).

   Then (as I describe in detail in Book I, Chapter 5) Microsoft asks you to let it take over your Web search engine and home page and keep track of all your Windows activities, sending the details back to Mother Microsoft (see Figure 5-2).

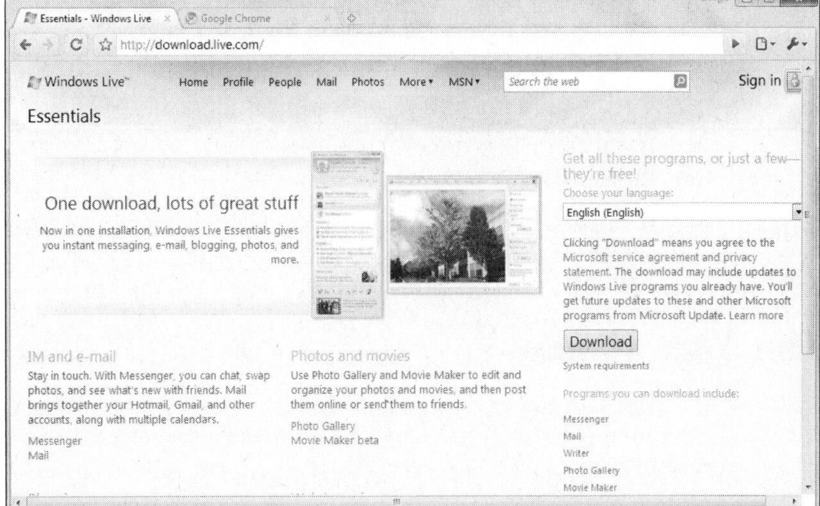

Figure 5-1: The Windows Live download page includes all of Microsoft's "Live" offerings.

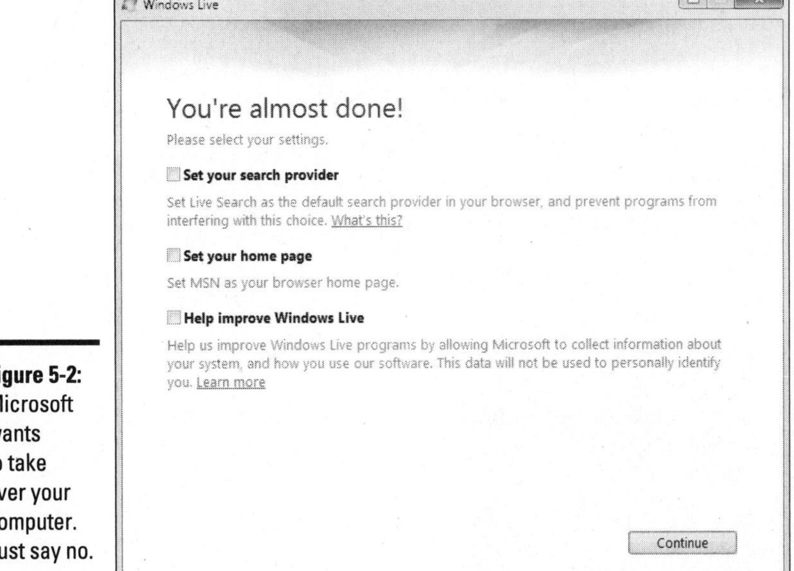

Figure 5-2: Microsoft wants to take over your computer. Just say no.

4. **Unless you have an overwhelming urge to help Microsoft attain world domination in this decade, deselect all three check boxes and click Continue.**

   The final screen asks you to sign up for a Windows Live ID.

5. **If you truly want a Windows Live ID and don't already have one, click Sign Up and follow the steps in Book V, Chapter 7 to create a completely bogus ID.**

   If you have a Hotmail ID, a Messenger ID, an old Microsoft Passport ID, or an Xbox Online ID, you already have a Windows Live ID.

6. **Click Close.**

   Windows Live Movie Maker is now installed on your computer. You can't see it yet, but it's there.

Meet Your Maker

To start Windows Live Movie Maker, choose Start➪All Programs➪Windows Live➪Windows Live Movie Maker. You see a blank screen like the one shown in Figure 5-3.

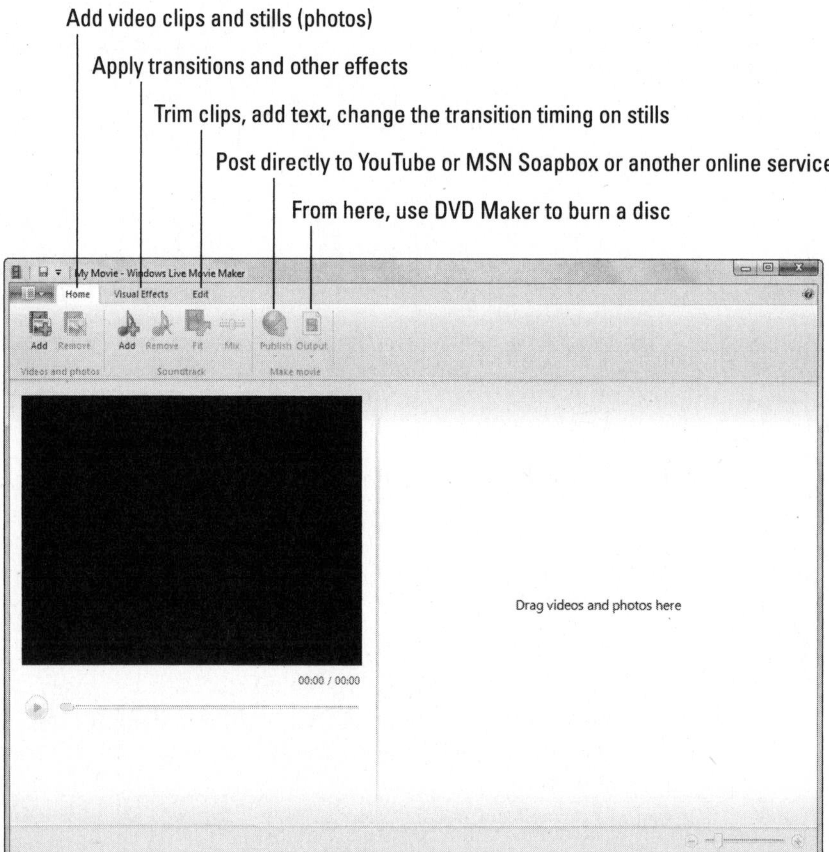

Figure 5-3: Windows Live Movie Maker as it starts.

Windows Dead Movie Maker

When this book went to press, around the time Windows 7 appeared on the market, Microsoft was having a horrible time making features work in Windows Live Movie Maker (WLMM). Because WLMM is part of Windows Live, it can be updated at any time, and you should definitely follow the steps in this chapter to see whether Microsoft has gotten its moviemaking act together. But if Windows Live Movie Maker leaves you cold, take heart in the fact that Microsoft has made the old version available — I call it Windows Dead Movie Maker — and you can use it with Windows 7.

You can download Windows Movie Maker (WMM) 2.6, the version originally developed for Windows Vista, from the Microsoft download page at `tinyurl.com/yp6gao`. WMM 2.6 was created for Vista users who have PCs that aren't powerful enough to handle the built-in Vista version of Windows Movie Maker, so it doesn't have all the visual bells and whistles. But it works fine on Windows 7.

For detailed instructions on using the old (and, many would say, vastly superior) Vista Movie Maker, see Book VII, Chapter 5 of my *Windows Vista All-in-One Desk Reference For Dummies* (published by Wiley).

Take a moment to become familiar with the parts of the window. At the top, you see these three tabs:

✦ **Home** lets you add or remove video clips, photos (or other picture files, collectively known as *stills*), and music. It also lets you post your movie directly on the Internet — probably with the help of a plugin — or save to a video file, which can subsequently be used by Windows DVD Maker to burn a DVD that plays in any DVD player.

✦ **Visual Effects** contains a bag full of visual tricks, divided into *transitions* (which come into play between clips) and *effects* (which, uh, affect the clips themselves).

✦ **Edit** holds tools for adding text, trimming clips, or stretching the transition time on stills.

If you used Vista's old Windows Movie Maker, you immediately notice that Windows Live Movie Maker in Windows 7 has no *timeline,* the feature that helps you sync music with the movie. (At least, the version of WLMM available this week has no timeline.) If you need the timeline — and many video editoristas do — you have to download and install Windows Dead Movie Maker (see the nearby sidebar).

Gathering Clips

Before you can edit video, you must get some clips into your computer. D'oh!

In general, you have five ways to acquire clips:

✦ **Use your camcorder.** WLMM helps you bring in movies from most digital video cameras. Whatever you can see on that tiny video screen will look great pulled into your PC — and because it's digital, the quality should be outstanding. Just plug in your camcorder and click the AutoPlay link labeled Import Pictures and Videos (or Import Video) Using Windows Live Photo Gallery.

Note that you import to Photo Gallery and then use the clips in Movie Maker.

Plan to spend about one-third of "real time" to transfer your clips into Photo Gallery: One hour of video should take about 20 minutes to pull off your camera. When the video comes in, Photo Gallery breaks the stream into clips that correspond to the time they were taken.

✦ **Shoot video on your digital camera.** If your digital camera produces files in MOV format, don't panic. See the following "Converting video formats" sidebar for details about a free conversion Web site, `media-convert.com`, that can convert your MOV into a WMV or AVI, both of which are understood by WLMM.

✦ **Use your Webcam.** It's hard to believe, perhaps, but a cheap Webcam can produce reasonably good video footage for your fledgling attempt at producing *Rocky VIII.* Don't expect high definition, but it's hard to beat the price. Use the capture program that came with your Webcam.

Converting video formats

Windows 7 may support some formats (such as MOV) in Windows Media Player or Windows Media Center, but offer very buggy support, or no help, in Windows Live Movie Maker. Why? WLMM is, uh, Live — it's not part of Windows itself — and thus doesn't necessarily tap into all the conversion goodies available to the mainstream Windows 7 programs.

If you need to convert video formats, and you have an hour or two to spare, a fantastic, free Web site does all the heavy lifting. Go to `media-convert.com` and follow the instructions to upload your video. Then choose the format you want — WMV and AVI work well with Windows Live Movie Maker. You may have time for a latté or two or three, but when the site finishes, it points you to your converted file and lets you download it with a click.

Very slick. Incredibly versatile. And absolutely free.

Don't shake yer booty

Did you shoot a lot of video back before image stabilizers became all the rage — and came down in price? Yeah, me too.

If your movies shake like a Willy's in four-wheel drive (sorry, Jerry), help is at, uh, hand. Goodervideo (`goodervideo.com`) offers the truly amazing program SteadyHand, which takes the shakes out. Feed SteadyHand an ASF, AVI, or MPEG file filled with jerks and jitters, and the clip you get back looks like it was taken on a tripod bolted to the base of Cheyenne Mountain. At $66.66, SteadyHand ain't cheap, but your old videos are worth it, aren't they?

It's almost as easy as saying, "Lights! Camera! Action!" except that you don't have to worry about blowing a $100 million budget, overrunning a 32-day shooting schedule, or keeping your stars out of each other's trailers.

- **Use Windows Media Center to record your favorite shows.** You can't burn "protected" material onto a DVD, but many TV shows can be used as WLMM fodder. (Find out all about Windows Media Center in Book IV, Chapter 4.)
- **Buy, beg, borrow, or steal existing clips.** The Web is full of video clips you can use. No doubt your friends have marvelous cute clips of Little Dufous spilling ice cream on his blue suede shoes. They're all fair game: any AVI, MPG, WMV, or other video file, including DVR-MS files generated when you record a TV show in Windows Media Center, and VOB files from certain kinds of camcorders; any MP3, WMA, WAV, or other audio file; and any BMP, GIF, JPG, PNG, TIF, or other type of picture file.

You can mix and match clips from all those sources.

If you don't have all the camera gadgets you need — or don't know how to operate them — ask your dealer for assistance.

Assembling a Movie

A *project* is a file that contains your work on a movie. In effect, a project is a movie, either completed or in development. A *clip* is a piece of a movie (or music or a still picture). In the preceding sections, I mention a bunch of ways to gather clips. When the clips are ready, you assemble the clips to create a project.

Creating a project

Here's how to put together a project — er, a movie:

1. **Choose Start⇨All Programs⇨Windows Live Movie Maker to start Windows Live Movie Maker. Immediately choose File⇨Save Project, give your movie a name, and click the Save button to save the project.**

   Your project is ready to go.

2. **Choose a clip from one of your collections, or from anywhere else on your computer or network, and drag it to the storyboard at the bottom of the window.**

   Alternatively, you can click the Add icon in the upper-left corner and WLMM goes to your Videos library (see Figure 5-4). From there, you can navigate anywhere you like and pick the clips that interest you.

   Alternatively (you have lots of ways to skin the cat, eh?), you can choose the photos or clips you want in Windows Live Photo Gallery and then choose Make⇨Make a Movie.

   However you choose them, images of the clips appear in the upper-right part of WLMM — a location known as the *storyboard* (see Figure 5-4).

Figure 5-4: Drag a movie clip or still picture to the storyboard to start the project.

3. **Drag one or two more clips to the unoccupied part of the storyboard.**

   An image of each one appears in the workspace.

   Unless you change things, still photos dragged to the storyboard appear in the final movie for three seconds.

   You can easily use Windows Live Photo Gallery to locate video clips and still photos (see Book IV, Chapter 5). If you find something you want to put in your project, click it in the Photo Gallery, drag it into Windows Live Movie Maker, and drop it wherever you want the clip or still to be inserted in the storyboard.

   You can insert a clip between two existing clips. Just drag it between the two clips.

4. **To move a clip to a different location in your movie, click the clip, drag it to the place where you want to insert it, and release the mouse button.**

   When you need to move a clip a long way, dragging can be clumsy and error-prone; the cutting-and-pasting technique is more convenient. To cut and paste, right-click the clip you want to move and choose Cut. Then right-click the clip after which you want to place this clip and select Paste.

   To delete a clip from the workspace, right-click the clip and choose Remove.

5. **To save your project, choose File (the little icon to the left of the Home tab) and then Save.**

   Congratulations! You're well on your way to becoming a film legend.

Playing a clip or a movie

To play a clip, double-click it in the storyboard (see Figure 5-5).

WLMM picks up the movie starting with the clip (or still) that you double-clicked. When you've seen enough, click the Pause button to stop the playback.

As you play a clip, the slider underneath the monitor moves across the bar to show how far the monitor has progressed through the clip. The number near the monitor's lower-right corner shows the elapsed play time for the entire movie, to the nearest hundredth of a second, and the total time for the movie.

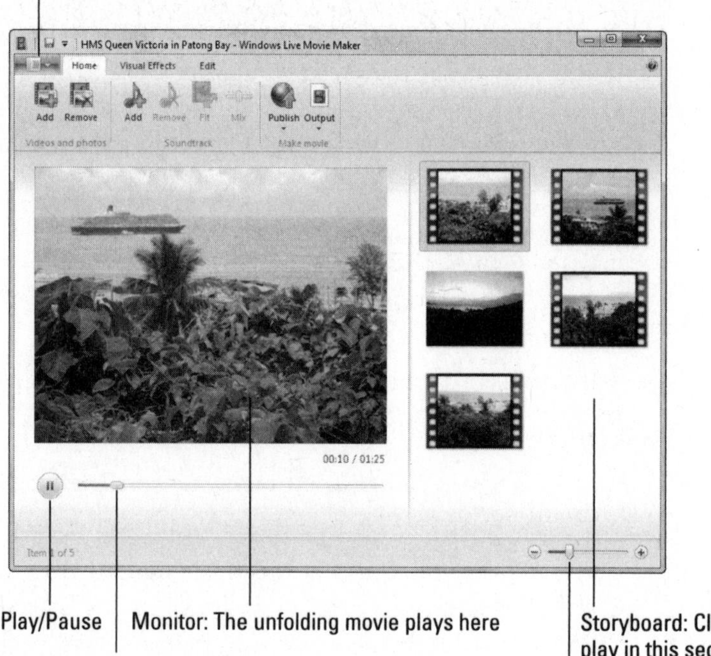

Figure 5-5: Playing a clip in the monitor.

Making transitions and adding effects

Windows Live Movie Maker gives you several ways to manage the transition from one clip to the next. You can fade out the end of one clip while fading in the beginning of the next clip. You can slide the new clip down on top of the old one, or you can hatchet-chop slides, in a maneuver Microsoft calls a *roll.*

Laissez les bons temps rouler, eh?

Best of all, adding a transition to a movie takes only a few clicks. Here's the easiest way:

1. **Get your movie put together in the sequence you like.**
2. **Click the Visual Effects tab.**

   WLMM shows you the Transitions and Effects options, at the top of the screen (see Figure 5-6).

Figure 5-6: Adding a transition.

3. **Click on the clip (or still) that you want to have a transition.**

   Alternatively, you can Ctrl+click to select several clips or stills that should have the same transition.

4. **Choose the transition from the scrolling list in the upper-left corner.**

   The transition you choose is an "entrance" or "intro" transition — it's the transition that takes place just before the clip plays in the movie.

Use the Storyboard to start at any point in the presentation and check how your presentation's transitions look in the grand scheme of things. Don't like your handiwork? You can delete a transition by clicking the clip, clicking the Visual Effects tab, and choosing the first transition — the one labeled No Transition.

In addition to adding the transitions available in Windows Live Movie Maker, you can change the appearance of an individual clip or still. WLMM includes automatic effects to turn a clip into black-and-white or to apply color filters, including an old-fashioned sepia toning.

To apply an effect to a clip, click the clip (or still), bring up the Visual Effects tab, and choose whichever effect you like from the list in the upper-right corner. Click the Play button to preview the result and see what you think!

Trimming a clip

Windows Live Movie Maker lets you trim individual clips — remove pieces at the beginning or end of the clip, to make it shorter.

Here's how to lop off the beginning or end of a clip:

1. **Open the project containing the clip you want to trim. Click the Edit tab and then the Trim icon.**

   You see the Trim window, shown in Figure 5-7.

Figure 5-7: Use the slider to trim a clip.

2. **Click the clip you want to trim, and then click the Play button.**

   The clip starts playing normally, with the slider moving along as the clip progresses.

3. **When you reach the point where you want to trim, click the Pause button. Move either the starting or ending trim indicator against the slider, depending on whether you want to trim the beginning or end of the clip.**

   If you want to trim both the beginning and the end of a particular clip, click Play and then Pause at the point you want to trim at the beginning, and slide the left trim indicator so that it butts up against the play slider. Then click Play again and when you hit the end of the trimmed area, click Pause again. Slide the right trim indicator against the slider.

You can drag the slider left or right at any time. That makes it easier to locate the trim points precisely.

4. **When you have the beginning and/or end trim points set with the trim indicators, click the Save and Close icon in the upper-right corner.**

   Although you might think that WLMM would throw away the trimmed parts, in fact the clips are intact. If you ever change your mind and want to "un"trim the clip, repeat Steps 2, 3, and 4 but slide the trim indicator back to its original location.

To adjust the length of time that a still (photo) appears in the movie, click on the still, click the Edit tab, and in the Duration drop-down box, select the length of time that you want the still to appear.

Typing titles

Superimposing text over your clips ranks as the simplest of WLMM tricks, and you can use any font known to Windows. Here's how to add titles:

1. **Put your movie together first.**

   Adding titles is easiest when you know which clip comes first, which second, and which carries up the rear.

2. **Choose the Edit tab.**

   WLMM shows you its Edit view, as shown in Figure 5-8.

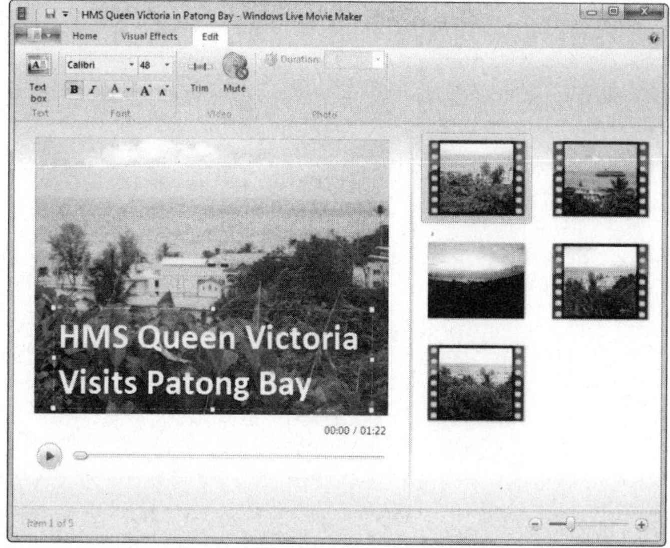

Figure 5-8: Adding text to your movie is only a few clicks away.

3. **Click the Text Box icon.**

   WLMM plants a resizable text box on your clip.

4. **Type the text that you want to appear on the clip.**

   It appears inside the text box. You can format the text by using the font drop-down list, font size, and Bold, Italic, and color button.

   If the text outgrows the size of the text box, click and drag the resizing handles. Click and drag to move the text box anywhere on the clip.

5. **When you're happy with the text, click outside the text box.**

   If you ever want to go back in and edit the text, click the Text Box icon again.

The text appears for the duration of the clip. When the movie moves on to the next clip, the text disappears.

Mixing in the sound

Clips are usually recorded with sound. If your clips have sound, the sound plays along with the clip, just as you would expect. Smash a few clips together into a movie, and the soundtrack on each clip becomes the soundtrack for the movie.

WLMM also lets you superimpose a music file over the top of the movie. If your clips have sound, you can adjust the *balance* — the relative volume of the sound recorded with the clip, and the volume of the added music file.

Here's how to get sound mixed in:

1. **Open the project into which you want to superimpose a music file. Click the Home tab.**

   You see the main WLMM screen (refer to Figure 5-8).

2. **In the Soundtrack area, click the Add icon.**

3. **Navigate to the sound file that you want to superimpose on the movie and click Open.**

   At least in the current version of WLMM, you get only one sound file. If the playing time of the sound file is shorter than the playing time of the movie, you don't hear any superimposed sound after the music file peters out. If the playing time of the sound file is longer than the playing time of the movie, the superimposed sound stops abruptly when the movie ends.

4. **Click the Mix icon.**

   WLMM shows you a mixer that lets you adjust the relative volume of the sound that was recorded with the movie (on the left) and the relative volume of the superimposed sound file (see Figure 5-9).

Slide left to increase the balance in favor of the sound in the original clip

Slide right to increase the balance in favor of the music file

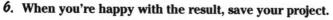

The name of the music file appears here

Figure 5-9: Add music, but you get only one music file per movie.

5. **Adjust the mixer to balance the original soundtrack and the music file.**

   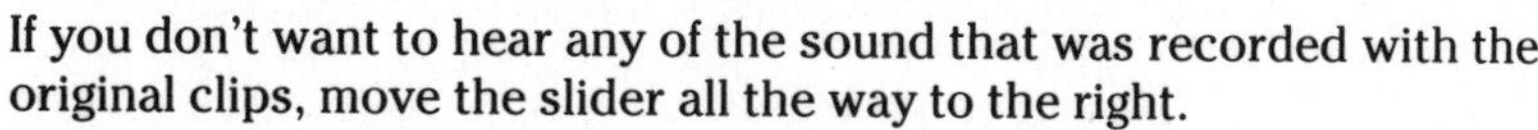

   WARNING!

   If you don't want to hear any of the sound that was recorded with the original clips, move the slider all the way to the right.

   The choice you make affects the entire movie: You can't mix individual clips or parts of clips.

6. **When you're happy with the result, save your project.**

   You're ready to make your movie available to the outside world.

TIP

You can use sound clips from any source — including those ripped by Windows Media Player from a CD.

Publishing a Movie

After you edit a movie to your satisfaction, you probably want to show it to other people. When you choose File➪Save Project or File➪Save Project As (File is the little icon to the left of the Home tab), Windows Live Movie Maker stores the movie as a Windows Live Movie project — a so-called WLMP file — that can be watched only in Windows Live Movie Maker. Blech. If you want your friends to be able to view it, either they have to run Windows Live Movie Maker or you have to convert the movie into a format they can use.

Finding the right publication method

If you want a friend to see your movie, you have four basic choices:

- **Give your friend a WLMP file.** You have to convince her to install Windows Live Movie Maker and play the movie on her PC (which has to be a Windows Vista or Windows 7 computer; Windows XP doesn't run WLMM). Yeah, sure. Like she doesn't have anything better to do with her life.

  To turn your project into a WLMP file, simply save the project.

- **Turn your movie into a WMV file.** You can then give the WMV file to your friend and, as long as she has access to Windows Media Player (or any box that plays WMV files), she's in good shape.

  To turn your project into a WMV file, on the Home tab, click the Output icon and choose either Windows Media DVD Quality (to churn out a low-quality 640 x 480 resolution WMV for Windows Media Player) or Windows Media Portable Device (to turn out a compact 320 x 240 resolution WMV for MP4 players).

  If you originally recorded your clips using a high-definition camera, the stuff you get out the back from WLMM looks like, uh, stuff you get out the back, if you know what I mean.

- **Turn your project into a DVD.** In this two-step process, you first save the file as a WMV file (see the preceding bullet point). Then you convert the WMV file into a DVD using Windows DVD Maker. (See the "Ripping, burning, and converting movies" section, at the end of this chapter.)

- **Publish your project directly to the Internet.** That's easy: See the next section.

Publishing directly to the Web

After you put together a movie, you can easily get it on the Web. WLMM ships with the ability to post to the Microsoft MSN Soapbox Web site — a service used by, oh, maybe 10 people in the whole world — 12, if you include Washington state.

Fortunately, plugins are available and improving almost daily that let you publish directly to all the well-known video sites: YouTube, Flickr, and the like. Microsoft developers have shown a particular interest in the plugin named LiveUpload to YouTube, at (`codeplex.com/liveuploadyoutube`), which may be ready for prime time someday.

Here's how to publish your movie on the Web:

1. **Make sure your movie is in final form. Then save it.**
2. **On the Home tab, click the icon marked Publish and choose from one of the available Web sites.**

   You can choose to add a plugin at this point so that you can publish to any of the well-known video sites. The quality of the plugins varies.

   In this case, I choose Publish on MSN Soapbox. What the heck? — now 13 people in the whole world use Soapbox.
3. **If you're prompted for a logon ID and password, type it or do whatever is necessary to sign in.**

   Soapbox presents you with the tagging dialog box shown in Figure 5-10.

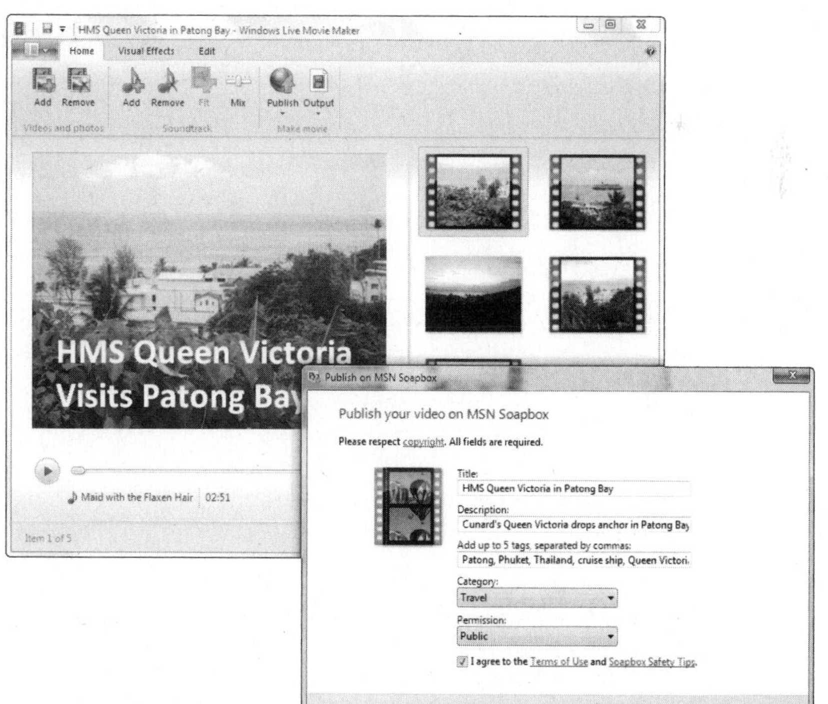

Figure 5-10: Type your tags here.

4. **Fill out whatever tag information the site requires, and then click Publish.**

   It may take five minutes to upload the movie, but when you're done, it's there.

Figure 5-11 shows my video posted on Soapbox.

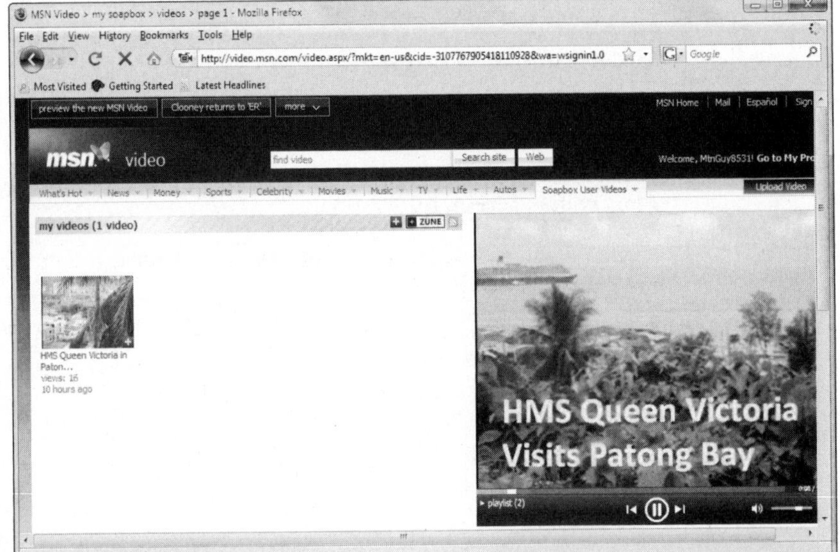

Figure 5-11: Your video shows up on Soapbox immediately.

Using Windows DVD Maker

Windows DVD Maker burns DVDs that can be played in DVD players. You generally feed Windows DVD Maker a WMV file created by Windows Live Movie Maker, but you can also use it to make a slide show of photographs, optionally using the Burns effect to move the photos slowly, panning and zooming, to add a bit of pizzazz. You can even set background music.

Windows Live Movie Maker and Windows DVD Maker operate completely independently — it's like they're from two different planets. For example, Windows DVD Maker lets you save your "project," which is a collection of movies and pictures. Windows Live Movie Maker lets you save projects, too. Predictably, a Windows DVD Maker project (MSDVD file) isn't anything like a Windows Live Movie Maker project (WLMP file). So, if you're in Windows DVD Maker and you choose File➪Open Project File, don't expect to see your Windows Live Movie Maker project. You can't open a Windows Live Movie Maker project in Windows DVD Maker (or vice versa, for that matter).

Making a DVD

Windows DVD Maker lets you choose the 4:3 or 16:9 aspect ratio, NTSC or PAL format, when (or whether) you will see a DVD menu, what text will appear on the menu, and what the menu looks like.

To let others view your movie, follow these steps:

1. **In Windows Live Movie Maker, click the Publish icon and publish your movie as a WMV file.**

   You tell WLMM where to put the WMV file.

2. **To get Windows DVD Maker going, choose Start⇨All Programs⇨ Windows DVD Maker.**

   After you click through quite a fancy but meaningless splash screen, you see the Add Pictures and Video to the DVD window, shown in Figure 5-12.

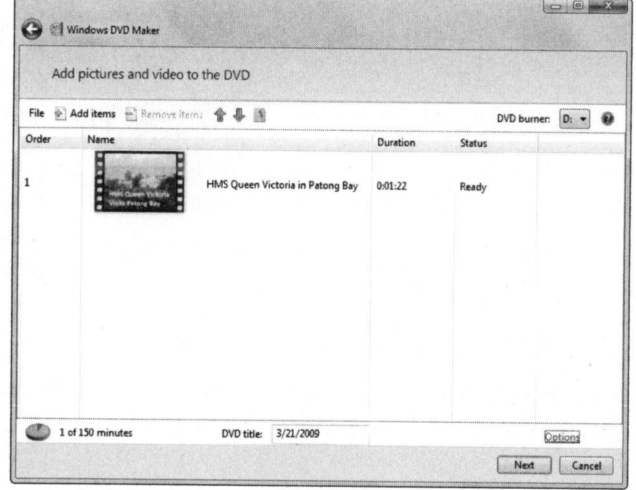

Figure 5-12: You can assemble multiple WMV files in Windows DVD Maker.

3. **Click the Add Items icon, navigate to the WMV (or AVI, MPG, or even picture) files you want to burn on the DVD and click Add.**

   You see a list of selected files in the Add Pictures and Video to the DVD window.

4. **In the lower-right corner of the Add Pictures and Video to the DVD window, click the link that says Options.**

   You see the DVD Options dialog box, shown in Figure 5-13.

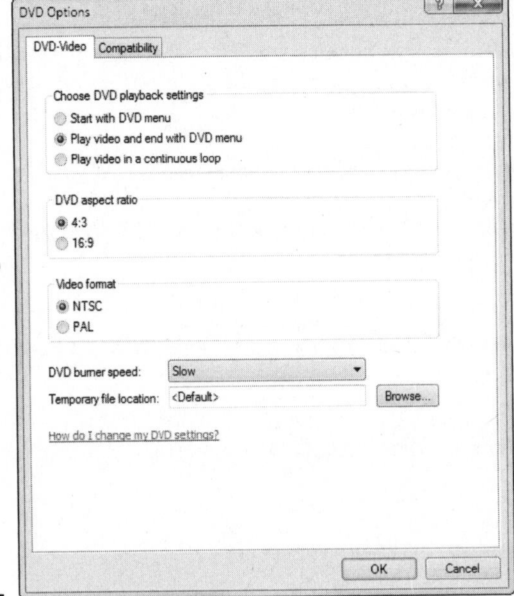

Figure 5-13: You can make your DVDs much easier to navigate by making judicious choices here.

5. **Consult Table 5-1 and choose the DVD menu method you want. Pick an aspect ratio (wide-screen is 16:9) and NTSC (for the United States) or PAL (for almost everywhere else). Set the DVD burner speed to Low, to minimize your chances of turning out useless coasters. Then click OK.**

   You return to the Add Pictures and Video to the DVD screen (refer to Figure 5-12).

6. **Put a DVD in the DVD drive and click Next.**

   Windows DVD Maker shows you the Ready to Burn DVD window (see Figure 5-14), which lets you choose some truly garish color casts, set menu text, and organize a slide show.

7. **Play with the settings, by all means — you can see the effect of what you do by clicking the Play Scenes link inside the preview — but don't expect too much.**

   The only exception: photo slide shows. Windows DVD Maker has many more capabilities than Windows Live Movie Maker — the aforementioned Burns effect; the ability to play more than one song in the background; and the ability to stretch out the slide show so that it lasts as long as the music.

8. **When you're happy with the result, click Burn.**

   Wait 10 or 15 or 20 or 30 minutes, and you should have a DVD that plays in any DVD player.

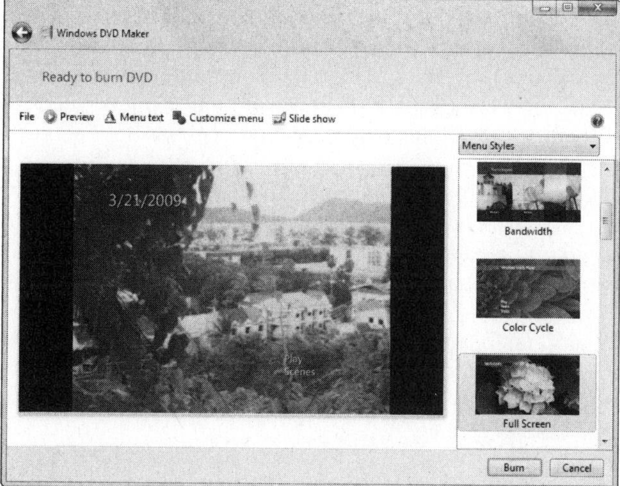

Figure 5-14: Windows DVD Maker gives you some control over menus and adds a few bizarre color overlays.

Table 5-1 DVD Playback Settings

Setting	*What It Means*
Start with DVD menu	When you insert the DVD into a DVD player, the first thing you see is a menu offering to show you individual "chapters" (corresponding to the files you burn) or to play the whole DVD.
Play video and end with DVD menu	When you insert the DVD into a DVD player, it starts playing. When the movie's completely done, you see the menu that lists the chapters on the CD, and gives you an option to play the entire CD. About 99 percent of the time, this is what you — and your viewers — want.
Play video in a continuous loop	This setting is good for kiosks, long staff meetings, or other places where user intervention is neither required nor desired.

Ripping, burning, and converting movies

The legal status of DVD ripping and burning seems clear: You can't make copies of commercial movies and hand them out to your friends; you can't rent a DVD and rip a copy for your later enjoyment.

On the other hand, the legal status of making backups of DVD movies you bought also seems quite clear: You can probably make a backup copy for your personal use. Maybe. At least, that's the theory. In practice, it may be illegal to sell software that makes it possible to rip movie DVDs. Or maybe not. Have your lawyer call my lawyer and let them bill each other for lunch.

Windows 7 doesn't rip any commercial DVDs. Period. End of story. It's against the Microsoft religion. You can play a DVD on any Windows PC, but Windows 7 won't pull a movie off a commercial DVD and stick it in your computer. If you want to rip a DVD, you have to look beyond Windows 7.

One company has been making ripping, burning, and file-format conversion software for many years. Xilisoft Corporation (`xilisoft.com`) may have just the converter you need — if it's still in business. Xilisoft also does iPod/MP4 player conversions.

By all means, try Windows Live Movie Maker or Windows DVD Maker to see whether you can convert and play video the way you want. But if you get frustrated, check out Xilisoft. Its products aren't cheap, but I've had good luck with them. Free trial versions are generally available from shareware sites such as `www.tucows.com`.

Chapter 6: Setting Up Media Center

In This Chapter

- **Figuring out where all those %$#@! wires go**
- **Getting Media Center adjusted**
- **Coercing your TV into submission**
- **Recording TV**

By the time you finish putting together your first Windows 7 Media Center (WMC) system, you may swear off assembling PCs ever again. If you can get it all in one box, you have it made. But the minute you start mixing and matching, adding home theater sound here, slapping around a set-top TV box there, and wedging that 120-inch LCD screen somewhere in the middle, you're going to find out a lot more than you ever wanted to know about Dolby 7.1, IR blasters, and DVI connectors.

In fact, one of the very best reasons for buying a WMC component system from a local store is that you can hire the company that sold you the unit to put it together for you.

Not long ago, a friend of mine told me that he was getting out of the computer business because it has just gotten too complicated. He made that announcement — you guessed it — immediately after assembling a Windows Media Center PC. Of course, he built it from scratch.

Media Center PCs combine all the frustrations of assembling a complicated PC with the joys of figuring out how to attach your satellite box, where to hook up the speakers, which stack of books to stick under the TV, how to keep all the wires from pulling each other out, and what to do with the subwoofer. The only saving grace? You don't have to worry about a video recorder. Probably.

Digital rights versus your rights

Windows Media Center sits at ground zero in the ongoing battle over digital rights management (DRM). When WMC blocked the recording of a broadcast *American Gladiator* installment on NBC in May 2008, recriminations flew fast and furious. Microsoft claimed it was only following the rules, acting as a gatekeeper. Some disputed that there was even a gate to keep.

DRM rules have changed, and they're changing even now — for example, at this moment, if you record certain TV programs using WMC and a CableCARD, you can't play them back on, oh, an MP4 player. Suffice it to say that your WMC challenges go beyond hardware — and they can change from day to day.

Determining Whether You Need Media Center

There are lots and lots of alternatives to Windows Media Center. It seems like every cable company these days offers devices that provide at least some of the features in WMC, and the latest incarnations of the TiVo deliver much more than the basics.

If you're only dabbling in the digital home entertainment arena to record TV, WMC rates as overkill. Consider:

- Most garden-variety digital video recorders (DVRs) — even the cheap ones rented by cable companies — can handle all the basics: skip advertisements, pause and rewind during a live broadcast, program recording schedules.
- The not-so-cheap DVRs from major electronic manufacturers also include high-definition (HD) support, advanced sound systems, and more.
- The newest TiVo — progenitor of the genre — includes CableCARD support (so that you don't need to buy a set-top TV box), multiroom viewing (record on one TiVo and play on another), online scheduling (so that you don't have to mess with that %$#@! remote), and two-tuner support.

More than that, if you're thinking about recording TV, you may be living in the past: Technology is fast catching up with the do-it-yourself recording fervor, and online movie rentals rock. Consider:

- If you live in the United States, head to Hulu (`www.hulu.com`), which has free, high-definition versions of a huge variety of TV shows and movies on NBC, ABC, Fox, and other networks. Hulu (shown in Figure 6-1) is a joint venture between NBC, Fox, and ABC/Disney, and it's growing by leaps and bounds.

  If you install PlayOn (`themediamall.com`) on your PC, you can stream Hulu recordings to any Xbox 360 or PlayStation 3 in your home.

- The TiVo Series 3 hooks directly into Amazon Video on Demand (see Figure 6-2), a service that offers many recent movies for $3.99 to $4.99. High definition, Dolby 5.1 — good stuff.

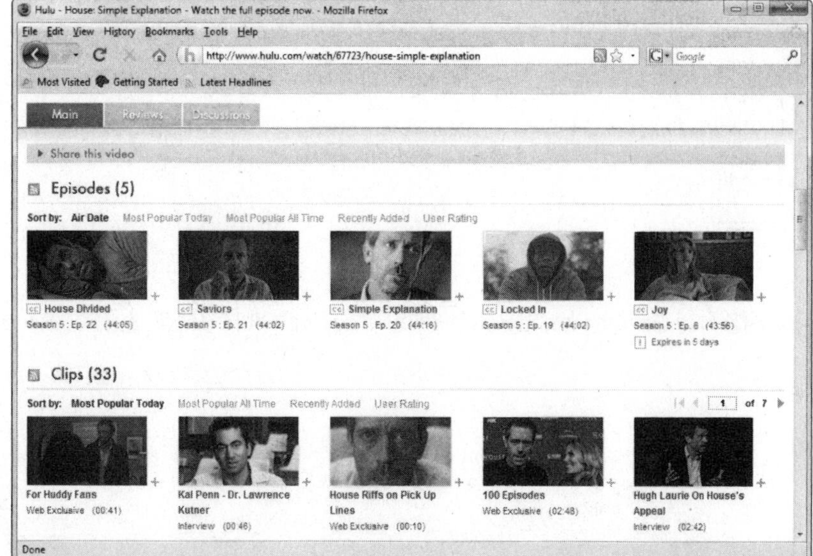

Figure 6-1: On Hulu, all the high-def *House* that's fit to print.

Figure 6-2: The TiVo interface with Amazon Video on Demand.

Media Center draws people in with its incredible interface; its power; its seductive, immersive multimedia capabilities; its position as the physical and logistical center of all your audio and visual equipment — and the ability to control all that and more from across the room by using a remote. With an Xbox 360, your game machine can tap into the full Windows 7 Media Center as well — and do it, uh, well.

Here's what Media Center offers that most people want:

- **All the TV recording and playback capabilities you can imagine:** Support for multiple CableCARDs is included.
- **A visual treat:** You receive full high-definition and lots of thumbnails and other visual cues. When the menus appear, they don't obliterate the current show (see Figure 6-3). If you start fumbling through the menus, the clip playing now appears in the lower-left corner, so it's one-click easy to go back from whence you came. You can fast-forward or reverse thumbnails, too.

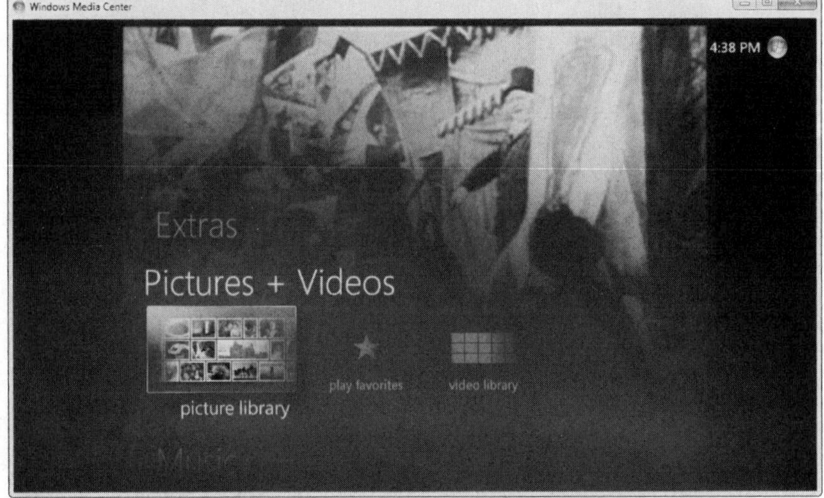

Figure 6-3: Menus don't take over the screen; Dr. Caligari continues to speak while the menu appears.

- **Full integration with Windows 7:** The Windows Media Center icon appears on the taskbar, and from there it's right-click easy to go to the TV Program Guide or play your recently viewed tracks. Windows 7 libraries get their full due, including the Pictures and Music libraries and even a Media Center desktop gadget.
- **Virtual channels available now — and more on the way:** Virtual channels let you easily hook into services such as Hulu and YouTube. WMC is the 800-pound gorilla of Internet video players, and content providers everywhere take that into consideration.

Media Center limitations

The biggest limitations of Windows Media Center center around digital rights management, and they aren't all exclusive to Media Center. If you record your favorite high-def TV show on your Media Center system, can you burn it to DVD and then watch the DVD on a neighbor's DVD player? On another PC? On your MP4 player? The answers aren't cut-and-dried. If they concern you, ask people who own and use Media Center (at, for example, `thegreenbutton.com`) before you buy.

Lots of people become confused about the difference between Media Center and Windows Media Player (WMP). Don't let the similarity in names cause any heartburn. In fact, Media Player (see Book IV, Chapter 1) is just one component of Media Center — it's the part of Media Center that plays music, movies, and recorded TV shows. Media Center doesn't look anything at all like Media Player (well, okay, you can show the WMP "visualizations" in Media Center), but every time you play a song or view a movie, WMP is running in the background.

Although you can find some Windows Media Player settings from inside Windows Media Center, using it to change WMP is a bit like trying to drive a Volkswagen with a bazooka.

Organizing the Normandy Invasion

So you have eight big boxes sitting on the floor of your living room (or dorm room or office), and the first debilitating pangs of buyer's remorse have set in.

That's normal. Not to worry. The following sections offer a handful of tips that can help you through the assembly process. Go ahead and benefit from others' experience.

Gathering the tools for an easier setup

The folks at the computer store sold you everything you need. But I can guarantee that they forgot a couple of items that you surely want. Before you assemble the beast, you need to run out and pick up what they forgot.

In particular, you need these items:

- **An uninterruptible power supply (UPS):** If the sales droid let you walk out of the shop without a UPS, he should be lashed. No, a surge protector isn't good enough. You need a UPS big enough to handle your computer and any other sensitive hardware that's hanging around: TV, audio equipment, network hub, DSL or cable modem, scanner, external drives, or USB hubs — the whole nine yards.

No, you don't need to plug your printer into a UPS — and you should never plug a laser printer into a UPS. Laser printers draw a tremendous amount of power; a laser printer will probably blow out your UPS when it starts, and even if your UPS doesn't end up as a heap of smoldering goo, if the power goes out, the UPS will die in seconds from the laser printer's power drain.

- **Lots of power strips:** The ones that plug into the UPS don't need surge protection, but any that plug straight into the wall should have surge protectors.

Anything with a "brick" that converts AC current to DC (which you commonly find with laptop computers, telephones, modems, and other devices) doesn't require a surge protector. But any brick located at the end of a power cord invariably takes up two (or even three) slots on a power strip.

- **A roll of masking tape and a fine-point permanent-ink marker:** You should mark the end of every cable as you connect it: Wrap a piece of tape around the wire and write down where it's going. That way, when you look at a power strip with five plugs in it, you can tell which one goes to your PC and which one goes to your TV. You can also tell your left-front speaker from the right-side and center-rear speakers without pulling the speaker cable out from under the rug.

If you save a snapshot of the final array of cables — even if you only use your Webcam — you have a good record of which cable went where, in case your 3-year-old nephew decides to pull a few cables off the back of the TV.

- **Those little plastic gizmos that bundle cables together:** They're cheap, and they keep you from going nuts. By the time you're done, the back of your PC will look like a wiring bundle down the fuselage of a 747.
- **Video cables that are long enough to go where they need to go:** Before you assemble the beast, block out precisely where the PC goes, where the monitor goes, and where the TV (if you have one) goes. Then figure out how long the video cables must be. Then dig into the box and see whether the cables you have are long enough. I bet they aren't, particularly if you're connecting a TV. When you go out shopping, make sure to buy the right kind of cables.

You can try to figure out whether you need an HDMI cable, an optical audio cable, a DVI cable, or a reversible 3-plug mini-DIN with imploded wombat RJ-945 squared cable, but why sweat the hard stuff? If you have any doubt about which kind of cable you need, haul out your digital camera or mobile phone and take close-up shots of the connectors on the back of your computer and on the back of your TV. Then schlep the camera to the shop and ask the salesperson to figure it out. Hey, that's what he's paid to do.

- **Remote hardware:** Some Media Center PC systems don't have keyboards or mice. I think that's a huge mistake. WMC includes an onscreen keyboard, but it's about as hard to use as T9 SMS on a mobile phone. At least until Microsoft brings more functions into the Media Center umbrella, occasional trips out to Windows itself are inevitable — and for those, you want a keyboard and mouse. If your Media Center PC sits in a cramped dorm room, running for the keyboard is no big deal, but if you have to get up off the couch and find a chair to put in front of the computer, it's a pain in the neck.
- **A nice bottle of wine:** Need I explain what this is for? Beer works in a pinch.

Getting Windows in gear

The first time you start your new Media Center computer, almost anything can happen. Why? Each manufacturer seems to have a different way of introducing you to the experience.

Making your video card acquiesce

If your Media Center PC came with its own TV set, if you're running videos on your computer monitor, or if you already have things set up so that video stuff shows up on your TV and computer stuff shows up on your monitor, breathe a sigh of relief and move on to the next section in this chapter to verify that your sound card is working right.

But if you want to connect both a TV and a computer monitor to your PC and you haven't yet figured out how to make movies play on the TV rather than in a window on your PC's monitor, you have a bit of work to do.

If you have a TV and a monitor plugged into your PC (or two monitors — one for Windows itself, the other for media) and you can't get Windows to show things on both of them, follow this procedure:

Old sounds can be good sounds

The folks who sold you that Media Center home theater setup probably want to sell you a new sound system, too. Don't hesitate to use your current sound system. Media Center works very well indeed with most modern surround sound systems — even better if you can get a fiber optic TOSLINK cable to reach from your PC to the amp.

1. **On the screen that works, right-click any blank place on the Windows desktop and choose Screen Resolution.**

   You see the Change the Appearance of Your Displays dialog box, shown in Figure 6-4.

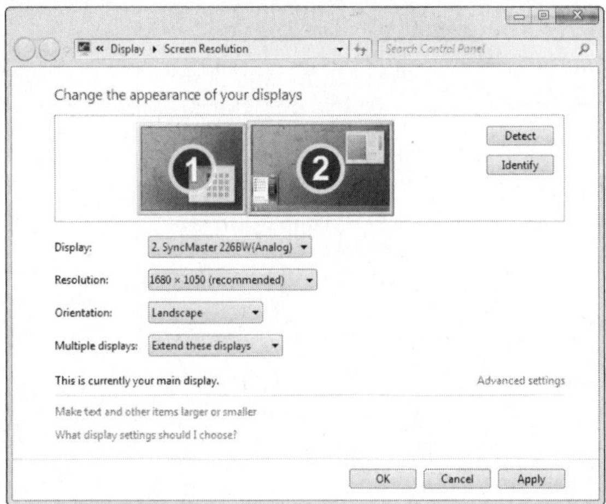

Figure 6-4: Get both your TV and your monitor working.

2. **Click the Identify Monitors button and Windows puts a `1` on the screen it considers to be the first, and a `2` on the second.**
3. **In the Multiple Displays box, choose Extend These Displays.**

   This step ensures that the Windows desktop extends across both displays, which is the easiest way to run Media Center.
4. **Click Apply.**

   Windows asks whether you want to keep the new settings.
5. **Click the Keep Changes button.**

   Congratulations! Your PC can now see double.

Setting sound straight

Modern audio chips produce phenomenal sound. If you have a home theater (that is, audio) system to provide the oomph, Media Center can rock your house off its foundation. Kinda adds a new dimension to the old adage "If this house is a-rockin'. . . ."

Setting up a sound system usually entails matching up the audio card outputs (pink, blue, lime green, black, orange, tutti-frutti) to the audio amp's inputs and then snaking a lot of wires over, under, around, and through the room. When you're done, the $64,000 question arises: Did you hook up the speakers correctly? Easy to ask. Not so easy to answer.

Every sound card works differently, but most of them can help you verify that the right plug on the back of the card is connected to the left, er, right speaker. For example, the SoundBlaster Audigy Audio chip, which ships on many inexpensive motherboards, can be tested in this way:

1. **Right-click the speaker in the notification area, near the clock, and choose Playback Devices.**

   Windows shows you the Sound dialog box (see Figure 6-5).

Figure 6-5: Typically, this list includes external speakers and headphones.

2. **Choose the speakers you're using and click the Configure button.**

   The Speaker Setup panel appears, as shown in Figure 6-6.

3. **Choose the kind of speaker setup you have.**

   The diagram changes based on your selection. For example, 5.1 Surround uses two front speakers, two back speakers, a center speaker, and a subwoofer. If you click Quadraphonic, you see four speakers.

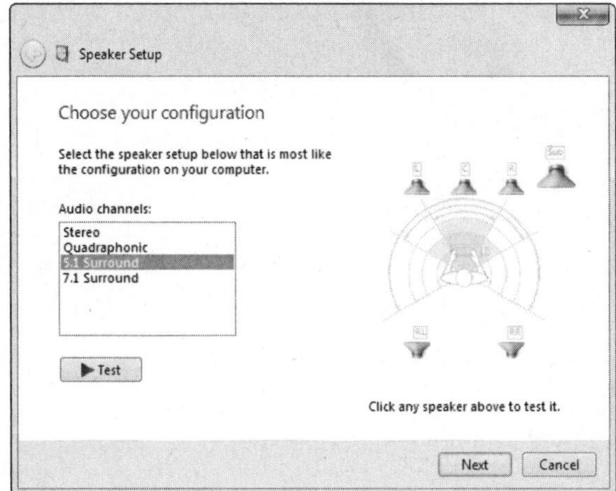

Figure 6-6: Test your speakers to make sure that they're hooked up properly.

4. **Click the Test button to test each speaker in turn, or click an individual speaker to make sure that it's properly identified.**

   If the wrong speaker sounds off, you probably messed up one of the color-coded connections on the back of the audio card. Rearrange the cables and try, try again.

5. **Click Cancel to close the Sound dialog box; then click the red X to exit the Control Panel.**

   You're now ready to faithfully reproduce the sound of "point-one" hand clapping, in full 5.1 (or 7.1 or, heck, 149.1) surround sound.

Gathering folders for libraries

Before you run the Media Center setup routine, you can make your Media, uh, Centering much easier if you take a few minutes to set up your Pictures, Music, and Videos libraries.

Though it's true that you can add folders to all three libraries from inside Windows Media Player, using the tools built into Windows Explorer simplifies things considerably.

Follow the nostrums in Book II, Chapter 1 to add any wayward folders — including folders accessible via your HomeGroup — to the Music, Pictures, and Videos libraries.

Setting Up Media Center

With Windows 7 finally cowed into subservience, at last you're ready to set up Windows Media Center. Here's how:

1. **Click the Start button on your remote (if your TV is set up) or choose Start⇨All Programs⇨Windows Media Center.**

   If this is your first time in the Media Center, you see a splash screen assuring you that WMC is "The best way to experience TV on your PC."

   If you already completed the setup and you want to do it all over again (perhaps to change some privacy-robbing settings), scroll to Tasks and choose Settings⇨General⇨Windows Media Center Setup⇨Run Setup Again. Yep, that's where they buried it.

2. **Click Continue.**

   You see the Get Started screen, shown in Figure 6-7.

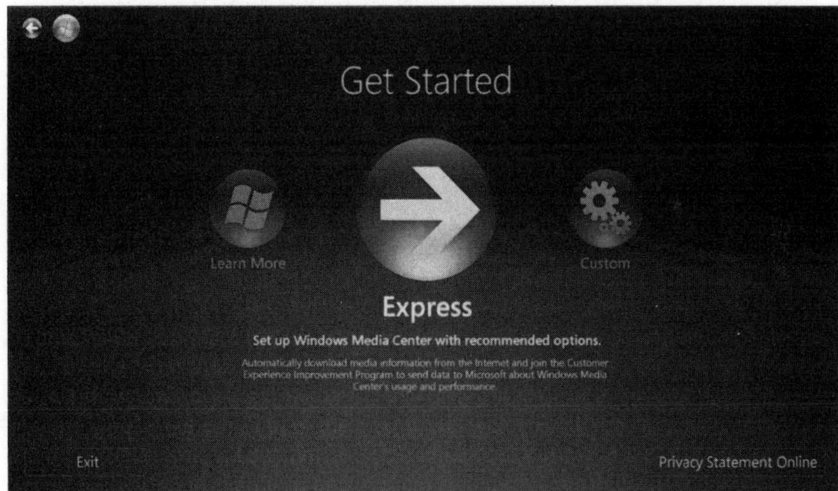

Figure 6-7: Don't take the Express setup.

3. **Click Custom.**

   WMC advises that it will take you through two sections: Required Setup and Optional Setup. Click Ho-Hum Next. WMC asks whether you want to help improve Windows Media Center by joining the Customer Experience Improvement Program (CEIP) and sending logs of all your WMC activity to the giant Microsoft database in the sky.

Like so many other offers from Microsoft, the Customer Experience Improvement Program claims to maintain your confidentiality, not collect personally identifiable information, and so on. As with so many other offers from Microsoft, you have to ask yourself whether you trust the company and everyone in it. If you have an always-on Internet connection, Microsoft can (and probably does) collect your Internet Protocol (IP) address, along with detailed information about the movies you watch, your music preferences and buying patterns, your favorite TV programs, and so on. I would bet that the remote even checks to see whether you pick your nose. It's none of Microsoft's business. Just say *no.*

4. **Select No Thank You and click Next.**

   WMC asks whether it's okay to connect to the Internet to find cover art for albums, music and movie information, and TV program guide listings. You may disagree — given Microsoft's track record, I wouldn't blame you — but I figure that the additional benefits are worth giving up some of my privacy, so I choose Yes.

5. **If you're like me, choose Yes and click Next.**

   WMP advises that you have completed everything you need for enhanced playback (whatever that might be), and asks whether you want to configure its Optional Setup.

6. **In most cases, WMP makes good guesses for configuring your TV tuner, so choose I Have Finished and click Next.**

   Media Player shows you a You Are Done! screen.

7. **Click Finish.**

While you're thinking about it, take a second to double-check your main privacy settings. Scroll to the Tasks menu and choose Settings➪General➪Privacy➪Privacy Settings. From the dialog box, shown in Figure 6-8, you can turn on or off the two privacy settings.

Here's what the settings mean:

✦ **Use the Guide and Send Anonymous Information:** You get to use the program guide, but Microsoft collects information about your use of it, including your IP address (which uniquely identifies your computer), customized TV listings, zip code, and television service provider. If you change a guide entry, Microsoft notes that, too, and uses the information to make the guide more accurate. The Microsoft privacy statement isn't clear, at least to me, about whether viewing information (such as which programs you watched and when) and guide use information (such as which stations you flip to from the guide) are sent to the mother database. Unless Microsoft comes out at some point in the future and denies that it's collecting this type of information, you should assume that selecting this check box gives Microsoft permission to track what you watch.

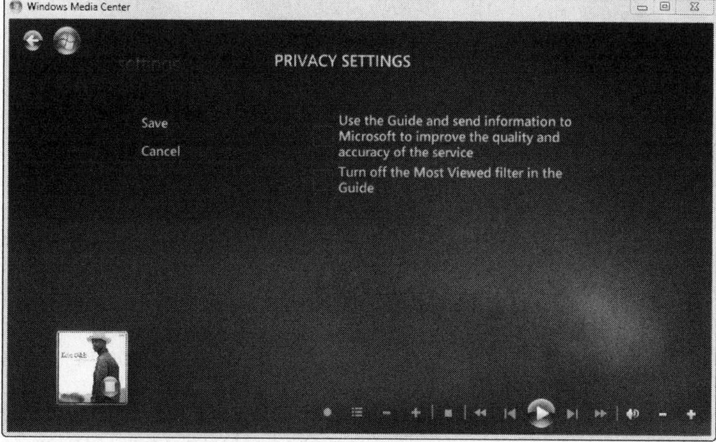

Figure 6-8: Don't send Microsoft any information that makes you feel uncomfortable.

✦ **Turn Off the Most Viewed Filter in the Guide:** Media Center keeps track of the shows you watch the most so that it can present the Most Viewed list as one of the categories in the guide, thereby narrowing the list of TV stations displayed in it. I can find no reference in the Microsoft privacy statement to the ways in which this information can be used. Unless Microsoft comes out at some point in the future and denies that it's collecting this type of information, you should assume that selecting this check box gives Microsoft permission to track what you watch. (Have you heard that one before?)

Beyond the Basics

After you set it up, most of Media Center is, simply, self-explanatory. The parts that work right require very little digging beyond the normal scope of a couch potato with a remote — which describes me perfectly when I'm tired of working and just want to relax.

Tackling the parts that don't work right takes an advanced degree in Cable Guy Engineering, a van stuffed with specialized electronic gizmos, and three martinis, in more or less that order.

Media Center can't — and won't — do some things. Unless laws in the United States change drastically, Microsoft will never offer a program that rips DVDs. Recording FM and AM radio seems arcane enough to the 'Softies that it'll never happen.

This chapter delves into the more advanced Media Center topics that seem to crop up over and over again. In some cases, you can "discover" the features easily in couch potato mode. But in a surprising number of cases, it really helps to know where the bodies are buried.

Playing recorded TV shows

Playing a TV show on the Media Center PC that recorded it couldn't be simpler. From the Media Center main menu, select the TV + Movies option (or press the TV button on the remote) and then choose Recorded TV (see Figure 6-9).

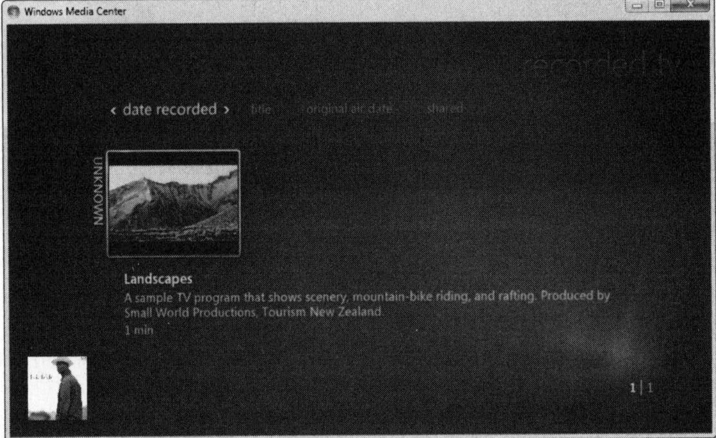

Figure 6-9: Playing a TV show on the PC that recorded it is easy.

The shows listed on the screen are all those you recorded. To play a recorded show, just click it.

Playing a recorded TV show on a PC other than the PC that recorded it can be interesting. The key problem: digital rights management.

Did you see my discussion of C.R.A.P. music in Book IV, Chapter 1? Every TV program you record with Media Center is in Microsoft's proprietary, protected format — so recorded TV is C.R.A.P., any way you slice it.

When Media Center records a TV show, it brands the recorded file with whichever restrictions the broadcaster imposes. For some shows, on some stations, it's no big deal. But for movie channels such as HBO, the restrictions can be considerable. As of this writing, that may include a restriction that you can play back the show only on the PC on which it was recorded — and you can "stream" the show to other PCs connected directly to your network, as well as media extenders such as the Xbox 360. Heaven only knows what kind of restrictions may be imposed in the future — will your device allow you to play a program only on alternating Thursdays or within a day of when it's recorded? Who knows. We ain't talkin' VHS videotape here.

What happened to DVR-MS?

If you recorded any TV shows in Windows Vista Media Center or Windows XP Media Center Edition, you ended up with files that bore the odd filename extensiondvr-ms. It seems that technology has fallen out of favor with Microsoft. When you record TV shows by using the Windows 7 Media Center, you create files in the `.wtv` format.

As was the case with files in the DVR-MS format, few products can handle WTV files. That may change over time, but at least for now, WTV files are great for playing on Windows 7 Media Center PCs, and that's about it.

To convert WTV files to other, more capable (but lesser-quality) formats, try running the free converter ToDVRMS, from Andy VT at `babgvant.com/files/folders/misc/entry12098.aspx`.

Despite these questions, Windows 7 Media Center adds the ability to share Recorded TV folders among PCs on a network (see Figure 6-10). To add the folders, choose Tasks➪Settings➪Media Libraries➪Recorded TV and select Add Folders to the Library.

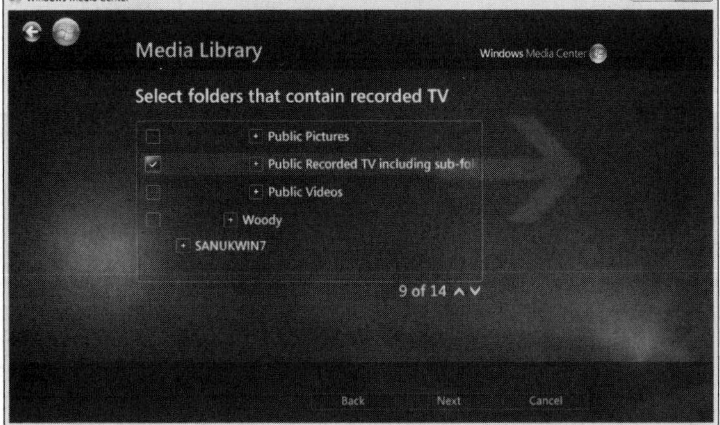

Figure 6-10: You can add recorded TV shows from other Media Center PCs to your Recorded TV library.

You can move the recorded TV file (it's a `.wtv` file, located in the Public Folder's Recorded TV folder) by any convenient method — burn it to a DVD, copy it across a network, send it by e-mail, or etch it on papyrus. After you place the file on a new machine, if it's going to play, it plays with Windows Media Player. In a pinch, you can also use Media Center.

The notorious broadcast protection flag

In early May 2008, thousands of Windows Vista Media Center users trying to record certain NBC shows, including *American Gladiator,* were greeted with this notification: "Restrictions set by the broadcaster and/or originator of the content prohibit recording of this program." Folks who used other video recorders — TiVo or anything other than Windows Vista Media Center — had no problem recording the shows.

What happened? Apparently, somebody on the NBC end accidentally set a "broadcast protection flag" for the shows. WMP detected the presence of the flag and cut off recording. Other manufacturers' hardware probably should have detected the flag and kicked out, too, but nobody had set the flag in recent history and the other hardware ignored it.

The moral of this story: If you think you should be able to do things with the TV show you recorded and you can't, chances are good that somebody is using DRM software to prevent you from doing it. Ka-ching!

Burning DVDs

Media Center uses the (truly underpowered) Windows DVD Maker to burn DVDs and CDs. Don't expect anything great, but you can burn a DVD with your Media Center remote.

To burn a data DVD, consider using Windows itself and drag the files you want to the DVD drive (see Book II, Chapter 1). To burn music — either as an audio CD or as a data CD with MP3 files — use Windows Media Player (see Book IV, Chapter 1).

If you're stuck with protected WTV files (recorded from, say, a movie channel) or if you can't get a mouse or keyboard hooked up to your PC, you can use Media Center to burn a DVD. Here's how:

1. **Stick a blank DVD (or CD) in your DVD drive.**

   Media Center wants a blank DVD or CD, so you might as well insert it first. If Media Center is running in full-screen mode, you see the Burn a CD or DVD message. If it isn't, scroll to Tasks and choose Burn CD or DVD.

   Media Player asks whether you want to burn an audio CD/DVD or a data CD/DVD or a DVD slide show, as shown in Figure 6-11.

2. **To create a DVD that can be played on your TV (as long as the files aren't protected), select the Video DVD or DVD Slide Show option and click Next.**

   Media Center asks you to type a name for the DVD. You can use the onscreen keyboard, if you press OK on your remote control.

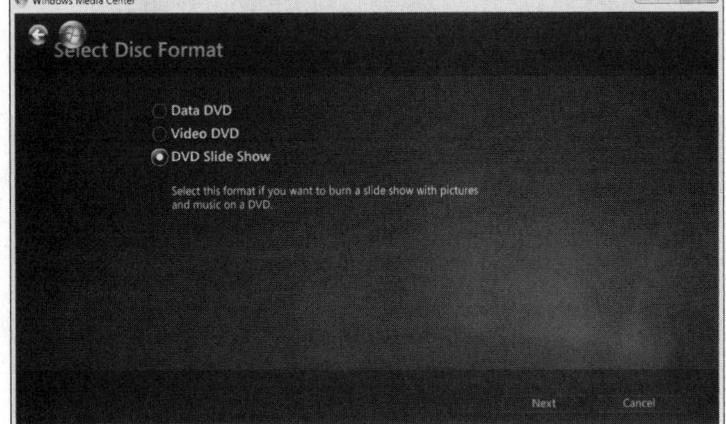

Figure 6-11: You have much easier ways to create a data DVD.

3. **Type a name for the DVD and click Next.**

   Depending on whether you chose a DVD slide show or a video, Media Center wants to know whether it should look in your Recorded TV or Videos library or in your Music or Picture library.

4. **Choose between Recorded TV, Videos, Pictures, or Music, and click Next.**

   Media Center presents you with a list of all your recorded TV shows (or videos) that pass digital rights management muster — you don't even see the recorded TV shows that are restricted. Media Center invites you to select the ones you want to burn, as shown in Figure 6-12.

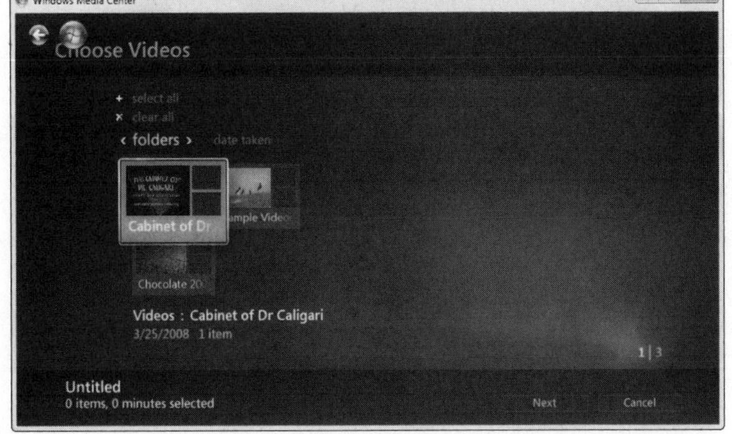

Figure 6-12: Choose the videos you want to burn.

5. **Select the check box in the lower-right corner of each recorded TV program that you want to record, and then click Next. Follow the prompts to add more, if you so desire.**

   When you're done, click Burn DVD.

   Media Center asks one last time whether you want to burn the chosen clips to DVD. Resist the temptation to click No, You Stupid Machine, I've Jumped through All These Hoops with a Lousy Remote Because I Needed the Practice.

6. **Click the Yes button and go grab a latté.**

   This step takes a while, especially if you have a long recorded TV show. Better yet, go to your favorite restaurant, order a seven-course meal, and don't forget the cognac and cigars when you're done.

   When Media Center comes back, you have a fully functional DVD, ready to pop into any DVD player.

Finding more information about Media Center

Windows Media Center rates as a world unto its own, with its own gurus, buzzwords, problems, and solutions and even a secret handshake or two.

In July 2008, Microsoft bought an online forum and WMC enthusiast site named The Green Button (`thegreenbutton.com`). It's still the preeminent source of Windows Media Center information on the Internet. Since the dawn of Media Center time, The Green Button has served as a bully pulpit for Media Center cognoscenti, with all sorts of amazing advice — some of which is distinctly, refreshingly, *not* Microsoft Party Line.

In late 2009, Michael Healy started the Hacking Windows 7 Media Center site, `Hack7mc.com`, and he has managed to amass an extensive, easily accessible collection of tricks, tips, and (surprisingly, given its name) tutorials. Highly recommended.

Book V

Windows 7 and the Internet

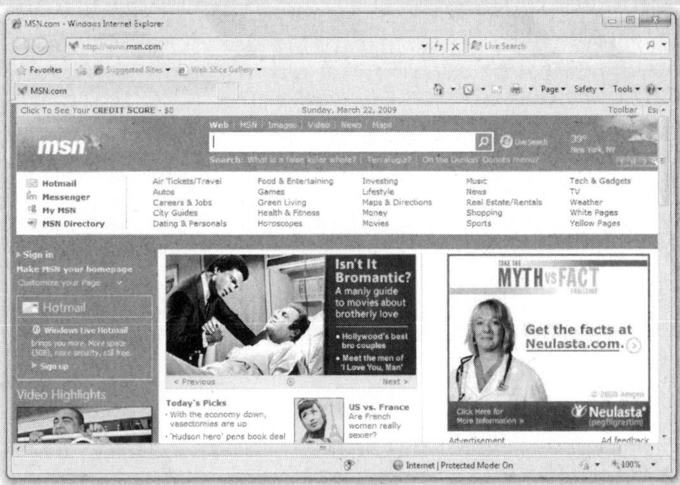

Contents at a Glance

Chapter 1: Getting the Most from the Internet

In This Chapter

- Getting a quick overview of the Internet
- Dialing with dollars
- Connecting with Broadband
- Setting up an Internet connection
- Finding important Internet resources

Internet this. Web that. E-mail today. Hair (or at least spam about hair products) tomorrow.

Windows 7 makes it easy to get online: You can dash off a quick message to your daughter, send a birthday card to your mom, pick up the latest baseball scores and news headlines, glance at the stock market, look up show-times and locations at a dozen local theaters, compare features and prices on the latest mobile phones, send a free SMS phone message, and check out the weather in my home town, Phuket, all in a matter of minutes — if your Internet connection is fast enough.

Five years from now (although it may take ten), the operating system you use will be largely irrelevant, as will be the speed of your computer, the amount of memory you have, and the number of terabytes of storage that hum in the background. Microsoft will keep milking its cash cow, but the industry will move on. Individuals and businesses will stop shelling out big bucks for Windows and the iron to run it. Instead, the major push will be online. Rather than spend money on PCs that become obsolete the week after you purchase them, folks will spend money on big data pipes: It'll be less about *me* and more about *us.* Why? Because so much more is "out there" than "in here." Count on it.

But what is the Internet? This chapter answers this burning question (if you've asked it). If you don't necessarily wonder about the Internet's place in space and time, know that this chapter also explains how to connect to the Internet. Of course, the easiest way to do that is by using Internet Explorer (IE), the Web browser that comes (surprise, surprise) packaged with your version of Windows. You can also use Firefox, the scrappy, free upstart that took on Goliath and showed the lumbering giant a thing or three.

I explain how to download and install Firefox — my browser of choice and free, to boot — in Book V, Chapter 2. I talk about Google's up-and-coming Chrome browser there, too.

Connecting with IE or Firefox is, thankfully, a straightforward process. You aren't likely to encounter many superhuman challenges along the way — perhaps an unrecognized modem or a misplaced password, or you might need to kick your cable guy, but nothing insurmountable. This chapter walks you through the basics of making that initial IE connection and helps you anticipate and, hopefully, avoid any potential trouble spots along your path.

You may already be an old hand at making Internet connections. If that's the case, go to the head of the class and move along to the next chapter.

What Is the Internet?

You know those stories about computer jocks who come up with great ideas, develop the ideas in their basements (or garages or dorm rooms), release their product to the public, change the world, and make a gazillion bucks?

This isn't one of them.

The Internet started in the mid-1960s as an academic exercise — primarily with the RAND Corporation, the Massachusetts Institute of Technology (MIT), and the National Physical Laboratory in England — and rapidly evolved into a military project, under the U.S. Department of Defense Advanced Research Project Agency (ARPA), designed to connect research groups working on ARPA projects.

By the end of the 1960s, ARPA had 4 computers hooked together — at UCLA, SRI (Stanford), UC Santa Barbara, and the University of Utah — using systems developed by BBN Technologies (then named Bolt Beranek and Newman, Inc.). By 1971, it had 18 (see Figure 1-1). According to the Web site `internetworldstats.com`, by the end of 2008, the Internet had more than 1.5 *billion* users worldwide.

Today, so many computers are connected directly to the Internet (including all of you who run digital subscriber line [DSL] or cable modems) that the Internet's addressing system is running out of numbers, just as your local phone company is running out of telephone numbers. The current numbering system — named IPv4 — can handle about 4 billion addresses. The next version, named IPv6 — and bundled in Windows 7 — can handle this number of addresses:

340,000,000,000,000,000,000,000,000,000,000,000,000

That should last us for a while, doncha think?

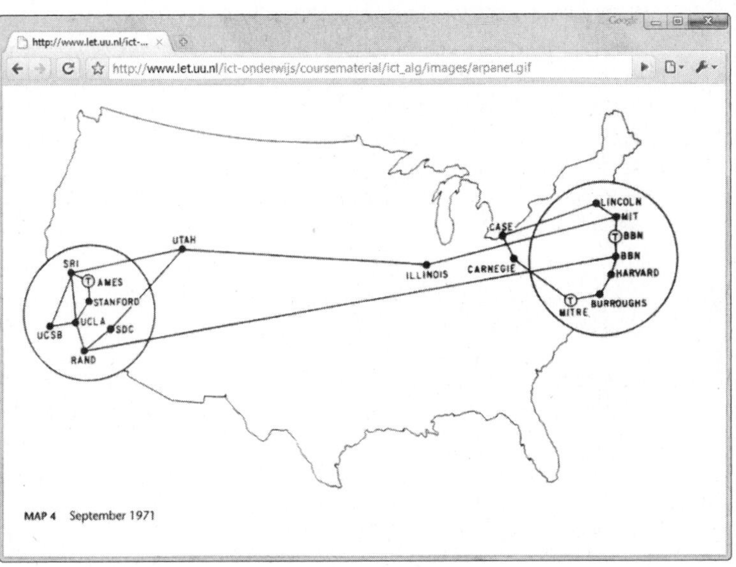

Figure 1-1: The original ARPAnet in September 1971, shown with the Google Chrome Web browser, from the University of Utrecht Web site in the Netherlands — times change, eh?

Ever wonder why you rarely see hard statistics about the Internet? I've found two big reasons: Defining terms related to the Internet is devilishly difficult these days. (What do you mean when you say "X number of computers are connected to the Internet"? Is that the number of computers up and running at any given moment? The number of different addresses that are active? The number that could be connected if everybody dialed up at the same time? The number of different computers that are connected in a typical day or week or month?) The other reason is that the Internet is growing so fast that any number you publish today will be meaningless tomorrow.

Getting Inside the Internet

Some observers claim that the Internet works so well because it was designed to survive a nuclear attack. Not so. The people who built the Internet insist that they weren't nearly as concerned about nukes as they were about making communication among researchers reliable, even when a backhoe severed an underground phone line or one of the key computers ground to a halt.

As far as I'm concerned, the Internet works so well because the engineers who laid the groundwork were utter geniuses. Their original ideas from 40 years ago have been through the wringer a few times, but they're still pretty much intact. Here's what the engineers decided:

- **No single computer should be in charge.** All the big computers connected directly to the Internet are equal (although, admittedly, some are more equal than others). By and large, computers on the Internet move data around like kids playing hot potato — catch it, figure out where you're going to throw it, and let it fly quickly. They don't need to check with some übercomputer before doing their work; they just catch, look, and throw. The distributed network concept looks like the mesh (C) shown in Figure 1-2.

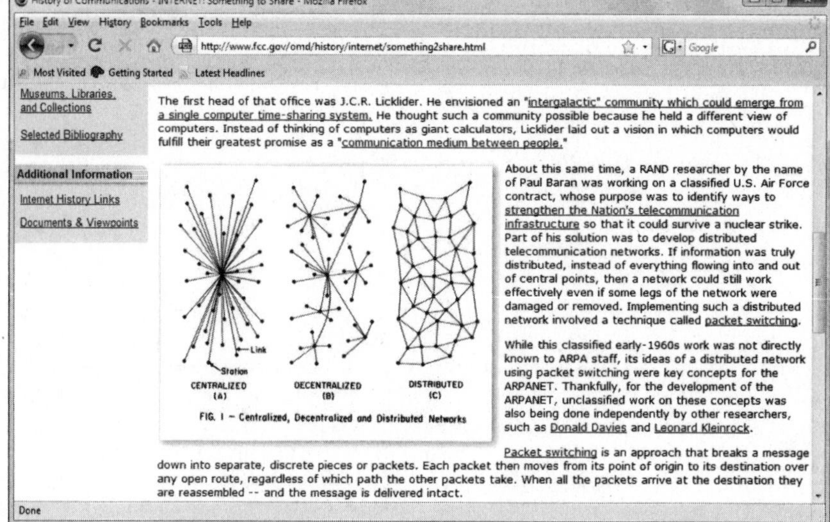

Figure 1-2: The U.S. Federal Communication Commission description of distributed networks.

- **Break the data into fixed-size packets.** No matter how much data you're moving — an e-mail message that just says "Hi" or a full-color, life-size photograph of the Andromeda galaxy — the data is broken into packets. Each packet is routed to the appropriate computer. The receiving computer assembles all the packets and notifies the sending computer that everything came through okay.

- **Deliver each packet quickly.** If you want to send data from Computer A to Computer B, break the data into packets and route each packet to Computer B by using the fastest connection possible — even if that means some packets go through Bangor and others go through Bangkok.

It's backbone-breaking work, but somebody's gotta do it

In January 2008, two underwater Internet backbone cables off the coast of Egypt were severed simultaneously. Much of south Asia, Egypt, and the Middle East had enormous problems with slow-as-molasses Internet for weeks, as the company that owned the cables searched to find and fix the break. In December 2008, four more were broken, in various incidents, wreaking havoc in major population areas all over the world (see the TeleGeography press release shown in the figure). Why, you may ask, didn't the Internet heal itself? After all, that's what the Internet is supposed to do — reroute around problems in the blink of an eye. It ends up that the problem had nothing to do with technology. It had everything to do with money.

This TeleGeography press release pinpoints the December 2008 Internet backbone cable breaks.

Internet service providers in Asia, Egypt, India, and the Middle East had contracts with one of the afflicted cable companies to provide big data pipes to their countries. In case of problems, several ISPs had backup contracts with the other afflicted cable company. When both lines went down, there were no contracts with alternative backbone providers and the ISPs didn't have enough money (or time) to sign on with other big backbones: Data had to limp out through various small connections.

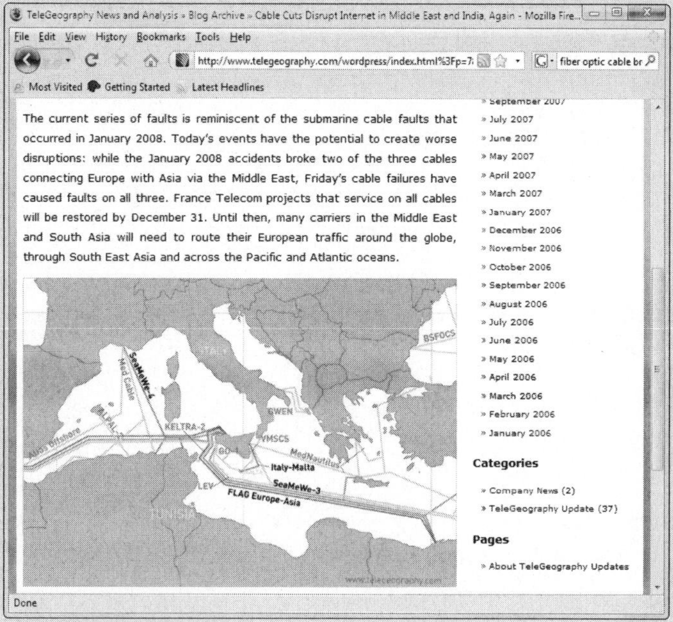

TeleGeography News and Analysis » Blog Archive » Cable Cuts Disrupt Internet in Middle East and India, Again - Mozilla Fire...

The current series of faults is reminiscent of the submarine cable faults that occurred in January 2008. Today's events have the potential to create worse disruptions: while the January 2008 accidents broke two of the three cables connecting Europe with Asia via the Middle East, Friday's cable failures have caused faults on all three. France Telecom projects that service on all cables will be restored by December 31. Until then, many carriers in the Middle East and South Asia will need to route their European traffic around the globe, through South East Asia and across the Pacific and Atlantic oceans.

Taken together, those three rules ensure that the Internet can take a lickin' and keep on tickin'. If a chipmunk eats through a telephone line, any big computer that's using the gnawed line can start rerouting packets over a different telephone line. If the Cumbersome Computer Company in Cupertino, California, loses power, computers that were sending packets through Cumbersome can switch to other connected computers. It all works quickly and reliably, although the techniques used internally by the Internet computers get a bit hairy at times.

Big computers are hooked together by high-speed communication lines: the Internet backbone. If you want to use the Internet from your business or your house, you have to connect to one of the big computers first. Companies that own the big computers — Internet service providers (ISPs) — get to charge you for the privilege of getting on the Internet through their big computers. The ISPs, in turn, pay the companies that own the cables (and satellites) that comprise the Internet backbone for a slice of the backbone.

If all this sounds like a big-fish-eats-smaller-fish-eats-smaller-fish arrangement, that's quite a good analogy.

What Is the World Wide Web?

People tend to confuse the World Wide Web with the Internet, which is a lot like confusing the dessert table with the buffet line. I'd be the first to admit that desserts are mighty darn important — life-critical, in fact, if the truth be told. But they aren't the same as the buffet line.

To get to the dessert table, you have to stand in the buffet line. To get to the Web, you have to be running on the Internet. Make sense?

The World Wide Web owes its existence to Tim Berners-Lee and a few co-conspirators at a research institute named CERN in Geneva, Switzerland. In 1990, Berners-Lee demonstrated a way to store and link information on the Internet so that all you had to do was click to jump from one place — one *Web page* — to another. Nowadays, nobody in his right mind can give a definitive count of the number of pages available, but it almost certainly exceeds 20 billion.

Like the Internet itself, the World Wide Web owes much of its success to the brilliance of the people who brought it to life. The following list describes the ground rules:

- **Web pages, stored on the Internet, are identified by an address, such as `http://www.dummies.com`.** The main part of the Web page address — `dummies.com`, for example — is a *domain name.* With rare exceptions, you can open a Web page by simply typing its domain name and pressing Enter. Capitalization doesn't matter: Typing `dUmMiEs.CoM` takes any Web browser to the same location as typing `http://www.dummies.com`. Spelling counts, and underscores (_) are treated differently from hyphens (-). Being close isn't good enough — there are just too many Web sites. As of this writing, DomainTools (`www.domaintools.com`) reports that about 110 million domain names end in `.com`, `.net`, `.org`, `.info`, `.biz`, or `.us`. That's just for the United States. Other countries have different naming conventions: `.co.uk`, for example, is the UK equivalent of `.com`.

- **Web pages are written in the funny language HyperText Markup Language (HTML).** *HTML* is sort of a programming language, sort of a formatting language, and sort of a floor wax, all rolled into one. Many products claim to make it easy for novices to create powerful, efficient HTML. Some of them are getting close.

- **To read a Web page, you have to use a Web browser.** A *Web browser* is a program that runs on your computer and is responsible for converting HTML into text that you can read and use. The majority of people who view Web pages use Internet Explorer as their Web browser, but more and more people (including me!) prefer Firefox (see `www.mozilla.org`). Unless you live under a rock in the Gobi Desert, you know that Internet Explorer is part of Windows 7 — today, anyway. Heaven only knows what the courts will do. You may not know that Firefox can run right alongside Internet Explorer, with absolutely no confusion between the two. In fact, they don't even interact — Firefox was designed to operate completely independently, and it does very well playing all by itself.

One unwritten rule for the World Wide Web: All Web acronyms must be completely, utterly inscrutable. For example, a Web address is a *Uniform Resource Locator,* or *URL.* (The techies I know pronounce URL "earl." Those who don't wear white lab coats tend to say "you are ell.") I describe the HTML acronym in the previous list. On the Web, a gorgeous, sunny, palm-lined beach with the scent of frangipani wafting through the air would no doubt be called SHS — Smelly Hot Sand. Sheeesh.

The best part of the Web is how easily you can jump from one place to another — and how easily you can create Web pages with hot links (also called *hyperlinks* or just *links*) that transport the viewer wherever the author intends. That's the *H* in HTML and the original reason for creating the Web so many years ago.

In July 2008, researchers at Google claimed that it had reached a new milestone, with 1,000,000,000,000 (that's one *trillion*) clickable links in its catalog. Heaven only knows how many pages the links pointed to.

Who Pays for All This Stuff?

That's the $64 billion question, isn't it? The Internet is one of the true bargains of the 21st century. When you're online — for which you probably have to pay EarthLink, Comcast, Verizon, NetZero, Juno, Netscape, Qwest, your cable company, or another Internet service provider a monthly fee — the Internet itself is free.

Internet Explorer is free, sorta, because it comes with Windows 7, no matter which version you buy. Firefox is free as a breeze — in fact, it's the poster child for *open-source* programs: Everything about the program, even the program code itself, is free. Google Chrome is free, too.

Most Web sites don't charge a cent. They pay for themselves in any of these ways:

- **Reduce a company's operating costs:** Banks and brokerage firms, for example, have Web sites that routinely handle customer inquiries at a fraction of the cost of H2H (er, human-to-human) interactions.
- **Increase a company's visibility:** The Web site gives you a good excuse to buy more of the company's products. That's why architectural firms show you pictures of their buildings and food companies post recipes.
- **Draw in new business:** Ask any real estate agent.
- **Contract advertising:** Google has made a fortune.
- **Use bounty advertising:** Smaller sites run ads, most commonly from Google but in some cases selected from a pool of advertisers. The advertiser pays a bounty for each person who clicks the ad and views its Web site — a *click-through.*
- **Use affiliate programs:** Smaller sites may also participate in a retailer's affiliate program. If a customer clicks through and orders something, the Web site that originated the transaction receives a percentage of the amount ordered. Amazon.com is well known for its affiliate program, but many others exist.

Some Web sites have an entrance fee. For example, if you want to use the *Oxford English Dictionary* on the Web (see Figure 1-3), you have to part with some substantial coin — $295 per year for individuals, the last time I looked. Guess that beats schlepping around 20 volumes.

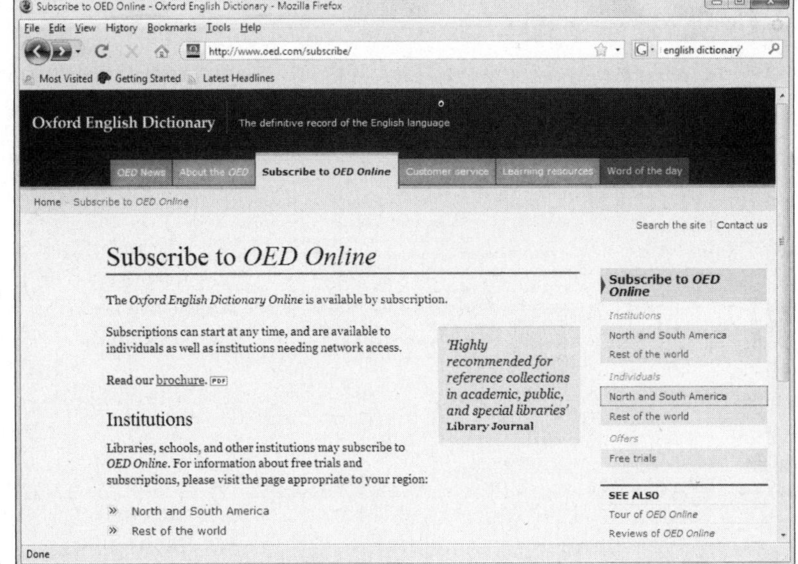

Figure 1-3: *The Oxford English Dictionary:* a venerable resource at a pricey Web site.

Connecting with Broadband

Digital subscriber line (DSL), asymmetric digital subscriber line (ADSL), integrated services digital network (ISDN), cable, and so on are known as broadband connections because they're faster than dialup modems — at least, theoretically. (Definition: A *broadband* connection is any Internet connection that's faster than the one you have. Heh-heh-heh.)

Here's the most important speed-up tip in this book: If you don't have a broadband line, get one. If you need an excuse, take a look at Google Earth or any of a hundred other data-sucking, marvelous, phenomenal free services that make sense only if you have data pipes big enough to handle them (see the "Uses and excuses for broadband" section, later in this chapter). Believe me, if you're reading this book, you'll get broadband sooner or later. It might as well be sooner.

The computer business is full of inscrutable terms, but the online world is even worse. If you need an accurate definition for a technical term or you want to compare acronyms such as ADSL and SDSL and xDSL and DSL (see Figure 1-4), your best bet is to hit Wikipedia (`wikipedia.org`). If you figure out the difference between ISDN/BRI and ISDN/PRI, let me know, okay?

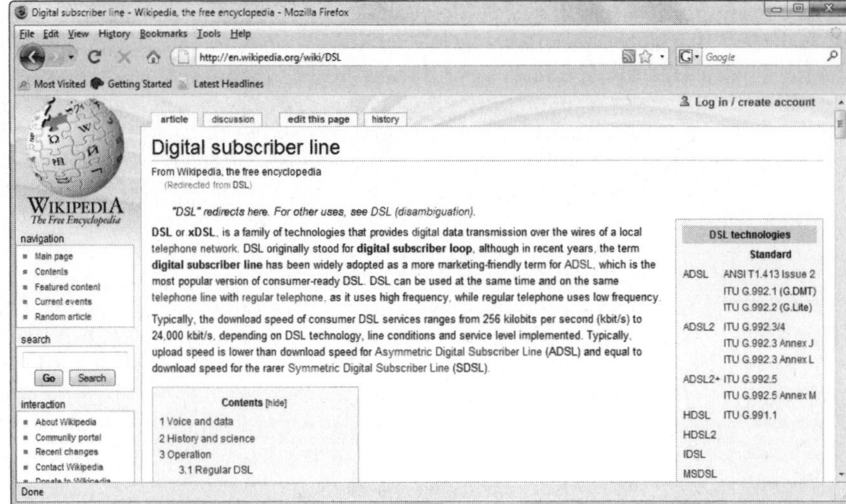

Figure 1-4: Wikipedia, the fount of all techie knowledge.

The last mile

The only real difference between DSL and a regular old dialup modem connection lies in the "last mile" between your house or office and the telephone switch. The phone and cable companies already use digital technology everywhere. If you use a dialup modem, your computer has to step back in history about a hundred years and contend with antiquated telephone technology.

Here's what's really happening. Your computer really, *really* wants to talk to other computers. If you hook up your computer to another computer with a fairly short cable, they can talk digitally, sending 1s and 0s over the cable to each other. Cool. But if your computer has to talk over the telephone line, that's another story entirely.

Back in the early days of telephones, all connections were analog: You talked into a mouthpiece, which caused a varying amount of electricity to travel through the telephone line; the earpiece on the other end of the telephone line picked up the electrical changes and converted the impulses back into sound. Those phones acted a bit like tying a piece of string to two paper cups — the sound pulses in the cup on one end made the string vibrate and the cup on the other end converted the vibrations back to sound.

Nowadays, telephone systems are entirely digital. (Well, almost entirely digital. I come back to that in a second.)

Computers are digital beasts — they talk in 1s and 0s. If you use your computer with a plain, old dialup phone line and a modem, the computer has to work like a telephone. Telephones are analog beasts — they want varying pulses. Modems bridge the gap. They convert digits into pulses and vice versa. Think of it this way: Your computer has a string of 1s and 0s that it wants to send to your friend Moe's computer — say, 11001. You and Moe, both game Dummies, decide to play modem. (Bear with me, okay?)

You call Moe and exchange pleasantries. When you're both ready, you both tell your computers to have at it. Your computer starts flashing the 1s and 0s on the screen that it wants to send to Moe's computer. You see a 1 on your computer's screen and yell into the telephone, "ONE!" Moe hears you say "one" and types a 1 into his computer. You shout "ONE" again, and Moe types another 1. Then you shout "ZERO" and Moe types a 0. "ZERO" again, 0 again. Then "ONE," and Moe types a 1. When your computer finishes, it flashes a message on the screen. You yell, "I'm done, Moe; did you get it?" Moe yells back, "Yep, I got it!"

That's what a modem does. When it's sending data, it takes the 1s and 0s that the computer wants to send and shouts into the phone line "ONE" or "ZERO." When it's receiving data, it listens for "ONE" and "ZERO" and relays the appropriate number to the computer. Some extra work is involved — exchanging pleasantries and making sure that all the data came through — but at its heart, a modem alternately yells and listens.

Here's the ironic part: Although the telephone system used to be entirely analog, these days it's almost entirely digital. The only analog part is the short distance — the *local loop* — from your house to the closest telephone switch. Nowadays, when you talk into the telephone, a varying amount of electricity (an analog signal) is sent on the phone line that goes only as far as the switch — typically, a few hundred yards. When your voice hits the switch, it's digitized and sent to the receiving switch, where it's converted back to analog so that it can travel the final few hundred yards to Moe's house. In essence, your slow-as-a-snail modem exists only to make the trip from your house to your local telephone switch. Everything else travels at blazing speeds.

DSL technology simply leapfrogs that final few hundred yards. Rather than convert your PC's digital 1s and 0s to analog ONEs and ZEROs, the DSL box makes sure that the digital data your PC generates gets patched directly into the already-digital network. Cable modems hook into the already-digital cable TV line that probably goes to your house. Easy, eh?

Uses and excuses for broadband

Need an excuse to get broadband? No doubt you already know that you can use a broadband connection to make free — or at least very cheap — high-quality, long-distance telephone calls. (See, for example, Skype, at `skype.com`, or Windows Live Messenger, which I discuss in Book V, Chapter 7.) You've probably struggled with some Web sites with stunning content (say, `nasa.gov` or `louvre.fr`) that make slow connections positively painful. Maybe you've heard about sites (say, `youtube.com` or `creativity-online.com`) with funny videos that beg for fast Internet access. Need a bigger excuse? Have you seen Google Earth?

Google Earth (`earth.google.com`) takes mapping into the third dimension, with incredibly detailed satellite photos all stitched together in a way that makes it easy to zoom in or out, pinpoint a location, or even — you have to see this to believe it — angling the view from the tops of buildings, down to look at the side, or even take in long vistas with mountains and rivers and trees and superhighways (see Figure 1-5). You'll be absolutely floored by the ability to, oh, type `Phuket, Thailand` in the Search bar and watch as the earth rotates, and gets closer and closer, until finally you can see . . . Phuket. Then you can "grab" the map and move down roads, identifying landmarks as you fly, and "tilt" the camera so that you see the tops or different angles of the fronts of buildings. Google Earth satellite photos cover most of the inhabited parts of the world. Most of Europe and North America boast incredibly high-resolution photos. If you like, metropolitan areas can have the outlines of roads superimposed on the photos, with road names clearly marked.

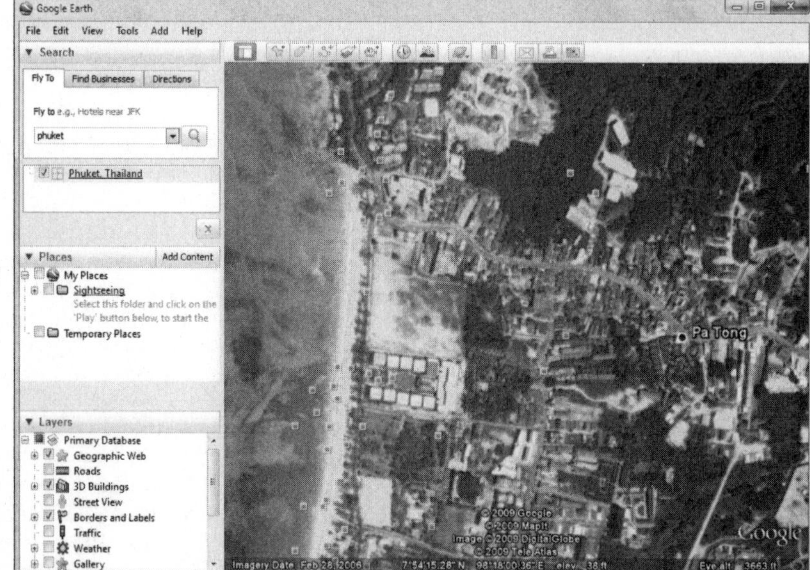

Figure 1-5: Google Earth — just one compelling reason to pay for a fast Internet connection.

For many people, Google Earth, all by itself, justifies the added expense of a broadband line. I would bet that you can find many more excuses.

Setting Up an Internet Connection

For most people, setting up an Internet connection is as simple as contacting an Internet service provider (commonly a phone company or cable TV company), arranging to have the Cable Guy come by at a time that you're home (good luck), sacrificing your credit card for a moment, and turning on your computer. If the installer did a good job, you don't have to sweat any of the details — Internet Explorer and, if you so choose, Firefox jump up and greet you when you double-click them.

It may go without saying, but don't let the Cable Guy (or whomever) leave your house until you turn on *your* PC, crank up IE or Firefox, and make sure that your Internet connection is working.

Dialup connections are a little trickier. You need a modem (your computer probably has a built-in one already), and a telephone cable that plugs into your computer and the phone jack on the wall. You also need to set up a subscription with a dialup service, which you can do at any store that sells computers.

The dialup service company (your ISP) has an instruction booklet that tells you precisely how to connect to its service. The ISP must give you a telephone number to dial, a logon ID, and a password.

You may also receive the names of the computers that accept and send out your mail (POP3 and SMTP servers), which you need in order to set up e-mail accounts that go through the ISP.

The booklet should step you through the rest of the process, but a few little details may be missing:

- **The Windows 7 Connect to the Internet Wizard can help you establish a dialup connection.** To open the Connect to the Internet Wizard, choose Start➪Control Panel, click the Network and Internet icon, and then click the Network and Sharing Center icon. In the Network and Sharing Center, click Set Up a New Connection or Network. Then double-click the Set Up a Dial-Up Connection link.
- **If you need to change details about the connection after you complete the Connect to the Internet Wizard, choose Start➪Control Panel, click the Network and Internet icon, and then click the Network and Sharing Center icon.** On the left, click the Change Adapter Settings link. Right-click the dialup connection and choose Properties. You see

a Dial-Up Connection Properties dialog box. There, you can change the phone number, pick a second modem (if you have one), control how often Windows 7 redials, or (as shown in Figure 1-6) make the dialup connection available to anybody logged on to your computer.

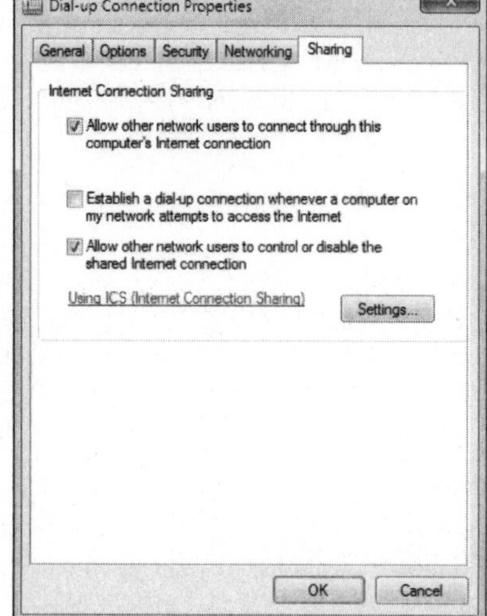

Figure 1-6: One of the many dialup options available in the Dial-Up Connection Properties dialog box.

If you need to change general dialup options after you complete the Connect to the Internet Wizard — for example, you suddenly realize that you need to dial 9 to get an outside line — follow the same steps but, on the General tab, select the check box marked Use Dialing Rules. Yeah, that's where it's hidden.

✦ **When all else fails, call your ISP and ask tech support to walk you through the connection process.** That's what tech support is for.

If you decide that you want to connect several computers by using either a wired or wireless network, I have detailed instructions in Book VII, Chapters 2, 3, and 4.

Finding Internet Reference Tools

I get questions all the time from people who want to know about specific tools for the Internet. Here are my choices for the tools that everyone needs.

Speakeasy speed test

Everybody, but everybody, needs (or wants) to measure her Internet speed from time to time. The site I use these days for testing is `speakeasy.net/speedtest`.

A million different speed tests are available on the Internet, and two million different opinions about various tools' accuracy, reliability, replicability, and other measurements. I used to run speed tests at DSLReports.com, but it blocked my Internet service provider. So I moved to Speakeasy and haven't looked back.

DNSStuff

Ever wonder whether the Web site BillyJoeBobsPhishery.com belongs to BillyJoeBob? Head over to `http://dnsstuff.com` (see Figure 1-7) and find out. You give DNSStuff a domain name and the site divulges all the public records about the site, commonly known as a *whois:* who owns the site (or at least who registered it), where the rascals are located, and whom to contact.

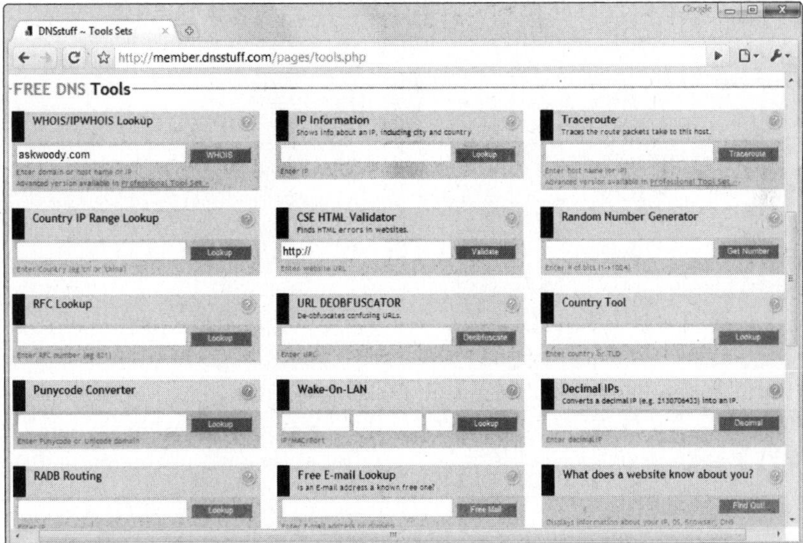

Figure 1-7: DNSStuff offers a wide array of Web- and Net-related tools.

DNSStuff also tells you the official "abuse" contact for a particular site (useful if you want to lodge a complaint about junk mail), whether a specific site is listed on one of the major spam databases, and much more.

3d Traceroute

So where's the hang-up? When the Internet slows down, you probably want to know where it's getting bogged down. (Not that it will do you much good, but you might be able to complain to your ISP.)

My favorite tool for tracing Internet packets is the free product 3d Traceroute, from German Holger Lembke in Braunschweig. You can download it at this Web site: `d3tr.de`. 3d Traceroute has no installer — it just runs. I like that.

When you run 3d Traceroute, you feed it a *target location* — a Web address to use as a destination for your packets. As soon as you enter a target, 3d Traceroute runs out to the target and keeps track of all the *hops* — the discrete jumps from location to location — along the way. It measures the speed of each hop (see Figure 1-8).

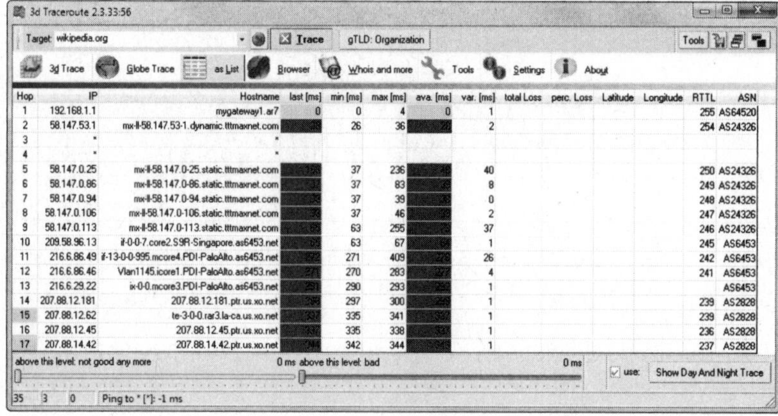

Figure 1-8: Why is the Internet so slow? 3d Traceroute pinpoints pileups.

If you look at the ASN column, on the far right end in Figure 1-8, you can see a list of AS numbers. Each number uniquely identifies a network operator. You can search for the AS number at `www.google.com` and see where your packets hit a roadblock.

Down for everyone or just me?

So you try and try and can't get through to Wikipedia or Hotmail has the hiccups: The browser keeps coming back and says it's timed out, or it just sits there and does nothing.

It's time to haul out the big guns. Hop over to `downforeveryoneorjust me.com` (no, I don't make this stuff up) and type the address of the site that isn't responding. The computer on the other end checks to see whether the site you requested is still alive. Cool.

The Wayback Machine

He said, she said. We said, they said. Web pages come and go, but sometimes you just have to see what a page looked like last week, or last year. No problem, Sherman: Just set the Wayback Machine for November 29, 1975. (That's the day Bill Gates first used the name Micro Soft.)

If you're a Mr. Peabody look-alike and you want to know what a specific Web page really said in the foggy past, head to the Internet Archive at `www.archive.org`, where the Wayback Machine has more than 85 billion Web pages archived and indexed for your entertainment (see Figure 1-9).

Figure 1-9: Everything old is new again with the Archive.org Wayback Machine.

Chapter 2: Finding Your Way Around Browsers

In This Chapter

- Recognizing that Internet Explorer ain't the only game in town
- Tabbing through the Internet Explorer window
- Protecting yourself from phishers
- Playing hide-and-seek with Internet Explorer, Firefox, and Chrome

For hundreds of millions of people, *the Web* and *Internet Explorer (IE)* are synonyms. It's fair to say that IE has done more to extend the reach of PC users than any other product — enabling people from all walks of life, in all corners of the globe, to see what a fascinating world we live in.

At the same time, IE has become an object of attack by spammers, scammers, thieves, and other lowlifes. As the Internet's lowest (or is it greatest?) common denominator, IE draws a lot of unwanted attention.

This chapter concentrates on showing you how to use Internet Explorer to do what you want to do. At the same time, it also gives you hints about using Firefox — the number-one competitor of Internet Explorer — and Google Chrome, which has advantages over the other two.

This chapter covers topics that are common to all three major browsers: IE, Firefox, and Chrome. (Most of the topics pertain to other browsers, too.) The next chapter delves deeper into the inner workings of IE, showing you how to customize and cajole the beast into behaving more in tune with your desires. The chapter after that helps you dig into Firefox.

Exploring Internet Explorer Alternatives: Firefox and Chrome

Let me make sure that you understand: You aren't stuck with Internet Explorer. Lots of good alternatives exist that many people (including me) prefer over IE. Why?

- **They ain't from Microsoft.**
- **They don't draw the lion's share of attention from malware writers.**

✦ **Using a product other than Internet Explorer prods Microsoft out of its developmental lethargy.** The IE alternatives keep competition alive and thriving, bringing fresh ideas and approaches into the mainstream. (See the nearby sidebar "The history of Internet Explorer.")

I use Firefox (see Figure 2-1) almost all the time, and I recommend that you do, too.

Figure 2-1: Mozilla Firefox, my choice for Web browsing.

The history of Internet Explorer

More than any other product, Internet Explorer reflects the odd and tortured Microsoft approach to the Web. After largely ignoring the Internet for many years, Microsoft released the first version of Internet Explorer in 1995, as an add-on to Windows. In 1996, Microsoft built Internet Explorer version 3 into Windows itself, violating antitrust laws and using monopolistic tactics to overwhelm Netscape Navigator.

Having illegally pummeled its competitor in the marketplace, Microsoft made almost no improvements to Internet Explorer between August 2001 and August 2006 — an eternity in Internet time. IE became the single largest conduit for malware in the history of computing, with major security patches (sometimes several) appearing almost every month.

And then there was Firefox. Dave Hyatt, Blake Ross (who was a sophomore at Stanford at the time), and hundreds of volunteers took on the IE behemoth, producing a fast, small, free alternative that quickly grabbed a significant share of the browser market. Microsoft responded by incorporating many Firefox features into Internet Explorer, ultimately releasing the version you now see in Windows 7.

I also use Google Chrome on occasion, just for a change of scene. One of these days, when Chrome matures a bit, I may switch permanently.

REMEMBER

No browser is completely safe, but some are better than others. For a breakdown of IE, Firefox, and Chrome weaknesses, see Table 2-1.

Table 2-1 Security Scorecard

Browser	*Achilles Heel*	*Security Status*
Internet Explorer	IE uses *ActiveX controls,* which are small programs that run on your computer, which are notorious as active conduits for infections and malware of myriad types.	Internet Explorer is the biggest kid on the block, and the number-one target for the bad guys. You can debate the imperviousness of all the browsers, but one fact stands out: More PCs have been infected by using Internet Explorer than any other program. Ever.
Firefox	Firefox doesn't touch ActiveX controls, but it runs with the same security privilege level as the user: If you use Firefox with an administrator account, the browser inherits your security clearance.	As Firefox gains market share, it attracts more attention from the bad guys, but the infection rate via Firefox is considerably lower than for Internet Explorer.
Chrome	Chrome runs in a "sandbox" that's isolated from the rest of Windows.	At least one expert browser hacker/cracker says that Chrome on Windows is now the most secure combination of browser and operating system available.

You can install Firefox without disturbing Internet Explorer — they coexist peacefully, and you can run either, or both, at any time. Here's how to get Firefox:

1. **Start Internet Explorer and go to `mozilla.com/en-US/firefox`.**
2. **Click the Download Firefox link.**
3. **Follow the instructions on the page to download and install the latest version of Firefox.**
4. **When you first start Firefox, it asks whether you want to make it your default browser (see Figure 2-2). I suggest that you select the Always**

Perform This Check When Starting Firefox check box and click the Yes button.

This step makes Firefox your browser of choice in almost all situations, except when Microsoft insists that you use Internet Explorer (for example, when checking for Windows or Office updates). The next time you run IE, it will ask if you want to make IE your browser of choice. Just deselect the box marked Always Perform this Check when Starting Internet Explorer and click No, No, a Thousand Times No!

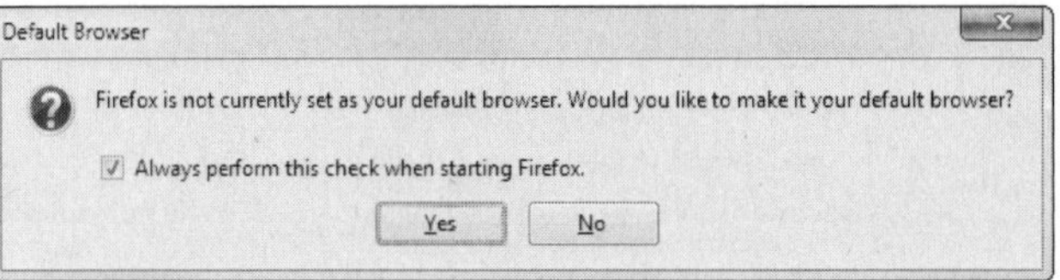

Figure 2-2: Making Firefox your default browser.

Downloading and installing Chrome involves similar steps, except that you start at `google.com/chrome`.

All the concepts — and many of the tips — that apply to Internet Explorer also apply to Firefox, and some of them also apply to Chrome. No matter which browser you use, follow along in this chapter. Where differences between Firefox, Chrome, and IE exist, I note them in parentheses.

Ready, Set, Browse!

As soon as you're connected to the Internet, you can begin browsing. To launch IE, click the Internet Explorer icon on the taskbar or choose Start⇨All Programs⇨Internet Explorer. (Firefox and Chrome probably have icons on the desktop. You can always click and drag those icons onto the taskbar.)

The first time you run Internet Explorer, it works through a convoluted setup routine. Here's how I respond:

1. **You see a setup splash screen that says** `Welcome to Internet Explorer 8`**. Oh, goody. Click Next.**

   The first question (see Figure 2-3) asks whether it's okay for Microsoft to keep records of all your Web browsing, all the time.

2. **Select the button marked No, Don't Turn On — unless you truly want to send your entire Web-surfing history to the giant Microsoft data mine in the sky. Click Next.**

   The setup program asks whether you want to take the default settings or choose Custom Settings.

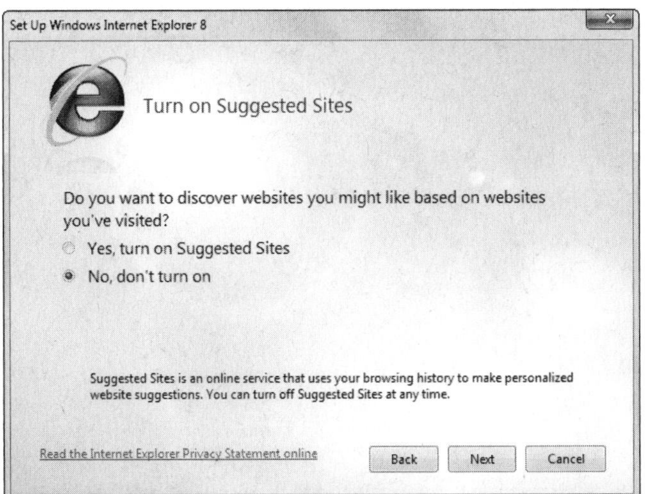

Figure 2-3: Suggested Sites involves sending Mother Microsoft a complete record of all the sites you visit.

3. **Of course you should choose Custom Settings. Click Next.**

   Setup asks whether you want to keep Microsoft's very own Live Search as your default search engine. Yeah, right.

4. **Select Show Me a Webpage after Setup to Choose More Search Providers and click Next.**

   Setup then asks whether it can download updates for your search provider.

5. **I select Yes because I trust Google to update without messing things up. Click Next.**

   Setup asks whether I want to choose more Accelerators (see Figure 2-4).

6. **I stick with the default Accelerators because I can easily add more. (See the section about exhilarating Accelerators in Chapter 3 of this minibook.) Click Next.**

   Internet Explorer wants to know whether it can become your default Web browser.

7. **If you don't yet have Firefox or Chrome (or one of the alternative browsers) installed, there's no harm in saying Yes. Deselect the check box that says Import Settings from My Other Browsers, and then click Next.**

   The setup routine wants to know whether you want to use Compatibility view updates. Compatibility view makes Internet Explorer 8 behave like Internet Explorer 6, so you can see Web sites that look funny in IE 8. From time to time, Microsoft updates the list of sites that don't work right with IE 8.

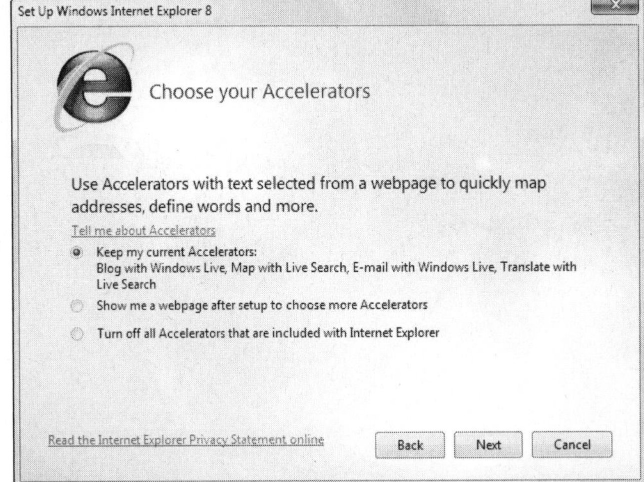

Figure 2-4: I don't add Accelerators at this point, but you may want to.

8. **I figure that Microsoft's updates to its Compatibility view list won't hurt, and might help, so I choose Yes, I Want to Use Updates. Your opinion may vary. Click Finish.**

   Internet Explorer comes up for air with three tabs: `msn.com` (unless the company that sold you the computer took over that screen), the Add Search Providers list, and a Welcome to Internet Explorer 8 screen.

9. **The Welcome to Internet Explorer 8 screen (see Figure 2-5) includes two worthwhile introductions: one to Accelerators and one for Web Slices. Take a few moments to follow the directions and see for yourself how these features work.**

   I cover Accelerators in the next chapter, in the section about exhilarating Accelerators. Web Slices appear to me to be relatively useless, but I talk about them in the following "What is (are?) Web Slices?" sidebar. Maybe you can find a use for them.

10. **Click the Add Search Providers tab.**

    You see the old Add Search Providers to Internet Explorer page, shown in Figure 2-6.

11. **On the left side of the page, click the Google link. Select the check box marked Make This My Default Search Provider, and click Add.**

    Congratulations! IE 8 is ready to roll.

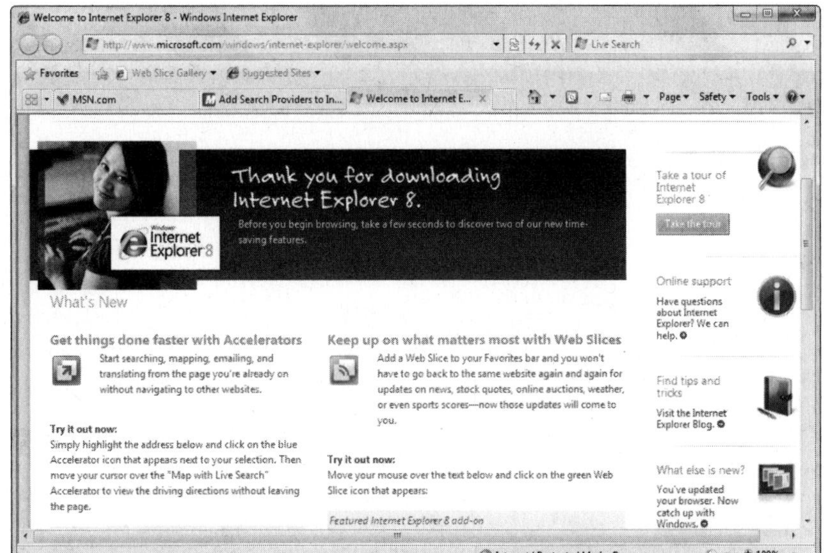

Figure 2-5: Take a minute to look at Accelerators — which you may find useful — and Web Slices.

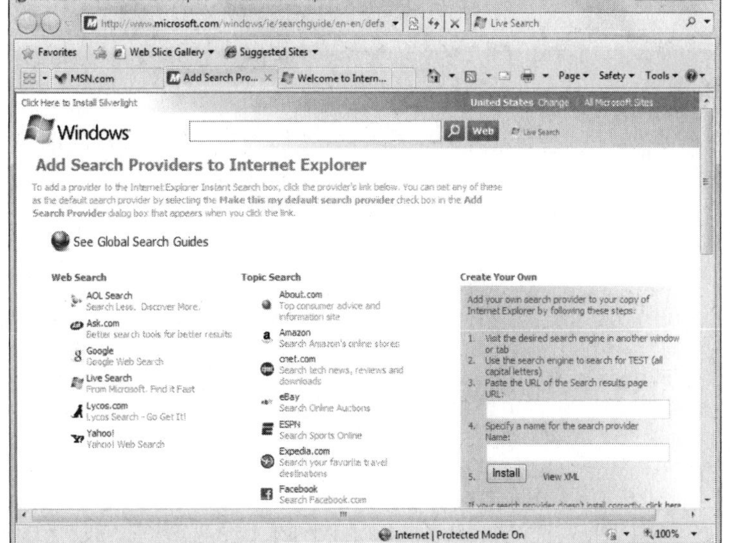

Figure 2-6: Microsoft's old Add Search Providers page.

Firefox and Chrome start with considerably less fanfare. Your primary choices are whether to import Bookmarks or Favorites from other programs (I rarely do) and whether you want to make the browser your default browser.

What is (are?) Web Slices?

In its never-ending battle to differentiate itself in an increasingly crowded Web browser market, Microsoft invented the *Web Slices* technology. If you go to a Web site that supports Web Slices (there are, oh, about ten of them at this point), you see a green Web Slices icon. Click the icon and you can add the Web site to your Web Slices collection.

All sites in your Web Slices collection appear as buttons on the Favorites toolbar. If you click one of the buttons, you see a thumbnail of the site, typically showing you just one item on the site. (That's where the "slice" comes from.) For example, a Web slice on an eBay page might show you a thumbnail of the bidding status for a single item. A Web slice for a retailer might show one specific item that's for sale. If the content for that particular item on the site changes, the Web Slices button turns bold and flashes red. So, if Lands' End suddenly discounts that shirt you want, you're notified immediately. Be still, my heart.

If Web Slices sound a lot like RSS feeds (see the section "Taking a walk around the Internet Explorer window," later in this chapter), well, they sound like that to me, too — except that they aren't as versatile, or as ubiquitous, as RSS. But for bidding sites such as eBay, they make some sense — as long as you want to watch every time somebody bids on an item.

Web site designers have to build hooks into their sites for Web Slices. I expect that you will see some big-name sites, prodded by Microsoft, supporting Web Slices, at some point.

Configuring your browser

No matter which browser you use, there's no reason to settle for the default settings. It's easy to change things around, so the browser works more like the way you want — yes, the dog *can* wag the tail.

Changing the default home page

After you have Internet Explorer, Firefox, or Chrome installed, the next time you start the program, it whirrs and after a relatively brief moment — how brief depends primarily on the speed of your Internet connection — a Web page appears. The information that page contains depends on whether your computer is set up to begin with a specific page known as a *home* page.

Microsoft sets up `msn.com` as the IE home page (see Figure 2-7) by default — a page best known for its phenomenally high density of ads. Most PC manufacturers set the Internet Explorer home page to display something related to their systems.

Firefox takes you straight to Google. Chrome, which is made by Google, shows you thumbnails of the sites you visit most often so that you can quickly choose among them (see Figure 2-8). I like that.

Figure 2-7: The MSN home page can be (ahem) long on advertising and short on useful information.

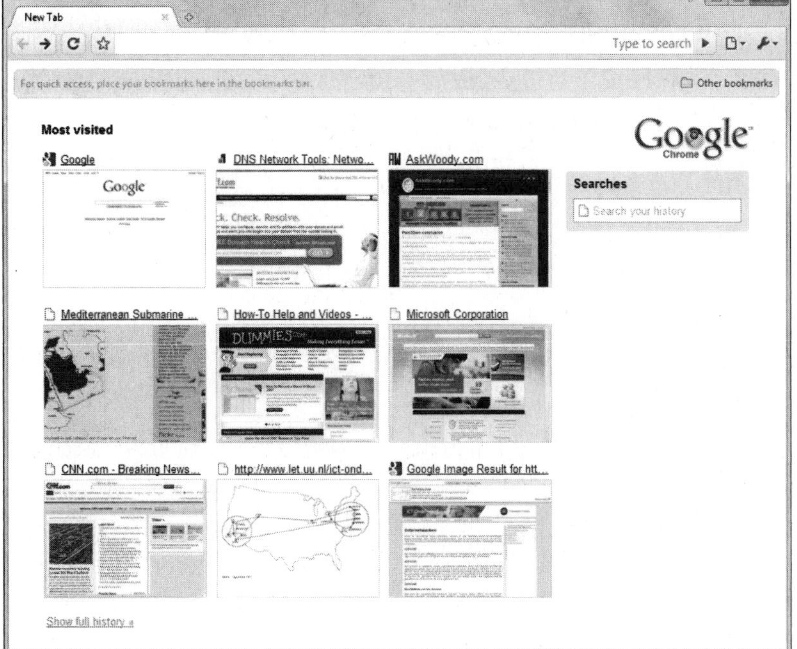

Figure 2-8: The Chrome default home page shows you thumbnails of the sites you visit most frequently.

If the ditzy, ad-laden MSN home page leaves you wondering whether P.T. Barnum still designs Web pages (there's one born every minute), or if your PC manufacturer's idea of a good home page doesn't quite jibe with your tastes, you can easily change the home page.

First, in your favorite browser, navigate to the Web page you want to use as your home page. If you're adept at using tabs (see the section "Pick a tab, any tab," later in this chapter), you can choose a group of pages as your home "page." Open new tabs for each of the pages.

Then follow the instructions for the browser you're using:

✦ **Internet Explorer:** Click the down arrow next to the Home icon on the IE taskbar and choose Add or Change Home Page. IE responds with the Add or Change Home Page dialog box, shown in Figure 2-9. Select the Use the Current Tab Set As Your Home Page button and click Yes to steer Internet Explorer away from its all-ads-all-the-time home page.

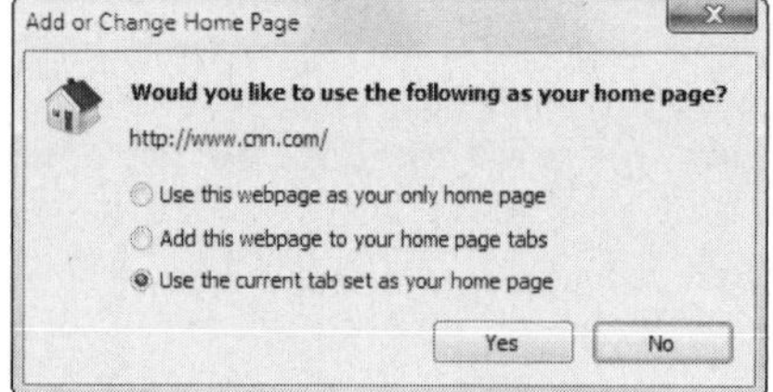

Figure 2-9: Steer Internet Explorer away from its ad-laden home page.

✦ **Firefox:** Choose Tools➪Options. In the Startup box, click the button marked Use Current Pages. Click OK.

✦ **Chrome:** Click the down arrow next to the icon of a wrench (that's a *spanner* for those of you in the United Kingdom) and choose Options. On the Basics tab, in the Home Page section, type the name of the home page you want to use. Click Close.

At least as of this writing, Chrome doesn't allow you to use a set of tabs as a home page.

The New Tab Page setting in Chrome refers to the page that has thumbnails of your most frequently visited pages (refer to Figure 2-8).

From that point on, whenever you start IE, Firefox, or Chrome, it loads the page or tabs you designated as "home."

If you don't want any home page — thus allowing your browser to appear on the screen faster, follow these directions:

- ✦ In **Internet Explorer**, click the down arrow next to the Home icon, choose Remove, and choose Home Page.
- ✦ In **Firefox**, choose Tools➪Options and select the Show a Blank Page option in the When Firefox Starts drop-down list.
- ✦ In **Chrome**, use the New Tab Page setting (refer to Figure 2-8). Chrome stores all necessary information on your computer anyway; when it starts, it doesn't need to go out to the Internet. Smart.

Switching the default search service

When you type something into the Search box in the upper-right corner of your browser, IE or Firefox runs out to your default Web search service, looks up what you typed, and presents you with the results, ready for you to click. Chrome doesn't have a separate search box because you can type your search terms into the address bar itself.

Firefox and Chrome use Google as their default Web search service. Unless the people who sold you your computer changed it or you followed my setup instructions the first time you ran IE, Internet Explorer uses Microsoft's own Bing Search site (you were expecting something else?). You may be one of the hundred-or-so people who prefer the Bing search engine, in which case you're home free. For the other 999,999,900 of us, it's easy to change:

1. **Click the down arrow on the Search bar — the one that probably says Live Search — and choose Find More Providers.**

   IE opens a page on `www.ieaddons.com` that lists available Web search providers (see Figure 2-10).

2. **Scroll wa-a-ay down the page — beyond Amazon Search and eBay Search and Social Search and Yahoo! Search Suggestions and ESPN Search — and, someday, you get to Google. Click the button next to Google that says Add to Internet Explorer.**

   Internet Explorer asks, "Do you want to add this search provider?"

3. **Click the button that says With 70% of the Search Market, You Should Provide Google As One of the Main Choices in the Search Box So that I Don't Have to Go Looking for It. Oh, wait a sec. I guess that isn't an option. Here it is: Select the check box that says Make This My Default Search Provider and click Add.**

   Google becomes your default search provider. You can verify that by looking at the text on the Search bar. It had better say *Google.*

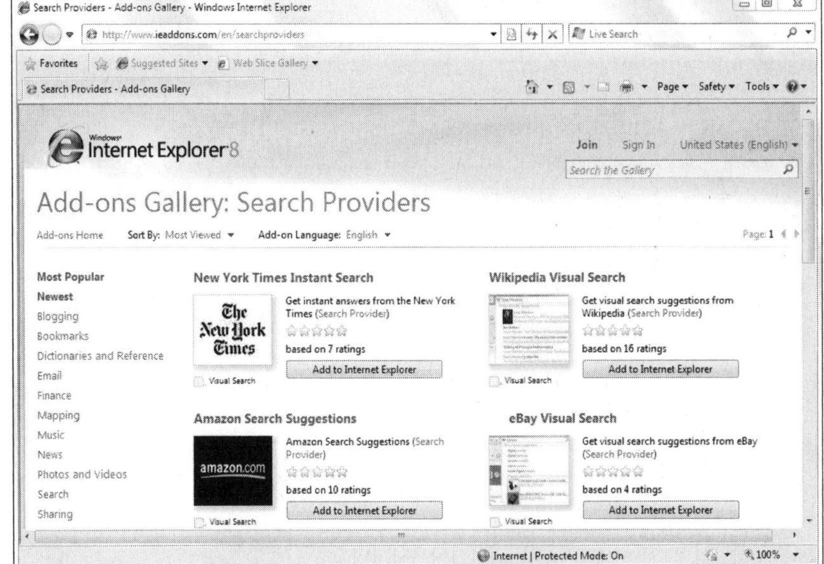

Figure 2-10: To make Google your default search engine, you have to go out and find it first.

Microsoft uses every (dirty) trick in the book to boost market share for Live Search — all the more reason to use Google, or one of the outstanding alternatives, such as Dogpile (`www.dogpile.com`) which automatically combines search results from Google, Yahoo!, Live, and Ask.

To change the default search engine in Firefox, click the down arrow inside the search box and pick a new search provider. The setting is "sticky" — it remains as your default search provider until you change it.

To change the default search engine in Chrome, click the down arrow next to the icon that looks like a wrench and choose Options. On the Basics tab, make a new selection from the Default Search box. Click Close.

Taking a walk around the Internet Explorer window

One great thing about Internet Explorer (and Firefox and Chrome) is that you can be an absolute no-clue beginner and, with just a few hints about tools and so on, you can find your way around the Web like a pro. Figure 2-11 gives you a diagram of the basic layout of the Internet Explorer window.

As you can see, IE packs lots of possibilities into that small space. The items you use most often are described in this list:

- **Address bar:** Enables you to type the Web address of a page that you want to move to directly.
- **Command bar:** Contains eight commands: Home, RSS Feed, Mail, Print, Page, Safety, Tools, and Help. If you have Microsoft Office installed, it has a ninth command: Research. Each menu includes a different set of commands related to working with Web sites. (See Table 2-2 for a description of the various commands, listed in the order in which they appear.)
- **Search box:** Includes tools you use to find your way around the Web and work with the Web pages you find. (See the preceding section for instructions on changing your default Web search engine.)
- **Status bar:** Displays information about Web pages, links, security, or actions that you can take while visiting a site.

Show Favorites list

Previous/Next

Add to Favorites

Type an address

If the site doesn't look right, click here

Reload page

Stop

Search

Command bar (see Table 2-2)

Status bar

Privacy report

InPrivate filtering

Security mode and Protected Mode

Zoom

Figure 2-11: The IE window includes everything you need to work on the Web.

Table 2-2 The Fare on the Internet Explorer Command Bar

Icon	*Description*
Home	Opens the home page (or pages). Click the down arrow to set a new home page.
RSS Feed	Opens the RSS (Really Simple Syndication) feed for the current site. (I talk about RSS in Chapter 3 of this minibook.)
Read Mail	If you have a registered e-mail program, clicking this button opens your e-mail program. (If the button doesn't work, click Start⇨Default Programs, click the link marked Set Your Default Programs, and then choose one.)
Print	Gives you some flexibility in printing Web pages. (See the "Saving and Printing Web pages" section, later in this chapter, for ideas.)
Page	Includes the ability to send a Web page by e-mail, turn it into a blog entry, edit the page, or view its HyperText Markup Language (HTML) source in all its glory. (See the "Saving and Printing Web Pages" section, later in this chapter, for details.)
Safety	Controls InPrivate browsing and InPrivate filtering and runs a SmartScreen Filter check for phishing. (See the "Thwarting Phishers" section, later in this chapter.)
Tools	Adjusts the built-in pop-up blocker, manages Internet Explorer add-ons, and more.
Research	Appears only if Office is installed; opens the Office Research pane, where you can look up words or phrases in dictionaries, thesauri, encyclopedias, and other references.
Help	Links to the Internet Explorer Help file.

Confusingly, the InPrivate filtering icon on the status bar doesn't have much to do with InPrivate browsing (commonly called Porn mode), which I discuss later in this chapter. (See Chapter 3 of this minibook for a discussion of InPrivate filtering.)

If you want to see the old-fashioned toolbar menus (File, Edit, View, and all the others) in Internet Explorer, press Alt. Yep, that's how you get to IE's inner workings.

Pick a tab, any tab

If you've never used browser tabs, you might wonder what all the fuss is about. It doesn't seem like there's much difference between opening another window and adding a tab (see Figure 2-12). But after you get the hang of it, tabs can help you organize pages and jump to the one you want.

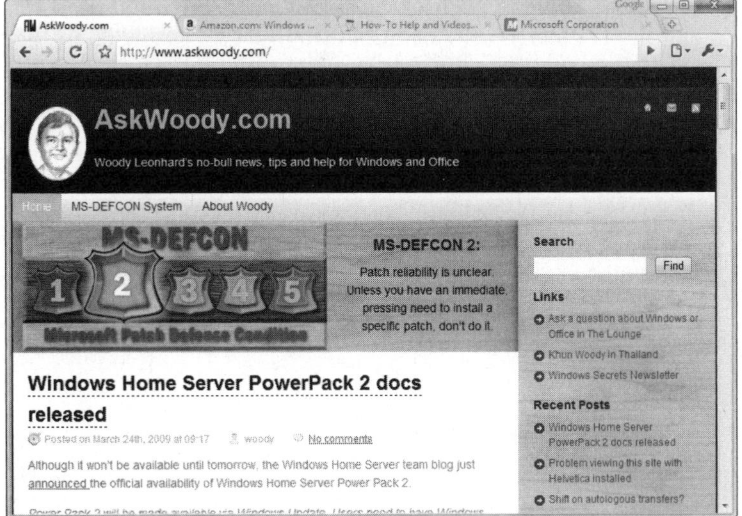

Figure 2-12: Chrome puts its tabs at the top of the window. IE and Firefox stick them down a little way.

Add a tab in any of the browsers in any of these ways:

- ✦ Ctrl+click a link to open the linked page in a new tab.
- ✦ Press Ctrl+T to start a new tab. When the tab is open, you get to navigate manually, just as you would in any other browser window.
- ✦ Click in the open area to the right of the rightmost tab.
- ✦ Right-click a link and choose Open in New Tab.

Internet / Protected Mode: On

The notification at the bottom of the Internet Explorer 8 window that says `Internet / Protected Mode: On` reflects two completely different settings.

Internet signifies that the Web page you see is in the Internet zone. Several different predefined security zones are in the IE 8 pantheon, and the Internet zone is the designated default for Web pages. Double-click the Internet link and you see that Web sites in the Internet zone require your approval to download programs and that unsigned ActiveX controls (refer to Table 2-1) aren't even downloaded.

To a first approximation, if you're browsing in "Protected mode," Internet Explorer kicks you down a security level. So, if you're running on an administrator account, the stuff that happens in Internet Explorer runs at a "standard" security level. If you have the User Account Control turned on (see Book II, Chapter 2), actions that would've gone unchallenged when you're using another program may trigger a UAC prompt when you're using IE.

Why do I like tabs? I can set up a single window with a bunch of related tabs and then bookmark the whole shebang. That makes it one-click easy to open all my favorite news sites, research sites, or financial sites. While my browser's out loading pages, I can go do something else and return to the tabbed window when everything's loaded and ready to go.

If I'm trying to research two different topics at the same time, I frequently start Firefox and create tabs to hunt down the first topic and then start Firefox again — start it in a different window, usually by Shift+clicking a link — and traipse through the second topic.

You can reorganize the order of tabs by simply clicking a tab and dragging it to a different location.

Kicking your browsing up a notch

No doubt you're familiar with basic browser functions. They're common to all three of the big browsers: Internet Explorer, Firefox, and Chrome. Type an address in the Address field to go to a Web page, click the Reload button to make sure that a page's information is the most up-to-date, click the Stop button if the page is taking too long to load and you want to move on, and click the Back (or Next) button to move back (or forward) to a page you already visited.

But you might not know about some of these finer points:

✦ **When you type on the address bar (Microsoft calls it a Smart Address bar), IE 8 and Firefox look at what you're typing and try to match it with the list of sites they have in their history lists and in your bookmarks.** Sometimes, you can get the right address (URL) by typing something related to the site. Watch as you type and see what IE 8 or Firefox comes up with.

Chrome works a bit differently. Chrome not only searches your history and bookmarks but also automatically sets up a Google search. If you type `dummies windows 7` in the address bar and press Enter, Chrome goes out to Google and performs a search on `dummies windows 7`. That speeds up your typing — you can change between a search of your history and a search of Google as you type. It also eliminates the need for a Search bar.

✦ **Click a link and the Web page decides whether you move to the new page in the current browser tab or a new tab appears with the clicked page loaded.** Many people don't realize that the Web page makes the decision about following the link in the same tab or creating a new one. You can override the Web page's setting.

- Shift+click and a new browser window always opens with the clicked page loaded.

- Ctrl+click and the clicked page appears on a new tab in the current browser window. (See the section "Pick a tab, any tab," earlier in this chapter.) Similarly, if you type in the Search bar and press Ctrl+Enter, the results appear in a new tab.

✦ **Even if the Web page "hijacks" your Backward and Forward arrows, you can always move backward (or forward) by clicking the down arrow next to the directional arrows and choosing the page you want.**

Rarely, a Web page manages to hide your Address bar and navigation buttons. If that happens, right-click the appropriate icon on the Windows taskbar and choose Close.

REMEMBER

You can bring up a history of all the pages you visited in the past few weeks by pressing Ctrl+H. You can also refer to all the Web addresses you entered, all your History, and all your Favorites, by clicking the down arrow to the right of the address box. The latter is particularly helpful if you want to make a small change in an address.

To search for a particular word or phrase on a page, press Ctrl+F.

Force your browser to *refresh* a Web page (retrieve the latest version, even if a version is stored locally) by pressing F5.

If you need to make sure that you have the latest version, even if the timestamps might be screwed up, press Ctrl+F5.

Saving space, losing time

Increasing or decreasing the number of days of browsing history that IE stores doesn't have much effect on the amount of data stored on the hard drive — even a hyperactive surfer will have a hard time cranking up a History folder that's much larger than 1MB. By contrast, temporary Internet files on your computer can take up 10, 50, or even 100 times that much space.

Those temporary Internet files exist only to speed your Internet access: When IE hits a Web page that it has seen before, if a copy of the page's contents appears in the `Temporary Internet Files` folder, IE grabs the stuff on the hard drive rather than wait for a download. That can make a huge difference in IE's responsiveness (particularly if you use a dialup modem), but the speed comes at a price: the 10, 50, or 100MB of space you have to give to IE's brain.

To clear out the IE temporary Internet files, hold down the Alt key and then choose Tools➪Delete Browsing History and click the Delete Files button. (In Firefox, choose Tools➪Clear Private Data, select the Cache check box, and click the Clear Private Data Now button. In Chrome, click the Wrench icon, choose Clear Browsing Data, select the Empty the Cache check box and click Clear Browsing Data.) You won't hurt anything, but revisited Web pages take longer to appear.

InPrivate Browsing: Porn mode

The easiest way to describe InPrivate Browsing? It's Porn mode. Yes, that's what the developers call it, too. If you're surfing someplace and you don't want to leave any records on your PC of where you dallied — doesn't matter whether it's a racy page, the political headquarters of a candidate you detest, or a squealing fan site for a sappy soap — turn on InPrivate Browsing.

Here's how to get into Porn mode:

1. **Start Internet Explorer. Choose Safety⇨InPrivate Browsing.**

   Internet Explorer starts a completely new window, which advises you that you're in InPrivate mode (see Figure 2-13).

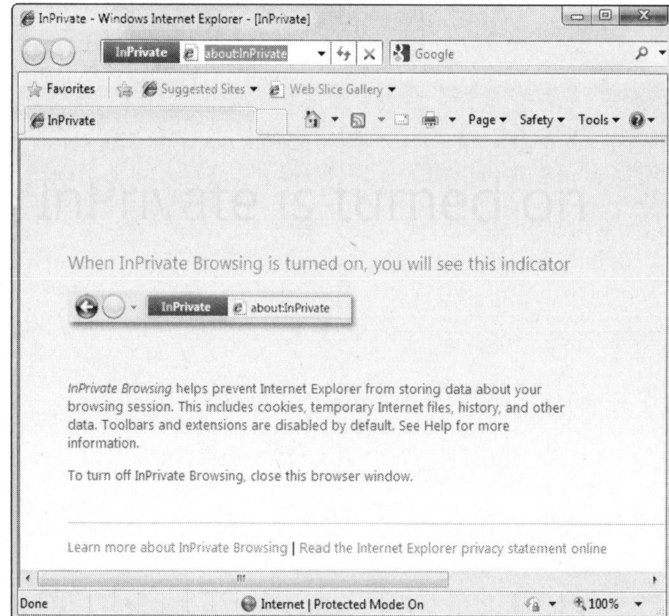

Figure 2-13: InPrivate Browsing keeps IE from depositing any record of your fling on your PC.

2. **To leave InPrivate Browsing, click the Close (X) button to close the Internet Explorer window.**

   There's no facility to turn off InPrivate Browsing. When you're done, just close the window.

The onion ring

Depending on which browser you use, InPrivate Browsing, Private Browsing, or Incognito keeps your browser from leaving any crumbs on your computer. But that doesn't keep your browsing activities private. Every Web site you visit can keep track of your IP address and a dozen other, lesser factoids about you.

Enter Tor, a program/system that uses "onion routing" to implement anonymous routing along its entire network — you're not only anonymous at the beginning and end of the network, but there's effectively no way to track your requests over the Internet. Tor Network started as a U.S. Naval Research Laboratory project, but in late 2004 the Electronic Frontier Foundation picked it up. It's now used by journalists, human rights workers, law enforcement officers, and normal people like you and me.

The official Tor home page (`torproject.org`) has details on the technology and the ways to make it work. The Firefox add-in, which you can use on a USB drive, works well.

Firefox has a similar cloaking mechanism: Private Browsing. Actually, Firefox has had a "private" capability for years, compliments of various add-ins. But starting with Firefox version 3.1, the feature is baked into Firefox itself. To switch Firefox into Private Browsing mode, choose Tools➪Begin Private Browsing. To get out of Private Browsing mode, just shut down Firefox.

Chrome calls it Incognito. To go incognito, click the down arrow next to the wrench icon and choose New Incognito Window. Chrome advises you with a message advising that "you've gone incognito," and it also puts a shady-looking character in the upper-left corner.

This kind of cloaking only keeps *your* PC clean. The sites you travel to can keep track of your Internet address (your *IP address;* see Book VII, Chapter 2 for details). Depending on how you connect to the Internet, your IP address can generally be traced to the router you're using to connect to the Internet. For more stealthiness, use Tor (see the nearby sidebar, "The onion ring").

Thwarting Phishers

Phishing is an attempt to acquire information — passwords, account numbers, or other personal factoids — fraudulently, usually via an e-mail message that appears to come from a reliable source but points you to a bogus Web site. (I talk about phishing threats in Book VI, Chapter 1.) Internet Explorer, Firefox, and Chrome all attack phishing with a vengeance.

Some phishing messages, like this one, make me roll my eyes:

> This e-mail was sent by the Wells Fargo server to verify your account information. You must complete this process by clicking on the link below and entering your account information. This is done for your protection, because some of our members no longer have access to their online access and we must verify it. To verify your identity and access your bank account, click on the link below.

But other phishing messages these days are so well-crafted that many a grizzled computer veteran (present company most certainly included) has been known to click through, stopping only at the last moment, when asked to type an account number and password.

How good are the phishing attempts? Take a look at Figure 2-14, which is a genuine PayPal survey logon page, and compare it to Figure 2-15, which no doubt originated with a pimply-faced, underachieving apparatchik in Kazbukistan — who's soon to become a *wealthy*, pimply-faced, underachieving apparatchik on the Kazbukistan Riviera.

As you can see in Figure 2-15, the latest version of IE second-guesses this site and displays a warning message. It's a feature known as SmartScreen Filter. Firefox and Chrome offer similar tools to combat phishing. Basically, these antiphishing tools enable you to provide immediate feedback about dubious destinations online; your feedback is aggregated with data from every other user who decides to use these tools.

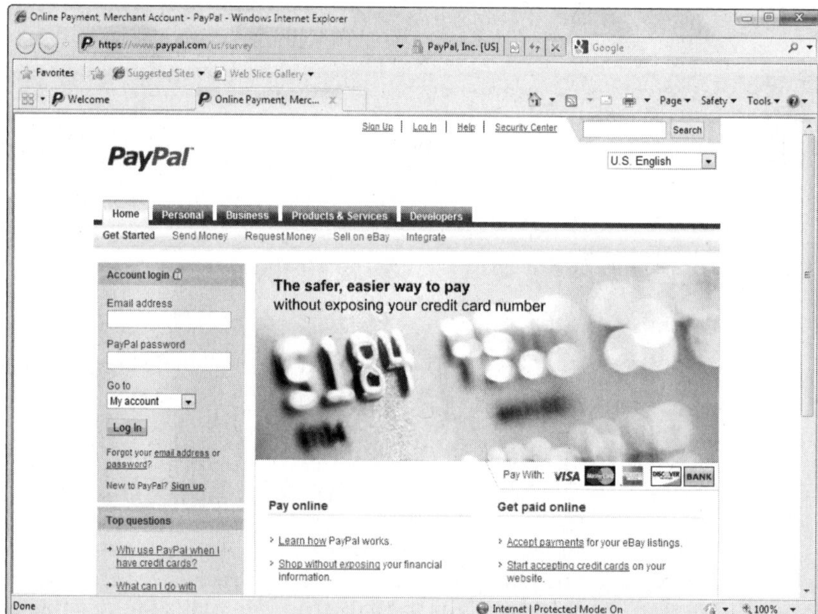

Figure 2-14: A genuine PayPal logon page.

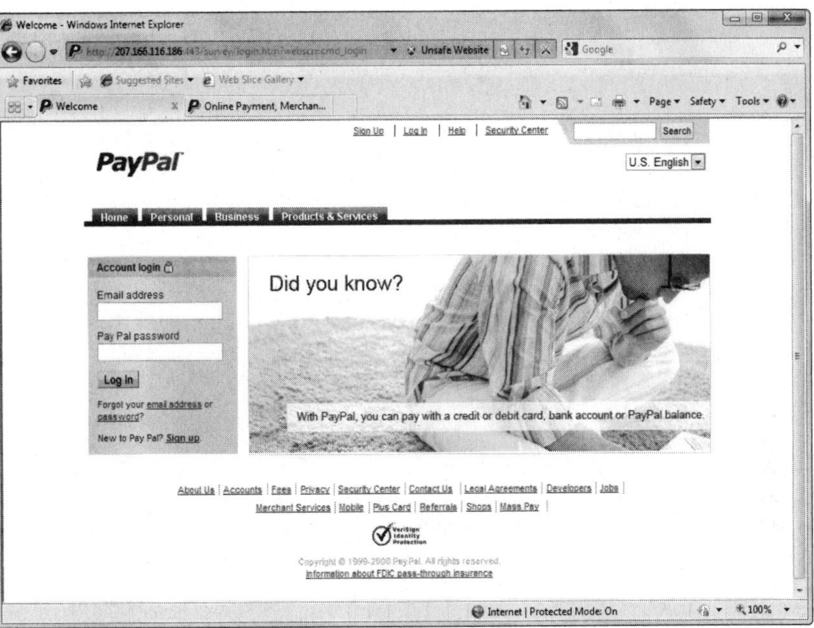

Figure 2-15: If it weren't for the Internet Explorer Unsafe Website warning, and the weird address, could you tell that this is a phishing site?

The most sophisticated phishing sites go up and come down in 24 hours or fewer — the perpetrators vanish that quickly. By automating the enormous task of identifying potentially dangerous sites, and employing the votes of thousands of would-be victims, Internet Explorer, Firefox, and Chrome have raised the phishing bar. These are important, albeit imperfect, tools. Your considered opinion may help save a naive person's tail. I strongly advise you to *not* disable the antiphishing features in any of the three browsers, and to report any obviously bad site by using the tools provided.

Back in the not-so-good-old days (which is to say, in the version of Internet Explorer immediately preceding the current one), turning on the IE phishing filter involved a leap of faith: You sent complete records of all your Web surfing activities to Microsoft, and the Mother Ship let you know if you were looking at a bad site.

Firefox led the charge to a much better phishing filter, one that protects you without violating your privacy. The same approach is now used by all three browsers. The Firefox-pioneered approach involves downloading a list of suspected sites periodically — which isn't the fastest way to keep on top of these fleeting flimflammers, but it alleviates any privacy concerns. Firefox doesn't need the whole database: It downloads changes (*deltas,* to those of you with white lab coats), only about once every 30 minutes.

As you surf, Firefox compares the addresses you're using with its internal database. If the site you seek isn't in the database, you're allowed through. On the other hand, if you try to go to a site that's in the database, Firefox phones home (actually, it contacts `www.google.com`) and verifies that the site is still considered bad. If the address still sets off alarms, you see the message shown in Figure 2-16.

If you click the link labeled Ignore This Warning (heaven help ya!), you see a site that looks a lot like a genuine Bank of America login page. Firefox thoughtfully puts a big red line at the top that says Reported Web Forgery! (see Figure 2-17).

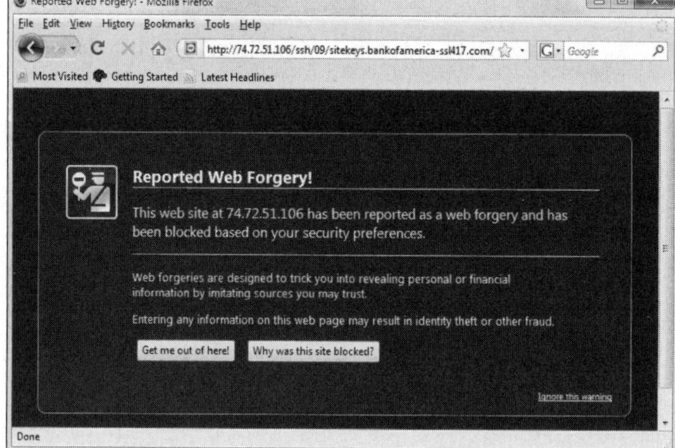

Figure 2-16: Firefox figures that you really aren't at the Bank of America Web site.

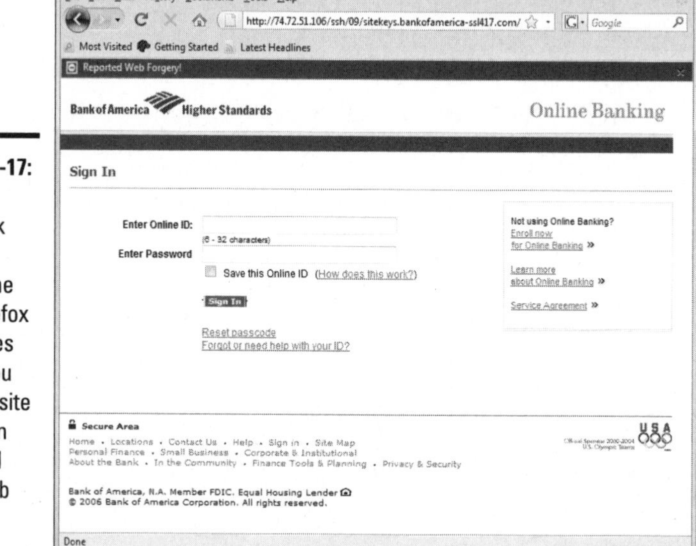

Figure 2-17: Even if you click through to see the site, Firefox continues to tell you that the site has been reported as a Web forgery!

What happened to pop-ups?

A *pop-up* is a browser window — typically containing advertising — that's spawned when you simply go to a Web site. Internet Explorer, Firefox, and Chrome include sophisticated blockers that prevent most obnoxious Web sites from plastering pop-ups all over your screen.

The pop-up filters in IE, Firefox, and Chrome work so well that it's getting harder to find a site with the temerity to put an advertising pop-up on the screen. Far more frequently, Web sites use pop-ups in ways that may actually be beneficial: The pop-up on `www.cnn.com`, for example, allows you to choose between U.S. and International editions; many download sites use pop-ups to start downloads.

If IE, Firefox, or Chrome detects a pop-up, it blocks the pop-up and displays a bar across the top of the page, inviting you to manually allow the pop-up. If you're looking at a reputable site, you might want to unleash the pop-up, just to see whether it does something that you want it to!

Internet Explorer and Chrome behave in similar ways. You can see the IE warning earlier in this section (refer to Figure 2-15).

Saving and Printing Web Pages

Viewing Web pages is easy. Working with them is hard. Nawwww. Not really. Not if you know the tricks.

Saving Web pages

If you find one of those invaluable articles that backs up every argument you've ever made about buying quality running shoes (ammunition guaranteed to convince your mate), by all means, save it! Or, if you finally find that sparkling New! icon you've seen on other people's sites, you can capture it to use on your own pages by saving the image to a file. This section explains how to save pages — and graphics items — for your own use later.

Saving to a file

There's no mystery to saving a Web page. It's not a whole lot different from saving any document in any program anywhere. Ready for the process? Don't blink — you may miss it:

First, regardless of which browser you're using, navigate to the Web page you want to save. Then follow the instructions for the browser you're using:

- **Internet Explorer:** Choose the Page button and then Save As. Pick a location, give the saved file a name, and click Save. Internet Explorer saves the whole page in an MHT file. *MHT* is a Microsoft-proprietary format, which means that you can open the file only by using Internet Explorer.
- **Firefox:** Choose File⇨Save As. Pick a location, give the saved file a name, and click Save. Firefox saves an HTM file — a regular HTML file, which can be opened with any browser — and a folder full of ancillary files.
- **Chrome:** Click the "page" icon to the right of the address bar and choose Save Page As. Pick a location, give the saved file a name, and click Save. Chrome, like Firefox, saves an HTM file and folder of component files, which can be opened by any browser. In theory, you can open the HTM file in Word and other programs, but in practice the results you see may leave your eyes begging for mercy.

Saving an image

Suppose that you run across a picture you really love, an icon you must have, or a banner you want to remember. You can save the image to your hard drive by following these steps:

1. **Right-click the image you want to save and choose Save Picture As. (In Firefox and Chrome, it's Save Image As).**

   Windows opens the Save Picture dialog box, shown in Figure 2-18.

   All browsers allow you to save the file in its original format (typically, JPG or GIF), but IE also lets you save as a bitmap (BMP) file. Avoid saving pictures as bitmaps — the quality isn't any better than the original, and the file size can expand greatly.

2. **Navigate to the folder in which you want to save the file.**
3. **Enter a name for the file, if needed.**
4. **Click the Save button to save the file.**

A word about copyright laws: If you didn't create the picture, it doesn't belong to you. Taking images from the Web may be fine for your personal use (sending a picture in a recipe to Aunt Edna is probably okay), but if you use images, text, ideas, pages, diagrams, music, or other elements as part of your business or as part of something you intend to make money on, you may be in danger of copyright violation. When in doubt, check it out: `benedict.com/info/info.aspx` is a great place to find more information on copyrights, fair use, and legal restrictions.

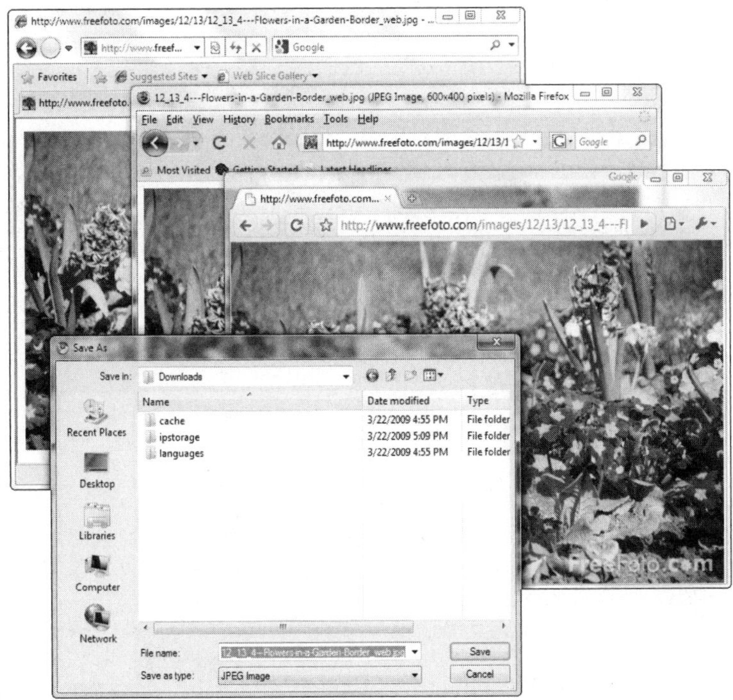

Figure 2-18: All three browsers save pictures similarly.

Printing Web pages

When you display a page that you want to print, don't click the Print icon. You probably won't like the junk that comes out of your printer. The printed version of a Web page rarely bears any resemblance to what you see on the screen. Look at Figure 2-19 and you can see what I mean.

Rather than go directly to the Print icon, click the down arrow next to the Print icon and choose Print Preview. (In Firefox, choose File➪Print Preview.) From the Print Preview window (refer to Figure 2-19), you stand a fighting chance of figuring out how to manipulate IE or Firefox into printing only the information you want. Given the price of color printer cartridges, this tip alone could pay for this book in a week!

Chrome doesn't even have Print Preview mode.

Can't get Internet Explorer (or Firefox) to print exactly what you want? Select the stuff you want, press Ctrl+C, and copy the good stuff to Word or WordPad. It's much easier to, say, delete an unwanted advertisement or squish a graphic down to size inside Word — especially if you're used to working in these programs.

Figure 2-19: Any resemblance between a Web page and the printed version of a Web page is entirely coincidental. If you print this Dummies.com page in IE, for example, you don't even see the Dummies logo.

Playing Favorites

As your surfing savvy increases, you'll begin to find pages that are keepers — Web sites with information that you know you want to be able to find later. Internet Explorer gives you an easy way to collect and organize those sites in the Favorites feature. (In Firefox and Chrome, the feature is named Bookmarks.)

When you start Internet Explorer for the first time and click the Favorites "star" just below the Address bar, you may notice that Microsoft or the company that sold you the computer splays a whole slew of folders covering a variety of topics, from home and health to banking and sports (see Figure 2-20). You may also see a number of strategic alliances represented there: Many third-party vendors involved in "partnering" with Microsoft and hardware manufacturers have their links built right into the default Favorites folders — and they pay dearly for the privilege.

Firefox ships with a handful of predefined Bookmarks, all associated with learning and using Firefox. Chrome ships with none.

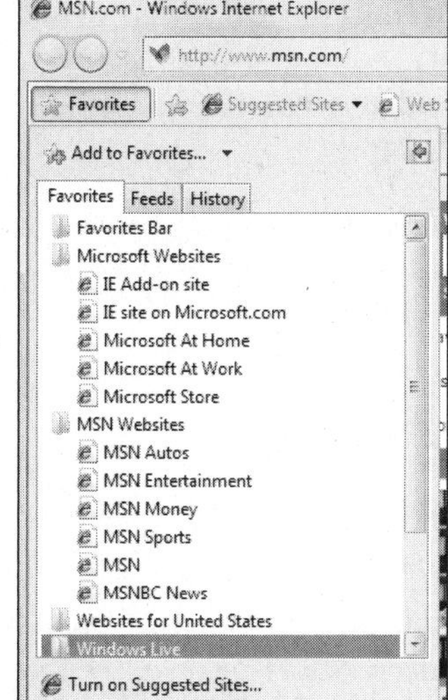

Figure 2-20: Microsoft salts its Favorites list with all sorts of junk you never use.

The steps for displaying, selecting, adding, and organizing Favorites all work the same way, no matter how many preset Favorites you find in your folders.

To explore the Favorites that Microsoft or your hardware manufacturer has, uh, thoughtfully arranged for you, follow these steps:

1. **Start Internet Explorer.**
2. **Click the Favorites "star" button just below the Address bar, and then click the Favorites tab.**

   A list of Microsoft-and-your-hardware-manufacturer's Favorites folders appears (refer to Figure 2-20).
3. **Right-click any of *their* Favorites that aren't *your* Favorites, and choose Delete.**

   It's your Favorites menu. Give all the slimy advertisers the boot.
4. **Click any folder that interests you.**

   A submenu of sites appears. Right-click any of them that deserve to go into the bit bucket, and choose Delete for them, too.
5. **If you see a site that you think might be useful, click its name in the Favorites list.**

   Internet Explorer goes to the site. If you click the right-facing arrow to the right of the site's name, it opens in a new tab.

Adding Favorites or Bookmarks of your own

When you find yourself viewing a site that you want to go back to later, you can add the site to your Favorites folder, or the Favorites toolbar. (In Firefox and Chrome, they're known as Bookmarks.)

Internet Explorer, the most cumbersome of the three browsers when it comes to using bookmarks, enables you to add sites to the preset folders, or you can create a new folder that is specific to your needs.

Say that you want to create a new Favorites folder named News and add `www.bbc.co.uk` to it. Here's what you have to do:

1. **Go to the Web site that you want to stick in your Favorites list.**

   In this case, bop over to the "beeb," at `www.bbc.co.uk`.

2. **Click the Add to Favorites Bar button, the one that looks like a star with a superimposed arrow. (Alternatively, you can click the Favorites button and then click the Add to Favorites button.)**

   A button for BBC appears on the Favorites bar, as shown in Figure 2-21.

Add to Favorites Bar button

New button for the BBC

Figure 2-21: Start by putting a button on your Favorites bar.

3. **Right-click any of the buttons on the Favorites bar (except the Favorites button and the Add to Favorites Bar button) and choose New Folder.**

   Internet Explorer shows you the Create a Folder dialog box (refer to Figure 2-21).

4. **Type a name for your new folder in the Folder Name box. Click Create.**

   In this case, I want a Favorites folder named News, so I type `News` in the Folder Name box.

   Internet Explorer creates a new button on the Favorites bar, named News.

5. **Click and drag your new button into the new folder.**

   In this case, I drag the BBC–Homepage button over to the new News button and release it. Internet Explorer removes the BBC button from the Favorites bar and puts it in the News drop-down list (see Figure 2-22).

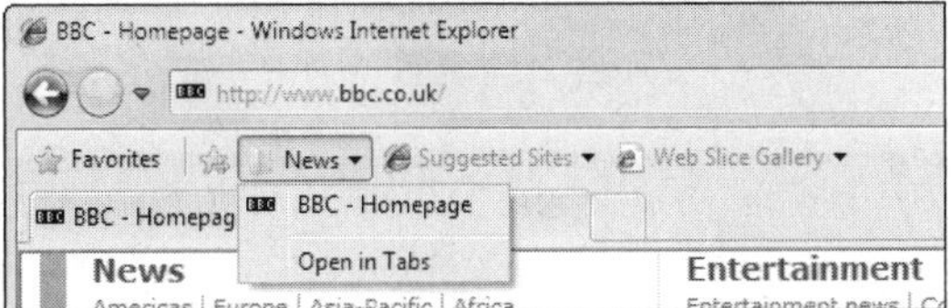

Figure 2-22: The BBC site appears in the News drop-down list.

Firefox behaves similarly. I talk about manipulating bookmarks in Firefox, and a feature named SmartFolders, in Book V, Chapter 4.

Chrome makes bookmarking easier still: Click the star to the left of the address bar. The bookmark is added to the Bookmarks bar, and an edit window appears that lets you control where to put the bookmark.

Chrome hides its Bookmarks bar by default. To make the Bookmark toolbar appear, click the down arrow to the right of the wrench icon and select Always Show Bookmarks Bar.

You can even apply tags to your Firefox and Chrome bookmarks. If you tag a bookmark with, oh, `Dummy`, any time you type `Dummy` in the address bar, Firefox and Chrome offer the bookmark as a quick alternative.

Organizing your Favorites or Bookmarks

Sometimes, surfing presents you with so many exciting things to look at that you may simply save pages right and left without taking the time to put them in folders. Over time, this method creates a mess of pages on your Favorites menu and forces you to go scrolling through many pages to find the page you want.

To straighten out your folders and your life, follow these steps:

1. **On the IE toolbar, click the Favorites button and then choose Add to Favorites⇨Organize Favorites.**

   The Organize Favorites dialog box appears, as shown in Figure 2-23.

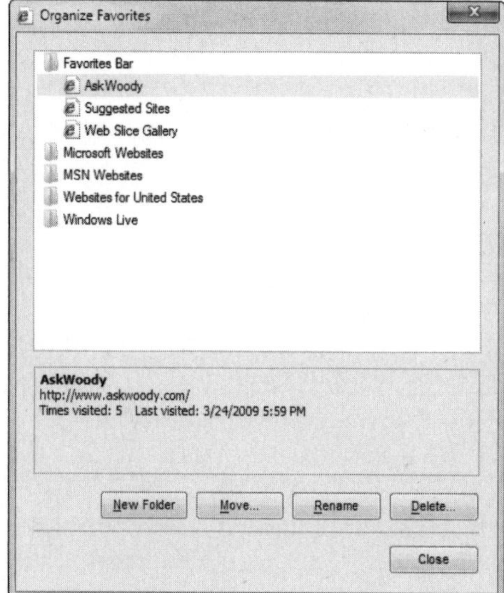

Figure 2-23: You can add your own folders and reorganize entries in the Organize Favorites dialog box.

2. **In the folder list, select the folder containing the links that you want to change.**
3. **Click and drag entries to move them into and among folders. Alternatively, click one of the command buttons described in this list:**
   - *New Folder:* Create a new folder to store the page. A new folder appears in the list; type the name for the folder and press Enter.
   - *Move:* Choose a new location for the link. The Browse for Folder dialog box opens so that you can select the folder to which you want to move the link.
   - *Rename:* Enter a new name for the link (or folder). The link you selected appears with its name highlighted; simply type a new name and press Enter.
   - *Delete:* Remove the link (or folder). The Confirm Folder Delete message box appears so that you can confirm that you want to delete the selected link. Click the Yes button to continue.
4. **Click the Close button.**

Chapter 3: Making Internet Explorer Your Own

In This Chapter

- **Making Internet Explorer work your way**
- **Turbocharging your surfing**
- **Speeding things up with Accelerators**
- **Hardening Internet Explorer 8**
- **Digging up the truth about cookies and InPrivate filtering**
- **Understanding RSS feeds**

I hear the same questions over and over again about making Internet Explorer, or IE, run faster (you can't do much); bypassing some of the more, uh, idiosyncratic IE behavior (a few solutions exist); clobbering cookies (why?), and knowing whether RSS is worth the effort (if you regularly read a "newsy" site, the answer is a resounding Yes).

In Book V, Chapter 2, I talk about getting Internet Explorer going for the first time. I also discuss topics that are common to the three major browsers — IE, Firefox, and Chrome: specifying a home page (you aren't stuck on MSN.com, right?), changing your default search engine (***Hint:*** Microsoft Live isn't the world's most popular search engine), waltzing around the IE window, surfing on the sly in Porn mode (er, InPrivate Browsing), using tabs, preventing phishing attacks, and working with Favorites (better known as Bookmarks in Firefox and Chrome).

In Chapter 4 of this minibook, I show you how to put lipstick on the Firefox pig (not a disparaging remark!). If you use Firefox — I do — or if you use Chrome, you should read this chapter first: Many of the tricks here work in Firefox and Chrome, too.

In this chapter, I take you through the tricks that can help you get the most out of IE (and, in some cases, Firefox and Chrome). I fill you in on RSS, from an IE point of view. I tell you the truth about cookies. I show you how to customize IE. And, if all else fails and you make a mess of things, you can return your IE settings to the way they were before you made all the modifications; at the end of this chapter, I tell you how.

Getting the Most from Internet Explorer

A handful of Internet Explorer tricks can make all the difference in your productivity and sanity. Every IE (and Firefox and Chrome) user should know these shortcuts:

- **You rarely need to type www in the Address bar at the beginning of an address, and you never need to type** `http://`**.** People who build Web sites these days are almost always savvy enough to let you drop the use of the www at the beginning of the Web site's name. Unless the site you're headed to was last updated in the late 17th century, you can probably get there by simply typing the name of the site, as long as you include the part at the end. So, you can type `http://www.dummies.com` if you want to, but typing `dummies.com` works just as well.

  If you come across a site that forces you to type www at the beginning of an address — say, if you type `someplace.com` and see a "Page not found" error — write to the Webmaster (in this case, send an e-mail to `webmaster@someplace.com`) and tell him that he needs to get into the 21st century. It's a sign of sloppy Web site design.

- **IE automatically sticks** `http://www.` **on the front of an address you type and** `.com` **on the end if you press Ctrl+Enter.** So, if you want to go to the site `http://www.dummies.com`, you only need to type `dummies` in the Address bar and press Ctrl+Enter.

- **With rare exceptions, address capitalization doesn't matter.** Typing either `AskWoody.com` and `askwoody.com` gets you to my Web site — as does `asKwoodY.cOm`. (The file or path info after the first slash in an address may be case sensitive, especially on poorly designed Web sites where the Web master isn't paying attention: `badsite.com/hello` may be different from `badsite.com/Hello`.) On the other hand, hyphens (-) and underscores (_) aren't interchangeable: `some-site.com` and `some_site.com` are two completely different sites. Similarly, the number 0 isn't the same as the letter *o,* the number 1 isn't a letter *l,* and radishes aren't the same as turnips. Or so my niece tells me.

- **Sometimes you want IE to open a new tab and leave your current tab where it is so that you can easily refer to it.** Usually, the Web page you're on has control over whether clicking a link opens a new tab, but you can override the page's setting. To make IE open the linked page in a new tab, hold down Ctrl when you click a link. To make IE start a whole new copy of itself, hold down Shift when you click a link. Alternatively, you can right-click a link and choose Open in New Tab or Open in New Window.

- **Depending on the size of your monitor and the quality of the display, the Web content you see may be a bit of a strain to read.** Some site designers try to cram as much information as possible on a page, crushing ten pounds of text into a five-pound space. If you have a mouse with a scroll wheel, you can zoom in on the page by holding down the Ctrl key and scrolling the wheel. Alternatively, you can choose Page⇨Zoom and select a zoom level that looks good to you.

  One trade-off when you zoom is that less information fits on the screen, so you have to do more scrolling to read through articles that capture (and hold) your interest.

- **If you find yourself working on pages with lots of content, you might want to flip your browser into Full Screen view, thus minimizing the amount of overhead impinging on the good stuff.** To do so, press F11 or choose Tools⇨Full Screen (press View⇨Full Screen in Firefox). When you want the navigation buttons back in IE, slide your mouse to the top of the screen.

Keeping track of passwords rates as the single biggest pain in the neck in any browser. You have passwords for, what — a hundred different sites? If you haven't yet discovered Roboform (`roboform.com`), you need to. Roboform memorizes the passwords of all your sites, stores them securely, automatically recognizes password-requesting pages when you get to them, and fills in the user ID and password with just a click. Whereas you had to memorize (or write down) a hundred different user IDs and passwords before Roboform, after you install the (free!) package, you need to provide only the single Roboform password and everything else gets filled in automatically.

Can you really turn off IE?

Windows 7 includes the ability to turn off several core Windows programs, and Internet Explorer is the number-one choice on everyone's list. It's particularly popular at Microsoft because the ability to turn off IE helps the 'Softies defend against antitrust attacks.

To turn off IE, choose Start⇨Control Panel. Click the Programs icon and then, under Programs and Features, click the link labeled Turn Windows Features On or Off. You see a list of Windows programs, including Games, Windows Media Player, DVD Maker, and several more. Deselect the Internet Explorer 8 check box and click OK. Windows reboots twice, but in the end the Internet Explorer program, `iexplore.exe`, is banished from your computer.

IE is buried deep inside Windows. It isn't clear to me how Windows removes IE and keeps on ticking, and for that reason I don't recommend that you turn it off completely. But it's nice to know the facility's there, if you should ever feel malevolently inclined.

Making Internet Explorer Run Faster

In general, if you want Internet Explorer to run faster, you need to get a faster Internet connection. Beefing up your computer, adding more memory, getting a larger hard drive — none of that stuff does much to make Web surfing faster. The bottleneck is your Internet connection. In this section, I show you three ways you can speed up IE.

Turning off graphics

If you're stuck with a slow connection and you're a bit desperate, one trick can speed up IE — but at a price. You can turn off graphics. When you tell IE to load a page without its graphics, the browser displays an empty box where the image is supposed to be. That's a bit like going to the Louvre and seeing only empty picture frames, but if you want to get through Web pages quickly, it may help.

Here's how to turn off graphics in IE:

1. **In Internet Explorer, choose Tools⇨Internet Options.**
2. **Click the Advanced tab.**

   You see the advanced options, shown in Figure 3-1.

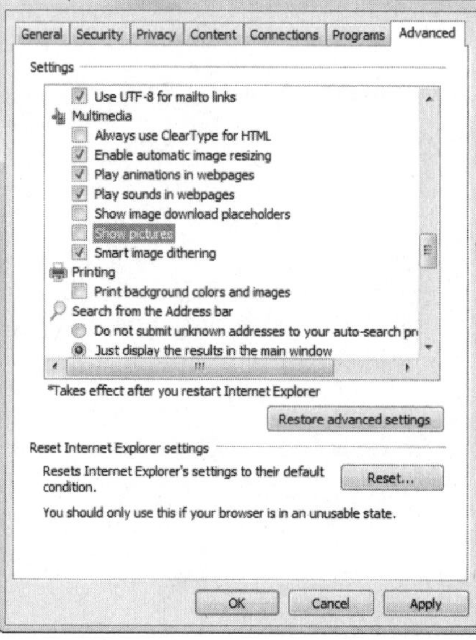

Figure 3-1: If speed is your thing, you can disable the graphics display to allow text to download quickly.

3. **Down in the Multimedia section, deselect the check box marked Show Pictures.**
4. **Click OK.**

   The next page you surf to appears without any pictures, as shown in Figure 3-2.

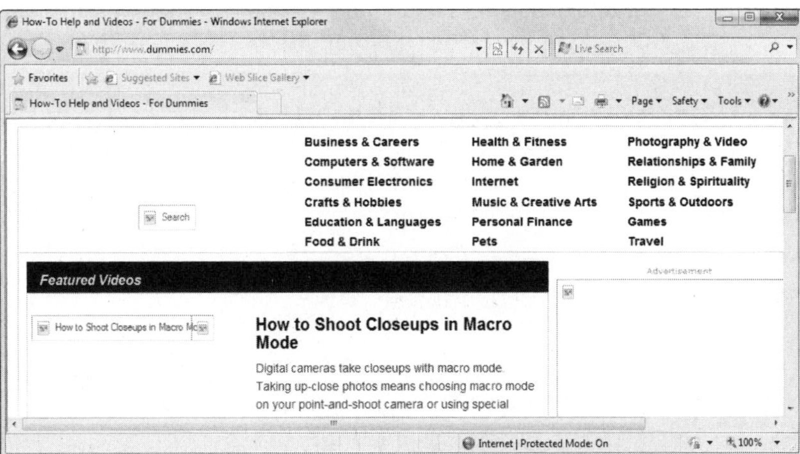

Figure 3-2: A no-pictures `dummies.com` loads much faster than the one with pics. Don't worry: The Dummies Man won't mind.

In Firefox, you can block images, too: Choose Tools➪Options➪Content and deselect the Load Images Automatically check box.

Even after you turn off the display of pictures, you can still view a picture, if you choose. When the Web page appears, simply right-click the image placeholder (which is usually a box with a small icon and some substitution text). When the shortcut menu appears, choose Show Picture, and the image appears on the page.

You turned the display of graphics back on, but they still aren't appearing. What gives? Press F5 to refresh the display, and IE reloads the page, which includes downloading the graphics as expected.

Turning off animations and sounds

If you're interested only in information, you can further reduce download times by deselecting the Play Animations in Webpages and Play Sounds in Webpages check boxes in the Advanced Options (refer to Figure 3-1). This action reduces your Web pages to straight text information, which may not be much fun but makes surfing much faster.

Increasing your storage space

Another way to boost IE performance is to increase the amount of storage space allowed for those temporary Internet files. I have never been able to feel a difference when I jack up the amount of space — that's my criterion for a good performance boost — but your results may vary. Here's how to increase your storage space:

1. **In Internet Explorer, choose Tools⇨Internet Options, and in the middle of the General tab, in the Browsing History area, click the Settings button.**

   You see the Temporary Internet Files and History Settings dialog box, shown in Figure 3-3.

Temporary Internet Files and History Settings

Temporary Internet Files
Internet Explorer stores copies of webpages, images, and media for faster viewing later.
Check for newer versions of stored pages:
Every time I visit the webpage
Every time I start Internet Explorer
Automatically
Never
Disk space to use (8-1024MB) (Recommended: 50-250MB) 100
Current location:
C:\Users\woody\AppData\Local\Microsoft\Windows\Temporary Internet Files\
Move folder... View objects View files

History
Specify how many days Internet Explorer should save the list of websites you have visited.
Days to keep pages in history: 20

OK Cancel

Figure 3-3: More room for temporary Internet files means that IE doesn't have to download Web pages as frequently, thus saving you (a small amount of) time.

2. **Crank up the number of megabytes allotted in the Disk Space to Use box.**

   If you have a lot of room on your hard drive, you can afford to let IE get a little sloppy. But remember that the gains you experience, day to day, aren't that great.

3. **When you're happy with your choice, click OK twice.**

   IE starts using the extra space the next time it goes to a new Web page.

Putting the Pedal to the Metal: Working with Accelerators

Internet Explorer 8 introduces the concept of *Accelerators,* quick lookup links that let you take data from a Web page and run with it, without going through a laborious copy/find-the-page/paste routine.

For example, you can highlight an address on a Web page, right-click it, and choose Map with Live Search. It may take a little refinement to get the address in a form that Live Search Maps can understand, but with very little effort, you see a map of the location, complete with offers for driving instructions and traffic reports (see Figure 3-4).

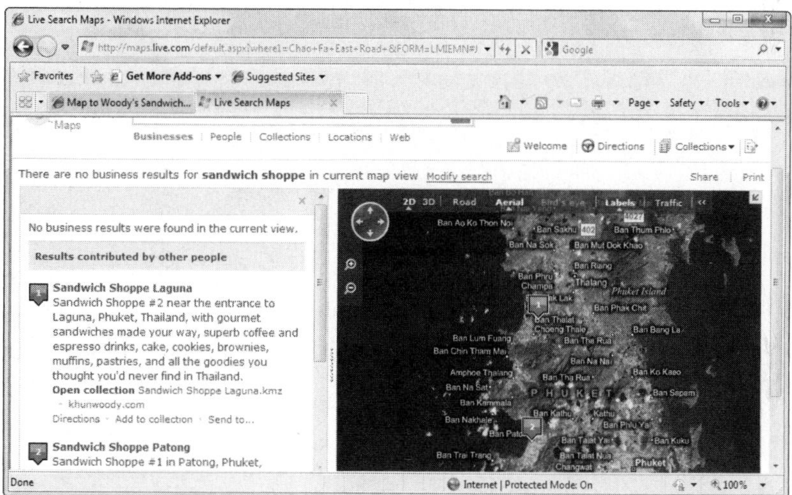

Figure 3-4: Rather than copy and paste an address into, say, Google Earth, in IE 8 you can simply highlight an address, right-click it, and look it up in Live Search Maps.

The number of Accelerators is growing exponentially. As of this writing, you can find Accelerators for performing these tasks:

- **Translate languages (see Figure 3-5):** Highlight a phrase in English and choose either Live Search Translator or Google Translate and an automatically generated translation of the phrase appears in the chosen language. You can switch From and To languages by clicking a link.
- **Read dictionaries, Wikipedia, and other references (such as music and movie site lookups).**

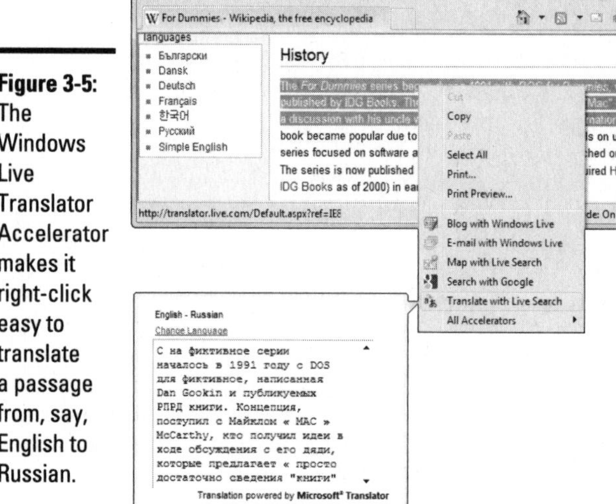

Figure 3-5: The Windows Live Translator Accelerator makes it right-click easy to translate a passage from, say, English to Russian.

- **Check out news and sports headlines.**
- **Experiment with torrents and file sharing services, videos (such as YouTube), and live TV.**
- **Shop at sites such as eBay and Newegg.**
- **Study your financial information, currency converters, stocks, and charts.**

If you aren't yet using Accelerators, try them: positively addictive. To work with Accelerators, choose Page➪All Accelerators➪Manage Accelerators. If you then click the link to Find More Accelerators, you can add such luminaries as a Bing Maps Accelerator, or a Share on Facebook Accelerator.

Hardening Internet Explorer 8

Microsoft extols the new, enhanced security on offer in IE 8, the version of Internet Express that ships with Windows 7. Of course, the 'Softies have been doing that for years: Internet Explorer 3.01 sported three advanced security levels that rode herd on *ActiveX controls* (the programs on Web sites that IE can run, sometimes to deleterious effect). IE 4 introduced *security zones* (which figure prominently in IE 8). IE 7 featured *Protected mode,* designed to restrict the sandbox in which ActiveX controls are run — and the cretin community managed to toss the sand all over the place. IE 8 now boasts a *SmartScreen Filter* (see Book V, Chapter 2), which looks and acts like a phishing filter — the main difference is that in IE 8, Microsoft has adopted the Firefox approach to maintaining phishing blacklists. IE 8 also runs in *Data Execution Protection* (DEP) mode, which should reduce the chances of being zapped by a smart online program that ventures outside its normal confines; with DEP, a program that tries to jump out of its sandbox gets slapped down.

It remains to be seen whether the cracking community can break IE 8 with the dexterity and alacrity applied to IE 6 and IE 7. One thing's for sure: It couldn't get much worse.

Here are the primary culprits:

- **ActiveX** (formerly known as Object Linking and Embedding, or OLE) is used by Web pages to run programs on your computer. As with scripting (see the next bullet), a Web site can call on ActiveX or install its own ActiveX *controls* (programs) to perform limited actions on your computer. A very large percentage of IE security breaches occur when an ActiveX control is used in ways that the IE designers never intended.

  Firefox and Chrome don't recognize ActiveX. Never have. Never will.

- **Scripting,** whether by JavaScript or VBScript, uses IE to run programs that sit inside Web pages. Both JavaScript and VBScript are updated frequently to deal with newly discovered security holes.

  Firefox and Chrome do run JavaScript. They're both vulnerable to JavaScript bugs, although the way they constrain JavaScript generally makes it considerably more difficult for bad guys to get inside your computer.

- **.NET Framework** (pronounced "dot net framework") is a big collection of program pieces that Web site designers can stitch together to create programs. .NET is built into windows Vista and Windows 7, but has to be separately downloaded and installed in Windows XP. .NET Framework springs security holes from time to time, although not on the same grand scale as ActiveX and JavaScript.

None of these technologies is bad in and of itself, but all of them present an invitation to malware writers intent on breaking into your system.

You may be thinking, "Hey, why do I care? I don't surf to weird Web sites. The warez guys and crackers don't draw me in. I'm not going to get stung." Unfortunately, "bad" sites are just part of the problem.

- **Many "good" Web sites have, in the past, hosted advertisements that harbored malicious code.** The ads are pulled in from a pool supplied by a vendor, and if one of the ads is modified surreptitiously, a perfectly legitimate Web site can start planting malware on your machine.

- **Some "good" Web sites have been *hacked* (altered) by slimeballs who stick destructive programs on otherwise legitimate pages.** Unless the people who maintain the page are on the lookout, hacked pages can go undetected for a long time.
- **Internet Explorer works behind the scenes, and it can be subverted in seemingly innocuous ways.**

From time to time, you may see recommendations from Microsoft about "locking down" certain Internet Explorer behaviors. Frequently, the advisories come out quickly, before Microsoft can release a full-fledged patch. Most IE lock downs take a similar approach:

1. **Start Internet Explorer. Choose Tools⇨Internet Options and click the Security tab.**

   You see the Internet Options dialog box, shown in Figure 3-6.

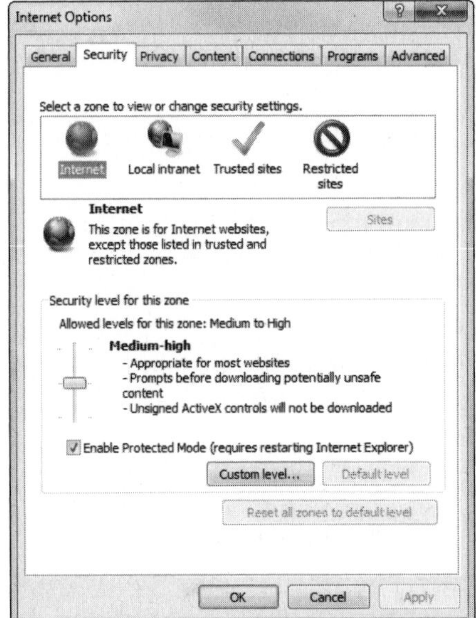

Figure 3-6: Lockdowns in the Internet zone.

Most lockdown advisories work in the Internet zone because that "zone" covers almost all your Internet interactions. The Security Level for This Zone box should show Medium High, and the check box marked Enable Protected Mode (Requires Restarting Internet Explorer) should be selected.

2. **Click the Custom Level button.**

   Internet Explorer shows you the Security Settings–Internet Zone dialog box (see Figure 3-7).

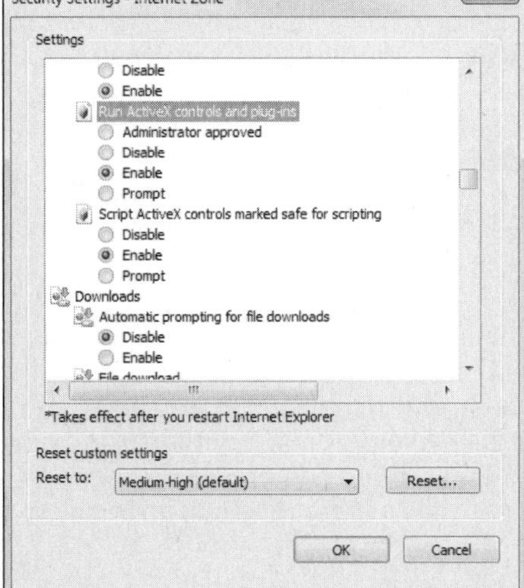

Figure 3-7: Most lockdowns involve making changes to the settings in this dialog box.

3. **Follow the lockdown instructions to restrict the activities of various parts of Internet Explorer.**

   By far the most common recommendation is to disable ActiveX. To do so, under the Run ActiveX Controls and Plug-ins heading, choose Disable. Many, many additional options are available in this dialog box, and you may well be advised to turn off other components of IE.

   I generally advise *against* turning off features willy-nilly because they can severely limit your ability to work with IE. For example, disabling ActiveX controls will make it impossible to have Microsoft's Update site scan your computer.

4. **When you finish making any recommended changes, click OK. When IE asks whether you're sure, click Yes.**

   You have to shut down IE and restart it for your new settings to take effect.

Don't lock down IE unless you have concrete recommendations from a source you trust. More often than not, you're safer switching to Firefox or Chrome and leaving IE to sort out its own problems, with an update in a day or a week or a year. We cover lockdowns periodically on AskWoody.com.

Dealing with Cookies

A *cookie,* as you probably know, is a text file that a Web site stores on your computer. The Web site can put information inside its own cookie (say, the time and date of your last visit or the page you were last viewing or your account number). At least in theory, a Web site can look at and change only its own cookies: The cookie provides a means for an individual Web site to store information on your computer and to retrieve it later, using your browser.

Of course, nothing ever goes precisely as planned. Bugs have appeared in the way Internet Explorer, in particular, handles cookies and, historically, it's been possible for rogue Web sites to retrieve information from cookies other than their own.

Because of ongoing problems, sound and fury frequently raised by people who don't understand, and concomitant legislation in many countries, "first party" cookies these days rarely include any interesting information. Mostly, they store innocuous settings and perhaps a randomly generated number that's used to track a customer in the company's database. To a bad guy, the data stored in most cookies varies between banal and useless.

By contrast, *third-party* cookies (or *tracking* cookies) aren't as bland. They have significant commercial value because they can be used to keep track of your Web surfing. Here's how. Say ZDNet (`zdnet.com`) sells an ad to Doubleclick. When you venture to a page with a Doubleclick ad on it, both ZDNet and Doubleclick can stick cookies on your computer. ZDNet can retrieve only its cookie, and Doubleclick can retrieve only its cookie. Cool. Doubleclick might keep information about you visiting a ZDNet site that talks about, oh, an Android phone.

Now say that DealTime (`dealtime.com`) sells an ad to Doubleclick. You go to a page on DealTime and both DealTime and Doubleclick can look at their own cookies. DealTime might be smart enough to ask Doubleclick whether you've been looking at Android phones and offer you a bargain tailored to your recent surfing.

Multiply that little example by 10, 100, or 100,000 and you begin to see how third-party cookies can be used to collect a whole lot of information about you and your surfing habits. There's nothing illegal or immoral about it. But some people (present company certainly included) find it disconcerting.

I don't get worked up about cookies these days. If you've ever worked with them programmatically, you're probably at the yawning stage, too.

Deleting cookies

Cookies don't have anything to do with spam — you receive the same junk e-mail even if you tell your computer to reject every cookie that darkens your door. Cookies don't spy on your PC, go sniffing for bank accounts, or keep a log of those <ahem> artistic Web sites you visit. They do serve a useful purpose, but like so many other concepts in the computer industry, cookies are exploited by a few companies in questionable ways. I talk about cookies extensively in Book VI, Chapter 1. If you're worried about cookies and want to know what's really happening, that's a great place to start.

In Internet Explorer, to delete all cookies, choose Tools⇨Delete Browsing History. You see the Delete Browsing History dialog box, shown in Figure 3-8. Select the check box marked Cookies (and any other items you want to clear out) and click Delete. IE deletes all your cookies.

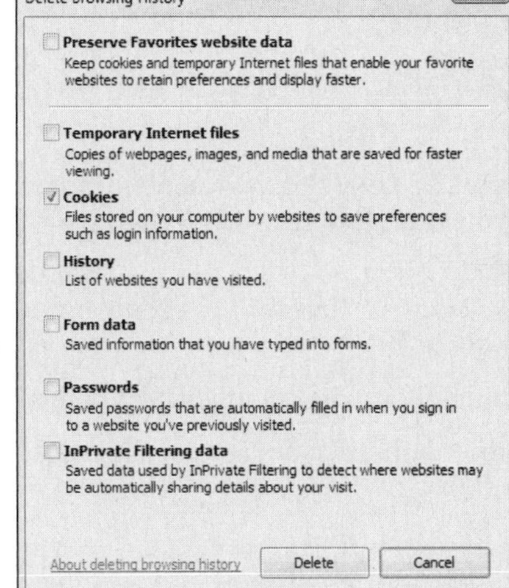

Figure 3-8: Delete all cookies on your PC by using this box.

In Firefox, choose Tools⇨Clear Private Data. Make sure that the Cookies check box is selected and click the Clear Private Data Now button. In Chrome, choose Tools⇨Options, click the Under the Hood tab and, in the Security part, Cookies Settings section, click the Remove All button.

InPrivate Filtering

In Internet Explorer, you can easily block all cookies, or all third-party cookies. Here's how:

1. **In Internet Explorer 8, choose Tools➪Internet Options.**

   You see the Internet Options dialog box (refer to Figure 3-6).

2. **On the Privacy tab, click the Advanced button.**

   IE shows you the Advanced Privacy Settings dialog box, shown in Figure 3-9.

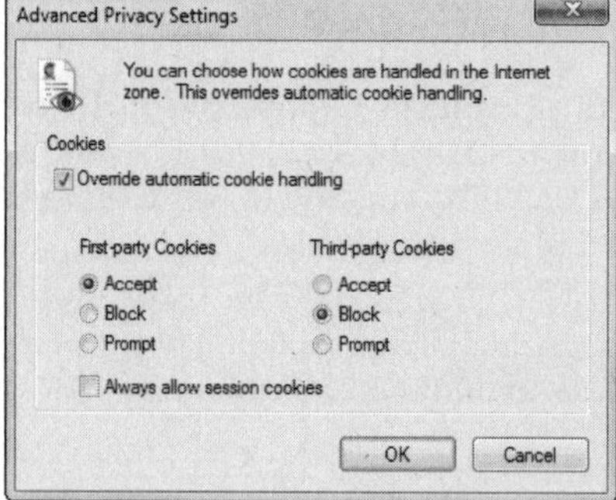

Figure 3-9: Block first-party or third-party cookies here.

3. **Select the check box marked Override Automatic Cookie Handling, and then tell IE what you want it to do with first-party cookies and with third-party cookies.**

   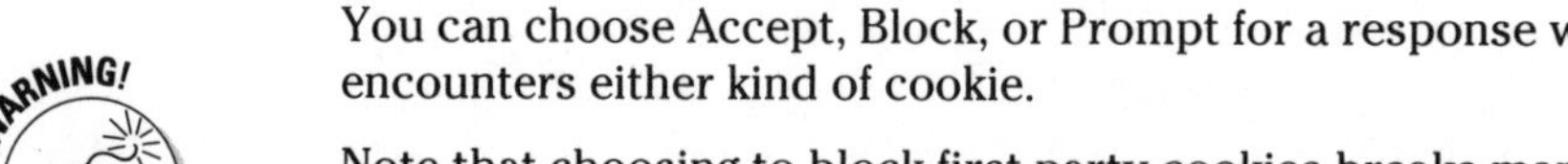

   You can choose Accept, Block, or Prompt for a response when IE encounters either kind of cookie.

   Note that choosing to block first-party cookies breaks many Web sites.

4. **When you're comfortable with your decisions, click OK.**

   The change takes effect at the next Web site you hit.

Internet Explorer 8 has a feature that watches as you surf the Web and counts how frequently third-party cookies from specific sites are deposited on your computer. If IE sees that you're accumulating a lot of cookies from a specific source, it starts blocking all cookies from that source.

The default trigger number is ten. For example, if you surf to ten sites with Doubleclick ads on them and you have InPrivate Filtering enabled, IE starts blocking Doubleclick cookies.

Though I'm absolutely certain that no attempt was made to block the business activities of any specific advertising companies, it's worth noting that Microsoft's longtime nemesis Google owns Doubleclick.

Despite the similarities in name, InPrivate Browsing (also known as Porn mode; see Book V, Chapter 2) has almost nothing in common with InPrivate Filtering. InPrivate Browsing prevents IE from storing any information about where you've been. InPrivate Filtering exists only to track and delete frequently occurring cookies.

To turn on InPrivate Filtering, choose Safety⇨InPrivate Filtering. InPrivate Filtering stays active only for as long as IE is running. As soon as you shut down IE, InPrivate Filtering flips off and you have to turn it on again manually.

You can easily see which advertisers have stuff buried on a specific Web page: Choose Safety⇨Webpage Privacy Policy and IE pumps out a list of all sites that could be putting third-party cookies on your computer from that Web page. For example, in Figure 3-10, I surf to `zdnet.com` and check out the privacy report. You can see that `doubleclick.net`, `2mdn.net`, `questionmarket.com`, and `com.com` (a ZDNet affiliate) are all cramming ads on that page and could all be planting cookies. (In fact, they aren't planting cookies, because the column in Figure 3-10 marked Cookies is empty.)

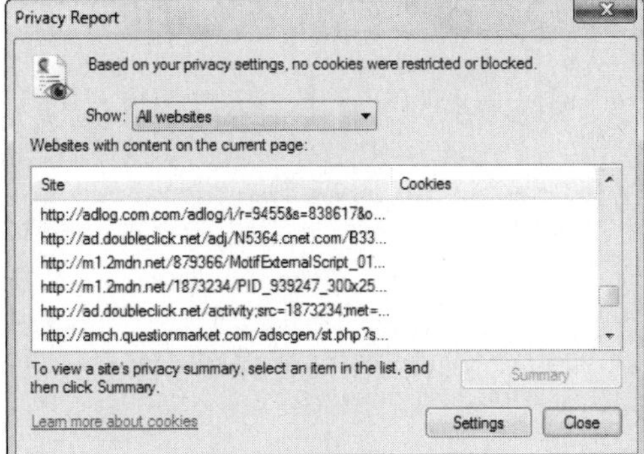

Figure 3-10: ZDNet has lots of advertisers, any or all of which could be planting third-party cookies on your computer.

Although you can't see it in the screen shot, on this particular day, the `zdnet.com` main page was also serving up "content" from `zedo.com`, `bnet.com`, and `revsci.net`. That's six independent potential third-party cookie factories appearing on *just one page*.

You might be surprised to learn that Microsoft uses Doubleclick, or at least it did as of this writing. Look at almost any of the sites that are linked directly from MSN.com. Betcha never would've thought.

To fine-tune InPrivate Filtering, you can choose Safety⇨InPrivate Filtering Settings. You see a dialog box like the one shown in Figure 3-11. Set the spinner for any number between 3 and 30 and the InPrivate Filter shows you how many cookies have been accepted for each advertiser, er, content provider.

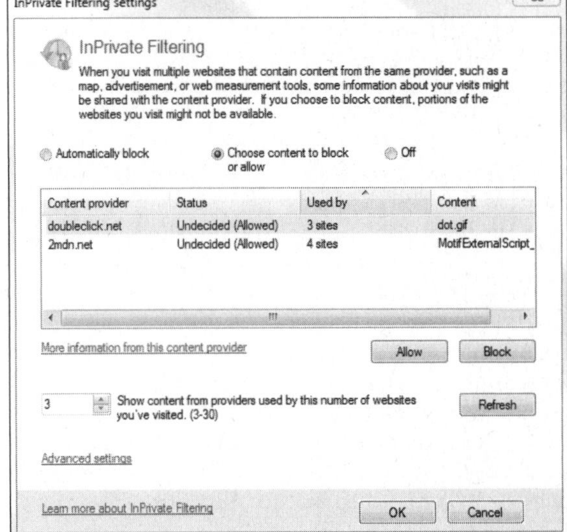

Figure 3-11: Fine-tune InPrivate Filtering settings here.

Adobe Flash's hidden third-party cookies

Adobe Flash — the program that runs animated sequences on Web sites — doesn't use cookies. At least, it doesn't use the kind of cookies you've come to know and love. Flash maintains its own text files, named *Local Shared Objects (LSOs).* Though LSOs sure do look and act like cookies, they're quite different.

Just for starters, cookies are limited to 4KB of text; LSOs are, by default, limited to 100KB. Cookies are controlled by your browser; LSOs are controlled by Flash, using settings that are tucked away in an obtuse location (`macromedia.com/support/documentation/en/flashplayer/help/settings_manager06.html`). When you clear all cookies on your computer, or block them, absolutely nothing happens to LSOs. You can easily see a list of all the cookies on your computer, but coming up with a list of LSOs is anything but straightforward.

LSOs can be set and read by Web pages, even if you can't see a Flash animation on the page. In fact, many Web page designers and programmers use LSOs when they want to store a whole bunch of data on your computer. I've seen tips for using LSOs to store small databases that can be scanned on demand, without having to refer back to the main database on the Internet. One of my friends says his bank stores data in an LSO, even though the bank's Web site doesn't have any (visible) Flash animations.

Just like regular third-party cookies, Flash LSOs can be used by third-party advertisers to track your movements online. By default, Flash accepts all third-party LSOs.

Working with RSS Feeds

At the risk of repeating myself repetitively, RSS — Really Simple Syndication — is, uh, really simple. There. Did that clear up any confusion you might have? Actually, RSS is a whole lot easier to see than it is to explain.

If you've ever used Firefox, you've seen RSS in action. The Latest Headlines Live Bookmarks button on the Bookmark toolbar uses an RSS feed from the BBC. In Figure 3-12, I clicked the Latest Headlines Live Bookmarks button, and I can read the headlines of the most recent news items posted on the BBC Web site.

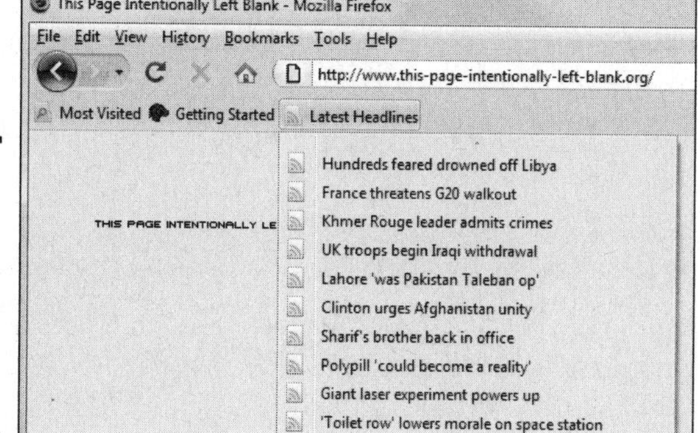

Figure 3-12: The Firefox Live Bookmarks feature works with RSS feeds.

If I click a headline from the Latest Headlines drop-down list, Firefox heads over to the BBC Web site and brings up the corresponding BBC news articles.

It's really just that simple.

Internet Explorer is a little more clunky than Firefox. (I talk about Firefox RSS feeds in Book V, Chapter 4.)

Here's how to get an RSS feed going in IE:

1. **Go to a Web site with an RSS feed. I just happen to have one handy: AskWoody.com. (Seriously, most newsy sites these days have RSS feeds, as do sites featuring continually changing information.)**

   If the site has an RSS feed, the "radio wave" button to the right of the Home icon turns orange. In Figure 3-13, AskWoody.com raises its RSS hand by turning on the orange radio wave button.

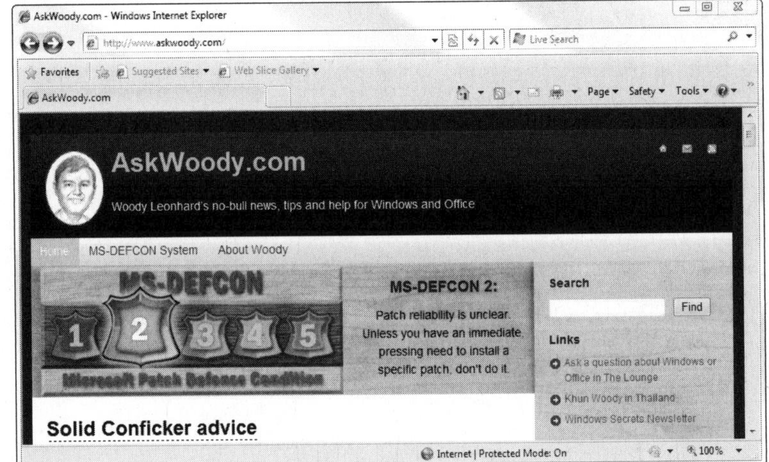

Figure 3-13: AskWoody.com has an RSS feed, which you can see by the orange "radio wave" button.

2. **Click the orange radio wave button.**

   IE shows you the most recent items available on the site's RSS feed and invites you to Subscribe to this Feed, as shown in Figure 3-14.

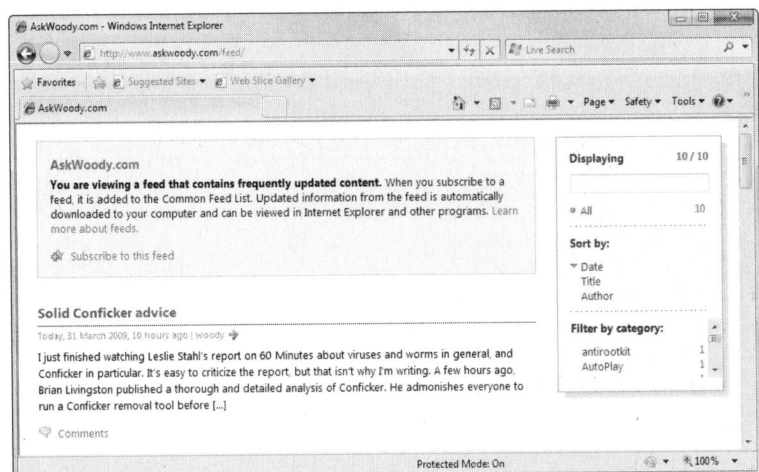

Figure 3-14: Subscribing to an RSS feed is easy.

3. **Click the link that says Subscribe to This Feed.**

   IE shows you the Subscribe to This Feed dialog box, shown in Figure 3-15.

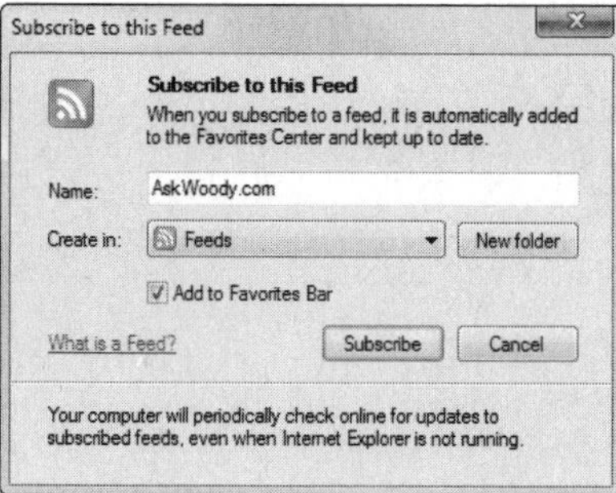

Figure 3-15: Put the RSS feed on the Favorites bar so that it's easy to access. Or, better, use iGoogle, as described in Chapter 4 of this minibook.

4. **If you want to be able to get at the feed easily, select the check box marked Add to Favorites Bar and click Subscribe.**

   Internet Explorer puts on the Favorites bar a button that's similar to the Latest News feed in Firefox (refer to Figure 3-12). Anytime you want to check the latest stories from that particular Web site, click the button.

RSS feeds can save you gobs of time, first by allowing you to peek at headlines without opening a Web page and second by showing you all the new stuff so that you don't have to scroll through the flotsam (never mind the jetsam). Fortunately, you have a much easier way to set up many feeds (see Book V, Chapter 4 for details).

Chapter 4: Using Firefox: The Advanced Course

In This Chapter

- **Putting Firefox to work**
- **Using bookmarks the Firefox way**
- **Creating Smart Folders**
- **Finding a better way to work with RSS feeds**
- **Gathering the best Firefox add-ons**

Hey, you can use Internet Explorer if you want to. Without doubt, IE has a few features that other browsers can't match — Web Slices, InPrivate Filtering, and Accelerators come to mind. If those ring your chimes, you need to play the IE game.

I use Firefox. I've used it for years, and I've recommended it in my books for years. Debating the relative merits of Web browsers soon degenerates to a fight over the number of angels that can stand on the head of a pin. Suffice it to say that I feel Firefox is faster, more adaptable, and more secure, and it simply works better than IE.

If you decide to take Firefox out for a drive, don't worry about leaving IE back at home. Firefox and IE coexist peacefully: With rare exception, one doesn't even know that the other is installed on your computer. You should keep IE around, for the odd (very odd) page that doesn't show up correctly in Firefox. And, you should keep IE updated — patch after patch after patch — just in case a wily worm finds a way to infect your machine through Internet Explorer. But for everyday Web browsing, I strongly recommend that you use Firefox. Or Chrome — which is still the new kid on the block, although it shows great promise.

In Chapter 2 of this minibook, I cover topics that apply, more or less, to all three browsers. In Chapter 3 of this minibook, I take you into Internet Explorer, describing more advanced features, some of which are unique to IE. In this chapter I (finally!) get to tell you about the best browser of 'em all — and how to trick it out to work your way.

I don't mean to imply that Firefox is perfect. It isn't. The Firefox team releases security patches, too, and you need to make sure you keep Firefox updated. But I think you'll enjoy using Firefox more than Internet Explorer — and I would bet that you hit far fewer in-the-wild security problems with the Fox.

Installing Firefox

Installing Firefox couldn't be simpler. You don't need to disable Internet Explorer, pat your head, and rub your belly or jump through any other hoops — although clicking your heels and repeating "There's no place like home" may help. Just follow these steps:

1. **Using any convenient browser (even IE), go to `firefox.com` and follow the instructions to download and run the installer for the latest version of Firefox.**

   Chances are good that you need to click a big, green button and then click Run to get the installer going.

2. **On the installer's splash screen, click Next.**

   You see the Setup window, shown in Figure 4-1.

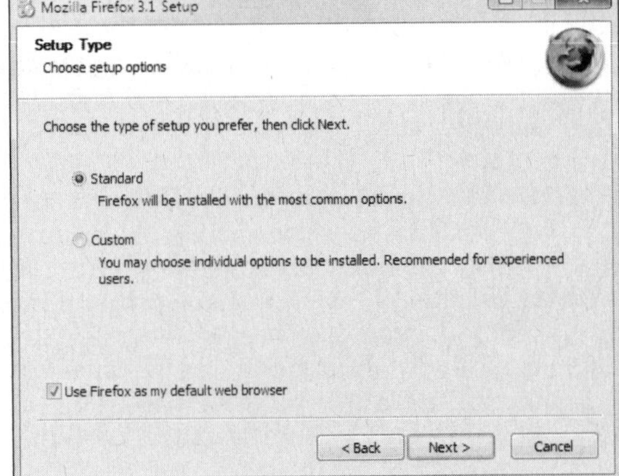

Figure 4-1: Go ahead and use Standard setup.

3. **Select the Standard button, select the check box that says Use Firefox As My Default Browser (if you feel so inspired), and click Next.**

   The standard options include generating icons for your desktop and the taskbar and for putting Firefox on the Start menu. You probably want all three.

4. **Click Install.**

   The installer takes a minute and installs Firefox and then asks whether you want to launch Firefox now.

5. **Click Finish and Firefox appears (see Figure 4-2).**

Depending on how you install Firefox, the first time you run it, you may be asked whether you want to import bookmarks from Internet Explorer. (I generally choose no because IE has so many useless Microsoft-centric built-in Favorites.) You may also be asked whether you want to make Firefox your default browser. (I choose Yes.)

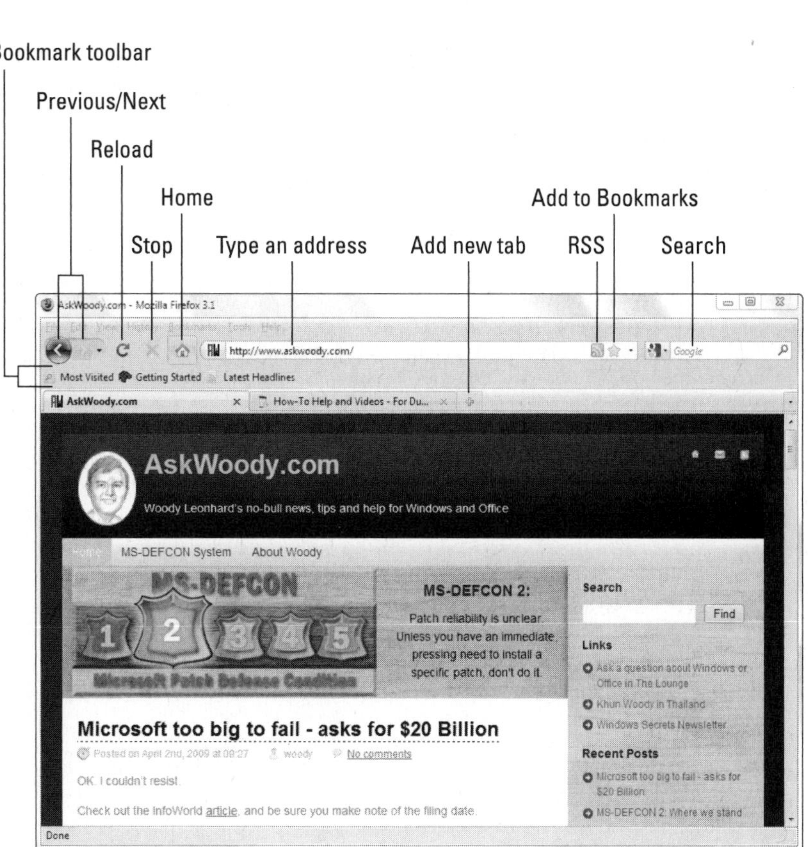

Figure 4-2: Firefox up and running with two tabs.

Firefox includes many of the controls you would expect from any browser — an address bar for typing Web addresses and a search box that hooks directly into your choice of search engines. But it doesn't have a lot of, uh, stuff that you find in Internet Explorer — you see no security zones, no privacy-sapping suggested sites, no Web Slices, no Protected mode. Firefox doesn't need them.

Most of all, the default home page in Firefox isn't the IE default, MSN.com. Some sanity persists in the universe.

Recapping Firefox Tips

In Chapters 2 and 3 of this book, I mention many speed-up tips that apply to Internet Explorer and Firefox. Permit me to recap those tips, this time presenting them with a Firefox twist and adding my favorite tips that are unique to Firefox:

- When you click a link, the person who designed the Web page determines whether the new page replaces the old one or whether the new page appears on a new tab, leaving the old page intact. You can override the Web page's commands. Ctrl+click to put the target site on its own, new tab. (If your mouse has a wheel, clicking with the wheel accomplishes the same thing.) Shift+click to start a new copy of Firefox and have the target site appear as the first tab in the new Firefox window.
- Similarly, you can Ctrl+click or Shift+click in the Search bar to have your search results appear on a new tab or in a new copy of Firefox.
- No need to type the `http://` or (in almost all cases) the www in a Web address: Typing `http://www.dummies.com` is the same as typing `dummies.com`. Press Ctrl+Enter and Firefox puts www. at the beginning and `.com` on the end: Type `dummies` and hit Ctrl+Enter and you go to `dummies.com`.

- Firefox performs several searches simultaneously when you type on the Address bar. (Firefox insists on calling it Smart Location Bar, which sounds to me like a pub next door to Molly Malone's. While this feature was in development, the programmers called it the Awesome bar. Uh, cool.) When you type, Firefox looks in your Bookmarks folder for matches, including tags. It also looks at your Web browsing history, giving higher preference to sites you visited recently or frequently. (To delete an item from the look-ahead list, press the down arrow to highlight the item and then press Del.) You can see the look-ahead capability in action in Figure 4-3.

  You can use the Firefox address bar just like the Search bar: Type your search terms, just as you would type them in Google, and press Enter, and Firefox then runs a Google search on the terms.

- Of course, you know the usual keyboard shortcuts that Firefox shares with Internet Explorer: Ctrl+F starts a Find search on the current Web page; F5 reloads the current page; and Ctrl+T starts a new tab, with your cursor in the address bar, ready to run.

- ✦ In Firefox, if you delete a tab by clicking the X on the tab itself or by clicking the scroll wheel on a scroll mouse, you can restore the just-deleted tab by holding down Ctrl+Shift and pressing T.
- ✦ In Firefox, Ctrl+L moves the cursor to the address bar and selects the whole address. That makes it two-clicks easy to copy the current address: Ctrl+L, Ctrl+C.

Most of those tricks don't work, or don't work the same way, in Internet Explorer.

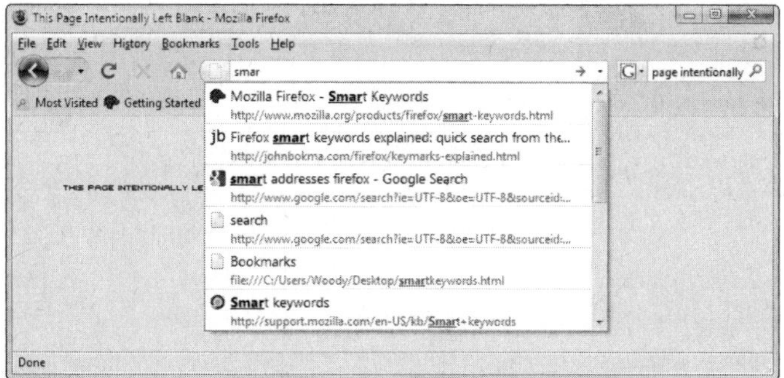

Figure 4-3: Firefox guesses at the site you want as you type.

Speeding Up Firefox

Firefox straight out of the box (er, straight off the Web) includes some settings designed to throttle it back a bit so that the Fox doesn't grab your Internet connection by the throat and hog all the bandwidth for itself.

That's great if you have to share. But if you have your own Internet connection and you want to let Firefox grab all the gigabyte gusto it can gather, here's how to convert it into a selfish, bratty, "just me" browser:

1. **Start Firefox. In the address bar, type** about:config **(no spaces) and press Enter.**

   Firefox warns that This Might Void Your Warranty! (Really. I don't make this stuff up.) Seriously, you're, uh, about to tamper with the Firefox configuration settings and if you aren't careful, you can mess things up royally.

2. **Click the button marked I'll Be Careful, I Promise!**

   Firefox shows you its configuration settings.

3. **In the Filter box, type** network.http **(no spaces) and press Enter.**

   Firefox brings up the configuration settings that include the text *network.http,* as shown in Figure 4-4.

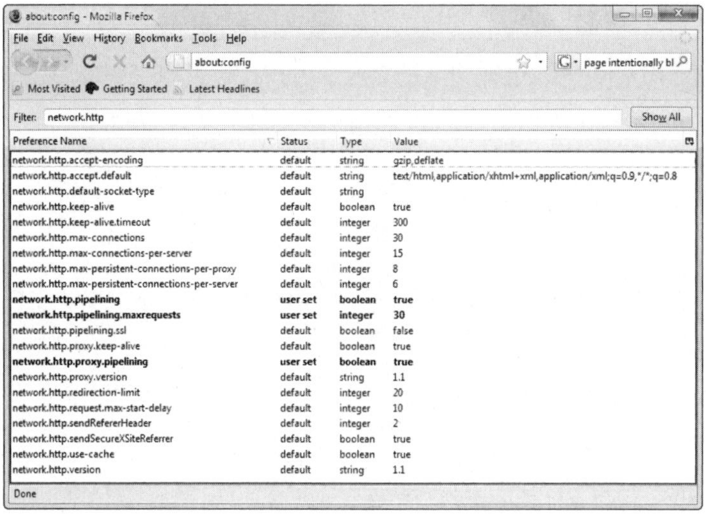
about:config - Mozilla Firefox
File Edit View History Bookmarks Tools Help
about:config
page intentionally bl
Most Visited Getting Started Latest Headlines
Filter: network.http
Show All
Preference Name Status Type Value
network.http.accept-encoding default string gzip,deflate
network.http.accept.default default string text/html,application/xhtml+xml,application/xml;q=0.9,*/*;q=0.8
network.http.default-socket-type default string
network.http.keep-alive default boolean true
network.http.keep-alive.timeout default integer 300
network.http.max-connections default integer 30
network.http.max-connections-per-server default integer 15
network.http.max-persistent-connections-per-proxy default integer 8
network.http.max-persistent-connections-per-server default integer 6
network.http.pipelining user set boolean true
network.http.pipelining.maxrequests user set integer 30
network.http.pipelining.ssl default boolean false
network.http.proxy.keep-alive default boolean true
network.http.proxy.pipelining user set boolean true
network.http.proxy.version default string 1.1
network.http.redirection-limit default integer 20
network.http.request.max-start-delay default integer 10
network.http.sendRefererHeader default integer 2
network.http.sendSecureXSiteReferrer default boolean true
network.http.use-cache default boolean true
network.http.version default string 1.1
Done

Figure 4-4: Speed up Firefox by using these settings.

4. **Double-click the highlighted line `network.http.pipelining`.**

   That changes the setting from False to True.

5. **Double-click the highlighted line `network.http.proxy.pipelining`.**

   That also changes the setting from False to True.

6. **Double-click the highlighted line `network.http.pipelining.maxrequests`. In the ensuing dialog box, type** 30 **and press Enter.**

   With the value set at 30, Firefox stops retrieving items on a page one at a time, and takes a shotgun approach, with up to 30 simultaneous requests.

7. **Right-click an empty place in the configuration settings and choose New⇨Integer. Create the new entry** nglayout.initialpaint.delay **and give it a value of** 0 **(that's the number zero).**

   That tells Firefox to wait zero seconds before retrieving whatever it needs to fill up a page.

8. **Click the X Close button to get out of Firefox.**

   The next time you start Firefox, it should load pages just a little bit faster.

Bookmarking with the Fox

Firefox handles bookmarks differently from Internet Explorer.

The easiest way to understand Firefox bookmarks? Start with the Unsorted Bookmarks folder.

If you hit a Web site that you want to bookmark, follow these steps:

1. **Click the Bookmark icon on the right edge of the Address bar. (Refer to Figure 4-2.)**

   This step bookmarks the page and puts the bookmark in a kind of All Other folder named Unsorted Bookmarks.

2. **If you'd rather stick your bookmark in a place where you can find it later or assign a tag to it, *double*-click the bookmark star on the right edge of the address bar.**

   Firefox opens its Edit This Bookmark dialog box, shown in Figure 4-5.

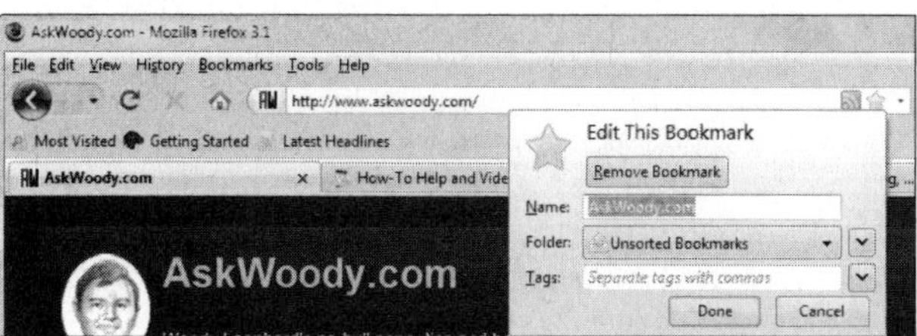

Figure 4-5: Pull your bookmark out of the Unsorted Bookmarks morass in this dialog box.

3. **Type any tags you want to associate with the bookmark in the Tags box, at the bottom.**

   Tags help you find things on the Address bar. For example, if you assign a Conficker tag to the bookmark, typing `conf` in the address bar brings up this particular bookmark.

4. **To organize your bookmarks into folders, or to place this bookmark on the Bookmark bar, click the down arrow to the right of the Folder box.**

   Firefox lets you choose the bookmark folder that should contain your new bookmark or create a new folder to hold the bookmark (see Figure 4-6).

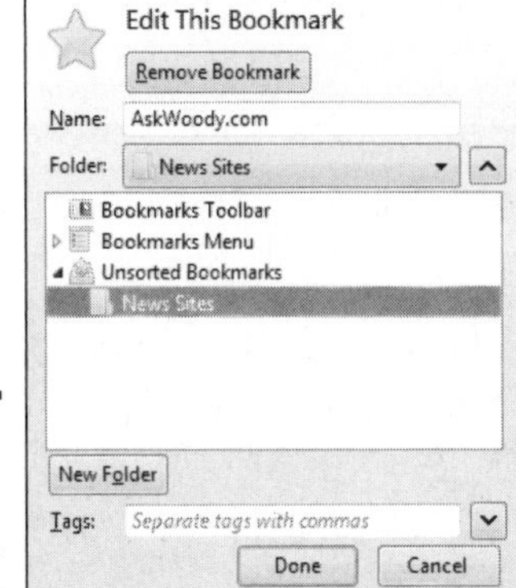

Figure 4-6: Add new folders here.

5. **If you create a new folder, you can leave it in the `Unsorted Bookmarks` folder, but if you want to make it more readily accessible from the Bookmarks menu, click and drag the new folder in the Edit This Bookmark dialog box so that the folder appears under the `Bookmarks Menu` folder.**
6. **If you want to put the new folder on the Bookmarks toolbar, to the right of the Latest Headlines button, click and drag it to the `Bookmarks Toolbar` folder (see Figure 4-7).**

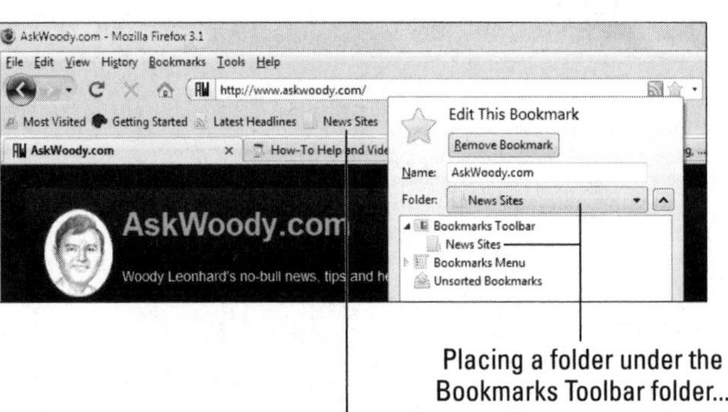

Figure 4-7: Put a button on the Bookmarks toolbar by dragging the folder under the `Bookmarks Toolbar` folder in the Edit This Bookmark dialog box.

After the folder has been created (and, optionally, located on the Bookmarks menu or the Bookmarks toolbar), you can place any bookmark in the folder by double-clicking the bookmark star.

You can rearrange the buttons on the Bookmarks toolbar by simply clicking and dragging.

Creating Smart Folders

Firefox *Smart Folders* work much like a saved search. You can save searches of your Bookmarks folders, or of your browsing history in Smart Folders, and they can be accessed from either the Bookmarks menu or the Bookmarks toolbar.

Here's how to set up a Smart Folder saved search:

1. **In Firefox, choose Bookmarks⇨Organize Bookmarks.**

   The Library appears, as shown in Figure 4-8.

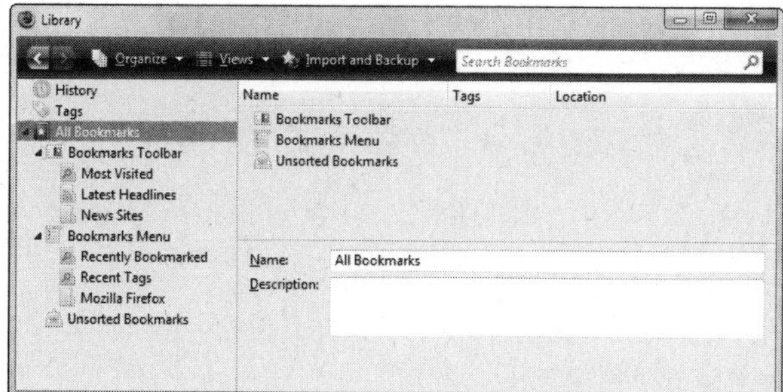

Figure 4-8: Organize your bookmarks, or add a Smart Folder, from this dialog box.

2. **On the left, choose which folders you want to search.**

   For example, you can search your browsing history by choosing the `History` folder, or you can search all bookmarks by choosing `All Bookmarks`. You can also narrow the scope of the saved search by clicking a lower-level folder, such as `News Sites`.

3. **In the upper-right corner, click in the Search box and type the items you want to locate.**

   In Figure 4-9, I search `All Bookmarks` for the term *windows.*

4. **Just below the Search box, click Save.**

   Firefox prompts you for a name for your saved search, er, Smart Folder.

5. **Type a name for your search and click OK.**

   Firefox creates a folder with the name you provided in Step 5 and puts the folder on the Bookmarks menu.

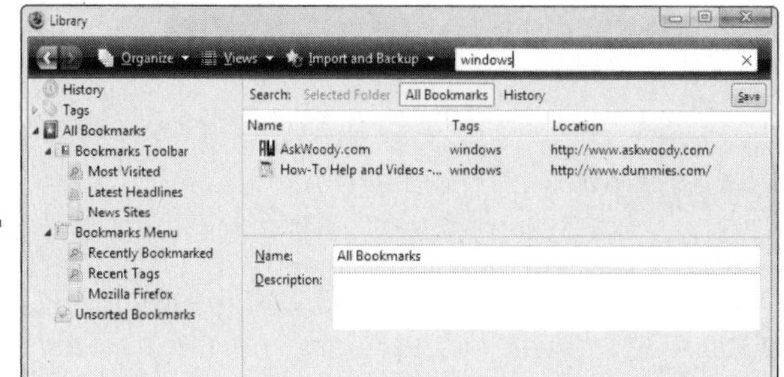

Figure 4-9: Set up your search.

6. **If you want to put the Smart Folder/saved search on the Bookmarks toolbar, click and drag the new folder under the `Bookmarks Toolbar` folder.**

   The new Smart Folder acts just like any other folder. If you open the folder on the Bookmarks menu, or click the button on the Bookmarks toolbar, Firefox runs the search and delivers the result.

Working with RSS Feeds — the Real Way

In Chapter 3 of this minibook, I talk about RSS feeds in Internet Explorer, but I had to bite my tongue, er, stifle my typing fingers. Though IE can handle RSS feeds all by itself, there's a much better way, using the Web site `igoogle.com`. Firefox makes it easy to add RSS feeds to your own, personalized `igoogle.com` page.

Here's how RSS, or *Really Simple Syndication,* works — really:

1. **A Web site (usually with "newsy" topics, but sometimes just a site that wants to get noticed) creates a specific kind of file, an *RSS feed.***
2. **When the Web site has, uh, new news, it adds a short new item to the beginning of the RSS feed file and drops the last item off the end.**

   Typically, the new item is just a few sentences long. That keeps the RSS feed short and simple and reasonably up to date.
3. **If you go to a Web site that maintains an RSS feed, Firefox can tell that it has an RSS feed, and a little orange box with "radio waves" appears to the right of the Web page's address.**

   You can see an example of the orange radio waves icon on the far right end of the address bar in Figure 4-2, at the beginning of this chapter.
4. **When you find a site with an RSS feed you want to follow, you *subscribe* to the feed.**

   It's kind of like subscribing to a newspaper or magazine.

5. **A program on your computer, an *RSS reader,* periodically looks at the RSS feeds for all Web pages on your subscription list, and keeps track of the latest items.**

Many different RSS readers are running around. If you like, you can use the RSS readers built into Internet Explorer, Firefox, or Chrome. Personally, I find all of them intrusive and hard to work with. My personal choice for an RSS reader is the iGoogle customized page from Google.

Here's how to set up a custom iGoogle page, with your own RSS reader:

1. **If you don't already have one, go to `gmail.com` and create a Gmail account.**

   Be creative. Your name is William Gates, right?

2. **In Firefox, go to `igoogle.com`.**

   You see a sign-up page like the one shown in Figure 4-10.

3. **Pick and choose the RSS feeds you want to see, and then click Save.**

   iGoogle shows you your initial iGoogle home page. After you have the page set up, you can add more RSS feed content by using the steps later in this section.

Figure 4-10: Get your own RSS reader going through iGoogle.

Feel free to use iGoogle as your browser's home page. I do.

With an iGoogle account set up, you have everything you need to keep on top of every site on earth. Here's how to start feeding your iGoogle page:

1. **In Firefox, navigate to the site that you want to add to your RSS reader.**

   You see the orange radio waves button to the right of the site's address.

2. **Click the radio waves button.**

   Firefox shows you the latest news items from the site and offers to set up a subscription to it, as shown in Figure 4-11.

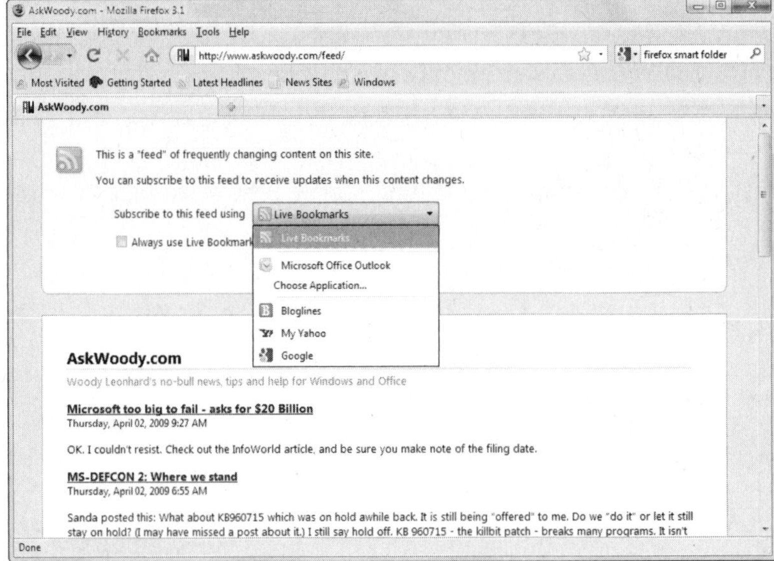

Figure 4-11: Choose Google to have the news from this site fed straight into your personal iGoogle page.

3. **Click the down arrow in the box marked Subscribe to This Feed Using, and choose Google. Then click the Subscribe Now button.**

   Google jumps in and asks whether you want to use your Google home page as the RSS reader (that's the iGoogle page you set up in the previous steps) or use Google Reader.

4. **Choose Add to Google Homepage.**

   If you're already signed in to Google, your personal iGoogle home page appears. (If you aren't already signed in, you have to type your username and password.) The RSS feed you choose appears in the upper-left corner of the page (see Figure 4-12).

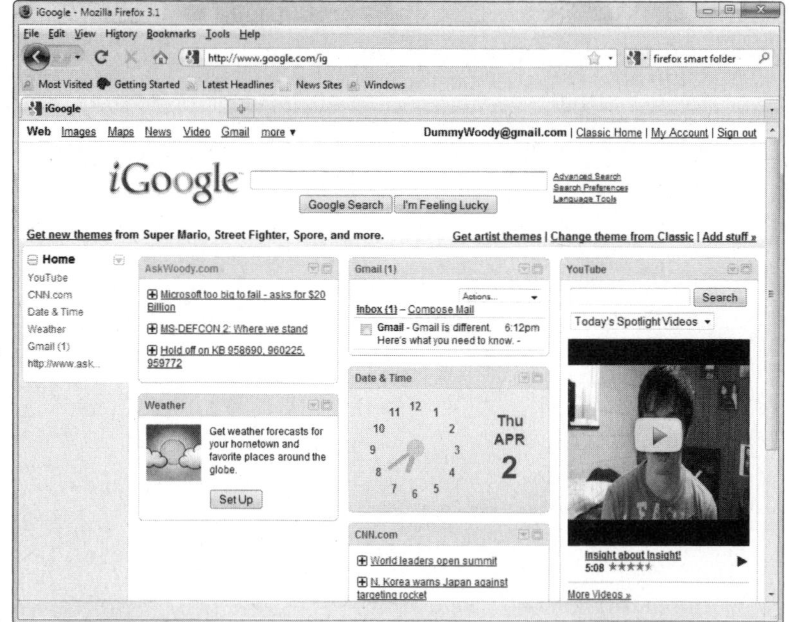

Figure 4-12: The RSS feed you chose appears in the upper-left corner of the page.

5. **You can click and drag the new RSS feed anywhere on the page.**

   Every few minutes, iGoogle reaches out to all sites on your iGoogle home page and retrieves the latest news from the sites' RSS feeds.

You can customize the Google home page till the cows come home. A series of tutorials is at `google.com/support/websearch/?ctx=web`.

If you don't want all of your RSS feeds served on your home page, try the Google Reader. With the Google Reader (`reader.google.com`), you have to click one additional time — typically on a Reader widget on your home page, or a Favorites or Bookmark icon — but the feeds contain more detail, and you have more control over the layout than with iGoogle.

Adding Firefox's Best Add-Ons

An enormous cottage industry has grown up around Firefox. The Firefox people made it relatively easy to extend the browser itself. As a result, tens of thousands of add-ons cover an enormous range of capabilities.

To search for add-ons, mosey over to `addons.mozilla.org/en-US/firefox` (see Figure 4-13). You can search for the add-ons recommended by Firefox itself or look for the most frequently downloaded add-ons.

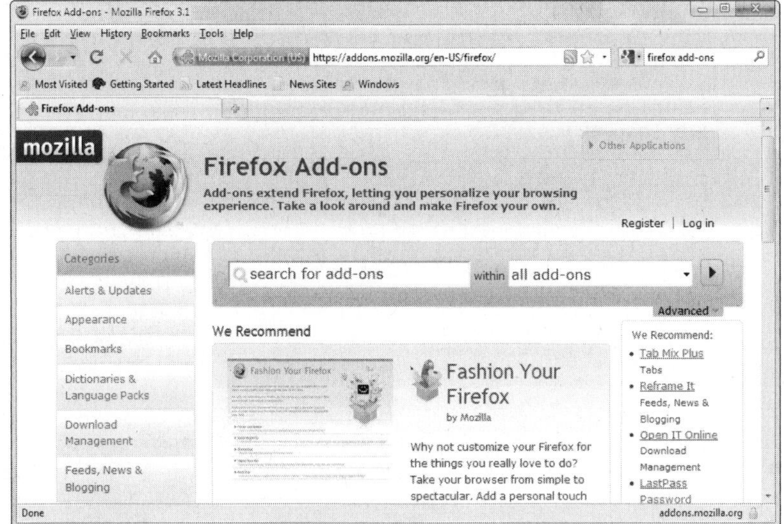

Figure 4-13: Firefox makes it easy to extend the browser with add-ons made by software developers all over the world.

Here are some of my favorites:

- ✦ **Adblock Plus** blocks ads. (What did you expect?) It doesn't work all the time — in the free version, you have to choose which ads you want to knock out — but it certainly speeds up download times. See a demo at `adblockplus.org/en`.
- ✦ **Greasemonkey** adds a customizable scripting language to Firefox. After you install Greasemonkey, you can download scripts from `userscript.org` that perform an enormous variety of tasks, from tweet assistance to downloading Flickr files.
- ✦ **Video Download Helper** makes it easy to download videos from the Web.
- ✦ **IETab** embeds Internet Explorer inside Firefox. If you hit a site that absolutely won't work with Firefox, right-click the link, choose Tools➪Open This Link in IETab, and Internet Explorer takes over a tab inside Firefox.
- ✦ **eBay Sidebar** watches your trades while you're doing something else.
- ✦ **DownThemAll** "scrapes" all downloadable files on a Web page and presents them to you so that you can choose which files you want to download. Click Start and they all come loading down.
- ✦ **NoScript** lets you shut down JavaScript programs, either individually or for a site as a whole. Many sites don't work with JavaScript turned off, but NoScript gives you a fighting chance to pick and choose the scripts you want.

- **Ghostery** keeps an eye on sites that are watching you. It tells you when sites contain "Web beacons" that can be used to track your surfing habits.
- **Linky** lets you open all links or images on a page, all at once, either on separate tabs or in separate windows. It's a helpful adjunct to Google image search.

To install the latest edition of any of these add-ons, go to `addons.mozilla.org/en-US/firefox` and search for the add-on's name.

Using Smart Keywords in Firefox

Imagine being able to type, oh, `news obama high tech` on the Firefox address bar and have the Google News site search for news with the words *obama high tech.* Imagine being able to type `tv star trek` and have TV.com search for *star trek.* Or, it might be `blogs conficker` and have Technorati search for *conficker.*

It's easy. Firefox calls them *Smart Keywords.* If you can find a Web site with a place to perform a search, you can create a Smart Keyword for that search.

Here's an example. I need to look up Google images all the time. It's a pain in the neck to go to `google.com` and click the Images link, or go to `images.google.com` and run a search for a specific image. Using Smart Keywords, I can tell Firefox to treat, oh, `im` as a Smart Keyword. That way, whenever I want to search Google images for, say, pictures of the ASUS Eee PC, I can type `im asus eee pc` and see all the hits in no time flat.

Here's how to set up the Smart Keyword:

1. **Go to a Web site that has a search box.**

   In Figure 4-14, I go to `images.google.com`.

2. **Right-click inside the search box and choose Add a Keyword for This Search.**

   Firefox shows you the New Bookmark dialog box, shown in Figure 4-15.

3. **In the Name box, type a name that reminds you of the purpose of the Smart Keyword. In the Keyword box, type the Smart Keyword you want to use. Click Save.**

   Your Smart Keyword takes effect immediately. Go ahead and try it.

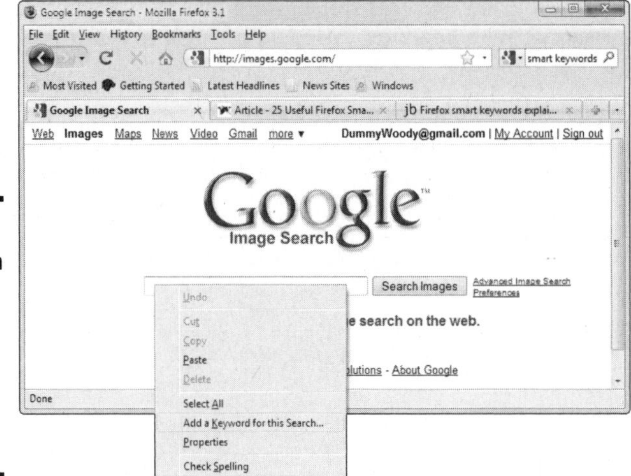

Figure 4-14: You can turn any search box, on any site, into a Firefox Smart Keyword.

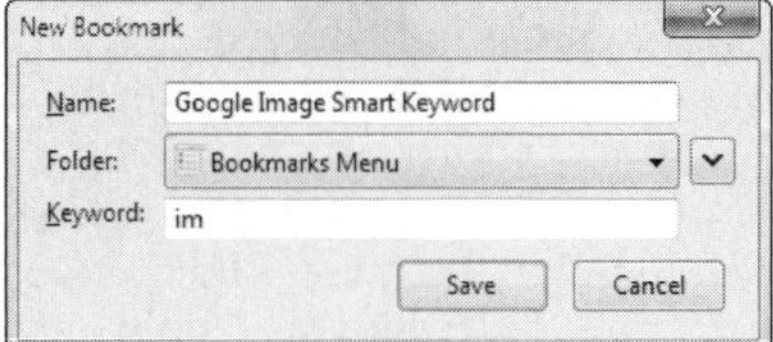

Figure 4-15: Smart Keywords are stored and handled just like bookmarks.

You can easily set up your own Smart Keywords by using this three-step process, but if you feel so inclined, you can import lists put together by other people. Take a look at `tucows.com/article/2094` for a collection of 25 Smart Keywords and instructions for importing them into Firefox.

Chapter 5: Searching on the Internet

In This Chapter

- Recognizing that Google ain't the only game in town — and neither is Microsoft Live Search or Bing
- Searching quickly and effectively
- Using Google pet tricks
- Posting on newsgroups with Google

Internet searching can be a lonely business. You're out there, on the Internet range, with nothing but gleaming banner ads and text links to guide you. What happens when you want to find information on a specific subject but you're not sure where to start? What if Google leads you on a wild goose chase? What if the Microsoft Bing "decision engine" takes the wrong turn?

Microsoft has been gunning for Google for years as though it's the only big search engine in town, but the fact remains that alternatives to Google abound. You don't need to develop a religious attachment to a single search engine. Look around and go with what works best for you.

We cover Google with near-religious fervor on `AskWoody.com`.

Even though everybody (outside of Redmond) says that Google is the best search engine, not everybody knows just how great Google is. Some of the engine's best parts are also its best-kept secrets. That's a shame, really, because folks who spend time searching the Web for information can save a lot of time and effort if they know how to use Google effectively. And, folks who don't spend time searching the Web for things should.

This chapter helps you get the most from Google, yes, but it also shows you many alternatives that can truly come in handy, whether you use Google or something else.

Understanding What a Search Engine Can Do for You

It ain't easy being the biggest, baddest search engine around. A decade or so ago, Google (then named BackRub) amounted to little more than a simple idea: If a lot of Web sites point to a particular Web page, the page being pointed to probably contains information that many people would find interesting.

Stanford grad students Larry Page and Sergey Brinn, the BackRub founders, scrimped together enough money to build a working prototype in a Stanford dorm room. By 1998, the (ahem!) PageRank system, which tries to assign a number that predicts the relevance of a page to a specific query, was generating a lot of interest on campus: Students could find the stuff they wanted without having to slog through endless lists of categories. In September 1998, Page and Brinn adopted the name Google and opened a real office with a cool $1 million in initial capital. Truth be told, the "office" was in a garage, which came with a washing machine, dryer, and hot tub. They blew all the money on computers — my kind of people.

Google has gone from one of the most admired companies on the Web to one of the most criticized — on topics ranging from copyright infringement to pornography to privacy and censorship — and the PageRank system has been demonized in terms rarely heard since the Spanish Inquisition. Few people now believe that PageRank objectively rates the "importance" of a Web page — millions of dollars and thousands of months have been spent trying to jigger the results. Like it or not, Google just works. The Google *spiders* (the programs that search for information), which crawl all over the Web, night and day, looking for pages, have indexed billions of pages, feeding hundreds of millions of searches a day. Other search engines have spiders, too, but Google's outspider them all.

As this book went to press, Google was worth about $140 billion, the verb *to google* had been embraced by prestigious dictionaries, the company was taking on Microsoft *mano a mano* in many different areas, and many other search engines offered decent alternatives to the once almighty Google.

In this section, I show you several kinds of searches you can perform with Google (and the other search engines). No matter what you're looking for, a search engine can find it!

Searching for text

One of the main reasons you use a search engine is to find textual information. For example, you might want to find out what the longest river in Asia is. You go to a search engine such as Google (`www.google.com`) and type **longest river in Asia** in the search field. Figure 5-1 shows the results of the Google search for *longest river in Asia.*

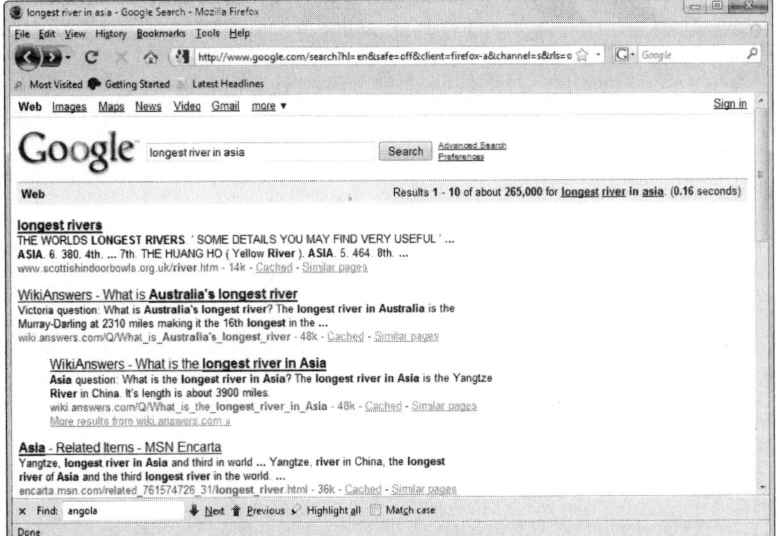

Figure 5-1: Google's search for the longest river in Asia.

The number-one result points to the Scottish Indoor Bowls Web site — surely a definitive source of information about rivers — which, indeed, delivers the correct answer: The longest river is the Yangtze (known locally as the Chang Jiang), at 6,380 kilometers, or 3,960 miles, long. The second Google response to the search phrase *longest river in asia* is an Answers.com entry for the longest river in Australia. Erp. The third result leads to the Microsoft MSN Encarta site, which has a thorough and accurate write-up.

If you don't find what you're looking for at Google, try one of these alternatives:

- **Dogpile** (`www.dogpile.com`) automatically combines the search results of Google, Yahoo! Search, Windows Live Search (formerly MSN Search), and Ask.com (formerly Ask Jeeves), with a proprietary ranking formula that frequently gives excellent results. As shown in Figure 5-2, the first two Dogpile results for *longest river in Asia* match Google's exactly, right down to the idiosyncratic choice of an indoor lawn bowling league as the preeminent authority on river lengths. The third result points to a kids' social studies page, but the fourth gets near the heart of the matter, with a link to the Wikipedia list of rivers by length.
- **Windows Live Search** (`search.live.com`) from Microsoft — which was merging with Microsoft Bing (`bing.com`) as this book went to press — covers much of the same ground as Google, although I find some of its proclivities irritating. For example, in Figure 5-3, you see how Live Search pulls the correct answer (with no details) from the Encarta Encyclopedia, but the next result links to the kids' social studies page, and the third link opens a list of books at Amazon.com — which isn't close to what I want. No doubt Microsoft has some sort of deal with Amazon.

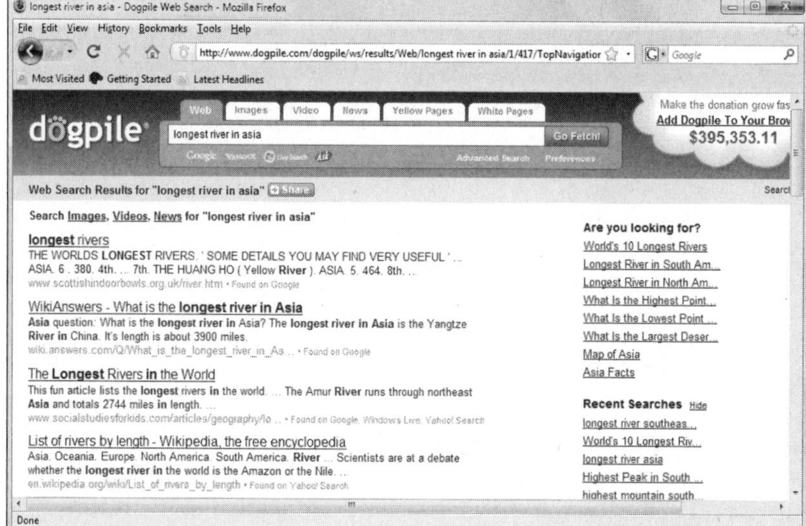

Figure 5-2: Dogpile's search results match Google's closely.

Bing carries on Microsoft's long-standing tradition for plastering Web pages with advertising. The "cashback" offers on Bing don't add up to much of a bargain — featured items cost 20% more than they do elsewhere, and Microsoft offers you a 5% rebate, delivered two months after you order. What's with that?

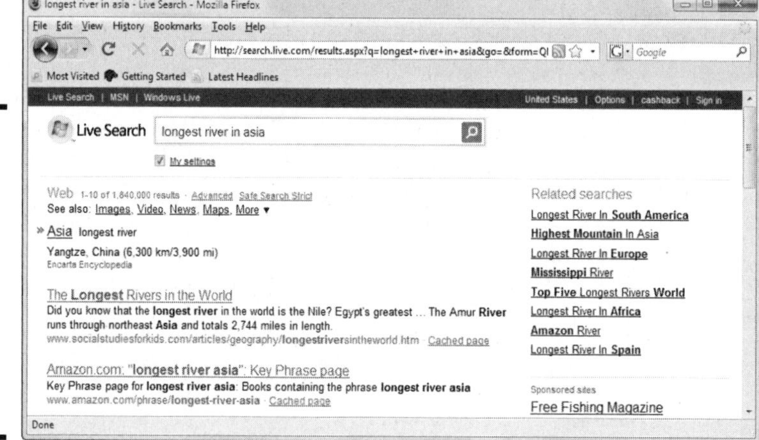

Figure 5-3: Microsoft Live Search nails the answer but doesn't give any useful links to more information.

✦ **Yahoo! Search** (`search.yahoo.com`) has an interesting and different history. Years ago, Yahoo! drew much acclaim for its directory — kind of an Internet Yellow Pages. In 2002, Yahoo! bought Inktomi, which had one of the best search engines at the time, and in 2003 it acquired AltaVista. The Yahoo! search site used the Google search engine until 2004, when it switched to a new engine based on the offerings from the acquired companies. As a result, Yahoo! frequently comes up with results that are significantly different from Google's — which may be good or bad, as you can see in Figure 5-4.

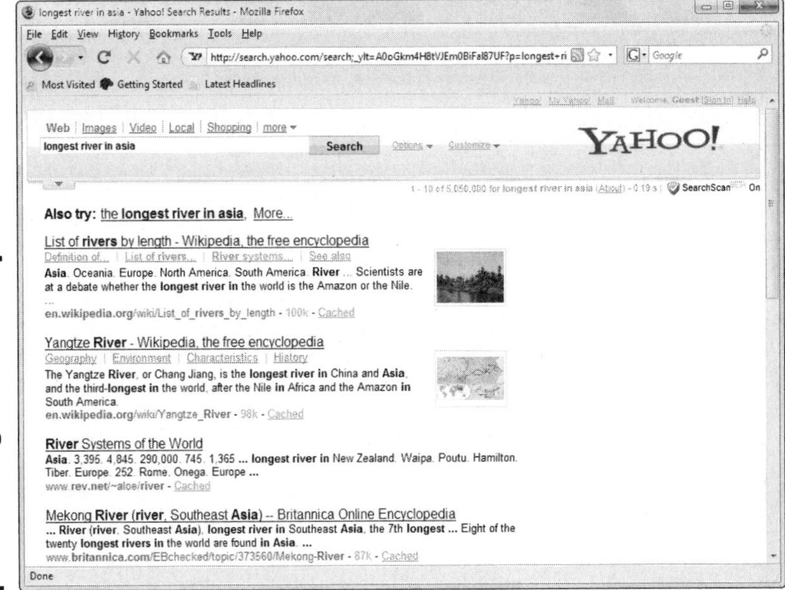

Figure 5-4: Yahoo! results range from excellent (the first two results) to desultory (the last two).

The number-one result from Yahoo! comes up with the list of rivers in Wikipedia, which matches the fourth entry in Dogpile. The second result hits paydirt: Yahoo! points to the Wikipedia entry for the Yangtze River, certainly one of the best sources of information about the Yangtze. The third result points to an individual's site, and the fourth doesn't pertain.

✦ **Ask** (`ask.com`), formerly Ask Jeeves, developed a small following because of its ability to work with natural-language questions. My search for the longest river in Asia (see Figure 5-5) yielded the best results of any of the engines I tested.

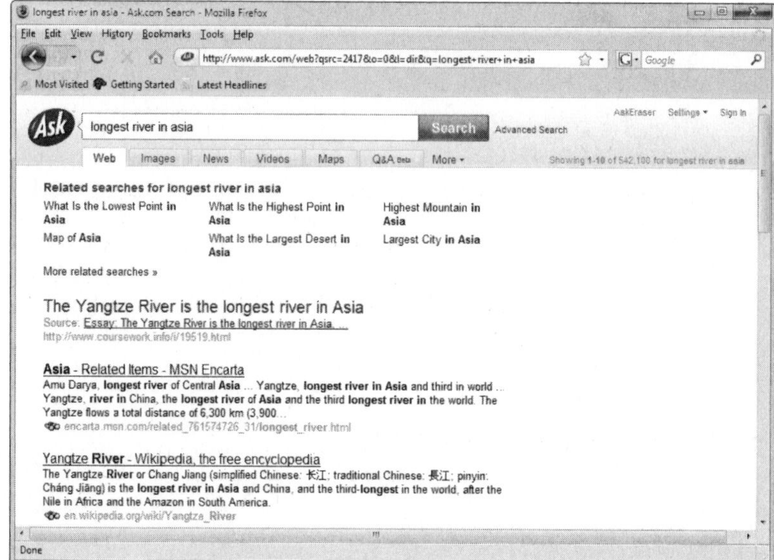

Figure 5-5: Perhaps surprisingly, Ask gave the most accurate results, with the correct answer appearing as number one.

So, which search engine is best? That's easy. None of them. If you don't find what you want in a few minutes, switch search engines. At the very least, you get a different perspective — and you might just find the answer you need.

I've gone back to using Google for almost all my searches. If I hit a snag, I'll try Dogpile. Microsoft's Bing doesn't seem to offer anything better than Google, although it's packed with advertising and abounds with offers for overpriced goods. And, I would have to be downright desperate to use Microsoft Live Search for images (see the next section).

Searching for images

If you search for images — photos, video clips, drawings — the capabilities of the various engines may surprise you. At least, they surprise me. For example, if I run the *longest river in Asia* search through the Google image engine (`images.google.com`), *all* the top search hits match my criteria (see Figure 5-6). That's quite remarkable.

The Windows Live Search image search (`images.live.com`) presents results in a unique, and very usable, way. Unfortunately, as you can see in Figure 5-7, the results have precious little in common with the search terms. The first item returned points to an eight-year-old CNN article about the Three Gorges Dam construction project, which was completed two years ago. The second result talks about a river in Malaysia, and the next dozen or more entries are all travel advertisements, some (but not all) of which actually talk about the Yangtze River.

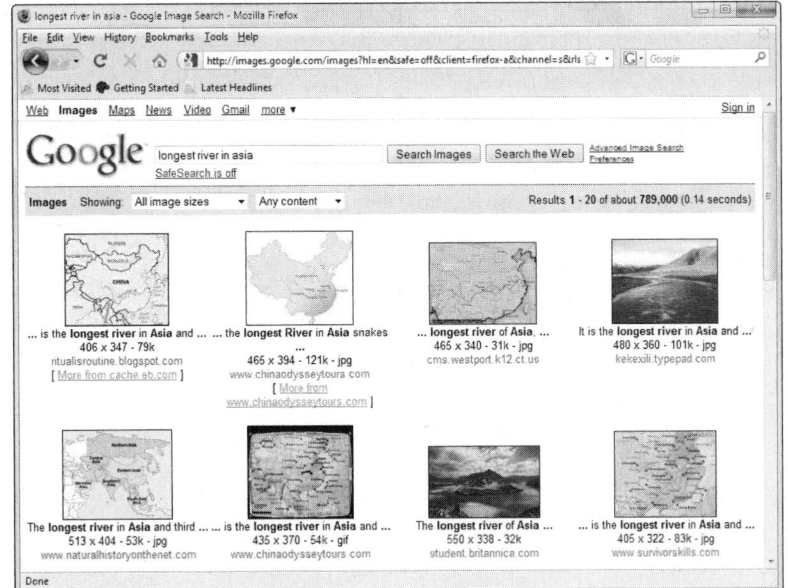

Figure 5-6: The Google image search engine scores a perfect 10 — far better than the text search engine.

Bing image search returns precisely the same results as Windows Live image search. Useless.

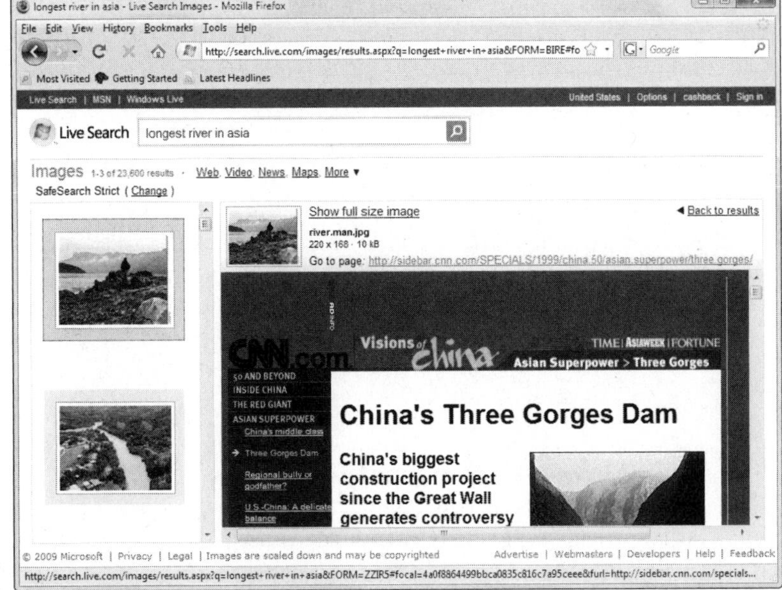

Figure 5-7: Microsoft Live image search comes up with a bunch of duds.

The Dogpile image results show a travel brochure, an elementary school site, and a river in South America. Blech. Yahoo!'s image search relies heavily on Flickr, which contains a substantial amount of unverified information. Ask's image search suffers from the same timeliness problems as Windows Live Search.

Searching for everything else: Blogs, news, and more

Other search engines, which rely more on audience participation than on automated scanning and gathering, are worth mentioning. Check out these examples:

- **Technorati** (`technorati.com`) specializes in indexing blog entries. It includes a kind of audience-participation engine that makes it easy to find the most popular blog entries: You're invited to vote for blog postings that ring your chimes. The emphasis is on technical topics.
- **Digg** (`digg.com`), like Technorati, relies on user votes to bring news stories and specific postings to your attention. Unlike Technorati, Digg doesn't scan or index entries — instead, it relies on submissions from the world at large. The Digg emphasis is on news, broadly defined, in the areas of technology, science, world, business, videos, entertainment, and games.
- **del.icio.us** (`del.icio.us`) makes it easy for you to bookmark sites and then leaf through other folks' bookmarks, with popularity rankings and affinity scores.

Finding What You're Looking For

Google has turned into the 800-pound gorilla of the searching world. I know people who can't even find AOL unless they go through Google. True fact.

The more you know about Google, the better it can serve you. Getting to know Google inside and out has the potential to save you more time than just about anything in Windows proper. If you can learn to search for answers quickly and thoroughly — and cut through the garbage on the Web just as quickly and thoroughly — you can't help but save time in everything you do.

Using the other Google engines

Google searches for much more than text. If you run a standard Google search using the search box, with the results shown earlier (refer to Figure 5-1), you're presented with a number of options above the Google search box:

✦ **Images:** I think Google has the best image search engine around. I talk about the image search engine in the "Searching for images" section, earlier in this chapter.

✦ **Maps:** Google Maps continues to amaze me. The direct connection here on the Google main page makes it quite easy to type search terms — no physical address necessary — and zero in on a location, anywhere in the world (see Figure 5-8).

Figure 5-8: Type any search criteria you like — it doesn't need to be an address — and Google Maps helps you find your destination.

✦ **News:** Google News aggregates news reports from 4,500 English language newspapers, wire agencies, and the like, all over the world. It's completely automated: no human intervention required. That's good and bad. It's good because you get to see a cross-section of how the news is being reported in many different places. It's bad because the automatic distiller ain't perfect.

I like searching Google News because it doesn't try to "spin" a topic, and the biases that show through tend to be biases shared by English-speaking people worldwide. You can sign up for Google News alerts via e-mail or SMS, and there's an RSS feed, so you don't need to search for the news — it can find you. (See the discussion of iGoogle and RSS feeds in Book V, Chapter 4.)

✦ **Video:** Google has pioneered the indexing and lookup of video clips, from sites all over the Web — YouTube, Picasa, AOL, MTV, NBC, Dailymotion, MySpace, and many more.

✦ **More/Groups:** Google owns newsgroups. If you're looking for Internet newsgroups — the largely unmonitored postings of millions of Internet users, on every topic under the sun — use the search box and then click More➪Groups. Google literally owns the newsgroup archives, to a first approximation, anyway. Google newsgroup tools and interface run rings around anything Microsoft can deliver. See the "Posting on Newsgroups" section, later in this chapter.

To keep on top of the latest specialized Google search engines, go to `google.com` and click first the More link and then Even More.

Searching wisely

You can save yourself a lot of time and frustration if you plot out your search before your fingers hit the keyboard.

Obviously, you should choose your search terms precisely. Pick words that will appear on any page that matches what you're looking for: Don't use `Compaq` when you want `Compaq S710`. That's true of any search engine.

Beyond the obvious, the Google search engine has certain peculiarities you can exploit. These peculiarities hold true whether you're using Google in your browser's search bar or you venture directly to `google.com`:

✦ **Capitalization doesn't matter.** Search for `diving phuket` or `diving Phuket` — either search returns the same results.

✦ **The first words you use have more weight than the latter words.** If you look for `phuket diving`, you see a different list than the one for `diving phuket`. The former list emphasizes Web sites about Phuket that include a mention of diving; the latter includes diving pages that mention Phuket.

✦ **Google shows you only those pages that include all the search terms.** The simplest way to narrow a search that returns too many results is to add more specific words to the end of your search term. For example, if `phuket diving` returns too many pages, try `phuket diving beginners`. In programmer's parlance, the terms are *anded* together.

✦ **If you type more than ten words, Google ignores the ones after the tenth.**

✦ **Google ignores a surprisingly large number of short words (such as *who, how, where, to,* and *is*) as well as single-digit numbers.** The results page tells you whether it ignored certain words. In Figure 5-1, at the beginning of this chapter, the underlines under the terms in the upper-right corner tell you that the terms *longest, river,* and *asia* were used in the search but *in* was not.

- **You can use OR to tell Google that you want the search to include two or more terms — but you have to capitalize OR.** For example, `phuket OR samui OR similans diving` returns diving pages that focus on Phuket, Samui, or the Similans.
- **If you want to limit the search to a specific phrase, use quotes.** For example, `diving phuket "day trip"` is more limiting than `diving phuket day trip` because in the former, the precise phrase *day trip* has to appear on the page.
- **Exclude pages from the results by putting a hyphen in front of the words you don't want.** For example, if you want to find pages about diving in Phuket but you don't want to associate with lowly snorkelers, try `diving phuket -snorkeling`.

  You can combine search tricks. If you're looking for overnight diving, try `diving phuket -"day trip"` to find the best results.
- **Google supports wildcard searches in quite a limited way: The asterisk (*) stands for a single word.** If you're accustomed to searches in, say, Word or Windows, the * generally indicates a sequence of characters, but in Google only stands for an entire word. You might search for `div*` and expect to find both *diver* and *diving* but Google won't match on either. Conversely, if you search for, oh, `email * * wellsfargo.com`, you find a lot of e-mail addresses. (The second * matches the at-sign (@) in an address. Try it.)

If you use Google to search for answers to computer questions, take advantage of any precise numbers or messages you can find. For example, googling `computer won't start` doesn't get you anywhere; but `two beeps on startup` may. If you're trying to track down a Windows error message, use Google to look for the *precise* message. Write it down, if you have to.

Using Advanced Search

Didn't find the results you need? Click the link to the right of the Google Search button to bring up the Advanced Search page.

If you need to narrow your searches — in other words, if you want Google to do the sifting rather than do it yourself — you should get acquainted with Google's Advanced Search capabilities. Here's a whirlwind tour:

1. **Run your search and, if it doesn't have what you want, click the Advanced Search link.**

   Google brings up its Advanced Search page (see Figure 5-9).

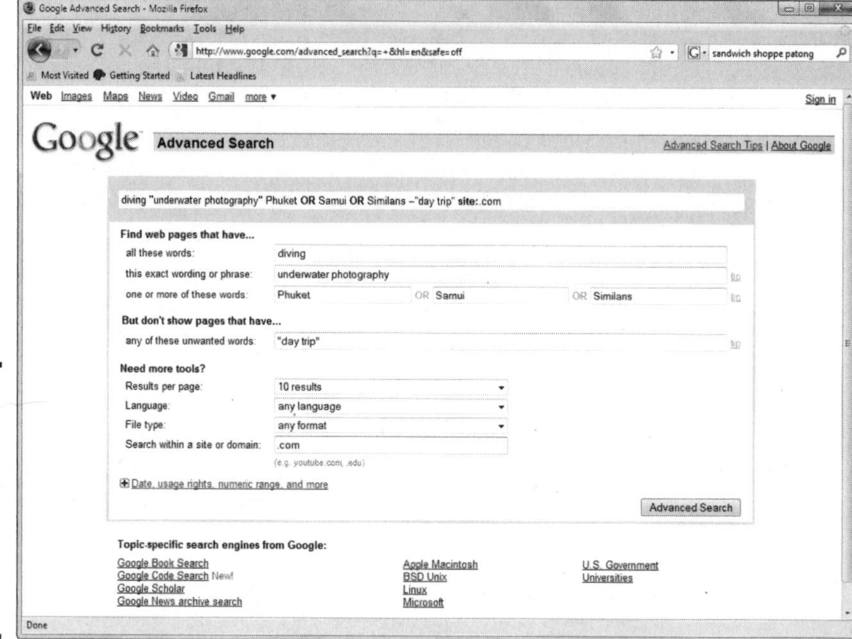

Figure 5-9: Advanced Search lets you narrow your Google search quickly and easily.

2. **Fill in the top part of the page with your search terms.**

   In Figure 5-9, I ask for sites that include the word *diving* and the exact phrase *underwater photography.* I also want to exclude the phrase *day trip* and return only pages pertaining to Phuket, Samui, or the Similans.

   Anything you can do in the top part of this page can also be done by using the shorthand tricks mentioned in the preceding section. If you find yourself using the top part of the page frequently, save yourself some time and brush up on the tricks (such as OR, -, "") that I mention in the earlier section "Searching wisely."

3. **In the bottom part of the Advanced Search Page, further refine your search by matching on**

   - The identified source language of the page (not always accurate)

   - A specific filename extension (such as `.pdf` or `.doc`)

     This setting is generally used for finding downloadable files — not Web pages.

   - The domain name, such as `dummies.com`

   You can also click the link at the bottom to limit the search to pages stamped with specific dates (notoriously unreliable), pages with specific licensing allowances (not widely implemented), and ranges of numbers.

4. **Press Enter.**

   The results of your advanced search appear in a standard Google search results window (see Figure 5-10).

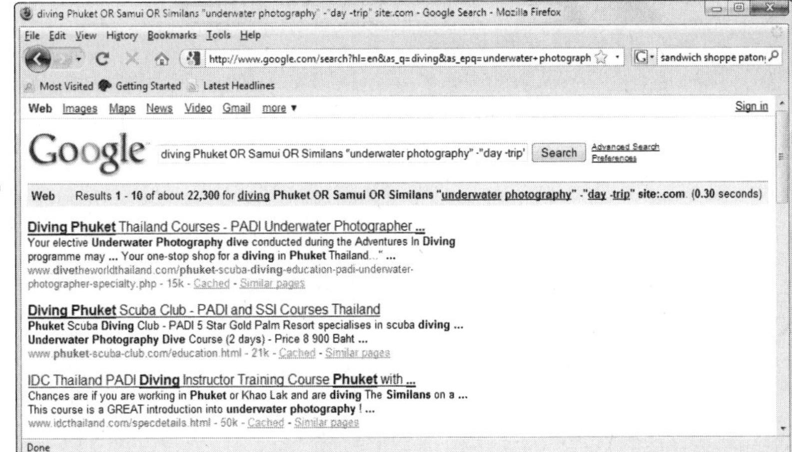

Figure 5-10: Running the stringent search specified in Figure 5-9 turns up 22,300 hits.

You can find more details about Google Advanced Search on the Google Advanced Search page, `google.com/help/refinesearch.html`.

Pulling out Google parlor tricks

Google has many tricks up its sleeve, some of which you may find useful — even if it's just to win a bet at a party. For example:

- **To find the status of your UPS, FedEx, or USPS delivery, just type the package number (digits only) in the Google search box.**
- **The search box is a stock ticker.** Type a symbol such as **MSFT** or **SCBSET**.
- **To use Google as a calculator, just type the equation in the Google search box.** For example, to find the answer to 1,234 × 5,678, type **1234*5678** in the search box. Or, to find the answer to 3 ÷ π, type **`3/pi`**. No, Google doesn't solve partial differentials or simultaneous equations — yet.
- **Google has a built-in units converter.** The word *in* triggers the converter. Try **10 meters in feet** or **350 degrees F in centigrade** (or **350 f in c**) or **20 dollars in baht** or (believe me, this is impressive) **.89 euros per liter in dollars per gallon**. You can also use *to*, as in **90 f to c**.
- **To find a list of alternative (and frequently interesting) definitions for a word, type** define, **as in** define booty.

- **You can see movie reviews and local show times by typing** movie **and then the name of the movie, such as** movie lincoln.
- **Try quick questions for quick facts. For example, try** height of mt everest **or** length of mississippi river **or** currency in singapore.

Posting on Newsgroups

One of the most important (but largely unknown and underutilized) Google gems is the ongoing archive of Usenet newsgroup postings. For many, many years, the Usenet newsgroups on the Internet served as a vital person-to-person link, with hundreds of millions of absolutely uncensored messages on every conceivable topic.

You may know newsgroups for their extensive collections of pictures, movies, songs, and other types of media. You may not know that the original reason for the newsgroups — providing a way for people to communicate with each other, about a bewildering number of topics — is still alive and well.

Google, being Google, has indexed the messages, built a credible viewer that shows you who replied to which message and when, and even assembled quite a serviceable front end so that you can post your own messages in the groups.

When you perform a standard Google search, frequently you find the results of a Google Groups search at the bottom of the search results page. Feel free to click the offered links and see what other people are saying!

To search for a message in the massive Google newsgroups archive, follow these steps:

1. **Start your favorite browser and go to `groups.google.com`.**

   Google shows you the Google Groups search page (see Figure 5-11).

2. **Type your search terms in the box and press Enter.**

   Google returns a list of all messages that meet your criteria. In Figure 5-12, I search for newsgroup messages that deal with Microsoft Knowledge Base (KB) article 960715.

   The results are normally presented to you in order of Google's calculated relevance. You may find it more enlightening to click the Sort By Date line at the top of the results list.

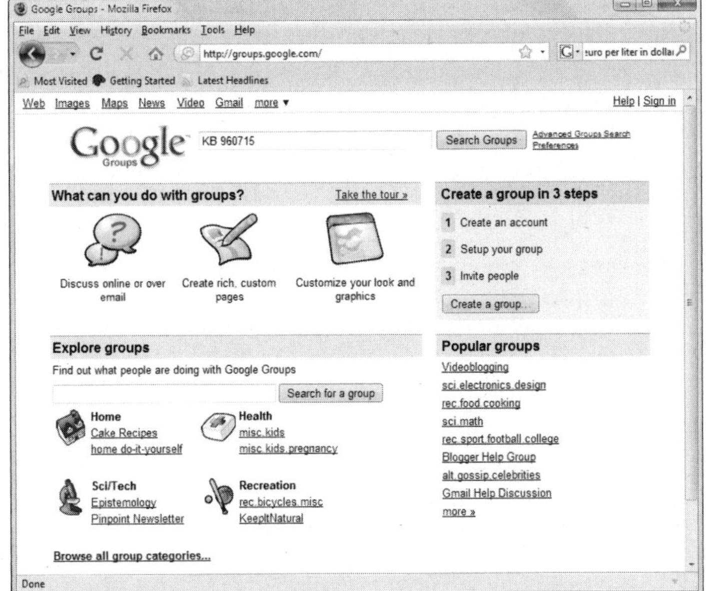

Figure 5-11: Search about a billion posted messages in the Mother of All Message Databases.

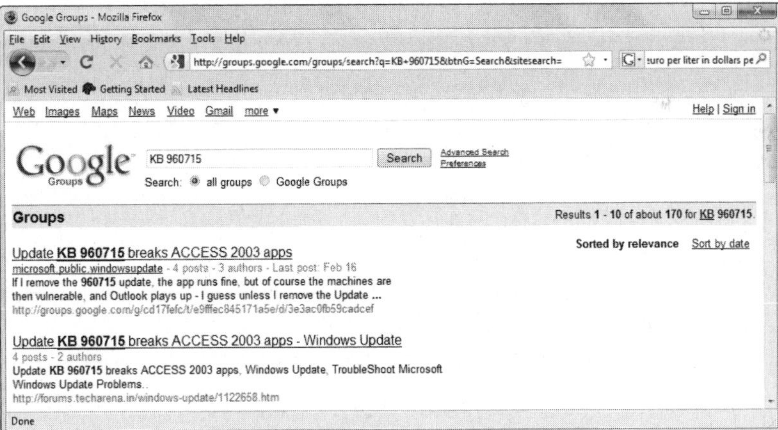

Figure 5-12: Messages posted on the newsgroups have bad things to say about the Microsoft security patch known as KB 960715.

3. **You almost always want to see the entire *thread* (the message itself, with all the messages that came before it and after it), so click the underlined link at the top of a message that interests you.**

   Google shows you the thread, as shown in Figure 5-13.

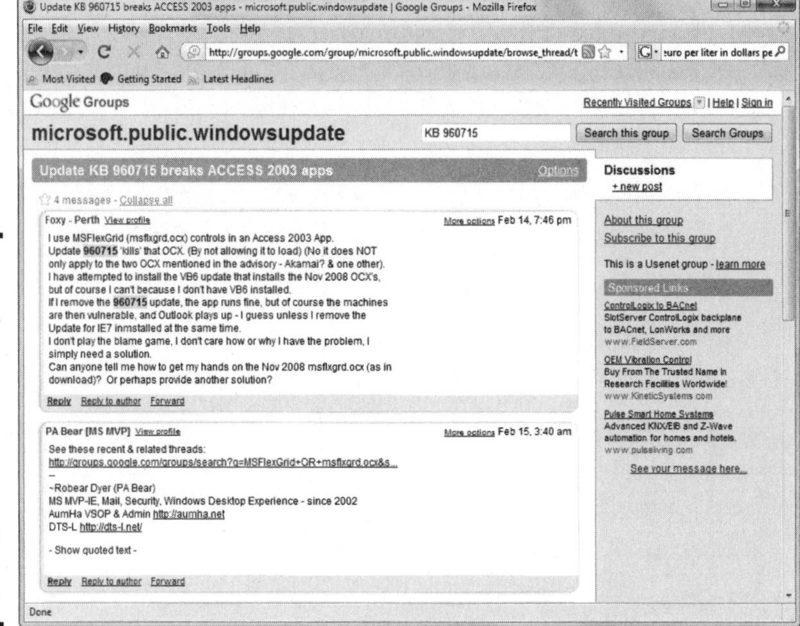

Figure 5-13: Google Groups shows you the message thread so that you can keep track of what was said and who replied.

4. **To reply to a message, locate and click a Reply link.**

   Generally, you can post on threads that are no more than 60 days old. You may need to sign up for a Google account, which takes only a few seconds. As soon as you're signed up, you see a Posting form.

5. **Type your message in the space provided and click Post.**

   Your message appears on the group in short order.

That's how hard it is to talk to anyone, on any subject, anywhere in the world.

Chapter 6: Sending Windows Mail Live

In This Chapter

- **Choosing the right e-mail program**
- **Whatever happened to [fill in the blank] mail?**
- **Using Windows 7's Live Mail Essential**
- **Putting together decent e-mail messages with a minimum of hassle**
- **Keeping on top of your contacts**

Q: What happened to Outlook Express?

A: Oh, it went away a long time ago. Outlook Express was the free e-mail program that shipped in Windows XP and almost all its predecessors. It's kaput. Bygones.

Q: What happened to Windows Mail?

A: It disappeared, too. Windows Mail was a barely warmed-over minor upgrade to Outlook Express. Microsoft shipped Windows Mail as the free e-mail program in Windows Vista. But Microsoft forgot about Windows Mail shortly after it shipped. Orphaned. Abandoned at birth.

Q: So what do we do for mail in Windows now?

A: Microsoft now actively encourages all Windows users — even those with Windows XP — to download and install Windows Live Mail, the latest and greatest incarnation of the Outlook Ex — er, Windows Mail line. Either that or you can buy Outlook, which is part of Microsoft Office.

Microsoft dropped all significant support for Outlook Express and Windows Mail years ago. Why? Because they don't make Microsoft any money. As "free" e-mail programs inside Windows, Microsoft couldn't charge for them, couldn't stick advertising in them, couldn't make a sou. Now, with the new, improved Windows Live Mail — which doesn't ship inside any version of Windows — Microsoft feels free to "monetize" its e-mail program. (I love the word *monetize* — it means that Microsoft can do just about anything it wants to turn a buck from the software, over and above what you paid for Windows 7.)

Q: Hey, I'm confused. What about Hotmail? I thought that was from Microsoft, too. How many different mail programs does Microsoft make? Which one should I be using?

A: Therein lies a tale. Told by a dummy, full of sound and fury. . . .

This chapter takes you through the choices you have in e-mail programs and, if you so decide, steps you through setting up Windows Live Mail, one of the vaunted Windows 7 Live Essentials.

Counting the Microsoft E-Mail Programs

Microsoft now has five — count 'em, five — *different* e-mail programs, with countless versions of each one: Hotmail, Outlook, Outlook Express, Windows Live Mail, and Windows Mail. None of those programs bears even a slight semblance to the others. And when you go on, beyond Microsoft, a great big world of e-mail awaits.

Two of these mail programs are obsolete: Windows Mail is a free program that shipped with Vista, and Outlook Express is the nearly-identical free program that shipped with Windows XP and earlier versions. If you know anyone who has technical problems with either or both of these programs, gently suggest to her that she's beating a long-dead horse and that she should consult the "Choosing an E-Mail Program" section for some good alternatives.

I cover the still-viable Microsoft e-mail programs in the following sections.

Outlook

Outlook, the e-mail program in Microsoft Office (see Figure 6-1), stands out as the granddaddy of e-mail programs. It's enormous. It's convoluted. It's expensive. Its pieces don't hang together well. It doesn't travel well unless you have a corporate Virtual Private Network (VPN) or Office Web Access (OWA), the latter of which truly should be counted as another Microsoft mail program. Most of the corporate world, and many normal folks (including yours truly), depend on it every day. Hundreds of versions of Outlook are used by tens of millions of people every day.

To further add to the confusion: Outlook was part of Office 2003 Student & Teacher Edition, the low-cost version of Office that sold like hotcakes. But the new, improved Office 2007 Home & Student Edition doesn't have Outlook. It's the price of progress, I guess.

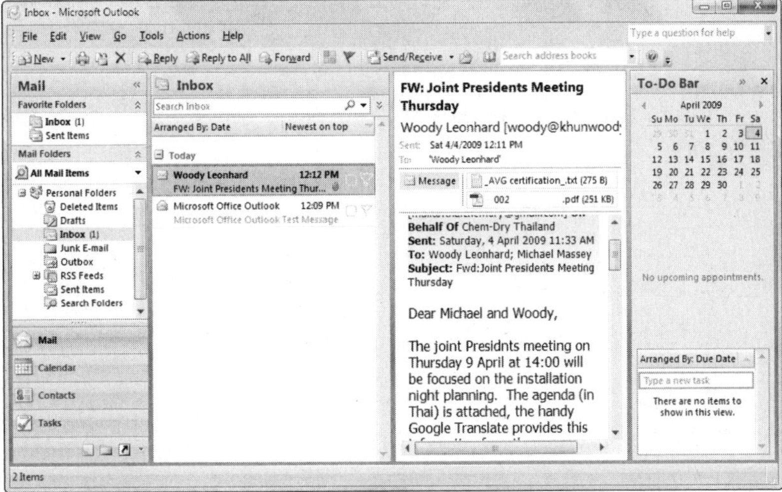

Figure 6-1: Outlook, the program inside Microsoft Office, includes an e-mail component, a calendar, a to-do list, contacts, and much more.

Hotmail

Hotmail is the online Microsoft e-mail service (see Figure 6-2). This week, the politically correct name for the product is Windows Live Hotmail — that could change next week — but everybody knows it as Hotmail. Hotmail once owned the online e-mail market. Every few months, Microsoft comes out with a facelift or a name change, each time promising that the new, improved Hotmail — er, Windows Live Hotmail — works "just like Outlook!"

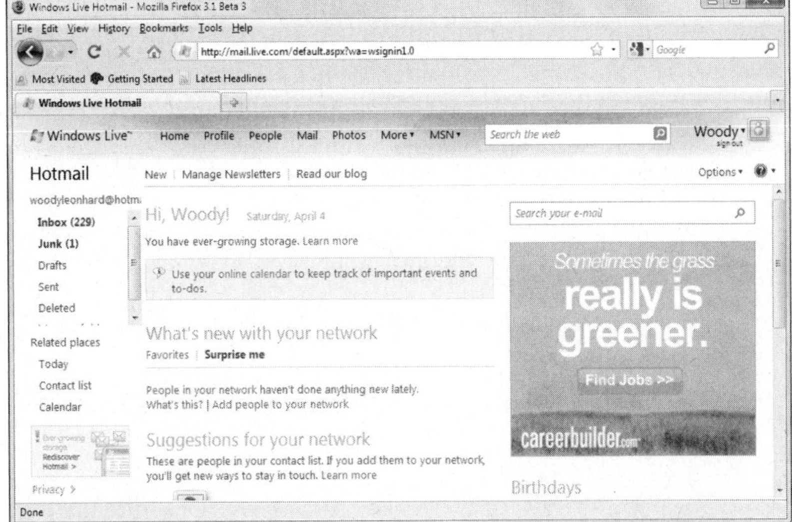

Figure 6-2: Windows Live Hotmail offers e-mail, an online calendar, and so-o-o many wonderful ways to spend money.

A brief history of Hotmail

Hotmail blazed new ground as the first free Web-based e-mail service when Sabeer Bhatia (a native of Bangalore and a graduate of both Caltech and Stanford) spent $300,000 to launch it in 1996. On December 31, 1997, Microsoft bought Hotmail for $400 million, and the service has never been the same. Microsoft struggled with Hotmail for many years, adding new users like flies, but always suffering from severe performance problems and crashes heard round the world. Ultimately, Hotmail was shuffled under the Microsoft Network (MSN) wing of the corporate umbrella, its free services were clipped, and its user interface was subjected to more facelifts than Dick Clark, which is saying something.

As MSN lost its luster and competitors such as Gmail and Yahoo! Mail battered at the, uh, Gates, the Hotmail subscription-based income model died almost overnight and the company's market share fell precipitously. Why pay for 20 MB of Hotmail message storage when Google gave away 1 GB for free? Hotmail became the number-one candidate for a "Live" makeover and the poster child for Microsoft's entire Live effort. It remains to be seen whether Hotmail, er, Windows Live Hotmail can survive another decade.

In fact, Hotmail doesn't work anything at all like Outlook. It can't. Hotmail stores all your messages on the giant Microsoft servers — none of it ever comes down to your desktop, unless you use a separate program to reach into Hotmail and pull mail down to your computer.

Windows Live Mail

Windows Live Mail, the primary topic of this chapter, is one of the Windows Live Essentials (which I talk about in Book I, Chapter 5). Windows Live Mail pulls mail down and stores it on your computer. Windows Live Mail gobbles up mail sent to your e-mail address, whatever your address may be, using traditional Internet e-mail computers *(POP3 servers).* It can also grab mail from Hotmail, Google's Gmail, Yahoo! Mail, and many other online mail services.

Choosing an E-Mail Program

You have three good reasons to use Windows Live Mail: inertia, inertia, and inertia. All the other reasons aren't convincing. If you're stuck with Windows Live Mail because you have a big collection of old Outlook Express (OE) or

Windows Mail (WM) messages, you have my sympathies. If you want to stick with Windows Live Mail because it looks and acts like OE or WM, at least at first glance, I s'pose that's a reasonable fear, er, justification.

But if you're willing to look beyond Windows Live Mail and Outlook Express and Windows Mail, you have all sorts of good options:

When you choose your own e-mail program, keep these points in mind:

- **If you don't want to carry your mail with you, use one of the many Web-based e-mail services.** Internet access is cheap, easy, and generally reliable all over the world. Recently, Google's Gmail (`mail.google.com`, see Figure 6-3), and Yahoo! Mail (`mail.yahoo.com`) have garnered the best reviews. Hotmail (er, Windows Live Hotmail, `hotmail.com`, or `mail.live.com`) and, perhaps surprisingly, AOL Mail (`discover.aol.com`) cover all the bases. It seems like the feature set and promotions change every week, so check each Web site to see what's best for you.

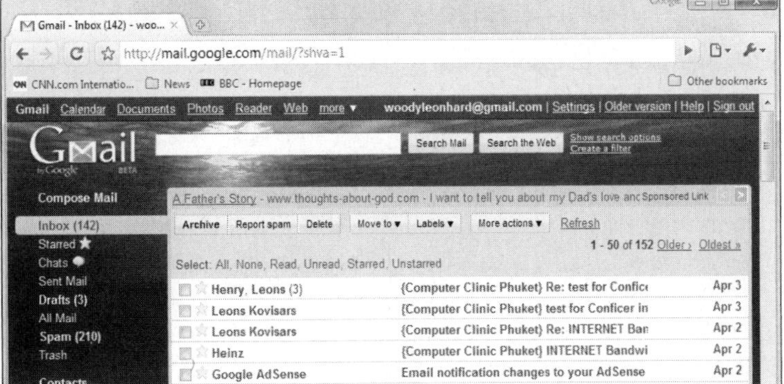

Figure 6-3: Google's Gmail is my favorite online mail program.

- **In my experience, people who rely on e-mail, and want to keep their mail on their own computer, ultimately gravitate to Outlook.** I know that's a heretical observation, but it's true. Outlook 2003 and 2007 combine hyperactive spam filtering and so-so antiphishing technology with the kind of industrial strength that many e-mail addicts need. It's also surprisingly easy to use — at least, the common e-mail actions are easy to find and run. The big downside? Outlook is expensive.

If you decide you want Outlook, keep several points in mind. Many companies get licenses for Outlook that come along for the ride when they buy Microsoft Exchange Server; your company may have a license for Outlook that's already paid for. If you have to buy a copy of Outlook, read up on the differences between Outlook 2003 and Outlook 2007. You may find that Outlook 2003 has everything you need — if you can find it — for a fraction of the 2007 price.

- **Several people I know use Mozilla Thunderbird (`mozillamessaging.com`), a lightweight, open source (free) mail program from the same foundation that brought us Firefox.** Most Thunderbird users I know are old Eudora fanatics; Thunderbird picked up where Eudora dropped dead in its tracks. Personally, I don't like Thunderbird; given a choice, I would always opt for one of the online services. But if you need to carry your messages with you and you don't like Windows Live Mail, it's a good alternative.

E-mail client, POP3, and bafflegab

Keeping up with all the e-mail buzzwords is difficult. Here's a quick little list that should get you through the major twists and turns of installing and using an *e-mail client* (an e-mail program that runs on your computer) and getting it to retrieve your mail.

In a traditional e-mail client, you type a message, list which addresses you want to receive the message, and then send it. When your computer sends the message, it connects to a specific kind of computer attached to the Internet: a *Simple Mail Transfer Protocol (SMTP)* server. The SMTP server is responsible for putting the message onto the Internet, destined for its intended recipient.

The Internet routes messages based on the e-mail addresses of the recipients. The last part of your e-mail address — the part after the @ sign — is your domain name. In `Woody@AskWoody.com` (yes, that's my e-mail address; no, capitalization doesn't matter), `AskWoody.com` is my domain name. A message sent to me ends up on a particular kind of computer, a *Post Office Protocol 3 (POP3)* server, that is tasked with handling messages sent to AskWoody.com.

When you tell your computer that you want to receive messages, it goes out to your POP3 server and downloads all the messages waiting for you in its queue. In most cases, after the messages are downloaded to your computer, they're deleted from the POP3 server.

Attachments to messages (pictures, files, and so on) travel as text, and your e-mail client (or the Web program you use to send and receive mail) takes care of the details using the specific set of rules named *Multipurpose Internet Mail Extensions (MIME)*.

Getting Started with Windows Live Mail

Windows Live Mail is one of those Windows 7 Live Essentials that is distributed independently of Windows 7. I talk about the Windows Live Essentials in Book I, Chapter 5.

Chances are very good that you can't see Windows Live Mail on your computer. Not to worry. Even if you have it installed, you'd be well advised to go out and download the latest version. Here's how to do it:

1. **Use your favorite Web browser to navigate to** `download.live.com`.
2. **Click Download.**

   The Windows Live Installer, `wlsetup-web.exe`, is transferred to your computer. Double-click it or do whatever you need to do (depending on your browser) to run it.
3. **Select the check box marked Mail and deselect the others. Then click Install.**

   The Windows Live installer downloads Windows Live Mail and sticks it on your computer. Time to grab a latté.

   Then (as I describe in detail in Book I, Chapter 5), Microsoft asks you to let it take over your Web browsing, uh, experience — and keep track of all your Windows activities.
4. **Deselect all the check boxes and click Continue.**

   The final panel asks you to sign up for a Windows Live ID.
5. **If you want to use one of the Microsoft online services and you don't already have a Windows Live ID, click Sign Up and follow the instructions in Book V, Chapter 7 to create a completely bogus ID.**

   If you have a Hotmail ID, a Messenger ID, or an Xbox Online ID, you already have a Windows Live ID.
6. **Click Close.**

   Windows Live Mail is now installed on your computer. You can't see it yet, but it's there.

Now you're ready to run Windows Live Mail (WLM) for the first time. Here's the easy way to start:

1. **Choose Start⇨Windows Live Mail.**

   WLM whizzes and gurgles for a bit and then shows you the Add an E-Mail Account dialog box, shown in Figure 6-4.

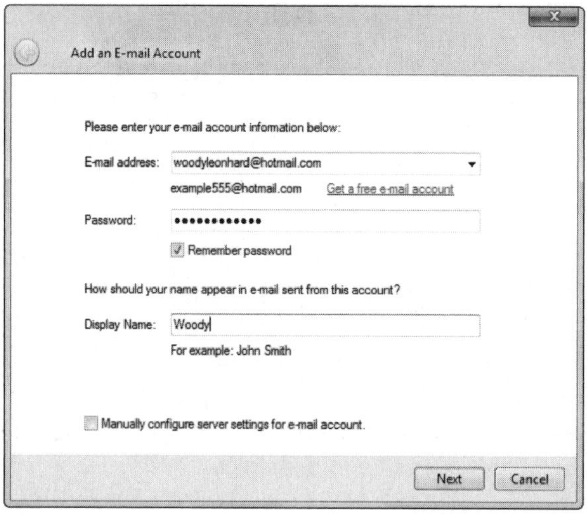

Figure 6-4: I add my Hotmail account to Windows Live Mail.

2. **If you have a Hotmail account and you want to use Windows Live Mail to access that account, fill out the Add an E-Mail Account dialog box with the information for your Hotmail account. Click Next and then click Finish.**

   Starting with a Hotmail account is a quick and easy way to get going with Windows Live Mail: WLM understands Hotmail, and you don't have to futz with any settings.

   On the other hand, you may want to use a conventional e-mail account, in which case you need to fill out the details (see the nearby sidebar, "E-mail client, POP3, and bafflegab"). Your Internet service provider (ISP) should've given you all that information.

   If you set up a Hotmail account, WLM advises that it needs to download the folders before you can read the messages in this account.

3. **Click Download.**

   WLM goes out to Hotmail (or whichever e-mail account you set up) and retrieves your Inbox. In the end you see your inbox, which looks more or less like the one shown in Figure 6-5. Yes, WLM blocks pictures, even if they come from the Microsoft Security Response Center. (See the nearby sidebar, "Why does Windows Live Mail block pictures?" for more information.)

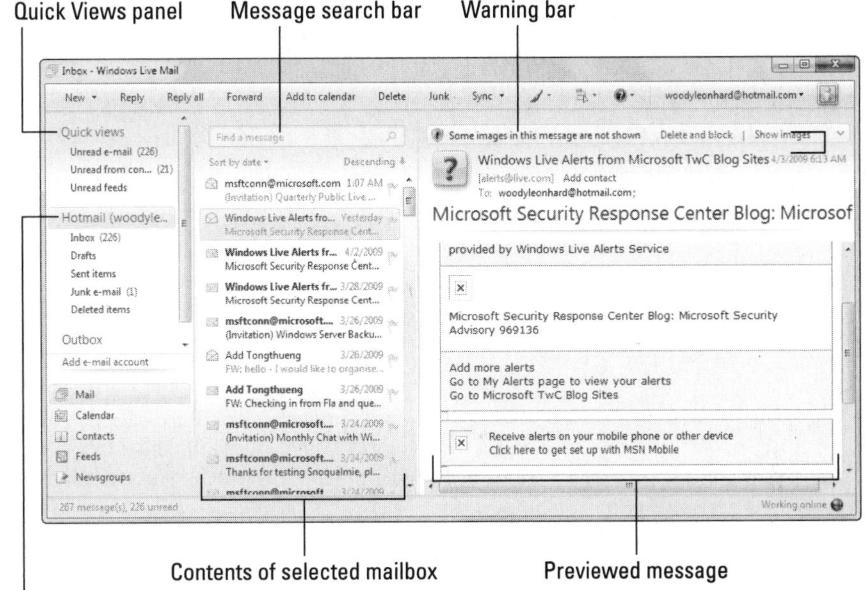

Figure 6-5: The Windows Live Mail inbox.

4. **You're ready to read, write, send, and receive, so you may as well.**

   See the next section for details.

The Windows Mail window (refer to Figure 6-5) is easy to figure out. Across the top is a traditional menu bar that changes depending on which Live Mail application you're running, plus icons for colorizing (adding a background color to the main window), "menus" (which behave much like a traditional Tools menu item, with a hodgepodge of settings underneath), and Help. (See Table 6-1 for a description of the menu items, from left to right, and what they do.)

Table 6-1 The Windows Live Mail Menu

Name	*What It Does*
New	Opens a window that lets you write a new message (see the "Conversing with E-Mail" section, later in this chapter). Also lets you create new events for the Calendar, a new contact for your Contacts list, or a new e-mail folder.
Reply	Opens a window that lets you write a new message. The e-mail address in the current message is used as the To address in the new message, and the contents of the current message are copied into the bottom of the new message.

(continued)

Table 6-1 *(continued)*

Name	*What It Does*
Reply All	Does the same thing as Reply, except that all the e-mail addresses in the selected message (both the From and To addresses) are copied into the new message.
Forward	Performs similarly to Reply, except that the To box is left blank.
Add to Calendar	Creates a new event, to go in your calendar, with the message subject used as the event's subject, and with a copy of the message in the text of the event. You have to add dates, times, and other information.
Delete	Moves the message to the Deleted Items folder, on the left.
Junk	Moves the message to the Junk e-mail folder, on the left. You're also given an opportunity to forward the message to Microsoft (and unnamed "third parties") for its giant junk collection.
Sync	Sends the mail in your outbox and retrieves mail for your inbox. This is the same as Send/Receive in Outlook.

In the upper-right area are tools that let you crank up Windows Live Messenger and change your Messenger persona. I talk about Windows Live Messenger in Book V, Chapter 7.

On the left, you see these items:

- **The Quick Views panel:** The Quick Views panel lets you filter your inbox quickly, so you see only Unread E-Mail, Unread E-Mail from Your Contacts, or Unread RSS Feeds.
- **All the different mailboxes for each e-mail account:** In Figure 6-5, I have only one e-mail account, so Windows Live Mail shows only my Hotmail mailboxes.
- **Links to the other Windows Live Mail applications.**

You may want to use Windows Live Mail to read your RSS Feeds, but I greatly prefer iGoogle, which is trivially easy to hook up with Firefox (see Book V, Chapter 4 for details). You may also want to use Windows Live Mail to read newsgroups, but for my money, Google Groups has the WLM program beat to pieces (see Book V, Chapter 5 for details).

In the middle, Windows Live Mail shows you the contents of the selected mailbox. In Figure 6-5, I select the inbox on the left, so the middle pane has a list of all messages in my inbox.

Why does Windows Live Mail block pictures?

Unless you specifically tell Windows Mail that you want it to download and show you pictures inside e-mail messages, it won't. There's a reason why — and it has nothing to do with all the, uh, shall we say, creative pictures floating around on the Internet these days.

Pictures can be put inside e-mail messages in one of two ways. Either the whole picture goes in the message, or a link to the picture goes inside the message. The link points to a place on the Internet where Windows Mail can retrieve the picture, if you ask it to. If the whole picture is inside the message, Windows Mail shows it. But if a link exists, Windows Mail doesn't retrieve the picture unless you tell it to.

Why? Because of a "Web beacon." Spammers learned long ago that they could put unique pointers inside e-mail messages, referring to pictures on their Web sites. When Windows Mail reaches out and grabs the picture, it leaves behind a trace of where it came from — and that trace can be linked to the e-mail address of the person who received the message. Spammers send out millions of messages with Web beacons, and they're rewarded with a list of all the e-mail addresses of the people who opened the messages.

Windows Mail doesn't follow the picture links — and thus it doesn't confirm the validity of your e-mail address to spammers — unless you choose Tools➪Options, click the Security tab, and deselect the Block Images and Other External Content in HTML E-mail check box.

On the right, you see a modified preview of the selected message. If Windows Live Mail has modified the message in some way, the notification appears in a bar at the top of the message. For example, in Figure 6-5, Windows Live Mail blocks pictures in the message. (For an explanation, see the following sidebar, "Why does Windows Live Mail block pictures?")

If you click the link marked Delete and Block on the message notification bar, Windows Live Mail deletes the current message and puts the sender on the Blocked Senders list. Then you never see another message from that sender ever again. If you accidentally click Delete and Block, you can bring the sender back from the blacklist: Click the down arrow on the "menus" icon, choose Safety Options, click the Blocked Senders tab, select the accidentally banished sender, and click the Remove button.

Conversing with E-Mail

If you grew up with e-mail, you're lucky. Windows Live Mail should behave more or less the way you expect. If you were born before, oh, 1999, you may not be so adept. This section scratches the surface of what there is to know about e-mail. It should suffice to get you started on the right foot.

Setting up mail accounts

The process of setting up mail accounts — and you can set up dozens, if you choose — is a simple one. Get your accounts in order and you're free to create, send, and receive e-mail messages at will. Or to Will.

How many e-mail accounts do you need? Many people have several e-mail addresses — perhaps one for work, one for school, and one for personal use.

I strongly recommend that you *not* add e-mail accounts for several people in Windows Live Mail. You can add a hundred accounts for yourself, but the minute you add an account for your significant other or your kids or your parents, things get sticky — not just because you all find yourselves reading each others' mail, but because replying, deleting, and forwarding other peoples' mail gets real hairy, real fast.

If more than one person is using Windows Live Mail, set up a separate Windows account for each person (see Book II, Chapter 2). That way, even if you don't put passwords on the accounts, you can keep the mail sorted out automatically. Little Billy won't accidentally delete Daddy's notification about winning the Irish lottery. Little Melinda won't accidentally leave her love letter in the family `Sent Items` folder.

To add other e-mail accounts or modify your existing one, follow these steps:

1. **Start Windows Live Mail.**
2. **On the left, above the list of applications, click the link marked Add E-Mail Account.**

   The Add an E-Mail Account dialog box, shown in Figure 6-6, appears. If you have a normal e-mail account, you probably need to select the check box marked Manually Configure Server Settings for E-Mail Account.
3. **If you're very lucky — or if you're adding a Hotmail, Gmail, or Yahoo! Mail account — just fill out the boxes and click Next. Windows Live Mail handles all the rest.**

   Windows Live Mail includes the Autodiscovery technology, which can automatically track down all your settings, based on your e-mail address. Microsoft has a big database of domain names (that's the part of your e-mail address to the right of the @ sign) and if your domain is in that big database, Windows Live Mail can guess at all the settings necessary to set up e-mail service.
4. **Unfortunately, in many cases you have to select the check box marked Manually Configure Server Settings for E-Mail Account and then click Next.**

If you choose to set up the account manually, you see the dialog box shown in Figure 6-7.

5. **Fill in the requested information and click Next.**

   Unfortunately, you have to get that information from the company that handles your e-mail service.

Someday it'll be easy to set up e-mail accounts. That day hasn't arrived yet.

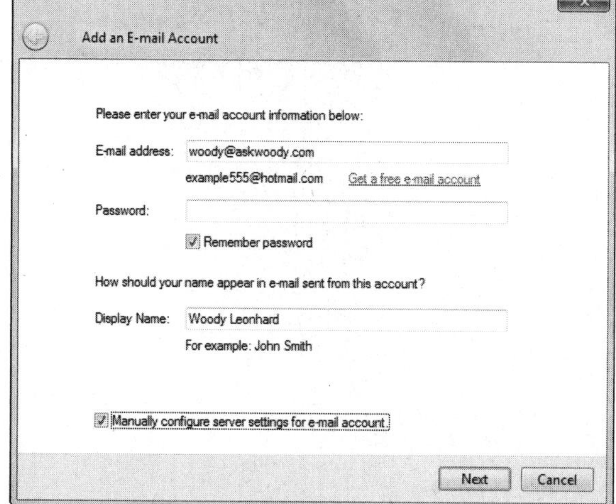

Figure 6-6: Manually configuring server settings for your e-mail account.

Add an E-mail Account
Where can I find my e-mail server information?
Incoming Server Information
My incoming mail server is a POP3 server.
Incoming server: someserver.com Port: 110
This server requires a secure connection (SSL)
Log on using: Clear text authentication
Login ID (if different from e-mail address):
woody
Outgoing Server Information
Outgoing server: someserver.com Port: 25
This server requires a secure connection (SSL)
My outgoing server requires authentication
Next
Cancel

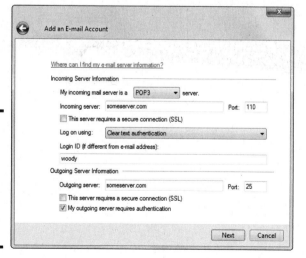

Figure 6-7: All this information has to come from your e-mail service provider.

Retrieving messages and attachments

When you want to check your e-mail, click the Sync link on the Windows Live Mail toolbar. A notice appears in the lower-right corner of the Windows Mail window, advising that you're receiving mail. Click the Receiving link in the lower-right corner of the Windows Live Mail main window and you can watch the details as Windows Live Mail uploads and downloads your massive missives (see Figure 6-8).

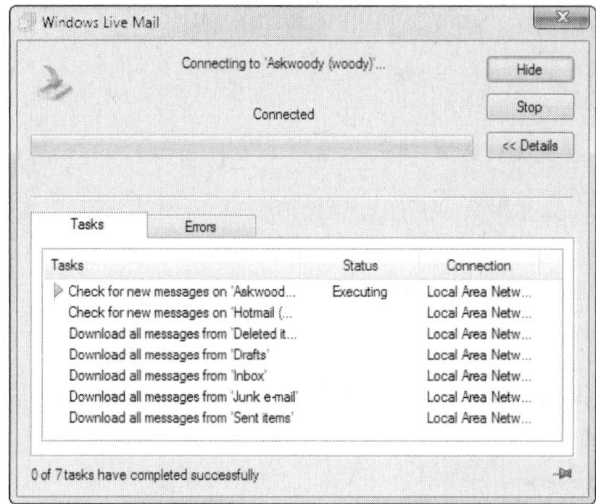

Figure 6-8: Checking for new mail.

In the normal course of events, you click an incoming message with an attached file, and a paper-clip icon appears at the top of the message body, indicating that a file is attached (see Figure 6-9). You can double-click the filename and open the attached file.

The latest version of Windows Live Mail blocks certain kinds of files, based on the filename extension of the attached file. (See Book II, Chapter 1 for a discussion of filename extensions — and why you need to make Windows show them to you.)

Of course, the concept of a "dangerous" filename extension is laughable. Until September 2004, the `.jpg` filename extension was considered "safe." Then somebody discovered that it was possible to stick a killer program inside a JPEG picture file and a filename extension that was once considered innocuous became, overnight, one of the world's Ten Most Wanted. Microsoft doesn't block `.jpg` files because that would make it impossible to receive photos.

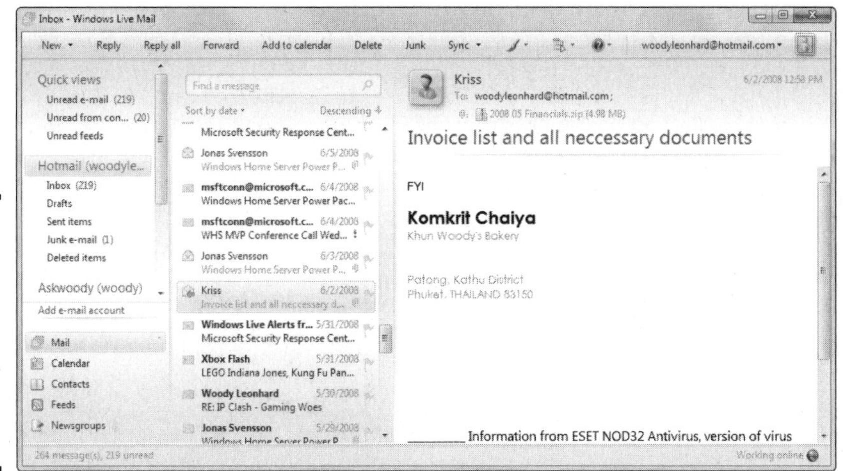

Figure 6-9: A file attached to a message appears as a paper clip next to the filename.

Similarly, Microsoft doesn't block `.doc` Word documents or `.xls` Excel spreadsheets or `.ppt` PowerPoint files, even though all of them have been used quite recently to carry 0day attacks, using previously unknown security holes. Danger is in the eye of the beholder, eh? (Turn to Book VI, Chapter 1 for more on 0day threats.)

If Windows Live Mail receives a message with a file attached to it and the filename extension of the attachment is in the following list, Windows Live Mail advises in a big red box (see Figure 6-10) that you have received a prohibited file type:

```
.ade  .adp  .app  .asp  .bas  .bat  .cer
.chm  .cmd  .com  .cpl  .crt  .csh  .exe
.fxp  .hlp  .hta  .inf  .ins  .isp  .its
.js   .jse  .ksh  .lnk  .mad  .maf  .mam
.maq  .mar  .mas  .mat  .mau  .mav  .maw
.mda  .mdb  .mde  .mdt  .mdw  .mdz  .msc
.msi  .msp  .mst  .ops  .pcd  .pif  .prf
.prg  .pst  .reg  .scf  .scr  .sct  .shb
.shs  .tmp  .url  .vb   .vbe  .vbs  .vsmacros
.vss  .vst  .vsw  .ws   .wsc  .wsf  .wsh
```

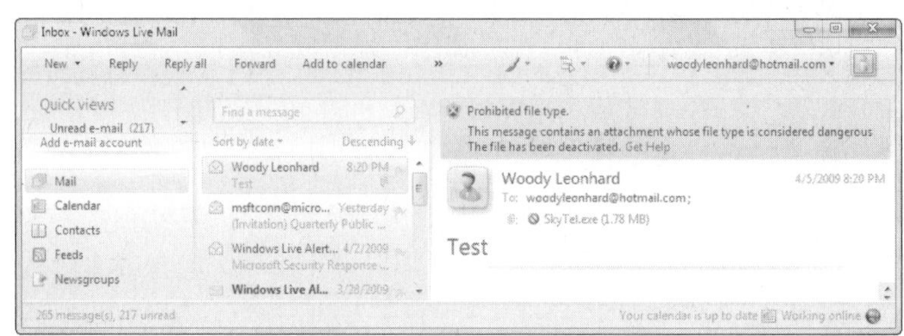

Figure 6-10: Windows Live Mail doesn't let you get to an `.exe` file unless you know the trick.

If you receive an e-mail message and you need to get at a blocked file attached to the message, here's how to do it:

1. **By far the safest, fastest, easiest way to get the attachment is to e-mail the person who sent you the message and ask her to zip the file and send it to you again.**

   If your friend is using Windows 7, Windows Vista, or Windows XP, have her choose Start➪My Computer and navigate to the file, right-click the file, and choose Send To➪Compressed (Zipped) Folder. Windows creates a compressed file with a `.zip` filename extension, which you can open immediately when you get it.

2. **If you can't get the file resent to you or you're in a big hurry, follow Steps 3 through 7, but be careful to finish all the steps.**

   In particular, make sure that you turn security on again when you're done, as I describe in Step 7.

3. **In the main Windows Live Mail window (refer to Figure 6-1), click the down arrow to the right of the Menus icon, and then click Safety Options and click the Security tab.**

   You see the Safety Options dialog box, shown in Figure 6-11.

4. **Deselect the check box labeled Do Not Allow Attachments to Be Saved or Opened that Could Potentially Be a Virus, and then click OK.**

   Windows Live Mail returns to the main window.

5. **Double-click the message containing the attachment that Windows Mail blocked.**

   You should be able to get at the file that was blocked. Be careful with it. There's a reason why Microsoft blocks attachments — they can harm your computer. Really.

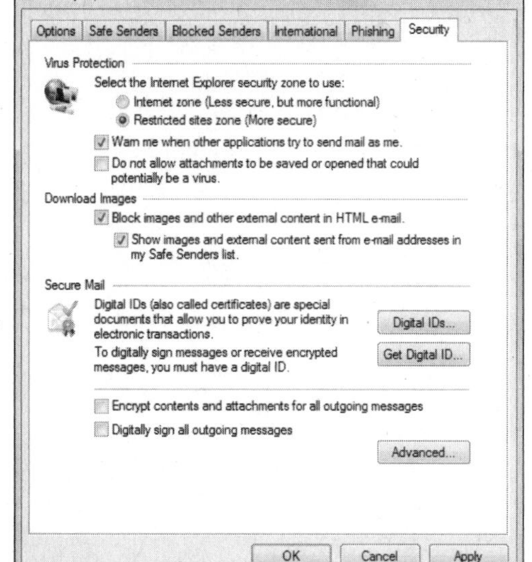

Figure 6-11: Turn off attachment scanning here — but only momentarily.

6. **At this point, you can click the file to run it or right-click the file and save it.**

   Be *very* cautious if you run the file by double-clicking it, okay? That's how machines become infected with viruses. It's far better to save the file and use your (recently updated!) antivirus program to scan the file, individually, before you open or run it. I warned you. . . .

7. **Turn attachment security back on. Repeat steps 3 and 4 but this time select the Do Not Allow Attachments to Be Saved or Opened that Could Potentially Be a Virus check box, and then click OK.**

   Don't forget this step. It's important.

Of course, you should never, ever, *ever* open or run a file attached to an e-mail message unless you know the person who sent it to you and you know that he truly did send it to you. If you have any doubt, send him a message and confirm that he sent you the file before you open it. If you receive confirmation, save the file and run your favorite antivirus package on it before you open it.

Remember that the return address on any e-mail message can be *spoofed* — a message from a cretin in Ripoffland can appear to be coming from Bill Gates or Koko the Gorilla, and there's no way to tell who really sent it.

Creating a message

When you're ready to create a message, follow these steps:

1. **Click the New link on the Windows Live Mail toolbar.**

   A message window appears, as shown in Figure 6-12, so that you can type your message.

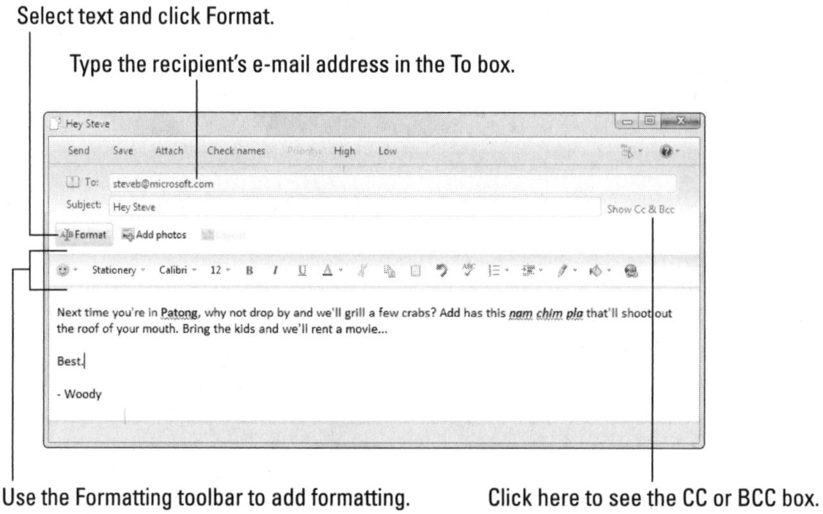

Select text and click Format.

Type the recipient's e-mail address in the To box.

Use the Formatting toolbar to add formatting.

Click here to see the CC or BCC box.

Figure 6-12: Writing a new message.

2. **Choose whom you want to send the message to.**

   You can enter the person's e-mail address in two different ways:

   - Type the e-mail address on the To line.
   - Click the Address Book icon to the left of the To line and select the recipient you want from the Address Book. (To select a recipient, click the contact from the list on the left, click the To button, and then click OK.)

3. **Enter a subject for your message. For best results, keep it fairly short and make it descriptive.**

4. **Type the body of your message.**

   You have a wide-open space to do just that. You can enter the words the way you want them without any fancy formatting, or you can change the look of the text by choosing a different font and size, changing colors, indenting information, and more.

See the following sections if you want to add a signature or attach files before you send.

Adding a signature

Many people like to append to the ends of their e-mail messages little catch phrases, business mottos, bon mots, snips of bathos, kinky double entendres, explicit — well, you get the idea. If you're into these kinds of signatures, you can let Windows Mail add a signature for you automatically. Here are the steps for adding a signature:

1. **Click the down arrow to the right of the Menus icon on the Windows Live Mail toolbar. Choose Options and click the Signatures tab.**

   You see the Signatures Options, shown in Figure 6-13.

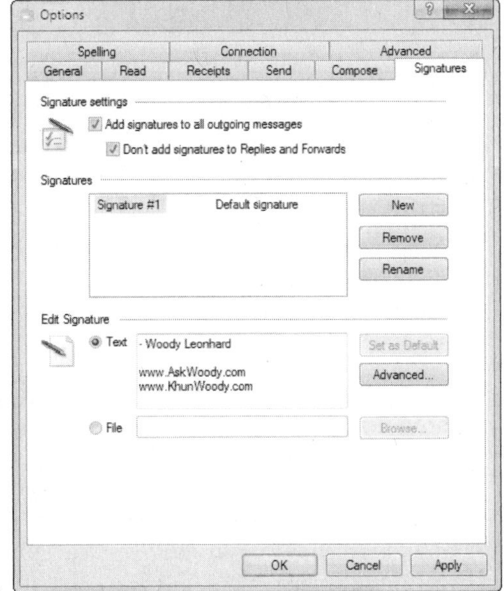

Figure 6-13: Set your default signature here.

2. **Enter your signature in the Edit Signature box or add the text file that you want to use as a signature by selecting the File option button and browsing to the file you want to use.**
3. **Select the Add Signatures to All Outgoing Messages check box to add the signature to all outgoing messages.**
4. **Click OK.**

   Your designated signature will be added to the bottom of all new messages you create.

After the signature is in the message, you can change it, edit it, delete it — the signature is just text.

You can create a formatted signature quite easily. Just use Word or any other program capable of saving an HTML file, and save your formatted signature as a .HTM file. In Step 2, select the File button and browse to the .HTM file. Just keep in mind that some e-mail programs munge fancy formatted signatures — entire messages, too, for that matter.

Attaching files

Want to piggyback a file on your message? No sweat. Just keep in mind that the person receiving your message may be under the same filename restrictions that you must endure (see the "Retrieving messages and attachments" section, earlier in this chapter) or maybe even worse.

When you want to simply attach a file, the process is simple. Follow these steps:

1. **Follow the steps earlier in this section to create your message.**
2. **If you want to attach a file to your message, click the Attach button on the Windows Live Mail toolbar, choose the file, and click Open.**

   If you want to send a file with a filename extension that's on the banned list (see "Retrieving messages and attachments"), convert it to a zip file first: Right-click the file and choose Send To➪Compressed (Zipped) Folder. Let Windows do its zipping thing. Then choose the zipped file before clicking Open.

On the other hand, if you want to use the Windows Live Mail Attach a Picture option, you need to understand how it works:

- **First and foremost, if you choose the Attach a Picture option, Windows Live Mail *doesn't* attach your picture (or pictures) to the message.** Your recipient doesn't receive your pictures. Instead, your recipient receives small thumbnail images.
- **If you attach a picture, you send your pictures *to Microsoft,* and the 'Softies post them on a Windows Live Mail server.**
- **Your recipient can click the thumbnails that were automatically generated and stuck in the message.** Clicking a thumbnail connects your recipient to the big Microsoft server in the sky and downloads the picture.
- **If your recipient wants to get full-size versions of all the pictures you sent, he has to click each thumbnail one by one and save the pictures one by one.** One exception: If your recipient has downloaded and installed Windows Live Mail, he can download all the pictures at the same time.
- **Your pictures disappear after 30 days.** Poof. If your recipient wants to look at your pictures 31 days after Windows Live Mail sent the thumbnails, he's out of luck.

If you can abide by the limitations of the Windows Live Mail Attach a Picture option, here's how to get it working:

1. **Write your message and then click the Add Photos button, above the Formatting toolbar.**

   Windows Live Mail invites you to gather picture files — `.bmp`, `.gif`, `.jpg`, `.png`, and a few lesser-known types. After you attach them all to the message, Windows Live Mail shows you a picture control bar, as shown in Figure 6-14.

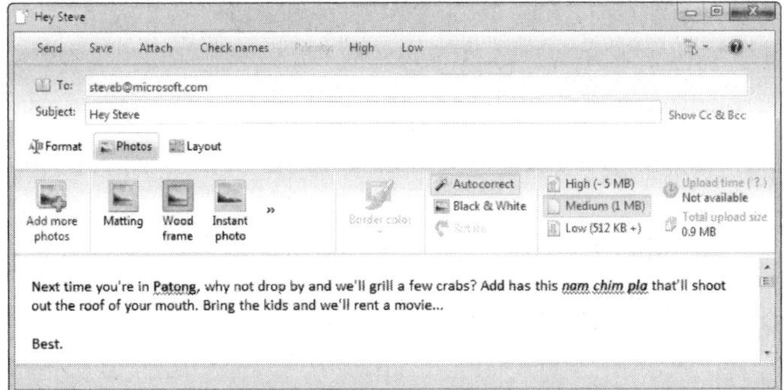

Figure 6-14: Windows Live Mail applies its shrinking technology to all pictures attached to the message.

2. **Choose one compression setting that applies to *all* attached pictures.**

   Realize that the compression you choose doesn't change the size of the message your recipient receives: She's going to receive only thumbnails, anyway. Instead, the compression affects the size of the picture file that's uploaded to the Microsoft Windows Live Mail servers. Your options:

   - *High* reduces each picture to 5MB or less. Few photos are 5MB, so the High setting means in general that your (giant!) photos and other pics go out in full high-definition resolution. Your recipient receives thumbnails, but if she decides to download a picture from the Windows Live Mail servers, it could take a while.
   - *Medium* reduces each picture to 1MB or less. If you're sending photos, this setting cuts the size in half or so. Your recipient doesn't have to spend as much time waiting to download her chosen pictures from the Microsoft server.
   - *Low* reduces each picture to half a megabyte or less. That can significantly reduce your "send" time. Recipients who decide to download the pictures will find that they're just fine for displaying on a computer, but fuzzy for printing copies.

3. **You can add eye candy — a wood frame or metal corners — and you can make fixes to the pictures, but those are much better performed (and much better controlled) with Windows Live Photo Gallery (see Book IV, Chapter 5 for details).**

The recipient sees a message like the one shown in Figure 6-15, with thumbnails at the bottom of the screen. Your recipient can click individual files to download them or view the pictures as a slide show on the Internet.

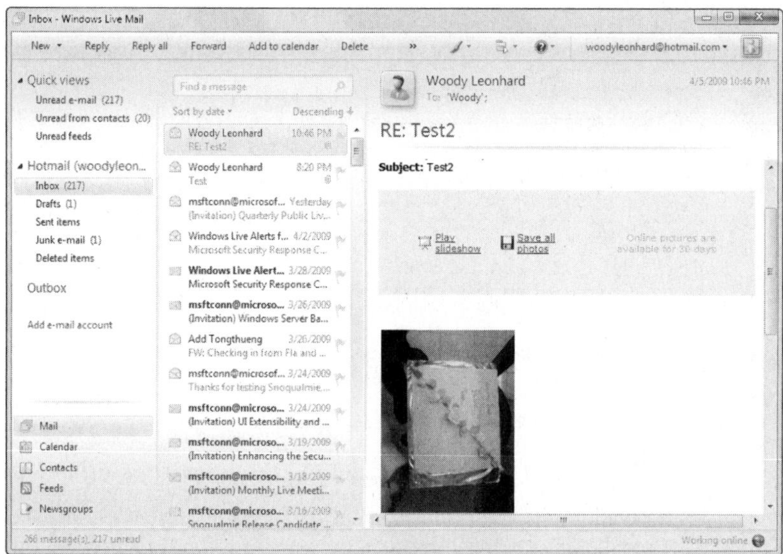

Figure 6-15: If you use the WLM Add Photos feature, your photos are posted on the Microsoft servers and your recipient sees thumbnails. Not what you expected, eh?

Sending a message

Okay. Ready, set, send! Just click the Send button in the mail window and your mail is sent immediately.

If you want to save a message and work on it again before you send it, click the Save button. This action places the message in your `Drafts` folder. When you want to continue working on it, simply open the `Drafts` folder and double-click the message.

Making Windows Live Mail wait to send and receive

As soon as Windows Live Mail starts, it looks for mail. If you haven't changed the out-of-the-box settings, Windows Live Mail continues to check for mail every 30 minutes, whether you want it to or not.

By default, Windows Live Mail is set up to send messages the moment you finish composing and click the Send button. I wish I had a nickel for every time I sent out a message and immediately wished that I could take it back. E-mail messages, like computer geeks, get better with age. At least, that's what I tell my significant other.

I think it's much better to force Windows Live Mail to wait until you click the Sync button before either receiving or sending any mail. Here's how:

1. **Click the down arrow to the right of the Menus button on the toolbar and choose Options.**

   You see the General tab, shown in Figure 6-16.

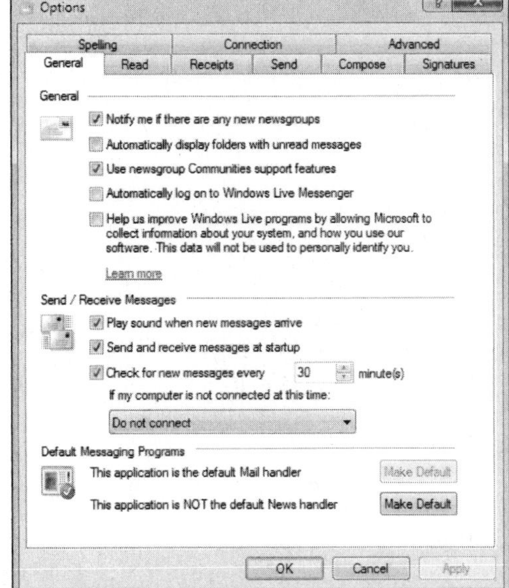

Figure 6-16: Keep Windows Live Mail from syncing auto-matically.

2. **Deselect the Send and Receive Messages at Startup check box and deselect the Check for New Messages Every . . . Minutes check box.**

   This step keeps Windows Live Mail from syncing immediately whenever you start the program, and it disables the automatic trolling for new messages.

3. **Click the Send tab.**

4. **Deselect the Send Messages Immediately check box. Click OK.**

   Your changes take effect immediately.

Chapter 7: Chatting with Windows Live Messenger

In This Chapter

- **Introducing Windows Live Messenger**
- **Using Messenger effectively**
- **Working with voice, pictures, and more**
- **Making Windows forget how to log you on automatically**

In the preceding chapter, I talk about the sorry state of Windows Live Mail: Microsoft now has five distinct mail programs, in dozens of versions, each with its own wrinkles and each with a basketful of pluses and minuses. And double minuses.

Instant messaging (IM) in the Microsoft milieu used to have the same problem. When Windows XP ruled the roost, we had Windows Messenger, MSN Messenger, and .NET Messenger, all from Microsoft, each with its own foibles and bumbles. Some versions of some Microsoft IM programs wouldn't even talk to others.

With Vista, some sanity returned to Microsoft's instant messaging mess: Starting with Vista, and continuing with Windows 7, exactly one (recent) offering exists, although it has a funny name — Windows Live Messenger — and you have to keep downloading and installing new versions. Never mind.

Like every Windows Live Essential application (see Book I, Chapter 5), Windows Live Messenger isn't part of Windows. It's an add-on program. Windows Live Messenger, more than any other Windows Live Essential, marches to the tune of its own drummer.

This chapter touches on the high points of Windows Live Messenger, particularly where the Messenger hooks into Windows 7 itself. I step you through installing Windows Live Messenger, give a few pointers about using it, and then — the most important step — show you how to turn the %$#@! thing off. Or at least tone it down.

It's a noisy, pushy, cacophonous world.

Exploring the Alternatives

What can I say? I don't use an instant messenger unless I have to. I find instant messaging intrusive, distracting, and disruptive — even more so than the phone, and few people have my direct phone number. E-mail is much better, for a lot of reasons.

But, truth be told, sometimes I *do* use IM — but only if I make an appointment with the other party in advance. Maybe I'm an old fuddy-duddy, but there are, oh, about a hundred thousand things I'd rather do than deal with IM interruptions all day. Oy!

If you must use an instant messaging program, you and the person you're talking to have a fairly limited number of options:

- **You can both use AOL Instant Messenger (AIM) or ICQ, which is owned by AOL.** AIM was the original instant messenger, although its market share had dwindled to 50 percent or so by 2006, and has headed sharply downhill since.
- **If one of you uses Windows Live Messenger, the other one can use Windows Live Messenger, MSN Messenger (some versions; see the nearby sidebar, "The historic Messenger mess"), Windows Messenger, or the latest version of Yahoo! Messenger with Voice.** Note that Windows Live Messenger is designed to run on Windows XP, Windows Vista, and Windows 7 computers.
- **If one of you uses the latest Yahoo! Messenger with Voice, the other can use Windows Live Messenger or any of the recent Yahoo! Messenger versions.**
- **If one of you uses Trillian, the other can most likely use just about any instant messaging program.** Trillian is the "universal donor," if you will, of the IM polyglot mess. Pidgin, another free program, also works well interacting with all the other IM networks.
- **If one of you uses Google Talk, the other can use any program that understands Jabber, the only more-or-less open, standards-based network.** Unfortunately, at this moment, only Google Talk and a handful of less-well-known programs speak Jabber.

Given the current deplorable polyglot state of affairs, I have several recommendations:

- **If you need to IM with someone who's already hooked up with a specific IM service, join that service.** That way, you get all the bells and whistles and smileys.

You don't need to use or pay for (yech!) AOL to run AIM. Drop by `aim.com` and download your free copy.

- **If you feel a general need to IM, go for Trillian (`ceruleanstudios.com`).** That gives you the maximum flexibility, although occasionally some IM services knock out Trillian. Trillian isn't the most exciting IM program, but it gets the job done.
- **Otherwise, Windows Live Messenger is your cup o' tea.**

The historic Messenger mess

Because so many Microsoft Messengers are floating around, it's hard to keep track without a scorecard. Unfortunately, if you're trying to communicate with different versions of Messenger, you might run into problems: They don't all talk to each other.

Over the past decade, we've seen the names Windows Messenger (now known as Windows Dead Messenger?), MSN Messenger, .NET Messenger, and most recently, Windows Live Messenger all applied to essentially the same product, its derivatives, and its plumbing. I'll forgive you if you don't get the names straight.

The original MSN Messenger first appeared in July 1999. Microsoft made it fully compatible with AOL Instant Messenger (AIM), which was the only messenger on the block. The folks at AOL didn't like Microsoft crashing its party, changed a few things, and rendered MSN Messenger incapable of talking to AIM customers. Lawsuits ensued. When the dust settled, AOL had its network, Microsoft had a different one, and Yahoo! had another. Google Talk came out with Jabber, an (arguably) open network. Trillian talked to all of them, to a greater or lesser extent. Microsoft apparently forgot its original court claims that IMing should be open to all and knocked Trillian off the MSN network repeatedly.

In 2001, Microsoft "forked" Windows Messenger, diverting that version from the MSN Messenger mainstream, to handle NetMeeting and videoconferencing in Windows XP. Windows Messenger was dependable, if boring. New versions appeared every year or two, whether we needed them or not.

MSN Messenger, the progeny of Microsoft's rapid-development, rapid-deployment crew, barreled ahead. We saw steady improvement in the product, delivered in a much more timely fashion. Too timely, in fact. New minor MSN Messenger versions seemed to roll out every week. Some versions of MSN Messenger didn't even communicate with Windows Messenger itself. Office 2003 hooked into Windows Messenger, not into MSN Messenger.

MSN Messenger 6.0, circa 2003, featured the (exciting!) Tic-Tac-Toe game and supported see-through windows, reminiscent of Aero Glass.

Then Microsoft started playing footsie with Yahoo!, and both Microsoft and Yahoo! released products that talk to each other (even though the latest versions may have trouble talking to earlier versions of their own programs). AOL bought Time Warner in 2000. Google bought part of AOL in 2005. Trillian got knocked out of a couple of networks, but has been fighting valiantly to get back into the ring.

What a mess.

Maybe Microsoft and Yahoo! can come up with compelling reasons for people to sign up for their advertising-laden proprietary services. I certainly haven't seen anything that would convince me, except that they're the biggest kids on the block.

I just love the WLM come-ons that tout its new, improved telephone (read: Skype-like) capabilities. Of course, you can use Windows Live Messenger to make a PC-to-PC or PC-to-phone call, but you've been able to do that since MSN Messenger version 3, a decade ago. Remember Net2Phone? Maybe Verizon is cheaper than Net2Phone, but we've been here, done that.

I wouldn't recommend Yahoo! Messenger to anyone. Why? Yahoo! has this infuriating habit of sticking other things in with the Yahoo! Messenger installer. Trying to get Yahoo! Messenger put on a machine without hauling in a ton of garbage is like trying to dry-dock the *QE2* without dragging along any seaweed. No, thank you.

Making Windows Live Messenger Work

Windows Live Messenger is one of the Windows 7 Live Essentials that are distributed independently of Windows 7. (I talk about the Windows Live Essentials in Book I, Chapter 5.)

Chances are very good that you can't see Windows Live Mail on your computer. That's okay. Even if you have it installed, you'd be well advised to go out and download the latest version.

Choosing one or more Windows Live IDs

Before you start, you need a Windows Live ID — Windows Live Messenger doesn't work without it. If you already have a Hotmail account, an MSN Messenger or Windows Messenger account, a .NET Passport, a Microsoft Passport, or an Xbox Live account, you already have a Windows Live ID.

I personally use more than one Windows Live ID. For example, I have three IDs that I use exclusively for Messenger, Hotmail (er, Windows Live Hotmail), and all the other Windows Live ID-rigged applications. Here's a list of user= ID-related things you can do to keep meaningless messaging to a minimum:

- **Choose a user ID for fun time.** Ideally, this ID is one that you don't mind sharing with the rest of the world. For example, I don't mind sharing with *you,* dear reader, that my fun-time ID is `AskWoody@hotmail.com`. I use it on alternating Wednesday mornings between 3:00 and 3:15, which are my allotted fun-time hours. Everybody knows about that ID. Now you do, too.

- **Choose a user ID for travel time.** Don't broadcast this ID. For example, try something like `WoodyOnTheRoad@hotmail.com` to minimize the amount of e-mail traffic coming in. Only a few people have the ID that I really use for this purpose. I encourage them to use it when they want to send e-mail to me, or chat with me, when I'm on the road.
- **Choose a user ID for first-tier friends.** From `SomeOtherID@live.com` to `NoneofYourBeeswax@hotmail.com`, this user ID is the one you hand out only to immediate family, close friends, and any essential work colleagues. That's the ID you use whenever you want to get some work done. No, you can't have mine.

You might've noticed that I don't use my regular e-mail address, `woody@AskWoody.com`, for Windows Live Messenger. I have many reasons why, but the fundamental sticking point is that I refuse to let my real IDs be assimilated by The Borg — er, I refuse to put my real IDs in the Passport database.

Signing up for an ID — or two

It's none of Microsoft's business what IDs you use. If you need a Windows Live ID to run Messenger — or to participate in an Office 2007 collaboration, open a locked Office document, or use any other piece of Microsoft software that you already bought and paid for — I say use one of Bill's free IDs, thank you very much.

Here's how:

1. **Figure out if you need one, two, or three (or more) IDs.**

   Most people can do quite well with two — one they hand out in general and one that's given to only a close circle of friends — but read the suggestions in the preceding section to see why you might want three.

2. **Sign up for free Hotmail accounts. Start your favorite Web browser and go to** `hotmail.com`**.**

   You see a Windows Live ID sign-in page similar to the one shown in Figure 7-1.

3. **Click the button to Sign Up for an account.**

   Hotmail shows you the sign-up sheet, per Figure 7-2.

4. **Fill out the sign-up sheet. Bonus points for creativity. (*Hint:* The zip code for the main Microsoft campus in Redmond is 98052, and BillG was born in 1955.) Enter the confirmation characters and click I Accept.**

   If you really want to read Microsoft's service agreement and privacy statement, go right ahead. I'm waiting for the *CliffsNotes* version.

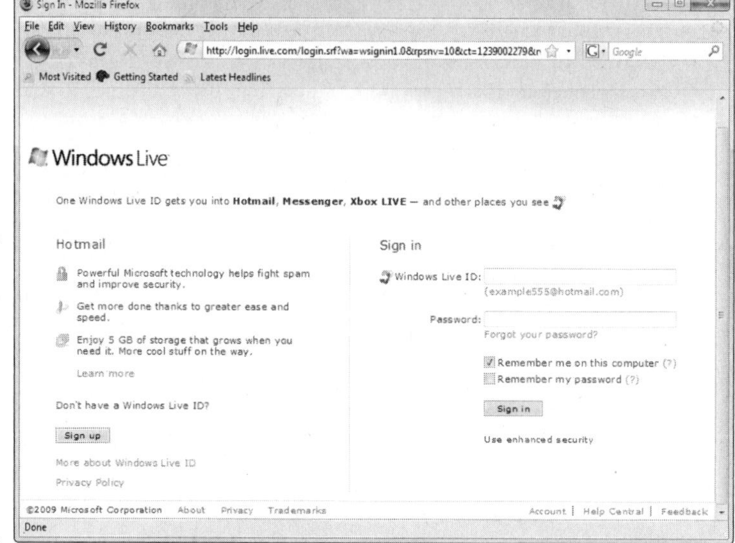

Figure 7-1: Sign up for a free Hotmail account and you automatically receive a Windows Live ID.

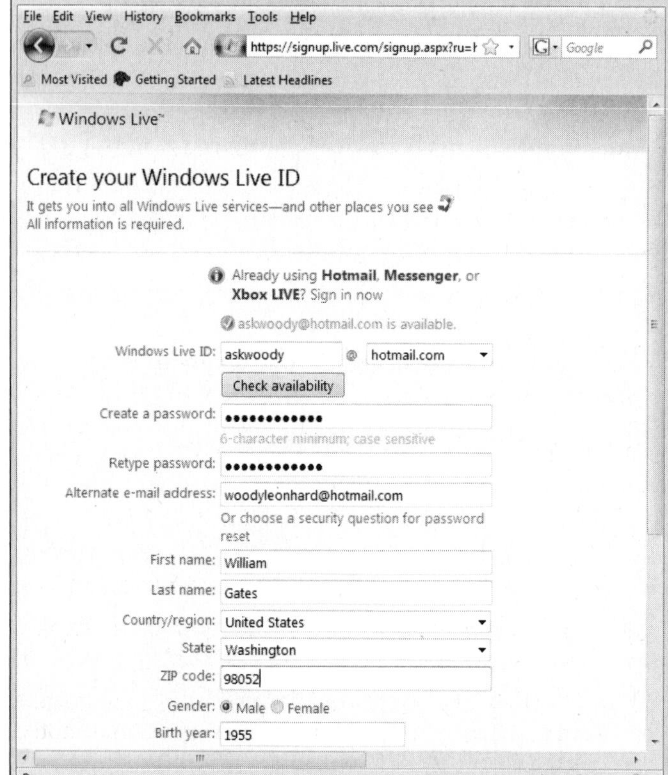

Figure 7-2: Don't worry — the Internet Police won't come knocking at your door, asking for identification. Creativity counts.

If all goes well, Hotmail — er, Windows Live Hotmail — appears (see Figure 7-3), you're logged in with your new e-mail address, and you can peruse the advertising on the right side of the window. Don't run out and pay for white teeth, okay?

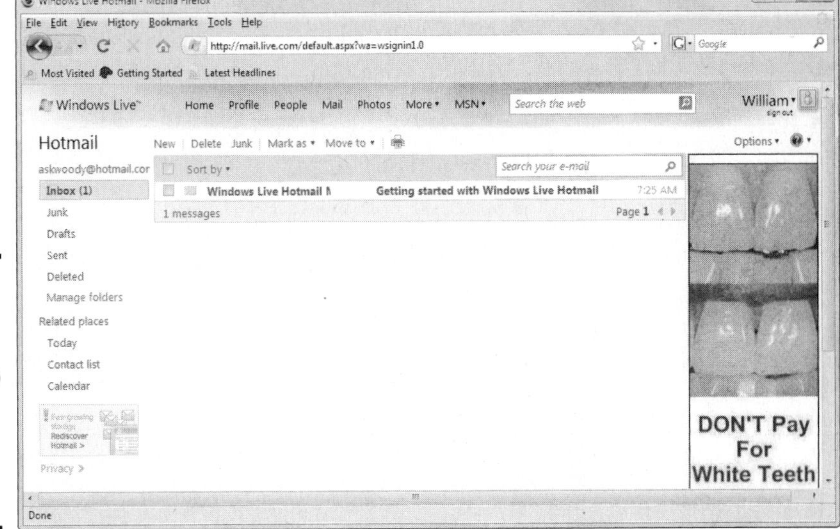

Figure 7-3: You know that you're all signed up when you can read the Hotmail ads.

5. **Repeat steps 2, 3, and 4 for each of the new Windows Live IDs you require.**

You have to log on to Hotmail (er, Windows Live Hotmail) or Windows Live Messenger at least once shortly after you create the IDs, and then once a month thereafter, to keep the IDs alive.

Installing Windows Live Messenger

When you're ready to talk, Windows Live Messenger is ready to listen. Or at least pass your voice (and video) along to the messaging masses. Here's how to get it going:

1. **If you don't yet have a Windows Live ID, follow the steps in the preceding section to get one (or two or three).**

   Windows Live Messenger doesn't work without a Windows Live ID.

2. **Use your favorite Web browser to navigate to `download.live.com`. Click Download.**

   You may get worried at this point that you're going to get all the Windows Live Essentials, whether you want them or not. Be of good faith. There's another step.

The Windows Live Installer, `wlsetup-web.exe`, is transferred to your computer. Double-click it or do whatever you need to do (depending on your browser) to run it.

3. **Select the box marked Messenger and deselect the others. Then click Install.**

   The Windows Live installer downloads Windows Live Messenger and puts it on your computer. That process can take a while.

   Then (as I describe in detail in Book I, Chapter 5), Microsoft asks you to let it take over your Web browsing experience — and keep track of all your Windows activities (see Figure 7-4).

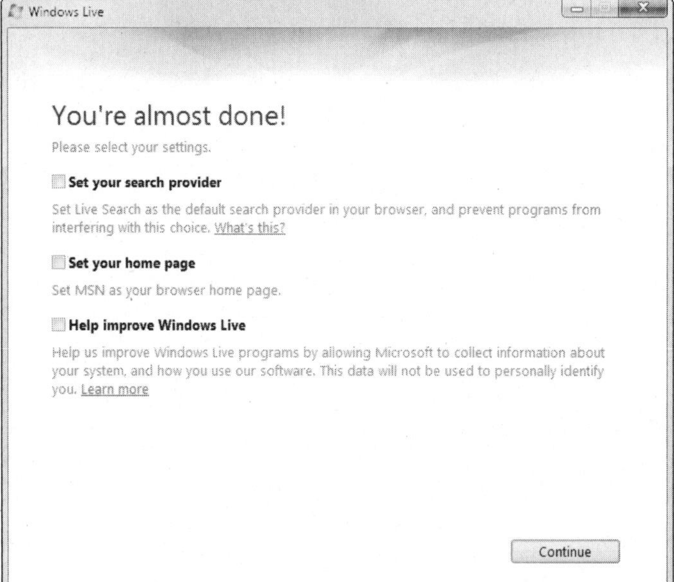

Figure 7-4: Microsoft wants to take over your search engine, set your home page to MSN.com, *and* keep track of all your Windows activities. Golly.

4. **Deselect all check boxes and click Continue.**

   The final panel asks you to sign up for a Windows Live ID.

5. **If you followed the steps in the preceding section, you already have one or two or three Windows Live IDs, so click Close.**

   Windows Live Messenger is now installed on your computer. It may take a minute or two, but ultimately you see the Windows Live Messenger sign-in window, shown in Figure 7-5.

Now you're ready to run Windows Live Messenger.

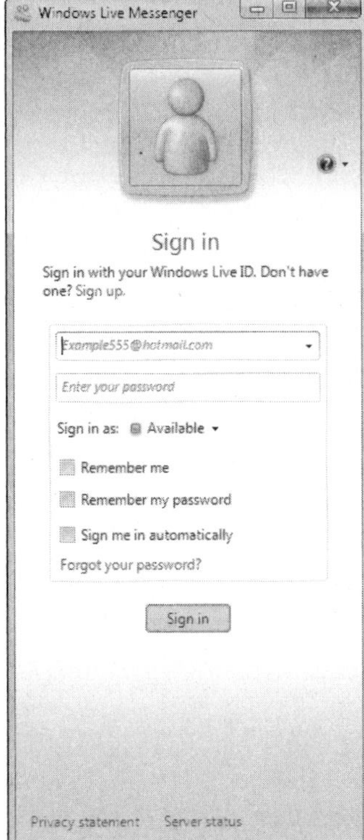

Figure 7-5: Home base — the Windows Live Messenger sign-in screen.

Starting Windows Live Messenger the first time

If you're careful when you first start Windows Live Messenger, you can save yourself a lot of time cleaning up afterward. Here's the easy, smart way to start:

1. **If you don't see the sign-in screen (refer to Figure 7-5), choose Start➪All Programs➪Windows Live➪Windows Live Messenger.**

   This step brings up the sign-in screen.

2. **Fill in the sign-in box with your "give it to anybody" Windows Live ID and your password. If you're using a computer in a public place, don't select any of the check boxes. But if you're at home or in a relatively secure office, select the Remember Me check box and think about selecting the Remember My Password check box (see the next paragraph), but do not select the Sign Me In Automatically check box. Click OK.**

If you select the Remember My Password check box, anybody who can get on your computer can start a Windows Live Messenger session and pretend to be you. If your computer's located in a room that's reasonably secure, or if you have a password on your Vista account, selecting the check box makes it easier to use Vista, but it isn't terribly secure. If you don't have a password on your Vista user account, think twice — three times — before you select this option.

You don't want WLM to sign you in automatically, because you want to make it easy to use different IDs, depending on how busy you are.

The two doughboys circle each like a blue hypothermic sumo wrestler taking on the green Incredible Hulk. A minute or two later, you see the Windows Live Messenger main screen, with a welcome screen to its right, as shown in Figure 7-6.

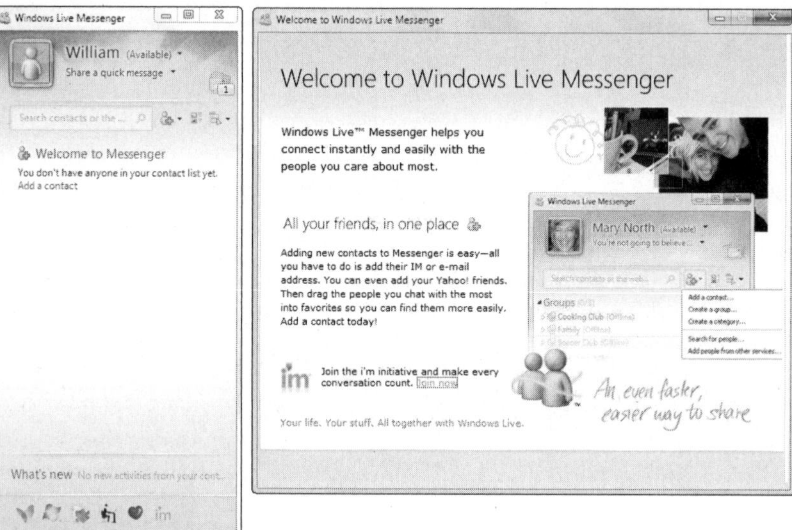

Figure 7-6: Windows Live Messenger springs to life.

3. **Click the Add a Contact link.**

   Messenger invites you to fill out the information for your messenger-enabled contact (see Figure 7-7).

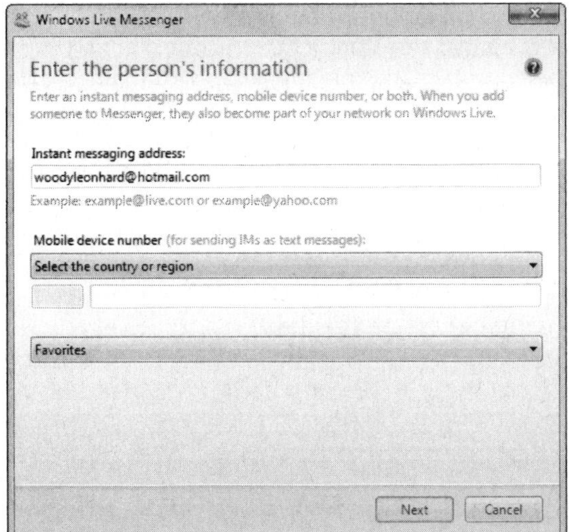

Figure 7-7: Enter contact information here.

4. **Fill out a contact's information and then click the Save button. It's even better if your contact is online and using Windows Live Messenger so that you can test things out.**

   When you add a contact and that contact doesn't yet have you on her buddy list, she sees a message like the one shown in Figure 7-8. The contact gets to choose whether she wants you to "see" her.

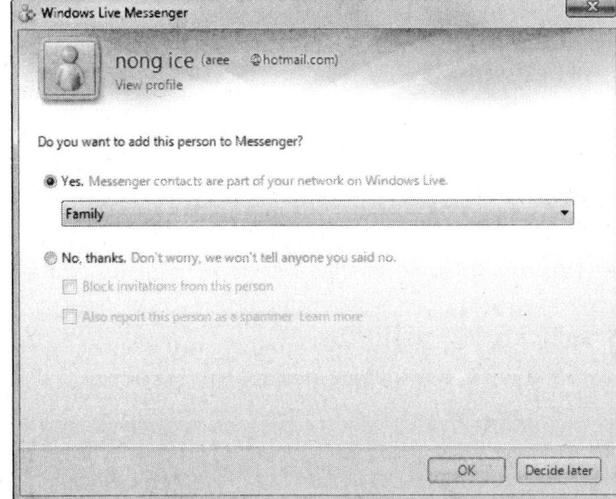

Figure 7-8: Your contacts must give permission before you can see them.

You can add someone to your Contact list, do everything properly, and have her show up on your Contact list — but you may never be able to connect to her because she told Messenger that she didn't want to be visible to you. Tough luck, eh?

To add more contacts, see the "Adding contacts" section, later in this chapter.

5. **To start a conversation, double-click the contact's name. Type your message in the box at the bottom of the Conversation window. When you press Enter or click the Send button, the message is sent to the designated recipient (or recipients).**

   A typical conversation is shown in Figure 7-9.

Figure 7-9: Woody and William have a little commercial conversation.

   Although you're limited in the amount of text you can type in the message box, if you press Enter, you can keep typing. You can copy text from just about anywhere and paste it into the message box: Windows Live Messenger treats it as though you typed it all out.

   For more tips on writing messages, see the "Making contact" section, later in this chapter.

6. **You can click the camera image next to your contact's picture and ask your contact whether it's okay to start the Webcam.**
7. **When you're done chatting with this contact, click the X (Close) button to exit the conversation.**

   Alternatively, you can click the down arrow to the right of the Show Menu icon and choose File➪Close.

8. **When all your conversations are over and you're done with Windows Live Messenger, click the X button or click the down arrow, and then choose File⇨Close.**

   Even if you closed Windows Messenger, it's still active — still lurking in the background and listening for incoming messages, still waiting to interrupt whatever you're doing with a ripply garururump sound. If you want to really turn the bloody thing off, right-click the Messenger icon in the Windows taskbar and choose Sign Out From Here.

The next time you start Windows Live Messenger, a companion window named Windows Live Today appears, offering you a stripped-down version of the "news" (if you can call it that) from MSN.com, along with wonderful opportunities to spend more money. You can safely click X to close that window at any point. If you want to turn off Windows Live Today, see the section "Stopping Windows Live Messenger from starting automatically," near the end of this chapter.

Working with Contacts

Contacts are people you can contact readily: Messenger knows about them, notifies you when they're signed in to Messenger, and lets you start a conversation with them by simply clicking their names.

The Contacts list isn't restrictive; anybody on the Contacts list who has your Messenger ID can start a conversation with you when you're online (unless you specifically block them: Right-click the contact's name and choose Block Contact).

Adding contacts

Messenger contacts aren't the same as Outlook or Windows Mail or Windows Live Hotmail contacts. They're completely separate entities, although from time to time you're given the opportunity to merge the lists.

After you follow the steps in the preceding section to get Windows Live Messenger going, you should set up your contact list. Here's how:

1. **In Windows Live Messenger, to the right of the box that says Search Contacts or the Web, click the Bubble Boy with a Plus Sign icon (patent pending) and choose Add a Contact.**

   A window marked Enter the Person's Information appears (refer to Figure 7-7).

2. **Fill in information about the contact. You need either an instant messaging address or a mobile phone number — everything else is optional. Click Next.**

It's helpful if the instant messaging address is a valid Windows Live Mail (or Yahoo! Messenger) address. If the contact's instant messaging address is for AOL Instant Messenger, for example, you can't get in touch with him.

Windows Live Messenger opens the invitation window, shown in Figure 7-10.

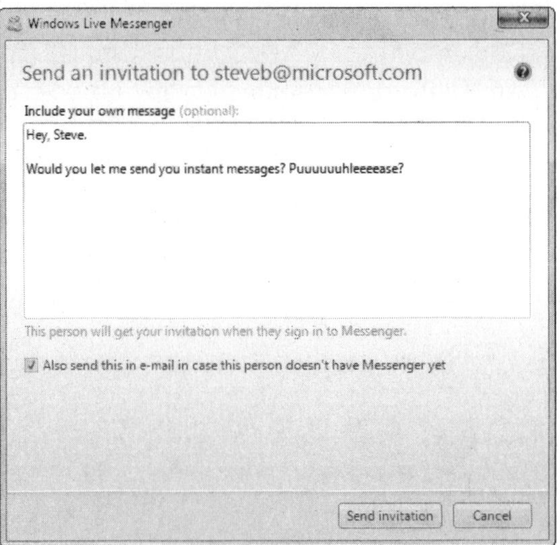

Figure 7-10: Make your case to convince your would-be contact that he should allow you to send him instant messages.

3. **Fill out the message that you want to deliver to your potential contact and then click Send Invitation.**

   When you click Send Invitation, Windows Live Messenger sends an instant message to your new contact, using the text you typed in Step 3 (refer to Figure 7-8). Your new contact can either accept or reject you. Summarily. And there's nothing you can do about it.

4. **Repeat Steps 1 through 3 for all the people you want to put in your Contacts list.**

   These people generally can bug you anytime they want.

As soon as you set up your "give it to anybody" Windows Live ID, click the down arrow to the right of the Show Menu icon (to the right of the doughboy) and choose File⇨Sign Out. Then log in with another Windows Live ID and repeat Steps 1 through 4 for each of your tightly held IDs.

Making contact

When one of your Contacts logs on, the square to the left of the contact's name turns green. To initiate a conversation with the person, double-click her name in the Messenger main window and a Conversation dialog box appears (see Figure 7-11).

Recipient's profile picture

Show Menu

Click to add an emoticon or wink

Type your message here.

Figure 7-11: Conversations are in the box.

To pick up on the conversation, follow these steps:

1. **Just type.**

   Whatever you type appears in the box at the bottom of the Conversation dialog box.

2. **You can edit what you type by clicking and pressing the usual keys: arrow keys, Delete, and others. When you're ready to send what you typed, press Enter or click the Send button.**

You also can cut, copy, and paste text, in the box at the bottom of the dialog box.

3. **To put a cute smiley face in your message, type** :) **or** :D. **Better, try** (A) **for an angel,** (6) **for a devil,** (b) **for a mug of beer, or** :[**for a very cool bat.**

   If you must, click the Emoticons button and choose from a bunch of icons or winks. (If you aren't cool enough to know already, *winks* are emoticons that move.)

   Golly gee, you can even go online and *buy* more emoticons and winks. How thoughtful. When you click the link for Featured Winks or Featured Emoticons, you're directed to a company that sells cute little icons, and you also see pop-ups that look like the one shown in Figure 7-12. Go looking for emoticons and you can contemplate such imponderables as Which Love Language Do You Speak? (***Hint:*** All it takes is money.)

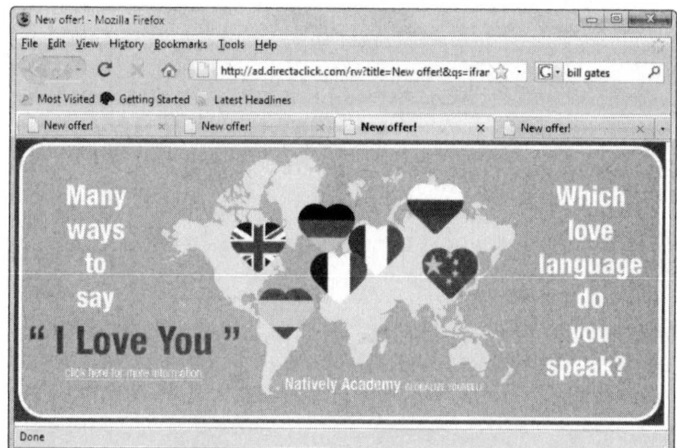

Figure 7-12: Which love language do you speak?

4. **When you're done with the conversation, click the X (Close) button to leave the Conversation dialog box.**

   Messenger returns you to the Messenger main window.

If you're done messaging and don't want to allow anyone to contact you, click the down arrow next to your name and choose Appear Offline.

One guess to how often I do that.

The first time you close a Conversation dialog box, Windows Live Messenger gives you the option of keeping transcripts of all your conversations. If you ever want to change your mind — either start keeping records or stop keeping them — in the main Messenger pane, click the little down arrow to the right of the Show Menus icon in the upper-right corner, choose Tools⇨Options, and click the Messages line on the left (see Figure 7-13).

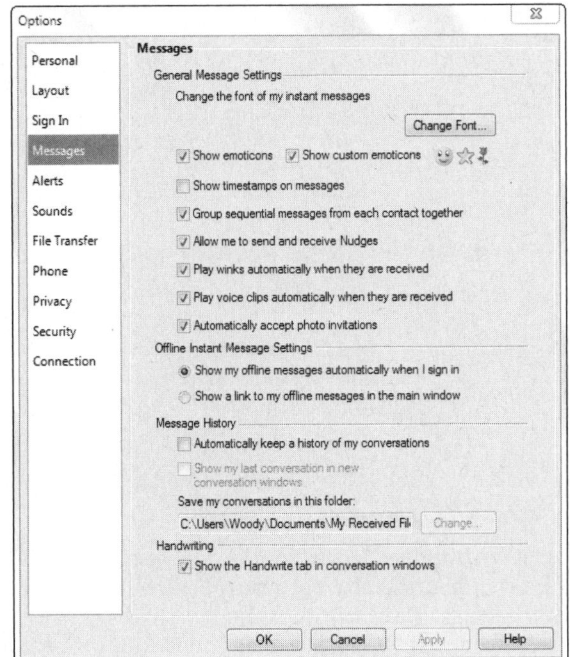

Figure 7-13: To save or not to save, that is the question.

Messenger records are usually kept in `c:\Users\<username>\Documents\My Received Files`.

Tweaking Settings in Windows Live Messenger

Windows Live Messenger has lots of settings, some of which actually make sense. To get to the mother lode, click the down arrow next to the Show Menu icon, on the right, and then choose Tools⇨Options. From that vantage point (see Figure 7-14), you can change your display name and choose from myriad additional settings.

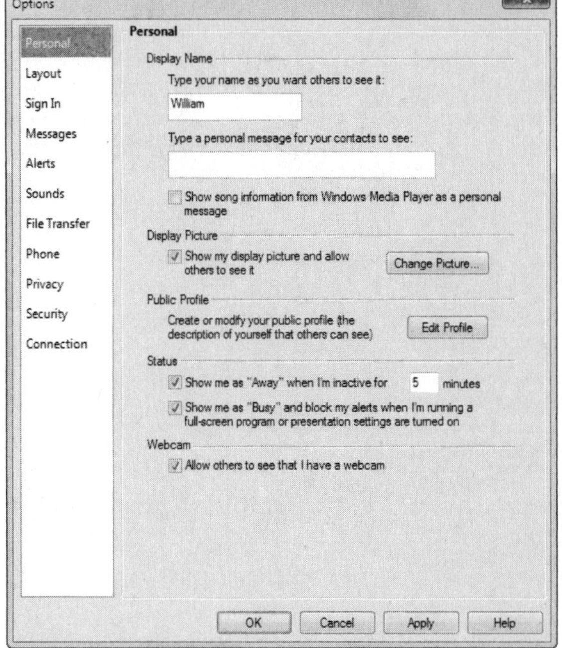

Figure 7-14: The Options settings for AskWoody @hotmail. com. Note that any or all of the information can be bogus.

Revealing your Webcam

The single most important setting in Windows Live Messenger — in my opinion, anyway — appears at the bottom of Figure 7-14. The check box says Allow Others to See that I Have a Webcam. If you allow other people to see that you have a Webcam, they can ask that you turn on your Webcam — all it takes is a click of the Webcam icon to the left of your photo in the message box (refer to Figure 7-9).

If someone wants to see whatever is in front of your Webcam — breathtaking scenery or bad hair day — you receive a message that requests your permission to start sending pictures from the camera to your correspondent. Press Alt+C and your Webcam kicks in, delivering a picture that looks like the one shown in Figure 7-15.

You may not feel comfortable broadcasting the fact that you have a Webcam, or you may be worried that you'll accidentally press Alt+C to turn on the camera at an inopportune time. Give it some thought and make your choice in the Options dialog box accordingly.

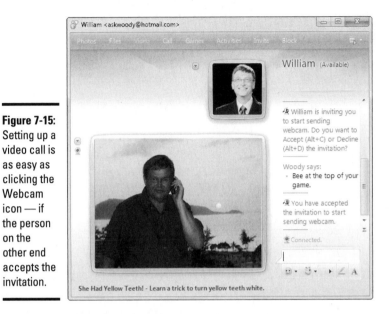

Figure 7-15: Setting up a video call is as easy as clicking the Webcam icon — if the person on the other end accepts the invitation.

Making Messenger forget your password

Have you already told Windows Live Messenger to sign you in automatically? Now that you understand how to use multiple accounts with Messenger, do you regret that choice?

Yeah. I know what you mean. Been there. Done that. Got the scars — or the arrows in the back.

If you have a Messenger ID that's set to sign in automatically, you can switch it back to manual. Here's how:

1. **Choose Start⇨Control Panel⇨User Accounts and Family Safety⇨User Accounts.**
2. **In the upper-left corner, click Manage Your Credentials.**

   You see the Credential Manager, as shown in Figure 7-16.
3. **Click the down arrow to the right of the name of the account you want to remove.**
4. **Click the link marked Remove from Vault, and then "X" out of the Credential Manager.**

   Windows develops a severe case of amnesia and cannot remember how to log you in to Windows Live Manager automatically.

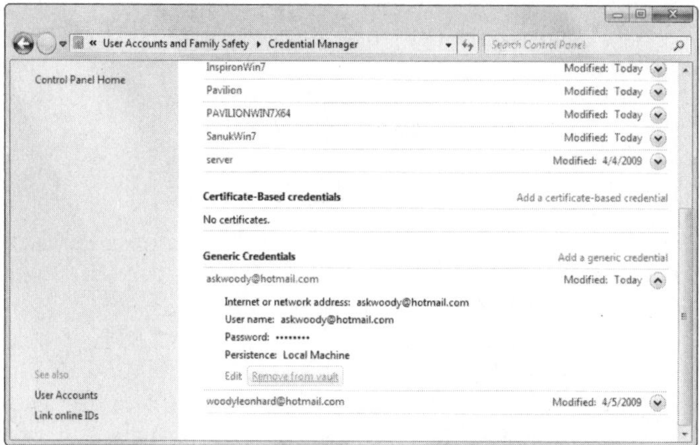

Figure 7-16: Make Windows Live Messenger forget your name and password here.

Stopping Windows Live Messenger from starting automatically

I have more requests for this single feature of Windows Live Messenger than all the others combined.

To put it bluntly: How do you turn off the lousy thing? Windows Live Messenger jumps out of the woodwork every time you log on to Windows. If you X out of Messenger, you see a helpful message that tells you "Windows Live Messenger will continue to run so that you can receive alerts and instant messages when you're signed in." Blech.

You can log off easily enough: Click the down arrow to the right of the Show Menu icon (to the right of the doughboy) and choose File➪Sign Out. But how do you keep Windows Live Messenger from starting every time Windows starts — so that you don't need to log off in the first place?

Turns out there are several ways to do it in Windows 7, but I think this one is the easiest:

1. **If you aren't signed in to Windows Live Messenger, use your Windows Live ID and sign in.**

   That's the hard part. To stop Windows Live Messenger, you need to start it first — kinda like clicking Start to Stop, if you know what I mean. Start by signing in to Windows Live Messenger. You can use any valid Windows Live ID.

2. **Click the down arrow to the right of the Show Menus icon (which is to the right of the doughboy with the plus sign) and choose Tools➪Options. Click Sign In, on the left.**

You see the sign-in options, shown in Figure 7-17.

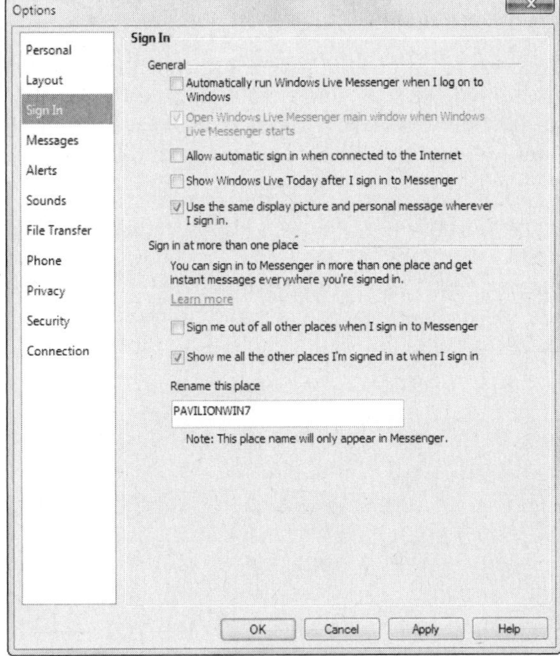

Figure 7-17: Sign-in options allow you to block Windows Live Messenger.

3. **To prevent Windows Live Messenger from starting automatically every time you start Windows, deselect the check box marked Automatically Run Windows Live Messenger When I Log On to Windows.**

   To keep Windows Live Messenger from showing the half-wit Windows Live Today screen every time you start Messenger, deselect the check box marked Show Windows Live Today after I Sign In to Messenger.

   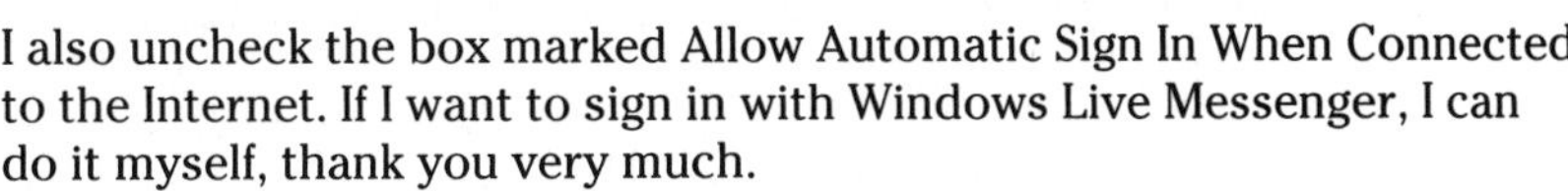
   I also uncheck the box marked Allow Automatic Sign In When Connected to the Internet. If I want to sign in with Windows Live Messenger, I can do it myself, thank you very much.

4. **Click OK.**

   Restart Windows just to make sure that you've driven a wooden stake through Windows Live Messenger's autostarting heart.

Using the fancier features

After you establish a conversation, you may have some success with the more advanced Windows Live Messenger features. These icons appear at the top of the Conversation window (refer to Figure 7-15):

- **Photos** invites you to select photos on your computer. Windows Live Messenger converts them to thumbnails and shows them on the recipient's computer.
- **Files** gives you two options:
  - If you choose to copy a file to the Internet, you're sent to the Microsoft Skydrive site, where you're guided through the steps to upload one to five files to a folder on Skydrive. You're limited to 50MB per file, and the file disappears after 30 days.

    At the end of the process, Skydrive has you fill out the information necessary to notify the recipient about the files and their locations. The notification goes out by e-mail (see Figure 7-18) — Windows Live Messenger doesn't do it for you. If you opt to share files over the Internet, the files are stuck in a "photo album" on Microsoft Skydrive and the recipient is notified by e-mail — not by instant message.

Figure 7-18: When your files are shared over the Internet, the recipient is notified by e-mail — not by instant message.

  - *Alternatively, you can send a file by way of Windows Live Messenger.* The recipient has to accept the offer. If you accept, Windows Live Messenger warns you that "Files may contain harmful viruses." You should ensure that your antivirus software has a chance to scan the file before you open it. The received file is placed in `c:\Users\<your name>\Documents\My Received Files`.
- **Video** sets up Webcams for both you and your recipient. You both get hit with a bunch of advertisements, after which a full two-way video session ensues. Of course, your Internet connection has to be capable of handling the demands of two-way video.

- **Call** opens Windows Live Call, a service from Telefonica Voype. (You can also start a call by choosing Start⇨Windows Live Call.) For more details, go to `live.us.telefonica.com`. Telefonica Voype initiates a Skype-like telephone call between your computer and either the recipient's computer or the recipient's telephone. You have to buy a $5, $10, or $20 credit before you can make calls. Make sure that you understand the billing amounts involved, and compare the charges to, for example, Skype's Skypeout (`skype.com/allfeatures/callphones`).
- **Games** lets you play games such as tic-tac-toe (which hasn't changed much since MSN Messenger 6; see the sidebar "The historic Messenger mess," near the beginning of this chapter). You play against the person you're chatting with.
- **Activities** brings up the Share Fun Activities options, which should be appealing to almost anyone under ten years old. The only exception: This is how you get into Remote Assistance, which I discuss in Book II, Chapter 5.
- **Invite** steps you through the process of inviting another person (or persons) to join your discussion. The only requirement is that they too must be running Windows Live Messenger.
- **Block** cuts off the current conversation and prohibits your recipient from contacting you.

Book VI
Securing Windows 7

"Well, the first level of Windows 7 security seems good—I can't get the shrink-wrapping off."

Contents at a Glance

Chapter 1: Lock Down: Spies, Spams, Scams, and Slams

In This Chapter

- **Taking responsibility for your computer's security — proactively**
- **Discovering how and why you're vulnerable**
- **Avoiding the best-engineered traps: scareware, botnets, keyloggers, and phishing trips**
- **Becoming part of the solution, not part of the problem**
- **Knowing when you've been bitten**

Windows XP had more holes than a prairie-dog field.

Vista was built on top of Windows XP. The holes were hidden better.

Windows 7 includes some truly innovative security capabilities. It's getting harder and harder to take out Windows. Of course, the bad guys are getting smarter and smarter — and they have more money these days.

The settings in Windows 7 focus on keeping the software itself intact: Firewalls, automatic updates, and user account restrictions — the Windows Security Holy Trinity — are all meant to keep the bad guys out of your computer. Windows Defender, bolted to the side of Windows 7, offers some spyware protection, but it's prone to problems of both omission and commission (see Book VI, Chapter 5). Dozens of software companies can sell you antivirus protection, but it can't cover *0day* assaults, malicious programs that take advantage of newly discovered security holes. (I tell you more about 0day assaults later in this chapter.)

Security goes deeper than the Windows 7 applications. Much deeper.

In this chapter, I explain the source of real threats. (More details follow in the next few chapters.) I also take you outside the box, to show you the kinds of problems we all face with our computer systems and to look at a few key solutions.

Most of all, I want you to understand that (1) you shouldn't take a loaded gun, point it at your foot, aim carefully and pull the trigger, and (2) if you're smart and can control your clicking finger, you don't need to spend a penny on malware protection.

Understanding the Hazards — and the Hoaxes

Not long ago, most PC viruses planted themselves on floppy disks. People spread infections by passing around infected disks. A machine got infected when it *booted* (started) with an infected disk in its disk drive. Infected machines subsequently put copies of the virus on every disk that had the misfortune of being stuck in the PC's disk drive.

Although *master boot record viruses* had a bit of competition from other types of viruses, they ruled the PC roost for several years. The most famous — er, infamous — boot record virus, Michelangelo, received an enormous amount of media publicity in early 1992. John McAfee became a TV talk-show celebrity, claiming that 5 million machines were infected, and his company made a fortune. If you were around at the time, you may recall that Michelangelo fell far short of the doomsayer's predictions, putting egg on the face of more than a few self-appointed "experts" who predicted the Demise of Computing As We Know It.

You'll find that it's a recurring theme.

One day, in the summer of 1995, somebody wrote a little virus using WordBasic, the macro programming language that's embedded within Microsoft Word. The virus didn't do much more than show the uninspiring dialog box shown in Figure 1-1. As a matter of fact, it's a wonder it even worked. But by the end of August 1995, a very large percentage of all the PCs on the Microsoft Redmond campus were infected with the Winword. Concept.A virus. Microsoft termed it a prank macro at the time and downplayed its significance. Boy, howdy — what a prank!

Figure 1-1: The Concept.A virus didn't work well.

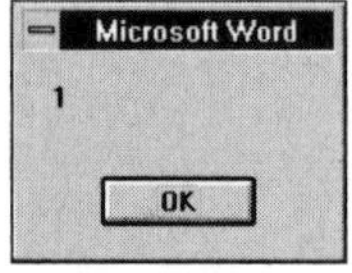

Winword.Concept.A spawned an entire industry — two of them, in fact: the virus writers (whom I generally call "the guys in black hats" or equivalently, "cretins") and the antivirus software folks ("the guys in white hats"). Nobody knows how much the cretins make, but the antivirus industry hauls in more than $5 billion per year.

Many of the best-known Internet-borne scares in the past decade — the Confickers, Mebroots, Bagles, Netskys, Melissas, ILOVEYOUs, Blasters and Slammers, and their ilk — work by using the programmability built into the computer application itself, just like good ol' Concept.A, or by taking advantage of Windows holes to inject themselves into unprotected machines (see Figure 1-2).

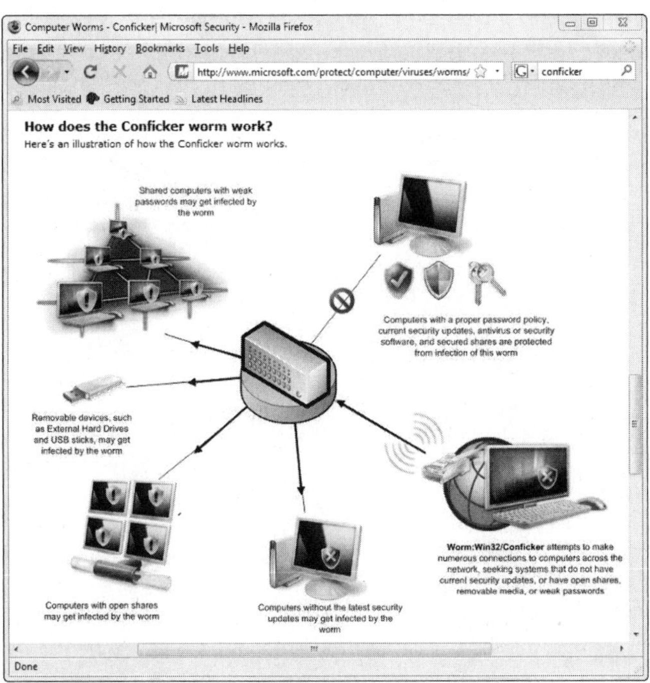

Figure 1-2: The Microsoft description of the many ways the Conficker worm can enter a computer, all employing programmability built into Windows, or security holes that had been patched months earlier.

Fast-forward a dozen years and the concepts have changed. The old threats are still there, but they've taken on a new twist: The scent of money has made cracking far more sophisticated. What started out as a bunch of miscreants playing programmer one-upmanship at our expense has turned into a profitable — sometimes highly profitable — business enterprise.

Where's the money? At least at this moment — and for the foreseeable future — the greatest profits are made by using botnets and phishing attacks. That's where you should expect the most sophisticated, most damnably difficult attacks.

Zombies and botnets

Every month, Microsoft posts a new Malicious Software Removal Tool that scans PCs for malware and, in many cases, removes it. In a recent study, Microsoft reported that 62 percent of all PC systems that were found to have malicious software also had backdoors. That's a sobering figure.

A *backdoor* program breaks through the usual Windows security measures and allows a cretin to take control of your computer over the Internet, effectively turning your machine into a zombie. The most sophisticated backdoors allow creeps to adapt (upgrade, if you will) the malicious software running on a subverted machine. And they do it by remote control.

Backdoors frequently arrive on your PC when you install a program you want, not realizing that the backdoor came along for the ride.

What's a buffer overflow?

If you've been following the progress of malware in general, and the beatings delivered to Windows in particular, you've no doubt run across the term *buffer overflow* or *buffer overrun* — a favorite tool in the arsenal of many virus writers. A buffer overflow may sound mysterious, but it is, at its heart, quite simple.

Programmers set aside small areas in their programs to transfer data from one program to another. Those places are *buffers.* A problem arises when too much data is put in a buffer (or if you look at it from the other direction, when the buffer is too small to hold all the data that's being put in it). You might think that having ten pounds of offal in a five-pound bag would make the program scream bloody murder, but many programs aren't smart enough to look, much less cry uncle and give up.

When too much data exists in the buffer, some of it can spill into the program itself. If the cretin who's stuffing too much data into the buffer is very clever, he/she/it may be able to convince the program that the extra data isn't data, but is instead another part of the program, waiting to be run. The worm sticks a lot of data in a small space and ensures that the piece that flops out will perform whatever malicious deed the worm's creator wants. When the offal hits the fan, the program finds itself executing data that was stuffed into the buffer — running a program that was written by the worm's creator. That's how a buffer overrun can take control of your computer.

Every worm that uses a buffer-overrun security hole in Windows takes advantage of a stupid programming error inside Windows. Programs inside Windows 7 should be checking their buffers all the time. Sorry, Microsoft, but that's a stone-cold fact, even if it means that Windows 7 runs slower.

Less commonly, PCs acquire backdoors when they come down with some sort of infection: The Conficker, Mebroot, Mydoom, and Sobig worms installed backdoors. Many of the infections occur on PCs that haven't been kept up to date with Microsoft security patches (see Book VI, Chapter 4) — buffer overflows are a favorite delivery mechanism. (See the nearby sidebar "What's a buffer overflow?") A look into the future shows that 0day ("zero day") exploits (see the section "0day exploits," later in this chapter) are likely to evolve into the delivery mechanism of choice.

A cretin who controls one machine by way of a backdoor can't claim much street "cred." But someone who puts together a *botnet* — a collection of hundreds or thousands of PCs — can take his zombies to the bank:

- A botnet running a *keylogger* (a program that watches what you type and sporadically sends the data to the botnet's controller) can gather all sorts of valuable information. The single biggest problem facing those who gather and disseminate keylogger information? Bulk — the sheer volume of stolen information. How do you scan millions of characters of logged data and retrieve a bank account number or a password?
- Unscrupulous businesses hire botnet controllers to disseminate spam, "harvest" e-mail addresses, and even direct coordinated distributed denial-of-service (DDoS) attacks against rivals' Web sites. (A *DDoS attack* guides thousands of PCs to go to a particular Web site simultaneously, blocking legitimate use.)

There's a fortune to be made in botnets.

The most successful botnets run as *rootkits,* programs (or collections of programs) that operate deep inside Windows, concealing files and making it extremely difficult to detect their presence.

You probably first heard about rootkits back in late 2005, when a couple of security researchers discovered that certain CDs from Sony BMG surreptitiously installed rootkits on computers: If you merely played the CD on your computer, the rootkit took hold. Several lawsuits later, Sony finally saw the error of its ways and vowed to stop distributing rootkits with its CDs. Nice guys. (The researchers, Mark Russinovich and Bryce Cogswell, were later hired by Microsoft.)

SRI published a thorough, eye-opening white paper about the Conficker worm and its botnet, at `mtc.sri.com/Conficker`. If you're curious about the inner workings of the infernal beasts, that's a great place to start. To date, Conficker is the most successful botnet ever, although Mebroot/Sinowal ain't no slouch. Certainly, the number of Conficker-infected Windows XP PCs runs over a million.

Mebroot the super Trojan

At its height, Mebroot (also known as Sinowal) was credited with stealing more than 500,000 pieces of financial information — bank account passwords, credit card numbers, and the like. Mebroot raised the bar in malware development: sneaky, slick, and quite professional. Although it has been around for years, its criminal tendencies came to light in late 2008.

At its core, Mebroot is a keylogger, and quite a clever keylogger. It watches unobtrusively as you type, kicking in and recording your keystrokes when you go to one of 2,700 Web sites — the list is controlled by the Mebroot creators and includes many of the world's most popular banking and investment sites. Mebroot can put ersatz information on your browser's screen, using the HTML-injection technique, prompting you to type an account number or a password whereas the authentic site doesn't. Of course, Mebroot gathers all the information and sends it back home — over a fancy, secure, encrypted connection.

Mebroot works by infecting the Windows XP master boot record (MBR) — it takes over the tiny program that's used to boot Windows. MBR infections have existed since the dawn of DOS. You'd think that Microsoft would have figured out a way to protect the MBR by now, but you'd be wrong. (Windows 7 blocks the simplest MBR access, but initial sectors are still programmatically accessible.) Mebroot works so well because it's sneaky, and it works in many different ways.

How sneaky? Consider this: Mebroot doesn't run straight out to your MBR and overwrite it. Instead, it waits for eight minutes before it even begins to analyze your computer and change the Registry. Dirty work on the MBR doesn't start until ten minutes after that. Mebroot erases all its tracks and then reboots the PC, using the adulterated MBR and new Registry settings, 42 minutes into the process.

After Mebroot is in a Windows XP system, it runs stealthily, loading itself in true rootkit fashion before Windows starts, flying under the radar by running inside the kernel, the lowest level of Windows. Mebroot sets up its own network communication system, with all its external data transmissions running 128-bit encryption. The people who run Mebroot have thousands of registered `.biz`, `.com`, and `.net` domains at their disposal.

Mebroot cloaks itself entirely: It has no executable files that you can see; changes to the Registry are extremely hard to find; no driver module is on the module list; and no Mebroot-related `svchost.exe` or `rundll32.exe` files are in the Task Manager Processes list. After Mebroot is running, using its own, internal communication software, it can download and run software fed to it by its creators, and the downloaded programs can run, undetected, at the kernel level.

Mebroot isn't so much a Trojan as a parasitic operating system that runs inside Windows.

Phishing

Do you think that message from Wells Fargo (or eBay, the IRS, PayPal, Citibank, a smaller regional bank, Visa, MasterCard, or whatever) asking to verify your account password (Social Security number, account number, address, telephone number, mother's maiden name, or whatever) looks official? Think again.

Did you get a message from someone on eBay saying that you had better pay for the computer you bought or else they'll report you? Gotcha. Perhaps a notification that you have received an online greeting card from a family member — and when you try to retrieve it, you have to join the greeting card site and enter a credit card number? Gotcha again.

Phishing — sending e-mail that attempts to extract personal information from you, usually by using a bogus Web site — has in many cases reached levels of sophistication that exceed the standards of the financial institutions themselves. Some phishing messages, such as the bogus message in Figure 1-3, warn you about the evils of phishing, in an attempt to persuade you to send your account number and password to a scammer in Kazbukistan (or New York).

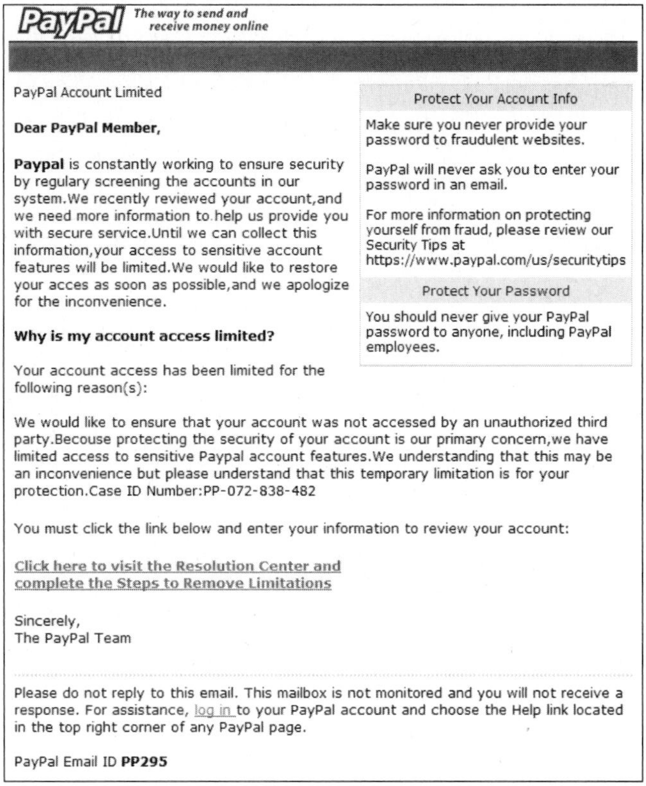

PayPal *The way to send and receive money online*

PayPal Account Limited

Dear PayPal Member,

Paypal is constantly working to ensure security by regulary screening the accounts in our system.We recently reviewed your account,and we need more information to help us provide you with secure service.Until we can collect this information,your access to sensitive account features will be limited.We would like to restore your acces as soon as possible,and we apologize for the inconvenience.

Why is my account access limited?

Your account access has been limited for the following reason(s):

We would like to ensure that your account was not accessed by an unauthorized third party.Becouse protecting the security of your account is our primary concern,we have limited access to sensitive Paypal account features.We understanding that this may be an inconvenience but please understand that this temporary limitation is for your protection.Case ID Number:PP-072-838-482

You must click the link below and enter your information to review your account:

Click here to visit the Resolution Center and complete the Steps to Remove Limitations

Sincerely,
The PayPal Team

Please do not reply to this email. This mailbox is not monitored and you will not receive a response. For assistance, log in to your PayPal account and choose the Help link located in the top right corner of any PayPal page.

PayPal Email ID **PP295**

Protect Your Account Info

Make sure you never provide your password to fraudulent websites.

PayPal will never ask you to enter your password in an email.

For more information on protecting yourself from fraud, please review our Security Tips at https://www.paypal.com/us/securitytips

Protect Your Password

You should never give your PayPal password to anyone, including PayPal employees.

Figure 1-3: If you click the link, you open a page that looks much like the PayPal page, and any information you enter is sent to a scammer.

Here's how it works:

1. **A scammer, often using a fake name and a stolen credit card, sets up a Web site. Usually it's quite a professional-looking site — in some cases, indistinguishable from the authentic site.**

   The Web site asks for personal information — most commonly, your account number and password or the PIN for your ATM card. See Figure 1-4 for an example.

Figure 1-4: This is a fake eBay sign-on site. Can you tell the difference from the original?

2. **The scammer turns spammer and sends out hundreds of thousands of bogus messages. The messages include a clickable link to the fake Web site and a plausible story about how you must go to the Web site, log on, and do something to avoid dire consequences. The From address on the messages is spoofed so that the message appears to come from the company in question.**

   The message usually includes official logos — many even include links to the real Web site, even though they encourage you to click through to the fake site.

3. **A small percentage of the recipients of the spam e-mail open it and click through to the fake site.**

   If they enter their information, it's sent directly to the scammer.

4. **The scammer watches incoming traffic from the fake Web site, gathers the information typed by gullible people, and uses it quickly — typically, by logging on to the bank's Web site and attempting a transfer or by burning a fake ATM card and using the PIN.**

   Within a day or two — or sometimes just hours — the Web site is shut down and everything disappears into thin ether.

Phishing has become hugely popular because of the sheer numbers involved. Say a scammer sends out 1 million e-mail messages advising Wells Fargo customers to log on to their accounts. Only a small fraction of all the people who receive the phishing message will be Wells Fargo customers, but if the hit rate is just 1 percent, that's 10,000 customers.

Most of the Wells Fargo customers who receive the message are smart enough to ignore it. But a sizable percentage — maybe 10 percent, maybe just 1 percent — will click through. That's somewhere between 100 and 1,000 suckers, er, customers.

If half the people who click through provide their account details, the scammer gets 50 to 500 account numbers and passwords. If most of those arrive within a day of sending out the phishing message, the scammer stands to make a pretty penny indeed — and she can disappear with hardly a trace.

I'm not talking about using your credit card online. Online credit card transactions are as safe as they are face to face — more so, actually, because if you use a U.S.-based credit card, you aren't liable for any loss caused by somebody snatching your card information or any other form of fraud. I use my credit cards online all the time. You should, too. (See "Using your credit cards safely online," later in this chapter, for more information.)

Here's how to fight against phishing:

✦ **Use Firefox version 3 or later or Internet Explorer 8 or later.** Both contain sophisticated — although not perfect — antiphishing features that warn you before you venture to a phishy site. (For more information, turn to Book V, Chapter 2.)

✦ **If you encounter a Web site that looks like it may be a phishing site, report it.** Use the tools in Firefox 3 or IE 8.

✦ **If you receive an e-mail message that contains any links to the Web, don't click them.** Nowadays, almost all messages with links to commercial sites are phishing come-ons. Financial institutions, in particular, don't send out messages with links any more — and few other companies would dare. If you feel motivated to check out a dire message — for example, if it looks like somebody on eBay is planning to sue you for something you didn't do — open Firefox (or Internet Explorer) and type the address of the company by hand.

✦ **Never include personal information in an e-mail message and send it.** Don't give out any of your personal information unless you manually logged on to the company's Web site. Remember that unless you encrypt your e-mail messages, they travel over the Internet in plain text form. Anybody who's "sniffing" the mail can see everything you've written. It's roughly analogous to sending a postcard.

✦ **If you receive a phishing message that may be new or different, check `www.millersmiles.co.uk` to see whether it's a well-known, uh, phish.** If you don't see your phish listed, submit a copy using the instructions at `millersmiles.co.uk/submit.php`. Hold on to the message for a while to see whether the authorities need a copy of the message header: If so, they'll send you instructions.

MillerSmiles (see Figure 1-5) has a wealth of information on phishing — 1.5 million samples of phishing messages, at last count — including an invaluable description of the steps you should take if you accidentally gave your personal information to a phisher. See `millersmiles.co.uk/identity theft/oah-6.htm`.

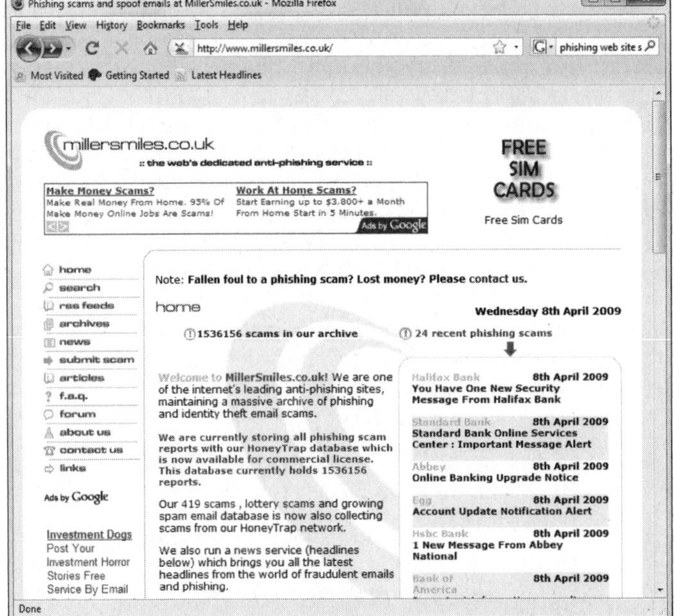

Figure 1-5: MillerSmiles maintains a huge database of phishing messages and offers sage advice about identifying, reporting, and recovering from phishing attacks.

0day exploits

What do you do when you discover a brand-new security hole in Windows or Office or another Microsoft product? Why, you sell it, of course.

When a person writes a malicious program that takes advantage of a newly discovered security hole — a hole that even the manufacturer doesn't know about — that malicious program is a *0day exploit*. (Fuddy-duddies call it "zero-day exploit." The hopelessly hip say "sploit.")

The security company iDefense Labs offers as much as $15,000 for certain newly discovered security holes in major software products. In addition, iDefense has an annual competition for "contributed vulnerabilities," offering a $50,000 grand prize every year for the "most significant" security hole of the year. To a first approximation, iDefense "buys" the security hole, works with Microsoft and other software manufacturers on a solution, and at the same time protects its customers from the threat, even before the software company releases the fix. (Details may change by the time you read this chapter. Got a hole to sell? See `labs.idefense.com/vcp`.) One enterprising cracker offered up his hole for sale to the highest bidder on eBay.

Rumor has it that several less-than-scrupulous sites arrange for the buying and selling of new security holes. Apparently, the Russian hacker group that discovered a vulnerability in the way Windows handles WMF graphics files sold its new hole for $4,000, not realizing that it could've made much more.

How do you protect yourself from 0day exploits? In some ways, you can't: By definition, nobody sees a 0day coming, although most antivirus products employ some sort of heuristic detection that tries to clamp down on exploits based solely on the behavior of the offensive program. Mostly, you have to rely on the common sense protection that I describe in the section "Getting Protected," later in this chapter. You must also stay informed, which I talk about in the next section.

Staying Informed

Botnets and sploits and phishing holes — oh, my!

When you rely on the evening news to keep yourself informed about the latest threats to your computer's well-being, you quickly discover that the mainstream press frequently doesn't get the details right. Hey, if you were a newswriter with a deadline ten minutes away and you had to figure out how the new Bandersnatch 0day exploit shreds through a Windows 7 TCP/IP stack buffer — and you had to explain your discoveries to a TV audience, at a presumed sixth grade intelligence level — what would you do?

Relying on reliable sources

Fortunately, some reliable sources of information exist on the Internet. It would behoove you to check them out from time to time, particularly when you hear about a new computer security hole, real or imagined:

- The Microsoft Security Response Center (MSRC) blog (`blogs.technet.com/msrc`) presents thoroughly researched analyses of outstanding threats, from a Microsoft perspective.

The information you see on the MSRC blog is 100 percent Microsoft Party Line — so there's a tendency to add more than a little "spin control" to the announcements. Nevertheless, Microsoft has the most extensive and best resources to analyze and solve Windows problems, and the MSRC blog frequently has inside information that you can't find anywhere else.

✦ SANS Internet Storm Center (ISC) (`isc.sans.org`) pools observations and analysis from thousands of active security researchers. You can generally get the news first — accurately — from the ISC.

✦ *Windows Secrets* newsletter (`windowssecrets.com`), the most-read Windows weekly ever, contains excellent recaps of all the latest problems. Also, my site, `AskWoody.com`, strives to present the latest security information in a way that doesn't require a Ph.D. in computer science.

Take a moment right now to look up those sites and add them to your Firefox bookmarks or Internet Explorer Favorites. Unlike the antimalware software manufacturers' Web sites, these sites have no particular ax to grind or product to sell. (Well, okay, Microsoft wants to sell you something, but you're already inured, yes?)

Microsoft releases security patches frequently (the second Tuesday of every month, as of this writing). You can get advance notice about upcoming patches on the MSRC blog. When the patches become available, they're described and presented in security bulletins bearing sequential numbers such as MS09-001, MS09-002, and so on. The patches themselves are attached to Microsoft Knowledge Base (KB) articles with numbers resembling KB 912345. Microsoft keeps the bulletins separate from the patching programs because a single security bulletin may have many associated patches.

From time to time, Microsoft also releases security advisories, which generally warn about newly discovered 0day threats in Microsoft products. You can find those, too, at the MSRC blog.

It's hard to keep all the patches straight without a scorecard. I maintain an exhaustive list of patches and their known problems and also the Microsoft patches of the patches (of the patches) on AskWoody.com.

Ditching the hoaxes

Tell me whether you've heard any of these:

✦ "Amazing Speech by Obama!" "CNN News Alert!" "UPS Delivery Failure," "Hundreds killed in [insert a disaster of your choice]," "Budweiser Frogs Screensaver!" "Microsoft Security Patch Attached."

- A virus will hit your computer if you read any message that includes the phrase "Good Times" in the subject line. (That one was a biggie in late 1994.) Ditto for any of the following messages: "It Takes Guts to Say 'Jesus'," "Win a Holiday," "Help a poor dog win a holiday," "Join the Crew," "pool party," "A Moment of Silence," "an Internet flower for you," "a virtual card for you," or "Valentine's Greetings."
- A deadly virus is on the Microsoft [or insert your favorite company name here] home page. Don't go there or else your system will die.
- If you have a file named [insert filename here] on your PC, it contains a virus. Delete it immediately!

They're all hoaxes — not a breath of truth in any of them.

Some hoaxes serve as fronts for real viruses: The message itself is a hoax, a red herring, designed to convince you to do something stupid and infect your system. The message asks (or commands!) you to download a file or run a video that acts suspiciously like an `.exe` file.

Other hoaxes are just rumors that circulate among well-intentioned people who haven't a clue. Those hoaxes hurt, too. Sometimes, when real worms hit, so much e-mail traffic is generated from warning people to avoid the worm that the well-intentioned watchdogs do more damage than the worm itself! Strange but true.

Do yourself a favor (me, too): If somebody sends you a message that sounds like the following examples, just delete it, eh?

- A horrible virus is on the loose that's going to bring down the Internet. (Sheesh. I get enough of that garbage on the nightly news.)
- Send a copy of this message to ten of your best friends, and for every copy that's forwarded, Bill Gates will give [pick your favorite charity] $10.
- Forward a copy of this message to ten of your friends, and put your name at the bottom of the list. In [pick a random amount of time], you will receive $10,000 in the mail, or your luck will change for the better. Your eyelids will fall off if you don't forward this message.
- Microsoft (Intel, McAfee, Norton, Compaq — whatever) says that you need to double-click on the attached file, download something, not download something, go to a specific place, avoid a specific place, and on and on.

If you think you've stumbled on the world's most important virus alert, by way of your uncle's sister-in-law's roommate's hairdresser's soon-to-be-ex-boyfriend (remember that he's the one who's a really smart computer guy, but kind of smelly?), count to ten twice and keep these four important points in mind:

- ✦ No reputable software company (including Microsoft) distributes patches by e-mail. You should never, ever, open or run an attachment to an e-mail message until you contact the person who sent it to you and confirm that she intended to send it to you.
- ✦ Chances are very good (I'd say, oh, 99.9999 percent or more) that you're looking at a half-baked hoax that's documented on the Web, most likely on the Snopes urban myths site (`snopes.com`) or the Trend Micro hoax site, at `threatinfo.trendmicro.com/vinfo/hoaxes`.
- ✦ If the virus is real, all the major news agencies will carry reports that (even if they're inaccurate!) are far, far more reliable than anything you get through e-mail. Check out BBC.com, CNET.com, or your favorite news site before you go way off the deep end.
- ✦ If the Internet world is about to collapse, clogged with gazillions of e-mail worms, the worst possible way to notify friends and family is by e-mail. D'oh! Pick up the phone, walk over to the water cooler, or send out a carrier pigeon and give your intended recipients a reliable Web address to check for updates. Betcha they've already heard about it anyway.

Try hard to be part of the solution, not part of the problem, okay? And if a friend forwards you a virus warning in an e-mail, do all of us a big favor: Shoot him a copy of the preceding bullet points, ask him to tape it to the side of his computer, and beg him to refer to it the next time he gets the forwarding urge.

Am I Infected?

So how do you know whether you're infected?

The short answer is this: Many times, you don't. If you think that your PC is infected, chances are very good that it isn't. Why? Because malware these days doesn't usually cause the kinds of problems people normally associate with infections.

Whatever you do, don't fall for the scamware that tells you it removed 39 infections from your computer but you need to pay in order to remove the other 179 (see "Shunning Scareware," a little later in this chapter).

Evaluating telltale signs

Here are a few telltale signs that might — *might* — mean that your PC is infected:

✦ **Someone tells you that you sent him an e-mail message with an attachment — and you didn't send it.** In fact, most e-mail malware these days is smart enough to spoof the From address, so any infected message that appears to come from you probably didn't. Still, some dumb old viruses that aren't capable of hiding your e-mail address are still around. And, if you receive an infected attachment from a friend, chances are good that both your e-mail address and his e-mail address are on an infected computer somewhere. Six degrees of separation and all that.

If you receive an infected message, look at the header to see whether you can tell where it came from. In Outlook 2003 and earlier, open the message and then choose View➪Options. In Outlook 2007, you have to open the message and then click the tiny square with a downward, right-facing arrow in the lower right corner of the Options group. A box at the bottom may (or may not!) tell you who really sent the message, as shown in Figure 1-6.

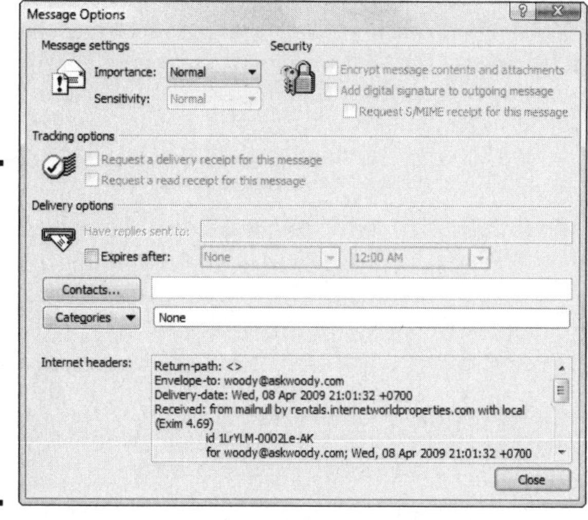

Figure 1-6: The box at the bottom contains the e-mail header, which may give you a clue to its origin.

✦ **You suddenly see files with two filename extensions scattered around your computer.** Filenames such as `kournikova.jpg.vbs` (a VBScript file masquerading as a JPG image file) or `somedoc.txt.exe` (a Windows program that wants to appear to be a text file) should send you running for your antivirus software.

Always, always, always have Windows show you filename extensions (see Book II, Chapter 1).

- **Your antivirus software suddenly stops working.** If the icon for your antivirus product disappears from the notification area (near the clock), something killed it — and chances are very good that the culprit was a virus.
- **You can't reach Web sites that are associated with antimalware manufacturers.** For example, Firefox or Internet Explorer works fine with most Web sites, but you can't get through to Microsoft.com or Symantec.com or McAfee.com. This problem is a key giveaway for a Conficker infection, but other pieces of malware do it, too.

What to do next

If you think that your computer is infected, follow these steps:

1. **Don't panic.**

   Chances are very good that you're not infected.

2. **DO NOT REBOOT YOUR COMPUTER.**

   This advice is particularly important in Windows 7 because of the way it takes snapshots of Last Known Good system configurations. If your machine gets infected and you reboot, and then Windows 7 mistakenly thinks that your infected system is "good," it may incorrectly update the Last Known Good configuration information. Resist the urge to press the Reset button until you exhaust all possibilities.

3. **Update your antivirus software with the latest signature file from the manufacturer's Web site; then run a full scan of your system.**

   If you don't have an antivirus package installed, run — don't walk — to the next section, and download and install AVG Free antivirus, or follow the instructions there to install Microsoft Security Essentials, the free new kid on the antivirus block.

4. **If your antivirus software doesn't identify the problem, follow your antivirus software manufacturer's instructions.**

   If you can't get into your manufacturer's Web site, beg, borrow, or steal another PC and log on to the manufacturer's Web site (see Table 1-1). All the major antivirus software manufacturers have detailed steps on their Web sites to take you through the scary parts.

   Note that some sites may have news posted hours before other sites — but it's impossible to tell in advance which will get the story first.

5. **If Step 4 still doesn't solve the problem, go to Jim Eshelman's AumHa site (`aumha.net/viewtopic.php?t=4075`) and post your problem on the Malware Removal forum.**

   Make sure that you follow the instructions precisely. The good folks at AumHa are all volunteers. You can save them — and yourself — lots of headaches by following their instructions to the letter.

6. **Do not — I repeat — do not send messages to all your friends advising them of the new virus.**

   Messages about a new virus can outnumber infected messages generated by the virus itself — in some cases, causing more havoc than the virus itself. Try not to become part of the problem. Besides, you may be wrong.

Table 1-1 Major Antivirus Software Vendors' Sites

Product	*Company*	*Breaking News Web Site*
AVG Anti-Virus	GRISoft	grisoft.com
F-Secure Antivirus	F-Secure	f-secure.com/virus-info
Kaspersky Antivirus	Kaspersky Lab	kaspersky.com
McAfee VirusScan	Network Associates	us.mcafee.com/virusInfo/default.asp
Norton AntiVirus	Symantec	securityresponse.symantec.com
Panda Antivirus	Panda	pandasecurity.com
Trend PC-cillin	Trend Micro	antivirus.com/vinfo

In recent years, I've come to view the mainstream press accounts of virus and malware outbreaks with increasing, uh, skepticism. The antivirus companies are usually slower to post news than the mainstream press, but the information they post tends to be much more reliable. Not infallible, mind you, but better. We also cover security problems at AskWoody.com.

Shunning scareware

A friend of mine brought me her computer the other day and showed me a giant warning about all the viruses residing on it (see Figure 1-7). She knew that she needed XP Antivirus, but she didn't know how to install it. Thank heaven.

Another friend brought me a computer that always booted to a Blue Screen of Death that said

```
Error 0x00000050 PAGE_FAULT_IN_NON_PAGED_AREA
```

It took a whole day to unwind all the junkware on that computer, but when I got to the bottom dreck, I found Vista Antivirus 2009.

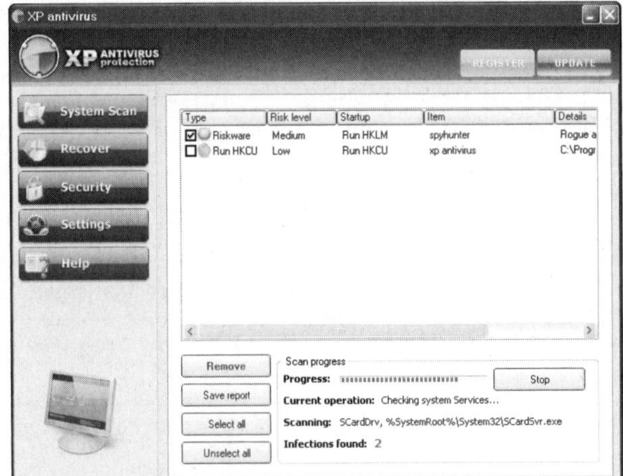

Figure 1-7: When is an antivirus product, in reality, a virus?

I've received messages from all over the world from people who want to know about this fabulous new program, Antivirus 2009 (or Vista Antivirus or XP Antivirus or MS Antivirus Security Center or Micro AV or similar wording). Here's what you need to know: It's malware, plain and simple, and if you install it, you're handing over your computer to some very sophisticated folks who will install key loggers, bot software, and the scummiest, dirtiest stuff you've ever seen on any PC.

Here's the crazy part: Most people install this kind of scareware voluntarily. One particular family of rogue antivirus products, named Win32/FakeSecSen, has infected more than a million computers; see Figure 1-8.

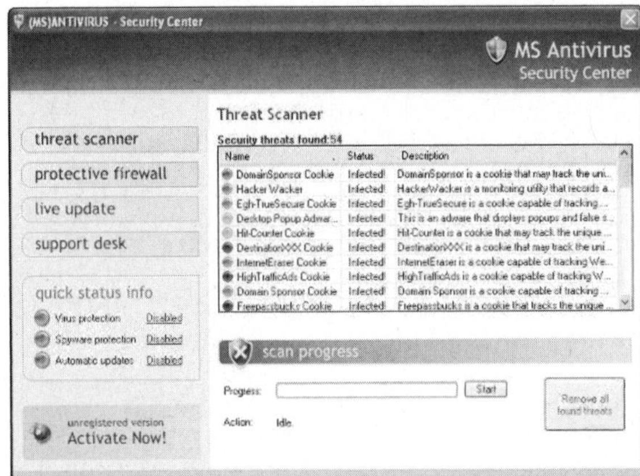

Figure 1-8: Win32/ FakeSecSen scares you into thinking you have to pay to clean your computer.

Typically you receive a spam message that invites you to install this wonderful new program named Antivirus something-or-another. You figure, hey, it couldn't be any worse than the big-name antivirus program you have now — the one that's no doubt bugging you every two days to cough up your credit card number to stay up-to-date — and figure it's worth a try.

Wrong.

Some people pick up Antivirus 2009 by clicking a link on a decent, well-known Web site. They just don't realize that people who run big Web sites frequently farm out their advertising, and sometimes the ads (which are delivered independently of the page itself) harbor threatening stuff. The SpywareRemove Web site reports (`tinyurl.com/55pjnk`) that, not long ago, Google was showing "sponsored" paid links that pointed directly to the Antivirus XP 2008 site.

The exact method of infection can vary, as will the payloads.

If you've got it, how do you remove it? For starters, don't even bother with Windows Add or Remove Programs. Any company clever enough to call a piece of scum Antivirus 2009 won't make it easy for you to zap it. The Bleeping Computer site has removal instructions at `tinyurl.com/6xxhyz`.

TECHNICAL STUFF

One of my favorite antimalware industry pundits, Rob Rosenberger, has an insightful analysis of this type of scareware in the article "Two decades of virus hysteria contributes to the success of fake-AV scams," at `vmyths.com/2009/03/22/rogue-av`.

Microsoft has an excellent review of rogue antivirus products in its Security Intelligence Report Volume 6, available at `microsoft.com/sir`.

Getting Protected

The Internet is wild and woolly and wonderful — and, by and large, it's unregulated, in a Wild West sort of way. Some would say it cannot be regulated, and I agree. Although some central bodies control basic Internet coordination questions — how the computers talk to each other, who doles out domain names such as dummies.com, and what a Web browser should do when it encounters a particular piece of HyperText Markup Language (HTML) — no central authority or Web Fashion Police exists.

In spite of its Wild West lineage and complete lack of couth, the Internet doesn't need to be a scary place. If you follow a handful of simple, common sense rules, you'll go a long way toward making your Internet travels more like Happy Trails and less like *Doom III*.

Protecting against malware

"Everybody" knows that the Internet breeds viruses. "Everybody" knows that really bad viruses can drain your bank account, break your hard drive, and give you terminal halitosis — just by looking at an e-mail message with *Good Times* in the Subject line. Right.

In fact, botnets and keyloggers can hurt you, but hoaxes and lousy advice abound. Every Windows 7 user should follow these tips:

- **Don't install weird programs, cute icons, automatic e-mail signers, or products that promise to keep your computer oh-so-wonderfully safe.** Unless the software comes from a reputable manufacturer whom you trust, and you know precisely *why* you need it, you don't want it. Don't be fooled by products that claim to clean your Registry or clobber imaginary infections.

  You may think that you absolutely must synchronize the Windows clock (which Windows 7 does amazingly well, no extra program needed), tune up your computer (gimme a break), use those cute little smiley icons (gimme a bigger break), install a pop-up blocker (both Internet Explorer and Firefox already do that well), or install an automatic e-mail signer (your e-mail program already can sign your messages — read the manual, pilgrim!). What you end up with is an unending barrage of hassles and hustles.

- **Buy, install, update, and religiously use one of the major antivirus software packages and one of the major antispyware packages.** It doesn't matter which one — all of them are good. Personally, I like free — the free versions of several antivirus products work just as well as the big-name, big-buck alternatives. (See Book VI, Chapter 5 for more on antivirus and antispyware software.)

  In spite of its name, antivirus software frequently looks for more than just viruses. Many 0day exploits can be nipped in the bud, shortly after their appearance, by a recently updated antivirus scan.

- **Never, ever, open a file attached to an e-mail message until you contact the person who sent you the file and verify that she did, in fact, send you the file intentionally.** After you contact the person who sent you the file, don't open the file directly. Save it to your hard drive and run your antivirus software on it before you open it.

- **Follow the instructions in Book II, Chapter 1 to force Windows 7 to show you the full name of all the files on your computer.** That way, if you see a file named `something.cpl` or `iloveyou.vbs`, you stand a fighting chance of understanding that it might be an infectious program waiting for your itchy finger.

- **Don't trust e-mail.** Every single part of an e-mail message can be faked, easily. The return address can be spoofed. Even the header information — which you don't normally see — can be pure fiction. Links inside e-mail messages may not point where you think they point. Anything you put in a message can be viewed by anybody with even a nodding interest — to use the old analogy, sending unencrypted e-mail is a lot like sending a postcard.
- **Check your accounts.** Look at your credit card and bank statements, and if you see a charge you don't understand, question it. Log on to all your financial Web sites frequently, and if somebody changed your password, scream bloody murder.

Using your credit card safely online

Many people who use the Web refuse to order anything online because they're afraid that their credit card numbers will be stolen and they'll be liable for enormous bills. Or they think the products will never arrive and they won't get their money back.

If your credit card was issued in the United States and you're ordering from a U.S. company, that's simply not the case. Here's why:

- **The Fair Credit Billing Act protects you from being charged by a company for an item you don't receive.** It's the same law that governs orders placed over the telephone or by mail. A vendor generally has 30 days to send the merchandise, or it has to give you a formal, written chance to cancel your order. For details, go to the Federal Trade Commission (FTC) Web site, `ftc.gov/bcp/edu/pubs/consumer/credit/cre28.shtm`.
- **Your maximum liability for charges fraudulently made on the card is $50 per card.** The minute you notify the credit card company that somebody else is using your card, you have no further liability. If you have any questions, the Federal Trade Commission can help. (See `ftc.gov/bcp/edu/pubs/consumer/tech/tec01.shtm`.)

The rules are different if you're not dealing with a U.S. company and using a U.S. credit card. For example, if you buy something in an online auction from an individual, you don't have the same level of protection. Make sure that you understand the rules before you hand out credit card information. Unfortunately, there's no central repository (at least none I could find) of information about overseas purchase protection for U.S. credit card holders: each credit card seems to handle cases individually. If you buy things overseas using a U.S. credit card, your relationship with your credit card company generally provides your only protection.

Some online vendors, such as Amazon.com, absolutely guarantee that your shopping will be safe. The Fair Credit Billing Act protects any charges fraudulently made in excess of $50, but Amazon says that it reimburses any fraudulent charges under $50 that occurred as a result of using its Web site. Many credit card companies now offer similar assurances.

Regardless, you should still take a few simple precautions to make sure that you aren't giving away your credit card information:

- **When you place an order online, make sure that you're dealing with a company you know.** In particular, don't click a link in an e-mail message and expect to go to the company's Web site. Type the company's address into Internet Explorer or Firefox, or use a link that you stored in your Internet Explorer Favorites or the Firefox Bookmarks list.
- **Type your credit card number only when you're sure that you've arrived at the company's site and when the site is using a secure Web page.** The easy way to tell whether a Web page is secure is to look in the lower-right corner of the screen for a picture of a lock (see Figure 1-9). Secure Web sites scramble data so that anything you type on the Web page is encrypted before it's sent to the vendor's computer. In addition, Firefox tells you a site's registration and pedigree by clicking the icon to the left of the Web address. In Internet Explorer, the icon appears to the right of the address.

  Be aware that crafty Web programmers can fake the lock icon and show an `https://` (secure) address to try to lull you into thinking that you're on a secure Web page. To be safe, confirm the site's address in the lower-left corner and click the icon to the left of the address at the top to show the full security certificate.

- **Don't send your credit card number in an ordinary e-mail message.** E-mail is just too easy to intercept. And for heaven's sake, don't give out any personal information when you're chatting online.
- **If you receive an e-mail message requesting credit card information that seems to be from your bank, credit card company, Internet service provider, or even your sainted Aunt Martha, don't send sensitive information back by way of e-mail.** Insist on using a secure Web site and type the company's address into Firefox or Internet Explorer.

Identity theft continues to be a problem all over the world. Widespread availability of personal information online only adds fuel to the flame. If you think someone may be posing as you — to run up debts in your name, for example — see the U.S. government's main Web site on the topic at `consumer.gov/idtheft`.

Click the icon to see the site's security certificate.

Confirm a site's address.

The lock icon indicates a secure site.

Figure 1-9: Firefox can tell you a lot about a secure site.

Defending your privacy

"You have zero privacy anyway. Get over it."

That's what Scott McNealy, CEO of Sun Microsystems, said to a group of reporters on January 25, 1999. He was exaggerating — Scott has been known to make provocative statements for dramatic effect — but the exaggeration comes awfully close to reality. (Actually, if Scott told me the sky was blue, I'd run outside and check. But I digress.)

I continue to be amazed at Windows users' odd attitudes toward privacy. People who wouldn't dream of giving a stranger their telephone numbers fill out their mailing addresses for online service profiles. People who are scared to death at the thought of using their credit cards online to place an order with a major retailer (a very safe procedure, by the way) dutifully type their Social Security numbers on Web-based forms.

Windows 7 — particularly through Microsoft Windows Live Essentials — gives you unprecedented convenience. That convenience comes at a price, though: Everything you do in Windows Live Mail, Messenger, Safety Center — or just about any commercial site on the Web, for that matter — ends up stored away in a database somewhere. And, as the technology becomes more and more refined, your privacy gets squeezed.

I suggest that you follow these few important privacy points:

✦ **Use work systems only for work.** Why use your company e-mail ID for personal messages? C'mon. Sign up for a free Web-based e-mail account, such as Gmail (`www.gmail.com`), Yahoo! Mail (`http://mail.yahoo.com`), or Hotmail (`www.hotmail.com`).

In the United States, with few exceptions, anything you do on a company PC at work can be monitored and examined by your employer. E-mail, Web site history files, and even stored documents and settings are all fair game. At work, you have zero privacy anyway. Get over it.

✦ **Don't give it away.** Why use your real name when you sign up for a free e-mail account? Why tell a random survey that your annual income is between $20,000 and $30,000? (Or is it between $150,000 and $200,000?)

All sorts of Web sites — particularly Microsoft — ask questions about topics that, simply put, are none of their dern business. Don't put your personal details out where they can be harvested.

✦ **Know your rights.** Although cyberspace doesn't provide the same level of personal protection you have come to expect in *meatspace* (real life), you still have rights and recourses. Check out `privacyrights.org` for some thought-provoking notices.

Keep your head low and your powder dry!

Keeping cookies at bay

A *cookie* is a text file that a Web site stores on your computer. Why would a Web site want to store a file on your computer? To identify you when you come back. It's that simple.

Consider the case of D. Dummy, D. Dummy's computer, and a Web site that D. Dummy visits — my hometown newspaper's site, `www.phuketgazette.net`, in this example. The *Phuket* (pronounced "poo-KET") *Gazette* uses cookies to keep track of when readers last visited its Web site so that readers can click a button and see what has happened since the last time they looked at the site. Nifty feature.

Here's how cookies come into the picture:

1. D. Dummy decides that he wants to look at the *Phuket Gazette* site, so he types `phuketgazette.net` in Firefox (or Internet Explorer) and presses Enter.

2. D. Dummy's computer starts talking to the Web site. "Howdy, y'all!" (Did I mention that D. Dummy's computer comes from Texas? Details, details.) "I'm D. Dummy, and I'd like to take a look at your main page."

3. The *Phuket Gazette* site, `phuketgazette.net`, starts talking back to D. Dummy's computer. "Hey, D. Dummy! Have you been here before?"

   Actually, the *Phuket Gazette* site is a whole lot more polite than that, but you get the idea.

4. D. Dummy's computer runs out to its hard drive and looks for a text file named (bear with me) `DDummy@www.phuketgazette.txt`. It doesn't find a file, so D. Dummy's computer says to the Web site, "Nope. I don't have any cookies here from y'all."

5. The *Phuket Gazette* site pulls off its shoes and socks, starts counting fingers and toes, and then says to D. Dummy's computer, "Fair enough. I figure you're user number 1578462. Store that number away, wouldja, so that I can identify you the next time you come back here? And, while you're at it, could you also remember that you were last here at 11:36 a.m. on December 14?"

6. D. Dummy's computer runs out, creates a new file named `DDummy@www.phuketgazette.txt`, and puts the values `1578462` and `11:36 a.m. on December 14` in it.

The *Phuket Gazette* site's main page starts to open on the screen. D. Dummy scans the headlines, and then heads off to do some shopping. Two hours (or days or weeks or months) later, dear old D. Dummy goes back to `www.phuketgazette.net`. Here's what happens:

1. D. Dummy types `phuketgazette.net` in Firefox (or Internet Explorer) and presses Enter.

2. D. Dummy's computer starts talking to the Web site. "Howdy y'all! I'm D. Dummy, and I'd like to take a look at your main page." (Texans.)

3. The *Phuket Gazette* site, `phuketgazette.net`, says to D. Dummy's computer, "Hey, D. Dummy! Have you been here before?"

4. This time, D. Dummy's computer runs out to its hard drive and finds a file named `DDummy@www.phuketgazette.txt`. D. Dummy's computer says to the Web site, "Gee whillikers. I have a cookie from you guys. It says that I'm user number 1578462 and I was last here at 11:36 a.m. on December 14."

5. That's all the *Phuket Gazette* Web site needs to know. It flashes a big banner that says "Welcome back D. Dummy!" and puts together a button that says "Click here to see everything that's happened since 11:36 a.m. on December 14."

The Doubleclick shtick

A Web site plants a cookie on your computer. Only that Web site can retrieve the cookie. The information is shielded from other Web sites. ZDNet.com (the PCMag Web site) can figure out that I have been reading reviews of digital cameras. Dealtime.com knows that I buy shoes. But a cookie from ZDNet can't be read by Dealtime, and vice versa. So what's the big deal?

Enter Doubleclick.net, which is now a division of Google. For the better part of a decade, both ZDNet.com and Dealtime.com have included ads from a company named Doubleclick.net. Don't believe it? Use Internet Explorer to go to each of the sites, press the Alt key, and select View⇨Web Page Privacy Policy. (In Firefox, you can do the same thing if you select Tools⇨Options⇨Privacy⇨Show Cookies and watch the bottom of the list.) Unless ZDNet or Dealtime has changed advertisers, you see Doubleclick.net featured prominently in each site's privacy report.

Here's the trick: You surf to a ZDNet Web page that contains a Doubleclick.net ad. Doubleclick kicks in and plants a cookie on your PC that says you were looking at a specific page on ZDNet. Two hours (or days or weeks) later, you surf to a Dealtime page that also contains a Doubleclick.net ad — a different ad, no doubt — but one distributed by Doubleclick. Doubleclick kicks in again and discovers that you were looking at that specific ZDNet page two hours (or days or weeks) earlier.

Now consider the consequences if a hundred sites that you visit in an average week all have Doubleclick ads. They can be tiny ads — 1 pixel high, or so small that you can't see them. All the information about all your surfing to those sites can be accumulated by Doubleclick and used to "target" you for advertising, recommendations, or whatever. It's scary.

Note that the *Phuket Gazette* site could also keep track of user 1578462 on the Web site's own computer — stick an entry in a database somewhere — and accumulate information about that user. (The site doesn't, but it could.)

No doubt you've been told that cookies are horrible, evil programs lurking in the bowels of Windows that can divulge your credit card number to a pimply teenager in Gazukistan and then slice and dice the data on your hard drive, shortly before handing you over, screaming, to the Feds. In fact, your uncle's sister-in-law's roommate's hairdresser's . . . and so on probably told you so himself. Well, guess what? A cookie is just a text file, placed on your hard drive by a Web page. Nothing sinister about it.

A cookie can be retrieved only by the same site that sent it out in the first place. So the *Phuket Gazette* can put cookies on my hard drive, but only the *Phuket Gazette* can read its cookies. There's a trick, though. See the sidebar "The Doubleclick shtick" for details.

To understand how cookies can pose problems, you have to take a look at the kind of information that can be collected about you, as an individual, and how big of a squeeze it puts on your privacy.

When you visit a Web site, the site can automatically collect a small amount of information about you. It can collect these bits and pieces:

- **Your computer's address (actually, the IP address, which identifies your computer on the Internet):** For most people with a DSL or cable connection, your address doesn't change often, if at all. That means a sufficiently persistent data-mining program can (at least in theory) track your activities over long periods.
- **The name of the browser you're using, its version number, and the name of your operating system:** In other words, the Web site will know that you're using Firefox 3 and Windows 7. No biggie.
- **The address of the Web page you just came from.**

There are other bits and pieces, which you can see by going to the Web site ShowIPAddress.com (see Figure 1-10).

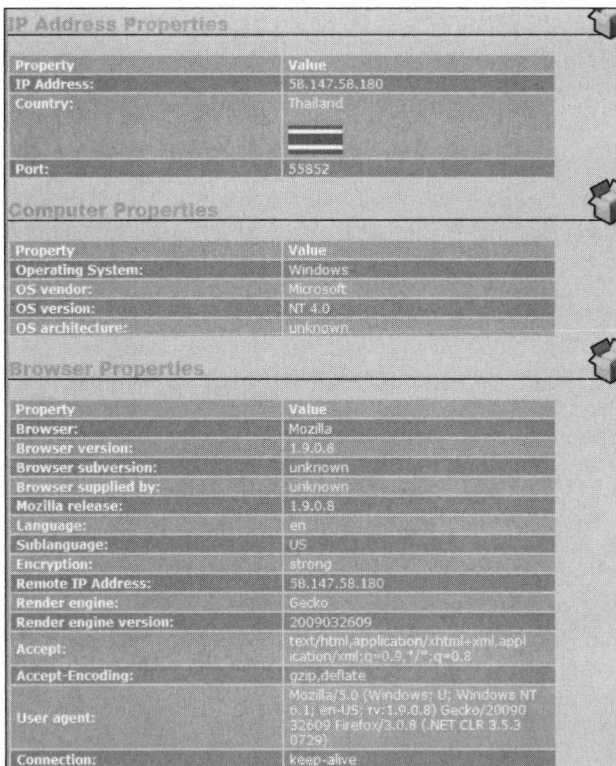

IP Address Properties

Property	Value
IP Address:	58.147.58.180
Country:	Thailand
Port:	55852

Computer Properties

Property	Value
Operating System:	Windows
OS vendor:	Microsoft
OS version:	NT 4.0
OS architecture:	unknown

Browser Properties

Property	Value
Browser:	Mozilla
Browser version:	1.9.0.8
Browser subversion:	unknown
Browser supplied by:	unknown
Mozilla release:	1.9.0.8
Language:	en
Sublanguage:	US
Encryption:	strong
Remote IP Address:	58.147.58.180
Render engine:	Gecko
Render engine version:	2009032609
Accept:	text/html,application/xhtml+xml,application/xml;q=0.9,*/*;q=0.8
Accept-Encoding:	gzip,deflate
User agent:	Mozilla/5.0 (Windows; U; Windows NT 6.1; en-US; rv:1.9.0.8) Gecko/2009032609 Firefox/3.0.8 (.NET CLR 3.5.30729)
Connection:	keep-alive

Figure 1-10: All the information sent by your browser to every Web site you visit.

That isn't a whole lot of information, but it comes along for the ride every time you visit a Web site. You can't do anything about it. When you're on a site, of course, the site can keep track of which pages you look at, how long you stay at each one, which buttons you click, and other information.

In addition, the site you're visiting can ask you for, quite literally, anything: the size of your monthly paycheck, your mother's maiden name, telephone numbers, credit card numbers, Social Security numbers, driver's license numbers, shoe sizes, and your dowdy Aunt Martha's IQ. If you're game to type the information, the Web site can collect it and store it.

That's where things start getting dicey. Suppose that you go to one Web site and enter your e-mail ID and credit card number and then go to another Web site and enter your e-mail ID and telephone number. If those two sites share their information — perhaps through a third party — it's suddenly possible to match your credit card number and telephone number. (Refer to the sidebar "The Doubleclick shtick" to see where all this is headed.)

Microsoft, of course, gathers an enormous amount of information about you in its Windows registration database, its Live ID database, the Windows Update database, and on and on. As of this writing, it doesn't appear that Microsoft has attempted to correlate the data in those databases. Yet.

For in-depth, knowledgeable updates on cookie shenanigans, drop by `cookiecentral.com`.

Reducing spam

Everybody hates spam, but nobody has any idea how to stop it. Not the government. Not Bill Gates. Not your sainted aunt's podiatrist's second cousin.

You think legislation can reduce the amount of spam? Since the U.S. CAN–SPAM Act (`www.fcc.gov/cgb/consumerfacts/canspam.html`) became law on January 7, 2003, has the volume of spam you've received increased or decreased? Heck, I've had more spam from politicians lately than from almost any other group. The very people who are supposed to be enforcing the antispam laws seem to be spewing out spam overtime (see Figure 1-11).

By and large, Windows is only tangentially involved in the spam game — it's the messenger, as it were. But every Windows user I know receives e-mail. And every e-mail user I know gets spam. Lots of it.

There are 600,426,974,379,824,381,952 ways to spell Viagra. No, really. If you use all the tricks that spammers use — from simple swaps such as using the letter *l* rather than *i* or inserting e x t r a s p a c e s in the word, to tricky ones like substituting accented characters — you have more than 600 septillion different ways to spell Viagra. It makes the national debt look positively tiny.

Figure 1-11: Typical politicians' spam. *Qui custodiet ipsos custodies?*

Hard to believe? See `cockeyed.com/lessons/viagra/viagra.html` for an eye-opening analysis.

Spam scanners look at e-mail messages and try to determine whether the contents of the potentially offensive message match certain criteria. Details vary depending on the type of spam scanner you use (or your Internet service provider uses), but in general the scanner has to match the contents of the message with certain words and phrases stored in its database. If you've seen a lot of messages with odd spellings come through your spam scanner, you know how hard it is to see through all those sextillion, er, septillion variations.

Spam is an intractable problem, but you can do certain things to minimize your exposure:

✦ **Don't encourage 'em.** Don't buy anything that's offered by way of spam (or any other e-mail that you didn't specifically request). Don't click through to the Web site. Simply delete the message. If you see something that might be interesting, use Google or another Web browser to look for other companies that sell the same item.

- **Opt out of mailings only if you know and trust the company that's sending you messages.** If you're on the Costco mailing list and you're not interested in its e-mail any more, click the Opt Out button at the bottom of the page. But don't opt out with a company you don't trust: It may just be trying to verify your e-mail address.
- **Never post your e-mail address on a Web site or in a newsgroup.** Spammers have spiders that devour Web pages by the gazillion, crawling around the Web, gathering e-mail addresses and other information automatically. If you post something in a newsgroup and want to let people respond, use a name that's hard for spiders to swallow: `woody (at) ask woody (dot) com`, for example.
- **Never open an attachment to an e-mail message or view pictures in a message.** Spammers use both methods to verify that they've reached a real, live address. And, you wouldn't open an attachment anyway — unless you know the person who sent it to you, you verified with her that she intended to send you the attachment, and you trust the sender to be savvy enough to avoid sending infected attachments.
- **Never trust a Web site that you arrive at by "clicking through" a hot link in an e-mail message.** Be cautious about Web sites you reach from other Web sites. If you don't personally type the address in the Internet Explorer address bar, you might not be in Kansas any more.

Ultimately, the only long-lasting solution to spam is to change your e-mail address and give out your address only to close friends and business associates. Even that strategy doesn't solve the problem, but it should reduce the level of spam significantly. Heckuva note, ain't it?

Chapter 2: Action Center Overview

In This Chapter

- Navigating the Action Center
- Troubleshooting in the Action Center
- Running a rootkit scan: what Action Center doesn't tell you
- Keeping out the bad guys

The Windows 7 *Action Center* may sound like the title of a Grade B movie or the locus of a local television news program, but it serves a simple and worthwhile purpose: Whenever Windows wants to get your attention, it nags you through the Action Center.

The Action Center consolidates security warnings — the purview of the old Windows Vista Security Center, Action Center's progenitor — with status notifications about updates, backups, and various troubleshooting tips. The center's most important work revolves around security, and that's why this chapter appears among the security chapters.

In theory, the Windows 7 Action Center offers one-stop shopping for all your security needs. In practice, it's a short stop indeed — and taking control of security settings that aren't accessible through the Action Center can be quite a headache.

But, hey, at least you don't see the notice "There are unused icons on your desktop" every time you boot Windows 7. See, there have been some real improvements since Windows XP.

In this chapter, I take you through a brief overview of the Windows Action Center — more details follow in the next few chapters. I also explain how the troubleshooting features can uncover unexpected problems — and in some cases, at least, fix them.

I also talk about free rootkit scanners. Rootkits don't draw the attention they deserve in the Action Center spotlight — in no small part because getting a rootkit to run in Windows 7 is a major challenge. You should nonetheless go the extra mile and make sure that your PC hasn't been subverted. (For a description of rootkits, see Book VI, Chapter 1.)

Entering the Action Center

If you go out looking for it, the Windows 7 Action Center sits buried in an obscure corner of the Windows infrastructure. But the Security "flag" sits up front and, uh, center. The easiest way to get to it: Click the flag down near the system clock and select Open Action Center from the pop-up menu. You see the Action Center in all its glory, which, if you've been a good Windows custodian, looks like Figure 2-1.

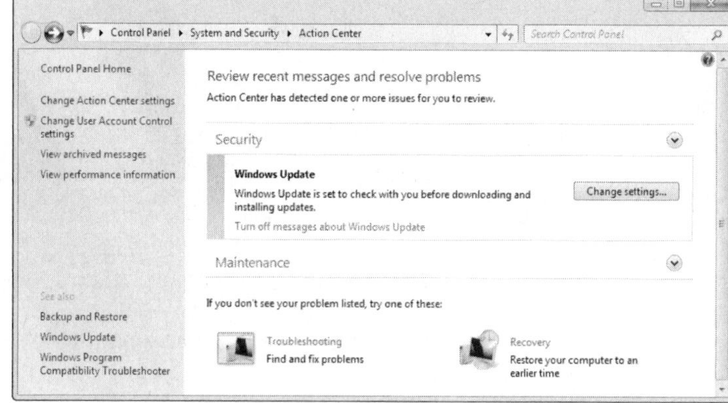

Figure 2-1: The Action Center, ready for — oh, you know.

The flag can take on three personas:

- **A plain, unfettered flag means that you conform to Microsoft expectations.** You may have security messages waiting or troubleshooting tips available in the Action Center but, on the whole, you're doing fine and needn't upset the applecart.

  Surprisingly, refreshingly, Windows 7 shows you a flag without an overlay if you tell it to check for Windows Updates but don't download them. That's a big, big improvement over earlier versions of Windows, which would go into conniption fits if you prevented Microsoft from reaching into your machine and applying any change it deemed appropriate. (See Book VI, Chapter 4 for details.)

- **A yellow exclamation point means that a portion of Windows wants your attention, and you should attend to it rather quickly.** Important security releases that haven't been applied fall into this category — at least, updates that Microsoft feels are important — as do hardware problems that leave a piece of your computer out of order.

- **A red circle with an X through it (see Figure 2-2) means that something is wrong and you need to check it quickly.**

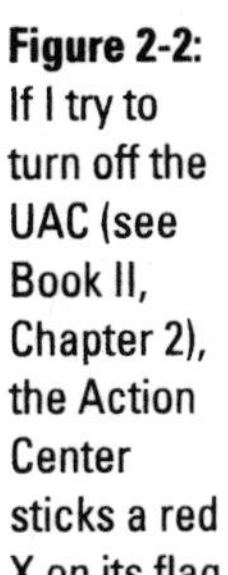

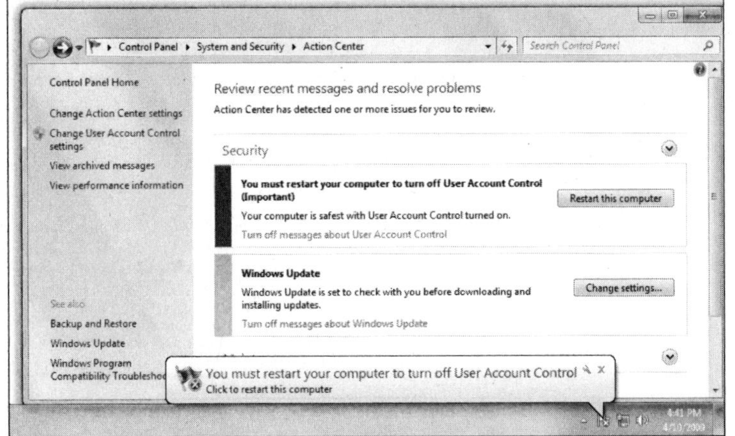

Figure 2-2: If I try to turn off the UAC (see Book II, Chapter 2), the Action Center sticks a red X on its flag.

In some respects, the Action Center works as a central clearing house for Windows problems: In many cases, if a Windows program hits a problem, the program notifies the Action Center and the Action Center talks to you. In other respects, the Action Center takes on a proactive stance: It actively goes out and checks to see whether something is wrong and reports on its findings.

Working with the Action Center

The Action Center itself consolidates a wide range of settings from many different parts of Windows — indeed, from places outside of Windows — all in one place.

Watching Security Settings

To see the monitored Security items, click the down arrow to the right of the Security heading in Figure 2-1. The Action Center monitors the status of the following elements (see Figure 2-3):

- **Windows Update (better known as Automatic Update):** Allows Windows to phone home and check for patches and patches to patches of patches. If you trust Microsoft, you can even allow Windows to patch itself, kinda like getting a license for self-administered lobotomies. (See Book VI, Chapter 4 for more about Automatic Updates.)

Fair warning: I firmly believe that automatic updating is for chumps. I've advised against using automatic updates since the feature first appeared in Windows Me, a decade ago.

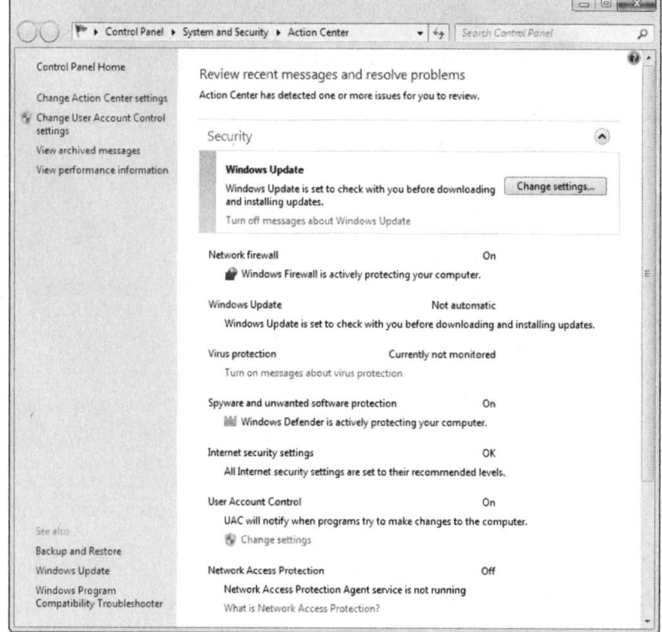

Figure 2-3: The security components of Action Center status reporting.

✦ **Network Firewall:** Blocks access to your computer from the Internet. (I talk about Windows Firewall at length in Book VI, Chapter 3.)

A *firewall* program insulates your PC (or network) from the Internet. At its heart, the Windows 7 inbound firewall keeps track of requests that originate on your PC or network. When data from the Internet tries to make its way into your PC or network, the firewall checks to make sure that one of your programs requested the data. Unsolicited data gets dropped; requested data comes through. That way, rogues on the Internet can't break in.

Windows 7 also has an outbound firewall, which is basically unusable. The Network Firewall line in the Action Center says On even if you don't have outbound firewall protection.

You may be using the Windows 7 Firewall, or you may have a third-party firewall installed. It's possible (but maddening) to run more than one firewall at the same time.

✦ **Virus protection:** Tells you whether you have a functional antivirus (AV) program, such as Microsoft Security Essentials, AVG Free, Avira AntiVir, Norton, McAfee, or Trend Micro PC-cillin, for example. (See Book VI, Chapter 5 for more about virus protection.)

- **Spyware and other unwanted software protection:** Looks at your computer and tries to determine whether you have spyware/scumware detection and blocking in force. Of course, Microsoft Windows Defender appears here — it's built into Windows 7 itself. But you may want to run an additional scum-busting program — two or more can usually run simultaneously without tripping each other up. Or you may want to replace Windows Defender with Microsoft Security Essentials, the new free anti-everything-ware program from Microsoft. (See Book VI, Chapter 5 for details.)
- **Internet security settings:** Refer only to your security settings in Internet Explorer. As of this writing, at any rate, the Windows Action Center doesn't tell you squat about any other browsers.
- **User Account Control:** Refers to Windows 7's effort to put dialog boxes like the one shown in Figure 2-4 on the screen. I explain how to control UAC in Book II, Chapter 2.

Figure 2-4: User Account Control settings trigger messages like this one.

- **Network Access Protection:** Covers a feature that works only in large, client-server domain networks. If you have a problem with your NAP settings, you need to contact your network administrator.

All these settings focus on preventing bad stuff outside your PC from getting inside — a noble goal, to be sure, but the baddies that lurk outside your box are only part of the problem. The other part? You.

To get — and keep — your security and sanity in Windows 7, you must understand how your PC can be attacked and what you can do to forestall those attacks, both from a computer point of view and by thinking "outside the box." (That's the theme of Book VI, Chapter 1.)

Checking Maintenance Settings

To see the general Windows programs that the Action Center monitors, click the down arrow to the right of the Maintenance heading. You see the following options (see Figure 2-5):

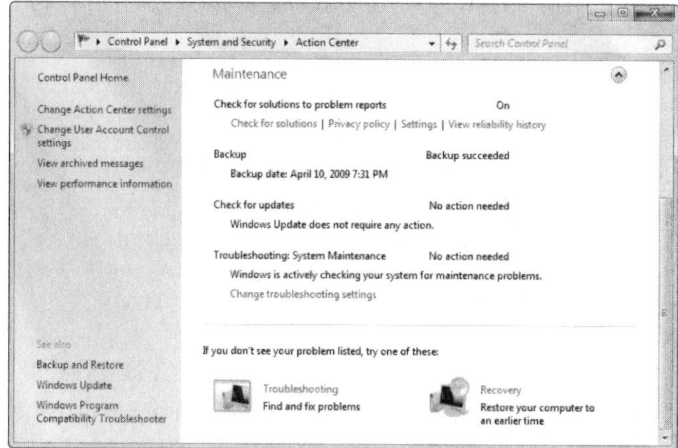

Figure 2-5: The maintenance components of the Action Center.

- **Check for Solutions to Problem Reports** is one of the passive settings — Windows Action Center monitors problem reports as they occur and keeps tabs on your reliability history.

  You can go back and see whether Microsoft has posted any solutions to problems that your computer has reported in the past. It's rare, but it does happen. If you want to see which problems your computer has reported, click the link on the left that says View Archived Messages.

  If you click the View Reliability History link, you see the Reliability Monitor, as shown in Figure 2-6. (I talk about the Reliability Monitor in Book II, Chapter 5.)

- **Backup** gives you the current status of your Windows backups. (I talk about backups in Book II, Chapter 3.)
- **Check for Updates** tells you whether any outstanding Windows updates are available. (I talk about Windows Update in Book VI, Chapter 4.)
- **Troubleshooting** lets you know if you somehow disabled the Windows troubleshooter. If you want to go out and check for troubleshooting tips, click the Troubleshooting link at the bottom of the Action Center. (I talk about Windows Troubleshooting in Book II, Chapter 5.)

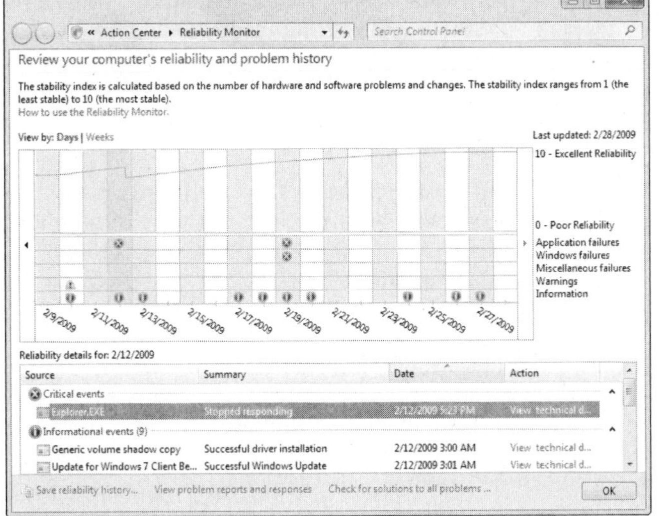

Figure 2-6: The Windows Reliability Monitor can help you pinpoint faulty software or hardware.

Rooting out Rootkits

One part of the Action Center bugs me: It makes sure that you have a firewall working, that you have an antivirus program running and updated, and that Windows Defender and/or other scumbusters (such as Microsoft Security Essentials) are on the lookout for malware.

That's good.

But the Action Center doesn't tackle — doesn't even consider — one key security question: Have you scanned for rootkits? *Rootkits* are programs, such as Mebroot (also known as Sinowal) or Conficker (also known as Downadup) that run underneath the Windows radar. (For a description of rootkits, see Book VI, Chapter 1.)

There are several reasons for the apparent oversight:

✦ **When Windows 7 was released, the rootkit writers were still focused almost exclusively on Windows XP.** Windows Vista rates as a tough nut for rootkit writers to crack. Windows 7 goes way beyond Vista, by setting up enormous hurdles that any rootkit would have to clear.

Nevertheless, somebody, somewhere, will likely — in fact, given the financial incentives, will almost inevitably — develop a very stealthy piece of malware, probably a rootkit, that will hitch a ride on Windows 7 systems. Just because it hasn't been done doesn't mean that it won't be done, if you know what I mean.

- **Good rootkits fly completely under the radar: They run underneath Windows in a way that Windows can't detect.** Some researchers contend that it's impossible to create a good rootkit scanner that runs on Windows. If a rootkit scanner doesn't run on Windows, it would be nearly impossible to have the Windows Action Center reliably track its actions, much less detect its presence.
- **Not enough real rootkit scanners are available.** Every Tom, Dick, and Hairless antivirus manufacturer claims to have a rootkit scanner, but it's generally useless — if not *completely* useless. Microsoft's own Security Essentials claims to scan for rootkits, but the results to date have been spotty at best.

Rootkits represent the way of the future for malware: A lot of money can be made by subverting PCs and turning them into botnets (see Book VI, Chapter 1). That's why I strongly recommend, in addition to working with the Windows 7 Action Center, that you scan all your machines specifically for rootkits — if you can find a good scanner.

The world of rootkits changes by the hour, so any recommendation I make now will be obsolete by the time the ink dries on this book. I suggest that you go to the Windows Secrets Web site (`www.windowssecrets.com`) and check the list of programs on the main page for a recommended free rootkit scanner.

At the moment, my favorite rootkit detector comes from the antivirus software manufacturer Trend Micro. Trend Micro RootkitBuster (see Figure 2-7) is, as of this writing, still in beta testing and supports only 32-bit versions of Windows 7. By the time you read this chapter, chances are good that it will be ready for prime time, and it may work with 64-bit versions.

Here's how to download, install, and run the Trend Micro RootkitBuster:

1. **Start your favorite Web browser and go to**

   `trendmicro.com/download/rbuster.asp`

   If TrendMicro has moved the RootkitBuster, try searching for *trendmicro rootkit* at `www.google.com`.
2. **Click the link to download RootkitBuster.**

   It's in a Zip file.
3. **Open the Zip file and then click and drag** `RootkitBuster.exe` **to your desktop.**

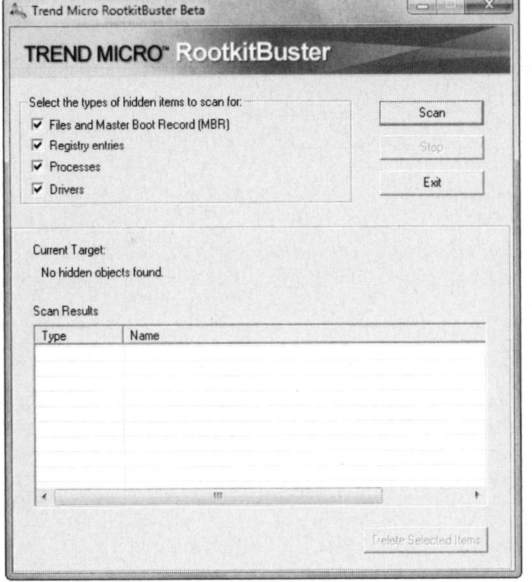

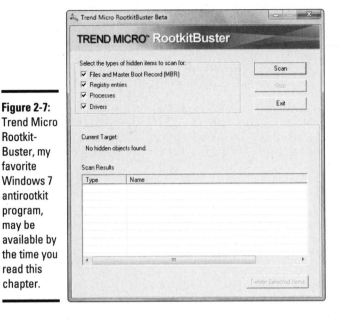

Figure 2-7: Trend Micro Rootkit-Buster, my favorite Windows 7 antirootkit program, may be available by the time you read this chapter.

4. **Right-click** `RootkitBuster.exe` **and choose Run As Administrator.**

   You may have to jump through one or more User Account Control dialog boxes.

   RootkitBuster appears (refer to Figure 2-7). There's no installer.

5. **Click Scan.**

   RootkitBuster can take 10 or 20 minutes or more, but in the end it reports any suspicious items it finds.

6. **If you find any potential problems, before you click the Delete Selected Items button, go back to the download site and click the Readme link. The Readme material may tell you about potential problems.**

   This step may prevent you from shooting yourself in the foot. Deleting the wrong Registry entry or file can be disastrous for your computer, so make sure that you know what you're doing before you click Delete.

Run RootkitBuster — or whichever rootkit detector you use — from time to time, and see what comes up.

Chapter 3: Windows Firewall

In This Chapter

- **Discovering what Windows Firewall can — and can't — do**
- **Knowing when Windows Firewall causes problems — and how to get around them**
- **Struggling with the bare-bones outbound Windows Firewall**
- **Making Windows Firewall work the way you want**

A *firewall* is a program that sits between your computer and the Internet, protecting you from the big, mean, nasty gorillas riding around on the information superhighway. An *inbound firewall* acts like a traffic cop that, in the best of all possible worlds, allows only "good" stuff into your computer and keeps all the "bad" stuff out on the Internet, where it belongs. An *outbound firewall* prevents your computer from sending bad stuff to the Internet, such as when your computer becomes infected with a virus or has another security problem.

Windows 7 includes a usable (if not fancy) inbound firewall. It also includes a snarly, hard-to-configure, rudimentary outbound firewall, which has all the social graces of a junkyard dog. Unless you know the magic incantations, you never even see the outbound firewall — it's completely muzzled until you dig into the Windows 7 doghouse and teach it some tricks.

Everybody needs an inbound firewall, without any doubt. Outbound firewalls are useful, but they can be quite difficult to understand and maintain. If you figure that you need an outbound firewall, try to use the one in Windows 7, and when you (inevitably) throw your hands up in disgust, take a look at Microsoft's competitors. This chapter helps you through the minefield.

Comparing Firewalls

The Windows 7 inbound firewall works reasonably well. It lacks many of the fancy features you can find in competing firewalls, but for most folks, it's good enough. One big bonus: The Windows 7 inbound firewall works hand in hand with Windows network settings (see Book VII).

On the other hand, the Windows 7 outbound firewall doesn't hold a candle to any of the commercially available firewalls. Here's why:

- **Competitive firewalls come with a built-in passel of outbound default settings that help you get started without being tripped up by the most common outbound traffic.** By contrast, the Windows 7 outbound firewall has exactly zero built-in settings.
- **You can "train" competitive firewalls by having them watch outbound traffic and then ask you to block or allow specific programs.** The firewall remembers your responses and, over time, reduces its level of intrusiveness. The Windows 7 outbound firewall, on the other hand, doesn't ask, doesn't learn, and doesn't care. If you've told Windows 7 to block something in particular, it doesn't get out of your PC; if you haven't told Windows 7 to block something, it goes through.
- **Competitors attempt to put a decent interface on their firewalls: The buttons and menus may be overly cute or convoluted, but at least they try to organize the outbound settings in a reasonable fashion.** As you can see in the section "Coping with the Windows 7 Outbound Firewall," later in this chapter, Microsoft has done almost nothing to make the Windows 7 outbound firewall easy to use. Quite the contrary: The inbound and outbound firewalls look like they came from two different planets — which they did.

Microsoft says that it disabled the Windows 7 outbound firewall because corporate customers demanded it. That seems mighty disingenuous to me because companies running Active Directory pull all the strings on their users' desktops anyway. I think Microsoft had many reasons for making the outbound firewall so infernally hard to use, not the least of which is the fact that enforcing almost any kind of outbound firewall would've driven Microsoft's support demands through the roof.

Hardware firewalls

Most modern routers and wireless access points include significant firewalling capability. It's part and parcel of the way they work, when they share an Internet connection among many computers.

Routers and wireless access points add an extra step between your computer and the Internet. That extra jump — named Network Address Translation — combined with innate intelligence on the router's part can provide an extra layer of protection that works independently from, but in conjunction with, the firewall running on your PC.

Many people in the software business feel that an outbound firewall is a must: It's the only way to tell whether your computer has been taken over, and it starts spraying your personal information to all corners of the Internet. I'm just ornery enough to disagree: I find outbound firewalls confusing, intrusive, and at most minimally effective. It's kinda like trying to steer a boat by looking at its wake.

If you're worried about monitoring the Internet traffic going out of your computer, though, there's no reason to spend a heap of money — or lose all your computer cycles — on one of those giant antivirus-antispyware-firewall packages. Instead, look into Comodo Personal Firewall (`personalfirewall.comodo.com`), which draws good reviews. Or, try ZoneAlarm Free Firewall (`zonelabs.com`). They're both absolutely free, and they work just as well as the high-priced spread.

Understanding Windows 7 Firewall's Basic Features

All versions of Windows 7 ship with a decent, capable — but not foolproof — *stateful* firewall named Windows Firewall (WF). (See the nearby sidebar, "What's a stateful firewall?")

The WF inbound firewall is on by default. Unless you change something, Windows Firewall is turned on for all connections on your PC. For example, if you have a LAN cable, a wireless networking card, and a modem on a specific PC, WF is turned on for all of them. The only way Windows Firewall gets turned off is if you deliberately turn it off or if the network administrator on your Big Corporate Network decides to disable it by remote control or install Windows service packs with Windows Firewall turned off.

What's a stateful firewall?

At the risk of oversimplifying a bit, a *stateful* firewall is an inbound firewall that remembers. A stateful firewall keeps track of packets of information coming out of your computer and where they're headed. When a packet arrives and tries to get in, the inbound firewall matches the originating address of the incoming packet against the log of addresses of the outgoing packets to make sure that any packet allowed through the firewall comes from an expected location.

Stateful packet filtering isn't 100 percent foolproof. And, you must have some exceptions so that unexpected packets can come through for reasons discussed elsewhere in this chapter. But a stateful firewall is quite a fast, reliable way to minimize your exposure to potentially destructive probes from out on the big, bad Internet.

In extremely unusual circumstances, malware (viruses, Trojans, whatever) have been known to turn off Windows Firewall.

You can change WF settings for inbound protection relatively easily. When you make changes, they apply to all connections on your PC. On the other hand, WF settings for outbound protection make the rules of cricket look like child's play.

WF kicks in before the computer is connected to the network. Back in the not-so-good old days, many PCs got infected between the time they were connected and when the firewall came up.

WF also has an inbound "lockdown" mode. By selecting two fairly easy-to-find Block All Incoming Connections check boxes (see Figure 3-1), you can lock down your computer so that it accepts only incoming data that has been explicitly requested by programs running on your computer. Any attempt by outside programs to communicate with your computer are rebuffed.

To see your Block All Incoming Connections check boxes, choose Start⇨Control Panel⇨System and Security⇨Windows Firewall, then on the left click the link to Change Notification Settings.

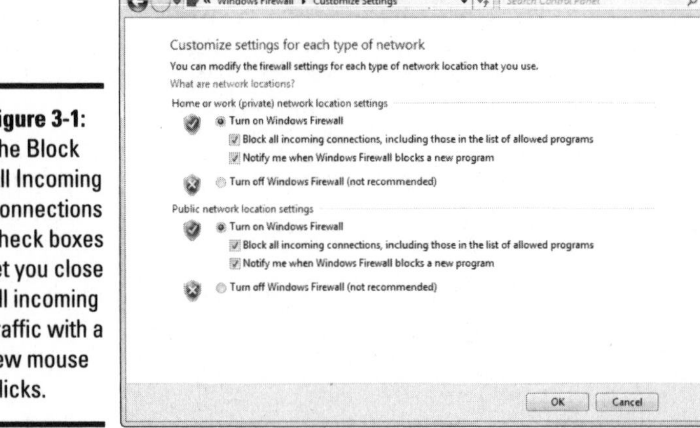

Figure 3-1: The Block All Incoming Connections check boxes let you close all incoming traffic with a few mouse clicks.

In practice, locking down your computer means that you can use Firefox or Internet Explorer or Chrome to look at Web sites, and you can send and receive e-mail and use instant messengers, as well as use printers and folders on your local network if you have one, but most other online functions are locked out. For example, if you use the Internet to play games with other folks who are online, or if you connect to your computer at work, locking down your PC prevents you from connecting. A lockdown even shuts down any connection to other computers or printers (or other shared devices) on the network. That's helpful if you're connecting in an airport and don't want other travelers to get at your `Shared Documents` folder. But it's a real pain in the neck in your home or office.

If you hear about a new worm making the rounds, you can easily lock down your computer for a day or two and then go back to normal operation when the worm stops ping-ponging over your company's network (or your home network, for that matter). You might need to deselect a Block All Incoming Connections check box long enough to print on a shared printer or to get at some data on your network, but you'll be essentially impenetrable whenever the Block All Incoming Connections check boxes are selected. If you're connecting to a strange network (say, using a wireless connection at a coffee shop or in a hotel), you can lock down while logged on and sip your latté with confidence.

Speaking Your Firewall's Lingo

At this point, I need to inundate you with a bunch of jargon so that you can take control of Windows Firewall. Hold your nose and dive in. The concepts aren't that difficult, although the lousy terminology sounds like it was invented by a first-year advertising student. Refer to this section if you become bewildered when wading through the WF dialog boxes.

As you no doubt realize, the amount of data that can be sent from one computer to another over a network can be tiny or it can be huge. Computers communicate with each other by breaking the data into *packets* (small chunks of data with a wrapper that identifies where the data came from and where it's going).

On the Internet, packets can be sent in two different ways:

- ✦ **User Datagram Protocol (UDP):** UDP is fast and sloppy. The computer sending the packets doesn't keep track of which packets were sent, and the computer receiving the packets doesn't make any attempt to get the sender to resend packets that vanish mysteriously into the bowels of the Internet. UDP is the kind of *protocol* (transmission method) that can work with live broadcasts, where short gaps wouldn't be nearly as disruptive as long pauses, while the computers wait to resend a dropped packet.
- ✦ **Transmission Control Protocol (TCP):** TCP is methodical and complete. The sending computer keeps track of which packets it is sent. If the receiving computer doesn't get a packet, it notifies the sending computer, which resends the packet. Almost all communication over the Internet these days goes by way of TCP.

Every computer on a network has an *IP address,* which is a collection of four sets of numbers, each between 0 and 255. For example, 192.168.1.2 is a common IP address for computers connected to a local network; the computer that handles the Dummies.com Web site is at 208.215.179.139. You can think of the IP address as analogous to a telephone number.

Peeking into Your Firewall

When you use a firewall — and you should — you change the way your computer communicates with other computers on the Internet. This section explains what Windows Firewall is doing behind the scenes so that when it gets in the way, you understand how to tweak it. (You find the ins and outs of working around the firewall in the "Making Inbound Exceptions" section, later in this chapter.)

When two computers communicate, they need not only each other's IP address but also a specific entry point called a *port* — think of it as a telephone extension — to talk to each other. For example, most Web sites respond to requests sent to port 80. There's nothing magical about the number 80; it's just the port number that people have agreed to use when trying to get to a Web site's computer. If your Web browser wants to look at the Dummies.com Web site, it sends a packet to 208.215.179.139, port 80.

Windows Firewall works by handling all these duties simultaneously:

- **It keeps track of outgoing packets and allows incoming packets to go through the firewall if they can be matched with an outgoing packet.** In other words, WF works as a stateful inbound firewall.
- **If your computer is attached to a home or work ("private") network, Windows Firewall allows packets to come and go on ports 139 and 445, but only if they came from another computer on your local network and only if they're using TCP.** Windows Firewall needs to open those ports for file and printer sharing. (See the later section "Using Public and Private Networks" for details about different network types.) WF also opens several ports for Windows Media Player if you've chosen to share your media files, as you might within a HomeGroup (see Book VII, Chapter 1), for example.
- **Similarly, if your computer is attached to a Home or Work ("private") network, Windows Firewall automatically opens ports 137, 138, and 5355 for UDP, but only for packets that originate on your local network.**
- **If you specifically told Windows Firewall that you want it to allow packets to come in on a specific port and the Block All Incoming Connections check box isn't selected, WF follows your orders.** You might need to open a port in this way for online gaming, for example.

- **Windows Firewall allows packets to come into your computer if they're sent to the Remote Assistance program (unless the Block All Incoming Connections check box is selected), as long as you created a Remote Assistance request on this PC and told Windows 7 to open your firewall (see Book II, Chapter 5).** Remote Assistance allows other users to take control of your PC, but it has its own security settings and strong password protection. Still, it's a known security hole that's enabled when you create a request.
- **You can tell Windows Firewall to accept packets that are directed at specific programs.** Usually, any company that makes a program designed to listen for incoming Internet traffic (Skype is a prime example, as are any instant messaging programs) adds its program to the list of designated exceptions when the program is installed.
- **Unless an inbound packet meets one of the preceding criteria, it's simply ignored.** Windows Firewall swallows it without a peep. Conversely, unless you've changed something, any and all outbound traffic goes through unobstructed.

Using Public and Private Networks

Windows 7 helps simplify things a bit by providing three different collections of security settings — actually, inbound Windows Firewall settings — each identified with a prototypical type of network (see Figure 3-2):

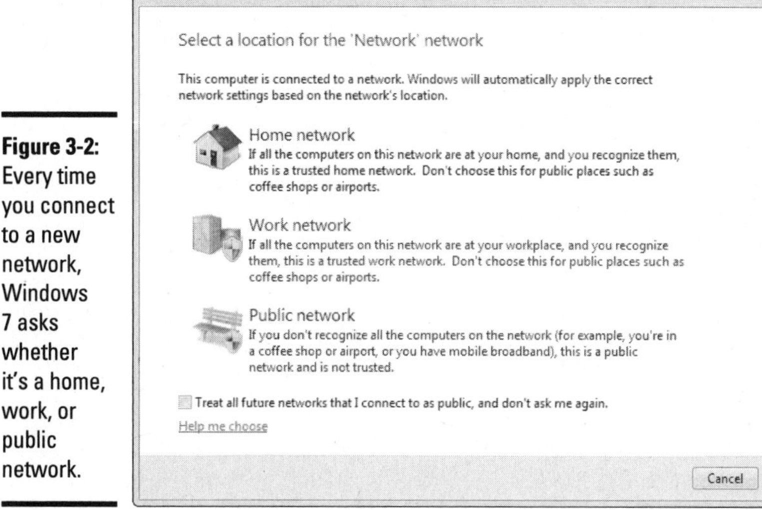

Figure 3-2: Every time you connect to a new network, Windows 7 asks whether it's a home, work, or public network.

- **Home networks** include peer-to-peer "workgroup" networks that are under your control (such as the kind you might set up following the instructions in Book VII, Chapter 2). You can let your hair down a little when you're on a private network. When you connect to a new network and identify it as a home network, Windows 7 lets you set up a HomeGroup or connect to an existing HomeGroup. That's a bit like handing you the keys to the house. (See Book VII, Chapter 1 for details.)
- **Work networks** are a lot like home networks, except that you can't establish a HomeGroup over a work network. Use a work network whenever you want to connect to a network and share things such as an Internet connection or specific folders or printers, but you don't want to share things like your music collection or your personal `Documents` folder.
- **Public networks** include networks that you don't control — airports, Internet cafés, hotels — where a very real chance exists that somebody else connected to the network could go snooping, or may try to shove infected files into your `Public` folder. When you connect to a new network, if you tell Windows 7 that it's a public network, Windows 7 knows that it shouldn't make your PC visible on the network and that you don't want to share printers and the like. Most of the time, you use public networks to connect to the Internet — and that's it.

There's a fourth kind of network, which you encounter only when you plug into a big company domain network. *Domain* networks are Big Corporate Networks — client/server "domains." If you take your laptop to the office and plug it in to a Big Corporate Network, Windows 7 recognizes the fact and automatically puts in place all the security that comes along for the ride. Unlike when you use home, work, or public networks, you don't get to tell Windows 7 which kind of network you're using when you connect into a domain.

I go into more detail about connecting to networks, setting the network type, and changing network types in Book VII, Chapter 1.

Making Inbound Exceptions

Firewalls can be absolutely infuriating. You may have a program that has worked for a hundred years on all sorts of computers, but the minute you install it on a Windows 7 machine with Windows Firewall in action, it just stops working, for absolutely no apparent reason.

You can get mad at Microsoft and scream at Windows Firewall, but when you do, realize that at least part of the problem lies in the way the firewall has to work. (See the "Peeking into Your Firewall" section, earlier in this chapter, for an explanation of what your firewall does behind the scenes.) It has to block packets that are trying to get in, unless you explicitly tell the firewall to allow them to get in.

Perhaps most infuriatingly, WF has to block those packets by simply swallowing them, not by notifying the computer that sent the packet. Windows Firewall has to remain "stealthy" because if it sends back a packet that says, "Hey, I got your packet but I can't let it through," the bad guys get an acknowledgment that your computer exists, they can probably figure out which firewall you're using, and they may be able to combine those two pieces of information to give you a headache. It's far better for Windows Firewall to act like a black hole.

Allowing designated programs to bypass the firewall

Some programs need to "listen" to incoming traffic from the Internet; they wait until they're contacted and then respond. Usually, you know whether you have this type of program because the installer tells you that you need to tell your firewall to back off.

If you have a program that doesn't (or can't) poke its own hole through the Windows Firewall, you can tell WF to allow packets destined for that specific program — and *only* that program — in through the firewall. You might want to do that with a game that needs to accept incoming traffic, for example, or for an Outlook extender program that interacts with mobile phones, or for a program that hooks directly into the Internet, like The Onion Ring (see Book V, Chapter 2 for a description).

Here's how to poke a hole in the inbound Windows Firewall:

1. **Choose Start⇨Control Panel. Click the System and Security link; click Windows Firewall.**

   You see the main Windows Firewall control window, as shown in Figure 3-3.

2. **On the left, click the link labeled Allow a Program or Feature through Windows Firewall.**

   Windows Firewall presents you with a lengthy list of programs that you might want to allow (see Figure 3-4): If a box is checked, it means that Windows Firewall will allow unsolicited incoming packets of data directed to that program and that program alone. The list varies depending on whether you're connected to a home or work network (a private network) or a public network.

   These settings don't apply to incoming packets of data that are received in response to a request from your computer; they apply only when a packet of data appears on your firewall's doorstep without an invitation.

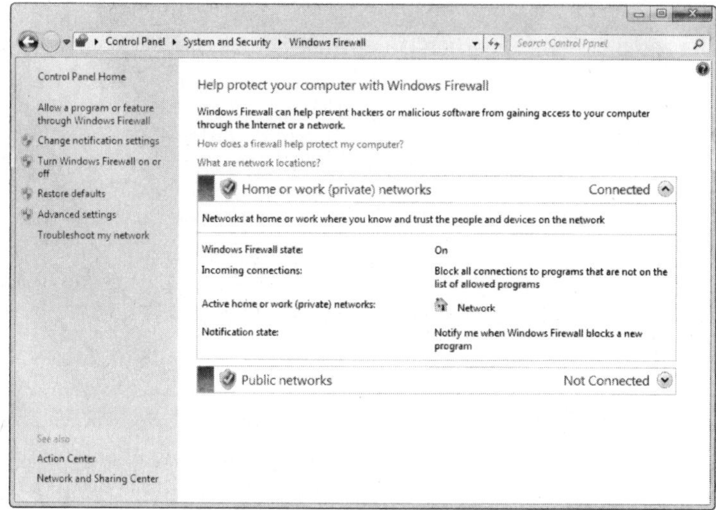

Figure 3-3: The Windows Firewall control window, as it appears when you're connected to a home or work network.

In Figure 3-4, you see that Skype is allowed to receive inbound packets whether you're connected to a home, work, or public network. Windows Media Player, on the other hand, may accept unsolicited inbound data from other computers only if you're connected to a home or work network: If you're attached to a public network, inbound packets headed for Windows Media Player are swallowed up by the WF Black Hole (patent pending).

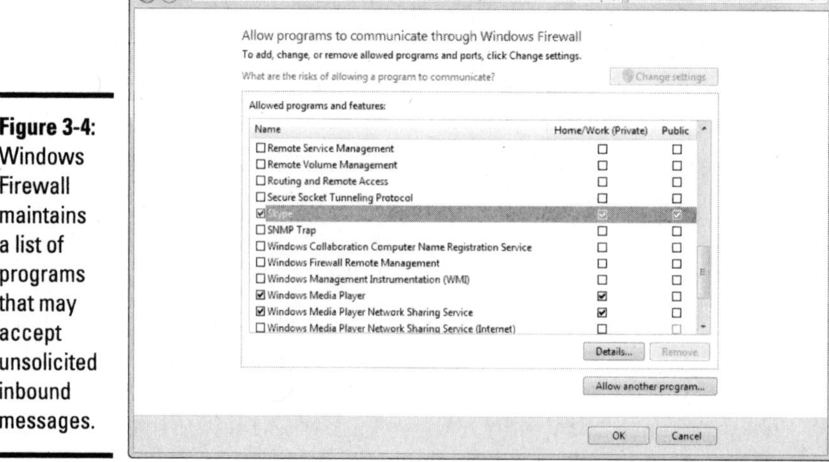

Figure 3-4: Windows Firewall maintains a list of programs that may accept unsolicited inbound messages.

3. **If you can find the program that you want to poke through the firewall listed in the Allow Programs list, select the check boxes that correspond to whether you want to allow the unsolicited incoming data when connected to a home or work network and whether you want to allow the incoming packets when connected to a public network.**

   It's rare indeed that you would allow access when connected to a public network but not to a home or work network.

4. **If you can't find the program that you want to poke through the firewall, click the Change Settings button at the top and then click the Allow Another Program button at the bottom.**

   You have to click the Change Settings button first and then click Allow Another Program. It's kind of a double-down protection feature that ensures you don't accidentally change things.

   Windows Firewall goes out to all common program locations and finally presents you with a list like the one shown in Figure 3-5. It can take a while.

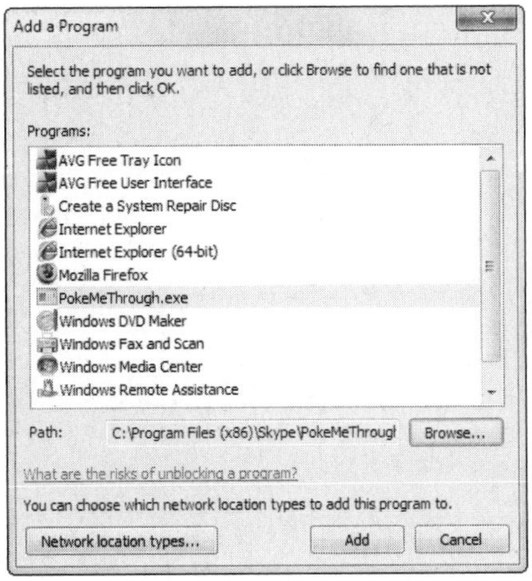

Figure 3-5: Windows Firewall suggestions for programs you might want to poke through it.

5. **If you can't find the program you want, click the Browse button and browse to the program's location. Select the program and click Open.**

   The program you chose appears on the Add a Program list (refer to Figure 3-5).

6. **Choose the program you want to add and click the Add button.**

Realize that you're opening a potential, albeit small, security hole. The program you choose had better be quite capable of handling packets from unknown sources. If you authorize a renegade program to accept incoming packets, the bad program could let the fox into the chicken coop. If you know what I mean.

In Figure 3-5, I choose `PokeMeThrough.exe` and click Add.

The program appears on the Allow Programs list. In Figure 3-6, `PokeMeThrough.exe` shows up on the list.

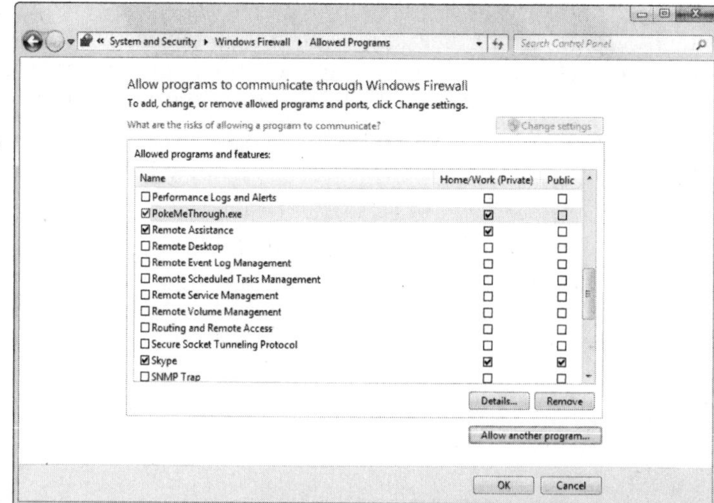

Figure 3-6: Your selected program appears on the Windows Firewall Allow Programs list.

7. **Select the check boxes to allow your poked-through program to accept incoming data while you're connected to a home or work network or a public network. Then Click OK.**

   Your poked-through program can immediately start handling inbound data.

In many cases, poking through the Windows Firewall doesn't solve the whole problem. You may have to poke through your modem or router as well — unsolicited packets that arrive at the router may get kicked back according to the router's rules, even if Windows would allow them in. Unfortunately, each router and the method for poking holes in the router's inbound firewall differs. Check the site `portforward.com/routers.htm` for an enormous amount of information about poking through routers.

Opening specific ports

Windows Firewall lets you open specific ports, so the inbound firewall stops monitoring incoming data on those ports.

Adding a port to the exceptions list is inherently less secure than adding a program. Why? Because the bad guys have a hard time guessing which programs you left open — they have a whole lot of programs to choose from — but probing all ports on a machine to see whether any of them let packets go through is comparatively easy.

Still, you may need to open a port to enable a specific application. When you select the check box to allow Remote Desktop, for example, you're opening port 3389. (Remote Desktop lets others — typically, system administrators — work directly on your computer.) That's the security price you pay for enabling programs to talk to each other.

Follow these steps to open a port:

1. **Choose Start⇨Control Panel. Click the link System and Security and then click Windows Firewall.**

   You see the main Windows Firewall control window (refer to Figure 3-3).

2. **On the left, click the Advanced Settings link.**

   You see the Windows Firewall *sanctum sanctorum*, shown in Figure 3-7.

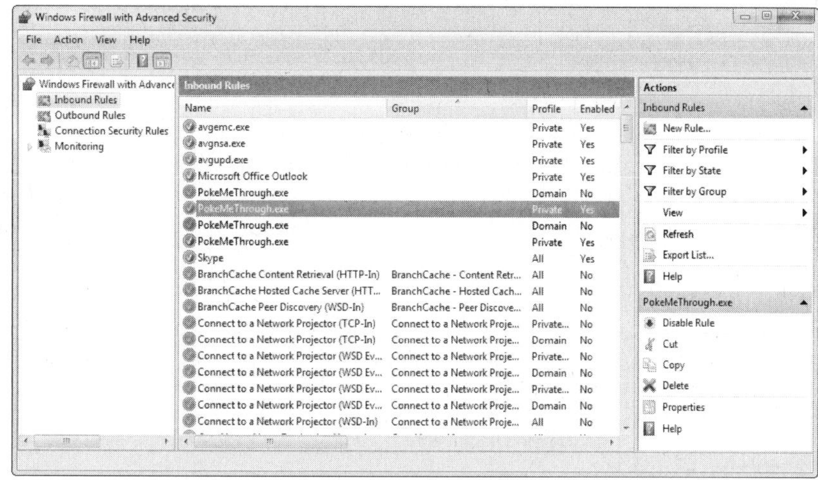

Figure 3-7: The complete list of Windows Firewall rules.

How do you know when you have to open a port?

Most first-time firewallers are overwhelmed by the idea of opening a port. Although you need to treat ports with care — an open port is a security threat, no matter how you look at it — sometimes you truly need to open one. Usually, you get a phone call like this:

"Dude. My game won't hook up with your game. You got a firewall or somethin'?"

"Uh, yeah. I'm running Windows Firewall."

"Pshaw, man. If you want to play Frumious Bandersnatch, you gotta open ports 418, 419, 420, an' 421."

"Does Frumious use UDP or TCP?"

"What's TCP? Some kinda disease? I dunno, man. I just read in the instruction book that ya gotta have 418, 419, 420, an' 421 open. Don'tcha ever read the manual, dude?"

At that point, you guess that Frumious Bandersnatch uses TCP (that's the most common choice), you run through Windows Firewall to liberate the four ports, and you have the game working in 30 seconds flat.

In general, if you need to open a port, the documentation for the program (game, torrent downloader, file sharer) will tell you. Assuming you read the frumious manual.

After you're done playing the game or transferring files, you should consider shutting down the port. A well-written game or file-sharing program won't let any creepy-crawlies into your computer, but bugs can and do happen.

3. **On the left, click Inbound Rules. Then, on the right, under Actions, click the New Rule link.**

   Windows Firewall shows you the New Inbound Rule Wizard, as shown in Figure 3-8.

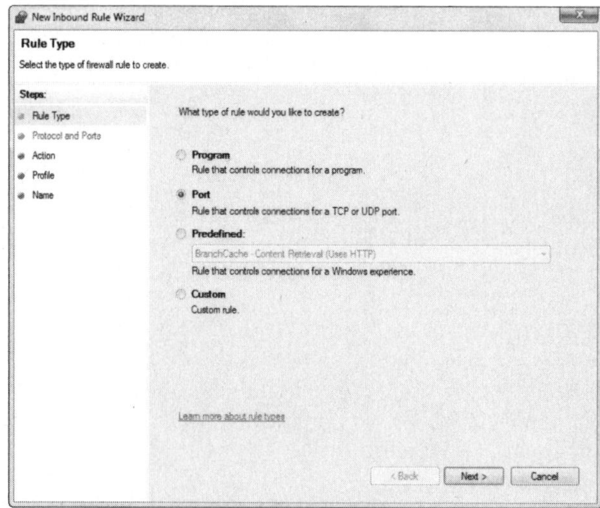

Figure 3-8: Open a port by using the Rule Wizard.

4. **Select the option marked Port and click Next.**

   The wizard asks you to specify which ports.

5. **In the Specific Local Ports box, type the ports you want to open, separated by commas, and then click Next.**

   In this case, Frumious Bandersnatch requires TCP ports 418, 419, 420, and 421, so I type those in the box.

   The wizard wants to know what action should be taken, if the firewall receives data on those ports.

6. **Choose Allow the Connection and click Next.**

   The New Inbound Rule Wizard wants to know whether it should apply this rule if you're connected to a domain network, a private network, or a public network. (*Public* means at either home or work). Typically, when I open ports, I only want them open when my computer is on at my home or home office (private) network. In other situations, I assume the network can't be trusted.

7. **Check the boxes for Domain, Private, or Public, and then click Next.**

   The wizard asks that you give the rule a name and, optionally, a description.

8. **Type a name (in this case, I call the rule that unblocks the port Frumious Bandersnatch, to make it easier to remember). Click Finish.**

   Your new rule appears in the Inbound Rules list (see Figure 3-9). It takes effect immediately.

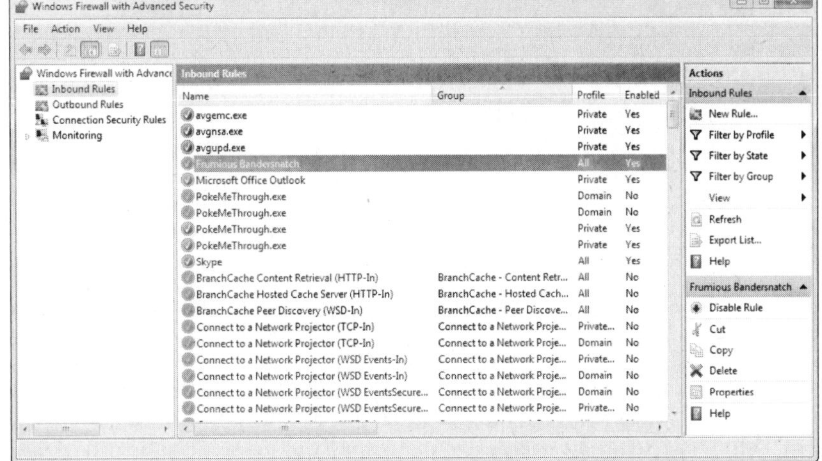

Figure 3-9: The new rule Frumious Bandersnatch appears.

Every port that you open to the outside world is a potential location for an attack. Open ports sparingly, and when you're done, close them by choosing them in the Inbound Rules list and, in the lower-right corner, clicking Disable Rule.

Coping with the Windows 7 Outbound Firewall

The Windows 7 outbound firewall doesn't work, look, or behave anything like the inbound firewall. Basically, it's there and it's on, but it doesn't block a thing, unless you tell it to. Whereas the inbound firewall offers the different levels of settings and enables you to further tweak those settings, the outbound firewall has only two basic functions: to block a program (or port or something else) that you select and to unblock a program you previously blocked.

To show you how the outbound firewall works, let me step you through an example. Consider that (another) security hole has been discovered in Internet Explorer (IE) and that you want to ensure that IE isn't allowed to connect to the Internet. Perhaps you use Firefox and you want to make sure that Windows 7 (or Windows Media Player or Outlook or Windows Update) doesn't surreptitiously crank up IE and turn it loose on the Web.

In firewall terminology, I want to block IE from making any *outbound* connection. Here's how to do it:

1. **Choose Start⇨Control Panel. Click the System and Security link, and then click Windows Firewall. On the left, click the link marked Advanced Settings.**

   You see the Windows Firewall with Advanced Security settings (refer to Figure 3-7).

2. **On the left, click Outbound Rules. Then, on the right, under Actions, click the New Rule link.**

   Windows Firewall shows you the New Outbound Rule Wizard, as shown in Figure 3-10.

3. **For this example, I want to block a program, Internet Explorer, so I make sure that the Program option is selected and then click Next.**

   The Outbound Rule Wizard asks you to choose the program.

4. **Click Browse. Navigate to** `c:\Program Files\Internet Explorer\iexplore.exe` **and click the Open button.**

   This step tells the wizard that you want to block Internet Explorer (which is the program `iexplore.exe`). The Wizard panel should look like Figure 3-11.

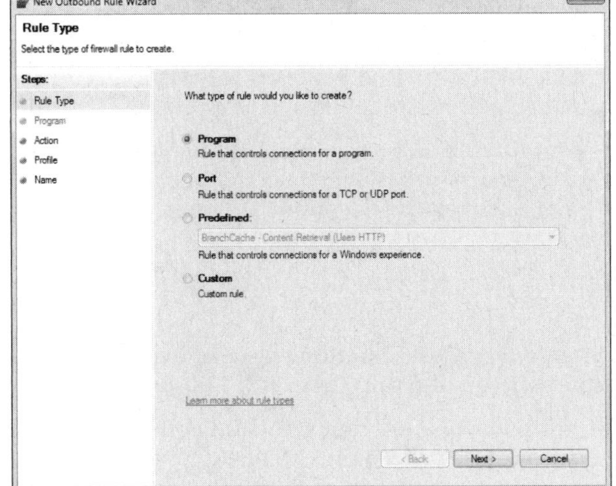

Figure 3-10: A wizard helps guide you through the creation of an outbound firewall rule.

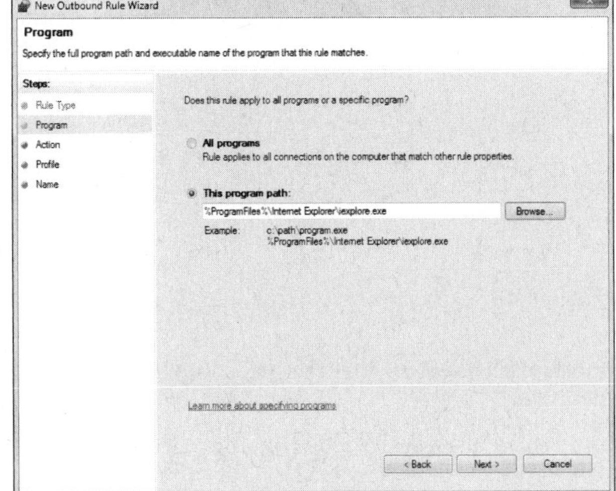

Figure 3-11: You must choose the specific program you want to block.

5. **Click Next.**

   The wizard asks whether you want to allow the program to go through the firewall, whether you want to allow it if it obeys something called an IPsec rule, or whether you want to prohibit the program from getting out.

6. **Click the Block the Connection button and click Next.**

   The wizard wants to know whether this rule applies to private networks, public networks, or domain networks (or all three). See the "Using Public and Private Networks" section, earlier in this chapter.

7. **If you want to keep IE from working while you're connected to a home or work network, select the Private check box. To block IE when you're connected to a public network, select Public. Ditto for a domain network. Then click Next.**

   The last step of the wizard asks you for a name for the rule and gives you space to type a description.

8. **In the Name box, type something descriptive, such as Block IE. Type a description if you like, and then click Finish.**

   The wizard puts your new rule at the top of the list (see Figure 3-12). The new block takes effect immediately.

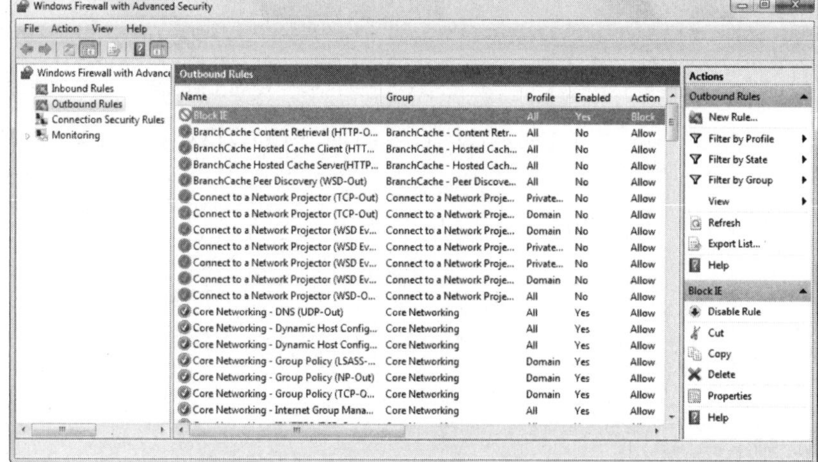

Figure 3-12: The rule blocking IE appears at the top of the Windows Firewall list.

9. **Go ahead and try it. Try to get Internet Explorer to work. I dare ya.**

   No way. IE gives you the notice "Internet Explorer cannot display the webpage." Heh-heh-heh.

10. **To get rid of the rule, right-click it and choose Delete. When Windows Firewall asks whether you're sure you want to delete the rule, click Yes.**

    Try Internet Explorer again, and it works like a champ.

Imagine setting up rules like this, manually, for every program you want to block from going out on the Internet. Now you know why I say that the Windows 7 outbound firewall is an ornery, snarly piece of software.

Individual program blocking is only part of the story, of course. If you set the outbound firewall to trap everything headed out of your machine, you'd probably spend most of your waking hours for the next ten years writing exceptions similar to this one, to allow "good" programs to get out.

Decent commercial firewalls have long lists of good programs. If they detect the presence of one, they poke a hole through the firewall for you. You're left with a brief (but intense) training period, where you have to approve each new, unidentified program that's trying to get out — and where you have to track down every outbound request that looks suspicious. It isn't easy, but it is tractable.

The Windows 7 firewall doesn't work that way. You get to do all the heavy lifting. And, you get to perform that work with a user interface that has been known to bring accomplished system administrators to tears.

If you have a specific program that you want to block, Windows Firewall can do the job. But for anything other than blocking the outbound actions of a small number of targeted programs, the Windows 7 outbound firewall rates as a marketing point ("Yes, Windows 7 has an outbound firewall!") and little more.

Chapter 4: Patching and Plugging

In This Chapter

- Getting the whole story about Windows Update
- Deciding which level of Automatic Update (if any) is right for you
- Making Windows Update work the way you want
- Retrieving a declined update

Windows Automatic Update is for *chumps.*

I've taken a lot of flak over the years for advising people to turn off automatic updating. I think you should tell Windows 7 to advise you when patches are available and then wait and see whether the patches do more harm than good before applying them to your PC.

Let's face it. You have to patch, sooner or later. Patching isn't like brushing your teeth, where you can ignore it for a year or two and things turn smelly and then gradually rot and fall out. If you don't patch today, by next month your computer can look and act and feel like toast. The bad guys know what's been patched, and they prey on people who don't get their updates.

On the other hand, you don't need to follow Microsoft's dictates and apply patches the moment they're available. More than a few Dummies have seen their computers melt down because of a bad patch that has been force-fed to them by the Automatic Update mechanism.

Almost everyone — certainly, anyone reading this book — needs to check out the latest Microsoft missives before applying updates. Blindly updating Windows can lead to all sorts of problems.

Windows Update stinks. Massively. Permit me to elaborate: Both the security patches that Microsoft dribbles out to users and the method by which Microsoft delivers those patches to users stink. Massively. But you can still keep your system patched while working around the worst that these patches and Windows Update have to offer.

If you're setting up a Windows computer for someone else to use, and they show no interest at all in keeping their system safe, by all means set them up with Automatic Updates. Sooner or later, everybody should patch. But if you're savvy enough to be reading this book, and concerned enough to check the Internet from time to time, you can save yourself a whole lotta headache by waiting for other people to shake out the problems with new patches. Let them get the arrows in their backs. Patch in haste: repent in leisure. Wait until Microsoft has had a chance to test their monthly patches on ten million PCs — and zapped a few hundred or tens of thousands along the way. It's easy. I explain it all in this chapter.

Patching Woes

Any large computer program has bugs. Heck, any *small* computer program has bugs. When a program grows as large as Windows — tens of millions of lines of code — the bugs start stacking up like planes at O'Hare in a snowstorm.

Microsoft issues hundreds of updates each year. Some updates fix bugs that make Windows crash. Many updates plug security holes. Most updates come in the form of *patches:* fixes to an individual Windows program that wasn't working right. Some patches are small. Most are big. Many Microsoft security bulletins, which appear to handle a single bug and its patch, in fact cover many big, frequently unrelated, patches.

Microsoft periodically releases security and "high priority" patches for Windows. Anyone with a recent copy of Windows (including Windows 7, Windows Vista, and Windows XP) who has taken the defaults when first running Windows, or chosen the option Install Updates Automatically (Recommended) gets those patches pushed, automatically, to their machines, as soon as the PC is connected to the Internet. You don't need to lift a finger: When automatic updating is turned on, you come in one morning and your PC has been patched and you never hear a word about it.

You can also download and install patches manually, any time they become available, by choosing Start⇨All Programs⇨Windows Update. The Windows Update Web site inspects your computer and recommends that you install whichever patches are on offer. (See the "Selectively Patching: A Panacea for Those Woes" section, later in this chapter.)

Most of the time, on most machines, the patches perform as advertised — they fix a defect in the product. Fair enough. Beats a product recall, I guess.

Sometimes, though, the patches don't work right or they offer bonus, uh, features that users neither asked for nor want. A few of my favorites:

✦ **The pretax predicament:** On April 11, 2006, a Tuesday, Microsoft released the Windows Explorer VERCLSID" patch, known cryptically as MS06-015. (For a description of the "MS06-XXX" patch numbers, see the "Decoding a security bulletin" section, later in this chapter.) Most Windows users in the United States didn't get the patch until Saturday or Sunday. Federal income tax returns were due on Monday, April 17. On the weekend before tax returns were due, thousands (possibly tens of thousands) of Windows consumers found themselves unable to navigate to their `Documents` folders, unable to open or save files, forced to type `http://` into Internet Explorer to keep it from freezing, and on and on. We consumers ultimately discovered that this patch messed up any machine with the older HP scanner program Share-to-Web and any machine with an older NVIDIA video driver.

✦ **The ghost in Windows 2000:** In April 2004, Microsoft released a slew of patches, one of which (MS04-014) locked up some Windows 2000 machines tighter than a drum. If you installed the patch on a Windows 2000 machine and you were unlucky, you couldn't boot the machine. The only solution was to haul out your installation CD and perform major brain surgery.

✦ **Windows Genuine Spyware:** In early 2006, Microsoft started using the Windows Automatic Update mechanism to push software that has absolutely nothing to do with security. Most notably, on April 24, 2006 — a day that will live in Windows infamy — Microsoft pushed a new version of the Windows Genuine Advantage program onto millions of PCs worldwide. Anyone foolish enough to have Windows Automatic Update enabled woke up one morning with a new piece of scumware, installed by Microsoft without their knowledge or consent.

That version of Windows Genuine Advantage — distributed as a "priority update" — included a component, named WGA Validation, that brands certain PCs with a notification that the PC is running a pirate copy of Windows. ("You may be a victim of software counterfeiting. This copy of Windows is not genuine and is not eligible to receive all updates and product support from Microsoft. Click Get Genuine now to get more information and resolve this issue.") A few days later, we discovered that a second component, named WGA Notification, "phones home" to Microsoft whenever the PC is rebooted or (apparently) once a day, whichever comes first. Of course, WGA couldn't be removed. After you got it, you were stuck with it.

Almost every batch of patches that Microsoft releases these days contains at least one stinker — a patch that, on a certain percentage of PCs, makes things much worse. It's like the cure is worse than the disease.

Patching non-Microsoft products

To keep your computer secure, you need to stay up-to-date on patches for all your programs. Microsoft takes the lion's share of the blame for messed-up PCs, but all too frequently malware sneaks in through Adobe PDF files, bad Java scripts, malicious Flash videos, and even (I hate to admit it) Firefox.

The bad guys frequently target these other programs because they're ubiquitous: Adobe claims that there are more computers that have Flash Player, for example, than there are computers running Windows — and they're probably right.

The best way I've found to stay on top of non-Microsoft patches is by using the free-for-personal-use, fast, and quite talented program Secunia Personal Software Inspector (`secunia.com/vulnerability_scanning/personal`). The security intelligence company Secunia makes PSI available free to advertise its other services. Secunia PSI knows about hundreds of programs. It scans your computer and advises you on which ones need security patches, and then it takes you by the hand and helps you install updates.

I've been at this business for a long time — I've used Windows since the days of Windows 286, which shipped on a single floppy disk, and I wrangled with DOS long before that. Of all the Microsoft features that I don't trust — and there are many — Windows Automatic Update rates as the single Microsoft feature that I trust the least. Microsoft has gone to extraordinary lengths over the past half-decade to reinforce my distrust and to demonstrate plainly and unambiguously that when it comes to updating Windows, Microsoft doesn't have a clue.

Choosing an Update Level

When you install Windows 7, or when you first start a new Windows 7 PC, Windows greets you with one of the most biased questions in all of computer-dumb, er, -dom. Windows asks whether you want to "help protect your computer and improve Windows automatically" with three truly bad choices (see Figure 4-1):

- **Use Recommended Settings:** You allow Microsoft to turn on Automatic Updates (more about that in this section), keep Windows Defender updated automatically, and generally let Microsoft have its way with your computer.

  Those may be the recommended Microsoft settings. They certainly aren't mine.

- **Install Important Updates Only:** You allow Microsoft to turn on Automatic Updates. See the theme here?

✦ **Ask Me Later:** This option is the one with a big red X and — you guessed it — my recommendation.

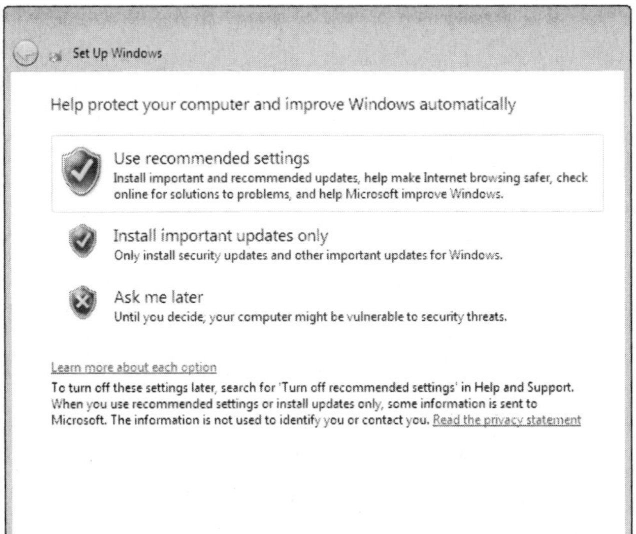
Set Up Windows
Help protect your computer and improve Windows automatically
Use recommended settings
Install important and recommended updates, help make Internet browsing safer, check online for solutions to problems, and help Microsoft improve Windows.
Install important updates only
Only install security updates and other important updates for Windows.
Ask me later
Until you decide, your computer might be vulnerable to security threats.
Learn more about each option
To turn off these settings later, search for 'Turn off recommended settings' in Help and Support. When you use recommended settings or install updates only, some information is sent to Microsoft. The information is not used to identify you or contact you. Read the privacy statement

Figure 4-1: A loaded question.

Microsoft wants you to turn on Automatic Updates. Heck, most Windows gurus suggest that you turn on Automatic Updates. One of those gurus says that it's better for Microsoft to automatically install its software on your PC than to leave your system wide open for some malicious kid to install his software on your PC.

He has a good point.

ASKWOODY.COM

Still, I disagree. I believe that Microsoft has proven conclusively that it can't be trusted to produce reliable security fixes. If Microsoft distributes an automatic patch that's so badly flawed that thousands or tens of thousands of PCs suddenly stop working, the people with those PCs won't have the slightest idea that the culprit was a bad patch from Redmond. In my opinion, savvy Windows users should let the Automatic Update service advise them when new patches are available — but they should wait to apply those patches until there's enough real-world experience with the patches to ensure that they solve more problems than they create. I cover the latest problems and recommend when to patch and when to hold off, on `AskWoody.com`. You can also get important, up-to-date analyses by subscribing to Windows Secrets Newsletter, `WindowsSecrets.com`.

No matter what you chose when you first started Windows, it's never too late to take back control of your computer. Here's how:

1. **Choose Start➪Control Panel, and then click the System and Security link. Then, under the Windows Update heading, click the link labeled Turn Automatic Updating On or Off.**

   You see the Choose How Windows Can Install Updates window, as shown in Figure 4-2.

2. **Windows Update lets you choose from four different levels of control so that you have some choice over what it does — or doesn't do — to your system. It's worth taking a few minutes to peruse Table 4-1, think through what Windows has to offer, and decide which approach works best for you.**

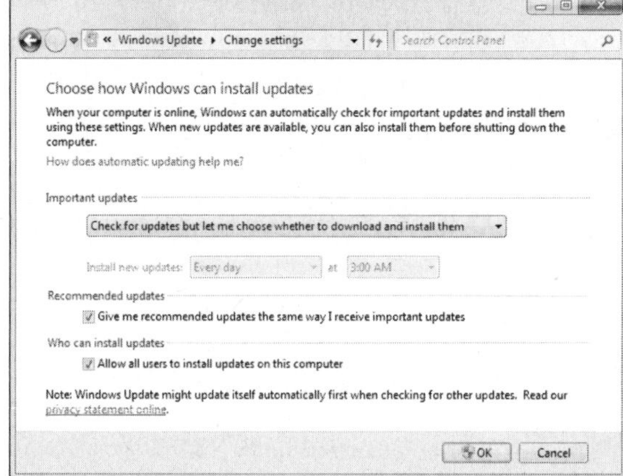

Figure 4-2: Control the way Windows updates itself.

While the gestation period for new worms is shrinking — the bad guys are picking up on the Microsoft security patches and figuring out how to exploit the holes shortly after the patches are announced — it's quite rare that a freshly patched security hole turns into an active exploit in a few days. And generally, word of botched security patches surfaces within a few days.

On the other hand, if Great-Aunt Mildred frets about breaking her computer if she plays a round of Solitaire, she's a good candidate for automatic updating. Go ahead and set it up for her — but as you do so, recognize your technological co-dependence: You're going to be bailing her out of patch problems for as long as she has your telephone number.

If you choose the Install Updates Automatically option, you can also specify whether you want Windows Update to check every day or once a week for updates.

3. **Select the check box marked Give Me Recommended Updates the Same Way I Receive Important Updates.**

   There's a very thin line between Important and Recommended in Microsoft parlance. (See the nearby "What's a 'critical' update?" sidebar.) As long as you have a chance to review the updates before they're installed, you might as well look at recommended updates, too.

4. **If the other people who use your computer can be trusted to exercise some diligence and discretion, select the check box marked Allow All Users to Install Updates on This Computer.**

5. **Take note of the, uh, note.**

   This dialog box warns you that Windows Update might update itself automatically first when checking for other updates. It's the Microsoft response to widespread criticism in August 2007, when it started changing Windows Update even if automatic updates were turned off.

   Microsoft feels that Windows Update has to be able to update itself, even without your permission: "Windows Update automatically updates itself from time to time to ensure that it is running the most current technology, so that it can check for updates and notify customers that new updates are available."

6. **When you're happy with your settings, click OK.**

   Your changes take effect immediately.

Windows Update versus Microsoft Update

Windows 7, right out of the box, only looks for updates to Windows — makes sense.

If you have Microsoft Office (or any of a small handful of additional Microsoft products) installed on your computer, the dialog box shown in Figure 4-2 takes on an additional option, marked Give Me Updates for Microsoft Products and Check for New Optional Microsoft Software When I Update Windows.

If you select that check box — and I recommend that you do — Windows Update starts looking for patches that apply to not only Windows but also Office (and, potentially, other modern Microsoft products). It also, annoyingly, starts offering you such stellar updates as Microsoft Silverlight and tries to force-feed you the Windows Live Essentials (see Book I, Chapter 5).

This supercharged pan-Microsoft version, dubbed Microsoft Update, works the same way as Windows Update: You can choose to notify but not download patches; uninstall patches; and in general do everything else mentioned in this chapter — applied to Microsoft Office.

The Windows Shutdown Conundrum

Both Windows XP and Windows Vista have easy ways to shut down your PC without installing downloaded patches: The Turn Off Computer window has a link that says Click Here to Turn Off without Installing Updates. Click the link and your computer shuts down without installing any downloaded patches.

Unfortunately, Windows 7 doesn't have any similar command: If you shut down Windows 7 normally, it automatically installs downloaded patches as part of the shutdown routine. The only way to avoid installing the patches? Pull the plug. Quite literally.

Many people (myself included) complained about the lack of a no-patch shutdown during the Windows 7 beta test cycle. For now, your only reasonable choice is to defer from downloading patches. Let Windows 7 notify you of new patches, but don't download them until you're ready to install them.

Table 4-1 Choosing a Windows Update Option

Option	*What It Does*	*Recommended For*
Install Updates Automatically (Recommended)	Windows checks with the Microsoft update site daily to determine when new updates are available, download them, and install them automatically for you — typically, in the middle of the night.	People who are easily confused by the process of telling Windows that it's okay to install new updates. It's also a good option if you don't have the time or inclination to look online to see whether a specific update has major problems, or if you have a PC located in a public place.
Download Updates, but Let Me Choose Whether to Install Them	Windows checks with the Microsoft update site daily to determine when new updates are available. If updates are available, WU downloads them and then asks your permission to install them.	Not recommended. Unfortunately, because of the way Windows 7 shuts down, you may be forced to install updates before you're ready.
Check for Updates but Let Me Choose Whether to Download and Install Them	Windows checks with the Microsoft update site daily to determine when new updates are available. If they are, Windows notifies you and asks for your permission to download and install them.	Folks who are willing to wait a week or two to install a new patch and who check online to see whether a patch is causing more harm than good.

Option	What It Does	Recommended For
Never Check for Updates (Not Recommended)	Windows Update is turned off.	Not recommended. (See, I can sound like Microsoft when I have to.) It's hard to imagine any situation where this option makes sense.

What's a critical update?

Microsoft has extremely strict definitions for its various levels of security patches. The official "severity rating system" defines these levels of security holes:

- **Critical:** "A vulnerability whose exploitation could allow the propagation of an Internet worm without user action."
- **Important:** "A vulnerability whose exploitation could result in compromise of the confidentiality, integrity, or availability of users' data, or of the integrity or availability of processing resources."
- **Moderate:** "Exploitability is mitigated to a significant degree by factors such as default configuration, auditing, or difficulty of exploitation."
- **Low:** "A vulnerability whose exploitation is extremely difficult, or whose impact is minimal."

In addition, Microsoft publishes an Exploitability Index that reflects the company's anticipation that some cretin will produce a piece of malware that can take advantage of the security hole in relatively short order. Here are the ratings:

- **Consistent Exploit Code Likely:** The Microsoft security team figures that somebody can come up with a piece of malware that uses the security hole to zap systems left and right.
- **Inconsistent Exploit Code Likely:** This rating also anticipates that somebody will be able to come up with a working program that takes advantage of the security hole, but the program probably won't work reliably.
- **Functioning Exploit Code Unlikely:** For any number of reasons, the security hole is well protected by other security settings, or it's so obscure that a big attack probably isn't in the cards.

Lest you truly believe that you should install critical updates before you install important updates — or that you can, say, ignore moderate updates — you need to realize that Microsoft's use of the terms is, in fact, quite arbitrary and at times highly debatable. Many "critical" patches don't address unassisted worm propagation. In at least one instance, the severity level of a security hole was changed after enough people complained. One critical update removed a symbol from one font in Office 2003. The assignment of a security level seems to reflect internal Microsoft politics more than anything else. So take the severity level and Exploitability Index ratings with a grain of salt, okay?

When Windows Update reaches into your computer to see what you have installed, which patches have been applied, and so on, it doesn't retrieve any personally identifiable information. It doesn't even retrieve your activation key. As far as I've been able to tell, Microsoft doesn't attempt to spy on your machine by using the Automatic Update program. So don't turn it off entirely unless you're really, really paranoid.

Selectively Patching: A Panacea for Those Woes

Microsoft really, really wants you to allow Windows 7 to automatically update itself. Unless you have much more faith in Microsoft than I do, you should seriously consider defying the Party Line and decide for yourself when (and whether!) patches should be applied. The Windows Genuine Spyware debacle alone (see the "Patching Woes" section, earlier in this chapter) amply demonstrates that Microsoft's automatic updating can't be trusted.

Let Microsoft notify you when it wants to install something on your computer, but don't blindly allow the 'Softies to install whatever they want. Wait until millions and millions of hapless Windows 7 customers unknowingly run the Microsoft patch beta tests and then install the patch after the cannon fodder has raised the alarm.

Microsoft officially releases new security patches on the second Tuesday of every month (except when it doesn't). If you hear of a security patch coming out on any date other than the second Tuesday of the month — an *out-of-band patch* — chances are good that a major security breach needs to get fixed fast. At least as of this writing, Microsoft also tends to release nonsecurity patches on the fourth Tuesday of the month. These patches generally aren't as interesting as the security patches, but they can still hose your system.

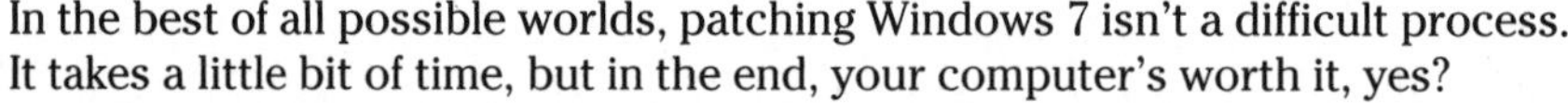
In the best of all possible worlds, patching Windows 7 isn't a difficult process. It takes a little bit of time, but in the end, your computer's worth it, yes?

Here's how I patch. You can do it, too, with a little help from your friends. Follow these steps:

1. **Make sure you've followed the steps in the "Choosing an Update Level" section, earlier in this chapter, so that the Windows 7 updater notifies you when a patch is available, but doesn't download or install it.**

   That's easy.

   Whenever a patch (or, more likely, a slew of patches) becomes available, you see a balloon in the notification area, near the clock, that says something like "Updates are available for your computer. Click here to download updates."

2. **When you have a few spare minutes, click the balloon.**

The exact terminology may change, but you see a notification that updates are ready. Don't worry if you can't get to the updates right away. If the balloon disappears, you can bring it back by clicking the flag in the notification area and choosing to read the message.

When you click the balloon or the flag, Windows Update shows you a notification box like the one shown in Figure 4-3.

3. **Don't click the Install Updates button. Instead, click the link on the left that says *X* Important Updates Are Available.**

   Windows 7 shows you the updates now on offer, as shown in Figure 4-4.

Figure 4-3: Updates are ready to download.

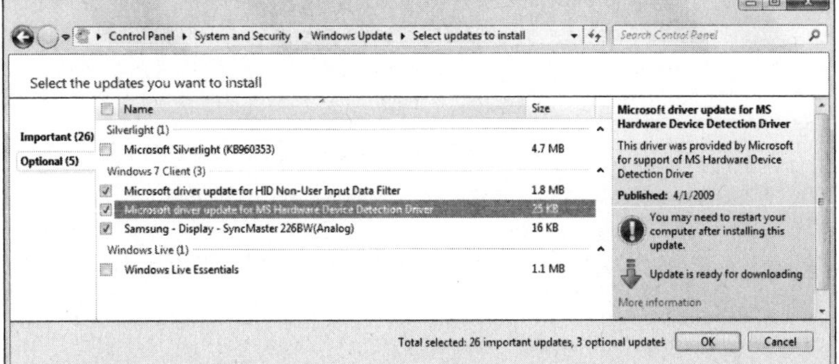

Figure 4-4: Windows Update offers details about each available patch.

4. **Check the boxes next to all the patches you want to install.**

   On the left, you can alternate between important and optional patches. Important patches are selected automatically. Optional patches aren't selected — you have to select the check boxes next to the ones you want.

You can click on any links in the update list, refer to the appropriate security bulletin or Knowledge Base article (see the "Getting What You Need from a Security Bulletin" section, later in this chapter), check my

MS-DEFCON status (see the “MS-DEFCON: Your guide to patch safety” sidebar, later in this chapter), look at your favorite security Web site, or consult that really wired astrologer who hangs out in the park. Bring your own tea leaves.

5. **Don’t be afraid to wait. You can click Cancel to get out of the list and come back at any time.**

The world may be jumping up and down. Heck, the U.S. Department of Homeland Security once issued an emergency bulletin recommending the immediate installation of a Microsoft security patch — a patch that turned into a dud. Keep your head while those about you are losing theirs.

Within a few days, problems with new patches appear — sometimes with disastrous vigor. The mainstream press frequently carries distorted, sensationalized reports either (a) warning you to patch immediately because the sky is falling (I call them Chicken Littles) or (b) describing disasters that didn’t really occur (I call them “he-said-she-said rumors” — or something distinctly less printable).

Windows 7 continues to pester you, mercilessly, with the same balloon warning, “Updates are ready for your computer.” That’s good. You need to hear the geese cackling.

6. **When you’re convinced that patching will cause more good than harm, click that infernal balloon (or click the flag), open the update details (refer to Figure 4-4), make sure that you want to take the plunge, and click the OK button.**

The Windows 7 update routine retrieves the updates and asks you for permission to install them. Go ahead and follow the prompts.

Downloading and installing updates can take anywhere from a few minutes to a few hours.

7. **When Windows 7 finishes installing the updates, restart your computer.**

Even if Windows 7 doesn’t require a reboot, it’s an excellent idea. Keep your eyes open for any problems and if you encounter one, check `AskWoody.com` or use your favorite search engine to get to the bottom of it. Follow the hints in Book V Chapter 5 to search intelligently.

MS-DEFCON: Your guide to patch safety

Big companies hire people — sometimes groups of people — to check the latest Microsoft patches, verify that they don’t break anything, and then deploy the patches, slowly, throughout the corporate network.

If you can afford to hire a patch-busting team, my hat’s off to you. But what are you — a typical Windows 7 user — to do? Where can you turn for understandable, unbiased reporting on Windows flaws and fixes — and flaws in the fixes?

I have a rating system on my Web site, `AskWoody.com`, that lets individual Microsoft consumers know when it's safe to install patches (see the nearby figure). I call it the Microsoft Patch Defense Condition Level — MS-DEFCON, for short. It's modeled after the U.S. Armed Forces DEFCON system, with the following levels:

The MS-DEFCON level advises you when it's safe to install patches.

- **MS-DEFCON 1:** Current Microsoft patches are causing havoc. Don't patch.
- **MS-DEFCON 2:** Patch reliability is unclear. Unless you have an immediate, pressing need to install a specific patch, don't do it.
- **MS-DEFCON 3:** Patch reliability is unclear, but widespread attacks make patching prudent. Go ahead and patch, but watch out for potential problems.
- **MS-DEFCON 4:** Isolated problems exist with current patches, but they are well known and documented on `AskWoody.com`. Check the site's latest entries to see whether you're affected, and if things look okay, go ahead and patch.
- **MS-DEFCON 5:** All's clear. Patch while it's safe.

Watch the MS-DEFCON level for an independent, somewhat jaundiced analysis of threats, from hackers and from Microsoft.

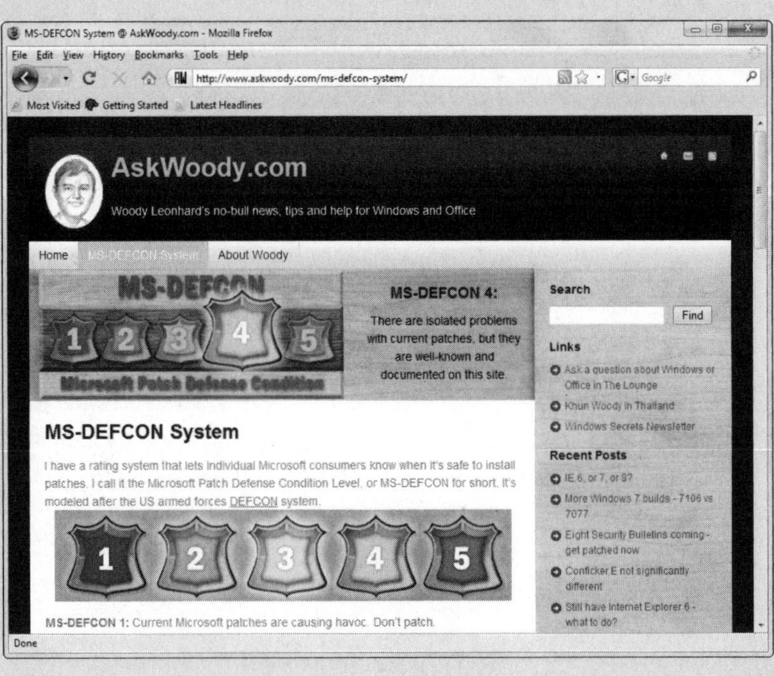

Once more, for emphasis: You have to keep Windows 7 patched. But you don't have to do it on Microsoft's terms. Take the bull by the horns, be mindful about the potential problems, and go out and do it your way.

Getting What You Need from a Security Bulletin

When Microsoft patches a security hole in Windows, it issues a security bulletin (like the one shown in Figure 4-5). A *security bulletin* gives you some brief information about a particular patch (or patches) and offers a way to download patches without Windows Update. Security bulletins contain official notice from Microsoft about things that go bump in the night. They're frequently laden with so much jargon that the interpreters need interpreters to translate them into plain English.

To find the latest security bulletins, check the Microsoft Security Response Center blog, `blogs.technet.com/msrc`. Notices of new or revised security bulletins frequently appear on the MSRC blog long before any of the other Microsoft delivery mechanisms get the word out.

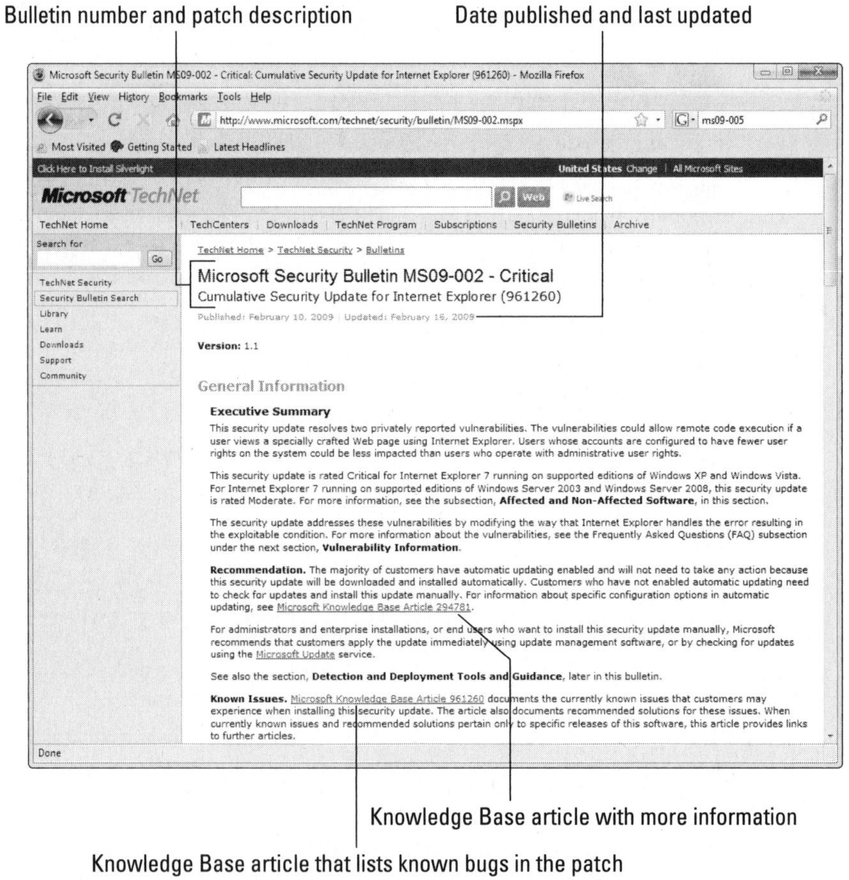

Bulletin number and patch description

Date published and last updated

Knowledge Base article with more information

Knowledge Base article that lists known bugs in the patch

Figure 4-5: Security Bulletin MS09-002.

Decoding a security bulletin

When you open a security bulletin, you need a few helpful pointers on interpreting what Microsoft has to say:

✦ **Security bulletins are assigned sequential numbers, such as MS09-002, denoting the second security bulletin issued in 2009.**

You might think that Bulletin MS09-002 would talk about the second security *patch* in 2009, but you'd be wrong. Microsoft bunches up security patches, sometimes releasing several completely unrelated patches in one security bulletin. Why? Because it knows that the world at large correlates the number of security bulletins with the relative "holiness" of its software. If Windows releases only 30 patches in a year and Linux releases 48, which operating system sounds more secure?

This particular security bulletin, MS09-002 (refer to Figure 4-5), includes 17 *different* patches, covering hundreds and hundreds of different programs.

✦ **Security bulletins are dated.** Usually they get revision numbers, too, but revision numbering seems to be, uh, subject to revision, if you know what I mean — the numbering can be a bit subjective. If you see a security bulletin that has been updated recently, there's a reason — usually something has gone wrong. If you see a security bulletin with a revision number such as 2.3 or 4.2, you know that problems bedevil the patches and that Microsoft has had to revise and re-revise (and re-re-revise) its explanations.

✦ **Each security bulletin refers to one or more Knowledge Base (KB) articles, which give further details about the patch.** The six-digit KB article number appears at the end of the description of the patch. (Refer to Figure 4-5, which refers to Knowledge Base article 961260.)

The Knowledge Base article number is important if you need to remove a patch. Frequently, this number is the only way you have to identify the patch. If you need to remove the patch because, say, it clobbers an important part of Windows, you need the KB article number. (See the "Checking and Uninstalling Updates" section, later in this chapter.)

✦ **Many patches have a second Knowledge Base article, referenced in the Caveats section, which exists solely to track the (acknowledged) bugs in the patch.** In Figure 4-5, Knowledge Base article 961260 contains a list of the bugs, updated as they are identified.

Getting patches through a security bulletin

Although you can use Windows Update to identify the patches your computer requires, download the patches, and even install them, you can download a patch manually and run it without Windows Update's interference, er, assistance. That can come in handy if you need to apply the same patch to numerous PCs or if you want to download the patch when your Internet connection isn't busy but wait to install the patch later.

To download and install a security bulletin patch manually, click the Download the Update link for Windows 7 in the security bulletin and then follow the instructions to download the patch.

Generally, it's much simpler to have Windows keep track of which patches are required and to download them automatically by using Windows Update, but if you need to apply the same patch to multiple machines, a manual download can save hours of trouble.

Checking and Uninstalling Updates

Want to know which patches have been installed? Do you suspect that a wayward patch has clobbered your machine, so you want to uninstall it?

As long as you don't mind wading through a bunch of Knowledge Base article numbers, getting to the list is easy. Here's how:

1. **Choose Start⇨Control Panel. Click the link for System and Security. Under the Windows Update heading, click the View Installed Updates link.**

   Windows Update presents you with a list of installed updates, as shown in Figure 4-6.

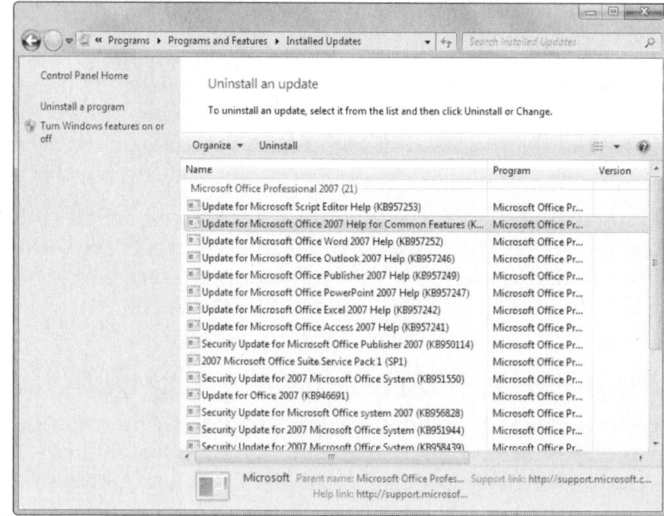

Figure 4-6: Installed updates appear with cryptic names and Knowledge Base article numbers.

2. **If you want to see details about a particular update, click once on the update and then, at the bottom, click either the Support link or the Help link.**

   Both take you to the Knowledge Base article for that particular patch.

3. **To remove a patch, double-click it, or click it once and then click Uninstall on the menu bar, at the top.**

   Note that some Windows 7 patches cannot be uninstalled — once you got 'em, you got 'em, and no amount of wailing or gnashing of teeth will tear them out of Windows 7.

4. **Click the X (Close) button to close the Uninstall an Update window.**

   Restart your computer to ensure that the uninstalled patch is truly uninstalled.

Chapter 5: Fighting Viruses and Other Scum

In This Chapter

- Understanding how antivirus products work with Windows
- Downloading and installing AVG Free, a free-for-personal-use antivirus program
- Using Windows Defender and other scumbusters
- Considering Microsoft Security Essentials, the latest member of the antivirus/antispyware/antimalware genre
- Reining in programs that start automatically whenever you start Windows 7

Every single Windows user should install, update, and religiously use an antivirus program — no exceptions, no excuses.

One question I hear all the time is, "Which antivirus program is the best?" My answer: They all work great. Pick one of the major packages and just do it. While you're worrying about whether this package scans better or that package blocks better or that another package costs a few bucks more or less, your system is at risk. Flip a coin, if you have to. But get your computer protected.

The second question I hear, right after the first: "Don't I need one of those fancy antivirus-firewall-spyware-kitchen-sink scanner packages? It's hard to find a simple antivirus program any more." Yes, it's true. The companies that used to sell antivirus software now offer monstrous Swiss Army knife mega-protection software, and they charge two arms and three legs for it.

I say *bah.* Actually, I say something a little less printable.

Although it's true that you need a firewall, Windows 7 has a perfectly usable firewall. (Yes, it's only a one-way firewall; see Book VI, Chapter 3 for details.) Windows 7 also has a capable anti-scumware program, Windows Defender, which I discuss in this chapter. Personally, I also run Spybot–Search & Destroy, right alongside Windows Defender. Spybot–S&D is free. I tell you more about that in this chapter, too.

These days, first-class antivirus software is available at no cost for personal use. You don't have an excuse any more. I show you how to install and use AVG Anti-Virus Free in this chapter. The free product from Avira named AntiVir Personal (`free-av.com`) and Alwil's Avast! Antivirus Home Edition (`avast.com`) work quite well, too.

As this book went to press, Microsoft was putting the final dollops on Microsoft Security Essentials, a free, real-time antimalware program that may take over the free antivirus niche. It remains to be seen if MSE will be able to hold its own against its more established rivals, but initial indications are that it performs well indeed. And it doesn't cost a sou.

The upshot: You don't need to spend the money or endure the hassle trying to figure out those fancy-schmancy anti-everything products. Your computer doesn't need to spend half its waking hours running the sludge. What you need is simple, fast, easy — and free. This chapter shows you how to put it all together.

Making Sense of Malware

Although most people are more familiar with the term *virus,* viruses are only part of the problem — a problem known as malware. *Malware* is made up of the elements described in this list:

- **Viruses:** A computer virus is a program that replicates. That's all. Viruses generally replicate by attaching themselves to files — programs, documents, spreadsheets — or replacing "genuine" operating system files with bogus ones. They usually make copies of themselves whenever they're run.

  You probably think that viruses delete files or make programs go belly-up or wreak havoc in other nefarious ways. Some of them do. Many of them don't. Viruses sound scary, but they really aren't. Most viruses have such ridiculous bugs in them that they don't get far "in the wild."

- **Trojans:** Trojans (occasionally called Trojan horses) may or may not be able to reproduce, but they always require that the user do something to get them started. The most common Trojans these days appear as programs downloaded from the Internet, or e-mail attachments: You double-click an attachment, expecting to open a picture or a document, and you get bit when a program comes in and clobbers your computer, frequently sending out a gazillion messages, all with infected attachments, without your knowledge or consent.
- **Worms:** Worms move from one computer to another over a network. The worst ones replicate very quickly by shooting copies of themselves over the Internet, taking advantage of holes in the operating systems (all too frequently, Windows).

The first truly big virus

The world changed when John McAfee appeared on the *Today* show in March 1992 and told Bryant Gumbel that the Michelangelo virus infected more than a million PCs. One week later, the PC world was supposed to end. All the major wire services ran alarming predictions — millions of dollars were forecast to be lost in the wake of the largest computer virus of all time.

The Big Day arrived and . . . nothing. A few thousand systems got clobbered, here and there, but Michelangelo turned into a dud of astonishing proportions. McAfee made millions. The wire services fell silent. We all got huckstered. Does history repeat itself in Internet time?

Some malware can carry bad *payloads* (programs that wreak destruction on your system), but many of the worst offenders cause the most harm by clogging networks (nearly bringing down the Internet itself, at times) and by turning PCs into zombies, frequently called *bots,* which can be operated by remote control. (I talk about bots and botnets in Book VI, Chapter 1.)

The most successful pieces of malware these days run as *rootkits,* programs that evade detection by stealthily hooking into Windows in tricky ways. Some nominally respectable companies (notably, Sony) have employed rootkit technology to hide programs for their own profit. Rootkits are extremely difficult to detect, and even harder to clean.

All these definitions are becoming more academic and less relevant, as the trend shifts to *blended-threat* malware. Blended threats incorporate elements of all three traditional kinds of malware — and more. Most of the most successful "viruses" you read about in the press these days — Conficker, Mebroot, and the like — are, in fact, blended-threat malware. They've come a long way from old-fashioned viruses.

Understanding Antivirus Software

Antivirus (AV) software protects your computer from viruses, right? Well, yes and no. Every AV product these days also protects your computer from other forms of malware — Trojans and lions and bears, oh my! Most AV products have turned into humongous "security suites" that ooze into every Windows pore, gumming up systems and giving you untold headaches, while demanding money on an all-too-regular basis. (Ever see *Little Shop of Horrors*? Think of the line, "Feed me, Seymour!" But I digress.)

Most AV software packages these days work in two very different ways:

- **Signature matching:** The antivirus software looks inside files to see whether any portion of the file matches a big database of known "bad" snippets of data. When a new virus or worm is discovered, characteristic parts of the infecting program are added to the signature database. Signature matching still forms the backbone of the antivirus industry, but the black-hat cretins are getting better at writing malware that modifies itself, rendering signatures useless.

Some industry pundits observe (rightly) that a steady flow of updated signature files drives revenue for the antivirus industry: If you drop your subscription, you don't get any new signatures. The antivirus software industry has one of the few software products that becomes nearly obsolete every few days. Powerful economic incentives exist to stick with the signature-matching model — which, by its very nature, works only after a new virus has been identified.

- **Heuristic analysis:** The antivirus software relies on the behavior (or the expected behavior) of a program to catch the destructive software before it has a chance to run. Although an enormous amount of research has gone into heuristic analysis, a black box that determines whether a file will mess up a PC is still a long way off. In fact, there are sound theoretical reasons why a perfect black box of that ilk can never exist.

When an AV program detects a bad piece of software, it normally asks whether you want to *quarantine* the offending file — stick it in an out-of-the-way place where the AV program can retrieve it if you need to — or simply delete it.

Microsoft Security Essentials

As this book went to press, Microsoft was finishing work on a completely new program called Microsoft Security Essentials (MSE). The 'Softies promise that MSE will cover the usual bases, by fighting viruses, scumware, rootkits, and Trojans. Installing Microsoft Security Essentials disables Windows Defender — Microsoft contends the MSE handles all of the Defender functions, and much more.

Like the Windows Live Essentials, Microsoft Security Essentials is free and available for download to anyone who has a validated copy of Windows. (See `Microsoft.com/security_essentials`.) There are some privacy concerns because MSE "phones home" to Microsoft, reporting on the software stored in your computer. Whether the hit to your privacy compensates for free antimalware features is an ongoing concern.

It remains to be seen whether Microsoft can or will deliver a free product that, uh, protects against defects in its own products, but stranger things have happened. Rest assured that we follow MSE diligently at `AskWoody.com`.

Antivirus software typically watches for infections (using both signature matching and heuristic analysis) in one of three ways, and each of the ways hooks into Windows in a different manner:

✦ **A complete scan:** Typically, you schedule full scans of all your files in the middle of the night, or shortly after you download a new signature file. The antivirus program runs a full scan as soon as it's up-to-date. A complete scan runs just like any other program.

✦ **On the fly:** When you open a file or run a program, Windows alerts your antivirus software, and the AV software kicks in to scan the file before it's run or opened. Similarly, if you download a program from the Internet or run a program on a Web page, Windows has your AV software check before you have a chance to shoot yourself in the foot.

✦ **Lurking:** Good antivirus software runs in the background, looking for specific events that may be indicative of an infection. Some AV packages include firewalls, spam blockers, and other components that take lurking to a higher level, but almost all AV software watches while you work, running as a separate Windows task in the background.

In addition, all AV software scans e-mail messages and attachments for infected files. Some scan before the mail reaches the e-mail program; others scan as you open attachments.

Identifying the challenges for antivirus software

Antivirus software manufacturers face many pressures, but aside from detecting all known viruses (and trying to catch some that aren't yet known), one top priority is performance. It takes time to scan a file, and computer folks, impatient by nature, don't like the idea of waiting while the AV software does its thing. The next time your computer goes out to lunch while you're trying to open a file, take heart: The PC you save may be your own.

Another problem facing antivirus software and its creators is the ever-changing nature of the game. Virus and worm writers can go to great lengths to hide their malicious creations. The polymorphic virus illustrates the point. A *polymorphic virus* changes every time it infects, so signature matching doesn't work well, if at all. One favored method for making a virus polymorphic: Encrypt it using a key that changes every time the virus infects. When the virus runs, its first job is to decrypt the main part of the virus. After it's decrypted, the main part goes out and infects, but the malicious code it passes on is encrypted with a different password. Thus, no two copies of the virus look the same, and signature-matching on anything but the (typically very small) decrypting part of the virus doesn't work.

Heuristic analysis of files to try to detect malware suffers from one near-fatal flaw. By its nature, heuristic analysis looks at a program's behavior or expected behavior and draws conclusions about the program based on what it looks like it'll do. There's no black-and-white, no signature-matching "AHA! I got a real one!" finality to the analysis. Instead, heuristic programs live in a world of shades of gray, where there's a 60 percent chance that *this* type of behavior is worm-like and a 78 percent chance that *that* behavior is worm-like. Antivirus software analysts have to turn that kind of soft data into an up-or-down "This is a virus" or "That isn't a virus" result. Frequently, the analysts (or, more correctly, their programs) don't guess right.

Understanding false positives

The bane of antivirus software's existence, a *false positive,* occurs when a perfectly good file is identified as infected. Most frequently, simply by chance, part of an uninfected file may contain the same sequence of characters as a virus, which triggers a signature match.

This all sounds like a gentlemanly mix-up, old chap, stiff upper lip and all that, until you come across a file that appears to be infected but isn't. One major antivirus package recently flagged a perfectly valid Windows file as infected — and of course, it wasn't. The vendor fixed the screwy signature file immediately, as you might imagine, but not before thousands of people dutifully deleted the Windows system file.

Oh yeah. It happens all the time, with all sorts of files.

Be aware of the fact that antivirus software isn't absolutely foolproof. Sometimes the identified bogeymen exist only as a figment of a pattern-matching program's imagination. Although you should take your antivirus program's recommendation as highly indicative of problems, remember that nothing is infallible. If you see a virus warning that doesn't make sense, quarantine the problematic file (don't delete it) and contact the company that created the file, to see whether something has run afoul of an errant antivirus program.

Caring for your antivirus software

McAfee calls them *DAT files.* Symantec (Norton) calls them *virus definitions,* as does Microsoft. F-Secure and Kaspersky both use the term *antivirus database,* whereas Grisoft (AVG) goes the other way, with *virus database.* Trend Micro (maker of PC-cillin) says *pattern file.* Panda uses *signature files,* and CA has *virus signatures.* For Sophos, they're *IDEs.* Microsoft Security Essentials calls them *virus and spyware definitions.*

No matter what you call them, the signature-matching database file lies at the center of every antivirus product's capabilities.

Ground zero

Most Windows worm outbreaks — including the Slammer worm, which infected at least 75,000 computers within ten minutes of its release in January 2003 — rely on a known, already-patched security hole in Windows. Conficker, which took the world by storm in early 2009, similarly used unpatched systems for its initial entrée. Systems that get infected are frequently vulnerable because the people who run the systems don't apply a patch that was readily available from Microsoft. (I discuss patching in Book VI, Chapter 4.) The cretins who write worms watch Microsoft patches closely and try to create programs that exploit the patched holes, knowing full well that a large percentage of all systems connected to the Internet aren't updated often.

Someday soon, that will change — and not for the better.

A *0day* worm (or *zero day* worm or *ground zero* worm) would use a previously unknown, and therefore unpatched, hole in Windows. If the really clever guys in black hats ever get smart enough to find a wide-open hole in Windows before Microsoft patches it, we're all in a world of hurt. We've already seen several 0day attacks, primarily based on Microsoft Excel, Word, and PowerPoint. But the first big 0day worm that goes for Windows will wreak havoc.

A precedent exists. Way back in November 1988, Robert Morris, Jr., a grad student at MIT, released a worm that brought down 6,000 Unix machines — quite a large percentage of all computers connected to the Internet, such as it was. By all accounts, Morris wasn't trying to hurt anything. He only wanted to see what would happen if a program could move from machine to machine. The "version 1.0" worm that got out had mistakes in it — programming bugs — that made it clog up every infected machine, and the rest is history. The Computer Emergency Response Team (CERT; `www.cert.org`) was created in response to Morris's worm.

Every antivirus software manufacturer now tries to protect against 0day attacks, primarily using heuristic analysis. The state of the art is evolving. Right now, your best protection is to stay patched (see Book VI, Chapter 4) and to keep your antivirus software up to date.

In normal use of your antivirus software, you should update its signature file daily. I suggest that you do it in the morning, just before you start to work. Most antivirus programs automatically run once a day. Here's the security schedule I recommend for most Windows 7 users:

- **Keep an eye on Microsoft updates to Windows 7, but don't install them automatically (see Book VI, Chapter 4).** Instead, wait until the other pioneers have arrows in their backs, and then make sure that your system won't end up in worse condition after the patch. Check the MS-DEFCON level on `AskWoody.com` for help.
- **Download antivirus signature files daily.** Your first job each morning should be to verify that your AV software has been updated properly and that the program's icon is visible in your system tray, next to the clock.

✦ **Check for massive new outbreaks daily.** Most AV software companies have e-mail newsletters that can warn you of major new problems. Checking your AV software manufacturer's home page every day to see whether any news is breaking is also worthwhile. Just keep in mind that your AV manufacturer has a vested interest in getting you to buy software.

Be leery of mainstream press reports of new, pending, or possible infections. The folks who write those breathless newspaper articles frequently don't know what they're talking about — they get the details wrong and hype nonexistent problems. It's far better to rely on more trustworthy news sources, such as the SANS Internet Storm Center, `isc.sans.org`, or Ryan Naraine's articles on ZDNet, `blogs.zdnet.com/security`.

✦ **If you think you have a virus, report it to your antivirus software manufacturer.** See the nearby sidebar "How to report a virus" for instructions.

✦ **If a major outbreak occurs, don't — I repeat, don't — send e-mail to all your friends.** That only makes the problem worse. Pick up the phone and call anyone who needs to know. Don't worry. If it's a big virus outbreak, they probably know already.

✦ **Use your antivirus program to run a complete scan of your system once a month.** If you have your signatures updated and your antivirus software is working properly, you don't need to do a full scan very often.

Antivirus software manufacturers create new versions of their programs from time to time, and, of course, they try to sell you the latest and greatest. In my experience, "old" AV programs with properly updated signature files are still effective six months or even a year after the "new" version comes out. You may get zapped by a completely new piece of malware, but then again, you might get zapped even if you're running absolutely the latest version of the antivirus software with up-to-the-second signature files.

Downloading and Installing AVG Free

What? You don't have an antivirus program? Are you tired of the Windows Action Center icon telling you "Windows did not find an antivirus program on this computer."? (See Figure 5-1.)

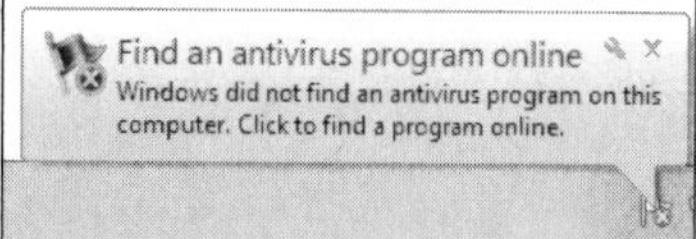

Figure 5-1: Click here and pay a pretty penny.

How to report a virus

Antivirus software manufacturers are constantly looking for new malware.

Unfortunately, at least 90 percent (and probably more like 99 percent) of what they receive is junk — requests for technical support, old hoaxes, viruses that have been around for a hundred years, and stuff that doesn't bear any resemblance to real, infectious programs.

If your computer has a new virus, your AV software manufacturer wants to hear from you. The instructions vary depending on the manufacturer (see the following list), but if you're sure that you found a new creepy-crawly, by all means submit it:

- AVG: virus@avg.com (Put the file in a password-protected Zip file and e-mail it.)
- F-Secure: analysis.f-secure.com/portal/login.html
- Frisk F-PROT: f-prot.com/virusinfo/submission_form.html
- Kaspersky: support.kaspersky.ru/virlab/helpdesk.html?LANG=en
- McAfee: vil.nai.com/vil/submitsample.aspx
- Symantec (Norton): symantec.com/avcenter/submit.html

You don't need to submit a new virus to more than one manufacturer. They all talk to each other, regularly, vociferously, and new viruses make their way rapidly from company to company. It's a credit to the AV industry that the lines of communication have been kept open, even among fierce competitors, and that samples of "real" viruses are made available to legitimate researchers, usually within hours of being identified.

You can also submit your suspected new virus to Virustotal (virustotal.com) and have it run scans of the infected file, using multiple antivirus products. Virustotal tells you whether your virus has been seen before.

Check your antivirus software manufacturer's site frequently. In fact, while you're thinking about it, bookmark it or add the site to your Web browser's Favorites list.

Hey, if it takes some nagging to get you with the program, so be it.

Personally, I use and recommend a powerful, capable, free-for-personal-use antivirus program — AVG Free from Grisoft. It goes in like a champ and coexists peacefully with Windows, and you can't beat the price: free for home users. Although Microsoft Security Essentials shows great promise, at this point I haven't seen enough empirical evidence and virus lab analysis to say for sure if it's any better than AVG Free. For now, I'll stick with AVG, the product I've used for years. But that could change in the not-too-distant future.

Here's how to download and install AVG Free:

1. **Go to the Grisoft AVG-Free Web site (`free.grisoft.com`).**

   The main page should look something like the one shown in Figure 5-2.

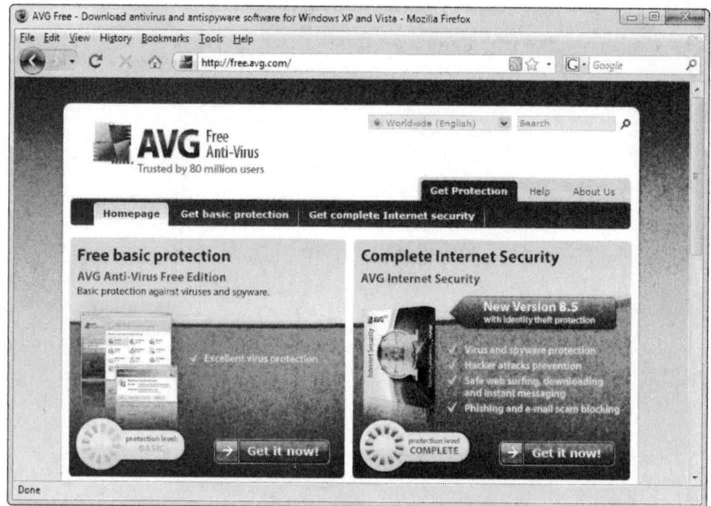

Figure 5-2: Start here to download AVG Free.

2. **Click the Get It Now link on the left side of the page.**

   The people who make AVG want you to buy the Complete Internet Security package. If you feel so inclined, by all means do so. But for most people, the free "basic" antivirus protection works just fine.

   Don't be confused by offers of a "free trial." You don't want a free trial of the AVG for-pay package. You want the free version, officially named AVG Anti-Virus Free Edition.

3. **At the bottom of the AVG Anti-Virus Free page, click the Free for Private Use Only/Download button.**

   AVG opens an advisor page, where you're once again given a choice between the Free Edition and a "free" premium package that has many strings attached (sponsored by TrialPay [`trialpay.com`]).

4. **Click the Download Now link to download the `AVG-Free .exe` file.**

   You may find yourself diverted to the CNET Web site (`cnet.com`). That's okay. Follow the instructions to download the software. When the download finishes, run the file, click through the User Account Control prompt, choose your setup language, and click the Next button.

5. **Accept the default settings (don't install any toolbars, of course — no need to add any more junk to your system), but when the installer asks whether you want to perform a standard or custom installation,**

choose Custom and click Next. Keep clicking Next until you see the Component Selection window, shown in Figure 5-3.

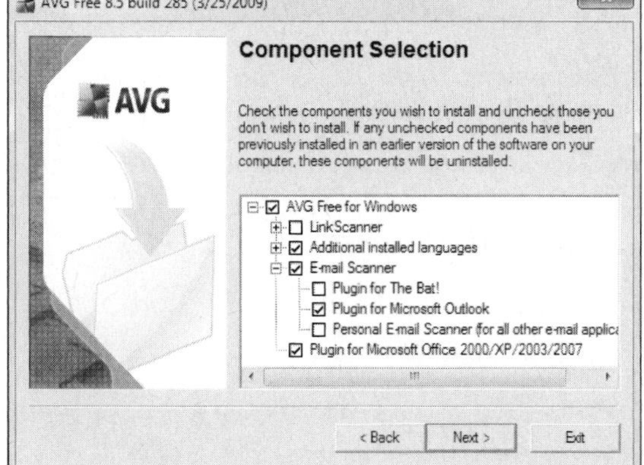

Figure 5-3: The Component Selection dialog box.

6. **In the Component Selection window, deselect the LinkScanner check box. Then click Next, and then Finish.**

   I don't like LinkScanner, so I suggest that you refrain from installing it. See the nearby sidebar "What is LinkScanner?" for my take on the situation.

   The AVG Free installer announces that it's complete, but it isn't.

7. **When you see the Installation Is Complete window, click OK.**

   AVG immediately starts its First Run Wizard, shown in Figure 5-4.

Figure 5-4: Installation isn't complete until you complete the First Run Wizard.

8. **Click Next. Follow along to set the time to update the signature files every day. If AVG asks, of course you don't want to provide information about detected threats to AVG. Check for the latest updates. Skip the Registration and you're done.**

   AVG Free starts running.

9. **In the notification area, to the left of the time display, click the up arrow and choose the AVG icon.**

   The main AVG Free window appears, as shown in Figure 5-5. You can click the X (Close) button, if you like, and AVG Free keeps running.

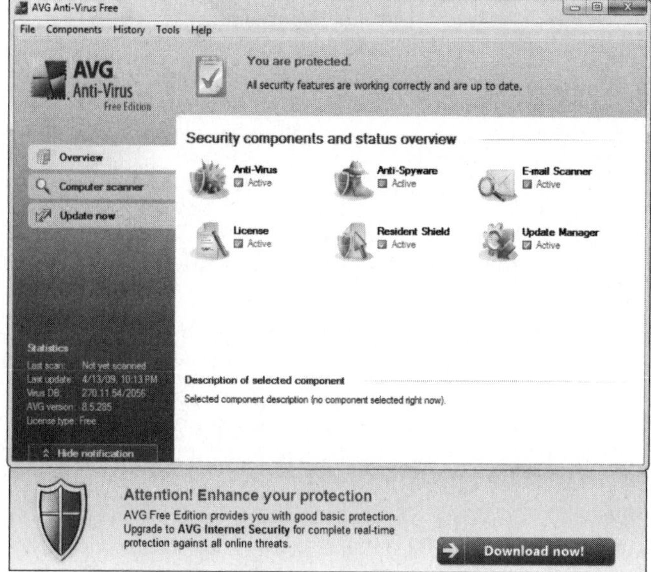

Figure 5-5: You can safely ignore the dire AVG warning at the bottom.

AVG Free always shows a dire warning at the bottom of its main window about how you need to enhance your protection, or how there are a zillion reasons why you need to pay for antivirus protection. If you want to believe the marketing, go right ahead.

If you messed up and installed the AVG Free LinkScanner by mistake, you can turn it off. Here's how:

1. **In the notification area, near the time display, click the up arrow and then double-click the AVG Free icon.**

If you have LinkScanner installed, a LinkScanner icon appears in the middle of the AVG control window, as shown in Figure 5-6.

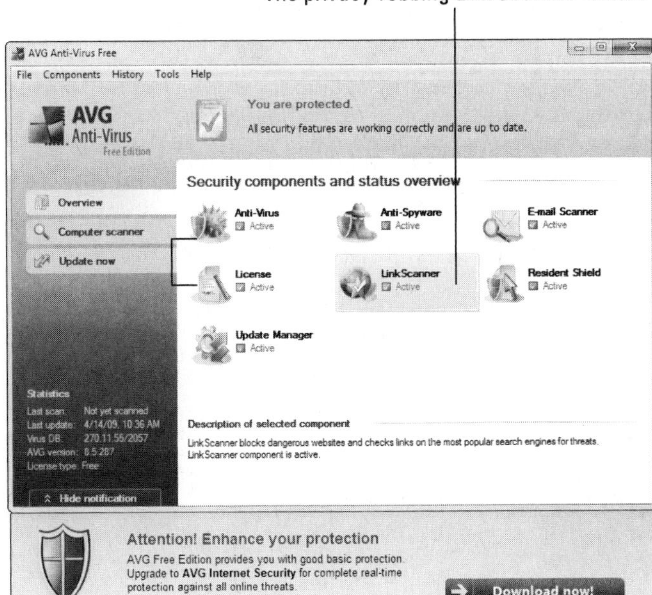

Figure 5-6: If you installed Link-Scanner, it appears in the AVG Free main window.

2. **In the main AVG control window, choose Tools➪Advanced Settings. In the Advanced Settings dialog box, on the left, choose LinkScanner.**

   You see the LinkScanner settings shown in Figure 5-7.

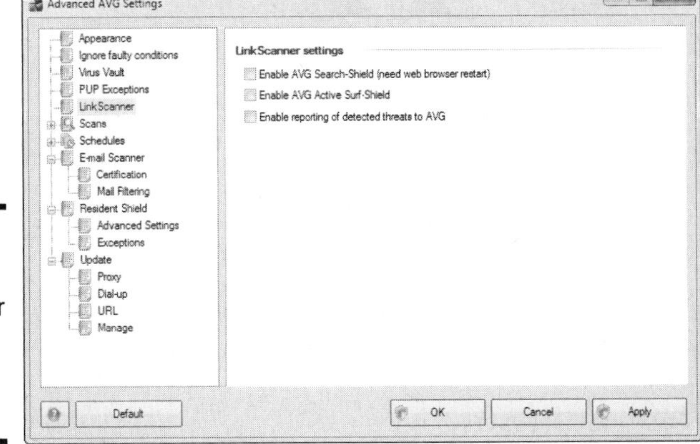

Figure 5-7: Disable LinkScanner by clearing all these boxes.

3. **Deselect the check boxes marked Enable AVG Search-Shield and Enable AVG Active Surf-Shield. Click OK.**

   You return to the main AVG Free control window, where you see the red warning message, `You may not be protected! Some components report an error. Oh me, oh my — how will you ever survive without LinkScanner?` (Okay, I fibbed about that last one.)

4. **In the main AVG control window (again), choose Tools⇨Ignore Faulty Conditions. On the right, in the component area, select the check box marked LinkScanner. Click OK.**

   AVG reports that you have decided to disable warnings about LinkScanner (see Figure 5-8), you naughty computer owner.

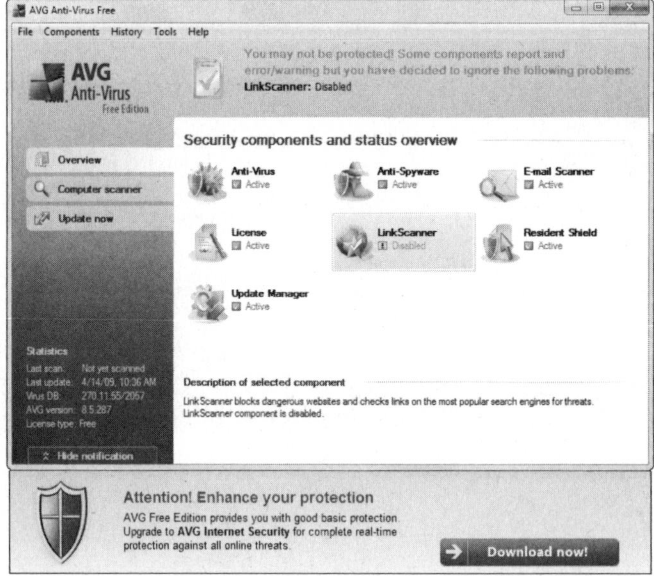

Figure 5-8: Mission accomplished — LinkScanner is both disabled and stifled.

5. **Click the X button to close the AVG control window.**

   Don't worry: AVG Free keeps working. The X only removes the control window; it doesn't stop AVG Free.

If you like AVG Free, tell your friends! Grisoft makes its money by selling corporate licenses and by peddling the regular version, which includes several additional features and a less-congested signature-file download site. While you're at it, tell your friends how to disable LinkScanner, too.

What is LinkScanner?

Grisoft, the company that makes AVG Free, bought the LinkScanner technology in December 2007 and incorporated it into AVG Free.

The concept behind LinkScanner is straightforward: Every time you run a search (say, through Google), LinkScanner kicks in, looks at all the Web sites returned by the search, and gives you a quick thumbs-up-or-thumbs-down take on each site, warning you if the site harbors malware.

Many Webmasters complained that LinkScanner was artificially inflating "hit" statistics for Web sites. Every time you looked at a new page of Google results, LinkScanner used to run out to all the Web sites and check them.

That changed in July 2008, when LinkScanner started using a blacklist that's downloaded to your PC. AVG says that it now scans links only as they're clicked, which means that LinkScanner harvests only part of your Web-browsing history — and AVG no doubt sells the logs to one of the major data-collection companies.

I don't like LinkScanner. It sends information about my Web-surfing history to AVG. It has caused problems in the past. Google itself now flags pages that are suspected to harbor malware. And Firefox does a better job in almost every respect, with little invasion of my privacy.

Dealing with Spyware

Windows 7 ships with the Microsoft antispyware program named Windows Defender. Although Windows Defender has many fine attributes, it has come under fire for errors of both omission and commission.

At the heart of the problem: What, precisely, is spyware? Microsoft has published a lengthy, detailed list of criteria that it applies when determining whether a specific program falls in the "spyware" category. You can see it at `microsoft.com/athome/security/spyware/software/msft/analysis.mspx`.

Whether Windows Defender follows those guidelines is the subject of heated debate. Five years ago, both CNET and the *New York Times* reported anonymous sources as saying that Microsoft was "in talks" to acquire Claria, a company best known for its scummy product Gator. About the same time, Windows Defender suddenly changed its treatment of Gator (see the *eWeek* story at `eweek.com/c/a/Security/Why-Microsoft-AntiSpyware-Is-Untrustworthy`). Was one related to the other? Who knows?

Here's the bottom line: Go ahead and use Windows Defender (it's already set up to run automatically every day), but don't rely on Microsoft to eliminate all programs that a reasonable person might find scummy. And don't get too dependent on Defender. Some day you may end up installing Microsoft Security Essentials (see the "Microsoft Security Essentials" sidebar earlier in this chapter). Doing so disables Windows Defender.

Where's Defender?

Although Windows Defender occupies a prominent place on the Windows XP and Vista Start menus, in Windows 7 it's buried.

If Windows Defender finds something wrong, it raises an alarm in the Action Center (see Book VI, Chapter 2). At that point, you can click a link and open Windows Defender.

If you just want to see how Defender's doing, it's hard to find. Here's how to open it:

1. **Choose Start, and then immediately type** defe **and press Enter.**

   Alternatively, you can choose Start⇨Control Panel, and in the upper-right corner, choose View By Large Icons, and then double-click Windows Defender.

   However you uncover Defender, it appears as shown in Figure 5-9.

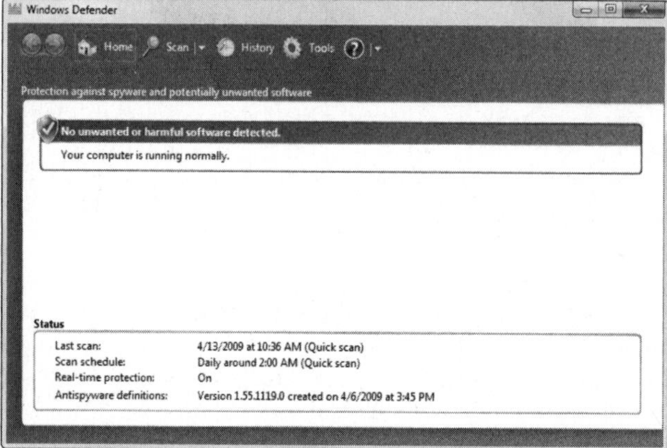

Figure 5-9: Windows Defender — if you can find it.

2. **To run a quick scan of your PC, click the Scan icon.**

   Windows Defender looks in the places that are most likely to harbor spyware and reports on its findings.

If Defender finds any dicey programs, it shows you a list of the offenders by alert level: Severe/High or Medium/Low. Windows Defender tells you where the spyware appeared and gives you the option to ignore, quarantine, remove, or always allow that item.

3. **To see the results of your most recent scans, click the History icon. To adjust the default settings, click the Tools icon (see Figure 5-10).**

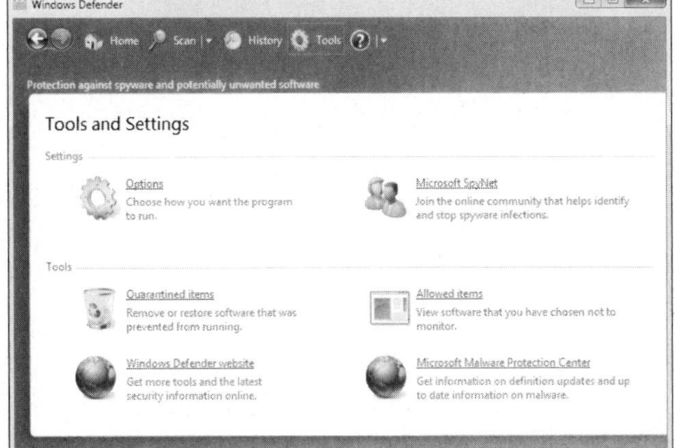

Figure 5-10: The Defender tools.

Inside Windows Defender you see several references to Microsoft SpyNet. At one time, SpyNet was a privacy-busting feature worth your attention and, uh, benign neglect. Nowadays, it seems to function primarily as a mechanism for collecting infection statistics — and even that role may be going away. If I hear of any problems with SpyNet, I'll raise the alarm on `AskWoody.com`.

4. **Click the X button to close Defender.**

   Windows Defender continues to work in the background.

Blocking spies with Spybot–S&D

Don't rely on Windows Defender alone to protect your computer from scummy programs. Microsoft has shown an alarming, shall we say, *flexibility* in the way it makes recommendations about quarantining or ignoring specific pieces of junkware.

As of this writing, the best "second" antispyware program I've found — which is to say, the anti-spyware program I use alongside Windows Defender — is Webroot SpySweeper (`webroot.com`), which costs $30 for one year or $40 for two years. It's thorough, capable, and unobtrusive; it can work side by side with Windows Defender; and the manufacturer has a long, strong record of protecting consumers from big, rich, powerful scum companies.

However, I use a Webroot SpySweeper competitor, Spybot–Search & Destroy. Why? It's free (for personal use), and it works pretty darn well. Even if I switch over to Microsoft Security Essentials, and thereby zap out Windows Defender, I still intend to run SpyBot–S&D from time to time. Two spyware heads are better than one.

Here's how to get SpyBot–S&D going with Windows 7:

1. **Crank up your favorite Web browser and go to `spybot.com`.**

   After selecting a country of origin, you're redirected to `safer-networking.org`, the home of Spybot–Search & Destroy (see Figure 5-11).

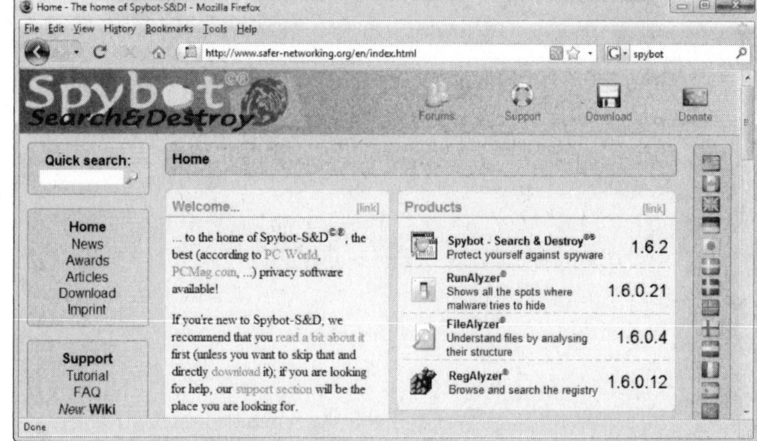

Figure 5-11: Spybot–S&D — my choice of (free!) antispyware programs.

2. **On the right, under Products, click the icon to the left of Spybot–Search & Destroy. On the next page, scroll down and click the link to download Spybot–Search & Destroy. On the *next* page, click one of the Download Here links. On the *next* page, click Download.**

   Whew. Are you still with me?

3. **Go through the usual machinations to download and run the installer.**

   Personally, I accept all the default settings, but you may not want TeaTimer. See the sidebar "Spybot–S&D options" for details.

   When the installer finishes, Spybot–S&D offers to create a Registry backup (which I decline), introduces the tutorial (which I strongly recommend), and shows you the main Spybot–Search & Destroy window, shown in Figure 5-12.

4. **Click the button marked Check for Problems.**

Spybot–S&D performs a full scan of your system. It can take an hour or more, so be patient. The report (see Figure 5-13) will surprise you — guaranteed.

5. **When you're done, click the X button to close the main window.**

   Be sure to take the tutorial. It introduces you to many Spybot–Search & Destroy capabilities, including rootkit detection — good stuff.

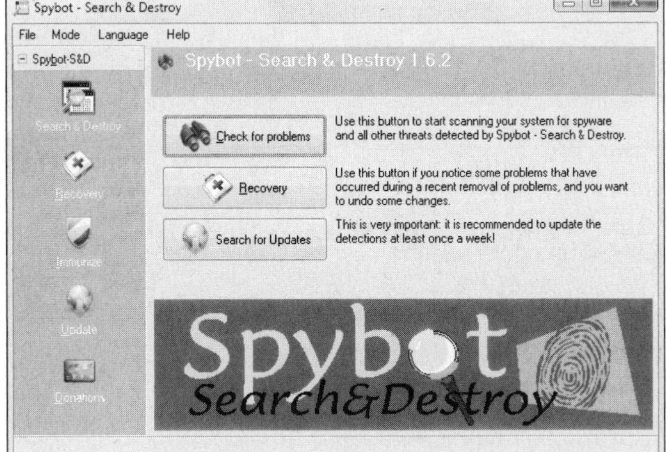

Figure 5-12: The Spybot–Search & Destroy command center.

Figure 5-13: Spybot–S&D finds a bunch of third-party "tracking" cookies.

Spybot–S&D options

When you install Spybot–S&D, you have a chance to install and run two ancillary applications. I run both, but you might not want to run TeaTimer, especially if you have a slower PC:

- **TeaTimer** is the *resident* part of Spybot–S&D. It runs all the time, in the background, looking as Windows programs start and comparing them to its blacklist of known scummy programs. TeaTimer takes a snapshot of important Registry settings and monitors those Registry keys as programs run. If a program tries to change one of the keys, TeaTimer tells you. It can restore the Registry to its earlier state, too, if you so choose.
- **Security Center Integration** makes Windows 7 aware of Spybot–S&D's presence, by hooking into the Action Center.

If you use Spybot–Search & Destroy, recommend it to your friends and don't forget to drop off a donation.

Blocking Bad Autostarting Programs

Windows automatically runs certain programs every time you start it, and those programs can prove cantankerous at times. So how do you prevent scummy programs from running every time you start Windows?

Both the Windows XP and Windows Vista versions of Windows Defender include the handy feature named Software Explorer, which lets you look at and, optionally, throttle any or all of the programs that start automatically, every time you boot Windows.

Unfortunately, Windows Defender in Windows 7 doesn't have a Software Explorer. Microsoft ditched it. Fortunately, there's a better way — from Microsoft, no less.

Microsoft distributes the `Autoruns.exe` program, which runs rings around the old Windows Defender Software Explorer. Autoruns started as a free product from the small company Sysinternals, and it owes its existence to Mark Russinovich and Bryce Cogswell, two of the most knowledgeable Windows folks on the planet. In July 2006, Microsoft bought Sysinternals. Mark became a Microsoft Demigod, er, Fellow. Microsoft promised that all the free Sysinternals products would remain free. And, wonder of wonders, that's exactly what happened. Autoruns is updated frequently and works like a champ — and it's still absolutely free.

To get Autoruns working, download `Autoruns.zip` from `technet.microsoft.com/en-us/sysinternals/bb963902.aspx`. Double-click the file and click and drag `Autoruns.exe` to your desktop. (The other program, `Autorunsc.exe`, is the command-line version of Autoruns. Chances are good that you'll never need it.)

Here's how to use Autoruns:

1. **Double-click** `Autoruns.exe`**.**

   You see a report like the one shown in Figure 5-14.

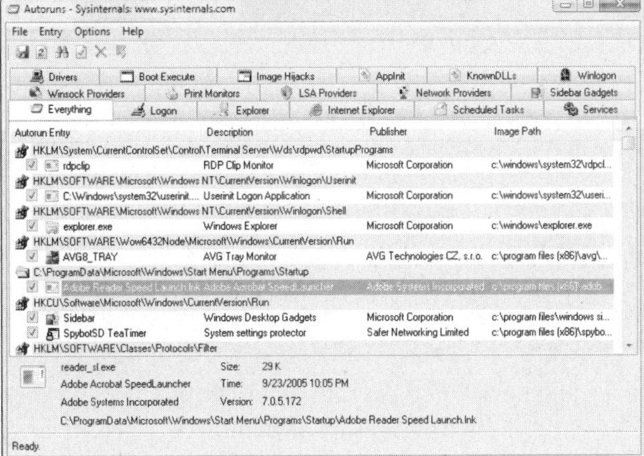

Figure 5-14: Autoruns lists all programs that run automatically in Windows, in the order they're started.

   The check box in front of each listed program controls whether Windows starts the program automatically: Deselect the check box, and the next time you boot Windows, that program gets left out.

2. **To see details about an individual program, click its name once.**

   Basic information about the program appears at the bottom of the window. For example, in Figure 5-14, I look at the details for the Adobe Acrobat SpeedLauncher.

3. **To find more information about an autostarting program, right-click it and choose Search Online.**

   This step runs a search on the program's name, using your default browser (in my case, Firefox) and its default search engine (in my case, Google).

   When I right-click the Adobe Acrobat SpeedLauncher and choose Search Online, the second Google result leads to the page shown in Figure 5-15.

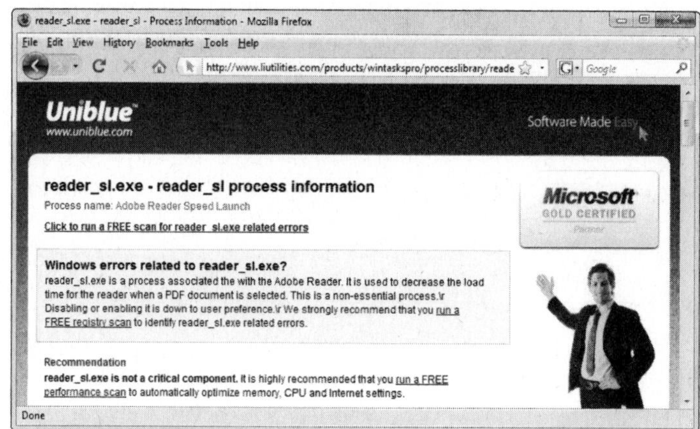

Figure 5-15: The liutilities.com Web site says that the Acrobat Speed-Launcher is a "non-essential" process.

4. **If you find an autostarting program that you want to prevent from launching automatically, deselect the check box in front of it.**

   Read the nearby "Don't kill these" sidebar before you squelch anything questionable.

5. **To hide all the Microsoft programs on the Autoruns list, choose Options➪Hide Microsoft and Windows Entries, and then click the Refresh icon.**

   You see an abbreviated list that includes only non-Microsoft products, as shown in Figure 5-16.

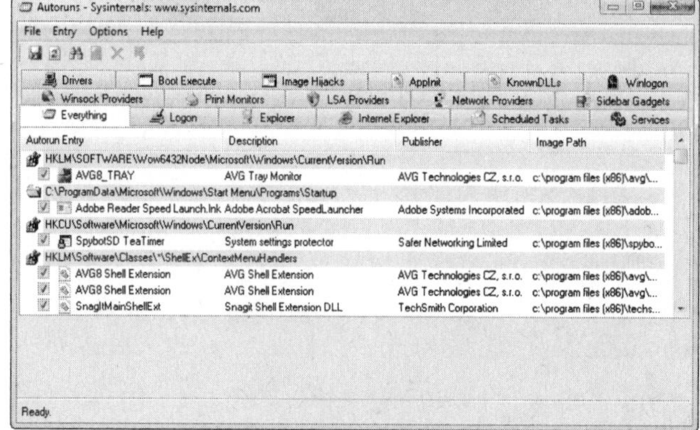

Figure 5-16: Autoruns lets you suppress the Microsoft programs.

6. **When you're done with Autoruns, click the X Close button to close it.**

   You have to restart Windows for your changes to take effect.

Don't kill these

Of course, you shouldn't disable an autostarting program just because it looks superfluous, or even because a blogger figures that it's contributing to global warming or slow startups, whichever comes first. As a general rule, if you don't know *exactly* what an autostarting program does, don't touch it. It's not nice to fool with Mother Nature.

You can find detailed, expert advice on what you should or should not touch with Autoruns at `forum.sysinternals.com/forum_posts.asp?TID=5226`.

As a general rule, when zapping auto-starting programs and background services, take out one at a time. That way when you reboot your machine, if something goes belly-up, you stand a good chance of identifying which program was the culprit.

In a nutshell, avoid messing with any of the system settings. You can play with items in the `\CurrentVersion\Run` Registry keys or the `\Start Menu\Programs\Startup` directories, but you can mess up your application programs if you zap entries willy-nilly. You can disable Internet Explorer browser objects if you think that they're causing problems, but be on the lookout for programs that go belly-up the next time you start IE.

Book VII

Networking with Windows 7

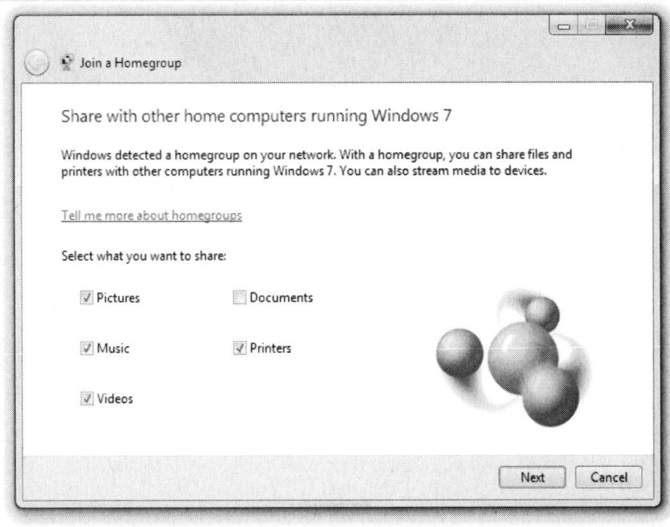

Contents at a Glance

Chapter 1: Attaching to a Network

In This Chapter

- Choosing between home, work, and public network types
- Getting your computer attached to an existing network
- Looking at how HomeGroups work
- Slicing and dicing your HomeGroup

Attaching your Windows 7 computer to an existing network rarely involves more than a few mouse clicks.

Correctly attaching your Windows 7 computer to an existing network requires a bit more.

Historically, Microsoft has had no end of problems with networking. Computers drop on and off the network like hyperactive jumping beans, for absolutely no reason other than that they've entered a new phase of the moon. Shared printers or folders appear and disappear at random intervals. A Windows Vista computer can see a Windows XP computer on the network, but not vice versa. Or the other way around.

I've lost more than a few pulled hairs trying to get my networks to network. I would bet you have, too.

Windows 7 brings a whole new approach to the networking game and, if you understand what it's supposed to do, it works. Unfortunately, if you have Windows XP computers or Windows Vista computers connected to your network, they'll likely continue to suffer the same slings and arrows that have always dogged them. But, in my experience, the Windows 7 computers on your network will work together nicely, and in most cases they play well with their less-endowed brethren.

This chapter takes you through the steps necessary to get your Windows 7 computer attached to an existing network — and to do a good job of it. Pay attention when you first attach it to a network and you can ignore the network afterward: It just works. Mess things up initially, and you may feel the ramifications of your choices days, weeks, or months from now.

This chapter also includes a section on playing Wi-Fi hide-and-seek — the steps you can take to ensure that your laptop connects to the correct network, the first time.

If you haven't yet set up a network, look at Chapter 2 in this minibook. Chapter 3 of this minibook explains how to expand your network. To set up a wireless network, see Book VII, Chapter 4. But if you already have a network in your home or office, or if you're trying to connect to a network in a coffee shop or airport, you're in the right place.

Before you set up a network connection in Windows 7, it helps a lot if you understand two pivotal concepts: network type and HomeGroups. Permit me to start this chapter with an explanation of both and then show you how to attach your computer to a network.

Choosing Between Home, Work, and Public

Are you connecting to a home, work, or public network?

That's the first question Windows 7 asks when you try to hook into a network (see Figure 1-1). It doesn't matter if you're using a Wi-Fi card, a LAN cable, or a piece of string attached to two cups — Windows wants to know whether you're in your house, at work, or in the public. It's downright eerie, eh? Kinda begs the question if you work at home.

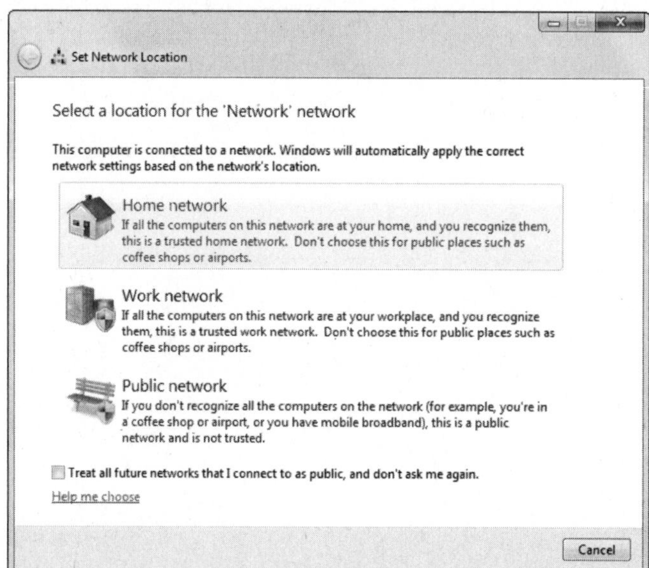

Figure 1-1: The Set Network Location dialog box.

It's also the number-one question I hear from Windows 7 networkers: What's the difference between home, work, and public?

Here's what's really going on with the three *network types*:

- **Public:** If you tell Windows 7 that you're connecting to a public network, it puts up your PC's shields. Windows Firewall plugs almost all its openings — the only ones left open are the ones absolutely necessary for Windows to communicate with the outside world. (See the discussion of Windows Firewall ports in Book VI, Chapter 3.) Windows 7 also starts the internal programs, or *services,* that are appropriate for running Windows connected to a potentially hostile network.
- **Work:** If you tell Windows 7 that you're connecting to a work network, it opens Windows Firewall so that you can communicate with other computers on your network and share folders, say, or use printers on the network. Windows starts the services that are appropriate for a computer running on a trusted network — services that look for and connect to other computers and make your computer visible on the network.
- **Home:** A home network behaves a lot like a work network, but when you choose Home, Windows 7 goes out and looks for other Windows 7 computers on the network. If it finds other Win7 computers and they already have a HomeGroup going (see the next section), Windows 7 invites you to join that HomeGroup. If it doesn't find one, Windows 7 asks whether you want to start one.

There's a big difference between a public network, on the one hand, and home or work networks, on the other. But the difference between home and work networks, at least to a first (and second) approximation, is that a home network supports HomeGroups, whereas a work network doesn't.

Or, to put it another way, if you want to use a HomeGroup for all Windows 7 computers in your office (see the next section), you *must* tell Windows 7 that you're on a home network. It doesn't matter whether you're in a home office, an office home, an office office, or the middle of a Faraday cage in the U.S. Embassy in Bishkek: If you want to set up or use a HomeGroup, you have to choose the home network type.

Windows remembers the network type, so if you switch networks (common with a laptop and unusual for a wired connection) and Windows can identify the new network, it doesn't ask again whether it's a public, work, or home network. It uses the old settings.

There's one additional network type, which you encounter only if you plug your computer into a big Corporate Network: a *domain* network. Central computers — the servers — completely control a domain network. Some domains can even support HomeGroups. If you want to know more about domain networks, see *Networking For Dummies,* 8th Edition, by Doug Lowe (Wiley). It's a whole different world.

Understanding HomeGroups

So you have a network, and two or more of the Windows 7 computers on the network say that it's a home network (see the preceding section). Good. Now you can start thinking about HomeGroups.

Don't be put off by the term *HomeGroup.* If you have a business and need to share information, a HomeGroup may provide exactly what you want.

As of this writing, anyway, HomeGroups work with only Windows 7 computers. You can have a zillion computers on your home network, running Windows and MacOS and Linux, laughing and printing and crashing together, but only the ones running Windows 7 with a designated home network type can participate in a HomeGroup. If you have computers that run something other than Windows 7 or you have Windows 7 computers that are set up with work or public networks, you can think of a HomeGroup as a clique inside your network.

The *HomeGroup* bundles a bunch of settings in quite a handy — I'm tempted to use the word *brilliant* — way. When your PC joins a HomeGroup, Windows strips away a lot of the hassle and mind-numbing details generally associated with sharing folders and printers and replaces the mumbo jumbo with a cookie-cutter method of sharing that works quite well, in almost all home and many small-business networks.

To connect to a HomeGroup, you need its password. Microsoft likens it to having a key to a house. At the risk of stretching a metaphor, if you have the key to the house (the HomeGroup password), you can get into anything in the house (printers, folders, and files inside those folders, in particular).

When you dig a little deeper, here's what you find:

- **A HomeGroup connects computers, not users.** If you attach a Windows 7 PC to a HomeGroup, all the people using that PC — all its user accounts — gain access to the data in the HomeGroup. Conversely, anyone accessing the HomeGroup from another computer gains access to the specified folders for all users on your PC.
- **Although you can override the default choices (see Figure 1-2), when you join your PC to a HomeGroup, you make all Pictures, Music, and Videos libraries on your PC available to other PCs in the HomeGroup; your printers are shared, too.**

  Note that I said *libraries*, not folders. (I talk about libraries in Book II, Chapter 1.) If you share the Pictures libraries on your PC with the HomeGroup, for example, all folders in all the Pictures libraries for all users on your computer are shared. If you add a folder from a Windows XP computer to your Pictures library and your PC is in a HomeGroup, that folder on the Windows XP computer becomes accessible to every user on every computer in the HomeGroup.

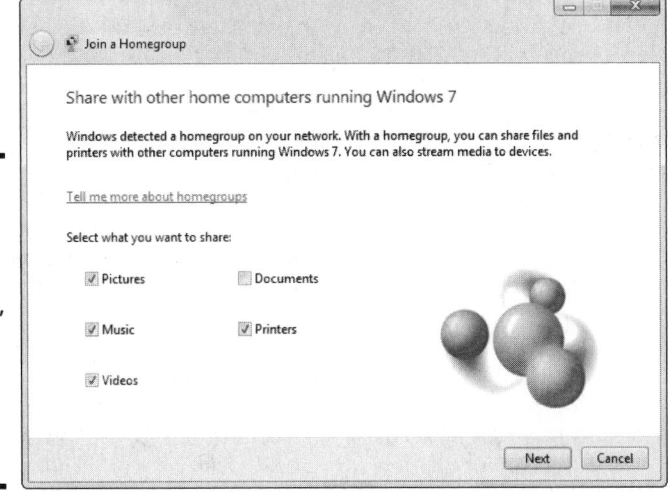

Figure 1-2: When your computer joins a HomeGroup, you can select which libraries to share.

More than that, you can put folders from other HomeGroup computers' libraries into your libraries. So if a computer in your HomeGroup has a Pictures library that includes a folder from a Windows XP PC, you can simply copy that folder into your Pictures library and it works like any other folder in your Pictures library. Combining HomeGroups and libraries leads to enormously powerful capabilities.

✦ **When you join your PC to the HomeGroup, you get to decide whether you want to share the Documents libraries for all users on your PC.** If you choose to share documents, the Documents library for every user on your computer gets shared. That may or may not be what you want, so consider your choice carefully.

When you share a file, it's important to understand whether other people in your HomeGroup can only open the file, modify its contents, or delete it. The default permissions level for HomeGroup-shared folders s a bit convoluted, but it makes sense. Unless you specifically modify the permissions (more about that in the "Caring for Your HomeGroup" section, at the end of this chapter), here's what you get:

✦ **Other users in your HomeGroup can open all files in your libraries (Pictures, Music, Videos, and, optionally, Documents).**

- **Other users in your HomeGroup cannot change files in your personal folders (your `\Pictures`, `\Music`, `\Videos`, and, optionally, `\Documents` folders).** But they can change or delete files in your computer's `Public` folders (`\Public\Pictures`, `\Public\Music`, `\Public\Videos`, and, optionally, `\Public\Documents`). They can also add new files to the public folders.
- **If you have other folders in your libraries, the folders inherit the restrictions that are set on the computer containing the folders.**

You can change the permissions level at any time — restrict access to folders or add new folders on your PC to the HomeGroup, for example. I show you how, in the section "Caring for Your HomeGroup," later in this chapter.

The easy way to add a folder to your HomeGroup? Go to any computer that's attached to the HomeGroup and drag the folder into the appropriate library. That's all it takes. After the folder sits inside one shared library, you can click and drag it into any other library on any computer that's attached to the HomeGroup.

When your computer is attached to a HomeGroup, you see a direct link to the HomeGroup on the left side of the Windows Explorer window (see Figure 1-3). From that jumping-off point, you can easily look at all shared folders on all computers in your HomeGroup.

Click here to start exploring all shared folders in your HomeGroup.

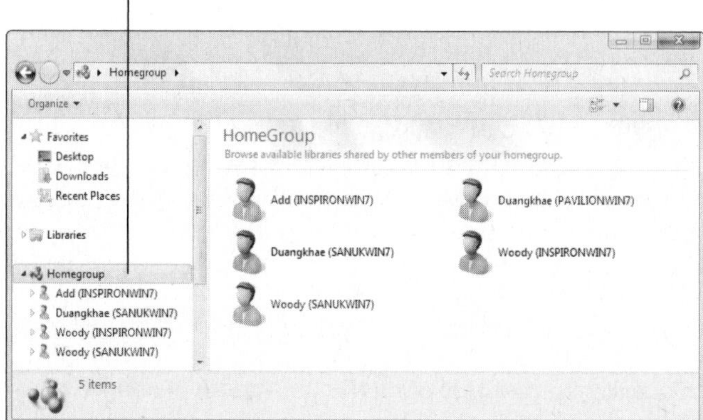

Figure 1-3: Your HomeGroup appears on the left side of the Explorer window.

HomeGroup links also appear in Windows Media Player (in the navigation pane on the left) and Windows Media Center (in the shared section of the browser).

Printers on a HomeGroup-connected computer are shared automatically with all other Windows 7 computers on the HomeGroup. You don't need to add a printer or install drivers. It just happens automatically, as long as the printer has the Windows logo — as do most of the printers made in the past few years.

Now that you know the inside story about HomeGroups, you may be tempted to switch your Windows 7 PCs from the work type over to the home network type so that you can set up a HomeGroup. Fortunately, that's easy to do — see the section "Caring for Your HomeGroup," at the end of this chapter.

Hooking Up to a Wireless Network

So you want to attach your computer to a wireless network? Good. You're in the right place. (If you want to connect to a network with a LAN cable, skip ahead to the "Hooking Up to a Wired Network" section.)

In this section I discuss hooking into a Wi-Fi (also known as an 802.11) network. I assume that the network is working and broadcasting its ID (known as an *SSID*) and that you know the password if the network requires one.

The method for connecting to WiMax networks, HSDPA, CDMA, and other kinds of networks is generally different from the steps listed here. You probably need to refer to the instructions that came with the WiMax or HSDPA service, your mobile phone, or CDMA network.

If you're connecting in a public place such as a hotel or a coffee shop, the people who run the network (or hotel or coffee shop) may have provided you with a user ID and a password. They may have charged you for the userID and password. Confusingly, that kind of user ID and password is different from a network password. If you have a user ID and password, follow along here but don't be surprised if you aren't asked for a password to connect to the network. They'll get ya after you're connected. Read on.

Here's how to get your PC going on a functional wireless network:

1. **Make sure your wireless chip or card is working.**

   Nine times out of ten, if you can't get Windows 7 to connect to a working Wi-Fi network, it's because you haven't turned on the wireless hardware inside your computer. Many laptops have a switch or a function (Fn) key combination that enables or disables the wireless hardware (see Figure 1-4). Most modern laptops have a light that glows when the wireless hardware is working. (Laptop manufacturers use switches so that you can turn off wireless and save battery power when you aren't using the network.) If you can't find the switch, consult the manual or ask your 8-year-old to find it for you. Kids seem to have a knack — and the eyesight — for spotting obscure switches.

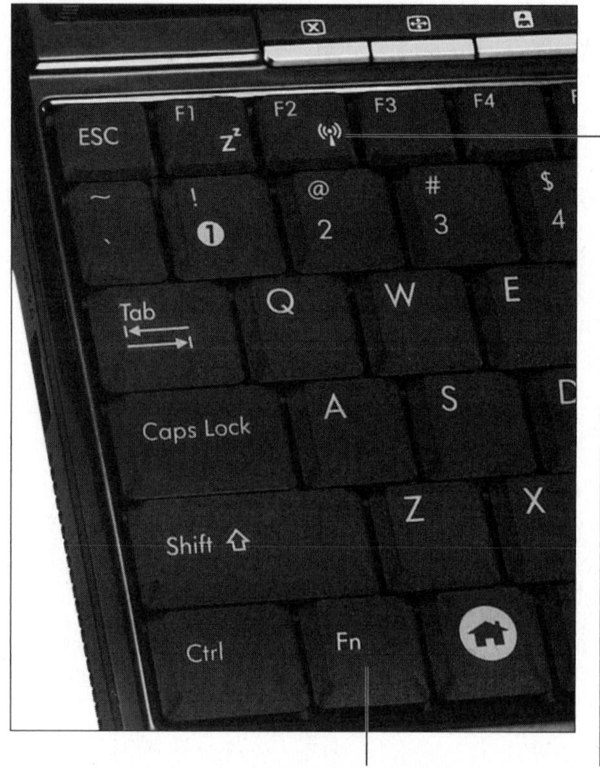
Hold down the Fn key...
...and press F2.

Figure 1-4: To enable (or disable) wireless on the Eee PC 1000H, hold down the Fn key and press F2.

2. **If wireless networks are available — broadcasting their IDs — the starburst on the stepladder "bar" icon in the notification area, near the clock, starts to glow and pulse. Click on it.**

   You see a list of all available networks, as shown in Figure 1-5.

3. **Click the name of the network you want to use. If you want to have Windows connect to the network automatically in the future, select the indicated check box. Then click Connect.**

The little starburst whirls and twirls and whistles an inaudible tune, and if the network has a password, it asks you to provide it. When it's done, you probably see the Set Network Location dialog box (refer to Figure 1-1). I say *probably* because if you've already chosen a network type for this particular connection, Windows is smart enough to use it again.

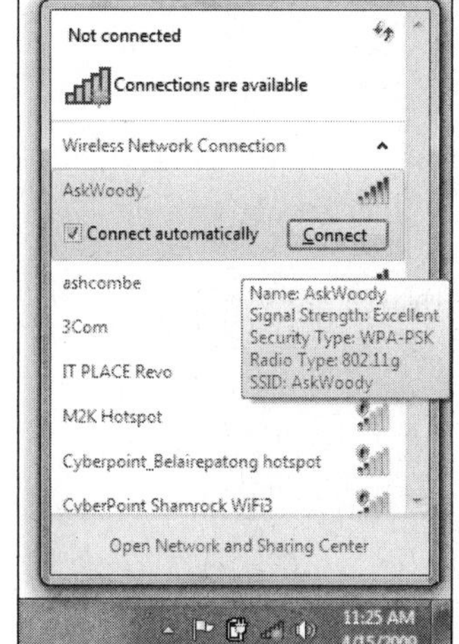

Figure 1-5: A list of all networks broad-casting their IDs.

4. **Take a look at the preceding section for a description of home, work, and public network types, and choose accordingly.**

   If you choose Public or Work, the computer connects, and after a minute or two you're done. Congratulations! Crank up Firefox or Internet Explorer and make sure you're connected to the Internet.

   This is where the user ID and password I mention at the beginning of this section may come in to play. If you're connecting to a network inside a hotel, or a for-pay network almost anywhere, the people who run the network may ask for a user ID and password. You know for sure if you get the wireless connection going, start your favorite browser, and see a logon screen like the one shown in Figure 1-6.

   The user ID and password may be free for hotel guests or coffee shop customers; it may cost two arms and three legs. You have to look or ask around.

   If you tell Windows that you're connecting to a home network, it runs out to see whether other Windows 7 computers are running on the network and whether any of them has a HomeGroup set up. If there's a

HomeGroup already, you see a message like the one shown in Figure 1-7. (If there's no HomeGroup, you see an offer to set up a new HomeGroup. See the later section "Hooking Up to a Wired Network" for details.)

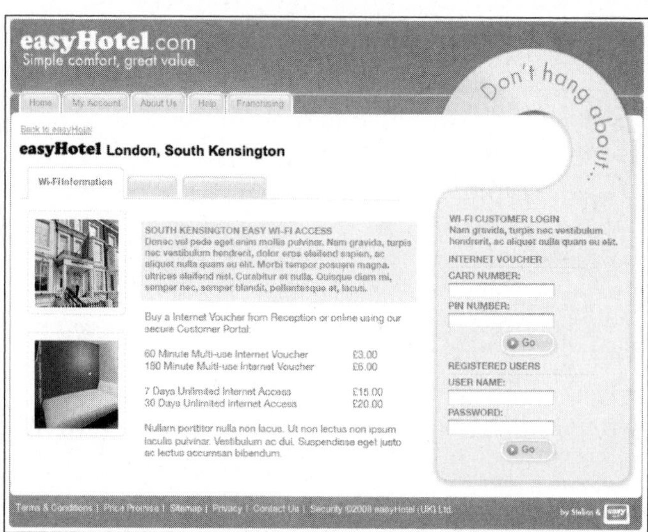

Figure 1-6: A typical hotel wireless login screen. Enter your user ID (card number) and password (PIN number) and you're riding on the Internet.

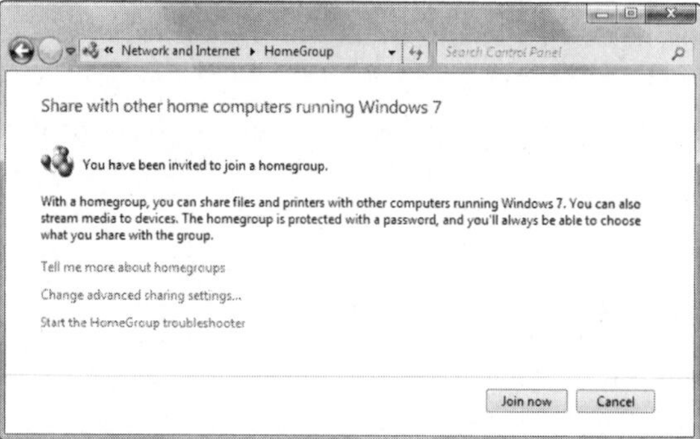

Figure 1-7: The invitation you receive the first time you connect to a network, if Windows finds a HomeGroup.

5. **If you want to join a HomeGroup (*Hint:* You probably do), click the button marked Join Now.**

   Windows wants to know which libraries to share with the HomeGroup and whether you want to share any printers attached to your PC (see Figure 1-8).

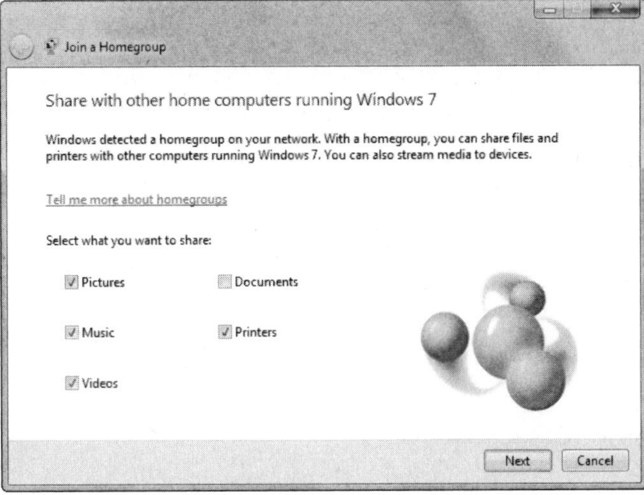

Figure 1-8: Carefully consider whether you want to share all Documents libraries on this computer.

6. **If you want to share all Documents libraries on the computer, select the Documents check box. Click Next.**

   In Figure 1-8, I decide that I don't want to share Documents libraries on this computer, so I leave the box deselected. You can always go back and change the sharing status of any folder. See the "Caring for Your HomeGroup" section, at the end of this chapter.

   Windows asks for the HomeGroup password, as shown in Figure 1-9.

Join a Homegroup

Type the homegroup password

A password helps prevent unauthorized access to homegroup files and printers. You can get the password from the person who set up your homegroup.

Where can I find the homegroup password?

Type the password:

Gg6pP5ji52

Next Cancel

Figure 1-9: To join the HomeGroup, you must have the password.

7. **If you don't have the HomeGroup password — the *passe-partout* of the networking world — go to any of the computers connected to the HomeGroup. Choose Start➪Control Panel. Under Network and Internet, click the link that says Choose HomeGroup and Sharing Options. Then click the link View and Print Your HomeGroup Password. Jot down (or print) the password.**

   Back in Figure 1-9, type the password and click Next.

   Windows advises that you have joined the HomeGroup.

8. **Click Finish.**

   All your Explorer windows start showing the HomeGroup item on the left (refer to Figure 1-3).

   Windows immediately offers you an opportunity to change your settings, as shown in Figure 1-10.

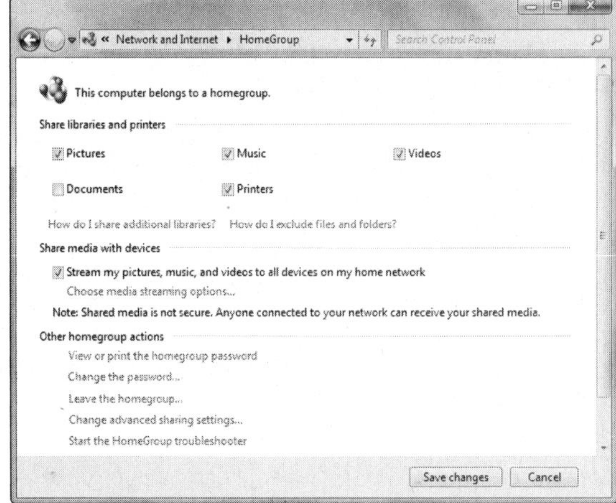

Figure 1-10: You can change your mind immediately, if you like.

9. **Select the Stream My Pictures, Music, and Videos to All Devices On My Home Network check box. Click Save Changes.**

   This step makes all media on this PC accessible to lesser computers on your network, including the Xbox 360 and other media boxes. It isn't exactly a HomeGroup setting, but what the heck.

   Windows leaves you in the Network and Sharing Center (see Figure 1-11), where you can bask in the glow of your newly established HomeGroup connection.

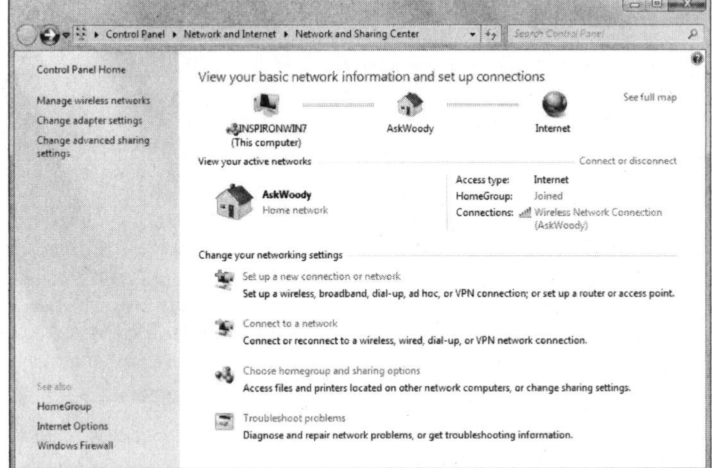

Figure 1-11: Your Network and Sharing Center shows that you're connected to a HomeGroup.

Hooking Up to a Wired Network

So you have a new Windows 7 computer and your network is up and running (see Book VII, Chapter 2). You're ready to plug the LAN cable into your router, and you wonder how to set things up right the first time.

Yep, this is where we go through the steps. Here's how to get connected the right way, the first time:

1. **Turn off your computer. Plug the LAN cable (also known as a Cat 5 or Cat 6 or RJ-45 or network cable) into the back of your PC and into the network's router. Turn on your computer.**

   In a cyberrendition of the "wazzup" Super Bowl commercial from a few years back, Windows figures out that it's connected to a network and shows you the rather unenlightening box shown in Figure 1-12.

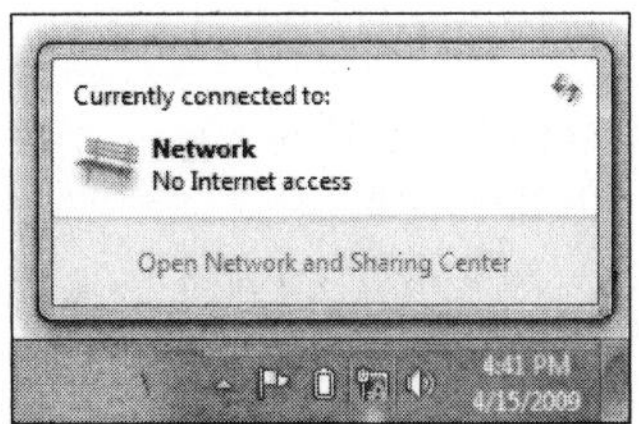

Figure 1-12: Windows discovers its wired network connection.

   If you wait a minute (or two or three), Windows shows you the Select Network Location window (refer to Figure 1-1).

2. **Consult the first section in this chapter, "Choosing Between Home, Work, and Public Networks" and choose the type of network you want to use.**

   If you choose Public or Work, Windows takes a minute or two to put everything in order and then hooks you up to the network.

   If you choose Home, on the other hand, Windows takes a look at the other computers on the network and discerns whether a HomeGroup is already on the network. If so, you see a series of dialog boxes like the ones that open in Steps 6 through 8 of the preceding section. On the other hand, if none of the computers on the network has a HomeGroup running (either they aren't running Windows 7 or they're set up as work computers or the person who set up the network didn't realize what a neat thing she would be missing if she passed on a HomeGroup), you see the invitation shown in Figure 1-13.

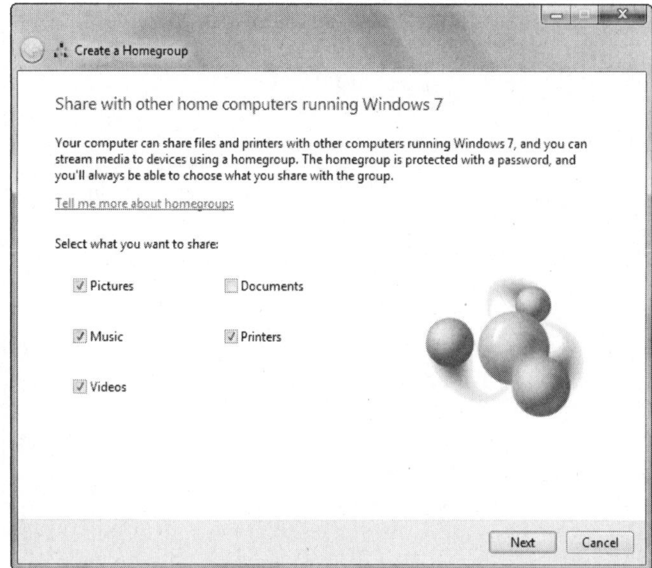

Figure 1-13: An invitation to start a HomeGroup.

3. **If you want to share all Documents libraries on the computer, check the box marked Documents. Click Next.**

   As you can see in Figure 1-13, I decided that I didn't want to share all Documents libraries on this computer.

   Windows bumps and grinds for a minute or two and then shows you the magic password for the new HomeGroup (see Figure 1-14). Although you can take the advice in the dialog box and write down the password, in fact it's quite easy to retrieve the password anytime you need it (see Step 7 in the preceding section).

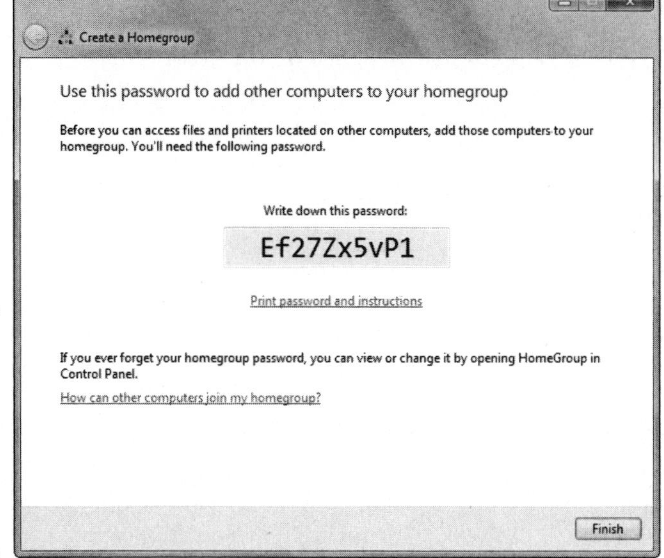

Figure 1-14: You can write down the HomeGroup password, if you like.

4. **Click Finish.**

   Et voilà — you have a new HomeGroup on this network. If you start Windows Explorer (choose, oh, Start⇨Computer), you can see the HomeGroup on the left side, as in Figure 1-15.

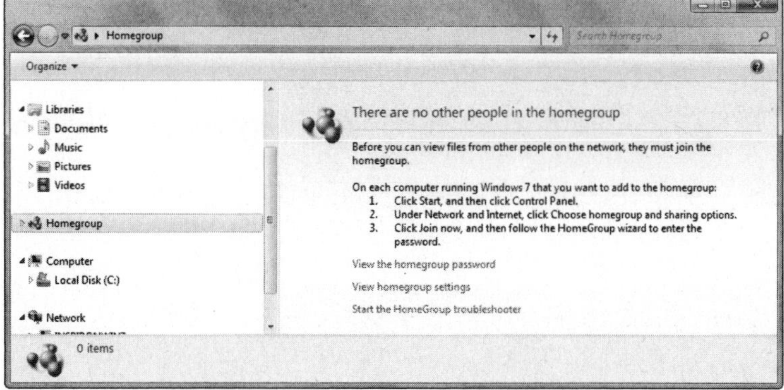

Figure 1-15: A brand-spanking-new HomeGroup, ready for Windows 7 PCs.

As far as I can tell, there's no way to set up more than one HomeGroup on a single network. Even if you could, it'd get mighty complicated, mighty fast.

HomeGroups work well with Windows Home Server. I introduce Windows Home Server in Book II, Chapter 3. *Windows Home Server For Dummies* (Wiley), which I also wrote, explains what you need to know to get WHS up and running.

Caring for Your HomeGroup

So you have a HomeGroup, with one or more PCs connected to it. This section explains how to change your HomeGroup so it suits you to a *T.*

Maybe you're just now admiring the abilities of HomeGroups, and you want to set one up. You're in the right place.

Changing your network type

HomeGroups work with only Windows 7 computers, attached to a network that you have identified as a home network. There's nothing particularly magical about it, and you can change from a work network to a home network — or from a public network to a home network — with just a few mouse clicks.

For that matter, if you want to put your shields up, you can change from a home network to a public network, by using the same procedure.

Here's how to change your network type:

1. **Choose Start⇨Control Panel and, under the Network and Internet heading, click the View Network Status and Tasks link.**

   Windows shows you the Network and Sharing Center, shown in Figure 1-16.

2. **In the box marked View Your Active Networks, click the link that mentions the network type you now have.**

   In Figure 1-16, I want to change from a public network to a home network, so I click the Public Network link. You may have a work network set up, if so, click the Work Network link.

   Windows shows you the Set Network Location dialog box, which you can see at the beginning of this chapter, in Figure 1-1.

3. **Consult the first section in this chapter to choose between home, work, and public networks, and choose the type of network you want to use.**

   But you're here because you want to change to a home network, right?

If you switch to a home network type, Windows invites you to either start a new HomeGroup (start at Step 3 in the "Hooking Up to a Wired Network" section) or, if a HomeGroup exists, join it (start at Step 6 in the "Hooking Up to a Wireless Network" section).

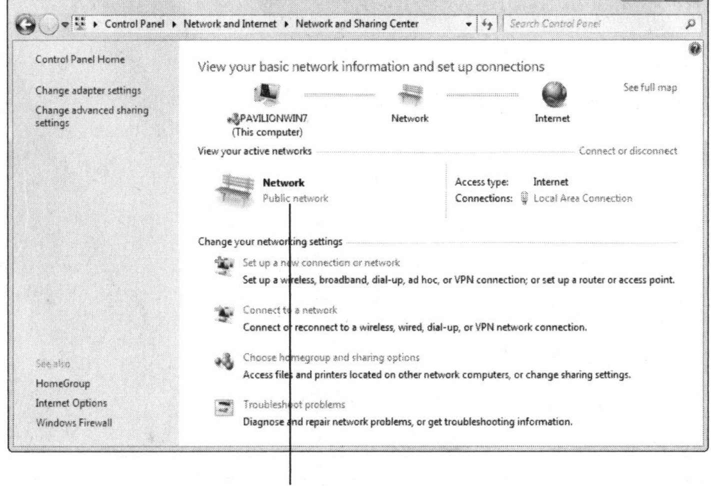

Figure 1-16: The Network and Sharing Center.

Click here to change the network type.

Changing the HomeGroup password

Want to know why Windows automatically generates that gargantuan password every time you start a new HomeGroup? Because early testers needed it. When Microsoft watched people trying to use HomeGroups for the first time, they discovered that many people would stop, worry, and fret about typing a password. In many cases, that's because the person setting up the HomeGroup uses only a small set of passwords, and they didn't want to hand the passwords out to everyone in the house or the company. So the testers spent quite a bit of time trying to figure out whether they should create a completely new password and, if so, which one to use. Brain overload.

To make your life easier, Windows assigns a somewhat arbitrary password when you create a HomeGroup. You're admonished to write it down, but in fact you can change it at any time, as long as all computers in the HomeGroup are turned on and you can log on to all of them.

To change the HomeGroup password, proceed thusly:

1. **Choose Start⇨Control Panel. In the Network and Internet section, click the Choose HomeGroup and Sharing Options link.**

   If you don't see Choose HomeGroup and Sharing Options, chances are quite good that your computer isn't connected to a HomeGroup.

   Windows shows you the Change HomeGroup Settings dialog box, shown in Figure 1-17.

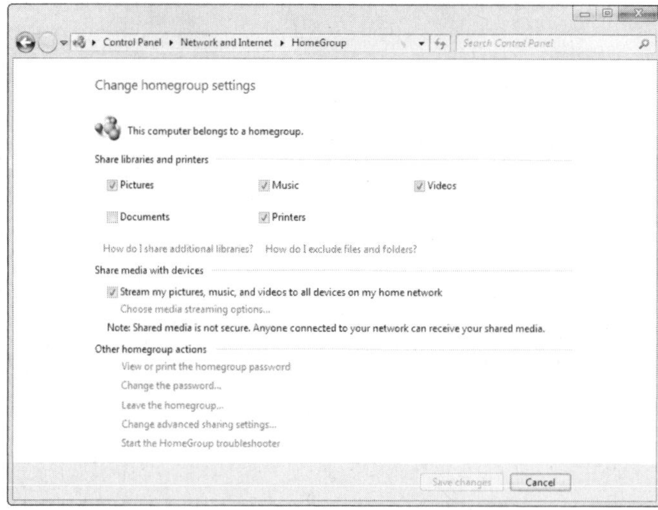

Figure 1-17: You can change most HomeGroup settings in this dialog box.

2. **Click the Change the Password link.**

   Windows presents you with the Change Your HomeGroup Password admonition, er, dialog box, shown in Figure 1-18.

3. **Make sure that all computers in your HomeGroup are awake (not hibernating or asleep), and make sure that you can log on to all of them. When you're ready, click Change the Password.**

   Windows offers a new password for you to use, or you can type one of your own.

4. **Click Next.**

   Your HomeGroup password is dutifully changed.

5. **One by one, go to each of the other computers in your HomeGroup and click Start⇨Computer. Then, on the left, click HomeGroup.**

   You see the warning shown in Figure 1-19. Some scurvy brigand has changed the password on your HomeGroup! Avast and alack, and buckle my swash. . . .

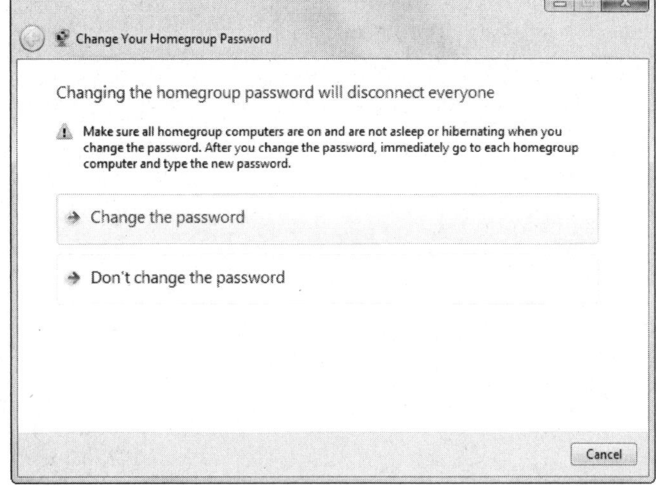

Figure 1-18: Change the password for the entire HomeGroup.

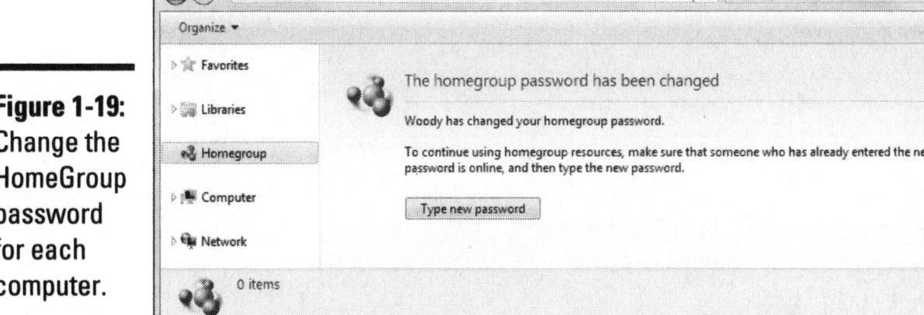

Figure 1-19: Change the HomeGroup password for each computer.

6. **Click the Type New Password button and do precisely that.**

   You reconnect to the HomeGroup.

If you have problems reconnecting to the HomeGroup, use the link shown earlier, in Figure 1-17, to leave the HomeGroup, and then click the Join Now button in the Share with Other Home Computers Running Windows 7 dialog box (Figure 1-7, earlier in this chapter), which appears automatically.

Adding or blocking folders in the HomeGroup

If you want to make a folder available to everyone in your HomeGroup, the simplest approach is to add it to one of your shared libraries. See Book II, Chapter 1 for details.

If you share your Documents library, for example, adding a folder to your personal Documents folder makes the folder available so that anybody attached to the HomeGroup can open and read the items in the folder. Adding the folder to your `Public Documents` folder allows everyone in the HomeGroup to read, modify, or delete the items in the folder.

Sometimes, though, you just want to make a folder available to the HomeGroup, and you don't want to go through the steps to add it to a shared library. For example, I like to share my `Downloads` folder so that other people in my HomeGroup can easily copy or run the files I download.

Here's how to add the `Downloads` folder to your HomeGroup, without adding the `Downloads` folder to any of your shared libraries:

1. **Navigate to the folder you want to put in the HomeGroup.**

   In Figure 1-20, I chose Start➪Computer and on the left, under Favorites, chose Downloads.

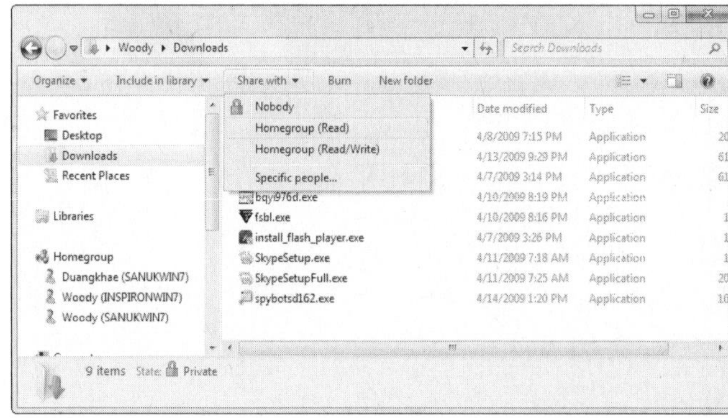

Figure 1-20: Adding a folder to your HomeGroup is easy, if you know the trick.

2. **On the menu bar, click the Share With button. Choose HomeGroup (Read) if you want to give everyone in your HomeGroup read access to the files. Choose HomeGroup (Read/Write) if you trust them not to delete or otherwise clobber the files.**

   It can take a few minutes, but eventually the shared folder becomes available all across the HomeGroup, as you can see in Figure 1-21.

Want to block a single folder that's in one of your shared libraries? Take a look at the line in Figure 1-20 that says Nobody. If you "Share With Nobody," you take away all access privileges for that particular folder — nobody but you can get into the folder — even if it's sitting inside a shared library.

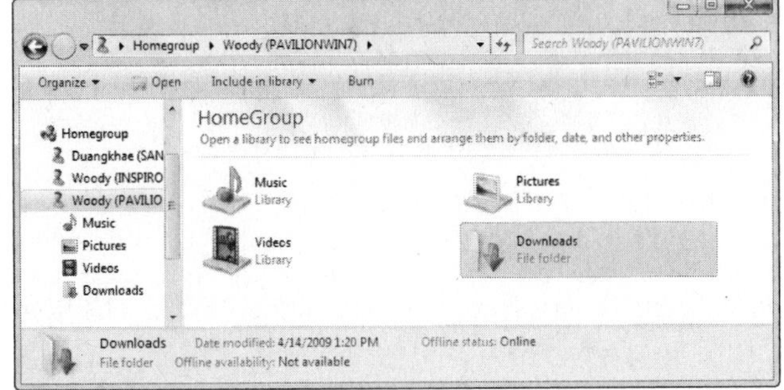

Figure 1-21: The `Downloads` folder becomes available on all computers that belong to the HomeGroup.

Chapter 2: Setting Up Your Own Network

In This Chapter

- **Finding out why you *do* want a network, at the office and at home**
- **Determining whether your office needs a Big Corporate Network (domain)**
- **Understanding how it all hangs together**
- **Networking for Neanderthals**

When businesspeople talk to each other, it's *networking*. When computers talk to each other, it's *pandemonium*.

This chapter tries to distill 30 years of advances in computer pandemonium, er, networking, into a succinct, digestible, understandable synopsis. I think you'll be pleasantly surprised to discover that even the most obnoxiously inscrutable networking jargon — some of which has made its way into Windows 7 — has its roots in simple concepts that everyone can understand.

Here's the easiest way to set up a network:

1. **Ask your neighbors which Internet service provider has the best deal on a fast Internet connection.**
2. **Call the Internet service provider and say, "I want a wireless router."**
3. **Pull out your credit card.**
4. **The end.**

As long as everything works right — and you don't want your network to do anything beyond the basics — that approach gets you a good, solid network and you don't have to understand anything other than the hook-up advice in Book VII, Chapter 1.

On the other hand, if something goes wrong, if a Windows 7 troubleshooter peters out on you, or if you want your network to advance beyond the cookie-cutter stage, you need to understand how networks network. I cover that topic in this chapter. In Chapter 3, I show you how to put together your own network, if you feel so inclined, and how to shoot beyond built-in troubleshooters.

Understanding Networks

Not long ago, networks were considered esoteric and intimidating, the province of guys in white lab coats, whose sole purpose in life was to allow you to print on the company's fancy laser printer or share that superfast company Internet connection but keep you from seeing your boss's personnel file or the company's budget. Those same guys (and they were always guys, it seems) often took it upon themselves to tell you what you could and couldn't do with your PC — which software you could use, how you could use it, where you could put your data, and so much more. They hid behind a cloak of mumbo-jumbo, initiates in the priesthood of "systems administration."

That situation has changed a lot. In Windows 7, a network is something that your 13-year-old can throw together in ten minutes. Mine did. (Your results may vary.)

The terminology doesn't help. Ask a network geek — or computer store salesperson — about the difference between a LAN and a WAN and you'll provoke a tirade of inscrutable acronyms so thick that you need a periscope to see out.

In the following sections, I cut through the bafflegab.

What a network can do for you

Do you need a network? The short answer: Yes. If you have two or more computers, one running Windows 7 and the other running Windows 98, XP, or Vista — or even a Mac or a Linux box — a network is well worth the hassle. You don't need a fancy one. But you do need one. Consider:

- **If you have a network and it's working properly, just about any piece of hardware attached to one computer can be used by the other.** That Blu-ray recorder on your desktop, for example, can be used by your laptop, the same way as if it were connected directly. A printer or (in some cases) a scanner attached to one computer can be shared by all computers.
- **You can use Windows 7 features on data from other machines, regardless of whether they're running Windows 7.** For example, you can stick a Windows XP computer's folders inside a Windows 7 library (and thus, if you like, a Windows 7 HomeGroup). You can use Windows 7 applications, such as Windows DVD Maker, on data from pre–Windows 7 computers.
- **You have an easy way to make backups.** The easiest, fastest, most reliable way to back up data is to copy it from the hard drive in one machine to the hard drive in another machine on the network.

✦ **You can share documents, pictures, music — just about anything — between the networked computers, with practically no effort.** Although few applications let you share individual files simultaneously — Word doesn't let two people on two different machines edit the same document at the same time, for example — sharing data on networked machines is still much simpler.

How a network networks

All you need to know about networks you learned in kindergarten. Here's the lowdown:

✦ **Good computers talk to each other over a network.** If your computer is on a network, it can play with other computers on the same network. If your computer isn't on a network, it can only sit in the corner and play by itself.

✦ **You can see all the computers on your network by looking at Mister Rogers' — uh, by choosing Start⇨Computer, and clicking the Network icon on the left, as shown in Figure 2-1.**

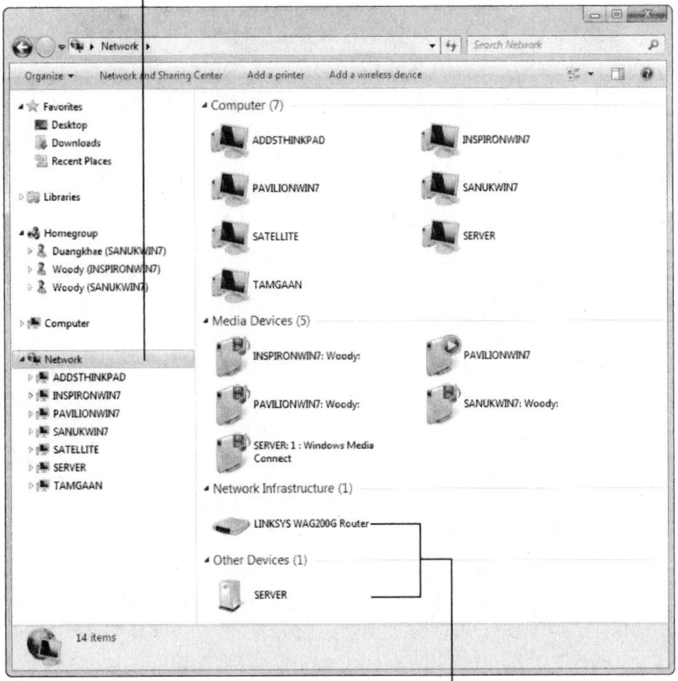

Click here to see all the network devices.

Figure 2-1: Windows 7 gladly lists all computers on your network.

The network router and Windows Home Server get separate icons.

- **Every computer in a network has its own name and number.** The number is an *IP address,* and all the names and numbers are different. You can keep track of the computers by their names. But the computers communicate by using their numbers — their *IP addresses.*
- **You can share stuff on your computer.** You have two different ways to share. The way you share depends on how the network — uh, kindergarten class — is organized:
  - If you have a mean teacher (a *network administrator*), she decides which information can be shared. When other kids want to borrow your stuff, they usually have to ask the teacher. I don't talk about this kind of network much because the teacher makes most of the decisions. Details are in the next section of this chapter.
  - On the other hand, if the kids are in charge of sharing, each kid can share his stuff. By far the easiest way to share stuff is by using a HomeGroup (see Book VII, Chapter 1).
- **Your network can share with other networks, just like kids in your class can share with kids in other classes.** The Internet is the biggest class of all. Yippie!
- **Unfortunately, some creeps are in other classes, and they may want to take things from you or share something that can hurt you.** You have to protect yourself.
- **When you run into trouble, the advice you hear over and over again (especially in the Windows 7 troubleshooters) is "talk to your teacher," uh, "contact your system administrator."** That advice is every bit as useless now as it was when you were 5.

When networks work right — which they do about 90 percent of the time in Windows 7 — they truly are simple.

Organizing Networks

To understand an abstract computer concept, nothing works better than a solid analogy. I use lots of them in this book: A document is like a sheet of paper; a CPU is like a car engine; a modem is like a high-tech hearing aid with a pronounced stutter set to Max at a Nine Inch Nails concert. You know what I mean.

That's the problem with configuring networks. No good analogies exist for all the bits and pieces. Yes, you can say that a server is like a gatekeeper or that a hub is like a collection of tap-dancing monkeys at a hyperactive organ-grinder's convention, but all the analogies fall flat in short order. Why? Because networks are different from what you experience from day to day. So, without the benefit of a good analogy, I shall forge ahead anyway.

Understanding servers and serfs

Two fundamentally different kinds of networks exist. They both use the same basic kind of hardware — cables, boxes, interface cards, and other elements. They both talk the same basic kind of language — Ethernet and something called TCP/IP, usually, but a few renegades speak in tongues. They differ primarily on a single crucial philosophical point.

In one kind of network, a leader, a top-dog PC, controls things. The leader is (you guessed it) a *server.* I still get shivers down my spine at the Orwellian logic of it all. In this kind of network, the lowly serf PCs are clients. Thus, this type of network gets the moniker *client/server.* Microsoft calls this network a *domain.* If you've ever wondered how in the realm of the English language a client could be all that much different from a server, now you know: In the topsy-turvy world of PC networking terminology, a server is really a master.

Client/server networks abound in large companies, where central control is crucial. Network administrators set up security rules, grant access wherever it's needed, allow new users to operate client PCs, and generally ride herd on the entire network. Usually, the servers hold important corporate files and backup copies of key files on the client computers. Usually, the major networked printers hang off the servers. Usually, all Internet access goes through the servers. Usually.

In the other kind of network, all the pigs, er, PCs are created equal. No single PC dominates — perhaps I should say *serves* — all the others. Rather, the PCs maintain an equal footing. This kind of network is called, rather appropriately, *peer-to-peer,* which sounds veddy British to me. Eh, wot? Microsoft calls them *workgroups,* which isn't nearly as classy.

The term *workgroup* has kind of fallen out of favor: You have to look hard in Windows 7 to find it. Windows 7 introduces the far more useful concept of *HomeGroups,* which are cliques of specific Windows 7 computers running inside a workgroup.

Peer-to-peer networking doesn't get hung up in the kind of security and central administration that client/server networks take for granted. For example, a typical user on a peer-to-peer network can share a disk drive so that anybody on the network can see it. On a client/server network, you have to call in the network administrator.

At the risk of oversimplifying, peer-to-peer networking works best in homes and small offices where security isn't a major concern. Client/server networking works best in larger companies with significant security needs — and a budget to match. Network administrators don't come cheap. So much for the overview. I now take a look at the details.

Introducing client/server networks

Client/server networks have one PC, a *server,* that's figuratively "on top" of all the others. Figure 2-2 shows a logical diagram of a client/server network. Do *not* take the diagram too seriously: It only shows the way client PCs are subservient to the server. It doesn't show you how to hook up a network.

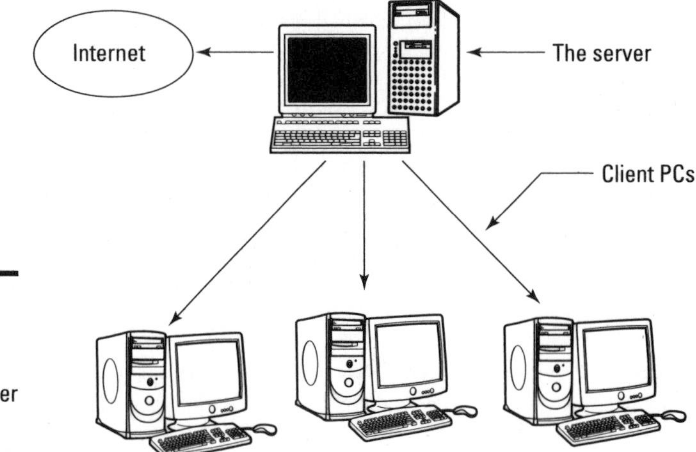

Figure 2-2: Logical view of a client/server network.

Client PCs have some, but not a whole lot, of autonomy in a client/server network. And, a bit of leeway exists in how much security a specific network or server enforces — some less-secure networks may allow guest accounts, for example, that don't require passwords. But by and large, client/server networks are set up to be secure. They exist to allow computers (and users and peripherals) to talk to each other. But strict limits are rigorously enforced on what individual users can do, where they can go, and what they can see.

Windows Home Server

Ready to get confused? Windows Home Server (WHS), the product from Microsoft, isn't a server in the client/server sense of the term. WHS was designed from the ground up to work in a peer-to-peer network. Although many people have had some success getting WHS to work in a Small Business Server network, the vast majority of WHS boxes run on regular, everyday home networks — peer-to-peer networks. I introduce some of the joys of Windows Home Server in Book II, Chapter 3. If you're interested in adding WHS to your network, check out *Windows Home Server For Dummies* (Wiley), which I also wrote.

Microsoft introduced a new umbrella security system in Windows 2000 Server: *Active Directory* is designed to put control of all client/server security activities in one place. Active Directory is quite a complex program — a world unto its own. If you have trouble talking to your network administrator in simple English, you may take some solace in the fact that he has to talk to Active Directory and the translation can be challenging. The African "click" languages pale in comparison.

In this book, I don't talk much about client/server networks (er, domains), simply because you don't have much control over them. If you use a client/server network, chances are good that somebody else in your company made the decision to go with client/server. She probably installed your copy of Windows 7 — most likely, Windows 7 Enterprise — or bought a new machine rigged to her specifications and configured it to work with your company's network. She also gets to fix things when your network connection goes bump in the night. Poetic justice, sez I.

I have to talk about client/server from time to time, though, for three big reasons:

- **You may have an existing client/server network that you want to convert to a peer-to-peer network.** Many Dummies (I raise my hand here) installed Windows Server 2003 or Windows Small Business Server networks in their homes or offices, and they rapidly grew tired of the constant hassles. They need to understand enough about client/server to get rid of it.

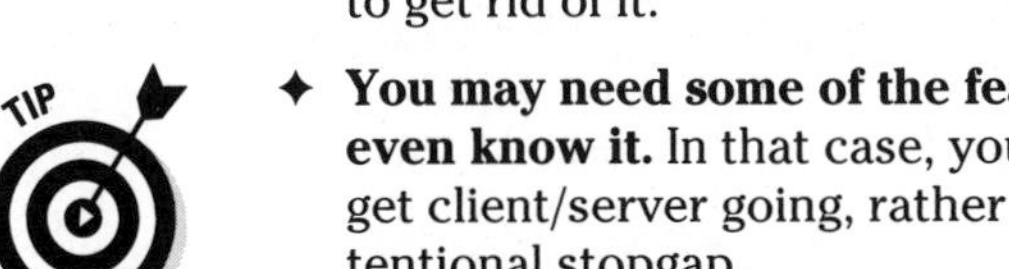

- **You may need some of the features that client/server offers and not even know it.** In that case, you're better off to bite the bullet now and get client/server going, rather than struggle with peer-to-peer as an unintentional stopgap.

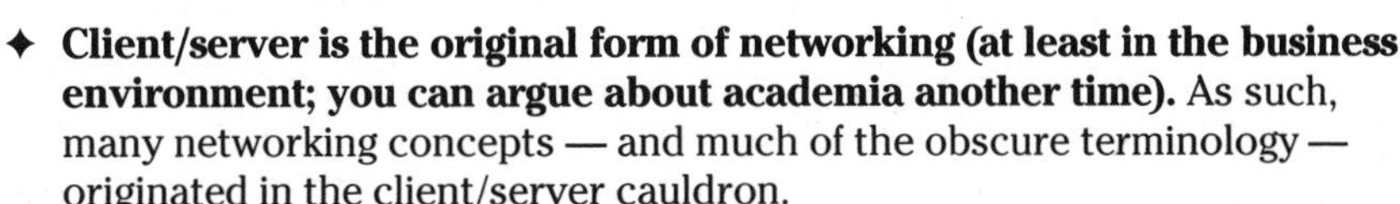

- **Client/server is the original form of networking (at least in the business environment; you can argue about academia another time).** As such, many networking concepts — and much of the obscure terminology — originated in the client/server cauldron.

Administrator accounts on client computers can make major changes to the client PC in question, but the real action is on the server. If you truly want to change things around, you need an administrator account on the server. That's the seat of power in the client/server milieu.

Introducing peer-to-peer networks

On the other side of the networking fence sits the undisciplined, ragtag, scruffy lot involved in peer-to-peer computing. In a peer-to-peer environment, all computers are created equal and security takes a backseat to flexibility. I like peer-to-peer networks (see Figure 2-3). Can you tell?

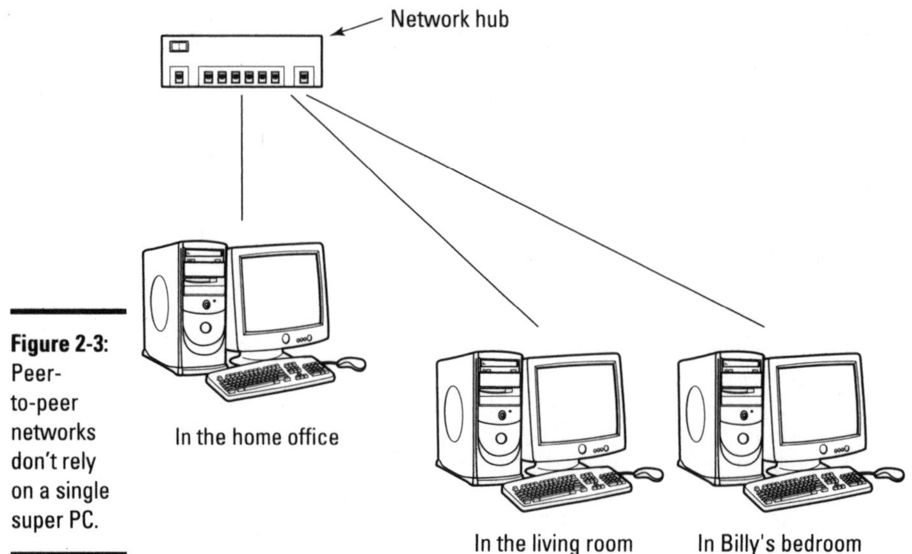

Figure 2-3: Peer-to-peer networks don't rely on a single super PC.

At different times, in different places, Microsoft refers to a peer-to-peer network by the following names:

- Workgroup or workgroup network
- Small-office network or small-business network
- Home network

The Windows 7 Help and Support Center also, on occasion, refers to peer-to-peer networks as, uh, peer-to-peer networks. They all mean the same thing.

Although the terminology is widely inconsistent, historically the term *HomeGroup* is used exclusively to refer to a specific kind of subnetwork on a peer-to-peer network. When you see the word *HomeGroup,* you know that Microsoft is talking about a HomeGroup. Refreshing, eh?

Traditionally, client/server networks (see the preceding section) dangled all shared peripherals off the server. Twenty years ago, your big office laser printer was probably connected directly to the server. The massive bank of 2GB hard drives no doubt lived on the server, too. Even now you hear references to print servers and file servers in hushed tones, as though only the server itself were capable of handling such massive processing demands.

Nowadays, you can buy a laser printer with funds from the petty cash drawer — although you had better have a line in the budget for toner and paper — and 1TB hard drives fit on the head of a pin (well, almost).

Peer-to-peer networks dispense with the formality of centralized control. Every authorized administrator on a particular PC (find out more about administrators in Book II, Chapter 2) can designate any drive, folder, or piece of hardware on that PC as shared, and thus make it accessible to anyone else on the network.

In a peer-to-peer network (a workgroup), any administrator on a given PC can share anything on that PC. If you're the least bit concerned about security, that fact should give you pause, high blood pressure, and intense anxiety attacks (not to mention apoplexy). Say you set up a work or home network using the standard Windows 7 settings. (See the discussion of work, home, and public networks in Book VII, Chapter 1.) The network that's installed is a peer-to-peer network, quite frequently with no passwords. That means anyone can walk up to a Welcome sign-on screen, click one of the usernames, and immediately designate every drive as shared, *even if you don't have a HomeGroup.* The entire process would take less than 30 seconds for an experienced Windows user. From that point on, anybody who can get to any computer on the network would have full control over all files on the shared drive — anybody can read, change, and even delete them permanently, without the benefit of the Recycle Bin.

The primary distinguishing factor among PCs in a peer-to-peer network lies in the shared hardware hanging off an individual PC. Refer to Figure 2-5 for example, and you see that only one PC has a scanner attached to it. Although you may be tempted to call this machine "the PC with the scanner hanging off it," in general parlance, you hear the PC referred to as the scanner's *host.*

Peer-to-peer networks are far more adaptable (computer nerds would say "more robust") than their client/server cousins because they don't rely on a single PC to keep the network running. In a peer-to-peer network, if the laser printer's host PC breaks down, you only need to schlep the printer over to a different PC and install it. You can immediately begin using the printer from any PC in the network. (If the autodetect feature kicks in properly, it's particularly simple: You only need to change the printer in the File➪Print dialog box.) In a client/server network, if the server PC breaks down, you can probably kiss your weekend good-bye.

To the outside world, your peer-to-peer network appears as though you have just one PC connected to the Internet — and it sits behind a big, scary firewall to fend off would-be attackers. To little Johnny, who's using the PC in his bedroom to download massive full-color pictures of anatomically correct Pokémon figures, his Internet connection works just as it always did: slow and cantankerous, with frequent dropped connections and unexplained outages. But at least everybody in the family gets bumped off the Internet at the same time.

Are you ready to be confused again? In a *peer-to-peer* network, different computers at different times can act a little like servers, and much too frequently they're called *servers*. Any computer that offers resources on a network (files, libraries, printers, USB back scratchers) can be considered a server. Even more confoundingly, you may encounter situations where software refers to itself as a server — Windows Remote Assistance, certain online gaming software, specific file sharing software — all act as servers at times. So don't be confused when you read about Remote Desktop Server or a multiplayer game server that's running on a peer-to-peer network. In those cases, the term *server* refers only to the actions of the software, not to the configuration of the network itself.

Comparing the p-pros and c-cons

If you need to decide between installing a client/server network (Microsoft calls it a *domain*) and a peer-to-peer network (which is installed automatically), you should read the two preceding sections for an overview of how each one works, and then weigh each of these factors:

- **The *c* in client/server stands for complicated, cumbersome, and costly.** You, or someone you hire, will spend a lot of time setting up a client/server network. If you have a small network with few employees and one or two applications, you know precisely which machines will be performing which tasks, and you know who needs access to which information and where it's stored, a real pro with extensive Active Directory experience can probably set up your client/server network using Windows Small Business Server in half a day. Beyond that, the sky's the limit — and plan on getting your network consultant's home telephone number because you're going to need it every time you hire a new employee, install a new computer, or maybe even begin using a new application.
- **Client/server networks can handle enormous volumes of data.** High-end servers can juggle hundreds (or even thousands or tens of thousands) of client PCs, with data transmission speeds that would bring tears to a lowly peer-to-peer network's eyes. The server can take on additional functions, such as handling e-mail for the entire network (most likely using Exchange Server, another cantankerous Microsoft product that's chock-full of features).
- **The *p* in peer-to-peer stands for powerful, painless, and potentially embarrassing.** If you persuade your Internet service provider to install a wireless network, you can have your network up and running in hours — and most of that time will be spent sweating over setting up a HomeGroup (see Book VII, Chapter 1). When it's up, the network is reliable and easy to use — and as exposed as a lobster in a glass tank. Unless you go to the trouble of setting up and rigorously using passwords on each PC's accounts (see Book II, Chapter 2), anybody who can

sit down at a PC and log on to an administrator account can make all the PC's contents available to anyone on the network, at any time. Except in extreme situations, not even Windows Firewall can help.

If you try to install and maintain a client/server network yourself — even with helper tools such as Microsoft Small Business Server — be aware that it's not nearly as simple as the marketing brochures would have you believe. Many Dummies, myself included, feel that installing and maintaining your own client/server network rates as a low-benefit, high-commitment time sink of the first degree.

Someday, secure networks will be easy to set up and use. That day hasn't arrived yet. Although networking in Windows 7 — including, notably, HomeGroups and libraries — has made simple networking a reality, truly secure networks — and really big networks — are still the province of guys in white lab coats.

Cutting through the Terminology

Peer-to-peer networks work well over wireless connections. If the people who sell you an Internet connection have a wireless box, get it. The installation folks plug the wireless router into the phone line or cable TV outlet, and every machine that has a wireless card gets on the Internet with a minimum of fuss.

Confused by the terminology? Don't be. Here's a quick reference:

- A *wireless router* (see Figure 2-4) combines the functions of a wireless access point, a DSL or cable "modem," and (usually) a hub. If you buy or rent a wireless router from your Internet company, you don't have to futz with any of the details — or any of the other terms in this list.
- A *wireless access point* is a fancy communication box with a pair of rabbit ears on top. PCs with wireless cards talk to the wireless access point.
- A *DSL modem* is a box that connects to your phone line and (usually) delivers always-on, fast Internet, most commonly using the asymmetric digital subscriber line (ADSL) technology.
- A *cable modem* is a box that does the same thing, but it connects to your cable TV cable.
- A *hub* is a box with a bunch of slots in the back that accept local-area network (LAN) cables. The hub connects all the PCs and other boxes that are plugged into it.
- A *LAN cable* looks like an extra-wide phone cable. It's used to connect PCs (usually ones without wireless cards) and other boxes.

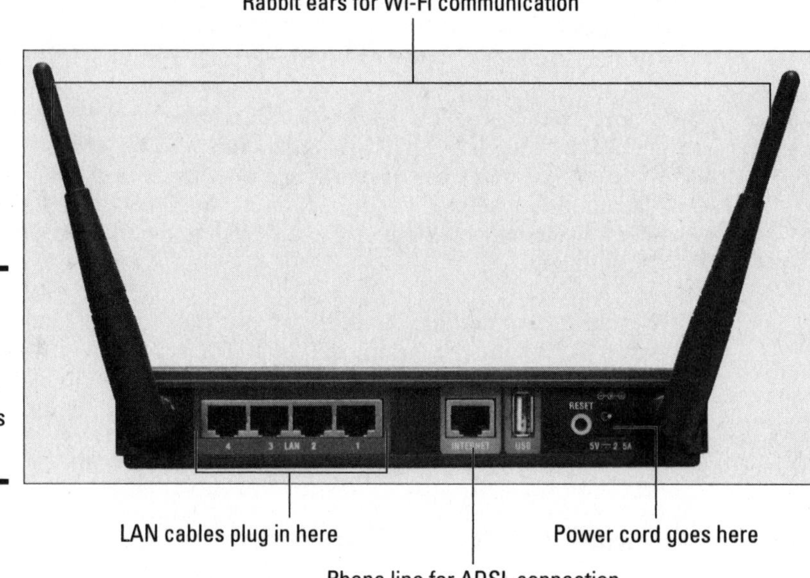

Figure 2-4: The back side of a D-Link DIR-628 wireless router.

Photo courtesy D-Link.

Wired and wireless connections aren't mutually exclusive. Almost every wireless network has the capability of attaching wired computers. In fact, most wireless networks you bump into every day have one or more computers running on wires. They all meet together at the router.

Further confusing matters, your ADSL company or cable company (or satellite company or HSDPC company or 20-mule team Borax ISP) probably bundles a wireless router, a WAP, a regular router, a hub, *and* a modem all in one box. The distinctions are blurring rapidly.

Making Computers Talk

Making computers talk to each other can be as simple as buying a box and some cables and plugging them all together, like you do with telephones — or as painful, expensive, and hair-challenging (as in pulling it out by the roots) as any computer pursuit you've ever encountered.

If you're setting up a new network, chances are good that you're looking at a wireless peer-to-peer (*workgroup*) network. That's an excellent choice. For the advanced course on wireless networks — surely the simplest kind of network to install — see Book VII, Chapter 4.

If you're going to get down and dirty with a wired network, you need to understand what Ethernet is all about. Read on.

Understanding Ethernet

The easiest, fastest, cheapest, most reliable, and most secure way to hook up a peer-to-peer network is also the oldest, least flexible, and most boring. If you want sexy, look somewhere else. If you want an old workhorse, hey, do I have a horse for you: It's Ethernet (see Figure 2-5), and it works like a champ.

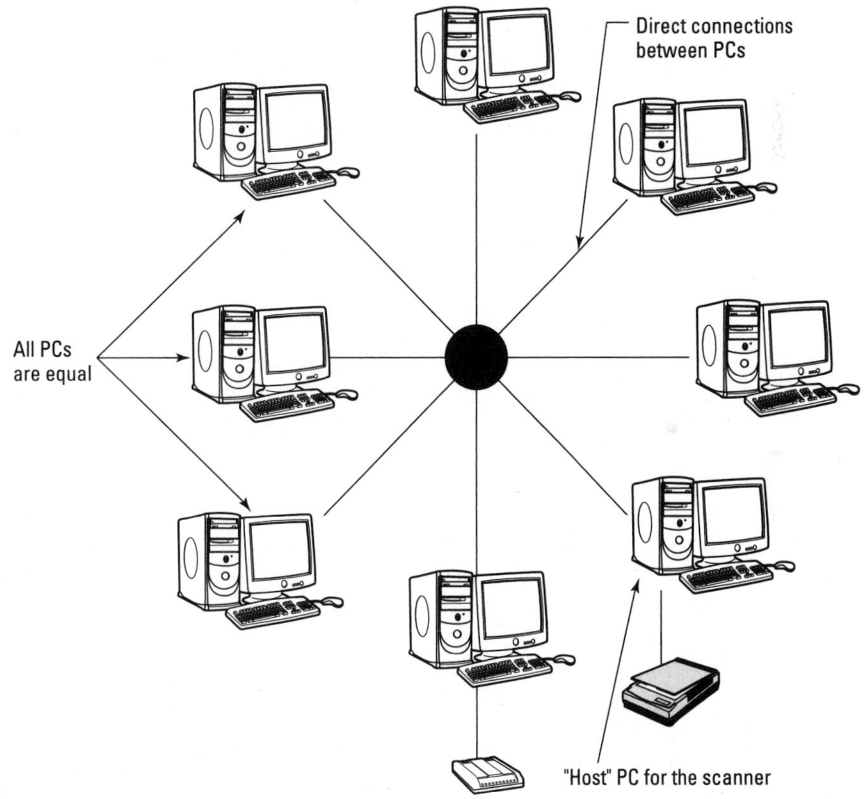

Figure 2-5: A typical Ethernet peer-to-peer network.

Ethernet isn't that complicated. In the early 1970s, Bob Metcalfe came up with an interesting new way to connect Xerox Alto computers. He called the technique *EtherNet.* The name stuck, give or take a capital *N.* So did the technology. By modern standards, Ethernet isn't sophisticated. Here's how it works:

1. All PCs on a network watch messages going over a wire.
2. When PC A wants to talk to PC B, A shoots a message out on the wire, saying something like, "Hey B, this is A," followed by the message.
3. PC B sees the message on the wire and retrieves it. Then it sends a message back to A, saying "Hey A, I got it."
4. PC A watches the wire for PC B's response. If A doesn't get a response in a reasonable amount of time, it just resends the message.

It's hard to believe, but with a few minor tweaks — such as what happens when two PCs try to send messages at the same time so that they're talking over the top of each other — that's all there is to Ethernet.

Here's what's even harder to believe: PCs using plain old Ethernet can send and receive messages at the rate of 10 Gbps, or 10 billion bits per second. Even garden-variety Ethernet systems work at 100 Mbps, or 100 million bits per second. (By comparison, a 2 Mbps ADSL line, under the best possible circumstances, receives data at slightly less than 2 million bits per second.) The action slows if many PCs are trying to talk to each other at the same time — they start talking over the top of each other — but for a typical peer-to-peer network, 100 Mbps (also called 100Base-T) works well.

Ethernet relies on a *hub* — a box (see Figure 2-6) — and cables running from the hub to each PC. The PCs need Ethernet ports so that you have a place to stick the cables. The PCs can be using any flavor of Windows since Windows 98. Plug it all together and run a setup program in Windows 7, and your network is ready to use.

That's the theory, anyway. Surprisingly, at least 90 percent of the time, it works. (I go into all the details in the next chapter.)

Figure 2-6: The Linksys EtherFast 4124, an Ethernet hub with 24 ports.

Photo courtesy Linksys by Cisco.

Adding wireless

What's the biggest problem with Ethernet? The cables. Unless your office or home has been wired with those big eight-wire Ethernet cables, you have to string them across the floor or under the rug, run them up and down staircases, or hang them out the window and pray that they don't blow away. Don't laugh — I've done all that and more.

Cables aren't all bad. If you have a desktop computer that sits next to a router (er, modem, wireless access point, hub — whatever), it's much easier to simply plug one end of a LAN cable into the computer and the other into the router. Wired connections are faster, cheaper, easier, more reliable, and more secure than wireless connections. Stringing another wire adds to the bundles of cables strewn on your desk but, hey, nobody ever looks at the back of your desk anyway, right?

Right?

Wireless networking relies on radio transmitters and receivers in place of Ethernet cables. You need a wireless access point (which goes by a lot of different names, most commonly WAP, as in, uh, Whap!), wireless receivers plugged into each PC (possibly by a card or connected via a USB adapter), or wireless built into the computer (common with laptops).

Wireless networks use the same kind of technology as everyday wireless telephones: The part that moves (the telephone handset) communicates with a base (the phone cradle) that stays put. Wireless connections suffer all the problems that you've no doubt encountered with portable telephones:

- ✦ The signal becomes weaker as you move farther away from the base station and at some point disappears.
- ✦ If the base becomes unplugged, everything goes bananas.
- ✦ Other people can eavesdrop on your conversations, unless you're cautious. Ain't no such thing as a free lunch.

I go into detail about wireless networking in Book VII, Chapter 4.

Chapter 3: Building Your Network

In This Chapter

- **Hooking together your own network**
- **Convincing Windows 7 that your network works**
- **Resolving conflicts — fighting mother hens**
- **Knowing what to do if one computer can't see another**

Sharing a printer. Transferring files. Freeing a phone line. Saving money. Those are useful reasons for setting up a network. Sno-o-o-ore.

I know that you want to get your office or house computers networked so that you can blister your coworkers or friends at *Far Cry 2* or *World of Warcraft*. Maybe you want to spend some quality time with your son one Sunday afternoon, spraying demons in *Doom IV*. Splat! Don't worry. I won't tell anybody.

By far the easiest, simplest way to install a network at your home or office involves talking to friends who live nearby, finding out which Internet service provider has the best deal, and then having the phone company or cable company (or satellite company or whoever) install your whole network, from the get-go. If you can't find the right person at the phone company, hire that ten-year-old next door to help. She'll figure it out.

Most ISPs will install an Internet connection and hook up a hub with four or more networking slots, for a pittance. The same ISP will no doubt install a wireless access point (see Book VII, Chapter 4) for a tiny bit more.

As long as everything works, you're in like Flynn. But the first time you go looking for your son's computer out on the network and you can't find it — whoa, Nelly. And, if the Windows 7 troubleshooter tells you to contact your network administrator, you might seriously consider tossing your PC out the, uh, windows.

In my experience, networks give rise to more troubleshooting problems than all other pieces of Windows put together. That's why I devote three chapters in this book to troubleshooting them.

This chapter steps you through the process of setting up your network, explains what's happening behind the scenes, and sets you up to shoot a whole lotta trouble in getting network problems solved.

Although this chapter deals with wired networks (see Book VII, Chapter 4 for the lowdown on wireless), you should check out this chapter even if you're going wireless. Why? Two reasons. First, the concepts and terms introduced in this chapter apply to wireless, too. Second, almost every wireless network uses at least one wired connection. So you're gonna get wired whether you want to or not. Can't win for losin', eh?

Planning Your Network

Yeah, you have to plan your network. Sorry.

You have a choice of lots and lots of ways to put together networks. The way I show you in this chapter is the way I recommend for first-time networkers who may or may not want to go wireless. It ain't cool. It ain't sexy. It ain't state-of-the-art. But it works.

Using a wired network

You have four good reasons for going with a wired network:

- **It's cheap.** You probably have all the hardware you need already, plus or minus a cable, and the phone or cable company handles the rest.
- **It's fast.** Wired connections work much faster than wireless. You don't see any difference if you're checking your Gmail or surfing a news site. But the minute you start slinging around big files, man, you can tell the difference.
- **It's reliable.** When you're hooked into a network cable, you're on. When you rely on wireless, you may be on or off or somewhere in between. The weather, your physical location, the interference emanating from a copy machine or a coffee machine — even sun spots, for heaven's sake — can clobber the connection.
- **It's secure.** Just about anybody with a nodding interest can listen in on a wireless connection. (It's another reason why you should use only secure Web sites — it's hard to unscramble what's being sent.) And, unless you lock down your wireless network (see Book VII, Chapter 4), even your next-door neighbor can go banging around your network. Tapping into a wired network is considerably more difficult.

If you're willing to take the wireless plunge, you should read through this chapter to understand the basic technology and terminology and how things hang together. Then, in the next chapter, I show you how to do the wireless thang — whether or not you tie your wireless network into a wired network.

In case you haven't had enough of the arcane terminology yet, this chapter shows you how to put together a 100Base-T Ethernet peer-to-peer network, using a router provided by an ISP. There. Now you can impress your friends and neighbors. Harrumph.

Follow the next sections in order, and you'll have your network up and networking in no time.

Blocking out the major parts

To set up a wired network, you need only a handful of parts:

- A network adapter inside your computer
- A hub, switch, or router
- Cables

The exact parts and quantities you need to get depend on how many computers you plan to network and what your existing system already has.

A few tricks lurk in the dark corners, as you may imagine, but all in all, if you stick to the simple, old-fashioned (cheap!) equipment, you'll be fine.

A network adapter

Each PC needs a *network adapter,* or *network interface card (NIC),* or *local-area network (LAN) adapter.* Every modern PC has a network adapter built in. If yours stops working (or no good Windows 7 driver for the NIC is available), see the nearby sidebar "Buying a network adapter" if you need to buy one.

Can't find your network adapter? Look at the back of the computer. If you see a place to plug in a cable with a receptacle that's about 50 percent wider than a telephone cable — it's for a LAN cable (also known as an RJ-45 or Cat 6 or Cat 5 cable; see the section "Cables," later in this chapter, for details) — you found it.

To confirm, crank up Windows 7, click the Start button, right-click Computer and choose Properties, and, in the View Basic Information about Your Computer dialog box, click the Device Manager button. Under the Network Adapters heading (see Figure 3-1), you should have an entry for your network adapter. Almost every entry for a network adapter says "10," "100," "1000," or some combination thereof — indicating the speed of the adapter, in millions of bits per second (Mbps). A "1000" speed adapter is also a "Gigabit" adapter.

Buying a network adapter

If your network adapter dies or you can't find a Windows 7 driver for your adapter, you need to buy a network adapter for your PC. Relax — they're cheap. Your first choice should be a USB network adapter. They're fast and easy, and they work like champs.

Sometimes, USB network adapters interfere with other USB devices. I have a laptop, for example, that works fine with a USB network adapter and works fine with a USB mouse, but starts acting like a jilted lover when I put the two together. The only solution I've found is to use the network or use the mouse, but not to use both at the same time.

Your network runs at the rate of the slowest card on the network. If all your adapters run Fast Ethernet (or 100 Mbps or 100Base-T), your network runs at 100 Mbps. If you have just one adapter card on the entire network that's capable of only the old, slow Ethernet speeds (10 Mbps or 10Base-T), the whole network runs at the lower speed unless you sink a lot of money into a hub or switch that sidesteps the differences. Gigabit cards are cheap (1 Gbps or 1000Base-T). Go ahead and splurge — one day you might buy a gigabit hub.

Faster network adapters speed up the exchange of data only between computers on your network. They don't do anything to speed up your Internet connection. Even the slowest network card these days can handle the bandwidth of any normal high-speed Internet connection.

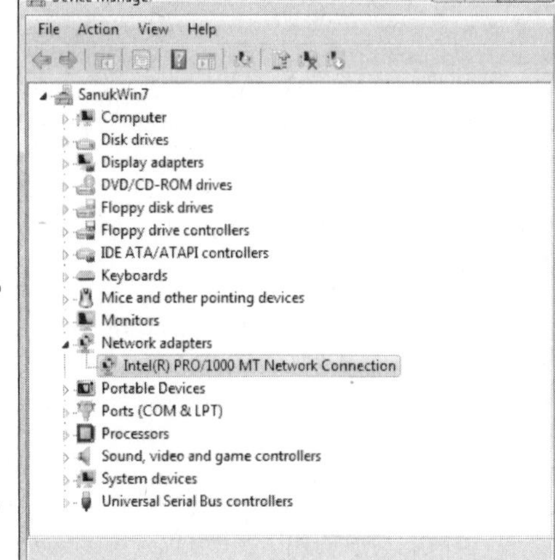

Figure 3-1: Network adapters invariably mention the speed — 10, 100, or 1000.

A hub, switch, or router

If you're going to have three or more computers in your network, you need a network *hub* or a *switch*. Chances are good that the cable modem or ADSL modem from your Internet service provider can act as a hub or switch: It probably has four or more *ports* on the back — slots where you can plug in a network cable.

A *hub* is nothing more than a box that connects all the wires in all the cables that are plugged into it. A *router* is a hub with an attitude. A *switch* is a hub that's stuck in its ways. And, *modems* — real modems — disappeared from the scene many years ago.

Before you get bogged down in semantic differences, you need to realize that when most computer geeks talk about hubs and routers and switches and modems, they use the terms interchangeably: Geek A may call a particular box a hub, Geek B may insist on calling it a router, Geek C might call the same box a switch, and Microsoft might call it a residential gateway. (A similar box in the wireless world could also be a wireless access point, a wireless hub, a wireless router, a wireless switch, or a hairless schnauzer.) In fact, differences exist between hubs, switches, and routers.

Give or take a dotted *i,* switches and hubs perform the same job and you can think of them interchangeably. Routers, on the other hand, have a bit of smarts inside their drab boxes. A broadband router (frequently, incorrectly, called a modem) is smart enough to handle a fast Internet connection on one end and your network on the other. Plug a cable or DSL modem into the wall, plug all your network cables into the other slots, turn on the router, and you're off to the races. The best technical description of broadband routers I've read is at `duxcw.com/faq/ics/diffrout.htm`.

Both hubs and switches are commonly identified by the speed of the connection: A 10/100 Ethernet switch, for example, handles both 10 Mbps and 100 Mbps network connections.

If you have a broadband router, you don't need a hub or a switch: The router has slots for network cables. Similarly, most wireless routers (or wireless access points) have built-in hubs. Look on the back of the box with rabbit ears to see whether you can find places to plug in network cables.

If you want to network only two computers, you don't need a hub (or a switch).

Cables

The cabling you get depends on how many computers you want to connect to your network:

- **If you're networking three or more computers to your wired network, you need cables to connect each PC to the hub or switch or router.** Take a cable. Plug one end of the cable into the PC's network adapter and the other end into an open slot on the hub. Repeat for each PC. Sounds like the instructions on a shampoo bottle, eh?
- **If you're connecting only two computers, and the two computers form the entire network, all you need is a special, *crossover* cable.** You can buy one — and you need only one — at any store that sells networking cables; just tell the salesperson that you want an RJ-45 crossover cable to network two PCs. Plug one end of the cable into the network adapter on one PC and the other end of the cable into the network adapter on the other PC, and you're ready to network. It's that easy.

Many modern network adapters are smart enough to use a regular LAN cable to hook up two computers directly. They can sense when you're trying to hook two computers together, and they compensate for your not having a crossover cable. Unfortunately, not all adapters are smart enough to know for sure — and if they don't work, they have no way of telling you that they didn't work. So, the safest approach is to use a crossover cable. It works every time.

Before you run out to buy cables, you need to think about how your installation will work so that you buy long enough cables. If you're thinking about stringing cables all over your house or office, set up a wireless system (see the next section). Stringing cables is a thankless job.

When you buy cables, get ones with decent connectors. I rarely encounter problems with Cat 5 or Cat 6 cables where the cabling itself went wonky, but I see snapped connectors all the time. And I, personally, wouldn't spend an extra farthing for Cat 6, which is supposedly better than Cat 5.

Using Internet Connection Sharing

For most people, most of the time, the easiest and fastest way to set up a network with a shared Internet connection entails nothing more than picking up the phone and calling the local phone company or cable company. They install a router, connect it to the Internet, and you can plug all your PCs into the back of the router — fair enough.

Sometimes, though, you have an Internet connection that's attached to just one PC and you want to share that connection with other PCs on the network. For example, you may have a fast wireless connection through your iPhone or an HSDPA or LTE card on a laptop and you want to share that connection across the network. You can do it with a Windows 7 feature known as *Internet Connection Sharing (ICS)*. For a schematic of ICS, see Figure 3-2.

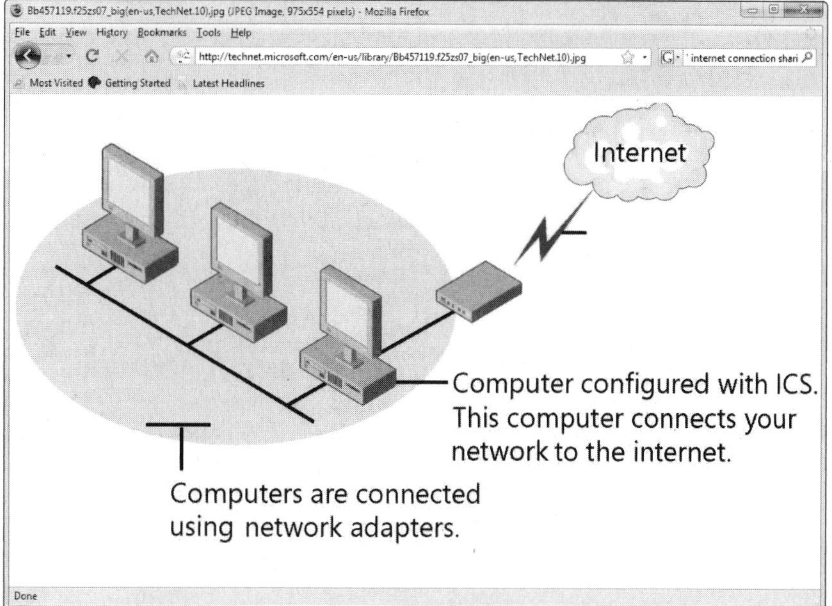

Figure 3-2: Microsoft TechNet demonstrates the connections in ICS.

The PC that runs Internet Connection Sharing must have *two* adaptors — one that connects to the Internet and one that connects to the network.

In the most common configuration, you plug your Internet connection (typically, a phone line, cable company line, or satellite connection) into a router and then run a cable from each PC to the router. The router turns into an Internet mother hen (that's a technical term). The computers on your network interact with the router, the router interacts with the cable or DSL modem, the modem talks to the Internet, and to the outside world you have only one connected PC. All the PCs on your network think they're connected directly to the Internet, thanks to the hardware mother hen.

But if you have only one computer connected directly to the Internet, ICS makes it easy to share that single computer's Internet connection among all computers on the network. ICS turns that lone PC into an Internet mother hen (there's that technical term again). The anointed ICS PC interacts with the Internet. All other PCs on the network interact with the ICS PC. To the outside world, you have only one connected PC. But all the other PCs in your network think they're on the Internet, too, thanks to the ICS mother hen. Clever — and effective.

Things get truly nasty when a network has two or more mother hens and they both believe that they're in control: One fights for all the chicks and the other fights for all the chicks, and then they both start looking at each other as chicks, and — all hell breaks loose. You think a catfight looks bad? You should see what these mother hens do to each other. At least 90 percent of all the confusion I've seen in setting up a network has to do with two or more mother hens fighting for control.

Okay, okay. Computer geeks don't call them mother hens. They're Dynamic Host Configuration Protocol (DHCP) servers. But they sure act like mother hens — mean ones, at that. More about battling mother hens in Book VII, Chapter 4.

I talk about setting up ICS in the next section.

Installing (or Reinstalling) Your Network

If you're setting up a new network, you're in the right place.

If you pulled out all your hair and still can't figure out how to get the %$#@! network working, tearing apart your network and reinstalling it from the ground up counts as a scorched-earth approach that may actually work.

So you have your PCs ready to go — network adapters installed and waiting. The hub's sitting in a box on the floor, or it has been attached to your cable TV or phone or satellite system by your friendly local DSL guy. All that cable makes quite a mess, and your spouse is starting to wonder, out loud, just what in the Sam Hill you expect to do with all of it. Yep. You're ready.

If you're going to set up a wireless network (see the next chapter), you need to start with this procedure to get your router going — typically, by plugging just one computer into the router with a regular LAN cable. When the router's working and you can connect that hardwired computer to the Internet, you're ready to start adding wireless computers.

If all the computers you're trying to connect are running Windows 7, you're almost done — plug in the cables and turn on the computers, and Windows 7 establishes the network for you. Piece o' cake. Run through the steps in Book VII, Chapter 1 to connect each Windows 7 computer to the network, and that's all she wrote.

On the other hand, if you have a mixed bunch of motley computers, you may have to set up the network manually and bring each computer online, one by one.

Here's a simple, ten-step process for getting your new network up and running with a minimum of fuss and hassle:

1. **Set up each PC.**

   Don't plug in the LAN cables yet. Connect the peripherals. Test each machine to make sure that it's working.

   If you're going to be sharing an Internet connection through one PC, using Internet Connection Sharing, get that PC connected to the Internet and make sure that everything is working fine.

2. **Turn off all PCs, unplug the router — from both the power outlet and the phone line/cable/satellite feed — and let everything sit for at least 30 seconds.**

   Yeah, this step sounds weird, but do it.

3. **With all the power off, put the router where it's going to go and connect all the LAN cables, at the hub and at each PC.**

   If you have a cable, DSL, or satellite modem, make sure that it's connected to the phone line or cable TV line and that it's plugged into the broadband router.

   Broadband routers have only one specific place where you can plug in a cable or DSL modem. That location frequently sits next to the "normal" slots, so read the documentation (or at least squint at the back of the hub!) to make sure that you plug your cable or DSL modem into the right slot.

4. **If you have a cable/DSL/satellite router (sometimes called a modem), stick the router's power plug in the wall, turn on the router, and wait for the lights to stop flashing.**

   This step establishes the DSL or cable or satellite modem as the mother of all mother hens. It also gives the modem a chance to run out to the Internet and gather anything it needs.

5. **If you have a wireless access point (with rabbit ears; see Figure 3-3) that's separate from your router, or if you have a second router, plug it in and wait for the lights to stop blinking.**

   Some people use more than one router on a network to add ports or to cut down the number of long cables necessary to hook up a many-PC network. See your router manufacturer's instructions for details, but in many cases you can just "daisy chain" routers together by stringing cables from one to the next.

   If the wireless access point or additional router wants to be a mother hen, it should work out its differences with the broadband router at this point.

Figure 3-3: The Linksys WRT54G, a workhorse wireless access point and router.

Photo courtesy Linksys by Cisco.

6. **Turn on one of the Windows 7 PCs.**

   Setting up a network in Windows 7 is easier — much easier — than setting it up with Vista or XP or any of those unmentionable alternatives.

   If you're going to use Internet Connection Sharing, turn on the ICS computer and start with it.

   Verify that the light on the hub for that PC comes on — in other words, make sure that the network adapter and cable for that PC are working okay. Now is the time to sort out connection problems: If the light doesn't go on, a cable is probably loose or an adapter card isn't installed correctly. Fix the problem now.

   When the light comes on at the hub, your Windows 7 PC installs any drivers it needs in order to connect to the hub and then looks for an existing network, or at least a working connection to the Internet.

7. **If no connection to the Internet is found — Internet Explorer doesn't work or you see a notification — click the network icon in the notification area (the one that looks like a trident superimposed on a computer screen) and choose Open Network and Sharing Center.**

If the Network and Sharing Center looks like Figure 3-4, Windows is trying to tell you that it can't find an Internet connection. If you find that you're connected to an "Unidentified network," check your Internet connection.

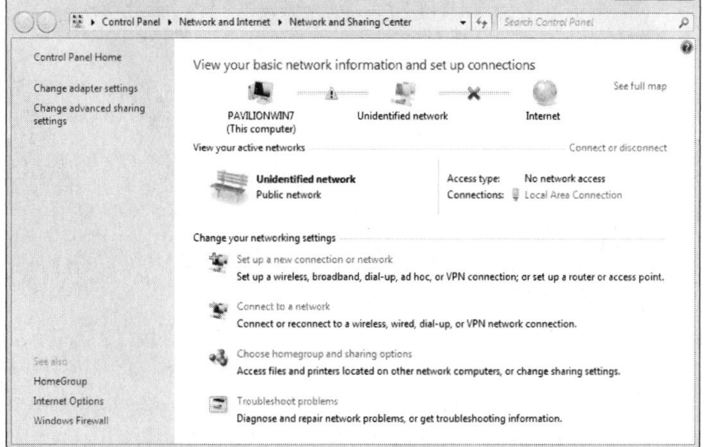

Figure 3-4: If Windows 7 can't find an Internet connection, it tells you that it has connected to an unidentified network.

If Windows 7 finds an Internet connection, it immediately starts you on the road to joining a network, with the Select a Location for the "Network" Network (is there an echo in here?) dialog box, shown in Figure 3-5.

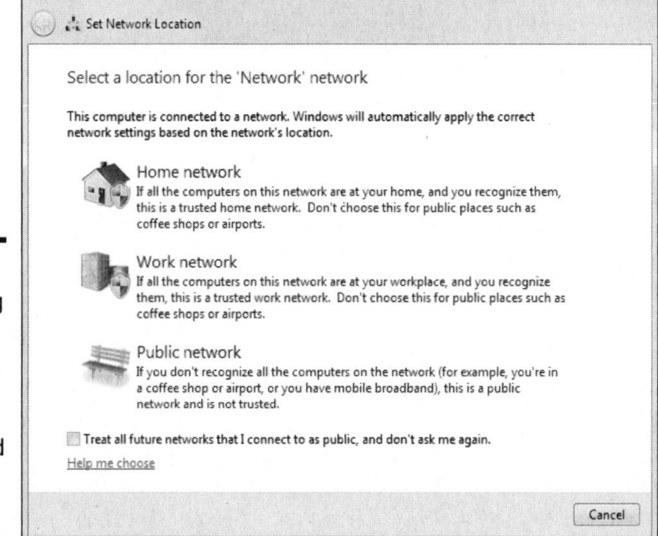

Figure 3-5: After finding an Internet connection, Windows 7 sets up a network and asks you which type.

From that point, Windows steps you through connecting to a network — even though it's a network with just one PC. Follow the instructions in Book VII, Chapter 1 to get things going. Pay particular attention to the discussion of HomeGroups.

8. **If you have an Internet connection and you want to set up this specific PC to share its Internet connection by way of Internet Connection Sharing, follow these substeps:**

You must have *two* adapters in the ICS system — one for connecting to the Internet and the other for connecting to the network.

   a. *Open the Network and Sharing Center (refer to Figure 3-5) by clicking the network icon, in the notification area, and choosing Open Network and Sharing Center.*

   b. *In the Network and Sharing Center, on the left, click the Change Adapter Settings link.*

   c. *Right-click the Internet connection — the adapter that's connected to the Internet — and choose Properties. Then click the Sharing tab.*

   Depending on whether you're sharing a wired or wireless Internet connection, you see the Network Connection Properties or Wireless Network Connection Properties, shown in Figure 3-6.

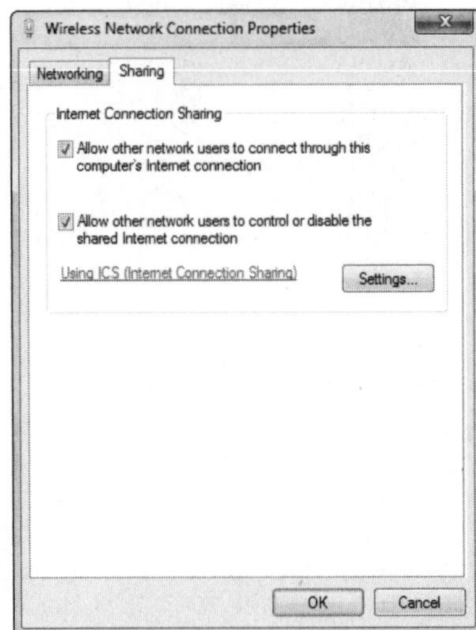

Figure 3-6: Sharing a wireless Internet connection (for example, a WiMAX, HSPA, or LTE broadband connection).

   d. Select the check box marked Allow Other Network Users to Connect through This Computer's Internet Connection. Optionally, you can allow other users to disable the shared Internet connection. Click OK twice and then "X" out of the Manage Network Connections dialog box.

The PC's Internet connection will be shared and accessible from other PCs connected to the network. If you already have other PCs attached to the network, you should reboot them so that they can find the new Internet connection.

9. **Continue to set up other computers on your network.**

   By starting with a Windows 7 computer, at least in my experience, you greatly increase the chances of getting your Windows XP and Windows Vista computers to talk with each other.

If you're adding Windows XP computers to your network, make sure that you have installed Windows XP Service Pack 2 or Service Pack 3, and then run the Network Setup Wizard. To open the wizard on a Windows XP computer, choose Start➪All Programs➪Accessories➪Communications➪Network Setup Wizard. Be prepared for some of the most confusing questions that any version of Windows has ever asked. I go into detail in my earlier book, *Windows XP All-in-One Desk Reference For Dummies,* 2nd Edition (published by Wiley).

Attaching a Vista computer to the network is considerably simpler, but you need to make sure that your Sharing and Discovery settings reflect the way you want to run the network. For details, look in Book IX, Chapter 2 of *Windows Vista All-in-One Desk Reference For Dummies,* also written by you-know-who, also published by — well, you get the idea.

When you're done, you're, uh, done. The network should be networking. Try choosing Start➪Network on any of the Windows 7 PCs and make yourself at home. Try printing on a networked printer. Betcha bucks to buckaroos that it sets itself up just that easily.

More Troubleshooting

I've encountered all sorts of problems with Windows XP and Windows Vista networks, but surprisingly few with Windows 7. In the following sections, I describe problems you may have connecting XP and Vista computers with your Windows 7 computers — and what you can do about them.

Networking on the road

Most of the time when I travel, I need to connect two PCs. I guess it's the writer in me, but I've spent hours — days, weeks — trying to pair up PCs in the field. Direct cable connect. Laplink. USB-to-USB adapters. A dozen other hardware and software kludges. I've resorted to e-mailing files to myself more times than I care to admit.

Suddenly, in Windows 7, it's easy. I mean, really easy.

If you're on the road and you need to plug your PC into a "foreign" network, there's nothing to it, as long as your laptop and the foreign network are running Windows 7, Vista, or XP networks. Plug a network cable into the laptop's network adapter, plug the other end into an available slot on the hub, turn on the laptop, and ba-da-boom-ba-da-bing, the whole operation takes maybe 30 seconds.

More than that, though, if I'm carrying two laptops that I need to network, all it takes is a crossover cable. (For a discussion of crossover cables — basically, an RJ-45 cable with one pair of wires crossed — see the section "Blocking out the major parts" earlier in this chapter.)

Whenever I pack two laptops, I carry a little 1-meter-long crossover cable. If I need to network the laptops, I plug one end of the cable into the network adapter on one laptop and the other end into the other laptop, and suddenly my Windows 7 network is right there with me. Everything I can do on the "big" network in my office works precisely the same way on the road. It's absolutely phenomenal.

Getting your computer to see another computer

Have you ever had two computers on a network suddenly stop talking with each other? One day you wake up and Computer A can't see Computer B, or vice versa. Both computers sit on the same network. Why can't they see each other?

Unfortunately, there's no specific way you can wring a computer by the neck and say, "Look, the other computer is sitting right here. Talk to each other, you stupid machines!"

Generally, the approach you have to take is slightly different depending on whether the noncommunicative machines are running Windows 7, Windows Vista, or Windows XP — and heaven help ya if you're trying to Mac a Mac or Penguin, er, Linux box play nicely.

My Windows 7 computer can't see a Windows Vista or Windows XP computer

So you have your network up and working — perhaps it's been working for a long time or maybe it's freshly built — and your Windows 7 computer can't see a Windows XP or Vista computer that you *know* is on the network.

It happens to me all the time. I don't know why, but Windows XP and (to a lesser extent) Vista computers drop out of sight for no apparent reason. It's frustrating, all the more so because the advice offered online — download this driver, upgrade that piece of software — rarely works.

There's a ritual I go through, with increasing levels of difficulty, to try to bring back the shy PC. This is school-of-hard-knocks stuff; I don't know of any official procedure to establish or reestablish communication with the missing computers. The fact that you're working from a Windows 7 computer increases your chances of hooking up to the other computer enormously. Windows 7 is much, much better than its predecessors.

Here's the way I tackle the problem:

1. **If you have any firewall other than Windows Firewall on either computer, disable it.**

   This step clears up the problem at least half the time. (Congratulations — you've hit one of the main reasons why I don't recommend firewalls from any company other than Microsoft.) If turning off the non-Microsoft firewall doesn't work, go to Step 2.

2. **Reboot the computer that you can't see.**

   Just walk over to the AWOL computer and restart it, from the ground up. (Don't just log off and log back on again, or switch users.) Wait a few minutes. Then try to get to it again from your Windows 7 computer. About 25 percent of the time, this technique clears up the problem. I have no idea why. If you still can't see the computer, it's time to try some tricky stuff: Go to Step 3.

3. **On the Windows 7 computer, choose Start➪Computer.**

   You see Windows Explorer with all your computer's drives listed, as well as all visible computers on the network (see Figure 3-7).

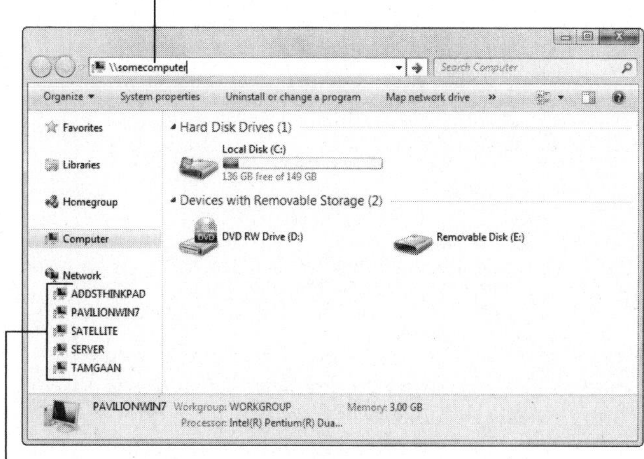

Figure 3-7: Try to establish a connection with a shy PC using Windows Explorer.

4. **In the address bar at the top, type \\ and the name of the missing computer and press Enter.**

   If you don't know the name of the missing computer, go over to it. If it's running Windows Vista, choose Start, right-click Computer, and choose Properties. The name appears near the bottom of the screen. If it's running Windows XP, choose Start, right-click My Computer, and choose Properties. In the System Properties dialog box, click the Computer Name tab. The name appears at the top.

   In Figure 3-7, I try to establish communication with a computer named `somecomputer`, so I type **\\somecomputer** in the address bar and press Enter.

   If that works, the hiding Vista or XP computer is having trouble with network discovery. I talk about network discovery settings for Vista in Book IX, Chapter 2 of *Windows Vista All-in-One Desk Reference For Dummies.* I realize that you might be tired of references to my earlier books, but this stuff is complicated and takes many pages to explain. Sorry. There isn't a network discovery setting in Windows XP — at least, nothing you can get at readily — but you can reset the settings that exist by working through the Windows XP Network Setup Wizard. See . . . oh, you probably guessed.

   If that doesn't work, you should start sweating. Go to Step 5.

5. **Run the Windows 7 Network Troubleshooter: Choose Start⇨Control Panel⇨System and Security and, under the Action Center heading, click the Troubleshoot Common Computer Problems link. Click the Network and Internet link and follow along from there.**

   If the troubleshooter says that you should contact your network administrator (see Figure 3-8), you have my permission to throw your computer out the window (or shoot the troubleshooter).

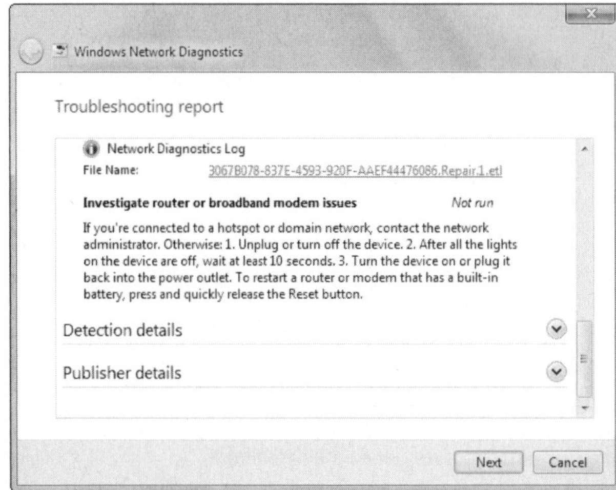

Figure 3-8: The Network Troubleshooter has several bad habits.

My computer can't see a Windows 7 computer

In my experience, Vista and Windows XP computers almost invariably find a properly configured Windows 7 computer — and I've never had a Windows 7 PC fail to find another Windows 7 PC. The devil's in the details, of course.

Here's the approach I take when one of my Windows 7 computers suddenly drops off the grid, or when a Windows 7 PC that's just been attached to a network doesn't show up on other computers on the network:

1. **If you have any firewall other than Windows Firewall on either computer, disable it.**

   I'm sorry if I start to sound like a broken record here. If turning off the non-Microsoft firewall doesn't work, go to Step 2.

2. **Make sure your Windows 7 computer is *supposed* to be visible. Click the network icon in the notification area — the one that looks like a trident in front of a computer screen — and choose Open Network and Sharing Center.**

   You see the Network and Sharing Center, which may look like Figure 3-9.

3. **If you identified your current network as a public network, Windows 7 protects you from the network: Other PCs can't see your PC, and they can't access anything on your PC.**

   Even the printers attached to a public-network-connected PC aren't available.

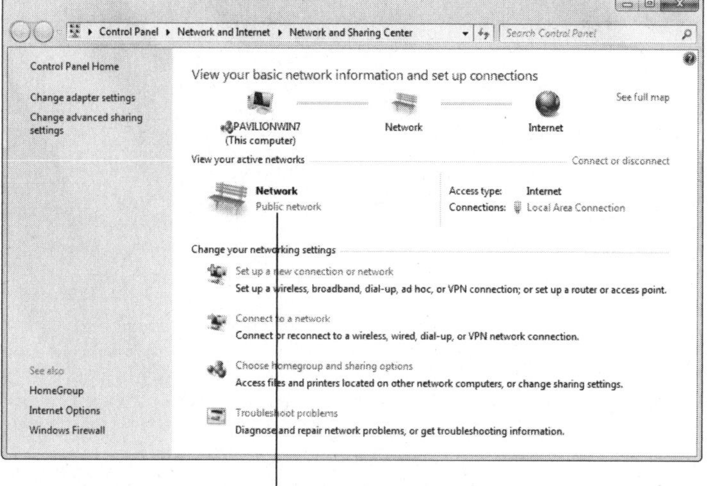

Figure 3-9: Windows 7 PCs on public networks aren't supposed to be visible.

4. **To identify your current network as a work or home network — and thus make your PC visible to other computers on the network — click the link marked Public network.**

   You see the Set Network Location dialog box (refer to Figure 3-5). From that point you can set the type of network, based on the discussion in Book VII, Chapter 1.

   If your network is already listed as Home or Work, go on to Step 5.

5. **Reboot the Windows 7 computer that you can't see.**

   That isn't exactly an act of desperation, but it's on a par with rubbing a lucky rabbit's foot.

6. **If you still can't see the Windows 7 PC, run the Network Troubleshooter on the Windows 7 PC.**

   See Step 5 in the preceding section.

Chapter 4: Putting the Why in Wi-Fi

In This Chapter

- **Setting up a wireless network**
- **Securing a wireless network**
- **Troubleshooting without wires**

I remember the first time I tried to install a wireless network in my home office.

It was an unmitigated disaster. I live in a three-story concrete town house. I put the *wireless access point* (the base station — the thing with rabbit ears on top) on the middle floor. It was one of the original Wi-Fi (pronounced "why-fie") base stations, which used the 802.11b protocol (more about that in the next section). As long as my laptop sat right next to the wireless access point, everything worked great. The minute I moved it downstairs or upstairs — or even walked into the stairwell — the connection died. Completely, totally, utterly gone. No amount of futzing with the rabbit ears helped. It's like the bunny turned belly up, and that's all she wrote.

That was a decade ago. Times change. The minute that the new, much-hyped 802.11g Wi-Fi equipment became available in my neck of the woods, I ran out and bought another wireless base station. And therein lies a story. . . .

I bought an 802.11g wireless broadband router and a plug-in card for the laptop. I paid less than $150 for the whole shootin' match. Installation was a breeze. I shut down every PC on my network, unpacked the router, unplugged my (very) old hub, plugged in the new hardware, started up the PCs — running Windows XP Pro Service Pack 2, at the time — and all my hardwired network cable connections worked. Fair enough, but that's not much of a big deal: I expected any replacement for the old hub to work right the first time.

So I plugged the wireless card into the laptop and powered it up. Windows XP Pro recognized it, installed the driver, told me the card was available — and it worked. I mean, right then and there, not having done a thing, Internet Explorer picked up the network connection, reached out across my peer-to-peer network, through my DSL modem, and started pulling pages off the Web — much to my amazement.

I took the laptop up and down the stairs and ran McAfee Speedometer (I've since switched to the Speakeasy test at `speakeasy.net/speedtest`) to judge how fast my Internet connection was running. Depending on my location, the speed was within 25 percent of the speed of the hard-linked connections. I couldn't believe it.

I thought I was in wireless hog heaven when, a couple of weeks later, a friend of mine asked whether I had just set up a new wireless access point. Why, yes, I said, how did you know? He told me he was sitting in a park about a half-mile away from my house, flipped on his laptop, went searching for wireless networks, and found one named AskWoody. He spent all of 15 seconds getting on my network to start using my Internet connection. It took him another 30 seconds to start looking at the files on my main machine's hard drive.

Oops.

Setting up a wireless connection is easy. Making your wireless network at least minimally secure takes only a few extra minutes — and it can save you untold grief — if you know the trick.

Choosing a Protocol

802.11g. 802.11n. It sounds so techy, doesn't it?

When your laptop's Wi-Fi chip talks with a wireless access point (see Figure 4-1), it speaks a specific language known as a *protocol.*

Figure 4-1: The Linksys WRT54G2, one of the most popular 802.11g wireless access points of all time.

Photo courtesy Linksys by Cisco.

If you're in the market for a wireless router — either one that you install yourself or one that comes along for the ride with your cable or ADSL Internet connection — you need to choose between two different protocols:

- **802.11g** is the more common, more reliable, less capable, and less expensive alternative. Computers that talk to each other using the 802.11g protocol can process more than 20 megabits per second, which means that it can keep up with most fast Internet connections, including fiber optic. Its indoor range runs a maximum of 100 meters, give or take a concrete wall or two.
- **802.11n** is the up-and-comer that still isn't standardized, so different manufacturers can offer slightly different (and at least theoretically incompatible) versions. The 802.11n protocol maxes out at about 100 Megabits per second, which makes it fast enough for full high-definition television. It can jump through three or more concrete walls, with a maximum indoor range around 300 meters.

See Table 4-1 for a full breakout of wireless protocols.

Table 4-1 Those 802 Numbers

Standard	*Rated (Theoretical) Speed (Mbps*)*	*Realistic Speed (Mbps*)*	*My Recommendation*
802.11b	10	4	Don't bother. The signal doesn't reach as far as 802.11g, and it's slower.
802.11g	50	20	The sweet spot. Backward compatible with 802.11b, so if you have an old wireless card, it works with your 802.11g base station. But it uses the same frequency range as many cordless phones.
802.11n	200+	100	Still a "draft standard," which means that it isn't standardized. If you buy 802.11n equipment, make sure to buy everything from the same manufacturer.

**Million bits per second*

All available 802.11g equipment can also communicate with wireless cards (and onboard laptop wireless chips) that speak only the older standard protocol, 802.11b.

What about Bluetooth?

Bluetooth is a horse of a different color. The wireless networks I talk about in this chapter are designed to replace wired local-area networks (LANs). They need to haul a lot of data over a fairly long distance — say, across a building or even many buildings.

Bluetooth, on the other hand, deals with relatively small amounts of data traveling over a short distance — perhaps 10 meters. It's built for connecting headphones to telephones, speakers to sound systems, cameras to laptops, or Bernie Madoff with his conscience.

To put it another way, if you want to transmit data from a dialup modem — perhaps a General Packet Radio Service (GPRS) modem in a mobile phone — to a nearby computer, Bluetooth works great. But if you want to send broadband across the room, you need to haul out the bigger Wi-Fi guns.

802.11n wireless access points have no problem handling 802.11g and 802.11b wireless cards, but one manufacturer's 802.11n may not support another manufacturer's 802.11n. For example, if you buy an 802.11n wireless router from, say, D-Link, it may not communicate with the built-in 802.11n Wi-Fi chip in your laptop at full 802.11n speed. Until the 802.11n standard is ratified (perhaps in 2010), you have no way to know for sure which manufacturers' products work with others'.

The term Wi-Fi encompasses all 802.11 protocols. Usually, when you hear this term, it specifically refers to 802.11b or g networks.

Installing a Wireless System

The easiest way to install a wireless system is to have the folks who sell you your Internet connection set it up. Every cable, ADSL, and satellite Internet service provider can come up with a wireless network in your home or office with relative ease.

On the other hand, if you already have an Internet connection and you don't want to pay your ISP a king's ransom to add wireless, doing it yourself is generally painless. Usually. Most of the time.

If you've never dealt with a network, read Book VII, Chapters 2 and 3 to make sure that you understand the basics. If you think of a wireless network as being similar to a "regular" wired network, with radio waves in place of network cables, you're pretty close to the mark.

Here we go with the stupid terminology again.

Wireless adapters and access points

Every computer in a wireless network must have a *wireless adapter,* which is just a radio receiver and transmitter, similar to the kind in cordless telephones. Most commonly, wireless adapters are built into laptops, but you can also stick a wireless adapter on a desktop computer. An adapter plugs into an ExpressCard port (typically on a laptop; see Figure 4-2), a USB port (which works with either a laptop or a desktop, see Figure 4-3), or a PCMCIA notebook port (the flat one, about the size of a pack of playing cards), or it goes inside the computer, screwed down as a PCI card.

Figure 4-2: The Linksys Wireless-N Express-Card.

Photo courtesy Linksys by Cisco.

Wireless networks use a *wireless access point* (WAP) that acts much like a base station for a cordless telephone. A WAP isn't technically necessary because you can instruct wireless adapters to talk to each other, much as you would use walkie-talkies. (See the Windows 7 Help and Support topic on ad hoc wireless networks.) If you plan to run much data over your wireless network, it's far better to run everything through a WAP.

Figure 4-3: A USB wireless adapter.

Photo courtesy Linksys by Cisco.

If you already have a wired network set up, adding a WAP is as simple as plugging one into your existing hub (router, switch, whatever) and adjusting the bunny ears. If you don't have a wired network already, I urge you to follow the advice in Book VII, Chapter 2 and start with a wireless broadband router.

The wireless router acts as a wireless base station, but it also has slots for regular wired network cables and a special slot to connect your cable or DSL or satellite modem (see Figure 4-4). Almost every wireless network starts out with a PC plugged into the back of the wireless router or access point — that's how you set up the WAP.

Figure 4-4: A wireless router has rabbit ears (in this case, three of them), slots for LAN cables, and a special slot for the Internet connection.

Photo courtesy Linksys by Cisco.

Location, location, location

The location of the wireless access point matters — the stronger the signal, the faster the data travels over the waves. Here are my suggestions:

- ✦ If you know which computers will use wireless the most, put the WAP as close as you can to them. If you don't know which computers will drive the largest volume (or you don't know where the high-volume computers will be located), put the WAP as close to the physical center of the coverage area as you can.
- ✦ Do not put the WAP right next to a wall. Move it away from the wall by at least 6 inches. Don't put one on the floor or directly attached to the ceiling, either.

- Remember that metal, water (read: fish tanks), and concrete affect signal strength. Wood and drywall don't matter much. Glass, brick, and stone sit somewhere in between.
- Try hard to connect your cable or DSL or satellite modem to the WAP by a regular network cable. Although it may be technically possible to go wireless, there's no reason to bog down the wireless system with the highest-volume link in your network.

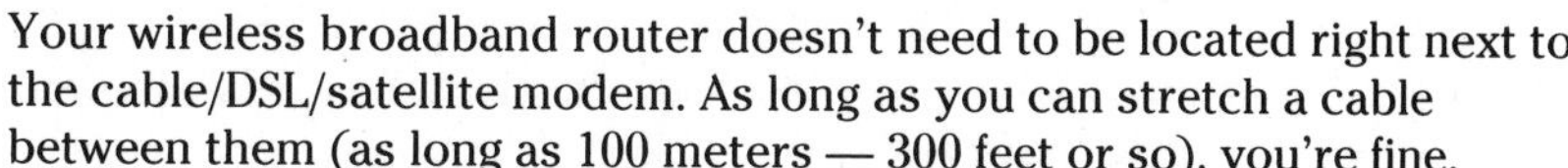

  Your wireless broadband router doesn't need to be located right next to the cable/DSL/satellite modem. As long as you can stretch a cable between them (as long as 100 meters — 300 feet or so), you're fine.

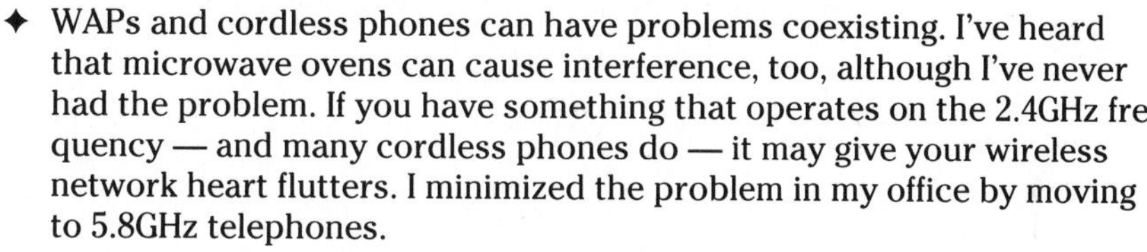

- WAPs and cordless phones can have problems coexisting. I've heard that microwave ovens can cause interference, too, although I've never had the problem. If you have something that operates on the 2.4GHz frequency — and many cordless phones do — it may give your wireless network heart flutters. I minimized the problem in my office by moving to 5.8GHz telephones.

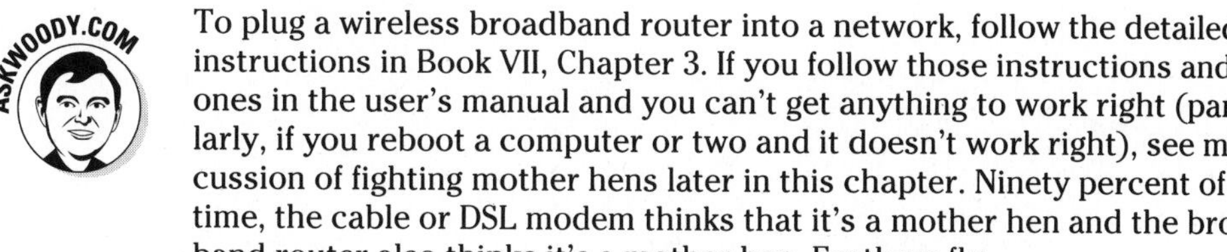

To plug a wireless broadband router into a network, follow the detailed instructions in Book VII, Chapter 3. If you follow those instructions and the ones in the user's manual and you can't get anything to work right (particularly, if you reboot a computer or two and it doesn't work right), see my discussion of fighting mother hens later in this chapter. Ninety percent of the time, the cable or DSL modem thinks that it's a mother hen and the broadband router also thinks it's a mother hen. Feathers fly.

Setting Up a Secure Wireless Network

Ya gotcher ears on, good buddy? Well, 10-4 that. Truckers do the wireless thang. You should, too.

If you paid to have your cable or ADSL or satellite company set up a wireless network, make sure that it set up something called *WPA Encryption* and that it gives you the WPA key. If your ISP has you going with a wireless box and it puts WPA security on it, you're all set. Move on to the next chapter. Don't go mucking around the inside of your wireless access point.

If your ISP installed a wireless network and didn't secure it with WPA Encryption (you can tell whether you can connect to the network without providing a password), call and chew an employee's ears off — both of 'em. In this day and age, it should be criminal to set up a wireless access point in a person's home or business without securing the setup.

If you're installing a wireless network on your own — or if you get stuck troubleshooting a wireless network that the ISP can't fix, or won't fix until a week from Tuesday (that's happened to me more than a couple of times), follow along with the rest of this chapter.

In the following procedure (the longest in this book!), I take you through the process of getting a wireless network up and running and then securing the network.

The first law of wireless networks pertains: *Any default installation of a wireless network is absolutely wide open and vulnerable to the most casual eavesdropping.* If you don't lock your wireless network down, somebody's going to blow it away.

Though it's true that you can set up a wireless access point by using a wireless connection, it's much simpler if you attach a Windows 7 PC directly to the wireless access point with a network cable. After you have the WAP set up and, uh, WAPping, you can unplug the cable and work wirelessly forevermore.

If all goes well, here's how to connect the first PC to your new wireless network and then harden the network so that it doesn't quack like a sitting duck:

1. **Before you set up anything, go on the Internet (or open your user manual) and make sure that you know the default username, password, and broadcast network name (usually called an *SSID*) for your wireless access point.**

   Run out to an Internet café if you can't find the user manual. Search `Google.com` for the model number of your WAP and default password.

   In this case, I configure a Linksys WRT54G. A quick trip to `Google.com` reveals that the default username is blank (yep, blank), the default password is `admin`, and the default SSID is `linksys`.

2. **Make sure that your WAP (broadband router, whatever) is plugged in and all its lights are blinking. For now, don't plug in your Internet connection.**

   Let's just work with the WAP for the moment.

3. **Connect a network cable from your Windows 7 PC to the WAP.**

   It's easier to set up a WAP using a cable, rather than trying to use a wireless connection. If you try to follow the rest of these steps using a wireless connection, you find that you have to reconnect several times. It can be done, but it's rather boorish.

When you plug in the WAP, Windows 7 identifies it as a new network. Tell Windows that you're on a public connection for now.

4. **Fire up Internet Explorer and go to `http://192.168.1.1`**

Most WAPs work fine with Firefox, but occasionally you run into some laggards that haven't kept up with the times.

Yes, that's a weird address. It's the address for the WAP.

Windows tells you that the WAP wants you to type the WAP's username and password, as shown in Figure 4-5.

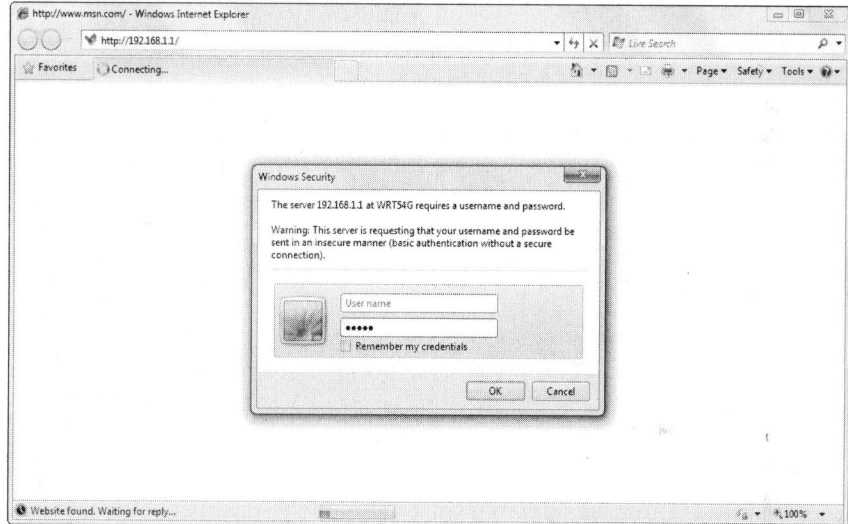

Figure 4-5: To get in, you must provide the WAP's username and password.

5. **Type the username and password you found in Step 1. In this case, with the WRT54G, the username is blank and the password is `admin`. Click OK.**

   You see the main Administration page. Each manufacturer has a slightly different design, but they all contain some information that's common to all access points.

Don't mess with anything you don't understand! Lots and lots of settings inside the router can render it useless — and you have to reset the whole machine to get it working again.

6. **Your first job is to change the WAP's password. On the Linksys router (see Figure 4-6), click the Administration tab. Type the new password twice.**

Enter the new password twice.

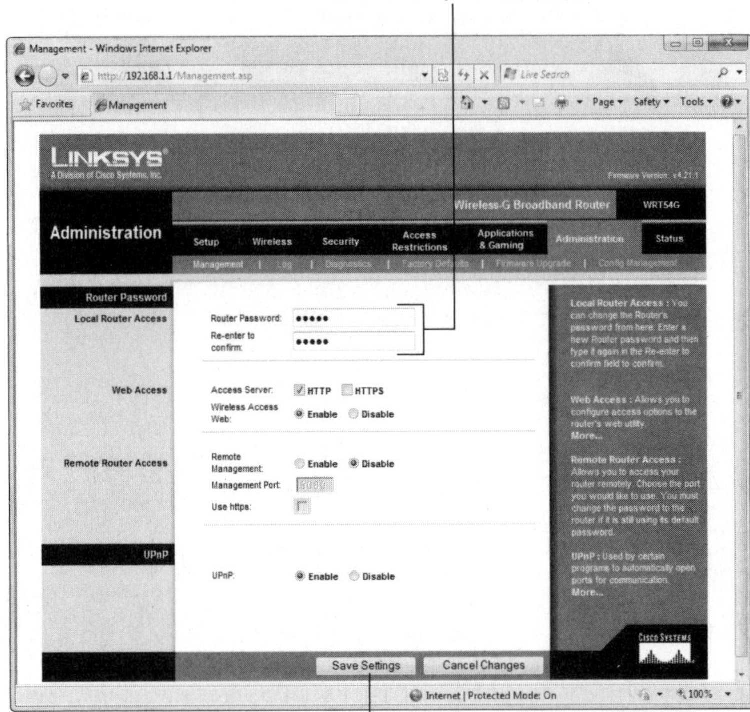

Figure 4-6: First change the WAP's password.

You must click Save Settings on each page.

Oddly, Linksys doesn't let you change the username (in fact, it doesn't even check it when you log on in Step 5). So, the security of your access point or router depends solely on the password.

7. **At the bottom of the page, click Save Settings.**

   Every manufacturer works differently, but in the Linksys world you have to click Save Settings at the bottom of *each page* in order to apply changes. If you go to a different tab without clicking Save Settings, your changes are thrown away.

   The access point or router reboots itself when you click Save Settings. When it returns to life, you see a logon screen quite similar to the one shown earlier, in Figure 4-5.

8. **Type the username and *new* password, and click OK.**

   You're back inside the access point or router.

9. **Your second job is to change the broadcast network name or SSID. On the Linksys router in the example, click the Wireless tab, and you see the network name settings shown in Figure 4-7.**

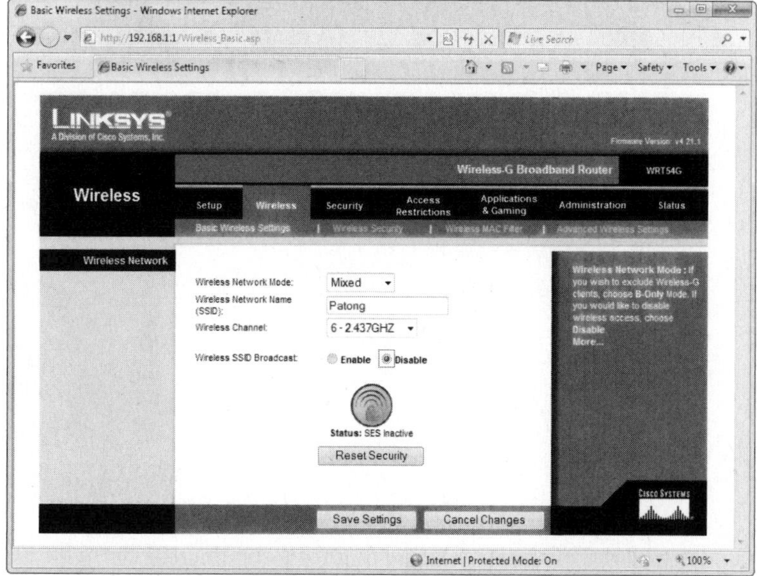

Figure 4-7: Give your wireless network a new name. To make it somewhat stealthy, don't broadcast its name.

The Wireless SSID Broadcast setting (which goes by different names on other access points and routers) controls whether the WAP "advertises" its presence by broadcasting its name so that computers with Wi-Fi cards can easily find it. On one hand, if you broadcast the name, it's easier to set up a network. On the other hand, if you don't broadcast the name, it's harder for somebody driving by in a '51 Chevy to pop onto your network. On a third hand, any savvy wireless dude with the right equipment can find your network anyway.

If you want to make your wireless network more secure, avoid using the common SSIDs listed at `wigle.net/gps/gps/Stat`.

10. **At the bottom of the page, click Save Settings.**

    Do what you need to do to get connected again.

11. **Your final task is to add encryption to your wireless connections. As with most security concerns, you have lots of inscrutable options, but most people using home or small-business networks do just fine with *WPA2* in *Pre-shared key* mode or *Personal* mode.**

For this Linksys router, I clicked the Wireless tab and then the Wireless Security subtab. I selected WPA2 Personal security mode and typed a shared key, as shown in Figure 4-8.

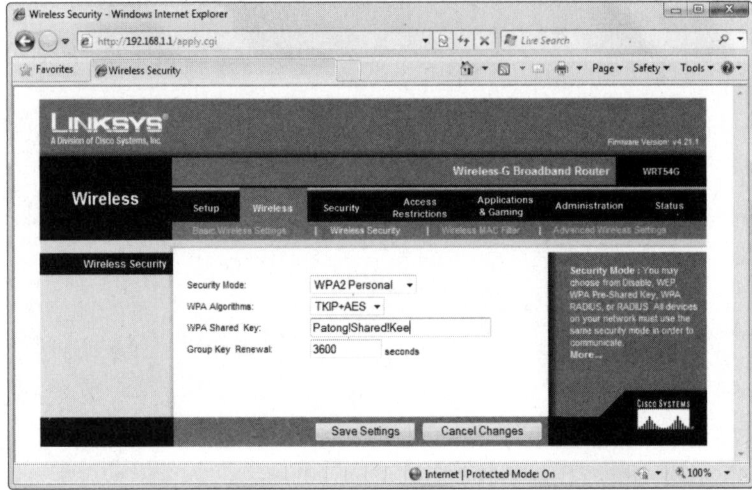

Figure 4-8: WPA2 Personal helps keep people off your network unless they know the password.

All the common security methods can be broken (heck, all the *un*common ones, too), but WPA2 Personal represents a good balance between security and dag-nab-it-I-hate-this-security-garbage sentiment.

12. **Write down the security mode and key, and then click Save Settings.**

    At this point, your wireless network is set up, secure, and ready to use. See the next section for details on how to connect your laptop — or any computer with a wireless connection — to the WPA2-protected network.

Before you "X" out of Internet Explorer, you might want to take a gander at the last section in this chapter, about two fighting mother hens, to see whether you should make one last, easy change inside the wireless access point or router that can keep the two chickens from each others' throats.

Connecting to a WPA2 Protected Network

In Book VII, Chapter 1, I cover everything you need to know about getting into a Wi-Fi network that's using minimal security.

Now for the advanced course.

If you followed along in the preceding section and set up your wireless network to use WPA2 PSK (also known as WPA2 Personal or WPA2 Pre-shared key) protection, here's how to get your laptop on the network:

1. **Fire up your laptop (or other Wi-Fi-capable computer) and make sure that your Wi-Fi connection is working.**

   Usually, a light goes on. You see the "bars" Wi-Fi icon in the notification area, down near the clock.

2. **If you click the Wi-Fi icon, you see that your semistealthy wireless network isn't listed (see Figure 4-9).**

Figure 4-9: The wireless network you set up in the preceding section doesn't appear on the list.

   It's hidden because you chose not to broadcast the SSID.

3. **Click the Wi-Fi icon and choose Open Network and Sharing Center.**

   The Network and Sharing Center shows that you aren't connected to the Internet, or to any network, as shown in Figure 4-10.

4. **Click the link that says Set Up a New Connection or Network. In the resulting dialog box, click the link that says Manually Connect to a Wireless Network.**

   Windows shows you the Manually Connect to a Wireless Network dialog box, shown in Figure 4-11.

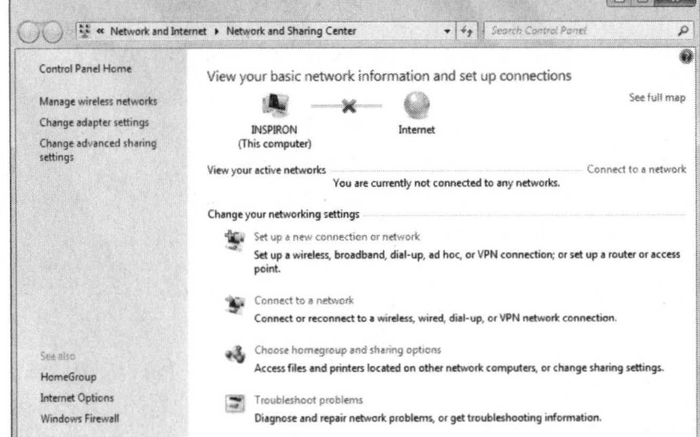

Figure 4-10: There are no network connections.

Figure 4-11: How to connect to a wireless network that you can't even see.

5. **Fill in the network name and choose the security type (WPA2-Personal), the encryption type (AES), and the security key you typed in Step 11 in the preceding section. Select the check box that says Connect Even If the Network Is Not Broadcasting, and then click Next.**

   Click the Wi-Fi icon, in the notification area. Your new network appears on the list of available networks, similar to the list shown earlier, in Figure 4-9, even though the wireless access point or router *isn't broadcasting its ID*.

6. **Click the Wi-Fi icon and then click your new network name.**

   Windows applies the WPA2 security key you provided and connects to the wireless access point or router, as shown in Figure 4-12.

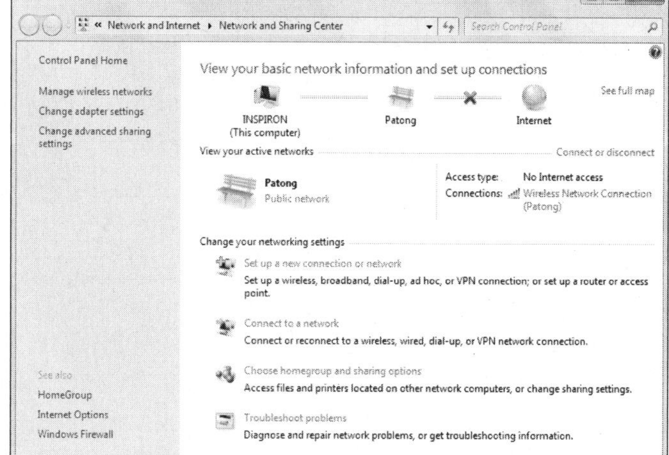

Figure 4-12: You can connect to the WAP/ router, even though it isn't broad-casting its ID.

Calming Two Fighting Mother Hens

Man, you ain't seen nothin' till you've seen two fighting mother hens.

If you have your telephone, ADSL, cable, or satellite company set up a wireless network in your home or office, you've got it made. If there's a problem, you just pick up the phone. And wait. And wait. And wait.

If you have only one router on your network — most likely, a broadband router — that connects directly to your phone line and has plugs for network cables and rabbit ears for wireless connections, you've also got it made. Those boxes have only one mother hen. If you listen closely, you can probably hear her clucking.

Many people let the phone company do its thing — attach a modem (actually, it's a router) to the ADSL line or cable or satellite — but they don't let the Cable Guy do the whole job. They let the phone company get one computer working, and then take over from that point. They might add another router or build a wireless network or run Internet Connection Sharing. Those folks — the ones with two routers or a modem and a wireless box — are the ones most likely to encounter battling mother hens. It's a frustrating, nearly invisible troubleshooting trip that can bring your network to its knees, sporadically, and with no visible cause.

The root problem: the *DHCP server.* More precisely, two of them.

Many cable, DSL, and satellite modems are set up as DHCP servers — mother hens, if you will — that expect to dole out IP addresses to each computer on the network. Many of these modems assign themselves an IP address of 192.168.1.1 and then hand out IP addresses starting in that range.

Unfortunately, many broadband routers and wireless access points are also set up as mother hens. They, too, expect to hand out IP addresses. Many of them assign themselves an IP address of 192.168.1.1 and expect to hand out IP addresses starting in that range.

What's wrong with this picture? Well, if you power up your modem and it assigns itself an address of 192.168.1.1 and then you power up your broadband router and it assigns itself an address of 192.168.1.1, you suddenly have an enormously unstable situation. It's as though two different clones of Jerry Springer were forced to sit down and talk to each other. And, when the unsuspecting PCs come up for air, seeking a mother hen to assign them an IP address, the feathers start flying.

Here's my favorite solution. Follow the instructions in the earlier section "Setting Up a Secure Wireless Network" to open the wireless access point or router that thinks it's a Mother Hen. Set the IP address of the mother hen, er, the access point or router to something other than 192.168.1.1 — say, 192.168.1.20, as I do in Figure 4-13.

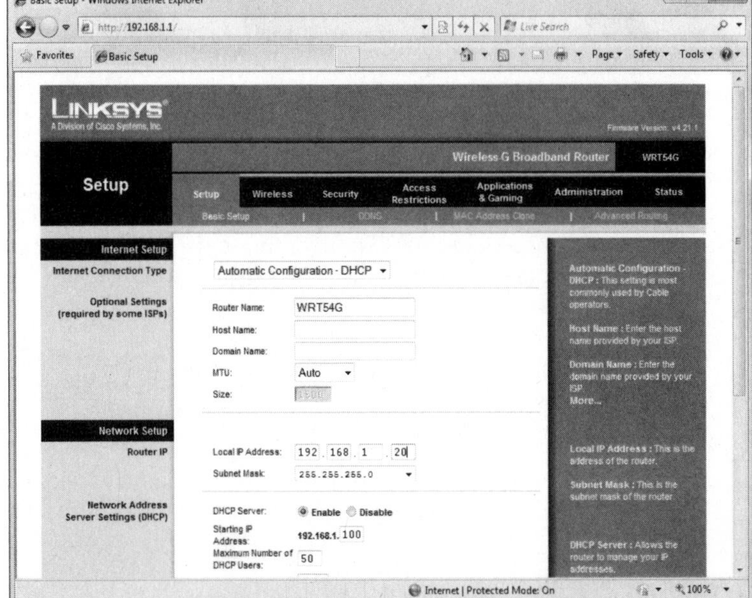

Figure 4-13: A quick and easy — and almost foolproof — solution to the problem of battling a mother hen.

Save the settings in the access point or router, and you're done. In the future, whenever one of the computers on your network goes looking for a Mother Hen, the closest one will answer the call and assign IP addresses accordingly.

Just one problem: Someday, you may need the IP address of the access point or router, and you may have forgotten that you changed it to 192.168.1.20 (or whatever). To minimize confusion, I stick a piece of masking tape on all my routers, modems, and access points and write the IP address on the top. Cheap and effective — I like it.

Although it's possible to go diving into the DHCP server settings on the router or on the modem, you don't need to. By setting the starting IP address on the router to something different from the starting IP address on the modem (and you aren't unlucky enough to choose an IP address that's being used for something else), you move each of the mother hens into her own, separate henhouse — end of fighting. All is right in the world.

Book VIII
Using Other Hardware

"Ms. Gretsky, tell the employees they can have Internet games on their computers again."

Contents at a Glance

Chapter 1: Finding and Installing the Hardware You Need

In This Chapter

- **Discovering what upgrades will improve your Windows 7 experience**
- **Making basic hardware upgrades**
- **Choosing a new monitor**
- **Troubleshooting new hardware installations**

Let's face facts: You don't need all the fastest, most expensive gadgets to get value out of your computer. On the other hand, equipment that fits your needs can help you do more and better work in less time.

You can spend a whole lot of money on toys and gewgaws that, ultimately, end up collecting dust. You can spend a pittance on items that you'll use every day. Unfortunately, it's hard to tell in advance whether a specific, fancy new WhipperSnapper II belongs to the former group or the latter.

This chapter reviews the common computer thingies now available to help you decide whether any of them would be valuable to you. I take a special look at the hardware that's supposed to make Windows 7 work faster.

I've had a great deal of luck in upgrading three- or four-year-old Windows XP PCs to Windows 7: In many cases, a little more memory (goose it up to 1GB) and a decent video card (widely available for, say, $50 or less) provide all the oomph necessary to get Windows 7 humming, on hardware that's more than a little past its prime.

In subsequent chapters, I take a specific look at hard drives, and printers and multifunction devices (you know, copier/scanner/faxer/coffee-warmer/foot-massager appliances). I also discuss Device Stage, a feature that debuted in Windows 7, which may make using hardware less, uh, hard.

Knowing What Windows 7 Wants

Do you have an old PC sitting in a corner, doing an uninspiring job of running Windows XP or (worse) Vista? Does your friendly local computer store advertise a pile of unsold computers, reduced in price because they're past their prime?

Not to worry, mate. That old hunk of iron may be usable yet.

In the course of writing this book, I tried running Windows 7 on all sorts of odd pieces of hardware. Here's what I found:

- Many systems that run like slugs under Vista perform significantly — noticeably — better with Windows 7.
- Fairly recent Windows XP desktop systems, when fed a little extra memory and a video card worthy of the name, can handle Windows 7 quite well.

- Old Windows XP laptops, on the other hand, don't do well with Windows 7. The primary culprit: lack of oomph in the video department.
- Almost any new system — even one that's been discounted heavily — runs Windows 7 very well. Get the memory up to 1GB or more and install a better video card, and you're done.

Let me tell you a story: Last month, I hopped down to my friendly local PC dealer, looking for a dirt-cheap PC to run Windows 7. I found a discontinued HP Pavilion — dozens of them — that the retailer had marked down to $225. Very basic stuff: Dual core Pentium, 1GB of memory, 160GB hard drive, integrated Intel GMA 3100 video driver, PCI Express slots.

Bravely pursuing Windows 7 enlightenment, I tore open the case and installed a used video card that I had lying around the office. It sports an NVIDIA GeForce 8600 GT chip with 256MB of memory. You can buy the same card at many discount shops for $50 or less.

I installed Windows 7 on the machine, and it proved positively snappy. The Windows Experience Index (see Book II, Chapter 4) came in at 5.3 (see Figure 1-1). That's a mighty good showing for a $300 PC.

A 5.3 score makes this discount Pavilion almost as fast as my (ridiculously expensive) two-year-old production machine. If anything, it feels faster.

Moral of the story: You don't need to spend a fortune to improve your PC's performance. As you work through the nitty-gritty details in this chapter, keep that simple fact in mind.

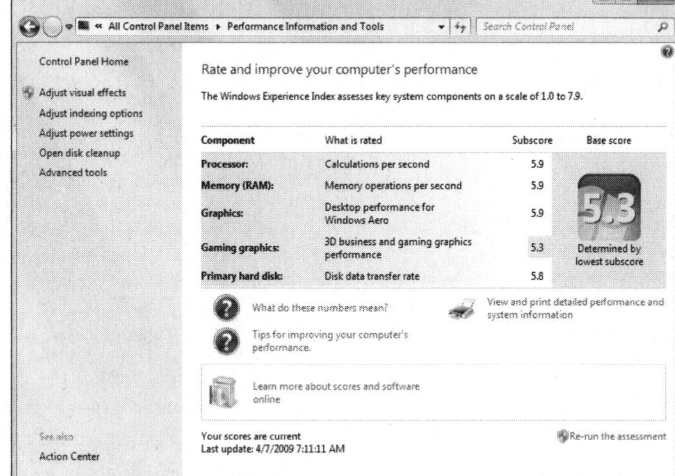

Figure 1-1: The Windows Experience Index score for a super-discounted $300 PC.

Upgrading the Basic Stuff

You probably have a printer, but it may not suit your needs — heck, photo-quality printers are so good and cheap nowadays that I'm frequently tempted to throw my old printer out the window. Your monitor may have died — or you might've noticed that gorgeous 29-inch flat-panel monitor winking at you across the aisle at your local Comput-O-Rama. Perhaps that giant 120GB hard drive you bought two years ago doesn't look so gigantic any more — particularly because the kids discovered how easy it is to transfer pictures taken on digital cameras.

Be of good cheer. For the most part, basic upgrades under Windows 7 are as slick as can be.

A few popular upgrades, such as adding a second (or third) hard drive and choosing a new printer, are beyond the scope of this book. You can find tips and basics for choosing and installing new hard drives (both internal ones and external ones) and printers at Dummies.com. Or check out *Upgrading and Fixing PCs For Dummies,* 7th Edition, by Andy Rathbone (Wiley) for more in-depth coverage.

Dealing with drivers

Most types of devices raise the question of compatibility: Will this gadget work with Windows 7? You can dissect that question a thousand different ways, but the real acid test is a simple one: Is a good driver available for the hardware? (A *driver* is a program that allows Windows 7 to interact with the hardware.)

In most cases, the answer is yes, simply because Microsoft now hounds hardware manufacturers who have the temerity to distribute bad drivers. Because Windows 7 is almost identical to Vista where the driver rubber meets the road, almost any driver that works for Vista is good for Windows 7, too. The same cannot be said for Windows XP drivers. If you're looking at a piece of hardware that has Windows XP support but no Vista support, pass it by. Windows 7 won't like it.

A high-level 'Softie I know once told me that 50 percent of all the tech support calls Microsoft has to answer deal with bad drivers. That's powerful incentive — and the main reason why Windows 7 wants to "phone home" when it crashes.

Most Windows 7 crashes, and a big part of the Microsoft Product Support team's workload, stem from bad device drivers — that Microsoft didn't write!

As hard as it may be to believe, that new piece of hardware you just bought may require no driver because its interface to the computer is completely standardized so that Windows 7 can operate any device of the same type. Most (but not all!) keyboards, monitors, and mice work like that. Any such device may have unique features that are available only with an appropriate driver, though.

Choosing a new monitor

Once upon a time, cathode ray tube (CRT) screens ruled the roost: They were hot enough to fry an egg and were prone to flicker and have wavy lines; the big ones weighed as much as an elephant — a *big* elephant. Nowadays, liquid crystal displays (LCDs) have taken over, and even newer technology appears just around the corner.

Before you buy a new monitor, make sure that you read an unbiased review (or ten) written by people who sit down in front of a bunch of monitors and compare them all side by side. I tend to look at CNET Reviews (`reviews.cnet.com`). You might also want to use Google.

If you opt for an LCD monitor — and most people do — consider the following information:

- **If you play games or work with fast-moving images, make sure that you can put up with a specific LCD's response time before you buy it.** LCDs are notorious for not keeping pace with some games, turning crisp images of, oh, smashing taxi cabs into mushy blobs of smashing taxi cabs. Come to think of it, maybe there isn't all that much difference.

  An LCD's *response time* is the amount of time it takes for a pixel to change from black to white and back to black, although some manufacturers measure the (much faster) time necessary to change colors. If you spend your working day, uh, working, a 10 or even 12 millisecond (ms) response time suffices. If you watch video or play games, look for 5 ms or better. Some people say that they can see a difference with 2 ms response times. If you think you might want 2 ms, make sure that you compare fast and (relatively) slow monitors side-by-side and see whether it's worth the difference in price.

- **The manufacturing process occasionally produces screens with dead pixels.** A dead pixel shows up as a black spot (or some other nonmatching color) in the image. Most manufacturers consider an LCD display functional if it has no more than three dead pixels, but a single dead pixel may drive you crazy, especially if it sits near the middle of the screen. If you look at a screen and immediately notice its dead pixel or pixels, pass it by or return it.

  Go to `gdargaud.net/Hack/DeadPixels.html` for a useful dead-pixel detector.

- **An LCD can be difficult to read from certain angles, particularly far from the screen's centerline.** This situation can be a problem if several people at a time have to watch the computer screen.

For more information on what to look for in a monitor, read on.

Eliminating the video card middleman

CRT monitors live in an analog world: They're controlled by signals that vary in strength, much as a television attached to a Nintendo gets driven by three cables controlling the red, green, and blue colors.

LCD monitors, on the other hand, are all digital, all the time. Internally, they control each dot on the screen with 1s and 0s, on and off, just like your computer.

The video card was invented specifically because the bits inside your computer needed to drive an analog monitor. The video card translated 1s and 0s inside the computer into varying-intensity red, green, and blue dots on the screen. In short, video cards served as digital-to-analog converters, feeding signals to CRT monitors.

Times have changed. It doesn't make any sense for the video card to translate bits into an analog signal, only to have an LCD monitor translate the analog signal back into bits. That's the crux of the Digital Visual Interface (DVI) plugs: Eliminate the video-card middleman.

More and more LCD monitors come equipped with DVI plugs. More and more video cards come equipped with DVI ports (see Figure 1-2). Unlike the old D-shaped VGA plugs, which have 15 round pins arranged in 3 rows of 5 each, the much larger and more rectangular DVI plugs have a single flat pin and (usually) 24 round ones, in an asymmetrical pattern.

Figure 1-2: The ATI Radeon HD 4890 offers two DVI ports and occupies a PCIe x16 slot.

Photo courtesy AMD Corporation.

If you have a choice, go with DVI. It's faster and more reliable than the old VGA interface — and the pins are less likely to get crunched when your ham-fisted cousin starts switching around monitors.

Choosing a screen resolution

A flat-screen monitor's *native resolution* is the number of image-forming dots, or pixels, that the monitor can display horizontally and vertically. Although you can adjust the resolution on CRT displays to infinitesimal sizes and squint with the consequences, for the most part, adjusting an LCD screen to any resolution other than its native resolution leaves your eyes begging for mercy.

The grid of dots in a flat-panel display is fixed — the modified screen resolution is a sleight of hand, performed by interpolating among dots on the grid. So it's important to choose a monitor with a native resolution you can live with.

Smaller and older screens conform to the 4:3 aspect ratio: 800 x 600 and 1024 x 768 resolutions are both 4:3 aspect ratios. (See the nearby sidebar, "Taking a look at aspect ratio," for more on aspect ratios.) Typical standard format (non-wide-screen) 17-inch and 19-inch screens run at 1280 x 1024, which isn't exactly 4:3 (it's actually 5:4), but you don't notice much distortion when viewing material meant to be seen at 4:3. For wide-screen measurements, see Table 1-1.

Table 1-1 Typical Wide-Screen Resolutions

Diagonal Measurement (Inches)	*Resolution*	*Aspect Ratio*
19	1440 x 900	16:10
22	1680 x 1050	16:10
23	2048 x 1152	16:9
24	1920 x 1080 (high-definition TV resolution)	16:9
24	1920 x 1200	16:10
27	1920 x 1200	16:10
30	2560 x 1600	16:10

I think the easiest way to understand the effect of changing screen resolution is to consider the effect of screen resolution on a plain-vanilla Excel 2007 spreadsheet:

- ✦ At 800 x 600 resolution, you can see cells A1 through L19 — or 228 cells — on a virgin spreadsheet.
- ✦ At 1024 x 768, you can see cells A1 through O27, or a total of 405 cells. That's 78 percent more usable cells than the 800 x 600 resolution offers.
- ✦ At 1280 x 1024, Excel 2007 shows cells A1 through S40, for a grand total of 760 cells. That's 88 percent more cells than at 1024 x 768 and more than three times as many as 800 x 600 offers.
- ✦ Jump to 1920 x 1200, and you see A1 through AC49, for a whopping 25,921 cells — 33 times as many as with a 1280 x 1024 screen, and very nearly 100 *times* as many as a spreadsheet at 800 x 600.

Taking a look at aspect ratio

If you've ever wondered why movies appear onscreen with a black band at the top and bottom, or why your photos get cut off a little differently on 8-by-10 prints as opposed to 6-by-9s, you've bumped into the effects of the aspect ratio.

The *aspect ratio* of a picture is the ratio of the picture's width to its height. For many years, televisions and (almost) all computer screens used the 4:3 aspect ratio, where the ratio of a screen's width to height is 4 to 3. In the following figure, you see a photo taken with a typical electronic camera. It produces pictures in a 4:3 aspect ratio.

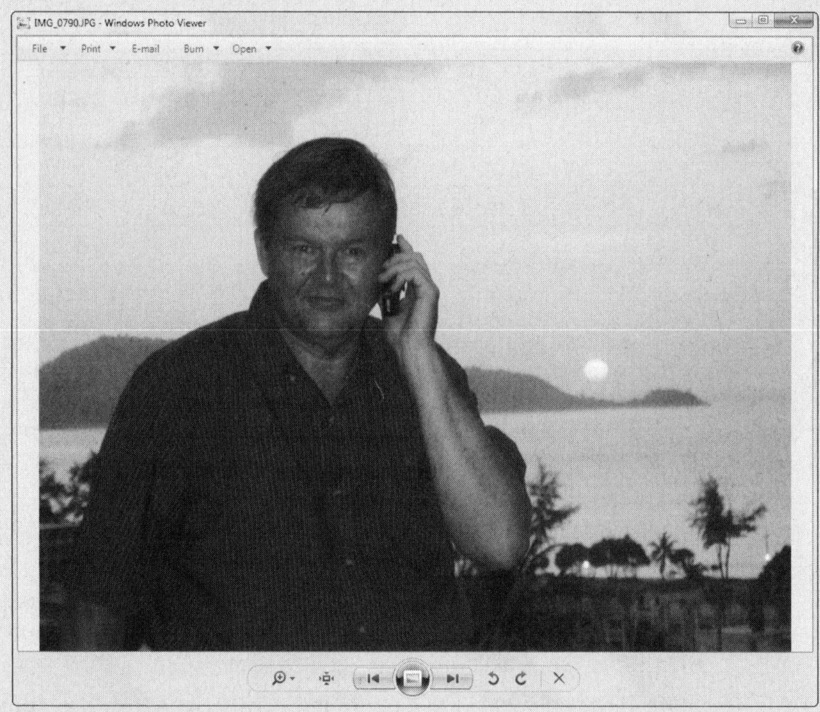

The earliest movies were shot at 4:3, but Hollywood quickly found that wider screens led to more spectacular films. Over time, the aspect ratio for movies changed, but TV stayed the same — and computer screens aped TV.

Nowadays, Hollywood movies use several different aspect ratios, but home theaters all over the world have mostly settled on the 16:9 aspect ratio (shown in the following figure), which has become the standard for high-definition TV (HDTV).

Although you probably won't spend most of your time sweating over 25,000-cell spreadsheets, this little comparison combined with a lot of experience leads me to a few simple generalizations:

- ✦ Any modern monitor you buy can handle 1280 x 1024 resolution just fine. If you're staring at a screen that has 1280 x 1024 resolution, you can see most of a page in Word or Excel. For most Windows users, that's good enough.
- ✦ If you go with a wide-screen monitor, you can put two spreadsheets on the monitor side-by-side, or see at least half of two different pages in Word, even at the lowest common resolution of 1440 x 900. Because of that, wide-screens make sense for most people who use a monitor all day long. They're also good for watching movies, but I digress.
- ✦ Really big screens make an enormous difference if you have less-than-stellar eyesight, suffer from eyestrain, or commonly work with full pages in Word or big spreadsheets in Excel. They're also quite handy if you want to let other people look at what you're doing.

You can also look into the possibility of running two monitors side by side — doubling the amount of screen you can see at the expense of exercising some neck muscles. Windows 7 makes setting up two monitors easy (see the next section), and most video cards these days will play along.

Do you own a monitor but you don't know its native resolution? As in so many other areas, Google is your friend. If you have a Samsung SyncMaster 226BW, for example, just run a Google search for *SyncMaster 226BW native resolution.* Bingo.

I use a 27-inch Dell wide-screen monitor on my production machine. I love it. My eyes love it. I consider it to be one of the best computer investments I've ever made — right up there with a good chair and an ancient keyboard (see "Upgrading keyboards," later in this chapter). You may not need that much real estate — and, yes, it's hard to justify the expense. But, oh, the views!

Changing resolutions and multiple monitors

To change your screen resolution (and set up a second monitor), follow these steps:

1. **Right-click in any blank place on the Windows desktop and choose Screen Resolution.**

   You see the Display Settings dialog box, shown in Figure 1-3, where you can set up multiple monitors.

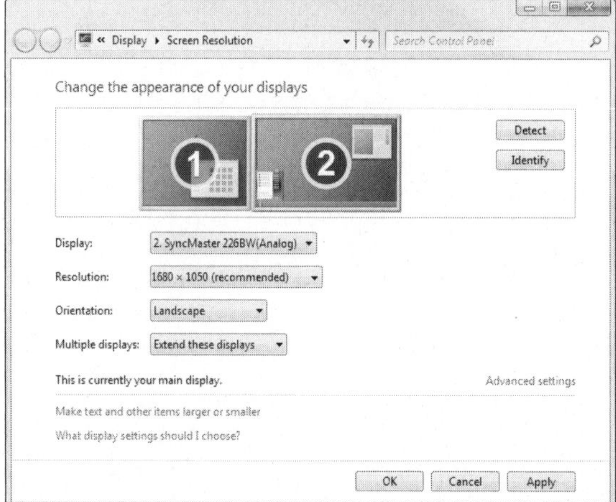

Figure 1-3: Set up one or more monitors.

2. **Click the 1 box to set up your first monitor and 2 to set up the second.**

   If you can't figure out which monitor is which, click the Identify Monitors button. Windows 7 puts a big *1* on Monitor 1 and a big *2* on Monitor 2.

3. **If you have more than one monitor, you can also choose where to show the desktop (see Table 1-2 for details).**

4. **To change the resolution on either display, click either the 1 monitor or the 2 monitor, and then adjust the resolution using the slider shown in Figure 1-4.**

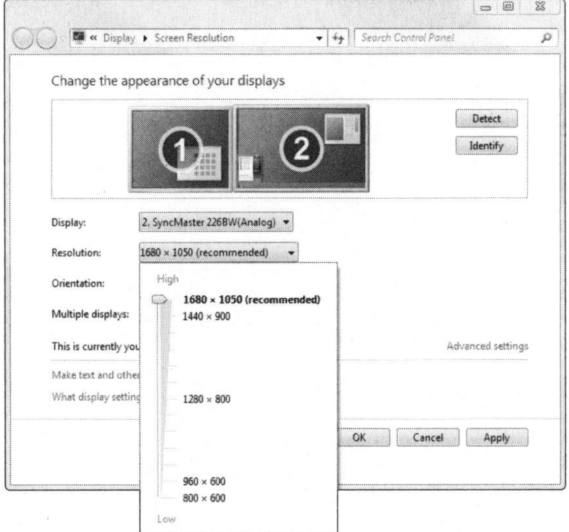

Figure 1-4: Adjusting the resolution on a correctly identified LCD monitor always results in fuzzy text.

If Windows 7 properly identified your monitor and you have a sufficiently powerful video card, this dialog box should already show the monitor's native resolution. Be intensely aware of the fact that lowering the resolution of your LCD screen, below its native resolution, only makes the text look worse. (See the preceding section to find your monitor's native resolution.)

If Windows doesn't let you set your monitor to its native resolution, you need to get a better video card. Some video cards can't support odd resolutions, and very high resolutions require capable cards. You're trying to pump 10 pounds of video from a 5-pound card.

5. **Click the Apply button.**

   Windows 7 changes the display's resolution and opens a dialog box that asks whether you want to keep the new settings.

6. **Click the Keep Changes button to keep the new settings or click Revert to return to the old ones.**

   If the display disappears or becomes unreadable, press Esc to return to the old settings. (Or, if you wait 15 seconds, Windows 7 returns to the old settings automatically.) If you can't read the screen, you chose a resolution that your monitor can't display.

7. **When you're done, click the OK button to close the Display Settings dialog box.**

Table 1-2 Multiple-Monitor Desktop Settings

Setting Name	*Shown on Monitor 1*	*Shown on Monitor 2*
Duplicate These Displays	The usual Windows desktop	Exactly the same as Monitor 1
Extend These Displays	The usual Windows desktop	A blank area where you can drag and drop anything you like; behaves as though it's to the right of Monitor 1
Show Desktop Only on 1	The usual Windows desktop	Nothing
Show Desktop Only on 2	Nothing	The usual Windows desktop

Picking a video adapter

Windows 7 places high demands on your video card. Many people find that upgrading their video cards delivers more noticeable punch than almost any other hardware improvement.

The best way to judge whether you need a new video card? Look at your Windows Experience Index (see Book II, Chapter 4). My score is shown at the beginning of this chapter (refer to Figure 1-1). If you don't play many games and your Graphics score falls much more than a point below all the other scores — or if you're a gamer and the Gaming Graphics score sits more than a point below the others — you're a good candidate for a video card upgrade.

To check out the latest in video card technology, offerings, and prices, I trust the reviews at Tom's Hardware (`tomshardware.com`).

When you choose a new video adapter, consider these points:

✦ **Superfast and superexpensive video cards don't do squat for most people.** Unless you're a fanatic gamer, look for video cards in the $100-and-under range.

✦ **If your monitor has a Digital Visual Interface, get a video card with a DVI port.** It's worth paying extra. Trust me. (For more on DVI, check out the "Eliminating the video card middleman" section, earlier in this chapter.)

✦ **Buy a card with a good fan.** Video cards generate a lot of heat. Dissipate, dissipate, dissipate.

Heat has become a major problem with video cards: hot cards get reliability problems. The generated heat can swirl around inside your PC and mess up other components. Some cards produce as much heat as the main computer chip on your motherboard. Most Windows 7–class video cards come with a built-in fan and heat sink, which draws away heat from the processing unit and video memory and dumps it into your computer's main case. If your computer is having heat problems — random screen freezes for no apparent reason or spontaneous reboots, for example — consider buying a dual-slot video card, with an oversize fan that forces air from the case, by way of openings in the second slot's mounting bracket.

If you're feeling handy, you can also buy and install a video card cooler, complete with its own heat sink, fan, and exhaust mounting bracket. For an example, see `driverheaven.net/guides/videocooling`.

In my experience, the single greatest source of frustration with Windows since its inception has been lousy video drivers. I've seen it happen year in and year out, in every version of Windows, with every video card manufacturer. Windows 7 is no exception. Video card manufacturers take a long time to produce decent drivers for their wares — and when they have stable drivers, the pressure to incorporate new features frequently leads to unstable newer versions. If you buy a new video card, make sure that you check the manufacturer's Web site for the latest Windows 7 driver before installing the card. And, always keep your old video card, just in case the new one simply doesn't work.

You can take solace in the fact that video drivers these days are as big and complex as Windows 98. Hard to believe, but true.

Upgrading keyboards

Face it: The keyboard that came with your computer wouldn't even make a decent boat anchor. Don't get me wrong. Those mushy, squishy, Tinkertoy keyboards would make fine Cracker Jack prizes, and casual computer users can get by with them for years. I wouldn't look down my nose at your flimsy, somnambulant, ludicrous excuse for a keyboard. Sniff.

Seriously, if you spend more than a few hours a day at the computer, you're probably wondering why your fingers hurt and why you make so many mistakes typing. There's a good reason: That keyboard you're using probably cost a dollar. Maybe less. Getting a new one can make a big difference in how well you type and can speed your computing enormously. You know — so that you can get a life. . . .

Several companies now make ergonomic keyboards, which are contoured to let you type with your hands in a position that (supposedly) reduces the stress on them; these keyboards take some getting used to, but some users swear by them. (Personally, I swear *at* them.)

If you've been using a "straight" keyboard, make sure that you can adjust to a split ergonomic keyboard before you buy one. I know a lot of people who have given up in disgust when their fingers couldn't adapt to the ergonomic split.

You can get a wireless keyboard. Keep in mind, though, that wireless keyboards have batteries that wear out. And, with regular wired keyboards, you don't have to worry about interference or blocked sensors. Sure, cables are ugly, but they're quite reliable.

You can also get a keyboard with a built-in pointing device to replace the mouse. Heck, you can probably get one that looks like Mickey Mouse.

If you're serious about replacing your tin-can keyboard, keep these points in mind:

- **Look for a keyboard that feels right.** Some folks like quiet keys. I like 'em loud. Some people prefer keys with short throws — ones you don't have to push very far. I like long throws. Some prefer minimal tactile feedback — when you push the key, it doesn't push back. I like lots of tactile feedback. Most current keyboards have a row of function keys across the top. I like mine on the left. Everybody's different, and the only way you're going to find a keyboard you like is to try dozens of them.
- **Expensive keyboards aren't necessarily better than cheap ones.** And, big-name keyboards aren't necessarily better than generics.
- **Heavy keyboards are better than light ones, unless you're going to schlep your keyboard with you on your travels through Asia.** Heavy keyboards with rubber feet stay put.

Benj Edwards at *PC World* has an excellent review and slide show of the inner workings of the IBM Model M keyboard — likely the best keyboard of all time — at `tinyurl.com/6hj6e4`.

Which keyboard do I use? An old Northgate OmniKey Ultra (see Figure 1-5), which is surely the Sherman tank of the keyboard biz. The beast weighs almost as much as a portable computer, and it costs just under $200. You can't find new ones any more — you have to buy them refurbished. It's ugly, it's retro, and it's decidedly unhip. But it keeps goin' and goin'. It's available from `northgate-keyboard-repair.com`, one of the few places that sell the classics.

For the brave of heart, eBay is full of good old clickity-clack ancient AT/IBM-PC style keyboards for less than half the price of the Northgate. Most of them require only an AT-to-PS/2 adapter (available at most computer stores) to plug into a modern computer.

Figure 1-5: Refurbished Northgate OmniKey Ultra.

Choosing a mouse — or alternatives

Mice are probably available in more varieties than any other computer accessory. You can find mice with special ergonomic profiles, colored mice, transparent mice, special mice designed for kids, and on and on.

Laser and optical mice now rule the roost. An optical mouse uses a light-emitting diode (LED) light source and sensor to detect movement over a flat surface. It has no rolling ball to slip or stick, and it rarely needs to be cleaned. You may find this model particularly helpful if you have furry pets and your mouse tends to get clogged by their hair. Laser mice use an infrared laser diode, but otherwise function in much the same way. They're significantly more sensitive than optical mice.

Right now, my favorite mouse is a Microsoft Natural Wireless Laser Mouse (see Figure 1-6). I never thought I'd convert to a wireless mouse, but this funny-looking critter fits my hand precisely, and the laser tracking works remarkably well.

Figure 1-6: My personal favorite: the Microsoft Natural Wireless Laser Mouse 6000.

Photo courtesy Microsoft Corporation.

Some folks prefer a trackball to a mouse. A *trackball* is a stationary device with a large ball resting in a cup on the top. You operate it by turning the ball with your palm or thumb. I hate 'em.

Some folks like to use a graphics *tablet* rather than or in addition to a mouse. You control software with a graphics tablet by touching its surface with a special stylus. Unlike a mouse, the graphics tablet detects position, not motion, so you can literally point at the item you want. You can even write or draw with the stylus. Graphics tablets are popular with serious users of photo editors and other graphics software, and they're becoming more popular since Microsoft started producing "digital ink" programs such as OneNote, which can read what you write, to a first approximation, anyway. Many of these applications have special graphics tablet support and can detect the amount of pressure you're applying to the stylus. Thus, you can press hard to draw a wide line, for example, or lightly to draw a thin line.

Tablet PCs — the kind that are designed to be used with a stylus and (almost invariably) OneNote — aren't for everyone. Some people love them. Most people don't get used to them. I count myself among the latter. If you ever think about buying a Tablet PC specifically for its note-taking capabilities, try to borrow one for a day or two before you plunk down the cash. You may find that the reality doesn't live up to the glitz. Or, you may find that you love it!

A *touchpad* is similar to a graphics tablet, but you control it with your fingertip rather than a stylus. Touchpads and belly buttons (er, pointer sticks) are common on notebook computers. You "click" by tapping the pad. A touchpad is convenient for moving the pointer around the screen, but because most people's fingers are less pointy than a stylus, it's not useful for drawing or writing. Touchpads usually are just a few inches long and wide, and cost $20 to $50, whereas graphics tablets are larger and cost $100 or more.

All mice designed for Windows computers are compatible with Windows 7. Specialized devices such as graphics tablets may require special drivers; make sure that the device you buy is Windows 7 compatible.

Key drives and ReadyBoost

Although Windows has been *prefetching* data — going out to the hard drive and loading certain files that the system feels are likely to be needed — since the days of Windows XP, Vista brought a new capability to the table. Windows 7 SuperFetch, like the Vista version, keeps track of the data and programs you commonly use on your machine and tries to load that data before it's used.

Prefetching doesn't help much if you don't have a lot of system memory: The stuff that's prefetched has a nasty habit of turning stale and getting shuffled off to Buffalo, er, sent back to the hard drive, thus negating any benefit of prefetching it. Windows 7 lets you use a USB key drive as kind of a scratch pad for prefetching: Rather than prefetch files from the hard drive and stick them in main memory before they're needed, Windows 7 can retrieve the files and store them on a dedicated chunk of real estate on a key drive. Because grabbing data from a key drive is about 10 or 20 times faster than pulling it in off a rotating platter, this *ReadyBoost,* as it's called, can make fetching work better. ReadyBoost also works independently of SuperFetch, as kind of a superfast cache.

The simple fact is that ReadyBoost doesn't help most PCs. After playing with it a bit, I've come up with a simple rule of thumb: If your computer has less than 512MB of memory and it would cost a fortune to add more memory, use a 512MB or 1GB key drive for ReadyBoost. Otherwise, fuhgeddaboutit.

Getting more out of USB

Your Windows computer probably has two, four, or six USB ports, but you can attach many more USB devices to it than that. In theory, you can attach 127 USB devices to one computer. If you keep that many devices, you probably have no space left to sit down!

To attach additional devices, you need the USB equivalent of a power strip to turn one connector into several. That device is a *USB hub.*

A USB hub has one USB connector to attach it to a computer and several connectors to attach it to devices. Hubs most often have either four or seven device connectors.

ASKWOODY.COM

If you run out of USB ports, get a *powered* USB hub — one that draws electricity from a wall plug (like the one shown in Figure 1-7). That way, you protect against power drains on your computer's motherboard. If possible, plug your USB hub into an uninterruptible power supply (UPS) so that a sudden loss of power doesn't cause a surge down the USB hub's power supply.

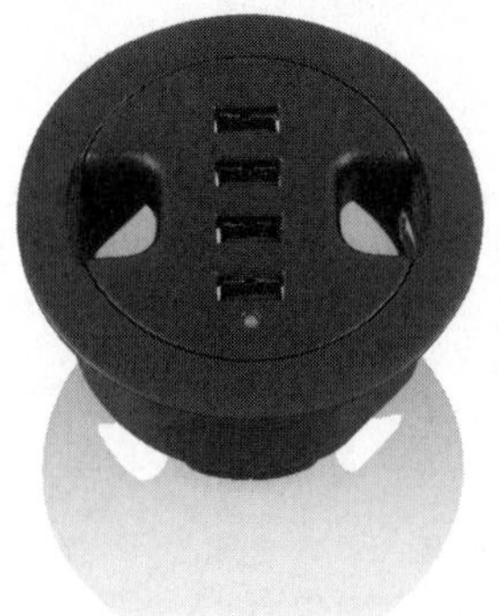

Figure 1-7: The Belkin In-Desk USB Hub fits into the hole in your desk, leaving room for cables.

Photo courtesy Belkin International.

You can plug one USB hub into another — *daisy-chain* them — to attach more devices than a single hub can support.

You can string USB cable forever and a day, but if you go much more than 16 feet (5 meters) with a single cable, you're stretching things thin. If you daisy-chain powered hubs, you can probably get away with a total run of 80 feet (25 meters) between the PC and the farthest-out USB-connected peripheral.

Understanding flash memory and USB key drives

Regular computer memory — random access memory (RAM) — needs a constant supply of power to keep going. *Flash memory* is a special kind of computer memory that doesn't self-destruct when the power goes out. Technically a type of Electronically Erasable Programmable Read-Only Memory (EEPROM), flash memory comes in many different kinds of packages.

If you spend any time using electronic cameras, you probably know all about memory cards — Secure Digital (SD), Compact Flash (CF), and Smart Media (SM) cards — and if you've been around Sony equipment, you also know about memory sticks. All of them rely on flash memory.

For us unrepentant computer types, flash memory also comes in a little package — frequently the size and shape of a pack of gum — with a USB connector on the end. You can call it a USB flash memory stick, a key drive, a USB drive, a key-chain drive (people really use them as key chains? I dunno — my favorite key chain looks like Watto from *Star Wars*), a pocket drive, a pen drive, a USB key, or a USB stick (that's what my cables do when they get old).

Here's how hard it is to use a USB drive in Windows 7:

1. **Plug the USB drive into a USB slot.**

   If the USB drive you stick in a USB slot has an AutoRun autostarting program on it, you see an AutoPlay notification, like the one shown in Figure 1-8.

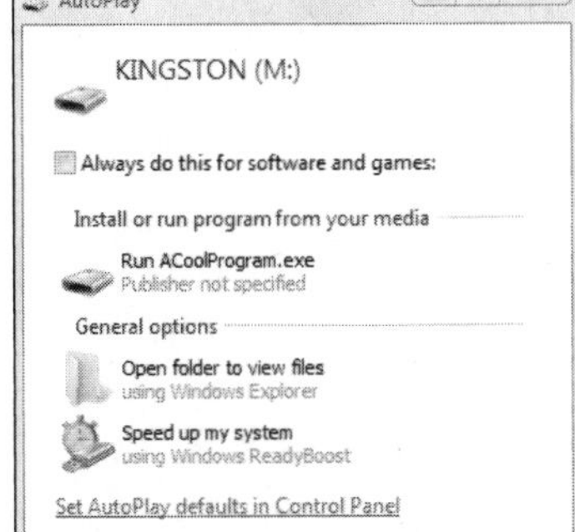

Figure 1-8: Your AutoRun options.

2. **Click one of the AutoPlay options.**

   You're done.

Some parts of the AutoPlay notification (refer to Figure 1-8) can be controlled by settings in files sitting on the USB drive itself. The Conficker worm, for example, takes advantage of AutoPlay programmability and tries to trick you into running the worm by using some clever wording. Figure 1-9 shows the AutoPlay notification that appears when you stick a Conficker-infected USB drive into a USB slot.

Figure 1-9: The entry marked Install or Run Program is bogus, generated by Conficker.

If you look closely at Figure 1-9, you see how Conficker can paste a folder icon in the Install or Run Program area. Conficker tries to trick you into running an infectious program by clicking the Open Folder to View Files link in the middle. I have details on how Conficker jimmies Windows into showing bogus AutoPlay entries in my Windows Secrets Newsletter article at `tinyurl.com/dbgndc` with further details at `tinyurl.com/mck9ys`.

When it comes to buying a USB drive, the salespeople would have you believe that it's cool to have color-coded sticks (I just put a sticker on mine), fancy encrypted memory (so that if somebody steals the stick, it takes him ten minutes, rather than ten seconds, to look at the data), designer outsides, and on and on. Here's what I say:

- ✦ Buy twice the amount of memory you think you need — you'll use it someday.
- ✦ Go for the lowest price.

If you need to read the other kinds of flash memory — memory cards, the kind normally used in cameras and MP3 players — buy a cheap, generic, USB multiformat memory card reader. It shouldn't set you back more than $10, and it can come in quite handy.

Installing New Hardware

If you have a USB device — a printer, hard drive, scanner, camera, flash memory card, foot massager, water desalination plant, or demolition machine for a new intergalactic highway — just plug the device into a USB port, and you're ready to go.

Okay. I exaggerated a little bit.

Two fundamentally different approaches to installing new hardware exist. It amazes me that some people never even consider the possibility of doing it themselves, whereas other people wouldn't have the store install new hardware for them on a bet!

Having the store do it

When you buy a new hard drive or video card, or anything else that goes inside your computer, why sweat the installation? For a few extra bucks, most stores can install what they sell. This is the easy, safe way. Rather than mess around with unfamiliar gadgets, which may be complicated and delicate, let somebody with experience do the work for you.

Different types of hardware present different levels of difficulty. It may make plenty of sense for you to install one type of device but not another.

At one end of the scale, installing a new video card or hard drive can be rather difficult and is best done by an expert. At the other end, speakers don't need any installation; you just plug them in and they work. The store can show you where the connectors go, but you have to plug them in yourself when you get home.

Here are some guidelines to help you judge how difficult an installation is likely to be:

- ✦ Any device that goes inside your computer is best left to the store unless you have experience with that specific kind of computer hardware.
- ✦ A device with a USB interface is usually easy; nine times out of ten, you just plug it in and it works.
- ✦ Most modern wireless networking systems are inserted with nary a hiccup.

A cable modem should be installed by the communication carrier's technician, if at all possible. Digital subscriber line (DSL) modems are easier to install, but you have to know whether your phone line is ready. The modem just plugs in, but the telephone line or cable may require configuration or rewiring to deliver the signal properly.

If you're unsure whether to install something yourself, ask the store which steps are involved. If you decide to try it but the instructions confuse you or scare you when you read them, don't be embarrassed to go back and ask for help. I do.

Doing it yourself

If you decide to install a device yourself, the job is more likely to go smoothly if you observe these guidelines:

- ✦ **Don't just dive in — read the instructions first!** Pay attention to any warnings they give. Look for steps where you may have trouble. Are any of the instructions unclear? Does the procedure require any software or parts that appear to be missing? Try to resolve these potential problems ahead of time.

  Having said that, I readily admit that I never install the software for a camera or a mobile phone. I just use the built-in Windows utilities, in Windows Live Photo Gallery and Windows Media Player. For my iPod, I follow the advice in Book IV, Chapter 2, and for other MP3 players, I just use Windows Media Player.

- ✦ **Back up your system before you start.** It's unlikely that your attempt to install a new device will disturb your system if it fails, but a backup is a good insurance policy in case something bad happens. You need to back up your data files. Windows 7 can create a system checkpoint and back up all the internal stuff.

- **Write down everything you do in case you need to undo it or ask for help.** This advice is particularly important if you're opening your computer to install an internal device!
- **If the device comes with a Windows 7 (or Vista) driver, check the manufacturer's Web site to see whether you have the latest version.** A company usually keeps drivers on one or more Web pages that you can find by clicking a Drivers, Downloads, or Support link. If you discover a version that's newer than the one packaged with the device, download it and install it instead.

  If you can't tell whether the version on the Web site is newer because you can't tell which version came with the device, you have two choices:

  - *Download and install the Web site's version just in case.* It's unlikely to be older than the one that came with the device!
  - *Install the one that came with the device.* Then check its date and version number. (See the next section). If the one on the Web site proves to be newer, download the newer one and install it. Read the instructions; you may need to uninstall the original driver first.

Checking a driver's version

To check the version number of a driver, follow these steps:

1. **Click the Start button. Right-click Computer and choose Properties. On the left, click the Device Manager link.**

   Windows 7 opens the Device Manager window, shown in Figure 1-10.

2. **Click the plus sign next to the heading that contains the device you want to check.**

   In Figure 1-10, I click the heading Display Adapters, and Windows shows me which display adapters are installed and recognized.

   You may have to try several headings to find the right one. If you guess wrong, just click again to collapse the heading you expanded.

3. **Double-click the device to open the Device Properties dialog box. Click the Driver tab to display details about the driver, as shown in Figure 1-11.**

   You should be able to identify the latest driver by its date or version number or both.

4. **Click the Update Driver button. When Windows asks, click to Search Automatically for Updated Driver Software.**

   Windows goes out to the big Microsoft driver database in the sky and retrieves and installs the latest driver.

Figure 1-10: The Device Manager window.

Figure 1-11: The driver date and version are easy to see.

Note that Windows does *not* automatically check the manufacturer's site for the latest drivers. Instead, it relies on the drivers that have been checked in to its driver database — and many of those drivers are weeks, months, or years out of date.

If you continue to have driver problems, go directly to the manufacturer's Web site and follow its instructions to download and install the latest.

Knowing what to do if anything goes wrong

If your driver installation goes belly-up, try these strategies in any order that makes sense to you:

- **Review the instructions.** Look for a section with a title such as "Troubleshooting" for suggestions on how to proceed.
- **Call or e-mail the manufacturer's technical support service for help.** The manual or the Web site can tell you how.
- **Call the store, or pack up everything and take it in.** If you happen to have a 7-foot-tall friend named Guido who drags his hairy knuckles on the ground, take him along with you. Moral support, eh?

If your computer no longer works correctly, restart Windows 7 with the last known good configuration. (See the instructions in the next section.)

Restarting with the last known good configuration

When you install a new device driver, you change the Windows 7 configuration. The next time you restart your computer, Windows 7 tries to use the new configuration. If it succeeds, it discards the old configuration and makes the new one current.

The whole process involves some smoke, a few mirrors, and the Windows Registry.

Sometimes, you install a new device driver and everything goes to heck in a handbasket. If that happens to you, restart Windows 7 and tell it to use the last known good configuration — which is to say, Windows should ignore the changes you made that screwed everything up and return to the state it was in the last time it started. That action effectively removes the new driver from Windows 7.

To start Windows with the last known good configuration, follow these steps:

1. **If your computer is working, click the Start button, click the right-facing arrow to the right of the little lock, and choose Restart.**

   Windows 7 restarts. Skip to Step 3.

2. **If your computer isn't operating, press the power button to turn it off. Wait a minute or so. Press the power button again to turn the computer back on.**

   If that doesn't work, try pressing the button again and holding it in for several seconds. If that doesn't work either, pull the power cord out of the back of the computer; wait a few seconds, and then plug it in again. If you're working with a laptop, you may have to remove the battery. Yes, it happens.

3. **As soon as the computer starts to come back to life, press and hold down F8.**

   Windows 7 displays a menu of special startup options you can choose.

4. **Use the up-arrow and down-arrow keys to move the menu's highlight to the option Last Known Good Configuration (Advanced), and then press Enter.**

5. **Finish the startup procedure as usual.**

If this procedure restarts your computer successfully, Windows 7 discards the "new" screwed-up configuration and returns permanently to the last known good configuration.

Installing USB hardware

Nine times out of ten, when you install a new USB device in a Windows 7 computer that has all the latest fixes, everything works easily. The general procedure works this way:

1. **Read the manual.**

   Some hardware installs automatically: Plug it in and it works. Most hardware needs a little help: You have to put a CD in the CD drive shortly after you plug it in and let Windows pull the driver off the CD. Some hardware, though, takes a little extra help, and you have to run an installation program from the product's CD before you plug it in.

   The only way to know for sure which approach works for the specific piece of hardware you bought is to read the furshlinger manual! Look for the section with instructions on installing the hardware on a Windows 7 computer. Failing that, look for Vista support. Follow the instructions.

2. **After you read the manual and do what it says, plug the USB device into any handy USB slot.**

   Windows realizes that you just installed a new USB device. Most of the time, Windows has a driver handy that will work and then installs it and notifies you that your new device is ready. In some cases, though, it brings up the Found New Hardware Wizard.

3. **Select the Yes, This Time Only link to let Microsoft see whether it has a new driver for the hardware.**

4. **Follow the rest of the steps in the wizard, and most times, you'll end up with a functioning device.**

5. **If you can't make the device work, check the Microsoft Knowledge Base articles for troubleshooting USB devices.**

   A good place to start: the old Vista tips for solving problems with USB devices, at `tinyurl.com/2vkuqv`.

Using Device Stage

If you're extremely lucky and you're installing a newer piece of hardware, you might have a gizmo that supports the Windows 7 standard known as Device Stage. If that's the case, pat yourself on the back, rub your lucky rabbit's foot (it won't do the rabbit any good), and move to the head of the class.

For more details about Device Stage, see Book VIII, Chapter 2.

Chapter 2: Using Device Stage

In This Chapter

- Understanding what Device Stage can — and cannot — do
- Controlling devices through Device Stage
- Connecting devices with Bluetooth

If you plug anything into your computer — printer, MP3 player, mobile phone, scanner, whatever — Device Stage can bring order to the chaos that has attended external devices since the dawn of the Windows age.

Before Windows 7, every printer manufacturer, every mobile phone manufacturer, every camera manufacturer had to come up with its own way of interacting with you, and its hardware, on your PC.

The problem doesn't lie so much with the drivers — some manufacturers make good drivers, and others make lousy ones, and that hasn't changed with Windows 7. The problem isn't with the custom applications that manufacturers offer — to retrieve photos from a camera, say, or set scanner preferences or adjust printer settings. (I rarely use a manufacturer's application when a built-in Windows application works just as well.)

The problem is that before Windows 7, every single lousy manufacturer had a completely different way of interacting with you, the user. Some placed pop-up messages or icons in the notification area. Others hooked into the AutoPlay box (see Book VIII, Chapter 1). More than a few expected you to know that you had to run their programs whenever you wanted to get things done.

Device Stage brings some structure to the problem. It isn't perfect — just for starters, each manufacturer has to build its own hooks into Device Stage, and applications and drivers remain the responsibility of the company that makes the machine, so quality can be iffy at best. But at least Device Stage represents a step in the right direction, giving us Windows consumers a single place to look and at least a little uniformity among the polyglot manufacturers.

This chapter explains how Device Stage *should* work — when manufacturers support it.

Getting a Grip on Device Stage

At the highest (some would say lowest) level, *Device Stage* is a gathering place for all the pieces of hardware you have stuck on your computer, plus any network devices that are accessible from your machine.

To see the collection, choose Start⇨Devices and Printers. Windows 7 presents you with the Devices and Printers list — known to the marketers as Device Stage (see Figure 2-1).

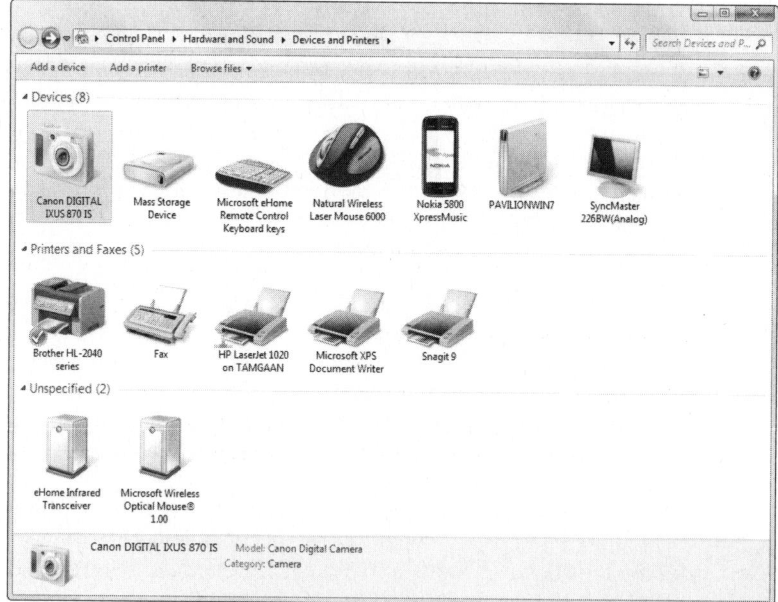

Figure 2-1: A gathering of devices.

Not all devices are Device Stage savvy, but the list of compatible products grows daily. You can tell whether your device works with Device Stage by double-clicking its name in the Devices and Printers folder and seeing whether any actions are specifically associated with it. For example, if I double-click the Nokia 5800 XpressMusic icon in Figure 2-1, I see the service page shown in Figure 2-2.

Depending on the device involved, the actions may include the ones in this list:

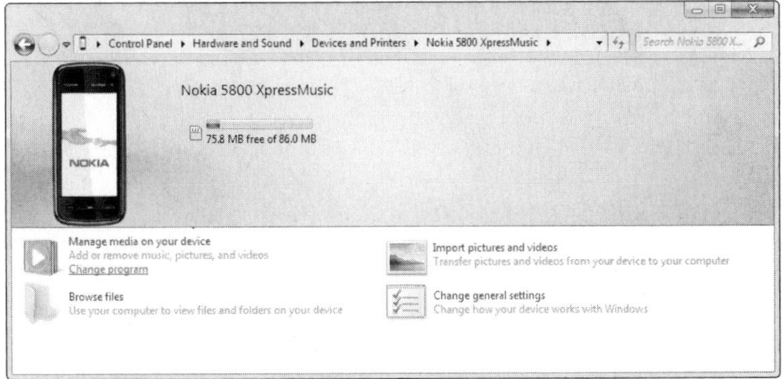

Figure 2-2: A Device Stage device has a service menu for manipulating it directly.

- ✦ Upload and download (syncing) music.
- ✦ Move pictures from the device to your PC.
- ✦ Adjust printer settings, such as the type and size of paper or the quality of the print.
- ✦ Download software updates for the device or for the programs running on your PC that support the device.
- ✦ Browse files on the device.
- ✦ Search the device's user manual.
- ✦ Choose among multiple functions for the device; stereotypically on multifunction printers, you would choose between print, scan, fax, and copy, for example.
- ✦ Run out to the Web for all manner of things.
- ✦ Change internal settings for the device, such as copy darkness or the way Windows reacts when you plug the device into your PC.
- ✦ Produce status reports that show, for example, the amount of memory being used (refer to Figure 2-2), the number of print jobs backed up, or the amount of ink left in the cartridges.
- ✦ Spend money on goodies for the device. (What? You didn't expect that one?)
- ✦ Make the device jump and sing and dance the boogaloo.

In addition, Device Stage–cognizant devices are rewarded for their technical acumen by having a picture of the device appear on the Windows taskbar. If you right-click the device, you see a jump list that includes all activities listed on the main menu, as shown in Figure 2-3.

Figure 2-3: The jump list.

Some Device Stage devices are added to the Windows right-click Send To menu. That makes it easy, for example, to send a music file to a mobile phone.

By contrast, when you double-click the names of devices that don't support Device Stage — such as the eHome Infrared Transceiver (refer to Figure 2-1) — you see the plain-vanilla Properties dialog box, like the one shown in Figure 2-4. That's the same Properties dialog box you see if you right-click the device and choose Properties. B-o-r-i-n-g.

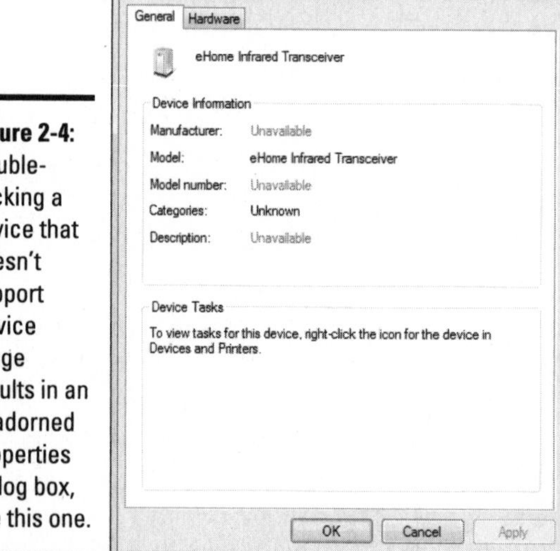

Figure 2-4: Double-clicking a device that doesn't support Device Stage results in an unadorned Properties dialog box, like this one.

Device manufacturers have to create a particular kind of file, an *XML* file, to make Device Stage work. The XML file is typically bundled with the driver. When you install a new device, Windows 7 looks for the driver and the XML file, and if it finds a well-constructed Device Stage–savvy package, you reap the benefits. Not all manufacturers feel compelled to provide Device Stage support, particularly for their older products. Hey, there's no money in it, right?

Taking Device Stage for a Spin

When things work the way they should, you can use Device Stage with a USB-attached device:

1. **Plug in the device.**

   Wait a while for the driver to be installed automatically.

2. **Choose Start⇨Devices and Printers.**

   You're done.

In many cases, you don't need to bother with Step 2 because an icon for your attached device shows up on the Windows taskbar. Life's tough, eh?

Many devices don't pin their icons to the Windows taskbar. If you want to see the icon all the time, you have to take the initiative. For example, the Brother HL-2040 printer, shown in Figure 2-5, has an icon but it disappears when the Devices and Printers window for the printer disappears.

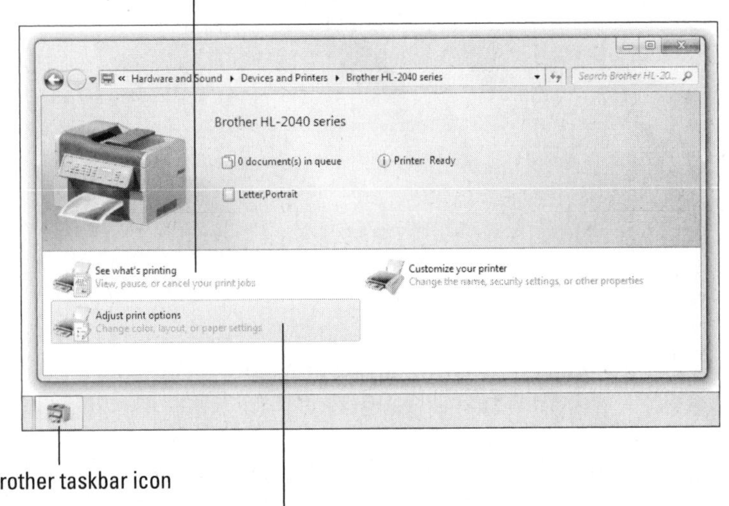

Figure 2-5: The Brother HL-2040, like most printers, doesn't put its icon on the Windows taskbar permanently.

Most devices work just fine with disappearing icons, but sometimes you want to keep an icon around — typically, for troubleshooting. I like to keep my printers up and directly available.

To permanently pin a Device Stage device's icon to the taskbar, follow these steps:

1. **In the Devices and Printers list (refer to Figure 2-1), double-click the device name to open the Devices and Printers service page for the device (refer to Figure 2-5).**

   The device's icon should appear on the Windows taskbar.

2. **Right-click the device's icon and (if the option presents itself) choose Pin This Program to Taskbar.**

   If you see the Pin This Program to Taskbar option, you're done.

   If you don't see an option to pin the program to the taskbar, the next best alternative is to put a shortcut to the printer on your desktop, just above the taskbar.

   Printer icons generally don't have a Pin This Program to Taskbar option.

3. **From the Devices and Printers list (refer to Figure 2-1), click the printer and drag it to the desktop.**

   You see a shortcut that can be moved anywhere you like.

If you can't get your device's drivers to install — as shown in Figure 2-6 — you should check these problem areas:

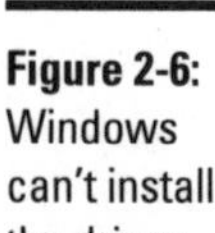

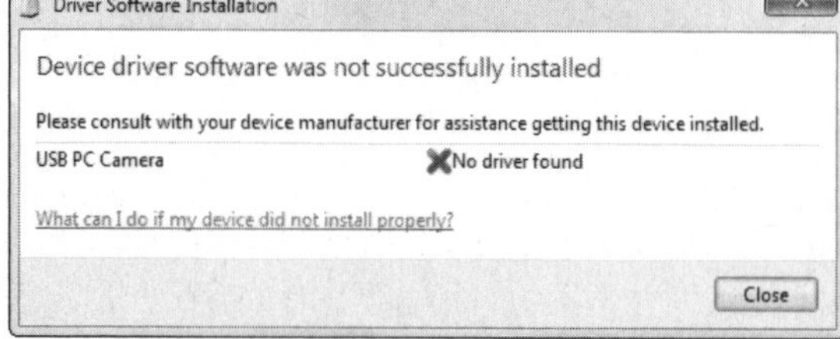

Figure 2-6: Windows can't install the driver.

- **Your Internet connection must work.** Unless you have an installation CD, if Windows doesn't have the driver already, it has to go out to the big Microsoft driver database on the Internet and look for one.
- **You have to turn on Windows Automatic Update.** But you turn it on only long enough to find the driver. The installer doesn't download or install a driver unless you have Automatic Update turned on. Refer to Book VI, Chapter 4 for details.

✦ **If that strategy doesn't work, go to the manufacturer's Web site and download the driver.** Make a note of which folder contains the driver, and then unplug the device and plug it back in again. When Windows asks, point it to the driver's location.

✦ **If all else fails, install the software that came with the device.** That's definitely a last-resort approach, but desperate times frequently call for desperate drivers, er, measures.

Before I could get my Nokia 5800 XpressMusic to work properly, I had to download and install the Nokia Ovi Suite — the programs that connect the phone to Windows. By the time you read this book, that download and installation may occur automatically. If it doesn't, and you're trying to make a Nokia phone o work with Device Stage, go to `ovi.com` and download the latest version.

Sometimes, rebooting makes things work: Choose Start, click the right-arrow next to Shut Down, and choose Restart. I'm not sure why, but rebooting can suddenly make things work right. I guess the gremlins inside your machine need a break from time to time.

Establishing a Bluetooth Connection

Device Stage isn't limited to USB-connected devices. The Device and Printers dialog box also shows you devices that are connected to your computer by way of Bluetooth and WiFi wireless connections. (As you probably know, *Bluetooth* is a short-range wireless way to connect two electronic products. Not too many years ago, Bluetooth had all sorts of problems. Nowadays, it usually works quite well.)

If you've never connected a Bluetooth device to your computer, here's how to do it:

1. **Verify that your PC has Bluetooth working — broadcasting — so that other Bluetooth devices can see it. How? Use Device Stage, of course. Choose Start⇨Devices and Printers and look for a Bluetooth device, like the one shown in Figure 2-7.**

   In Figure 2-7, you can see the Device Stage entry for the Bluetooth "radio" on one of my laptops.

2. **Right-click the Bluetooth device and choose Bluetooth Settings.**

   Windows shows you the settings shown in Figure 2-8.

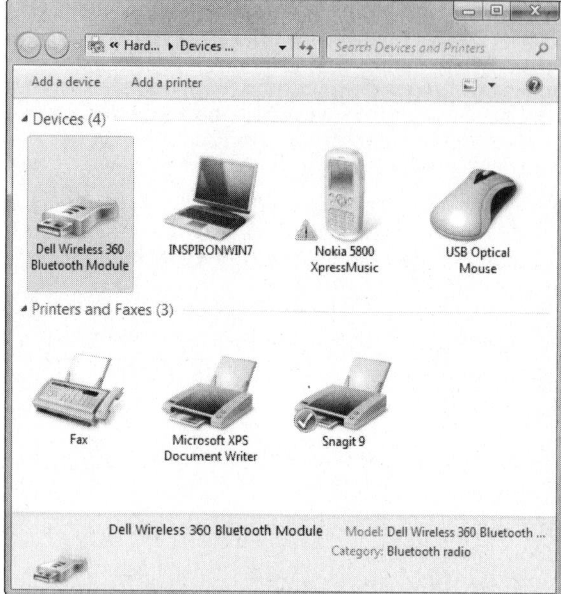

Figure 2-7: The Bluetooth transmitter on your computer shows up in the Device Stage list.

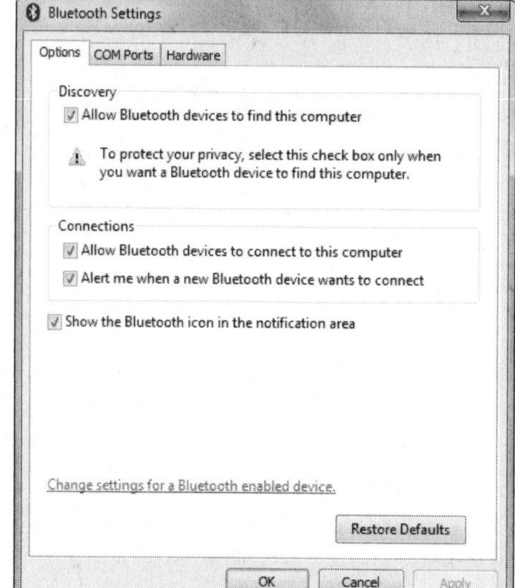

Figure 2-8: Make sure to enable Discovery on the computer side.

3. **Select the check box that says Allow Bluetooth Devices to Find This Computer, and then click OK.**

This step turns on the Bluetooth transmitter, which beams out a welcoming signal to every Bluetooth device in the area — generally 30 to 50 feet (or 10 to 20 meters) away.

4. **Make sure that Bluetooth is working on the device you want to connect.**

   That can be a monumental pain in the tooth.

   On the Nokia 5800 Xpress Music, which I use for this demo, I have to go through all the following hidden steps to enable Bluetooth. Your phone may be equally obtuse, particularly if it's a Nokia:

   - Tap the area next to the battery life indicator, and then click the two unmarked horizontal arrows. That action shows the Connectivity menu. (And you thought Windows 7 was confusing?)
   - Tap the Bluetooth link.
   - Tap the Off setting until it turns to On.
   - Tap Exit.

5. **Back in Device Stage, in the upper-left corner, click Add a Device.**

   If you enabled Bluetooth correctly on both your PC and the device, they should — *should* — start talking to each other. When they get past the handshake stage (that's the technical term for it), you see the results shown in Figure 2-9.

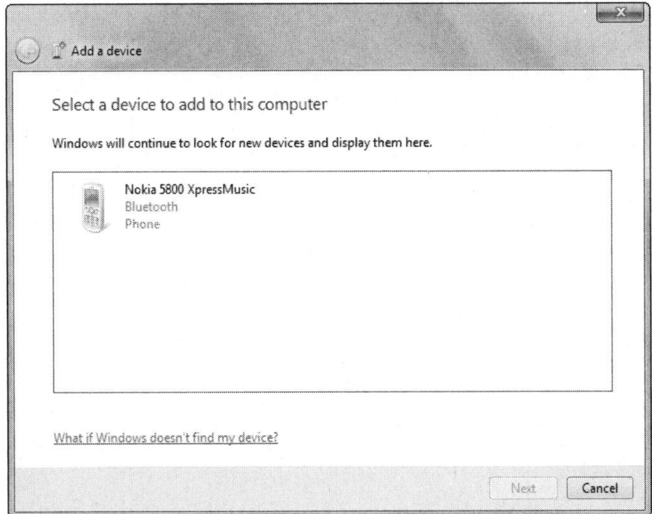

Figure 2-9: The phone is ready to connect.

6. **Double-click the phone (or headset or speaker or whatever).**

If your device requires authentication — all phones do — Windows 7 generates a random connection code and shows it to you, as shown in Figure 2-10.

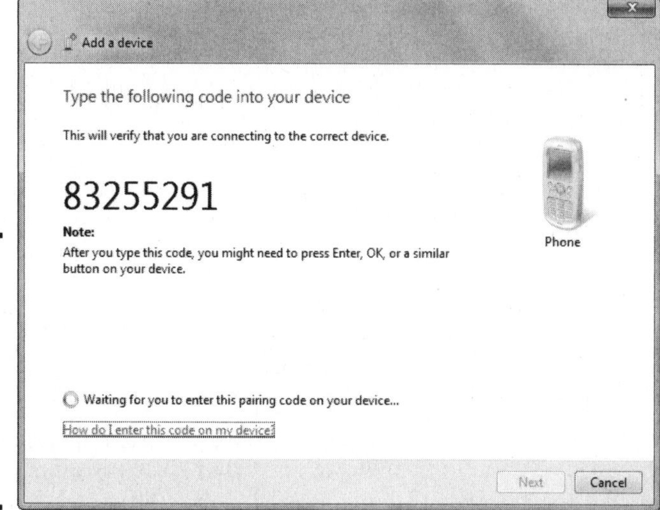

Figure 2-10: The connection code you have to enter into your telephone.

7. **At the same time, if all is working correctly, your telephone asks whether you want to accept a connection from your PC and then prompts you to enter the code shown on the PC's screen. Tap the code into your phone.**

   Windows advises that it has made the connection — but you have to wait a while (sometimes, quite a while) for the drivers to download. While you wait, you see the message shown in Figure 2-11.

   Be sure to keep your device turned on, and leave it within shouting range of your PC, while the drivers are installed. I've encountered problems with Windows retrieving the correct drivers if the connection with the device is broken.

   The normal rules for the automatic installation of drivers apply: You have to be connected to the Internet, and you have to have Automatic Update turned on (see the "Taking Device Stage for a Spin" section, earlier in this chapter).

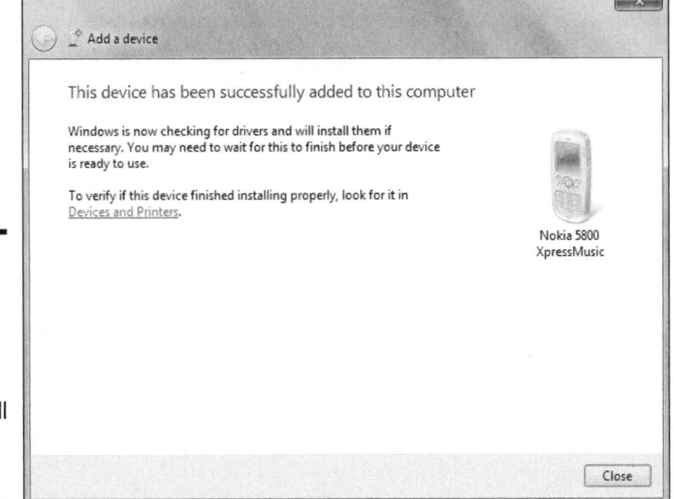

Figure 2-11: The device is connected, but may not work until all drivers are installed.

8. **Go back into Device Stage by choosing Start➪Devices and Printers. Wait until your new device appears on the screen without any swirly icons or yellow "warning" icons.**

   At that point, you can use the device — but you aren't done yet.

9. **Right-click the Bluetooth device and choose Bluetooth Settings. In the dialog box shown earlier (refer to Figure 2-8), deselect the check box labeled Allow Bluetooth Devices to Find This Computer, and then click OK.**

   Root around in your device and turn off Bluetooth there, too.

Good luck. Setting up Bluetooth can be challenging, but the results make it worth the effort.

Chapter 3: Printing (Almost) Effortlessly

In This Chapter

- **Attaching a new printer to your PC or network**
- **Solving print queue problems**
- **Considering other multi-function (print, scan, copy, fax) devices**
- **Troubleshooting other problems with printers**
- **Stopping a runaway printer**

Ah, the paperless office. What a wonderful concept! No more file cabinets bulging with misfiled flotsam. No more hernias from hauling cartons of copy paper, dumping the sheets 500 at a time into a thankless plastic maw. No more trees dying in agony, relinquishing their last gasps to provide pulp as a substrate for heat-fused carbon toner. No more coffee-stained reports. No more paper cuts.

No more . . . oh, who the heck am I trying to kid? No way.

Industry prognosticators have been telling us for more than a decade that the paperless office is right around the corner. Yeah, sure. Maybe around *your* corner. Around *my* corner, I predict that PC printers will disappear about the same time that *Star Trek* reruns go off the air. We're talking geologic time here, folks.

The biggest problem? Finding a printer that doesn't cost two arms and three legs to, uh, print. Toner cartridges cost a fortune. Ink costs two fortunes. That bargain-basement printer you can get for $65 will probably print, oh, about ten pages before it starts begging for a refill. And four or five refills can easily cost as much as the printer.

Gillette may have originated the razor-and-blades business model, but it took the likes of HP and Brother and Canon and Samsung to perfect it. Thank heaven Gillette hasn't figured out a way to put a microchip in the blades, to guarantee their obsolescence.

Windows 7 has excellent printer support. It's easy after you grasp a few basic skills.

Installing a Printer

You have three ways to make a printer available to your computer:

- ✦ Attach it directly to the computer.
- ✦ Connect your computer to a network and attach the printer to another computer on the same network.
- ✦ If the printer's capable of attaching directly to a network, connect your computer to a network and attach the printer directly to the network's hub, either with a network cable or by using a wireless connection.

Connecting a computer directly to a network hub isn't difficult, if you have the right hardware. Each printer controller is different, though, so you have to follow the manufacturer's instructions.

Although choosing a new printer is beyond the scope of this book, you can find free tips — inkjet or laser, basic or multifunction? — at `Dummies.com`.

Attaching a local printer

So you have a new printer and you want to use it. Attaching it locally — which is to say, plugging it directly into your PC — is the simplest way to install a printer, and it's the only option if you don't have a network.

All modern printers have a USB connector that plugs into your computer. In theory, you plug the connector into your PC's USB port and turn on the printer, and then Windows 7 recognizes it and installs the appropriate drivers. You're done. Figure 3-1 shows you that after Windows 7 recognizes my Brother printer and installs its drivers, the printer is ready to go — with no work on my part.

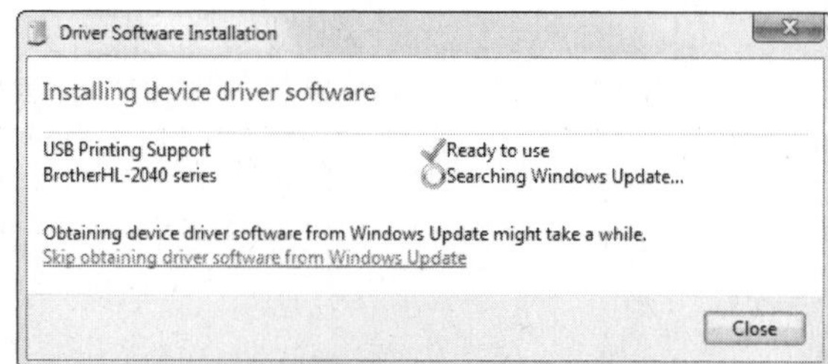

Figure 3-1: Letting Windows 7 do all the work.

Note that I *don't* recommend that you install the manufacturer's software, no matter what the instructions in the box with the printer may say. Most printers come with a CD loaded with . . . junk.

When the printer is installed properly, you can see the printer in your Device Stage device and printers window. (See Book VIII, Chapter 2 for details on Device Stage.) Choose Start➪Devices and Printers to open the Devices and Printers window, shown in Figure 3-2.

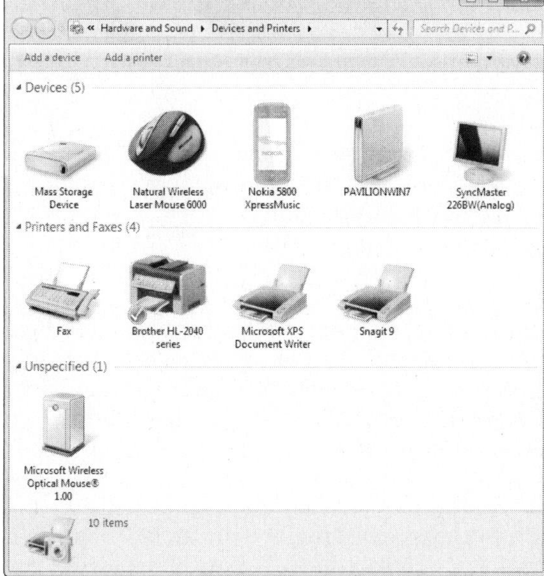

Figure 3-2: After my Brother printer is automatically recognized and installed, it appears in the Devices and Printers window.

Once in a very blue moon, and sometimes with very new models of printers, Windows may have trouble locating a driver. If that happens, you can use the CD that came with your printer or, better, go to the manufacturer's Web site and download the latest driver. See Table 4-1 for a list of Web sites.

Table 4-1 Driver Sites for Major Printer Manufacturers

Manufacturer	*Find Drivers at This URL*
Brother	`brother.com/E-ftp/info/index.html`
Canon	`usa.canon.com/html/conCprSupport.jsp`
Dell	`support.dell.com/filelib/criteria.aspx?c=us`

(continued)

Table 4-1 *(continued)*

Manufacturer	*Find Drivers at This URL*
Epson	`epson.com/cgi-bin/Store/support/SupportIndex.jsp`
HP	`welcome.hp.com/country/us/en/support.html`
Lexmark	`support.lexmark.com/cgi-perl/selections.cgi`
Samsung	`samsung.com/us/support/download/supportDownMain.do`

If you have to use an old-fashioned parallel or serial cable to connect your printer, make sure that you have the manufacturer's installation instructions handy, and follow its advice religiously.

Connecting a network printer

Windows 7 networks work wonders. I talk (and talk and talk) about them in Book VII. If you have a network, you can attach a printer to any computer on the network and have it accessible to all users on all computers in the network. You can also attach different printers to different computers and let network users pick and choose the printer they want to use as the need arises.

If you attach a printer to a computer in your HomeGroup, Windows automatically recognizes it and offers to make it accessible on your computer. You can turn off the automatic sharing of printers in your HomeGroup (see Book VII, Chapter 1), but unless you changed something, every printer attached to every computer in your HomeGroup is automatically identified and added to the Device Stage devices and printers list on every computer in the HomeGroup (see Figure 3-3). Very slick.

You can double-click the Device Stage icon and see all the information about the printer, as I describe in Book VIII, Chapter 2.

If you have printers attached to your network but not in your HomeGroup — for example, you may hang a printer on a Windows Vista or Windows XP machine — you can still add it to your collection of shared printers. Here's how:

1. **Choose Start⇨Devices and Printers.**

   You see the Device Stage list (refer to Figure 3-3).

2. **At the top, click the button that says Add a Printer.**

   Windows 7 asks whether you want to add a local printer or a network or wireless or Bluetooth printer, as shown in Figure 3-4.

Figure 3-3: This printer was automatically identified on my HomeGroup and made available to all the computers in it.

This icon indicates that the printer is shared.

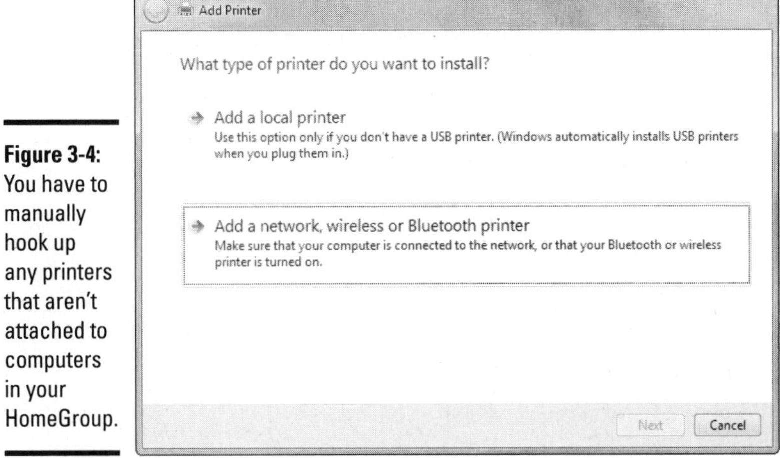

Figure 3-4: You have to manually hook up any printers that aren't attached to computers in your HomeGroup.

3. **Click the Add a Network, Wireless, or Bluetooth Printer paragraph.**

   Windows starts searching for printers (see Figure 3-5). Usually, it finds the printer you want. Sometimes it doesn't.

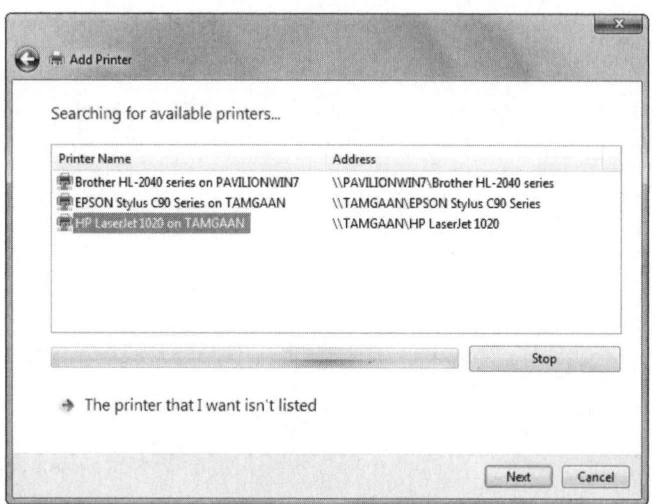

Figure 3-5: Windows searches all computers attached to your network, whether they're in your HomeGroup or not.

4. **If Windows doesn't identify the printer you want within a minute or two, click the Stop button and then click the link The Printer That I Want Isn't Listed.**

   From that point, click the Browse button and then locate the printer on your network. Select the printer, click the OK button, and then (refer to Figure 3-5) click the Next button.

   If the wizard doesn't display the printer you want to install, you can install it anyway, but you must type its name into the Printer text box under the Select a Shared Printer by Name option. The name has this form:

   ```
   \\host\printer
   ```

   Substitute for `host` the name of the host computer as it appears in the Shared Printers dialog box. Substitute for `printer` the share name of the shared printer (which you can find on the host computer's Printers list). You see something like this: `\\Dimension\LJ4`.

5. **If Windows *does* identify the printer, click the printer name and click Next.**

   Windows asks Do You Trust This Printer?

6. **Check to see whether a button says, "Golly, it's always been a good printer to me, but you never really know if it suddenly acquired subversive tendencies — right? — so how can I tell for sure?" If you don't find that button, click Install Driver.**

   Windows whirs and clanks for a while and then tells you that you've successfully added the printer.

7. **Click Next.**

   You're asked whether you want to make the new printer your *default* printer (the one that an application uses unless you explicitly tell it otherwise).

8. **Click Finish.**

   Your new printer appears in the Device Stage list, as shown in Figure 3-6.

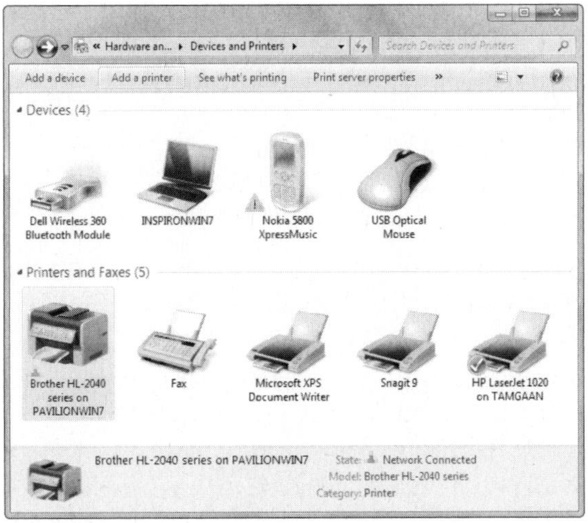

Figure 3-6: Windows 7 adds the LaserJet 1020 attached to Tamgaan (a Windows XP computer) to its Device Stage list.

File and printer sharing has to be allowed on both the host computer — the one with the printer physically attached to it — and on the other computer from which you want to be able to use the printer. To make sure that file and printer sharing is enabled, choose Start➪Control Panel and, under the Network and Internet icon, click the Set Up File Sharing link.

Using the Print Queue

You may have noticed that when you print a document from an application, the application reports that it's done before the printer finishes printing. If the document is long enough, you can print several more documents from one or more applications while the printer works on the first one. This is possible because Windows 7 saves printed documents in a *print queue* until it can print them.

If more than one printer is installed on your computer or on your network, each one has its own print queue. The queue is maintained on the host PC — that is, the PC to which the printer is attached.

Windows 7 uses print queues automatically, so you don't even have to know that they exist. If you know the tricks, though, you can control them in several useful ways.

Displaying a print queue

You can display information about the document that a printer is now printing and about any other documents in a printer's print queue by following these steps:

1. **If the printer is attached to a PC in your HomeGroup, go to any of the PCs in the HomeGroup and choose Start⇨Devices and Printers.**

   You see the Device Stage listing of devices and printers (refer to Figure 3-6).

2. **Right-click the printer and choose See What's Printing.**

   Windows shows you a list of all of the documents waiting to be printed — the *print queue* — as shown in Figure 3-7.

Brother HL-2040 series on PAVILIONWIN7 - Paused

Printer Document View

Document Name	Status	Owner	Pages	Size	Submitted
Microsoft Word - Renovation email.doc		HomeGroupUser$	4	1.08 MB	9:34:27 PM 4/27/2009
Microsoft Word - Test2.docx		HomeGroupUser$	1	1.63 KB	9:32:55 PM 4/27/2009
Microsoft Word - Mutual of America inquiry.doc		Woody	1	13.7 KB	9:32:32 PM 4/27/2009
Microsoft Word - Allow Bongkod to pick up Ad...		Woody	2	5.05 MB	9:31:24 PM 4/27/2009

4 document(s) in queue

Figure 3-7: The printer queue.

   The Owner column tells you which user put the document in the print queue. The jobs in the print queue are listed from the oldest at the top to the newest at the bottom. The Status column shows which job is printing.

3. **You can close the Device Stage window and keep the print queue window open for later use. You can minimize the print queue window and keep it in the taskbar.**

That can be quite handy if you're running a particularly long or complex print job — Word mail merges are particularly notorious for requiring close supervision.

Pausing and resuming a print queue

When you *pause* a print queue, Windows 7 stops printing documents from it. If a document is printing when you pause the queue, Windows 7 tries to finish printing the document and then stops. When you resume a print queue, Windows 7 starts printing documents from the queue again. Follow these guidelines to pause and resume a print queue:

- **To pause a print queue,** when you're looking at the print queue window, choose Printer➪Pause Printing.
- **To resume the print queue,** choose the same command again. The check mark in front of the Pause Printing line disappears, and the printer resumes.

Why would you want to pause the print queue? Say you want to print a page for later reference, but you don't want to bother turning your printer on to print just one page. Pause the printer's queue, and then print the page. The next time you turn the printer on, resume the queue, and the page prints.

Sometimes, Windows has a hard time finishing the document — for example, you may be dealing with print buffer overruns (see the "Troubleshooting Printing" section, later in this chapter), and every time you clear the printer, it may try to reprint the overrun pages. If that happens to you, pause the print queue and then turn off the printer. As soon as the printer comes back online, Windows is smart enough to pick up where it left off.

Also, depending on how your network is set up, you may or may not be able to pause and resume a print queue on a printer attached to another user's computer.

Pausing, restarting, and resuming a document

Why would you want to pause a document? Say you're printing a Web page that documents an online order you just placed and the printer jams. You already finished entering the order, and you have no way to display the page again to reprint it. Pause the document, clear the printer, and restart the document.

Here's another common situation where pausing comes in handy. You're printing a long document and the phone rings. To make the printer be quiet while you talk, pause the document. When you're done talking, resume printing the document.

Here's how these three different actions work:

- **Pause a document:** When you pause a document, Windows 7 is prevented from printing that document. Windows 7 skips the document and prints later documents in the queue. If you pause a document while Windows 7 is printing it, Windows 7 halts in the middle of the document and prints nothing on that printer until you take further action.
- **Restart a document:** When you restart a document, Windows 7 is again allowed to print it. If the document is at the top of the queue, Windows 7 prints it as soon as it finishes the document that it's now printing. If the document was being printed when it was paused, Windows 7 stops printing it and starts again at the beginning.
- **Resume a document:** Resuming a document is meaningful only if you paused it while Windows 7 was printing it. When you resume a document, Windows 7 resumes printing it where it paused.

To pause a document, right-click the document in the print queue and choose Pause. The window shows the document's status as Paused. To resume or restart the print document, right-click that document and choose Resume.

Canceling a document

When you *cancel* a document, Windows 7 removes it from the print queue without printing it. You may have heard computer jocks use the term *purged* or *zapped* or something totally unprintable.

Here's a common situation when document canceling comes in handy. You start printing a long document, and as soon as the first page comes out, you realize that you forgot to set the heading. Cancel the document and change the heading, and print the document again.

To cancel a document, select that document. In the print queue window, choose Document⇨Cancel. Or, right-click the document in the print queue window and choose Cancel. You can also select the document and press Delete.

When a document is gone, it's gone. No Recycle Bin exists for the print queue.

Conversely, most printers have built-in memory that stores pages while they're being printed. You may go to the print queue to look for a document, only to discover that it isn't there. (As I was walking up the stair / I met a doc that wasn't there. . . .) If the document has already been shuffled off to the printer's internal memory, the only way to cancel it is to turn off the printer.

Troubleshooting Printing

The following list describes some typical problems with printers and the solutions to those sticky spots:

- **I'm trying to install a printer. I connected it to my computer, and Windows 7 doesn't detect its presence.** Be sure that the printer is turned on and that the cable from the printer to your computer is properly connected at both ends. Check the printer's manual; you may have to follow a procedure (such as push a button) to make the printer ready for use.
- **I'm trying to install a printer that's connected to another computer on my network, and Windows 7 doesn't detect its presence. I know that the printer is okay; it's already installed and working as a local printer on that system!** If the printer is attached to a Windows XP or Vista PC, the printer may not be shared. To rectify the problem, right-click the printer and choose Sharing. (For details, see *Windows XP All-in-One Desk Reference For Dummies* or *Windows Vista All-in-One Desk Reference For Dummies,* both by yours truly and published by Wiley.)

  If the printer is attached to a Windows 7 PC and it's part of your HomeGroup, make sure that the HomeGroup is working. If it isn't part of your HomeGroup, read Book VII, Chapter 1 and get with the system!
- **I can't use a shared printer that I've used successfully in the past. Windows 7 says that it isn't available when I try to use it, or Windows 7 doesn't even show it as an installed printer any more.** This situation can happen if something interferes with your connection to the network or the connection to the printer's host computer. It can also happen if something interferes with the availability of the printer — for example, if the host computer's user has turned off sharing.

  If you can't find a problem, or if you find and correct a problem (such as file and printer sharing being turned off) but you still can't use the printer, try restarting Windows 7 on your own system. If that doesn't help, remove the printer from your system and then reinstall it.

  To remove the printer from your system, choose Start⇨Devices and Printers to open the Device Stage. Right-click the printer and choose Remove Device. Windows 7 asks whether you're sure you want to remove this printer. Click the Yes button.

  To reinstall the printer on your system, use the same procedure you used to install it originally. (See the "Connecting a network printer" section, earlier in this chapter.)

- **I printed a document, but it never came out of the printer.** Check the printer's print queue, over on the host PC (the one directly attached to the printer). Is the document there? If not, investigate several possible reasons:

  - *The printer isn't turned on.* Hey, don't laugh. I've done it. In some cases, Windows 7 can't distinguish a printer that's connected but not turned on from a printer that's ready, and it sends documents to a printer that isn't operating.
  - *You accidentally sent the document to some other printer.* Hey, don't laugh — oh, you've heard that one.
  - *Someone else unintentionally picked up your document and walked off with it.* Yes, dear, it was you. This is known, technically, as the-dog-ate-my-homework excuse.
  - *The printer is turned on but not ready to print, and the printer (as opposed to the host PC) is holding your whole document in its internal memory until it can start printing.* A printer can hold as much as several dozen pages of output internally, depending on the size of its internal memory and the complexity of the pages.

  If your document is in the print queue but isn't printing, check for these problems:

  - The printer may not be ready to print. See whether it's plugged in, turned on, and properly connected to your computer or its host computer.
  - Your document may be paused.
  - The print queue itself may be paused.
  - The printer may be printing another document that is paused.
  - The printer may be "thinking." If it's a laser printer or another type of printer that composes an entire page in internal memory *before* it starts to print, it appears to do nothing while it processes photographs or other complex graphics. Processing may take as long as several minutes.

    Look at the printer and study its manual. The printer may have a blinking light or a status display that tells you it's doing something. As you become familiar with the printer, you develop a feel for how long various types of jobs should take.
  - On the other hand, the printer's status display may tell you that the printer is offline, out of paper, jammed, or unready to print for some other reason.

Catching a Runaway Printer

This topic has to be the most common, most frustrating problem in printer-dumb.

You print a document and, as it starts to come out the printer, you realize that you're printing a zillion pages you don't want. How do you stop the printer and then reset it so that it doesn't try to print the same bad stuff, all over again?

Here's what I do:

1. **Pull the paper out of the printer's paper feeder.**

   This step stops the immediate problem, uh, immediately.

2. **Open the Device Stage window (choose Start➪Devices and Printers), right-click the printer, and choose See What's Printing.**

   You see the print queue (refer to Figure 3-7).

3. **Right-click the runaway print job and choose Cancel.**

4. **If Step 3 deletes the bad print job, good for you. If it doesn't delete the bad print job, wait a minute then turn off the printer and unplug it from the wall. (Really.) Reboot Windows. When Windows comes back, wait another minute, plug the printer back in, and turn the printer back on.**

   Your bad job should be banished forever.

Index

Numerics

A

B

C

D

E

F

G

H

I

J

K

L

M

N

O

P

Q

R

S

T

U

V

W

X

Y

Z

Business/Accounting & Bookkeeping

Bookkeeping For Dummies
978-0-7645-9848-7

eBay Business All-in-One For Dummies, 2nd Edition
978-0-470-38536-4

Job Interviews For Dummies, 3rd Edition
978-0-470-17748-8

Resumes For Dummies, 5th Edition
978-0-470-08037-5

Stock Investing For Dummies, 3rd Edition
978-0-470-40114-9

Successful Time Management For Dummies
978-0-470-29034-7

Computer Hardware

BlackBerry For Dummies, 3rd Edition
978-0-470-45762-7

Computers For Seniors For Dummies
978-0-470-24055-7

iPhone For Dummies, 2nd Edition
978-0-470-42342-4

Laptops For Dummies, 3rd Edition
978-0-470-27759-1

Macs For Dummies, 10th Edition
978-0-470-27817-8

Cooking & Entertaining

Cooking Basics For Dummies, 3rd Edition
978-0-7645-7206-7

Wine For Dummies, 4th Edition
978-0-470-04579-4

Diet & Nutrition

Dieting For Dummies, 2nd Edition
978-0-7645-4149-0

Nutrition For Dummies, 4th Edition
978-0-471-79868-2

Weight Training For Dummies, 3rd Edition
978-0-471-76845-6

Digital Photography

Digital Photography For Dummies, 6th Edition
978-0-470-25074-7

Photoshop Elements 7 For Dummies
978-0-470-39700-8

Gardening

Gardening Basics For Dummies
978-0-470-03749-2

Organic Gardening For Dummies, 2nd Edition
978-0-470-43067-5

Green/Sustainable

Green Building & Remodeling For Dummies
978-0-4710-17559-0

Green Cleaning For Dummies
978-0-470-39106-8

Green IT For Dummies
978-0-470-38688-0

Health

Diabetes For Dummies, 3rd Edition
978-0-470-27086-8

Food Allergies For Dummies
978-0-470-09584-3

Living Gluten-Free For Dummies
978-0-471-77383-2

Hobbies/General

Chess For Dummies, 2nd Edition
978-0-7645-8404-6

Drawing For Dummies
978-0-7645-5476-6

Knitting For Dummies, 2nd Edition
978-0-470-28747-7

Organizing For Dummies
978-0-7645-5300-4

SuDoku For Dummies
978-0-470-01892-7

Home Improvement

Energy Efficient Homes For Dummies
978-0-470-37602-7

Home Theater For Dummies, 3rd Edition
978-0-470-41189-6

Living the Country Lifestyle All-in-One For Dummies
978-0-470-43061-3

Solar Power Your Home For Dummies
978-0-470-17569-9

Available wherever books are sold. For more information or to order direct: U.S. customers visit www.dummies.com or call 1-877-762-2974. U.K. customers visit www.wileyeurope.com or call (0) 1243 843291. Canadian customers visit www.wiley.ca or call 1-800-567-4797.